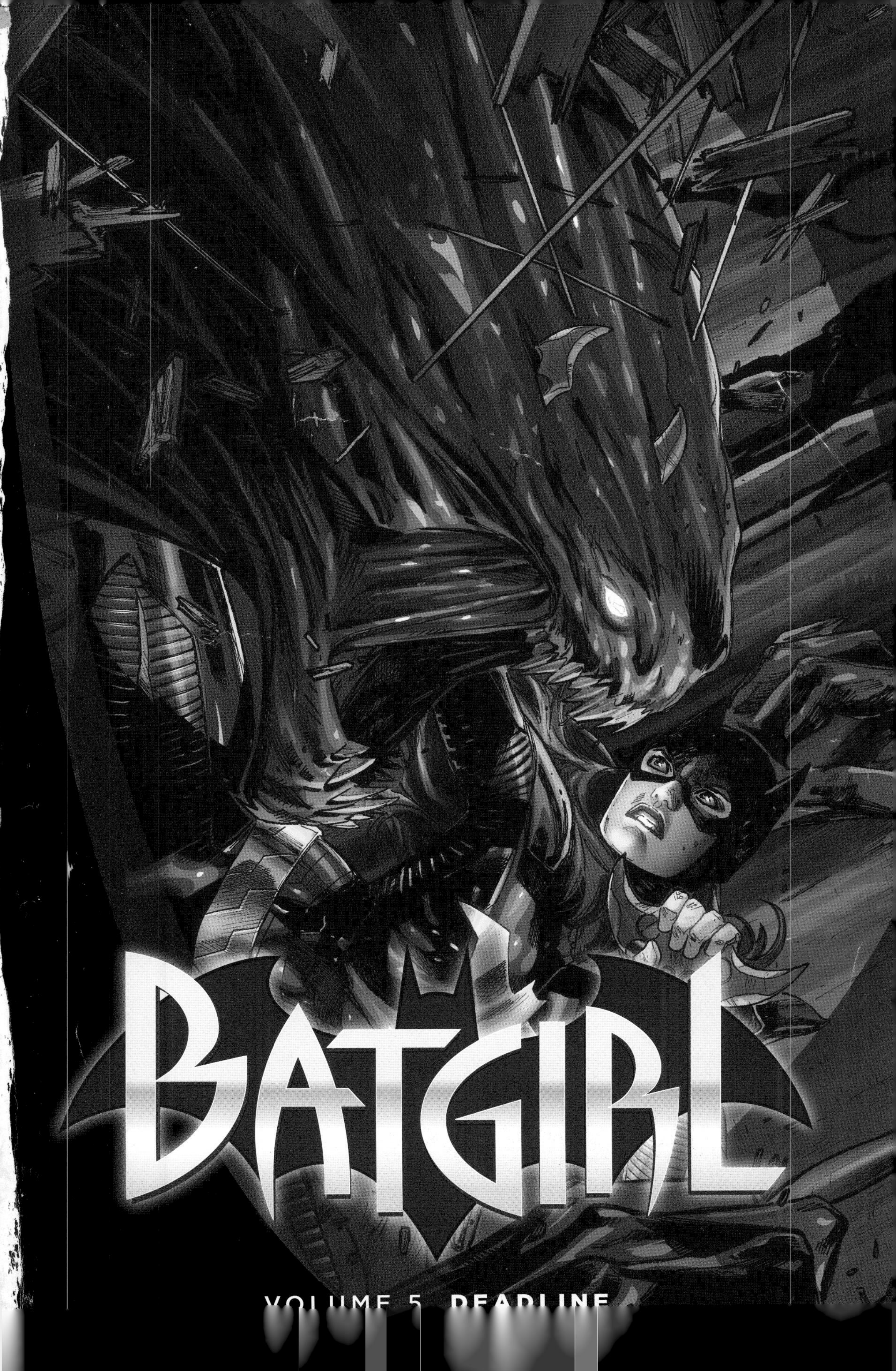
BATGIRL
VOLUME 5 DEADLINE

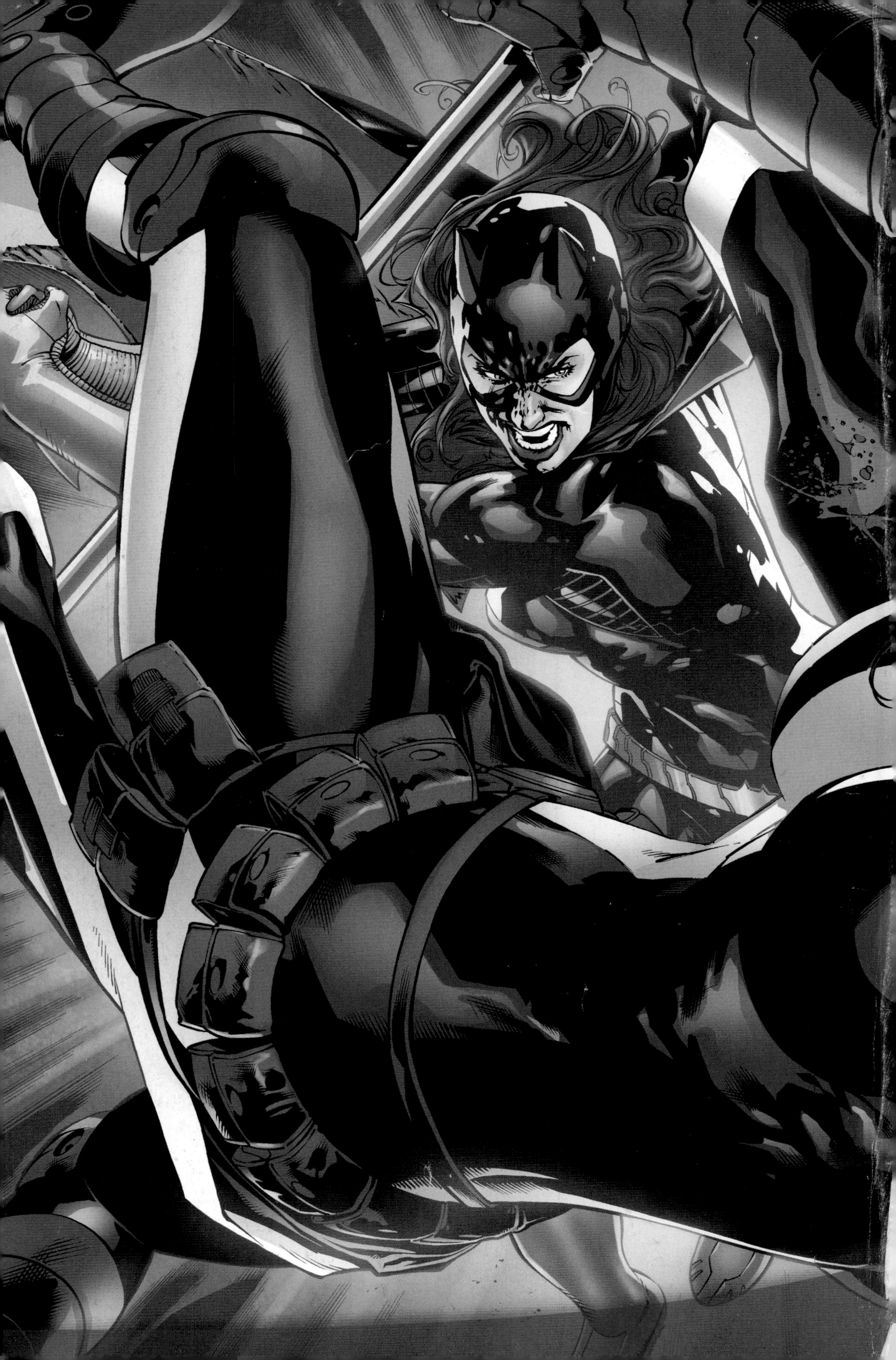

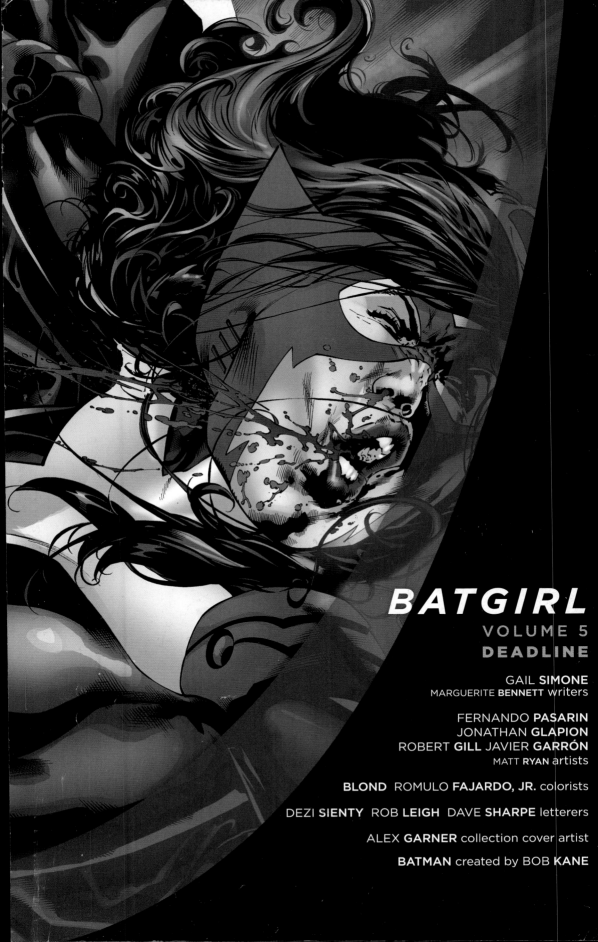

BATGIRL

VOLUME 5
DEADLINE

GAIL **SIMONE**
MARGUERITE **BENNETT** writers

FERNANDO **PASARIN**
JONATHAN **GLAPION**
ROBERT **GILL** JAVIER **GARRÓN**
MATT **RYAN** artists

BLOND ROMULO **FAJARDO, JR.** colorists

DEZI **SIENTY** ROB **LEIGH** DAVE **SHARPE** letterers

ALEX **GARNER** collection cover artist

BATMAN created by BOB **KANE**

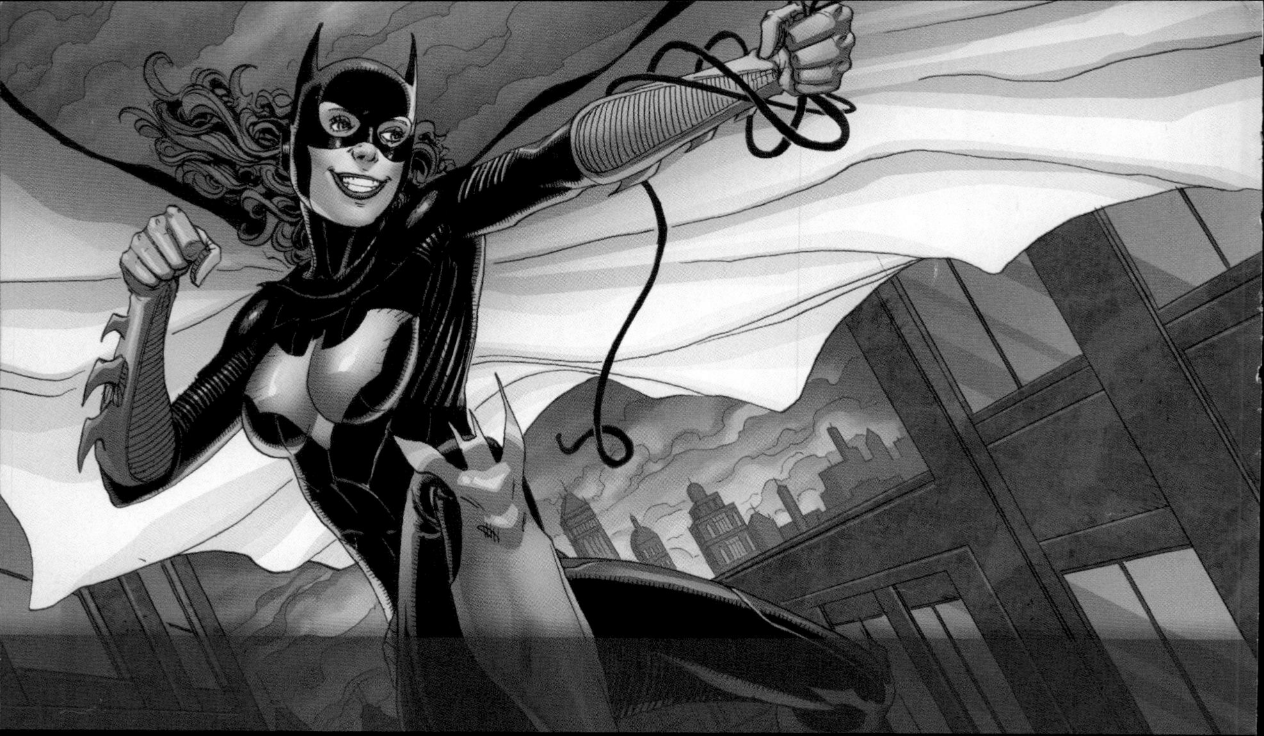

KATIE KUBERT CHRIS CONROY Editors - Original Series
MATT HUMPHREYS DAVE WIELGOSZ Assistant Editors - Original Series ROBIN WILDMAN Editor
ROBBIN BROSTERMAN Design Director - Books ROBBIE BIEDERMAN Publication Design

BOB HARRAS Senior VP - Editor-in-Chief, DC Comics

DIANE NELSON President DAN DIDIO and JIM LEE Co-Publishers GEOFF JOHNS Chief Creative Officer
AMIT DESAI Senior VP - Marketing and Franchise Management
AMY GENKINS Senior VP - Business and Legal Affairs NAIRI GARDINER Senior VP - Finance
JEFF BOISON VP - Publishing Planning MARK CHIARELLO VP - Art Direction and Design
JOHN CUNNINGHAM VP - Marketing TERRI CUNNINGHAM VP - Editorial Administration
LARRY GANEM VP - Talent Relations and Services ALISON GILL Senior VP - Manufacturing and Operations
HANK KANALZ Senior VP - Vertigo and Integrated Publishing JAY KOGAN VP - Business and Legal Affairs, Publishing
JACK MAHAN VP - Business Affairs, Talent NICK NAPOLITANO VP - Manufacturing Administration SUE POHJA VP - Book Sales
FRED RUIZ VP - Manufacturing Operations COURTNEY SIMMONS Senior VP - Publicity BOB WAYNE Senior VP - Sales

BATGIRL VOLUME 5: DEADLINE

DC Comics, 1700 Broadway, New York, NY 10019
A Warner Bros. Entertainment Company.
Printed by RR Donnelley, Salem, VA, USA. 11/14/14. First Printing.

ISBN HC: 978-1-4012-5041-6
ISBN SC: 978-1-4012-5511-4

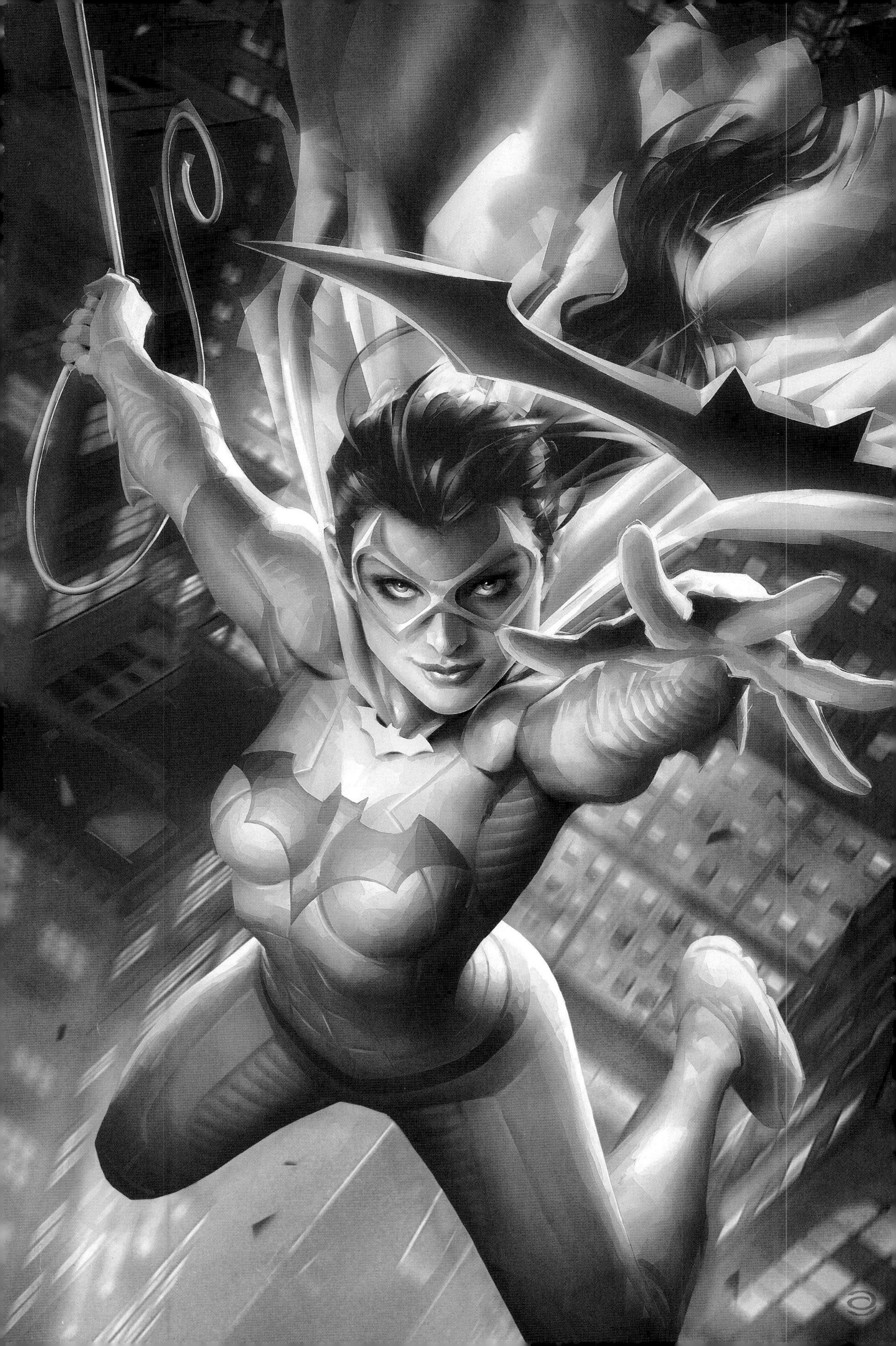

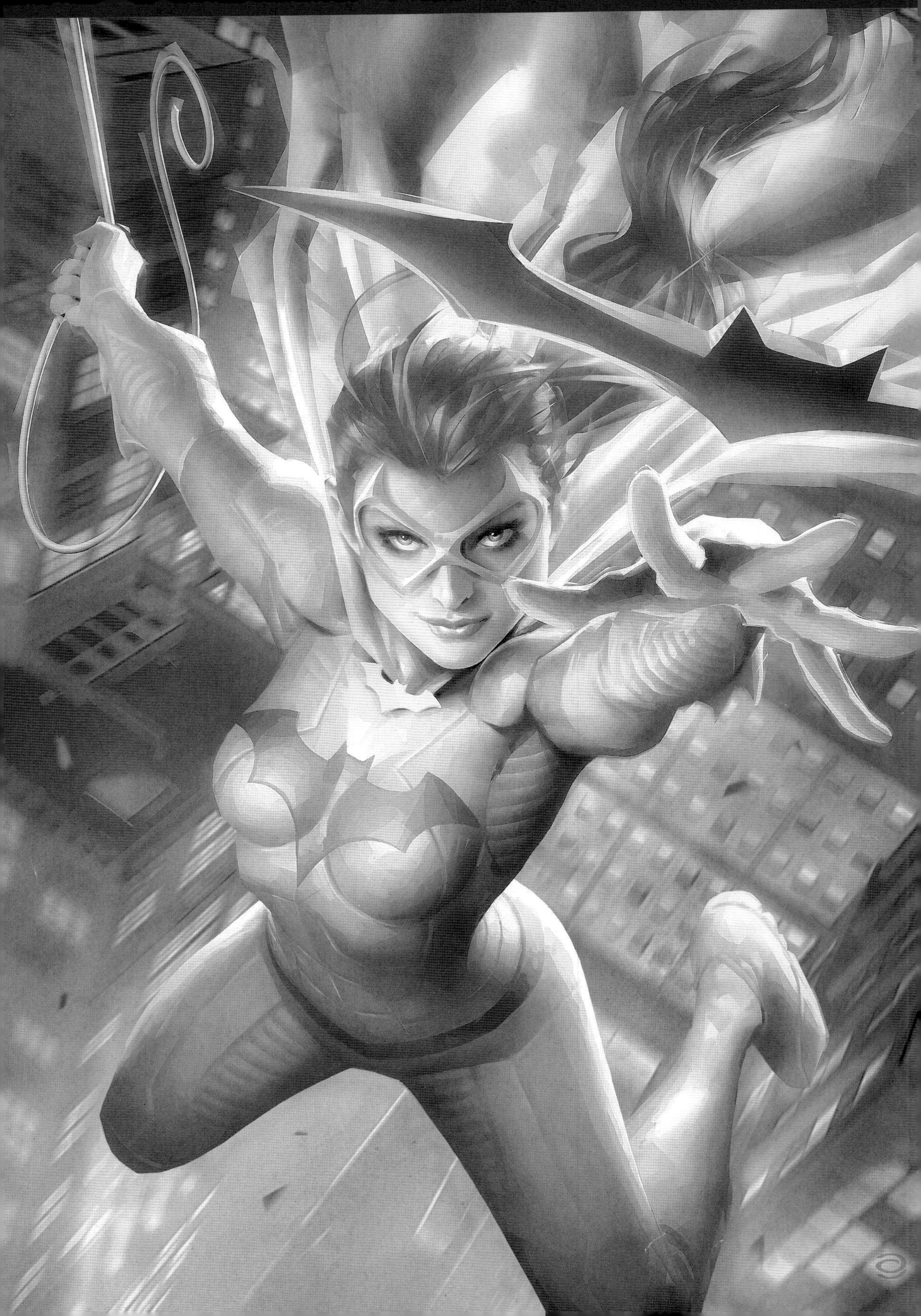

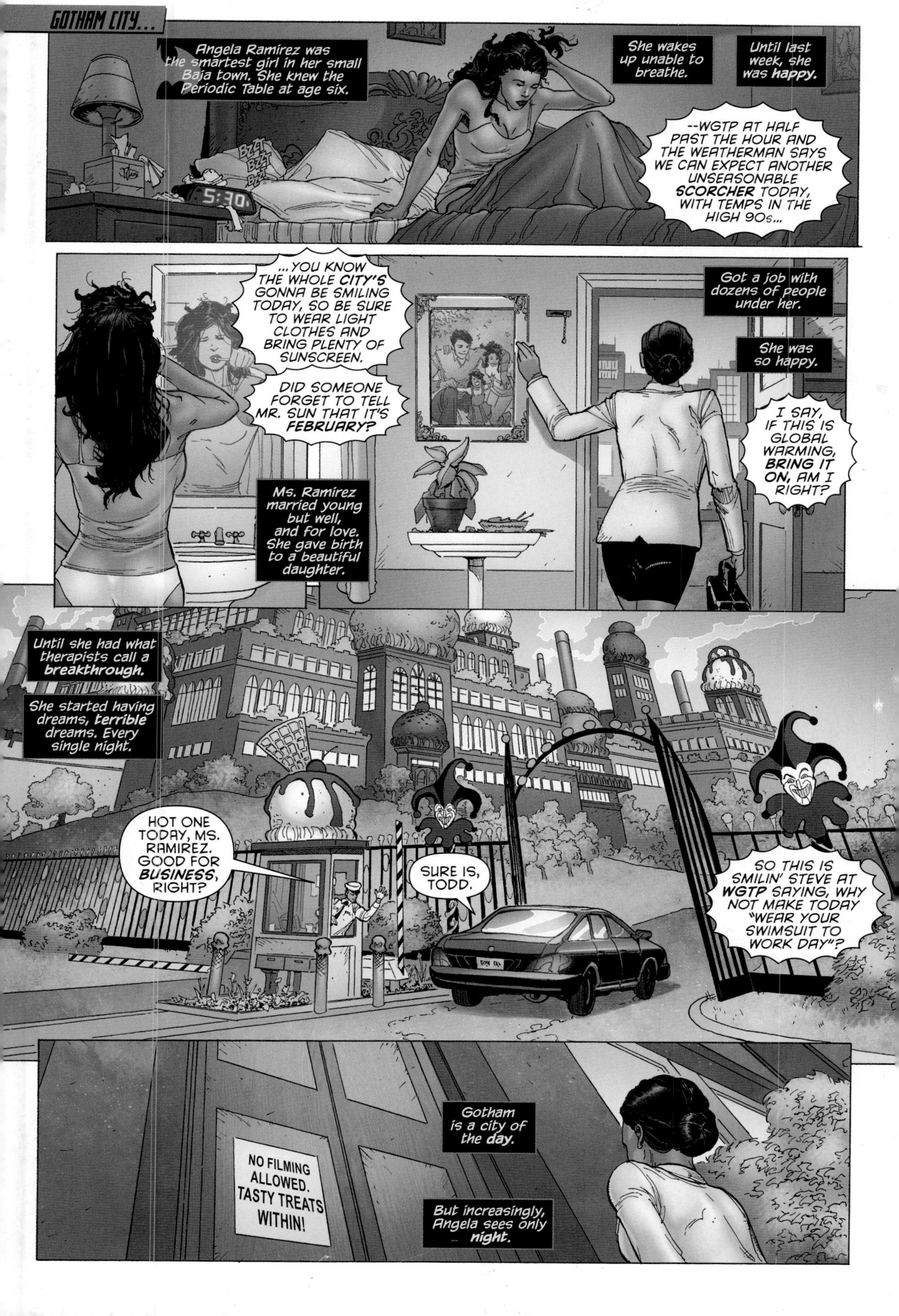
GOTHAM CITY...
Angela Ramirez was the smartest girl in her small Baja town. She knew the Periodic Table at age six.
She wakes up unable to breathe.
Until last week, she was happy.
BZZT BZZT BZZT
5:30
--WGTP AT HALF PAST THE HOUR AND THE WEATHERMAN SAYS WE CAN EXPECT ANOTHER UNSEASONABLE SCORCHER TODAY, WITH TEMPS IN THE HIGH 90s...
...YOU KNOW THE WHOLE CITY'S GONNA BE SMILING TODAY, SO BE SURE TO WEAR LIGHT CLOTHES AND BRING PLENTY OF SUNSCREEN.
DID SOMEONE FORGET TO TELL MR. SUN THAT IT'S FEBRUARY?
Ms. Ramirez married young but well, and for love. She gave birth to a beautiful daughter.
Got a job with dozens of people under her.
She was so happy.
I SAY, IF THIS IS GLOBAL WARMING, BRING IT ON, AM I RIGHT?
Until she had what therapists call a breakthrough.
She started having dreams, terrible dreams. Every single night.
HOT ONE TODAY, MS. RAMIREZ. GOOD FOR BUSINESS, RIGHT?
SURE IS, TODD.
SO THIS IS SMILIN' STEVE AT WGTP SAYING, WHY NOT MAKE TODAY "WEAR YOUR SWIMSUIT TO WORK DAY"?
NO FILMING ALLOWED. TASTY TREATS WITHIN!
Gotham is a city of the day.
But increasingly, Angela sees only night.

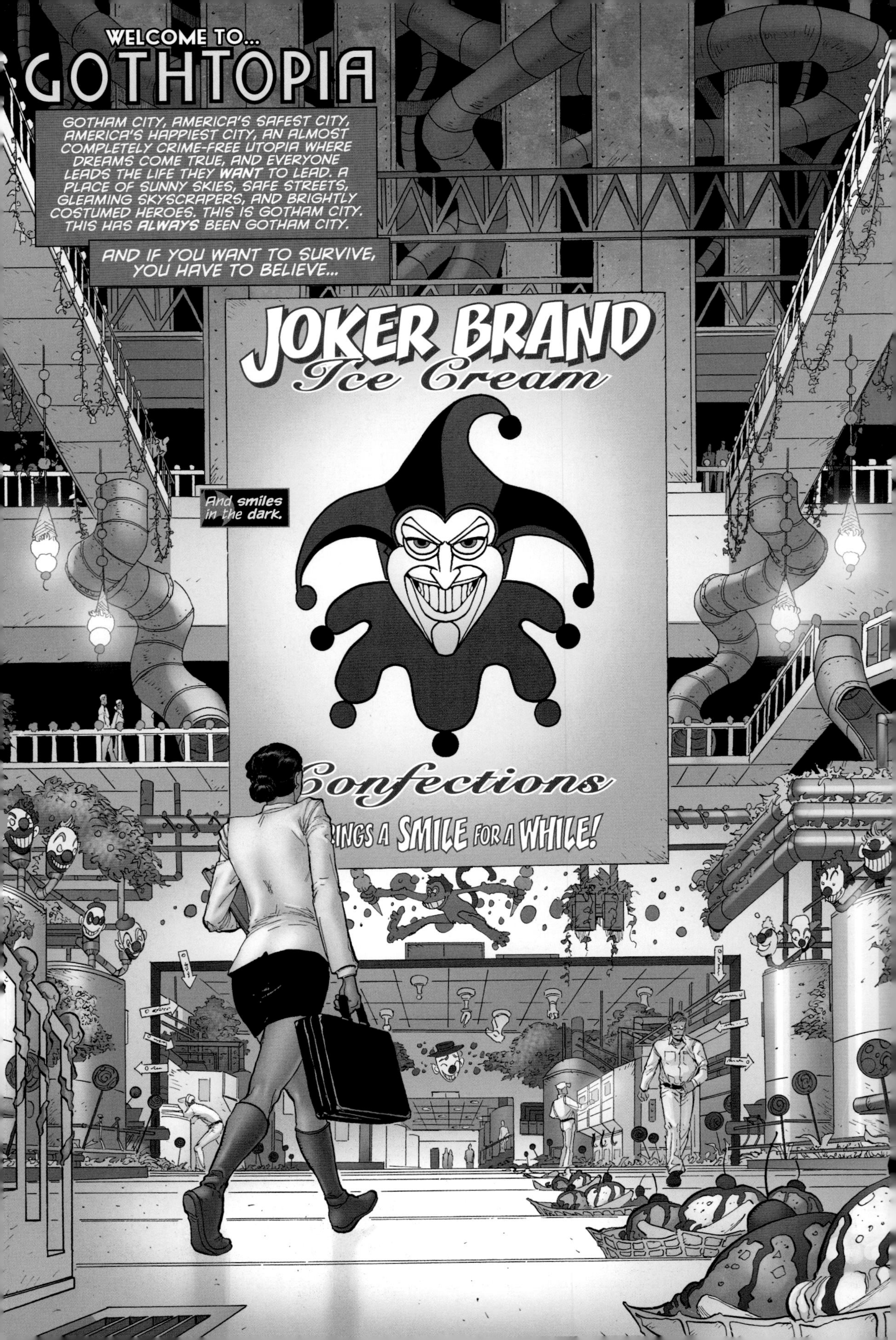

WELCOME TO...
GOTHTOPIA
GOTHAM CITY, AMERICA'S SAFEST CITY, AMERICA'S HAPPIEST CITY, AN ALMOST COMPLETELY CRIME-FREE UTOPIA WHERE DREAMS COME TRUE, AND EVERYONE LEADS THE LIFE THEY WANT TO LEAD. A PLACE OF SUNNY SKIES, SAFE STREETS, GLEAMING SKYSCRAPERS, AND BRIGHTLY COSTUMED HEROES. THIS IS GOTHAM CITY. THIS HAS ALWAYS BEEN GOTHAM CITY.
AND IF YOU WANT TO SURVIVE, YOU HAVE TO BELIEVE...
JOKER BRAND
Ice Cream
And smiles in the dark.
Confections
RINGS A SMILE FOR A WHILE!

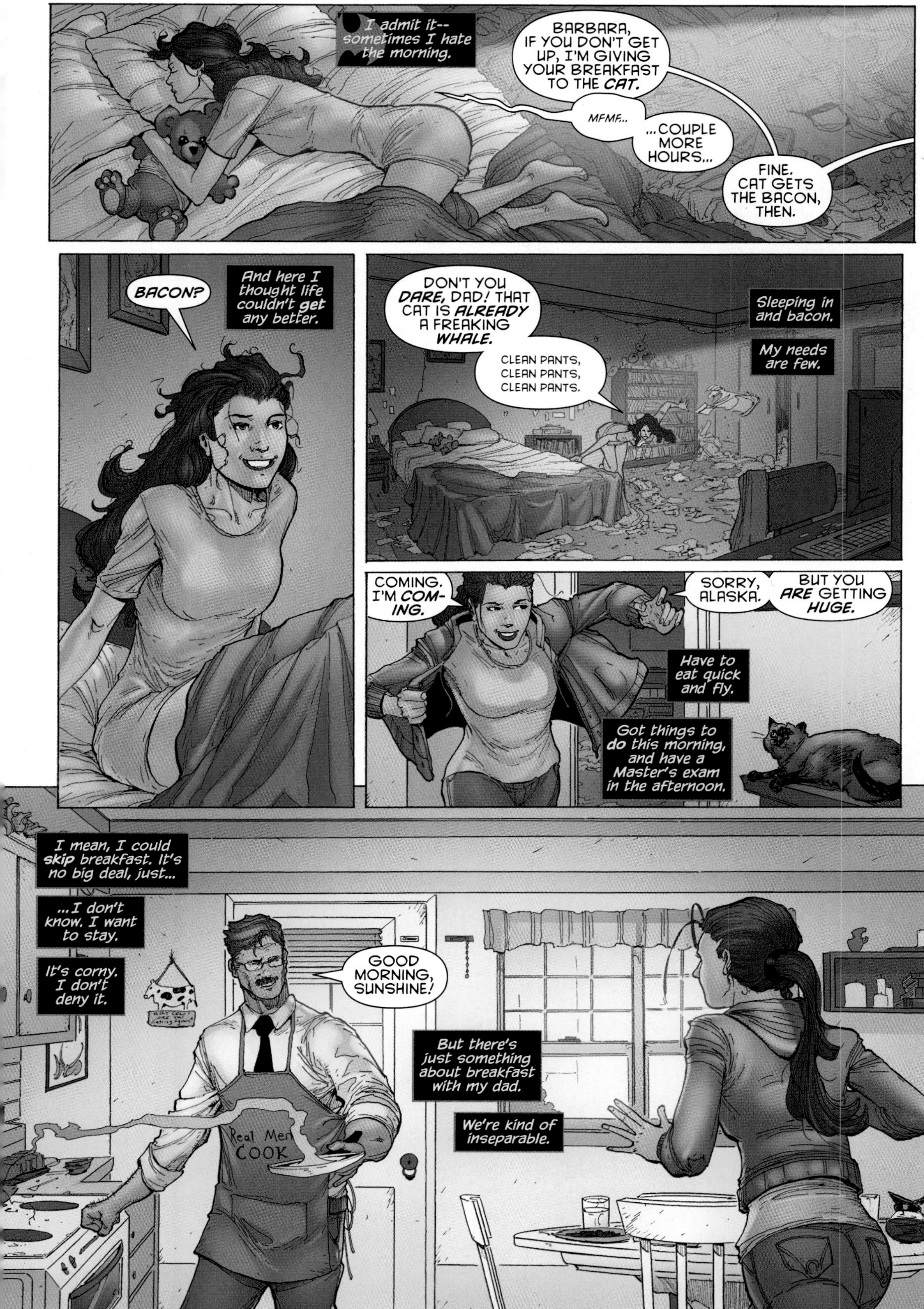
I admit it--sometimes I hate the morning.
BARBARA, IF YOU DON'T GET UP, I'M GIVING YOUR BREAKFAST TO THE CAT.
MFMF...
...COUPLE MORE HOURS...
FINE. CAT GETS THE BACON, THEN.
BACON?
And here I thought life couldn't get any better.
DON'T YOU DARE, DAD! THAT CAT IS ALREADY A FREAKING WHALE.
CLEAN PANTS, CLEAN PANTS, CLEAN PANTS.
Sleeping in and bacon.
My needs are few.
COMING. I'M COMING.
SORRY, ALASKA.
BUT YOU ARE GETTING HUGE.
Have to eat quick and fly.
Got things to do this morning, and have a Master's exam in the afternoon.
I mean, I could skip breakfast. It's no big deal, just...
...I don't know. I want to stay.
It's corny. I don't deny it.
GOOD MORNING, SUNSHINE!
Real Men COOK
But there's just something about breakfast with my dad.
We're kind of inseparable.

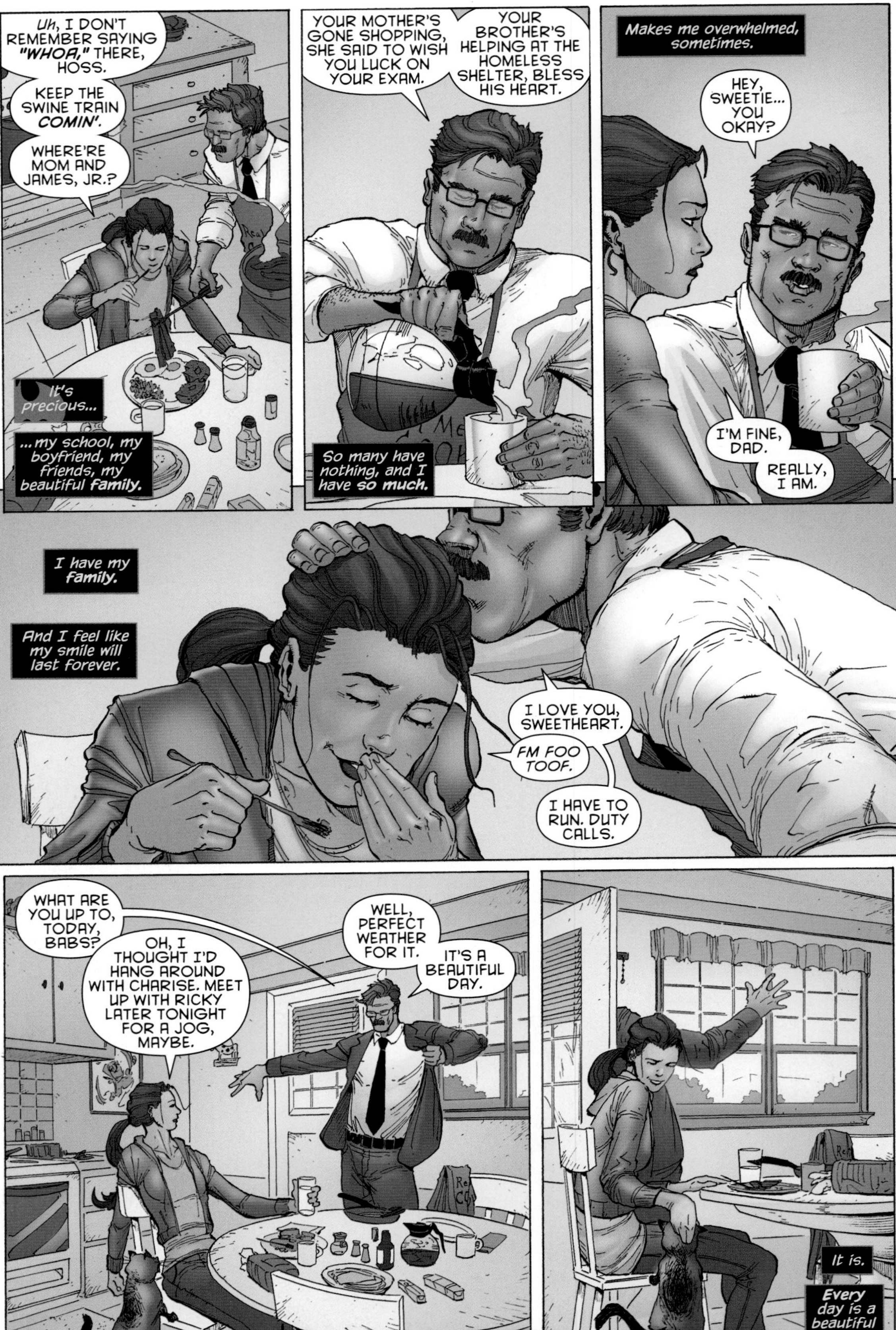

UH, I DON'T REMEMBER SAYING "WHOA," THERE, HOSS.
KEEP THE SWINE TRAIN COMIN'.
WHERE'RE MOM AND JAMES, JR.?
It's precious...
...my school, my boyfriend, my friends, my beautiful family.
YOUR MOTHER'S GONE SHOPPING, SHE SAID TO WISH YOU LUCK ON YOUR EXAM.
YOUR BROTHER'S HELPING AT THE HOMELESS SHELTER, BLESS HIS HEART.
So many have nothing, and I have so much.
Makes me overwhelmed, sometimes.
HEY, SWEETIE... YOU OKAY?
I'M FINE, DAD.
REALLY, I AM.
I have my family.
And I feel like my smile will last forever.
I LOVE YOU, SWEETHEART.
FM FOO TOOF.
I HAVE TO RUN. DUTY CALLS.
WHAT ARE YOU UP TO, TODAY, BABS?
OH, I THOUGHT I'D HANG AROUND WITH CHARISE. MEET UP WITH RICKY LATER TONIGHT FOR A JOG, MAYBE.
WELL, PERFECT WEATHER FOR IT.
IT'S A BEAUTIFUL DAY.
It is.
Every day is a beautiful day...

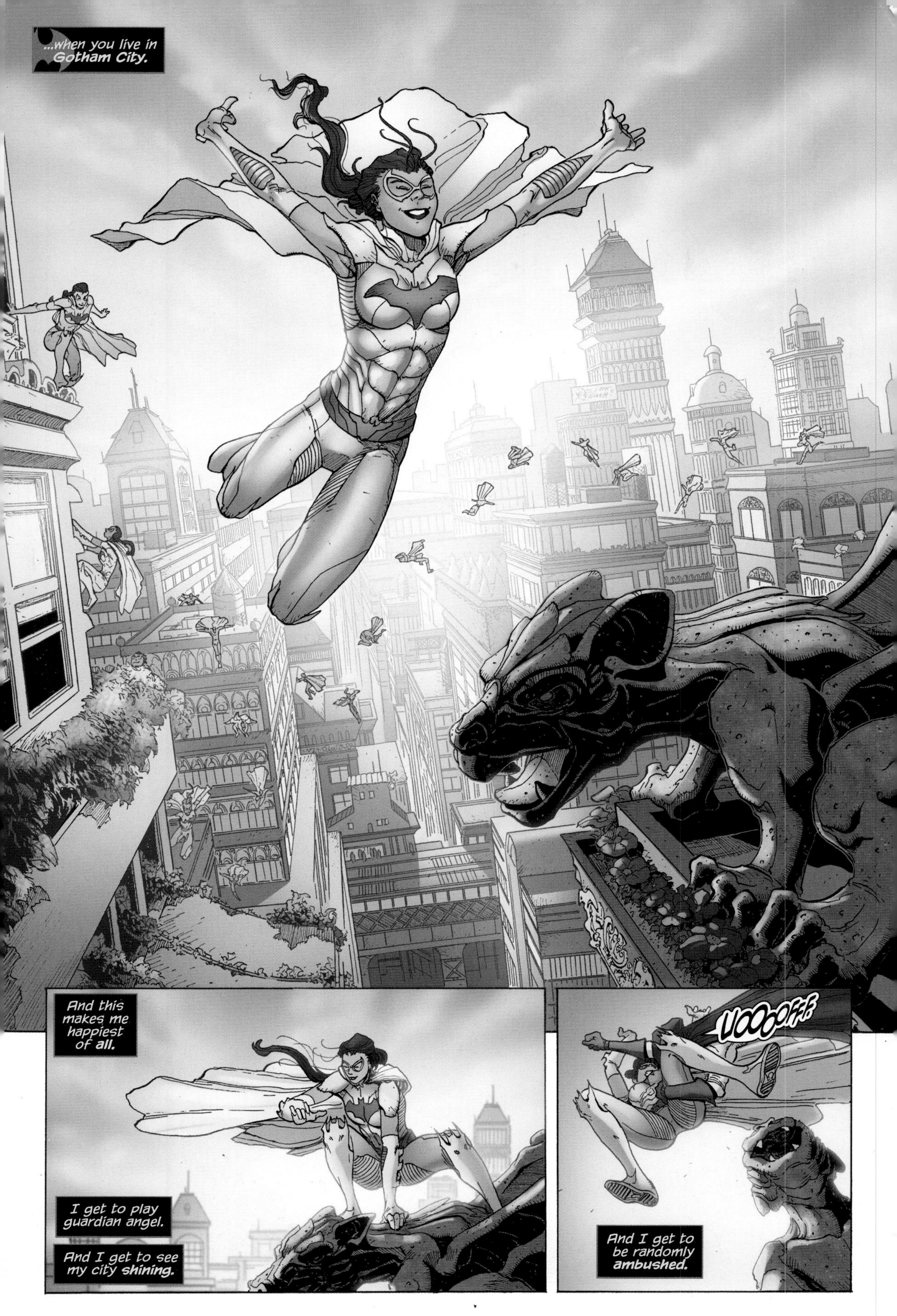

...when you live in Gotham City.
And this makes me happiest of all.
I get to play guardian angel.
And I get to see my city shining.
UOOOOFF!
And I get to be randomly ambushed.

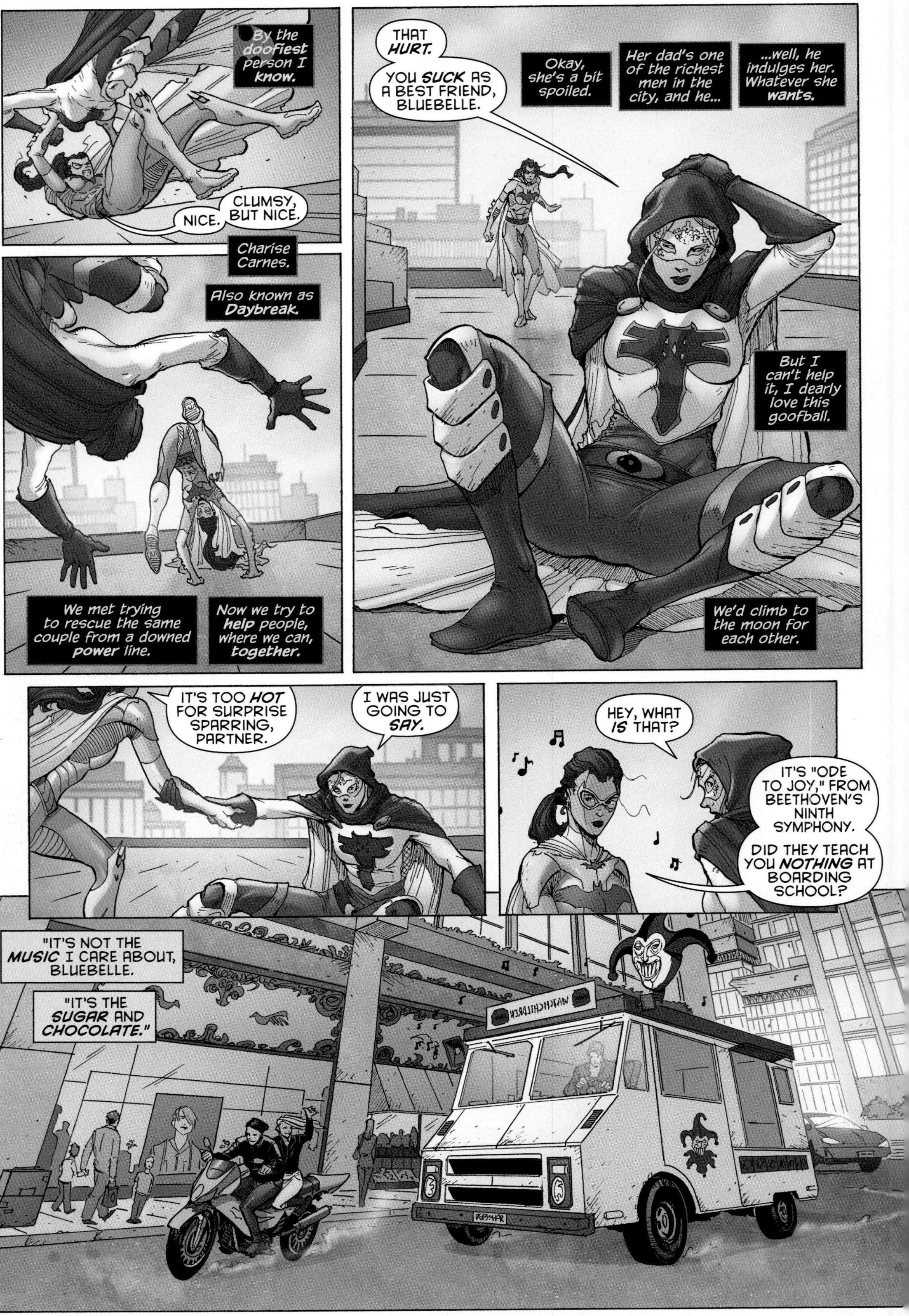
By the doofiest person I know.
CLUMSY, BUT NICE.
NICE.
Charise Carnes.
Also known as Daybreak.
We met trying to rescue the same couple from a downed power line.
Now we try to help people, where we can, together.
THAT HURT.
YOU SUCK AS A BEST FRIEND, BLUEBELLE.
Okay, she's a bit spoiled.
Her dad's one of the richest men in the city, and he...
...well, he indulges her. Whatever she wants.
But I can't help it, I dearly love this goofball.
We'd climb to the moon for each other.
IT'S TOO HOT FOR SURPRISE SPARRING, PARTNER.
I WAS JUST GOING TO SAY.
HEY, WHAT IS THAT?
IT'S "ODE TO JOY," FROM BEETHOVEN'S NINTH SYMPHONY.
DID THEY TEACH YOU NOTHING AT BOARDING SCHOOL?
"IT'S NOT THE MUSIC I CARE ABOUT, BLUEBELLE.
"IT'S THE SUGAR AND CHOCOLATE."

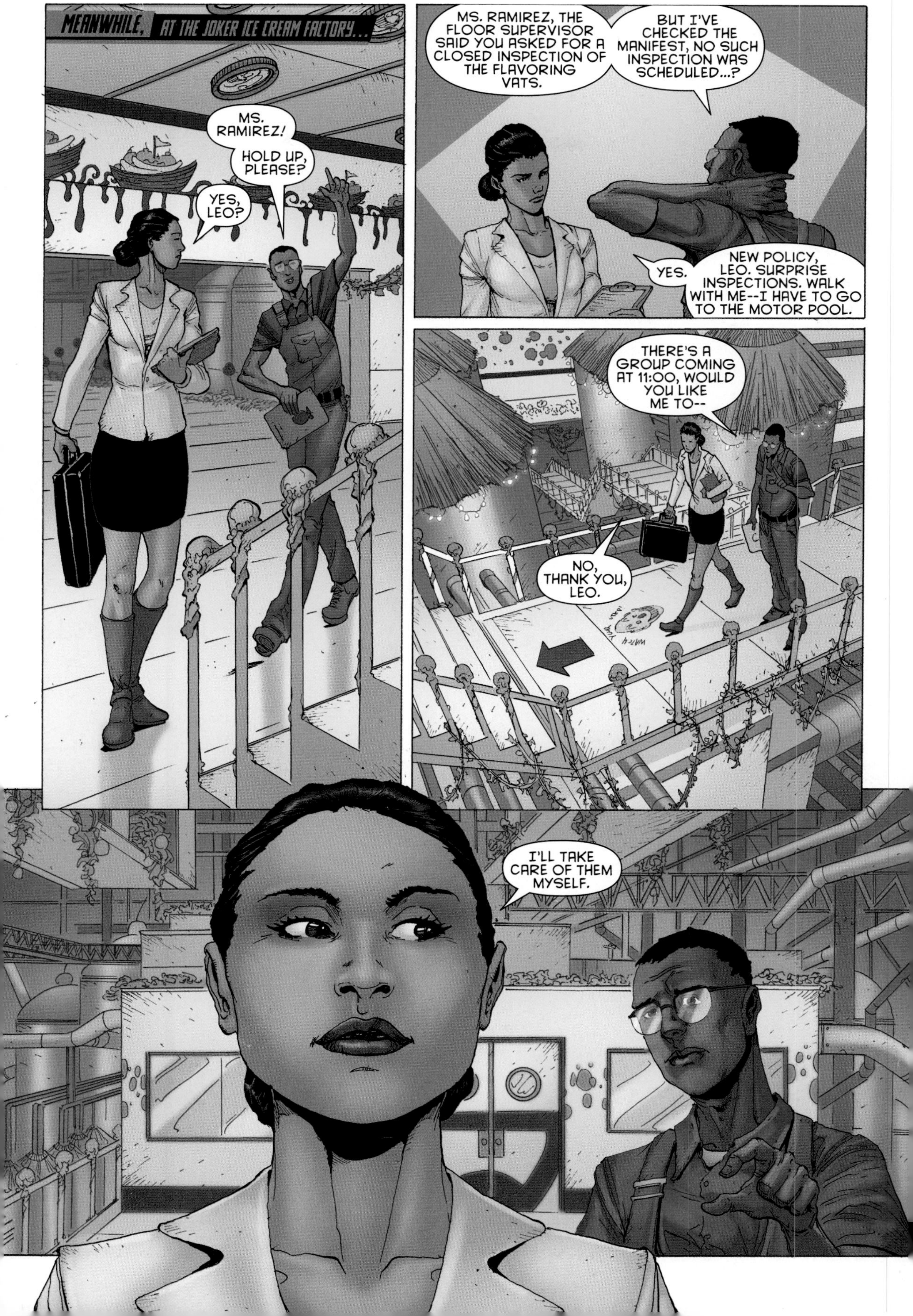
MEANWHILE, AT THE JOKER ICE CREAM FACTORY...
MS. RAMIREZ!
HOLD UP, PLEASE?
YES, LEO?
MS. RAMIREZ, THE FLOOR SUPERVISOR SAID YOU ASKED FOR A CLOSED INSPECTION OF THE FLAVORING VATS.
BUT I'VE CHECKED THE MANIFEST, NO SUCH INSPECTION WAS SCHEDULED...?
YES.
NEW POLICY, LEO. SURPRISE INSPECTIONS. WALK WITH ME--I HAVE TO GO TO THE MOTOR POOL.
THERE'S A GROUP COMING AT 11:00, WOULD YOU LIKE ME TO--
NO, THANK YOU, LEO.
I'LL TAKE CARE OF THEM MYSELF.

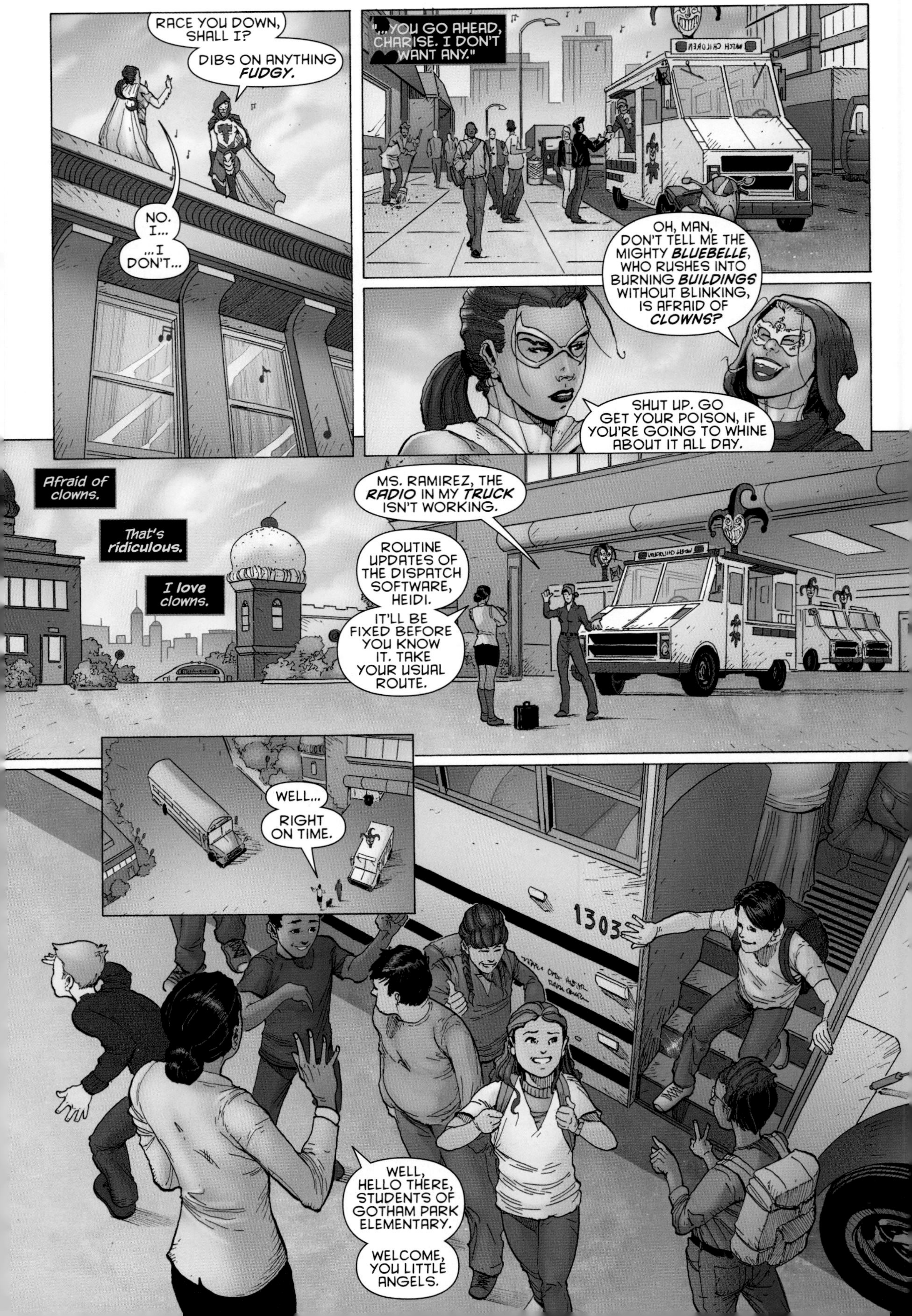
RACE YOU DOWN, SHALL I?
DIBS ON ANYTHING *FUDGY.*
NO. I...
...I DON'T...
"...YOU GO AHEAD, CHARISE. I DON'T WANT ANY."
OH, MAN, DON'T TELL ME THE MIGHTY *BLUEBELLE*, WHO RUSHES INTO BURNING *BUILDINGS* WITHOUT BLINKING, IS AFRAID OF *CLOWNS?*
SHUT UP. GO GET YOUR POISON, IF YOU'RE GOING TO WHINE ABOUT IT ALL DAY.
Afraid of clowns.
That's ridiculous.
I love clowns.
MS. RAMIREZ, THE *RADIO* IN MY *TRUCK* ISN'T WORKING.
ROUTINE UPDATES OF THE DISPATCH SOFTWARE, HEIDI.
IT'LL BE FIXED BEFORE YOU KNOW IT. TAKE YOUR USUAL ROUTE.
WELL...
RIGHT ON TIME.
1303
WELL, HELLO THERE, STUDENTS OF GOTHAM PARK ELEMENTARY.
WELCOME, YOU LITTLE ANGELS.

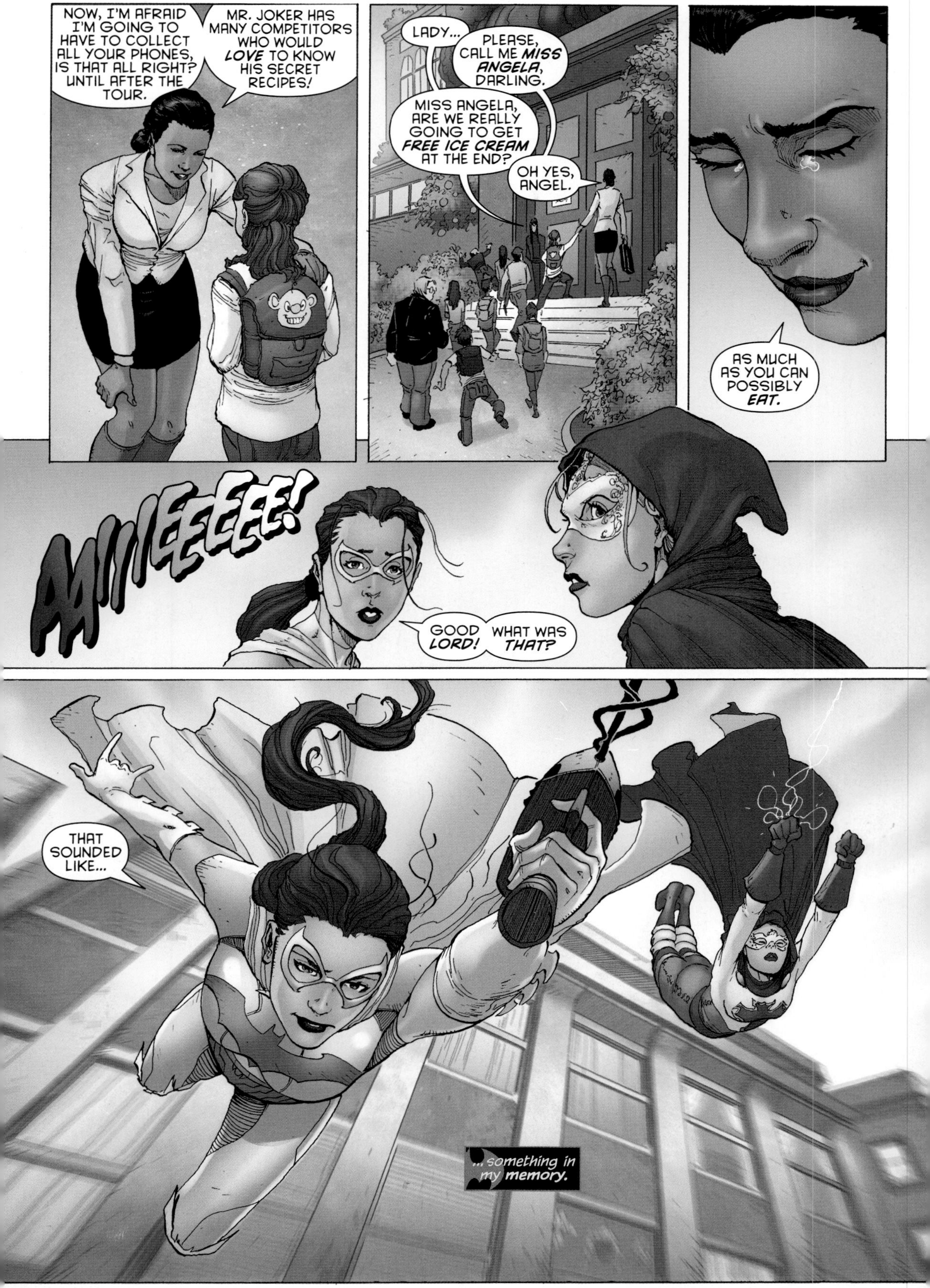
NOW, I'M AFRAID I'M GOING TO HAVE TO COLLECT ALL YOUR PHONES, IS THAT ALL RIGHT? UNTIL AFTER THE TOUR.
MR. JOKER HAS MANY COMPETITORS WHO WOULD LOVE TO KNOW HIS SECRET RECIPES!
LADY...
PLEASE, CALL ME MISS ANGELA, DARLING.
MISS ANGELA, ARE WE REALLY GOING TO GET FREE ICE CREAM AT THE END?
OH YES, ANGEL.
AS MUCH AS YOU CAN POSSIBLY EAT.
AAIIIEEEEEE!
GOOD LORD!
WHAT WAS THAT?
THAT SOUNDED LIKE...
...something in my memory.

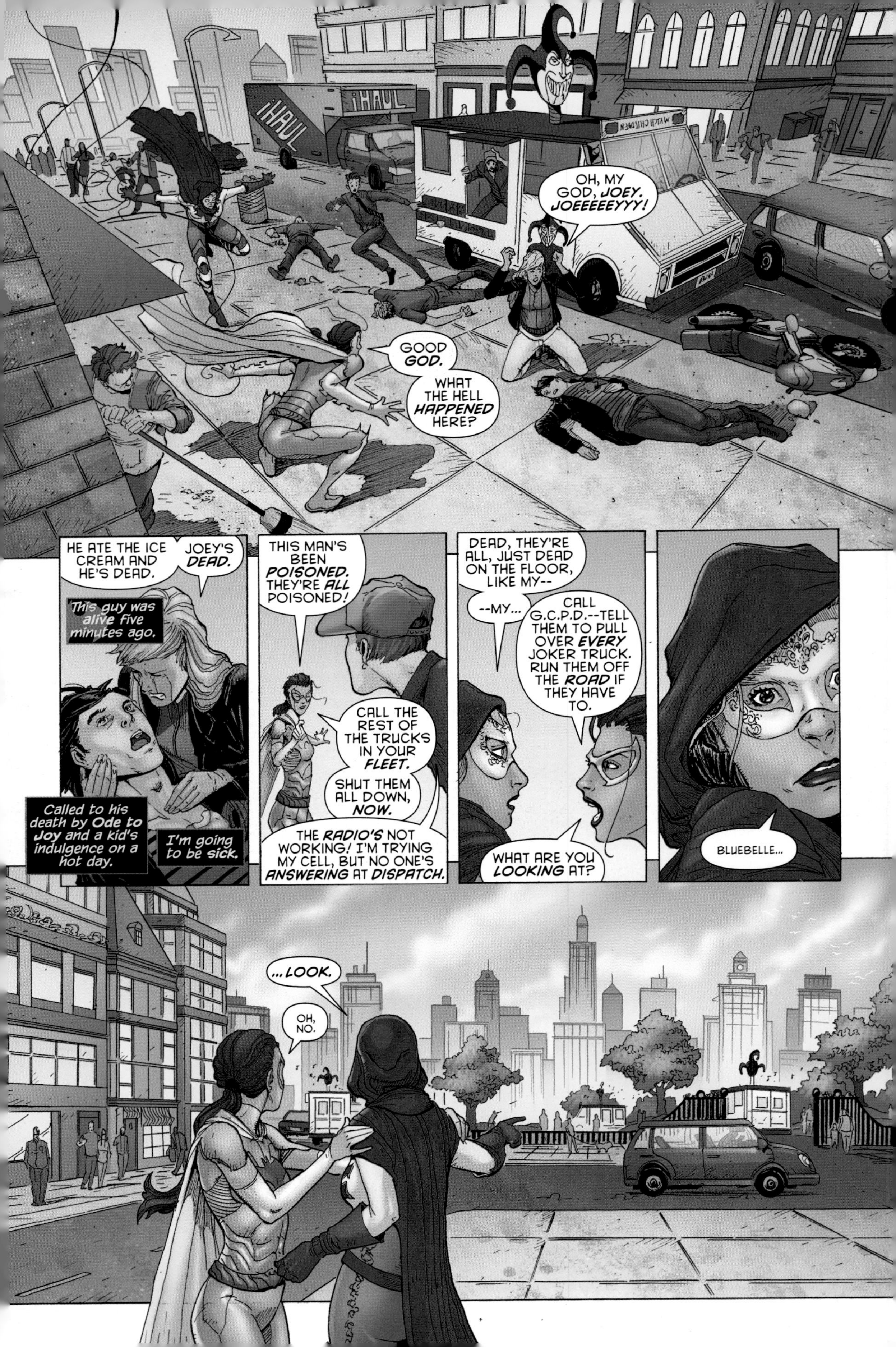
iHAUL
iHAUL
WATCH CHILDREN
OH, MY GOD, JOEY. JOEEEEEYYY!
GOOD GOD.
WHAT THE HELL HAPPENED HERE?
HE ATE THE ICE CREAM AND HE'S DEAD.
JOEY'S DEAD.
This guy was alive five minutes ago.
Called to his death by Ode to Joy and a kid's indulgence on a hot day.
I'm going to be sick.
THIS MAN'S BEEN POISONED. THEY'RE ALL POISONED!
CALL THE REST OF THE TRUCKS IN YOUR FLEET.
SHUT THEM ALL DOWN, NOW.
THE RADIO'S NOT WORKING! I'M TRYING MY CELL, BUT NO ONE'S ANSWERING AT DISPATCH.
DEAD, THEY'RE ALL, JUST DEAD ON THE FLOOR, LIKE MY--
--MY...
CALL G.C.P.D.--TELL THEM TO PULL OVER EVERY JOKER TRUCK. RUN THEM OFF THE ROAD IF THEY HAVE TO.
WHAT ARE YOU LOOKING AT?
BLUEBELLE...
...LOOK.
OH, NO.

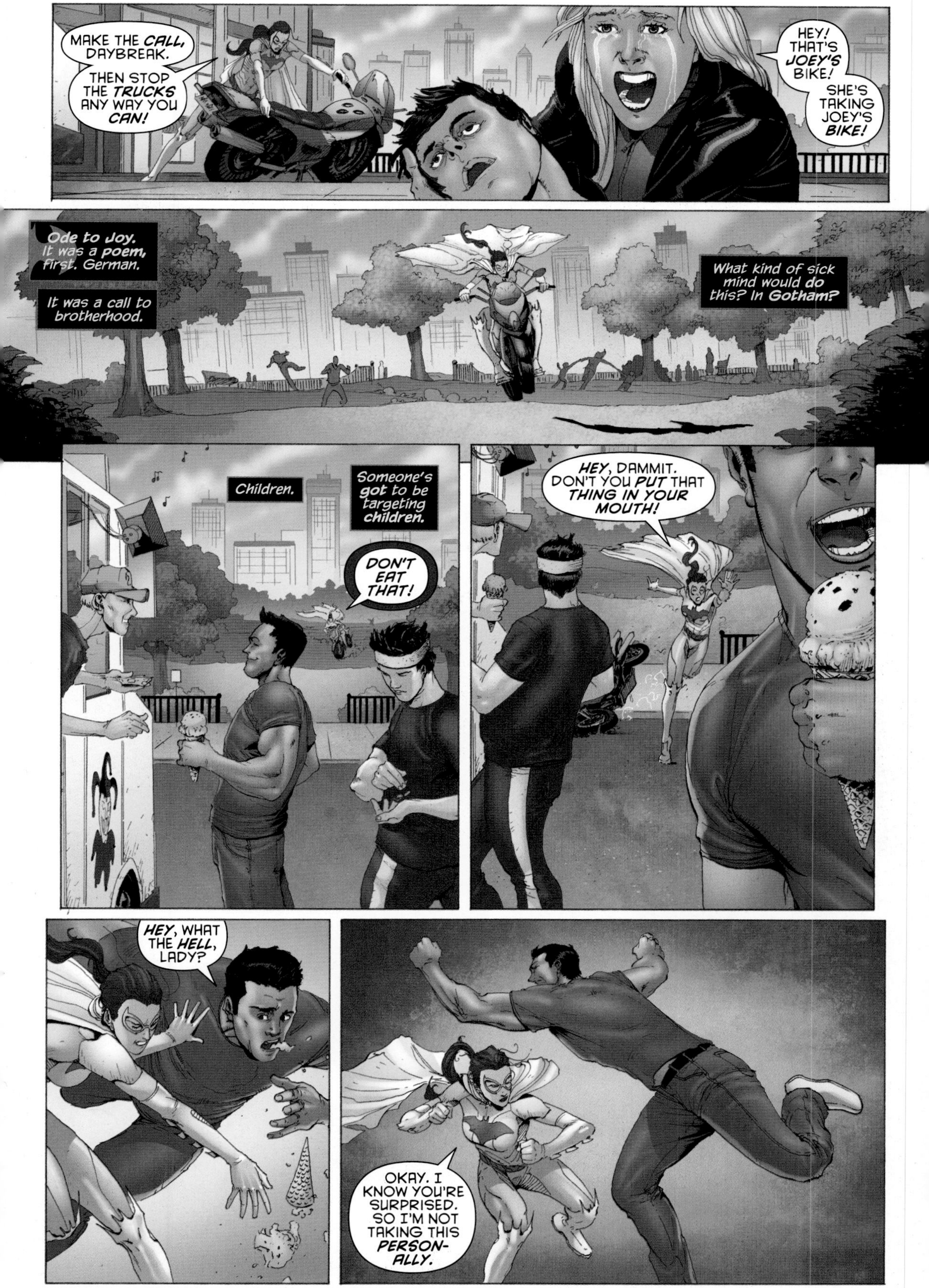
MAKE THE CALL, DAYBREAK.
THEN STOP THE TRUCKS ANY WAY YOU CAN!
HEY! THAT'S JOEY'S BIKE!
SHE'S TAKING JOEY'S BIKE!
Ode to Joy. It was a poem, first. German.
It was a call to brotherhood.
What kind of sick mind would do this? In Gotham?
Children.
Someone's got to be targeting children.
DON'T EAT THAT!
HEY, DAMMIT. DON'T YOU PUT THAT THING IN YOUR MOUTH!
HEY, WHAT THE HELL, LADY?
OKAY. I KNOW YOU'RE SURPRISED. SO I'M NOT TAKING THIS PERSON-ALLY.

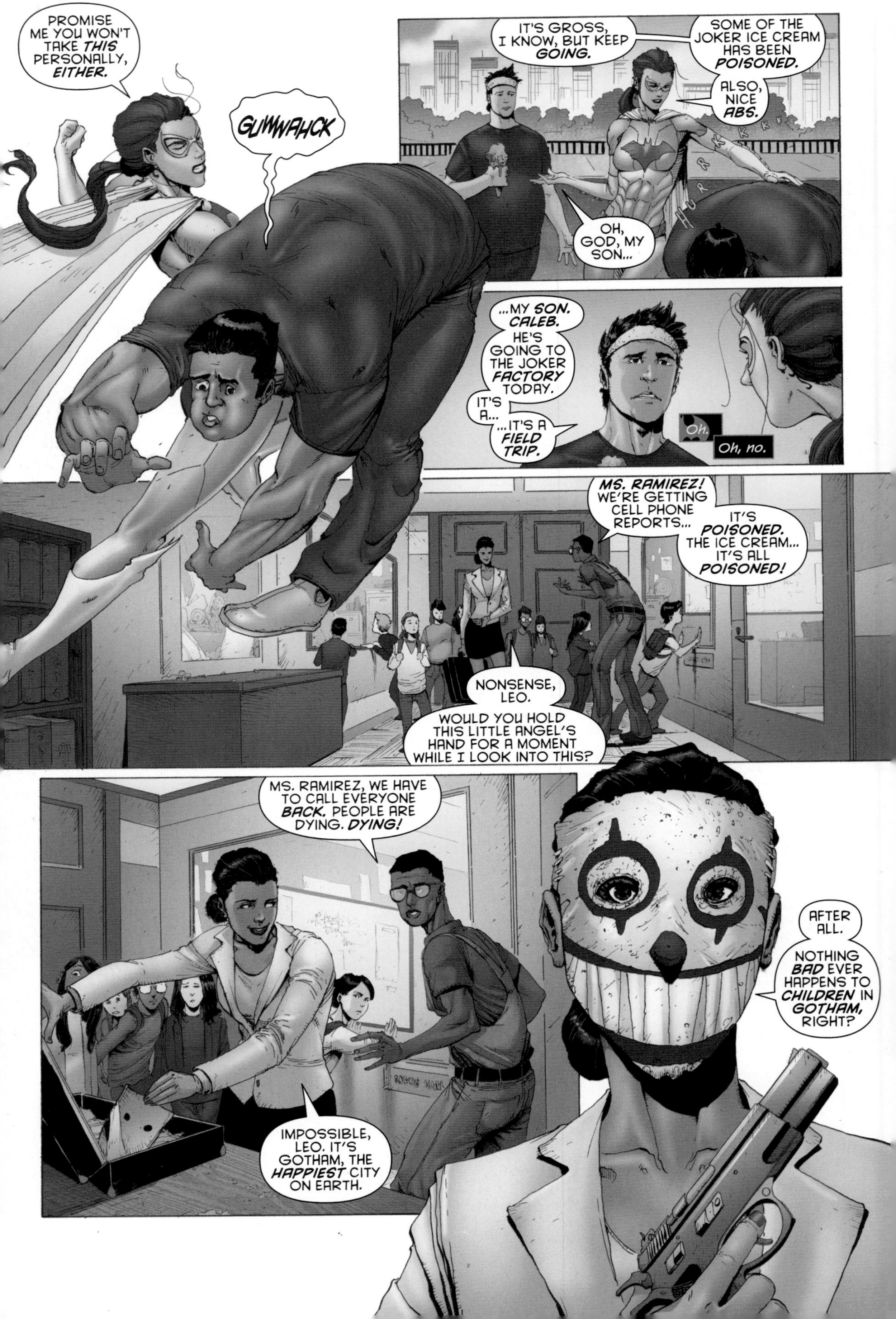

PROMISE ME YOU WON'T TAKE *THIS* PERSONALLY, *EITHER.*
GUMWAHCK
IT'S GROSS, I KNOW, BUT KEEP *GOING.*
SOME OF THE JOKER ICE CREAM HAS BEEN *POISONED.*
ALSO, NICE *ABS.*
OH, GOD, MY SON...
...MY *SON. CALEB.* HE'S GOING TO THE JOKER *FACTORY* TODAY.
IT'S A...
...IT'S A *FIELD TRIP.*
Oh.
Oh, no.
MS. RAMIREZ! WE'RE GETTING CELL PHONE REPORTS...
IT'S *POISONED.* THE ICE CREAM... IT'S ALL *POISONED!*
NONSENSE, LEO.
WOULD YOU HOLD THIS LITTLE ANGEL'S HAND FOR A MOMENT WHILE I LOOK INTO THIS?
MS. RAMIREZ, WE HAVE TO CALL EVERYONE *BACK.* PEOPLE ARE DYING. *DYING!*
IMPOSSIBLE, LEO. IT'S GOTHAM, THE *HAPPIEST* CITY ON EARTH.
AFTER ALL.
NOTHING *BAD* EVER HAPPENS TO *CHILDREN* IN *GOTHAM,* RIGHT?

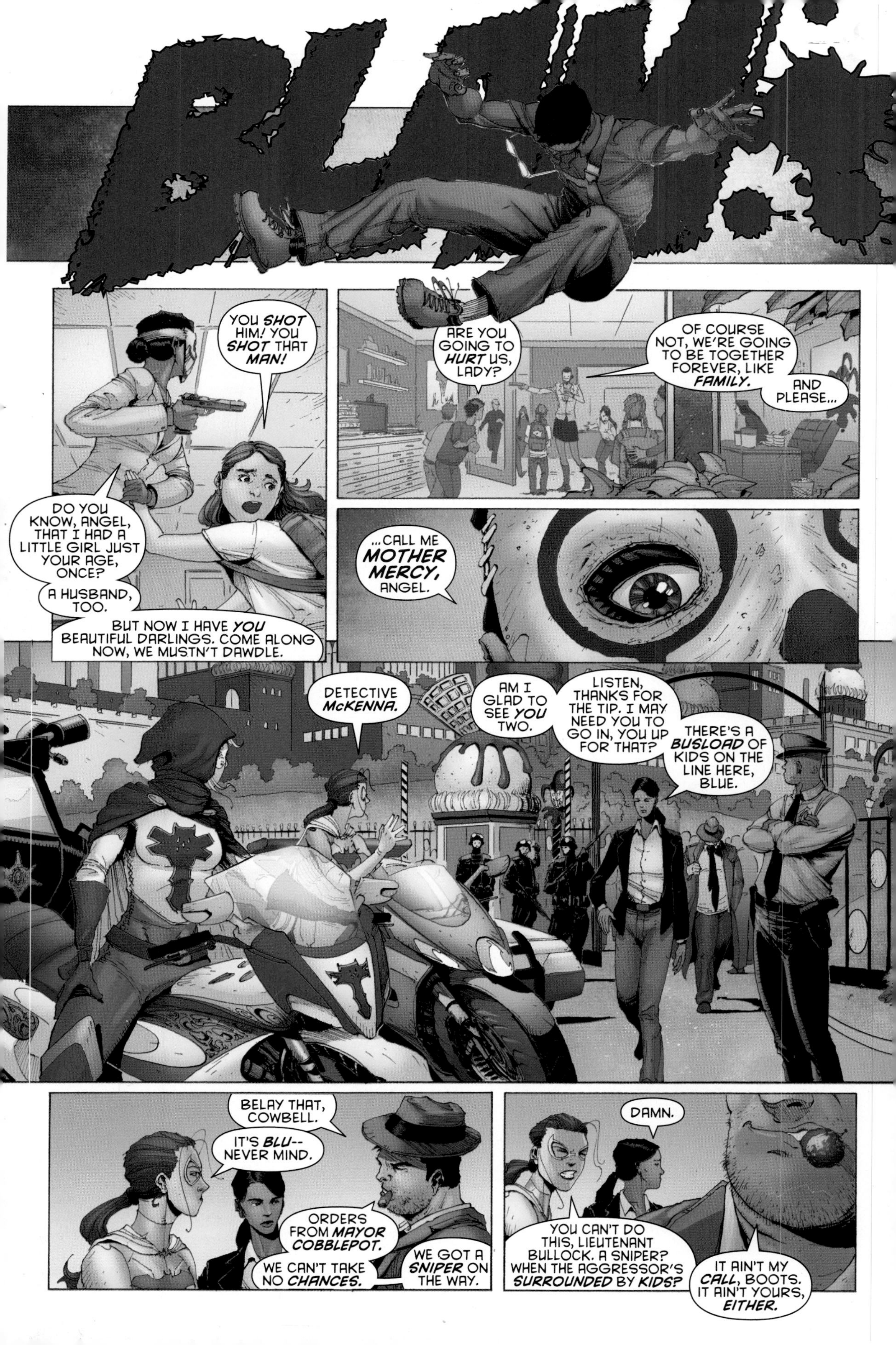

BLAM!
YOU SHOT HIM! YOU SHOT THAT MAN!
DO YOU KNOW, ANGEL, THAT I HAD A LITTLE GIRL JUST YOUR AGE, ONCE?
A HUSBAND, TOO.
BUT NOW I HAVE YOU BEAUTIFUL DARLINGS. COME ALONG NOW, WE MUSTN'T DAWDLE.
ARE YOU GOING TO HURT US, LADY?
OF COURSE NOT, WE'RE GOING TO BE TOGETHER FOREVER, LIKE FAMILY.
AND PLEASE...
...CALL ME MOTHER MERCY, ANGEL.
DETECTIVE McKENNA.
AM I GLAD TO SEE YOU TWO.
LISTEN, THANKS FOR THE TIP. I MAY NEED YOU TO GO IN, YOU UP FOR THAT?
THERE'S A BUSLOAD OF KIDS ON THE LINE HERE, BLUE.
BELAY THAT, COWBELL.
IT'S BLU-- NEVER MIND.
ORDERS FROM MAYOR COBBLEPOT.
WE CAN'T TAKE NO CHANCES.
WE GOT A SNIPER ON THE WAY.
DAMN.
YOU CAN'T DO THIS, LIEUTENANT BULLOCK. A SNIPER? WHEN THE AGGRESSOR'S SURROUNDED BY KIDS?
IT AIN'T MY CALL, BOOTS. IT AIN'T YOURS, EITHER.

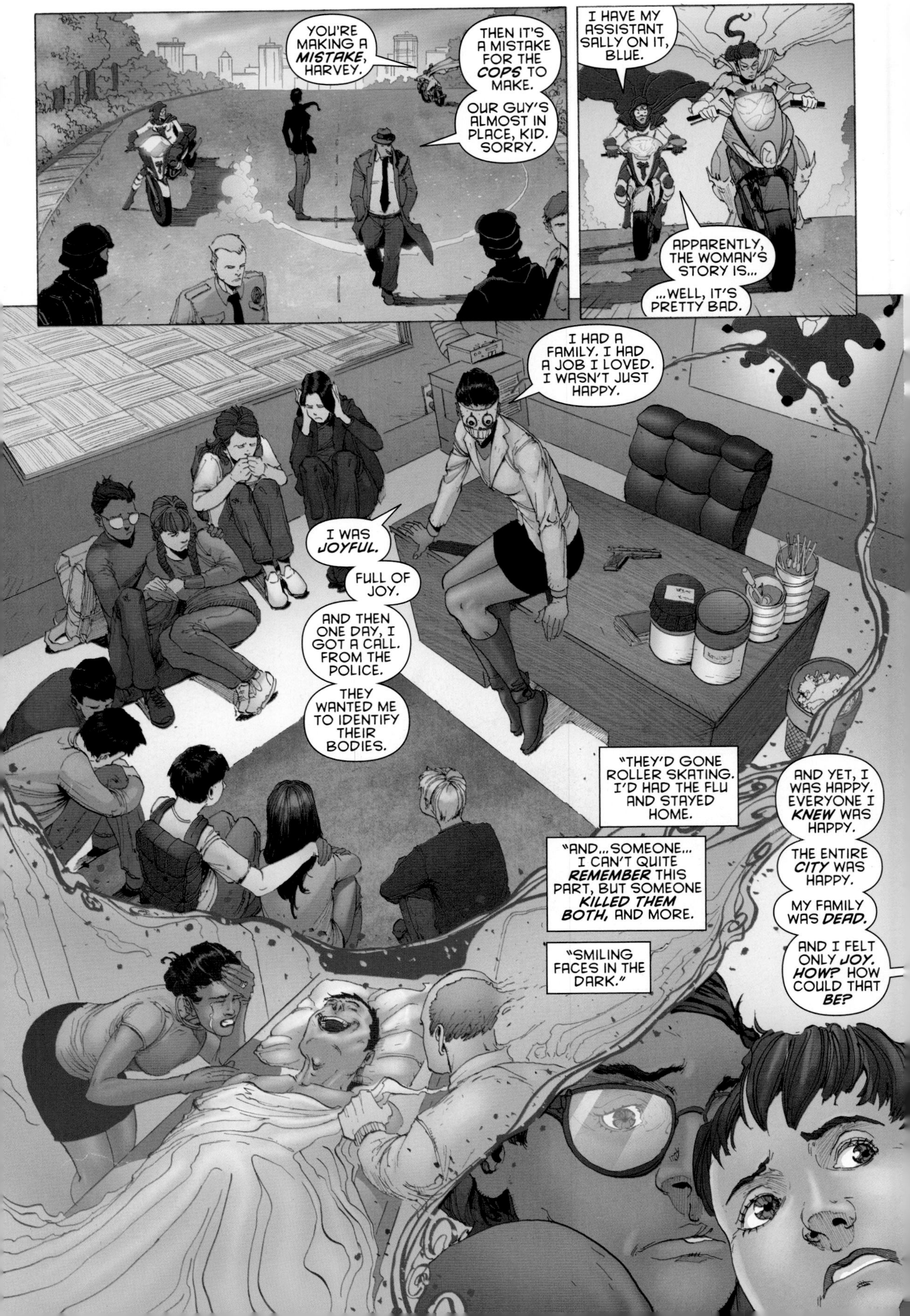
YOU'RE MAKING A *MISTAKE*, HARVEY.
THEN IT'S A MISTAKE FOR THE *COPS* TO MAKE.
OUR GUY'S ALMOST IN PLACE, KID. SORRY.
I HAVE MY ASSISTANT SALLY ON IT, BLUE.
APPARENTLY, THE WOMAN'S STORY IS...
...WELL, IT'S PRETTY BAD.
I HAD A FAMILY. I HAD A JOB I LOVED. I WASN'T JUST HAPPY.
I WAS *JOYFUL.*
FULL OF JOY.
AND THEN ONE DAY, I GOT A CALL. FROM THE POLICE.
THEY WANTED ME TO IDENTIFY THEIR BODIES.
"THEY'D GONE ROLLER SKATING. I'D HAD THE FLU AND STAYED HOME.
"AND...SOMEONE... I CAN'T QUITE *REMEMBER* THIS PART, BUT SOMEONE *KILLED THEM BOTH,* AND MORE.
"SMILING FACES IN THE DARK."
AND YET, I WAS HAPPY. EVERYONE I *KNEW* WAS HAPPY.
THE ENTIRE *CITY* WAS HAPPY.
MY FAMILY WAS *DEAD.*
AND I FELT ONLY *JOY. HOW?* HOW COULD THAT *BE?*

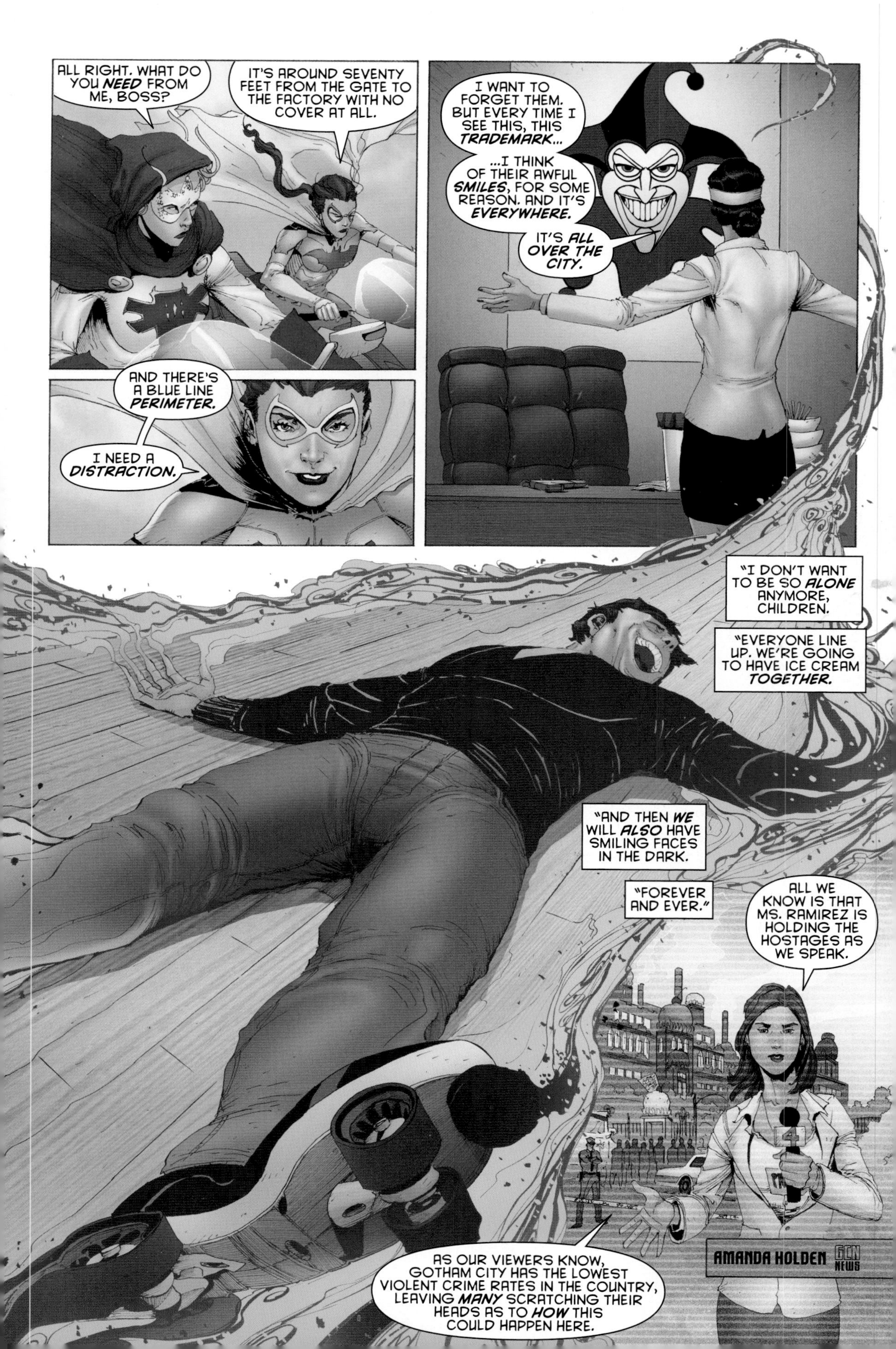
ALL RIGHT. WHAT DO YOU NEED FROM ME, BOSS?
IT'S AROUND SEVENTY FEET FROM THE GATE TO THE FACTORY WITH NO COVER AT ALL.
AND THERE'S A BLUE LINE PERIMETER.
I NEED A DISTRACTION.
I WANT TO FORGET THEM. BUT EVERY TIME I SEE THIS, THIS TRADEMARK...
...I THINK OF THEIR AWFUL SMILES, FOR SOME REASON. AND IT'S EVERYWHERE.
IT'S ALL OVER THE CITY.
"I DON'T WANT TO BE SO ALONE ANYMORE, CHILDREN.
"EVERYONE LINE UP. WE'RE GOING TO HAVE ICE CREAM TOGETHER.
"AND THEN WE WILL ALSO HAVE SMILING FACES IN THE DARK.
"FOREVER AND EVER."
ALL WE KNOW IS THAT MS. RAMIREZ IS HOLDING THE HOSTAGES AS WE SPEAK.
AS OUR VIEWERS KNOW, GOTHAM CITY HAS THE LOWEST VIOLENT CRIME RATES IN THE COUNTRY, LEAVING MANY SCRATCHING THEIR HEADS AS TO HOW THIS COULD HAPPEN HERE.
AMANDA HOLDEN
GCN NEWS

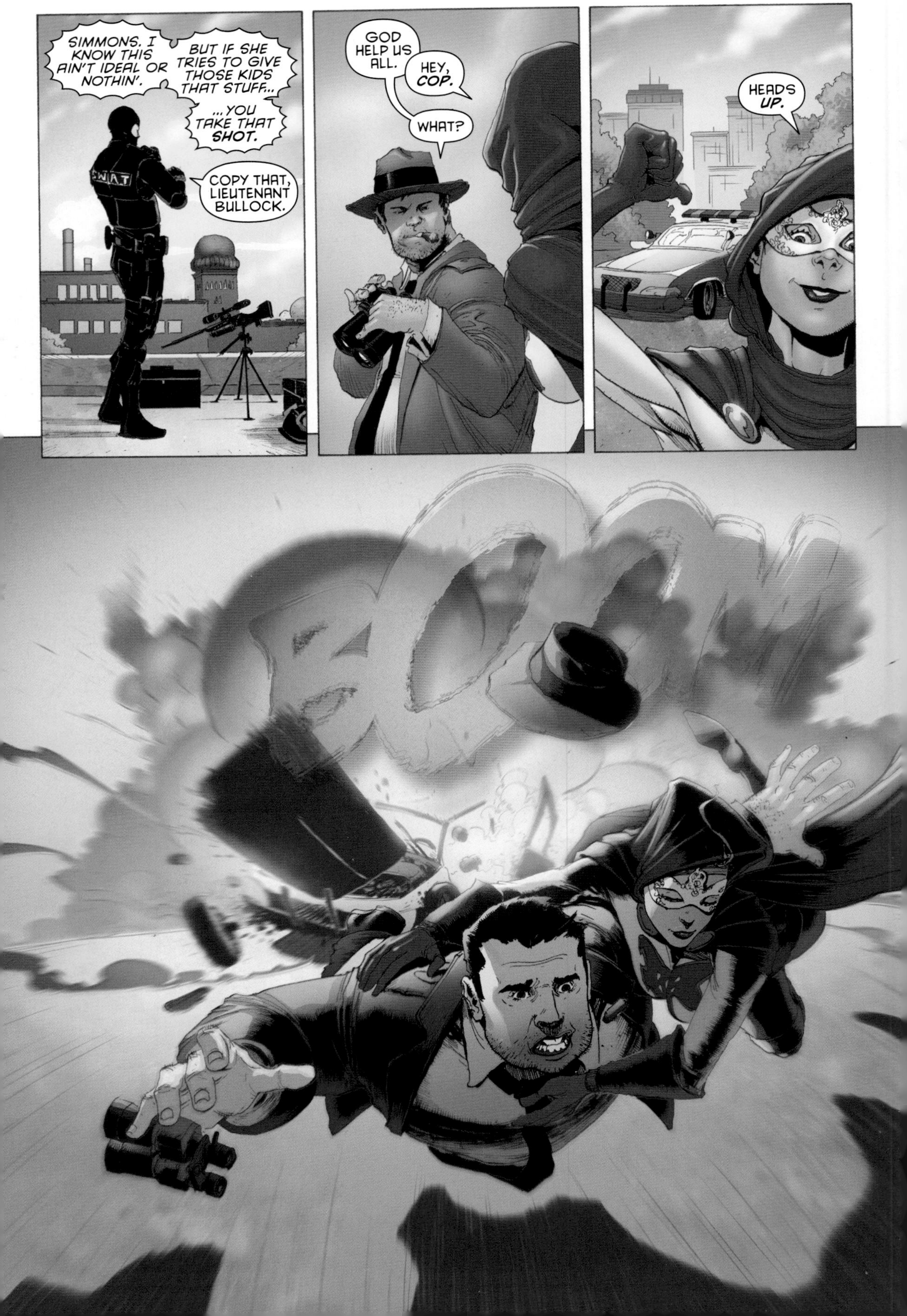
SIMMONS. I KNOW THIS AIN'T IDEAL OR NOTHIN'.
BUT IF SHE TRIES TO GIVE THOSE KIDS THAT STUFF...
...YOU TAKE THAT SHOT.
COPY THAT, LIEUTENANT BULLOCK.
GOD HELP US ALL.
HEY, COP.
WHAT?
HEADS UP.

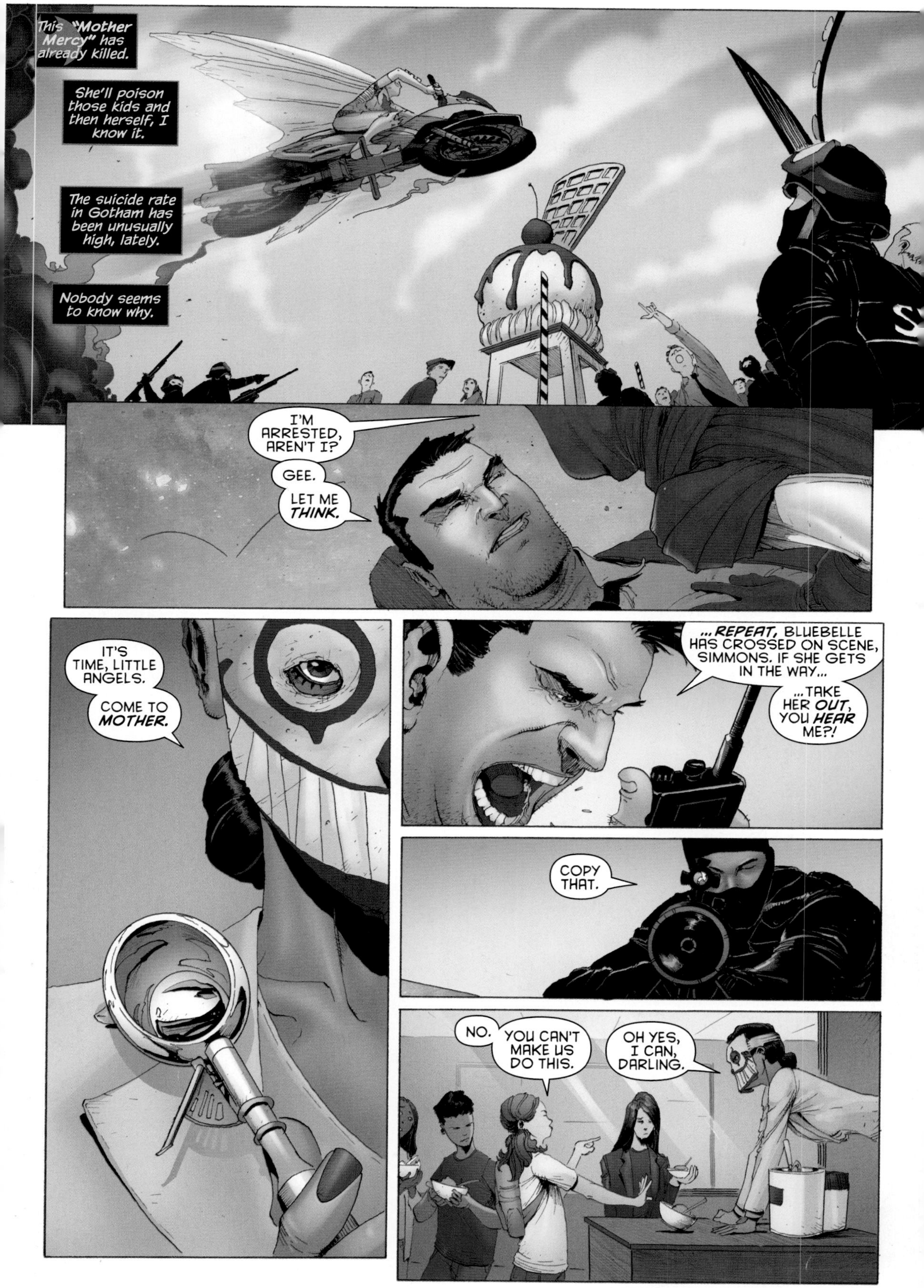
This "Mother Mercy" has already killed.
She'll poison those kids and then herself, I know it.
The suicide rate in Gotham has been unusually high, lately.
Nobody seems to know why.
I'M ARRESTED, AREN'T I?
GEE.
LET ME THINK.
IT'S TIME, LITTLE ANGELS.
COME TO MOTHER.
...REPEAT, BLUEBELLE HAS CROSSED ON SCENE, SIMMONS. IF SHE GETS IN THE WAY...
...TAKE HER OUT, YOU HEAR ME?!
COPY THAT.
NO.
YOU CAN'T MAKE US DO THIS.
OH YES, I CAN, DARLING.

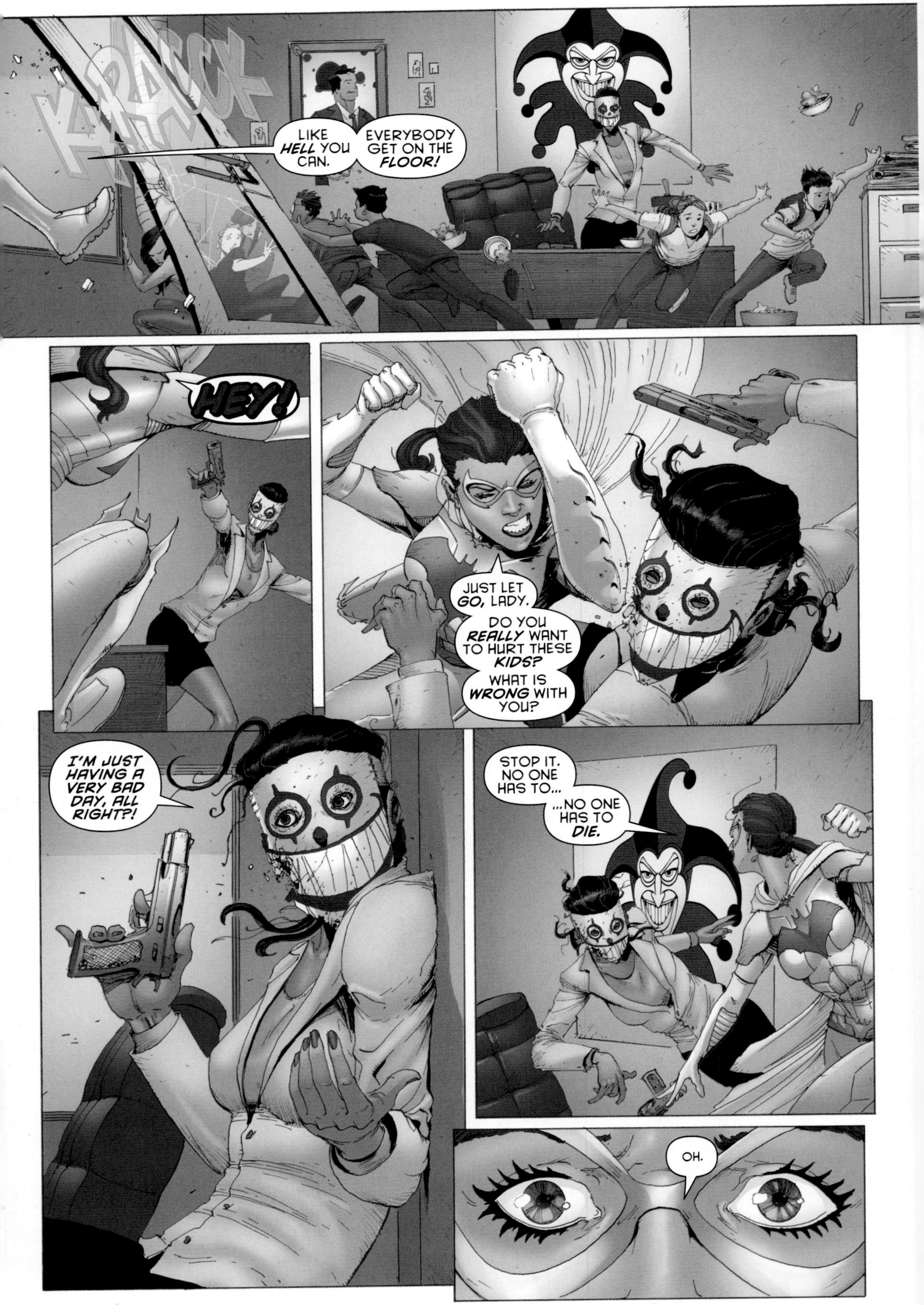
KRACK
LIKE HELL YOU CAN.
EVERYBODY GET ON THE FLOOR!
HEY!
JUST LET GO, LADY.
DO YOU REALLY WANT TO HURT THESE KIDS?
WHAT IS WRONG WITH YOU?
I'M JUST HAVING A VERY BAD DAY, ALL RIGHT?!
STOP IT. NO ONE HAS TO...
...NO ONE HAS TO DIE.
OH.

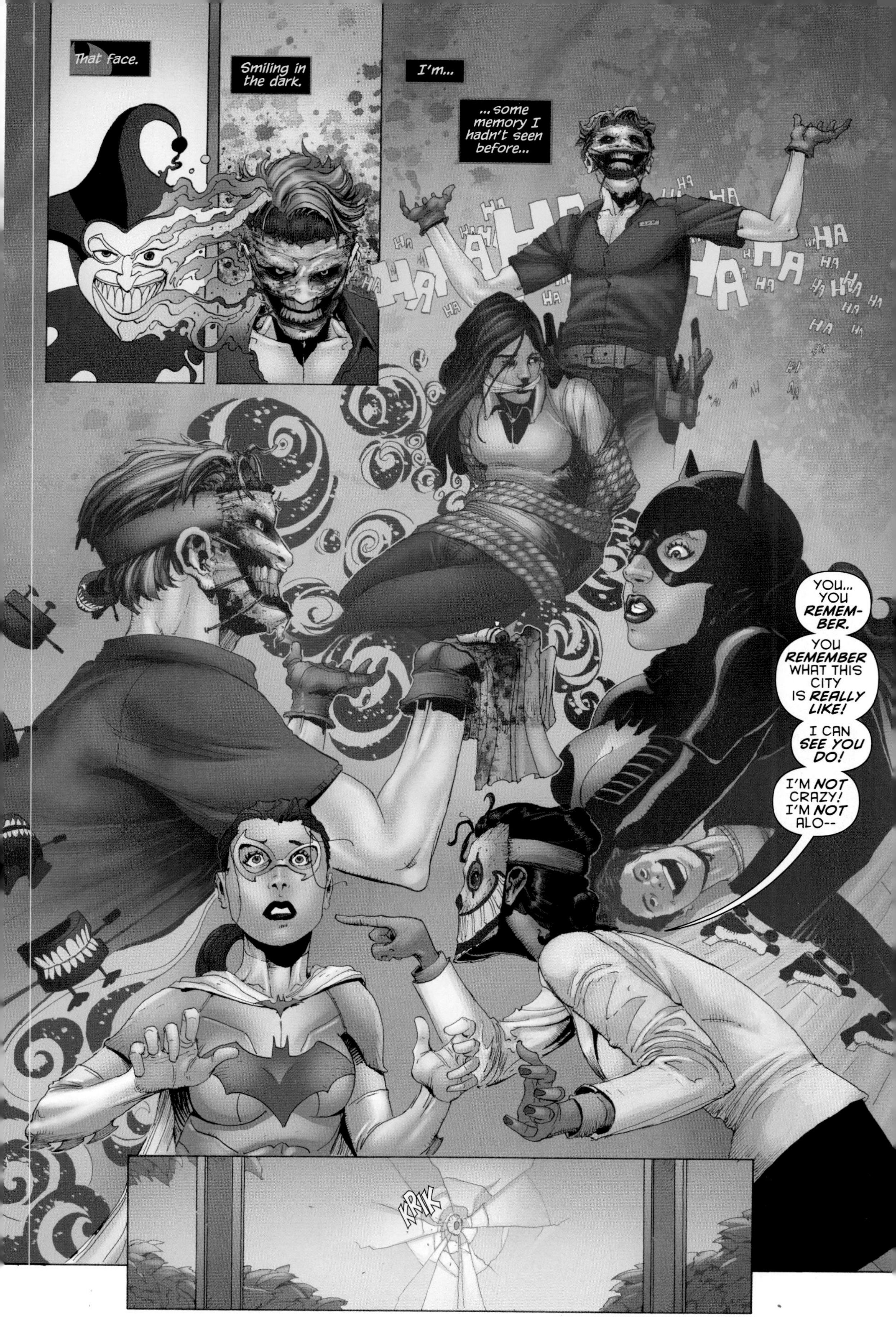

That face.
Smiling in the dark.
I'm...
...some memory I hadn't seen before...
HA HA HA HA HA HA HA HA HA HA HA HA HA HA HA HA HA HA HA HA
YOU... YOU REMEMBER.
YOU REMEMBER WHAT THIS CITY IS REALLY LIKE!
I CAN SEE YOU DO!
I'M NOT CRAZY! I'M NOT ALO--
KRIK

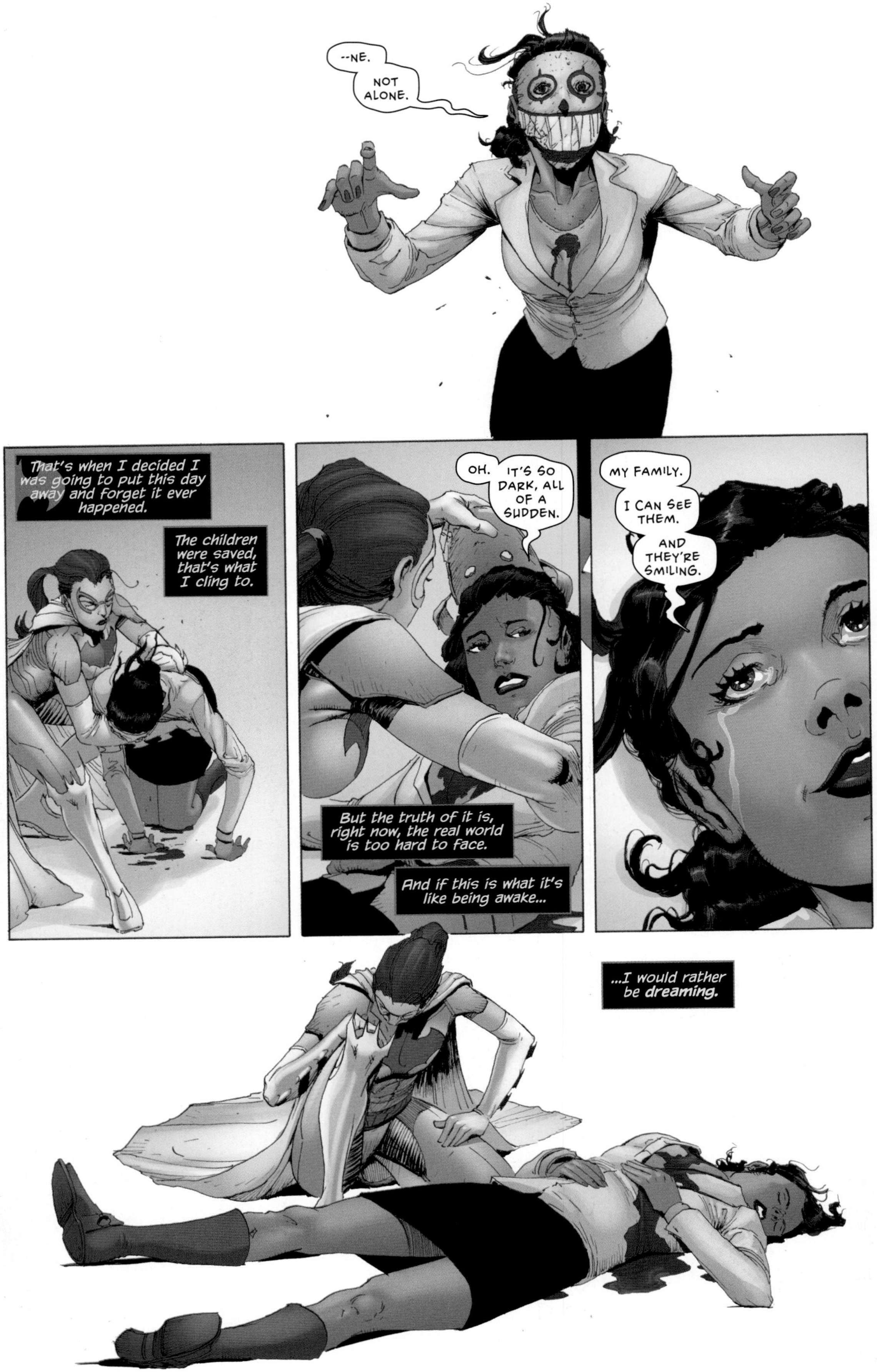
--NE.
NOT ALONE.
That's when I decided I was going to put this day away and forget it ever happened.
The children were saved, that's what I cling to.
OH.
IT'S SO DARK, ALL OF A SUDDEN.
But the truth of it is, right now, the real world is too hard to face.
And if this is what it's like being awake...
MY FAMILY.
I CAN SEE THEM.
AND THEY'RE SMILING.
...I would rather be ***dreaming.***

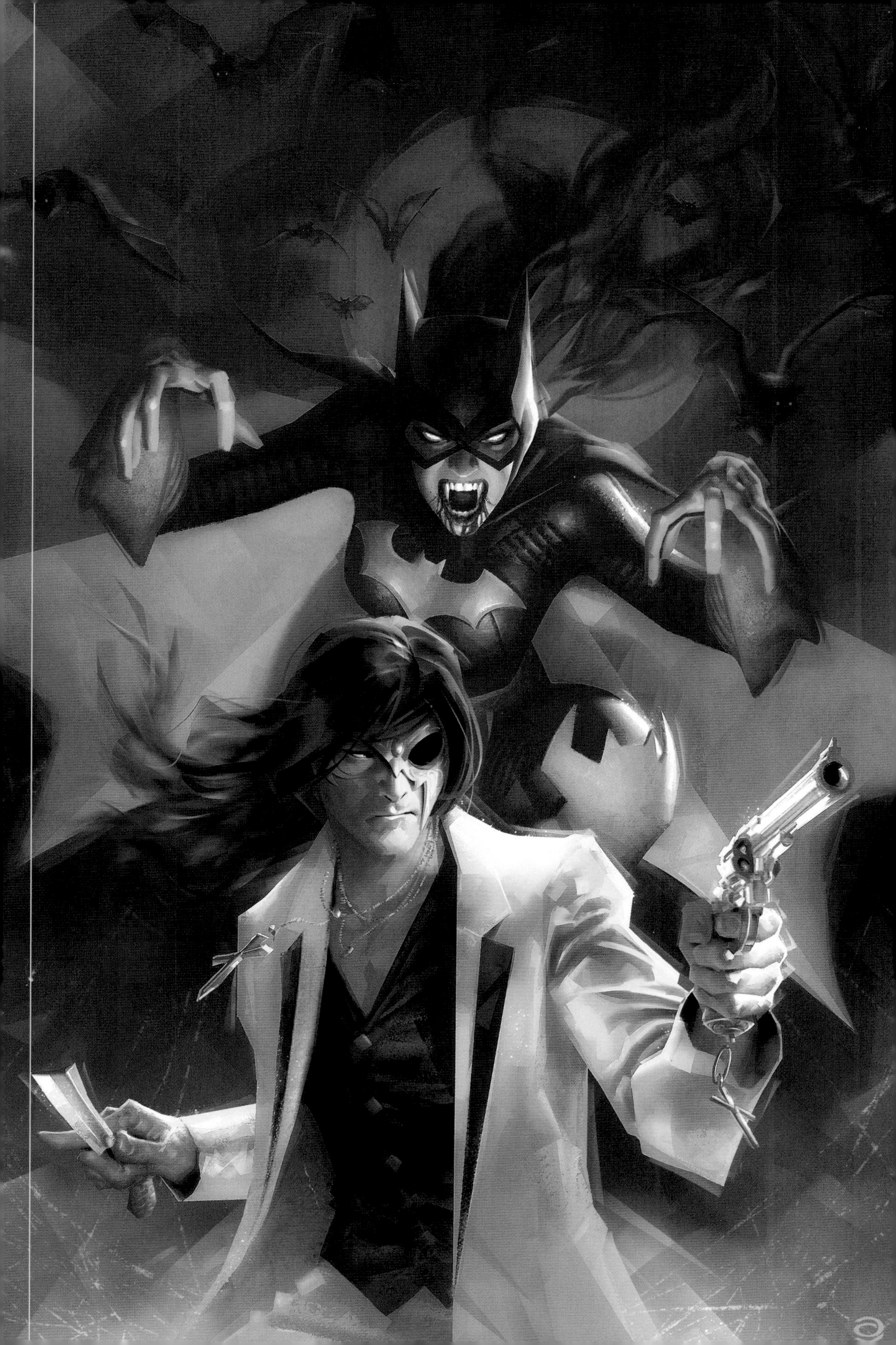

SIMONE writer FERNANDO PASARIN penciller JONATHAN GLAPION inker BLOND colorist ALEX GARNER cover artist

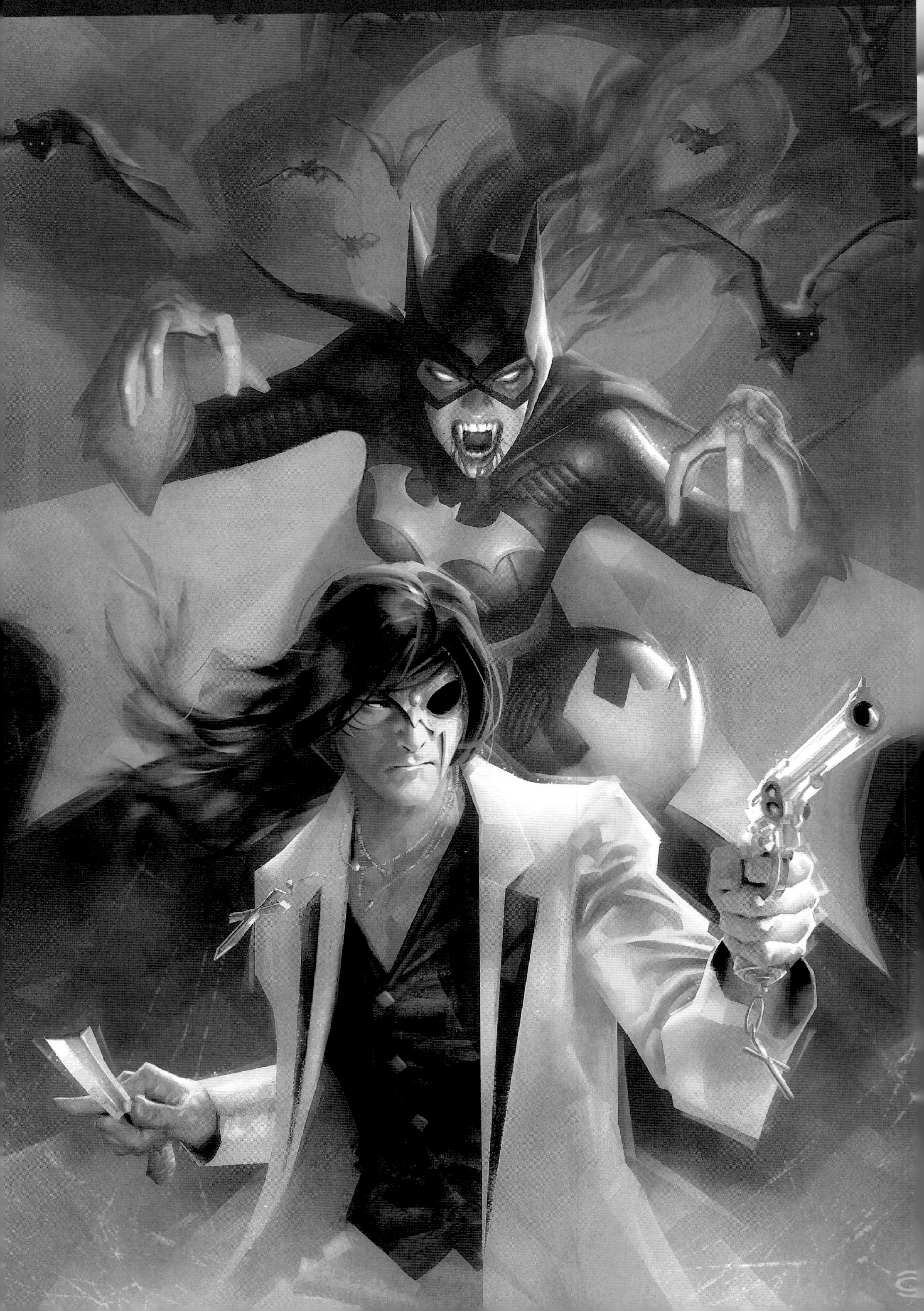

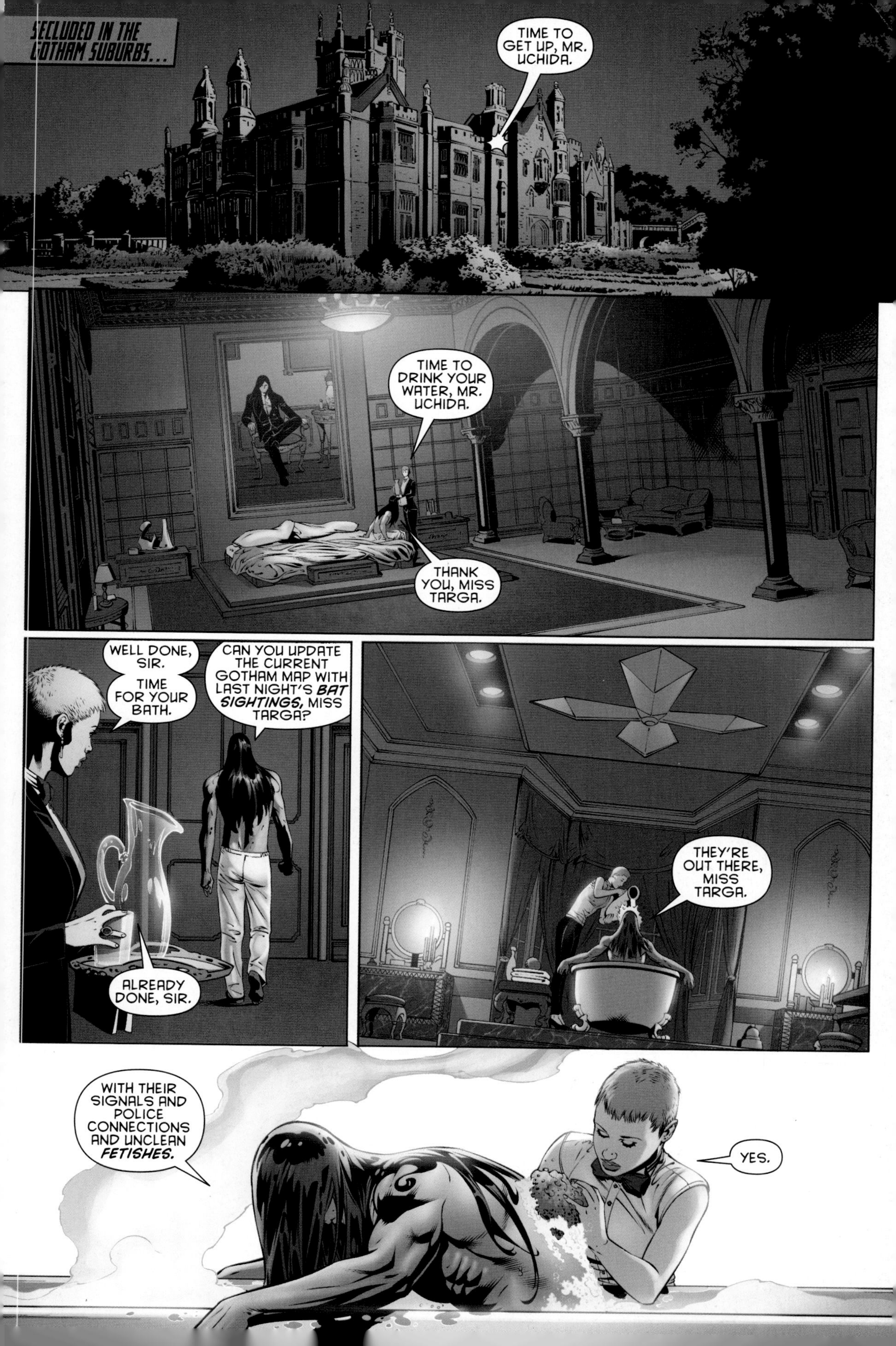
SECLUDED IN THE GOTHAM SUBURBS...
TIME TO GET UP, MR. UCHIDA.
TIME TO DRINK YOUR WATER, MR. UCHIDA.
THANK YOU, MISS TARGA.
WELL DONE, SIR.
TIME FOR YOUR BATH.
CAN YOU UPDATE THE CURRENT GOTHAM MAP WITH LAST NIGHT'S BAT SIGHTINGS, MISS TARGA?
ALREADY DONE, SIR.
THEY'RE OUT THERE, MISS TARGA.
WITH THEIR SIGNALS AND POLICE CONNECTIONS AND UNCLEAN FETISHES.
YES.

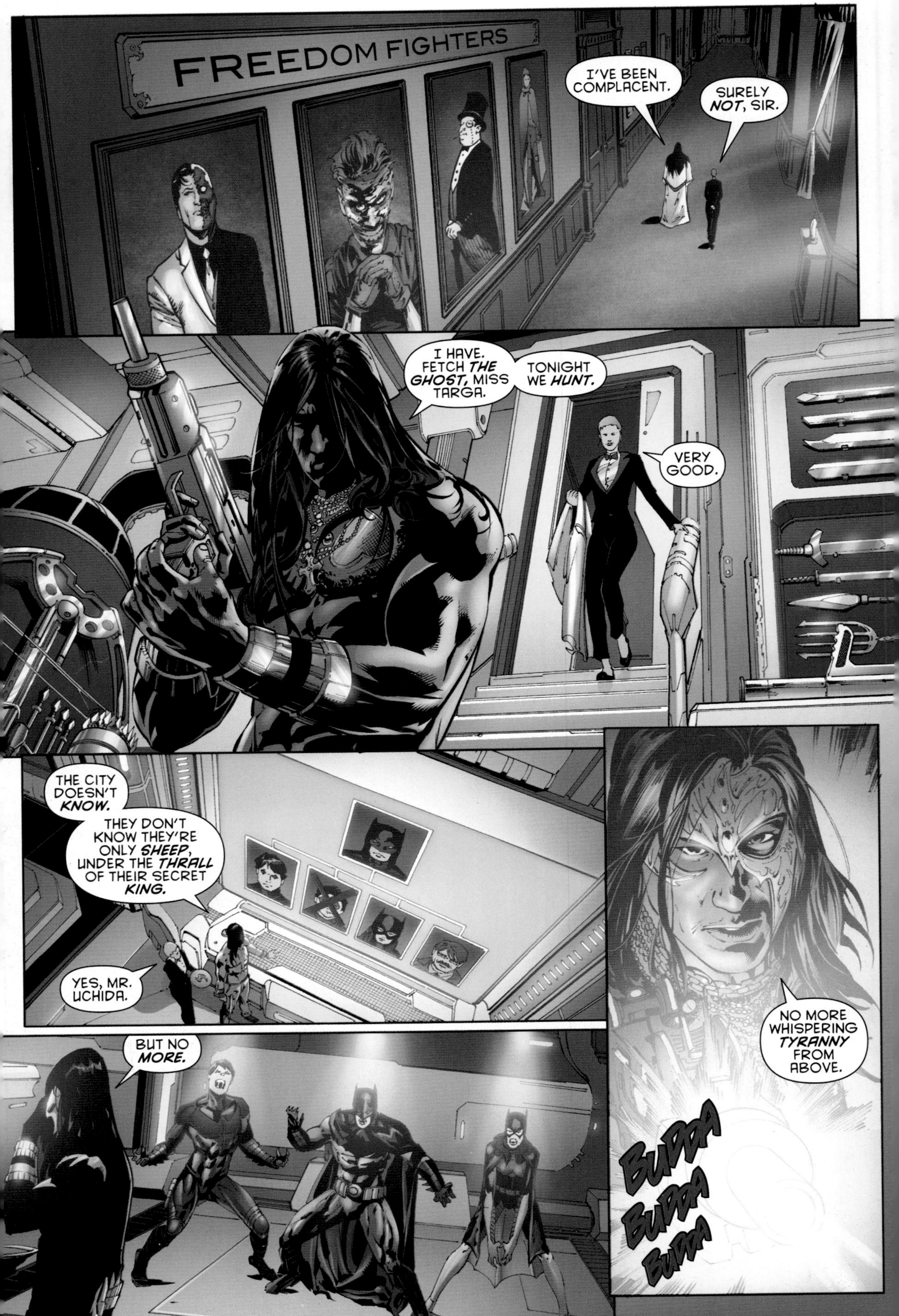
FREEDOM FIGHTERS
I'VE BEEN COMPLACENT.
SURELY NOT, SIR.
I HAVE. FETCH THE GHOST, MISS TARGA.
TONIGHT WE HUNT.
VERY GOOD.
THE CITY DOESN'T KNOW.
THEY DON'T KNOW THEY'RE ONLY SHEEP, UNDER THE THRALL OF THEIR SECRET KING.
YES, MR. UCHIDA.
BUT NO MORE.
NO MORE WHISPERING TYRANNY FROM ABOVE.
BUDDA BUDDA BUDDA BUDDA

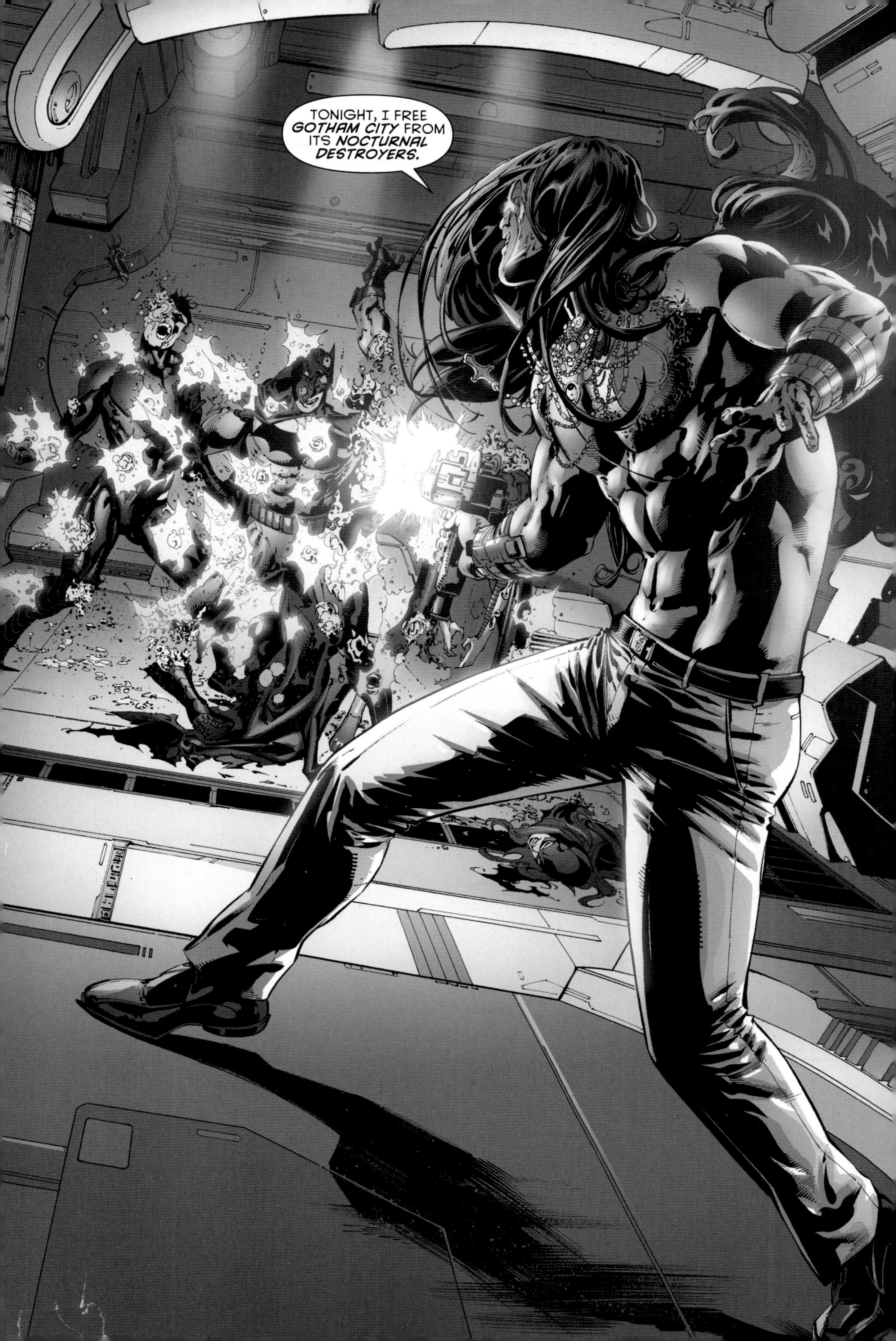
TONIGHT, I FREE GOTHAM CITY FROM ITS NOCTURNAL DESTROYERS.

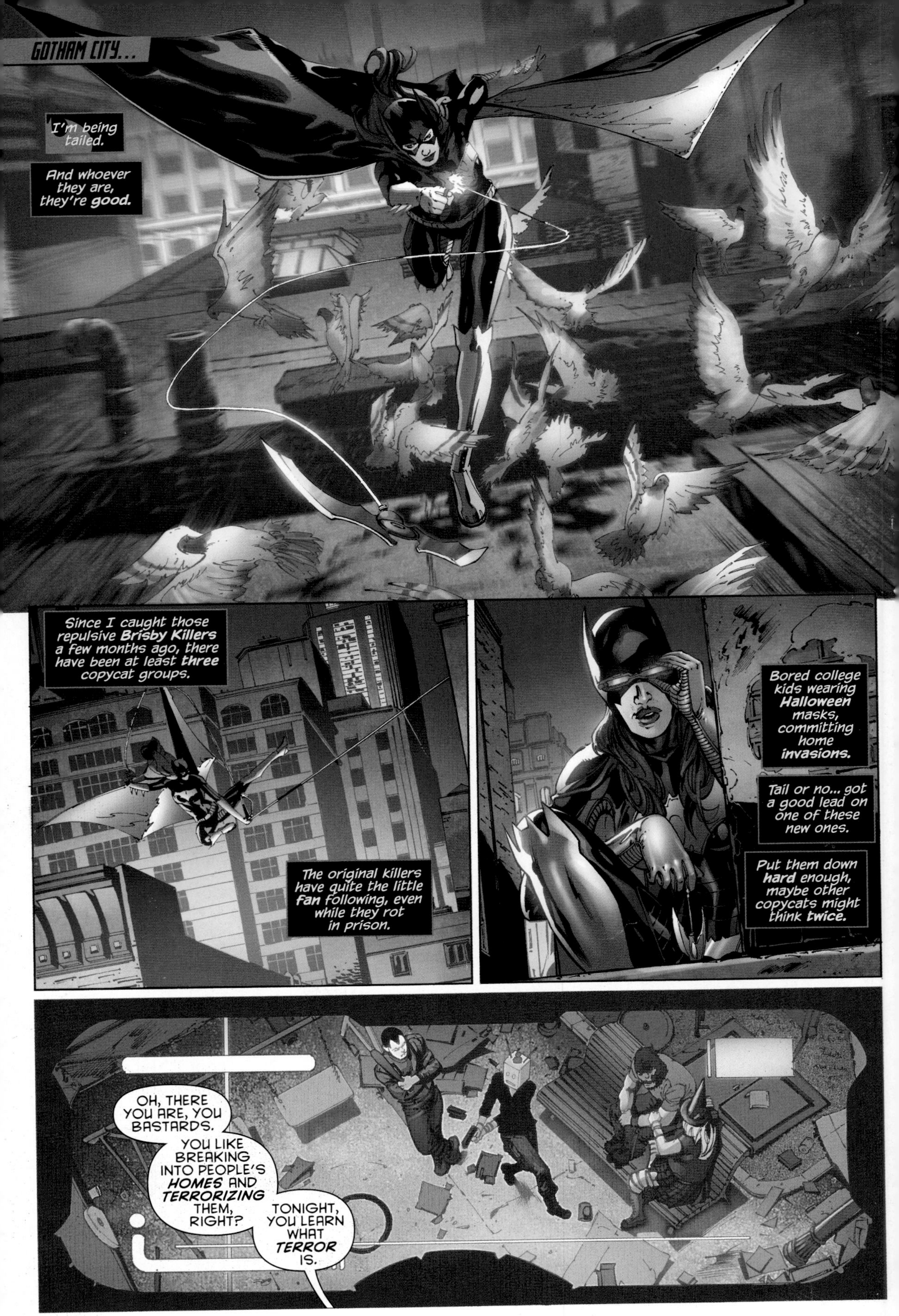
GOTHAM CITY...
I'm being tailed.
And whoever they are, they're good.
Since I caught those repulsive Brisby Killers a few months ago, there have been at least three copycat groups.
The original killers have quite the little fan following, even while they rot in prison.
Bored college kids wearing Halloween masks, committing home invasions.
Tail or no... got a good lead on one of these new ones.
Put them down hard enough, maybe other copycats might think twice.
OH, THERE YOU ARE, YOU BASTARDS.
YOU LIKE BREAKING INTO PEOPLE'S HOMES AND TERRORIZING THEM, RIGHT?
TONIGHT, YOU LEARN WHAT TERROR IS.

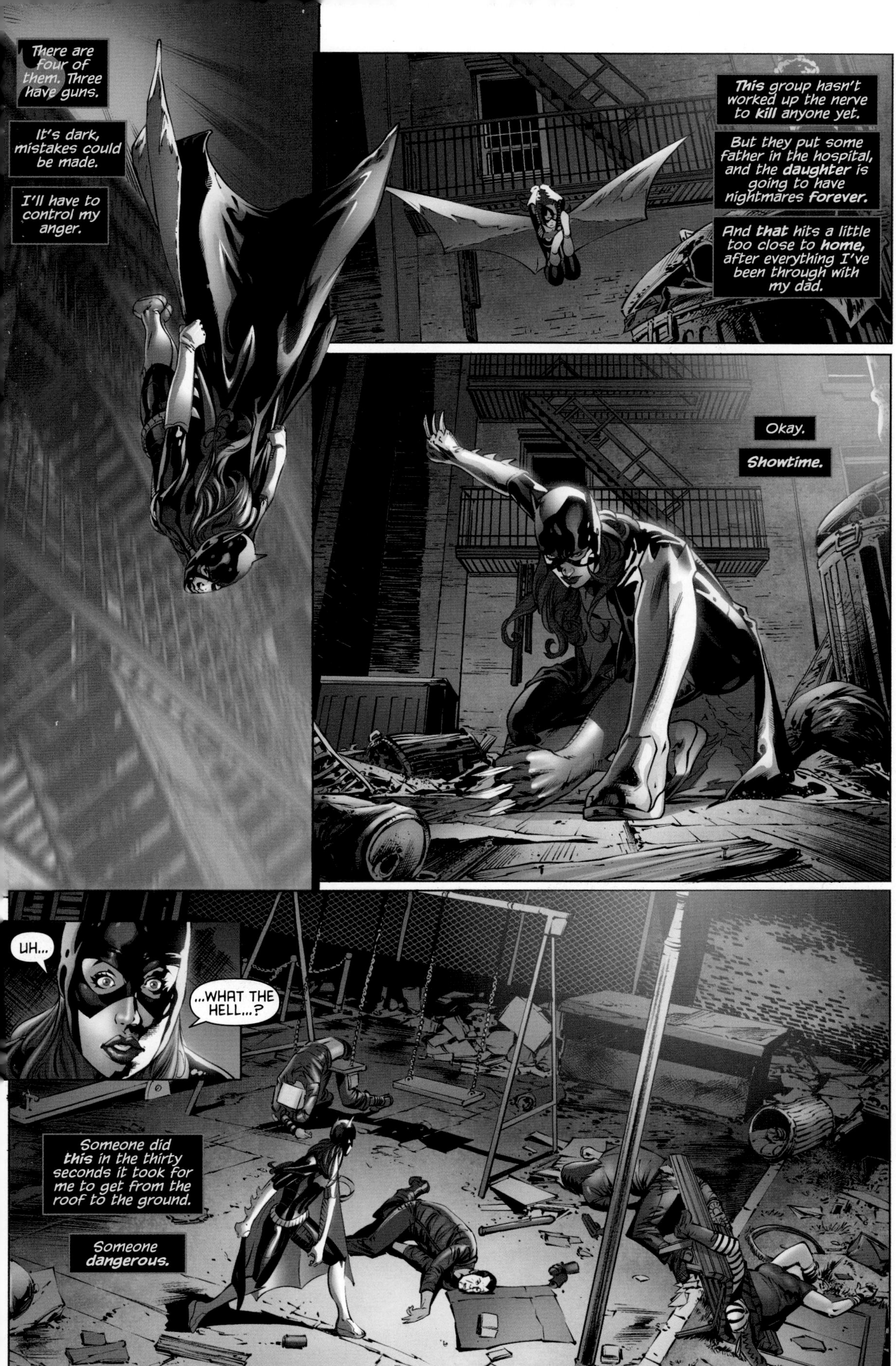
There are four of them. Three have guns.
It's dark, mistakes could be made.
I'll have to control my anger.
This group hasn't worked up the nerve to kill anyone yet.
But they put some father in the hospital, and the daughter is going to have nightmares forever.
And that hits a little too close to home, after everything I've been through with my dad.
Okay.
Showtime.
UH...
...WHAT THE HELL...?
Someone did this in the thirty seconds it took for me to get from the roof to the ground.
Someone dangerous.

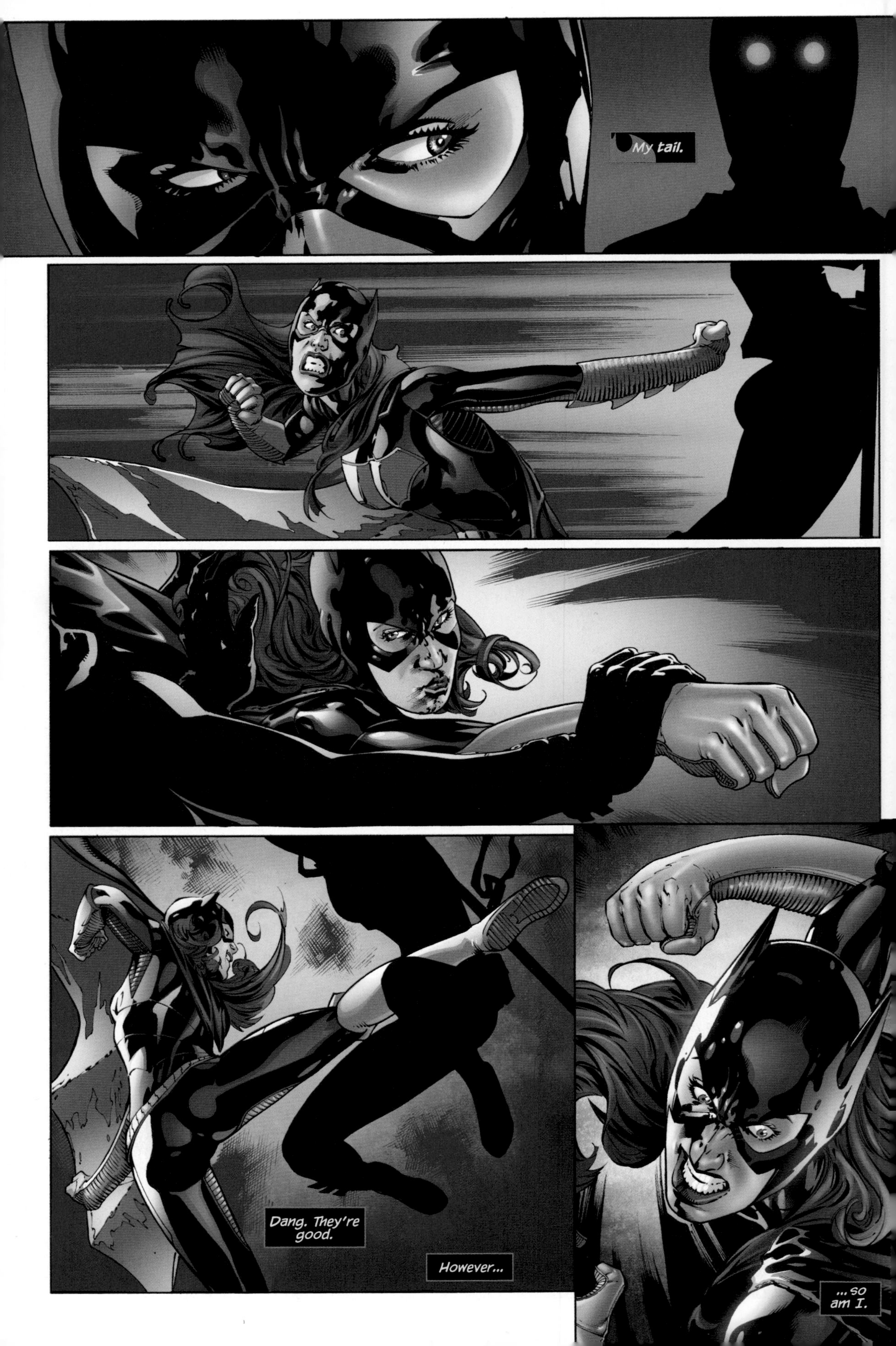
My tail.
Dang. They're good.
However...
...so am I.

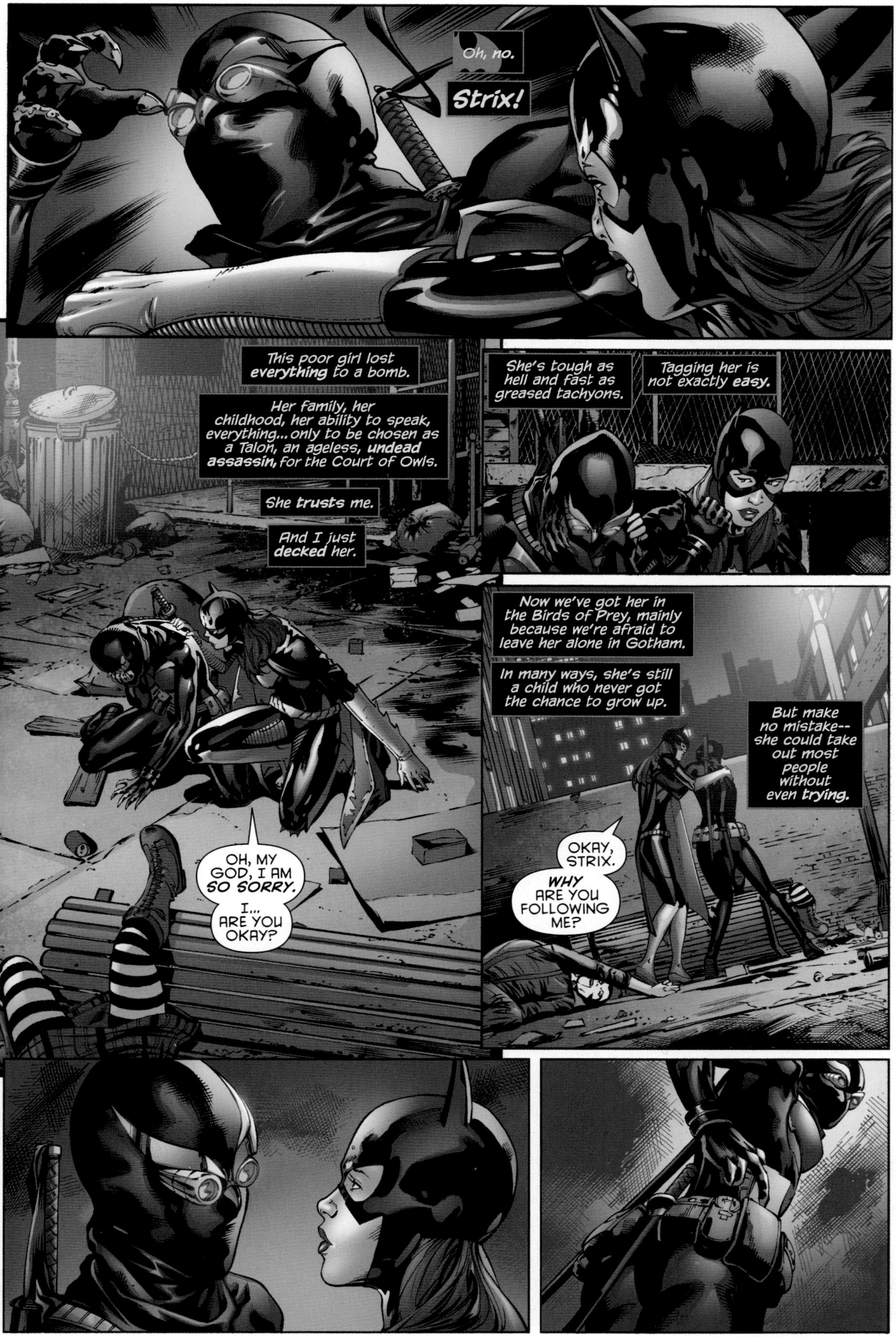

Oh, no.
Strix!
This poor girl lost everything to a bomb.
Her family, her childhood, her ability to speak, everything...only to be chosen as a Talon, an ageless, undead assassin, for the Court of Owls.
She trusts me.
And I just decked her.
She's tough as hell and fast as greased tachyons.
Tagging her is not exactly easy.
OH, MY GOD, I AM SO SORRY.
I... ARE YOU OKAY?
Now we've got her in the Birds of Prey, mainly because we're afraid to leave her alone in Gotham.
In many ways, she's still a child who never got the chance to grow up.
But make no mistake--she could take out most people without even trying.
OKAY, STRIX.
WHY ARE YOU FOLLOWING ME?

OH.

MISSING ~~CHILD~~
ABDUCTE~~D FROM~~
HOSPITAL
CISSY CHASTAIN

EIGHT-YEAR-OLD CISSY WAS TAKEN FROM ST.
FRANCIS HOSPITAL ON THE NIGHT OF JANUARY 13TH BY PER...
...KNOWN. HER MOTHER MISSES HER VERY M...

STRIX, I KNOW GOTHAM COPS DON'T HAVE THE BEST REPUTATION, BUT THEY ARE ACTUALLY *REALLY* GOOD AT RECOVERING LOST KIDS.

TAP TAP TAP

YOU WANT *ME* TO FIND HER.

WHY IS THIS SO IMPORTANT TO YOU?

DUE TO A FEVER IN HER INFANCY, CISSY IS UNABLE TO SPEAK. PLEASE HELP US BRING HER HOME. CALL: 555-1887.

TAP TAP TAP

OH. OH, HONEY.

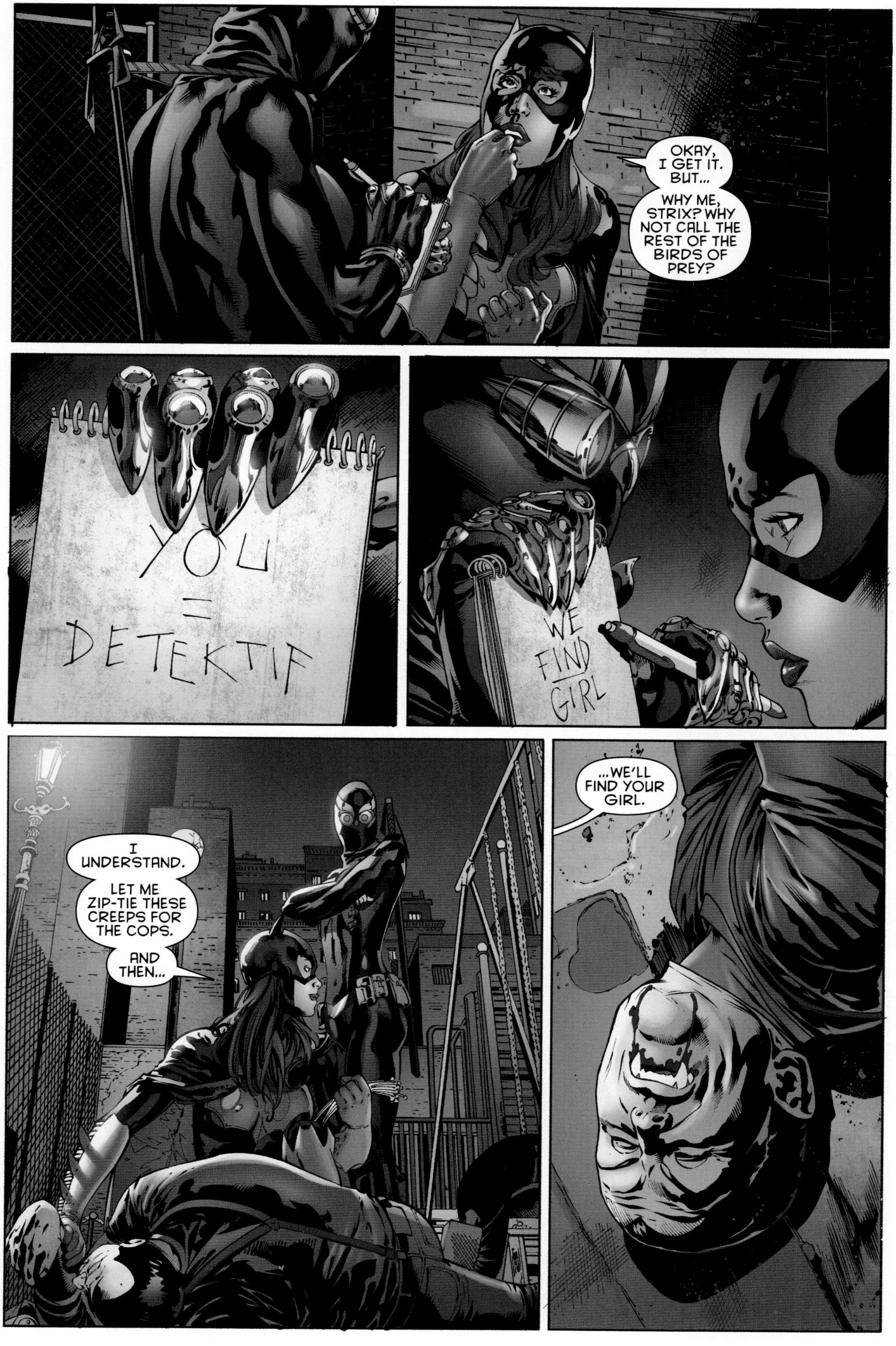

OKAY, I GET IT. BUT...
WHY ME, STRIX? WHY NOT CALL THE REST OF THE BIRDS OF PREY?
YOU = DETEKTIF
WE FIND GIRL
I UNDERSTAND.
LET ME ZIP-TIE THESE CREEPS FOR THE COPS.
AND THEN...
...WE'LL FIND YOUR GIRL.

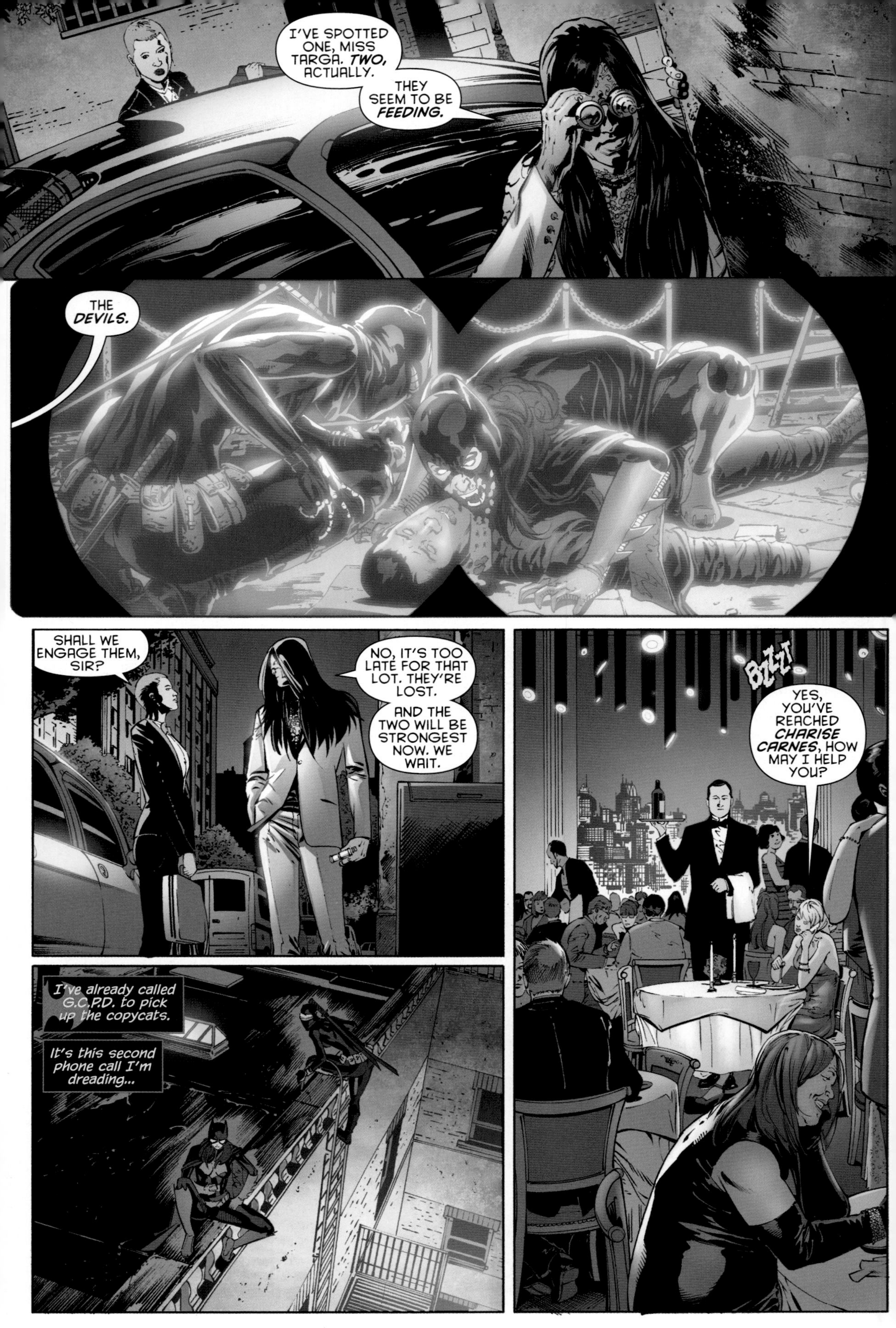
I'VE SPOTTED ONE, MISS TARGA. TWO, ACTUALLY.
THEY SEEM TO BE FEEDING.
THE DEVILS.
SHALL WE ENGAGE THEM, SIR?
NO, IT'S TOO LATE FOR THAT LOT. THEY'RE LOST.
AND THE TWO WILL BE STRONGEST NOW. WE WAIT.
BZZZT
YES, YOU'VE REACHED CHARISE CARNES, HOW MAY I HELP YOU?
I've already called G.C.P.D. to pick up the copycats.
It's this second phone call I'm dreading...

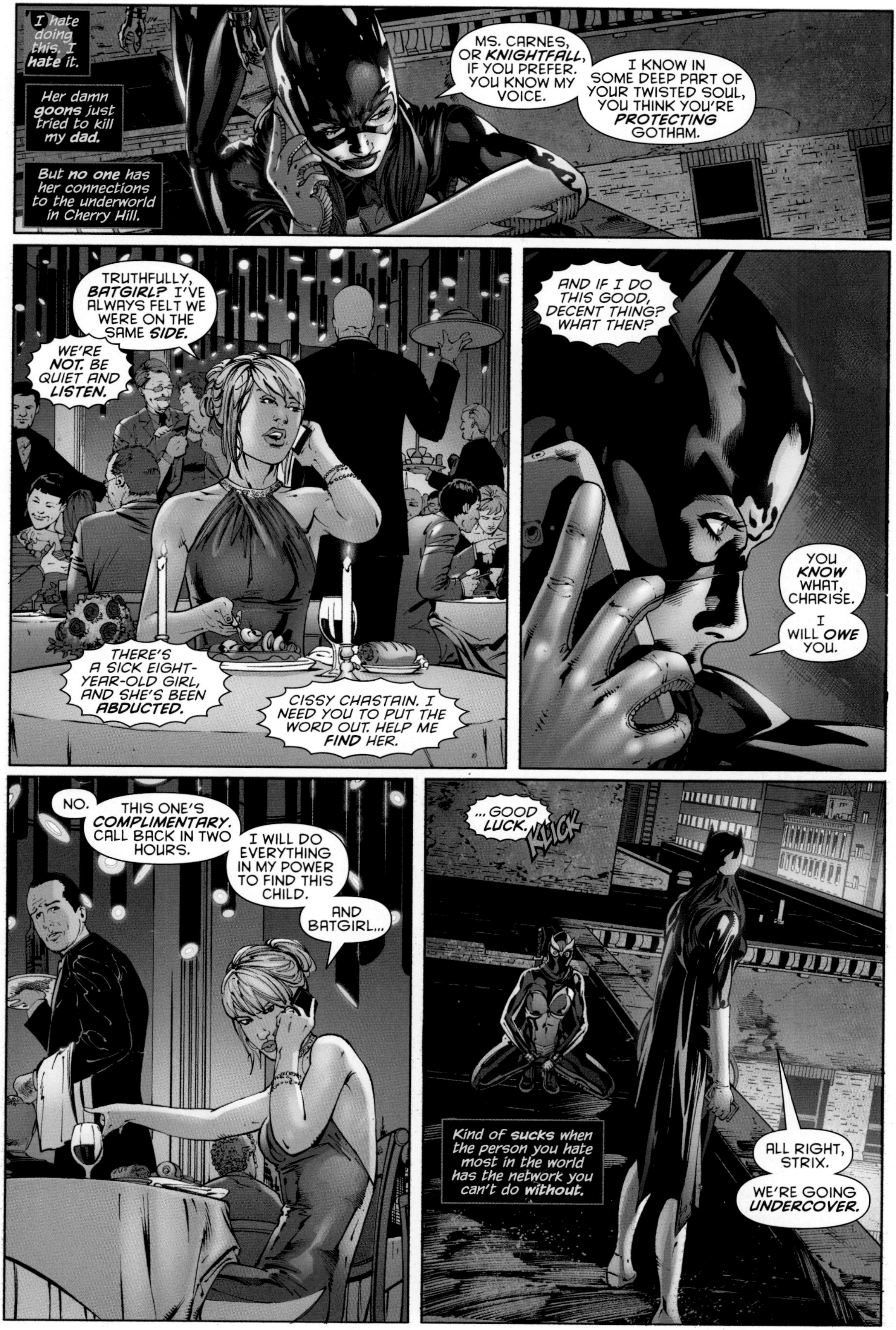

I hate doing this. I hate it.
Her damn goons just tried to kill my dad.
But no one has her connections to the underworld in Cherry Hill.
MS. CARNES, OR KNIGHTFALL, IF YOU PREFER. YOU KNOW MY VOICE.
I KNOW IN SOME DEEP PART OF YOUR TWISTED SOUL, YOU THINK YOU'RE PROTECTING GOTHAM.
TRUTHFULLY, BATGIRL? I'VE ALWAYS FELT WE WERE ON THE SAME SIDE.
WE'RE NOT. BE QUIET AND LISTEN.
THERE'S A SICK EIGHT-YEAR-OLD GIRL, AND SHE'S BEEN ABDUCTED.
CISSY CHASTAIN. I NEED YOU TO PUT THE WORD OUT. HELP ME FIND HER.
AND IF I DO THIS GOOD, DECENT THING? WHAT THEN?
YOU KNOW WHAT, CHARISE.
I WILL OWE YOU.
NO.
THIS ONE'S COMPLIMENTARY. CALL BACK IN TWO HOURS.
I WILL DO EVERYTHING IN MY POWER TO FIND THIS CHILD.
AND BATGIRL...
...GOOD LUCK.
KLICK
Kind of sucks when the person you hate most in the world has the network you can't do without.
ALL RIGHT, STRIX.
WE'RE GOING UNDERCOVER.

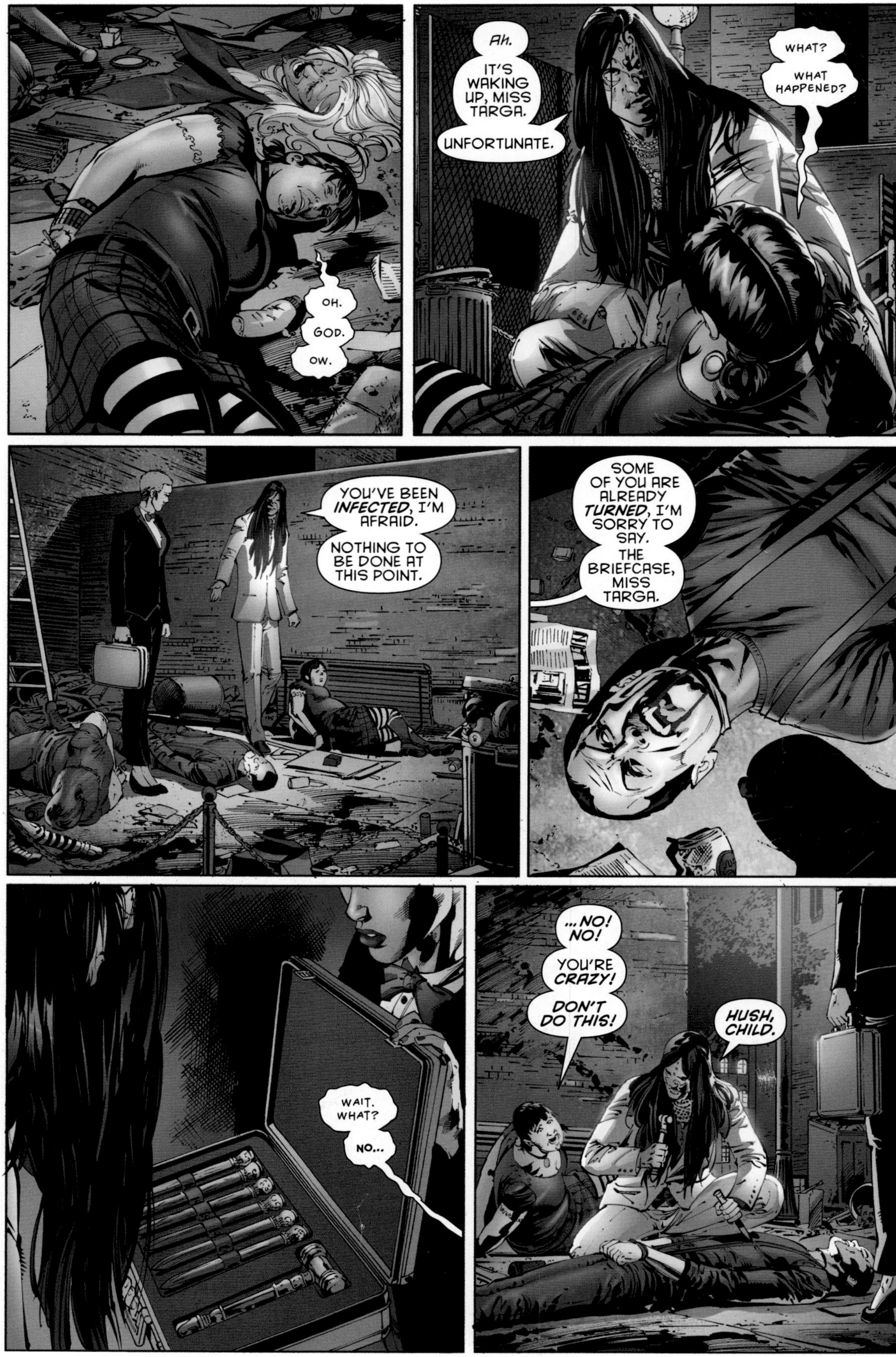
OH.
GOD.
OW.
Ah.
IT'S WAKING UP, MISS TARGA.
UNFORTUNATE.
WHAT?
WHAT HAPPENED?
YOU'VE BEEN INFECTED, I'M AFRAID.
NOTHING TO BE DONE AT THIS POINT.
SOME OF YOU ARE ALREADY TURNED, I'M SORRY TO SAY.
THE BRIEFCASE, MISS TARGA.
WAIT. WHAT?
NO...
...NO! NO!
YOU'RE CRAZY!
DON'T DO THIS!
HUSH, CHILD.

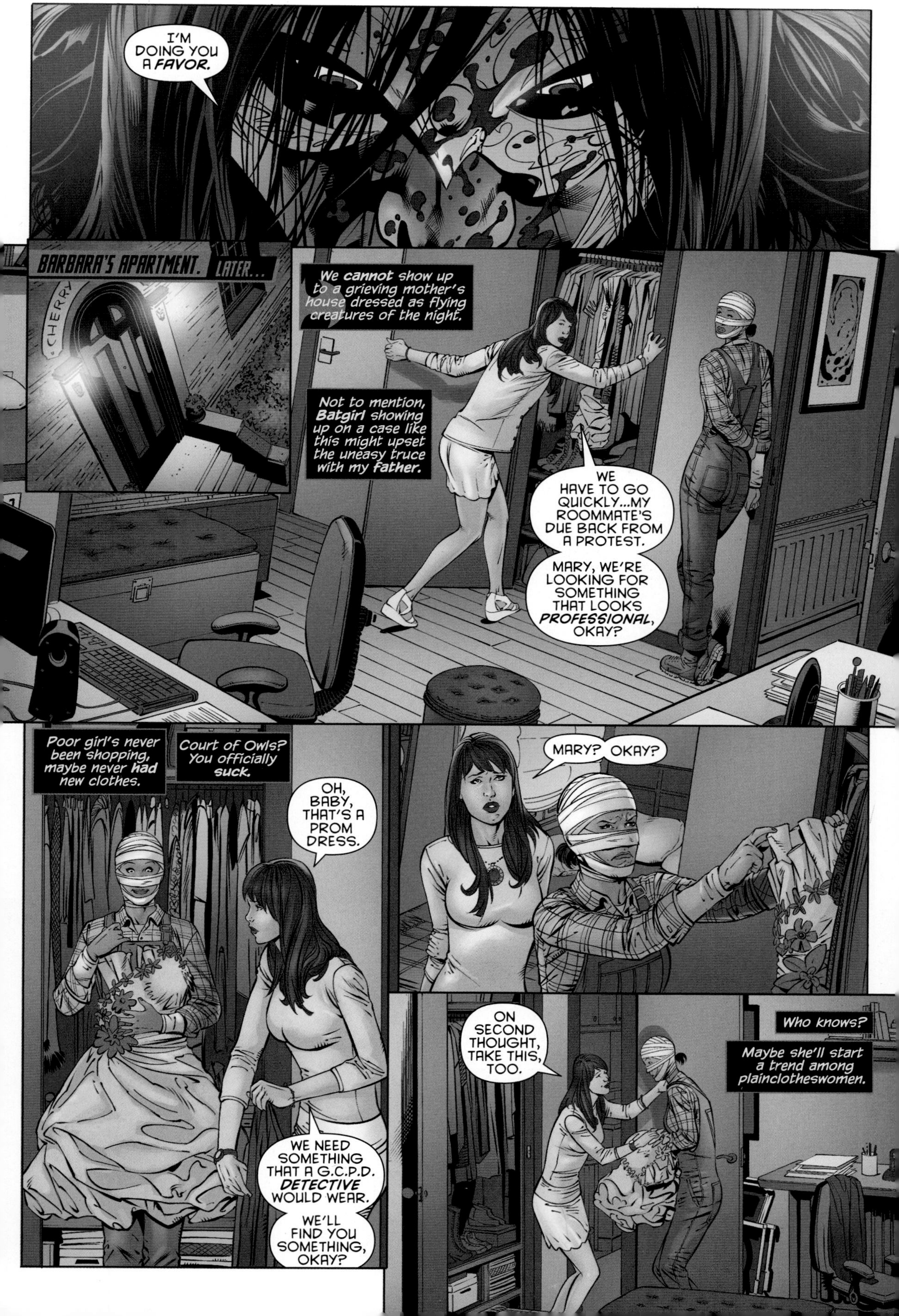

I'M DOING YOU A *FAVOR.*
BARBARA'S APARTMENT. LATER...
CHERRY
We **cannot** show up to a grieving mother's house dressed as flying creatures of the night.
Not to mention, **Batgirl** showing up on a case like this might upset the uneasy truce with my **father.**
WE HAVE TO GO QUICKLY...MY ROOMMATE'S DUE BACK FROM A PROTEST.
MARY, WE'RE LOOKING FOR SOMETHING THAT LOOKS ***PROFESSIONAL***, OKAY?
Poor girl's never been shopping, maybe never **had** new clothes.
Court of Owls? You officially **suck.**
OH, BABY, THAT'S A PROM DRESS.
WE NEED SOMETHING THAT A G.C.P.D. ***DETECTIVE*** WOULD WEAR.
WE'LL FIND YOU SOMETHING, OKAY?
MARY? OKAY?
ON SECOND THOUGHT, TAKE THIS, TOO.
Who knows?
Maybe she'll start a trend among plainclotheswomen.

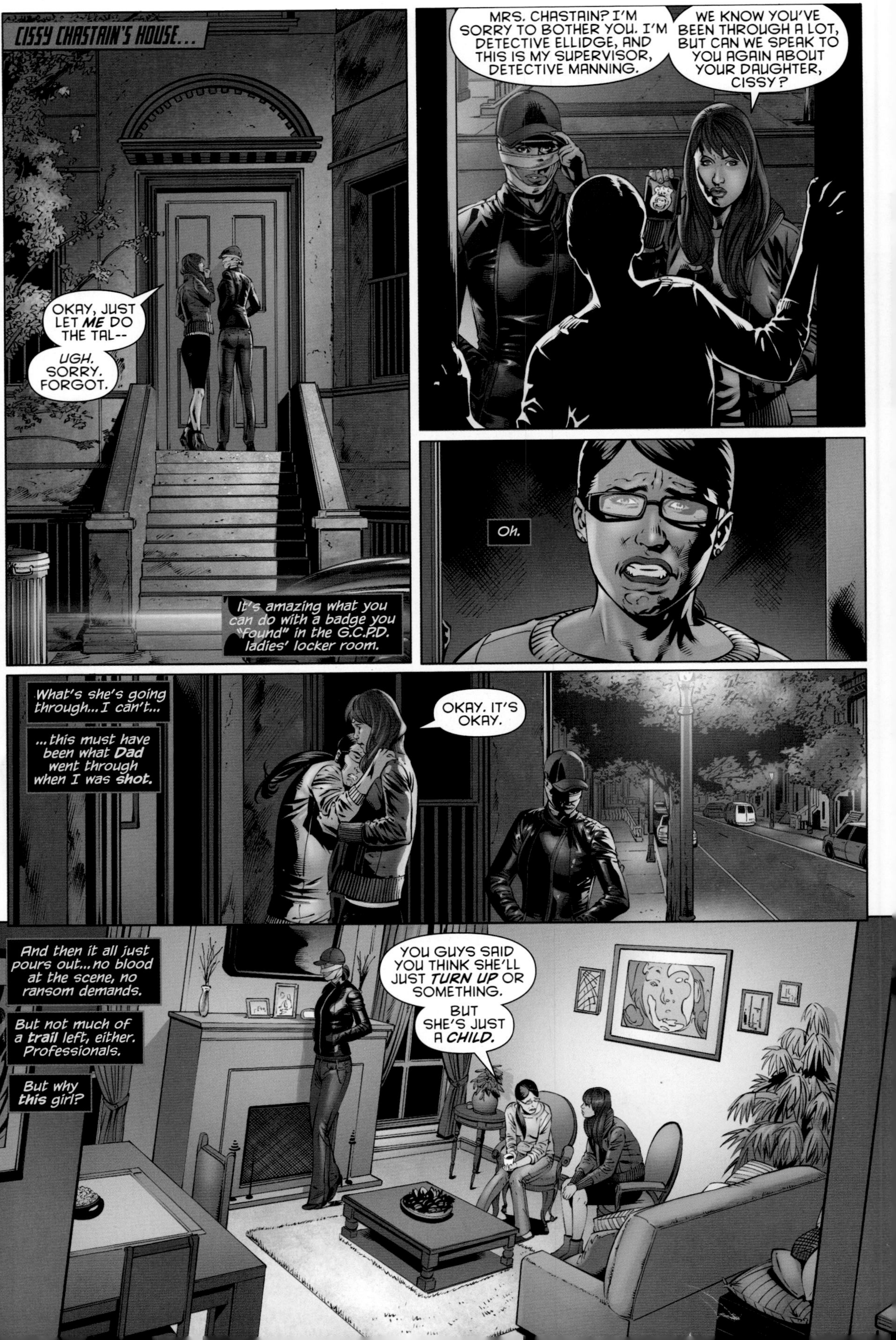
CISSY CHASTAIN'S HOUSE...
OKAY, JUST LET ME DO THE TAL--
UGH. SORRY. FORGOT.
It's amazing what you can do with a badge you "found" in the G.C.P.D. ladies' locker room.
MRS. CHASTAIN? I'M SORRY TO BOTHER YOU. I'M DETECTIVE ELLIDGE, AND THIS IS MY SUPERVISOR, DETECTIVE MANNING.
WE KNOW YOU'VE BEEN THROUGH A LOT, BUT CAN WE SPEAK TO YOU AGAIN ABOUT YOUR DAUGHTER, CISSY?
Oh.
What's she's going through...I can't...
...this must have been what Dad went through when I was shot.
OKAY. IT'S OKAY.
And then it all just pours out...no blood at the scene, no ransom demands.
But not much of a trail left, either. Professionals.
But why this girl?
YOU GUYS SAID YOU THINK SHE'LL JUST TURN UP OR SOMETHING.
BUT SHE'S JUST A CHILD.

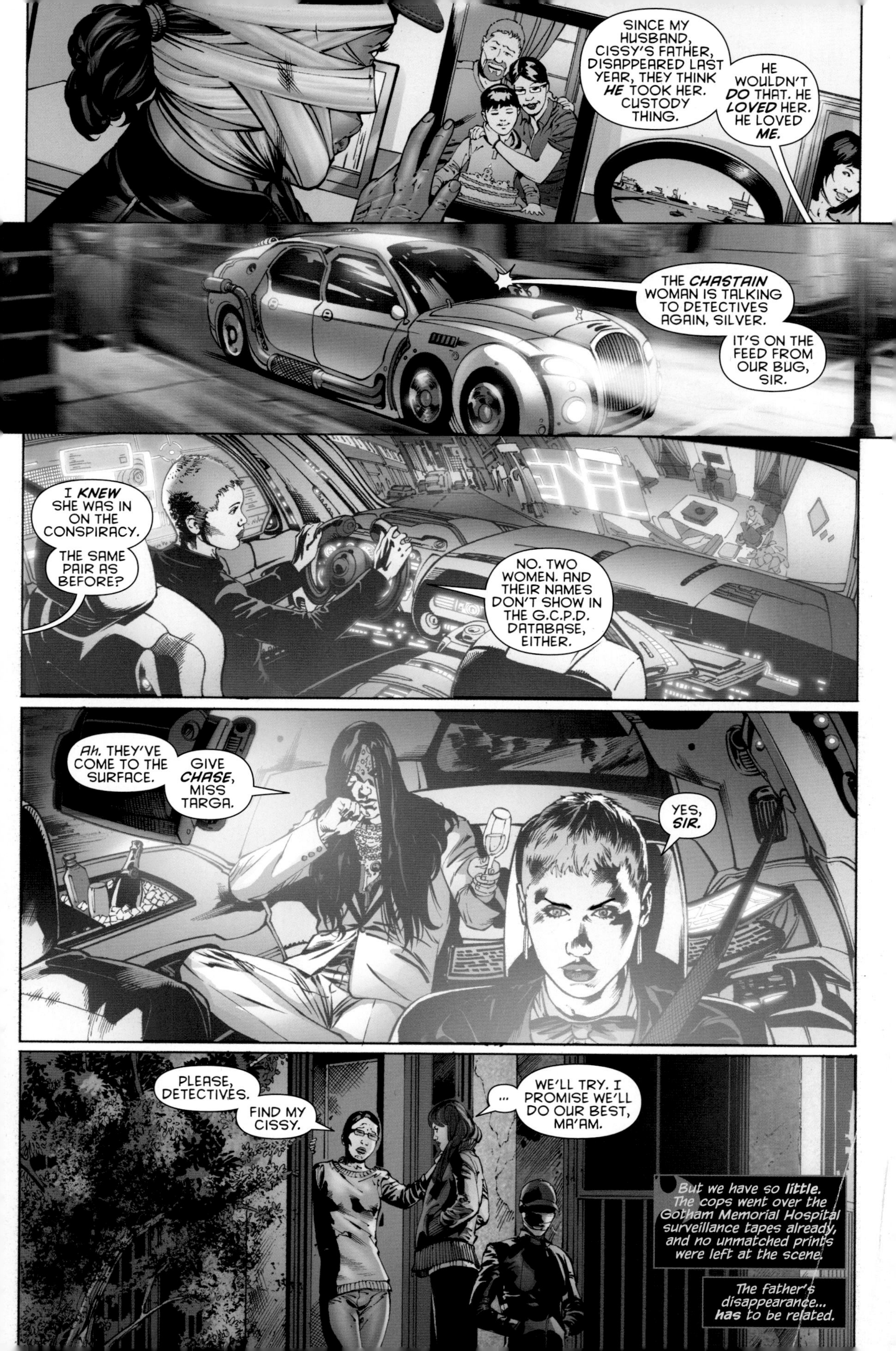

SINCE MY HUSBAND, CISSY'S FATHER, DISAPPEARED LAST YEAR, THEY THINK **HE** TOOK HER. CUSTODY THING.
HE WOULDN'T **DO** THAT. HE **LOVED** HER. HE LOVED **ME.**
THE **CHASTAIN** WOMAN IS TALKING TO DETECTIVES AGAIN, SILVER.
IT'S ON THE FEED FROM OUR BUG, SIR.
I **KNEW** SHE WAS IN ON THE CONSPIRACY.
THE SAME PAIR AS BEFORE?
NO. TWO WOMEN. AND THEIR NAMES DON'T SHOW IN THE G.C.P.D. DATABASE, EITHER.
Ah. THEY'VE COME TO THE SURFACE.
GIVE **CHASE**, MISS TARGA.
YES, **SIR.**
PLEASE, DETECTIVES.
FIND MY CISSY.
... WE'LL TRY. I PROMISE WE'LL DO OUR BEST, MA'AM.
*But we have so **little**. The cops went over the Gotham Memorial Hospital surveillance tapes already, and no unmatched prints were left at the scene.*
*The father's disappearance... **has** to be related.*

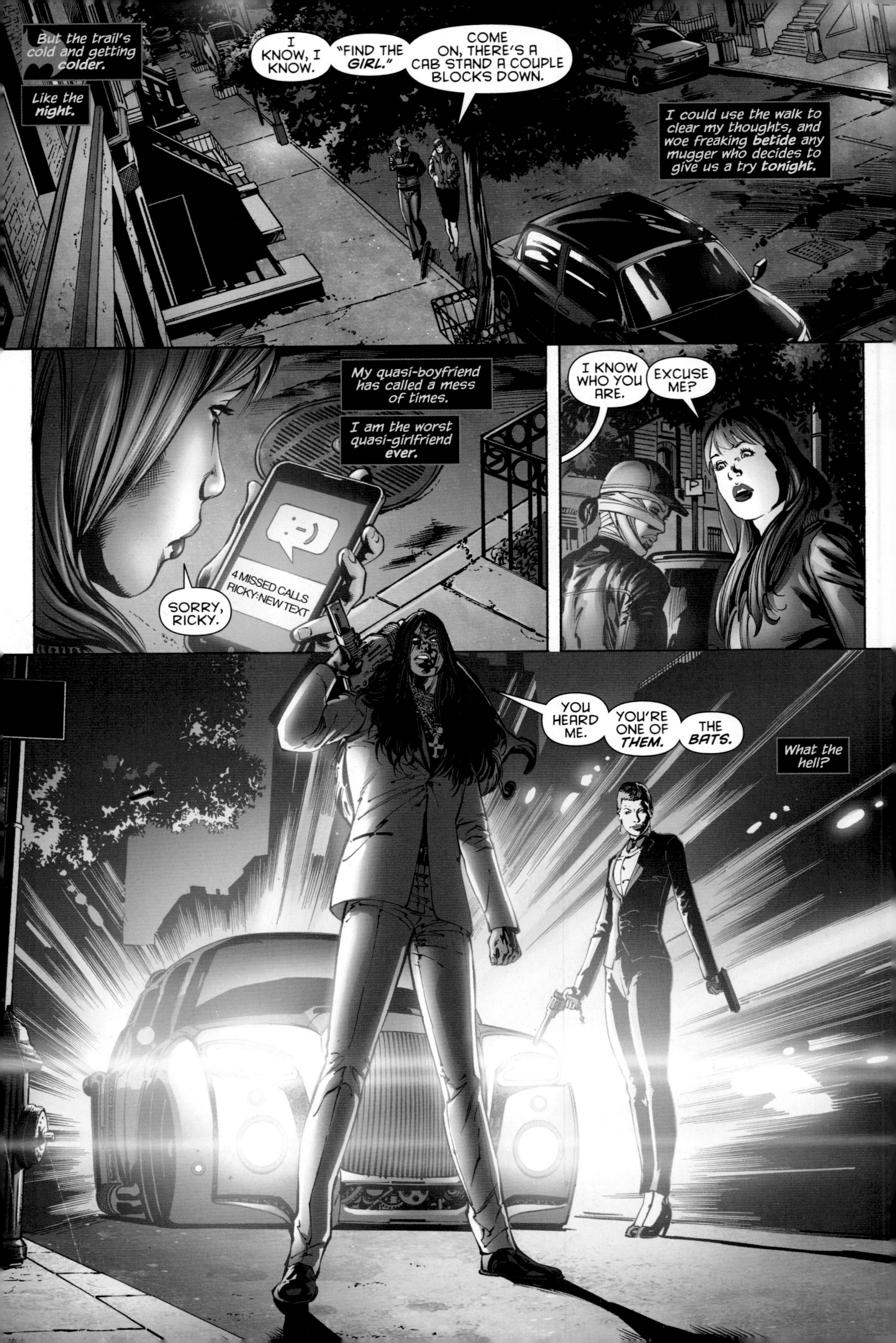
But the trail's cold and getting colder.
Like the night.
I KNOW, I KNOW.
"FIND THE GIRL."
COME ON, THERE'S A CAB STAND A COUPLE BLOCKS DOWN.
I could use the walk to clear my thoughts, and woe freaking betide any mugger who decides to give us a try tonight.
My quasi-boyfriend has called a mess of times.
I am the worst quasi-girlfriend ever.
:-)
4 MISSED CALLS
RICKY: NEW TEXT
SORRY, RICKY.
I KNOW WHO YOU ARE.
EXCUSE ME?
YOU HEARD ME.
YOU'RE ONE OF THEM.
THE BATS.
What the hell?

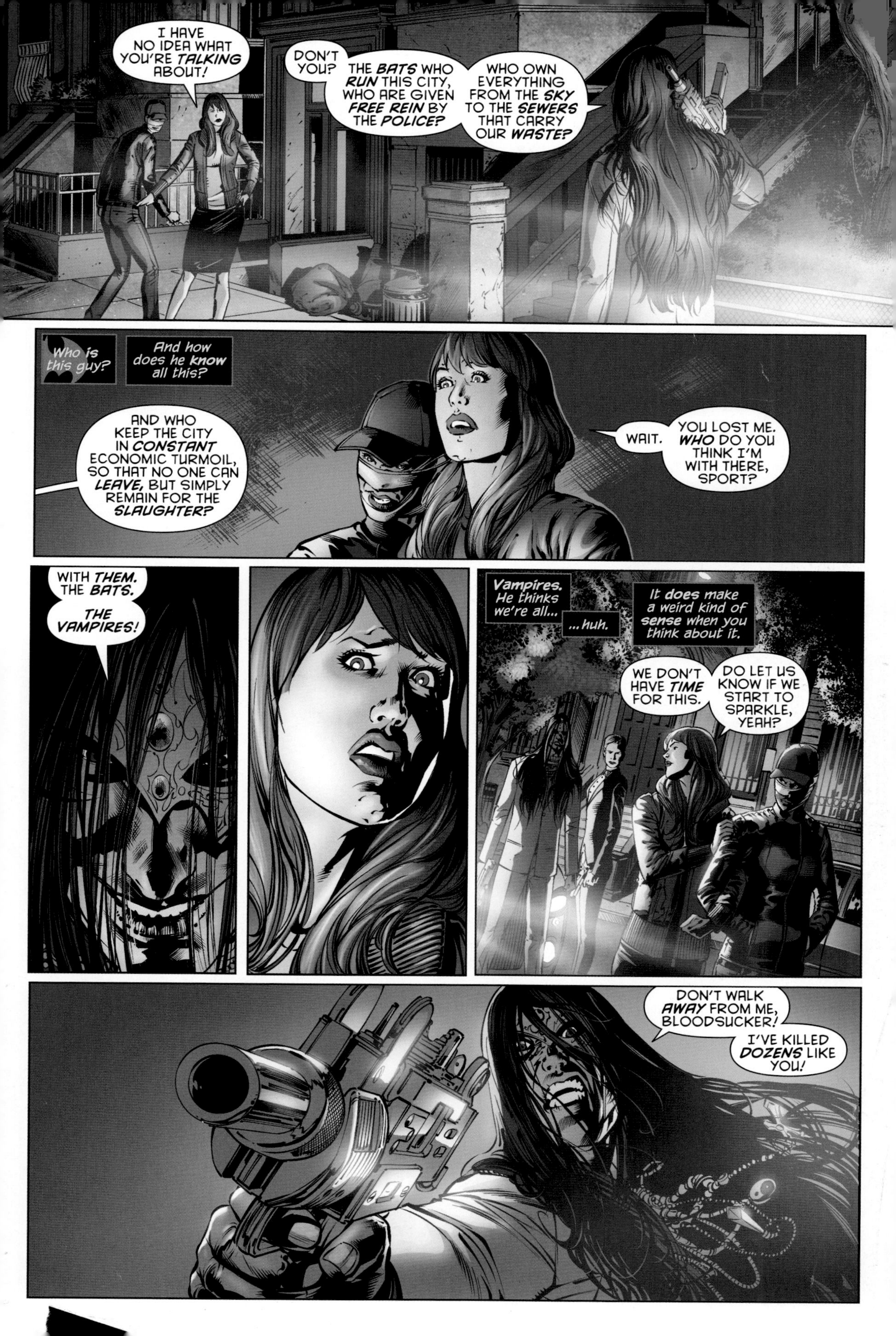

I HAVE NO IDEA WHAT YOU'RE TALKING ABOUT!
DON'T YOU?
THE BATS WHO RUN THIS CITY, WHO ARE GIVEN FREE REIN BY THE POLICE?
WHO OWN EVERYTHING FROM THE SKY TO THE SEWERS THAT CARRY OUR WASTE?
Who is this guy?
And how does he know all this?
AND WHO KEEP THE CITY IN CONSTANT ECONOMIC TURMOIL, SO THAT NO ONE CAN LEAVE, BUT SIMPLY REMAIN FOR THE SLAUGHTER?
WAIT.
YOU LOST ME. WHO DO YOU THINK I'M WITH THERE, SPORT?
WITH THEM. THE BATS.
THE VAMPIRES!
Vampires. He thinks we're all...
...huh.
It does make a weird kind of sense when you think about it.
WE DON'T HAVE TIME FOR THIS.
DO LET US KNOW IF WE START TO SPARKLE, YEAH?
DON'T WALK AWAY FROM ME, BLOODSUCKER!
I'VE KILLED DOZENS LIKE YOU!

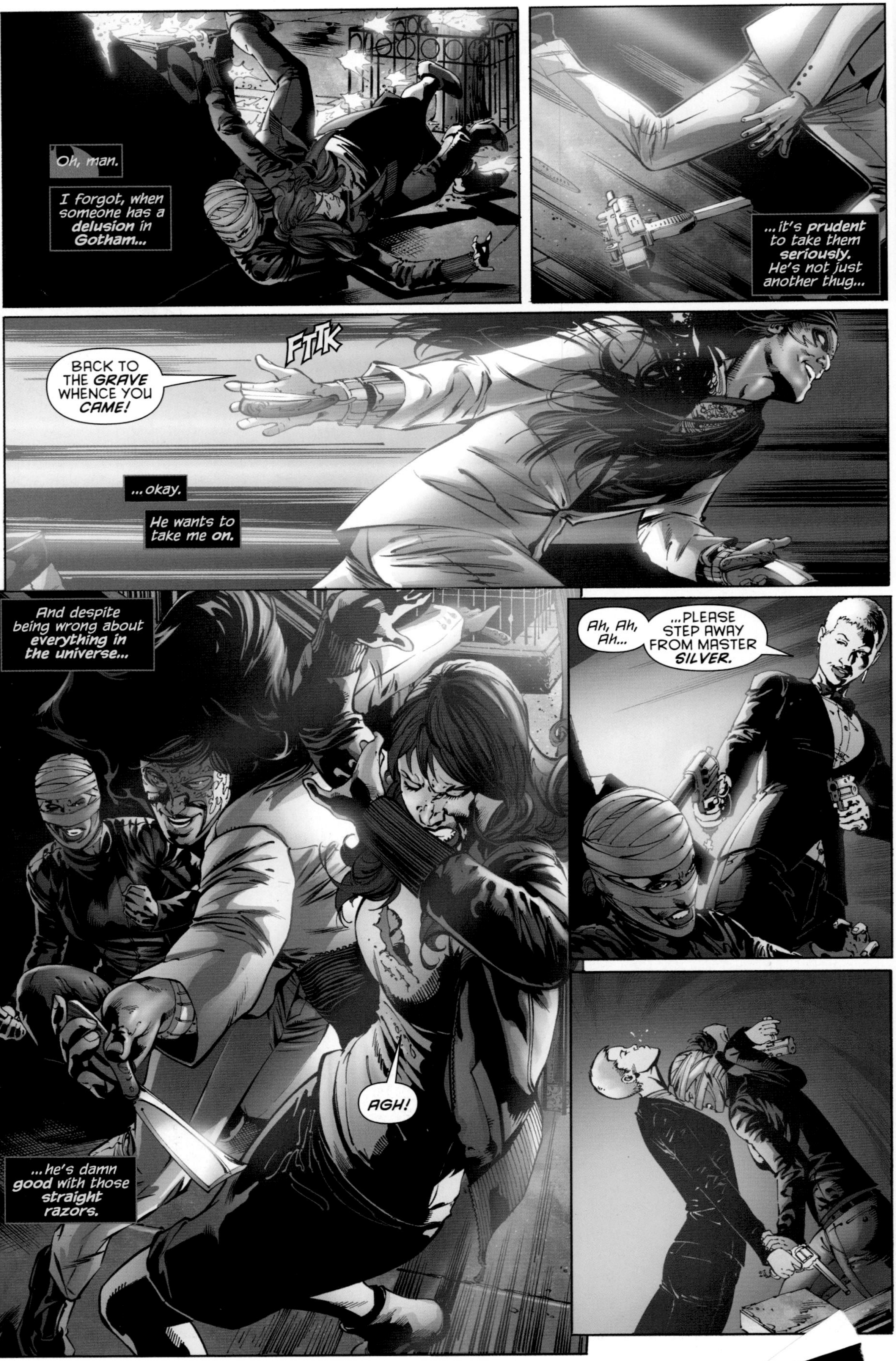
Oh, man.
I forgot, when someone has a delusion in Gotham...
...it's prudent to take them seriously. He's not just another thug...
FTTK
BACK TO THE GRAVE WHENCE YOU CAME!
...okay.
He wants to take me on.
And despite being wrong about everything in the universe...
AGH!
...he's damn good with those straight razors.
Ah, Ah, Ah...
...PLEASE STEP AWAY FROM MASTER SILVER.

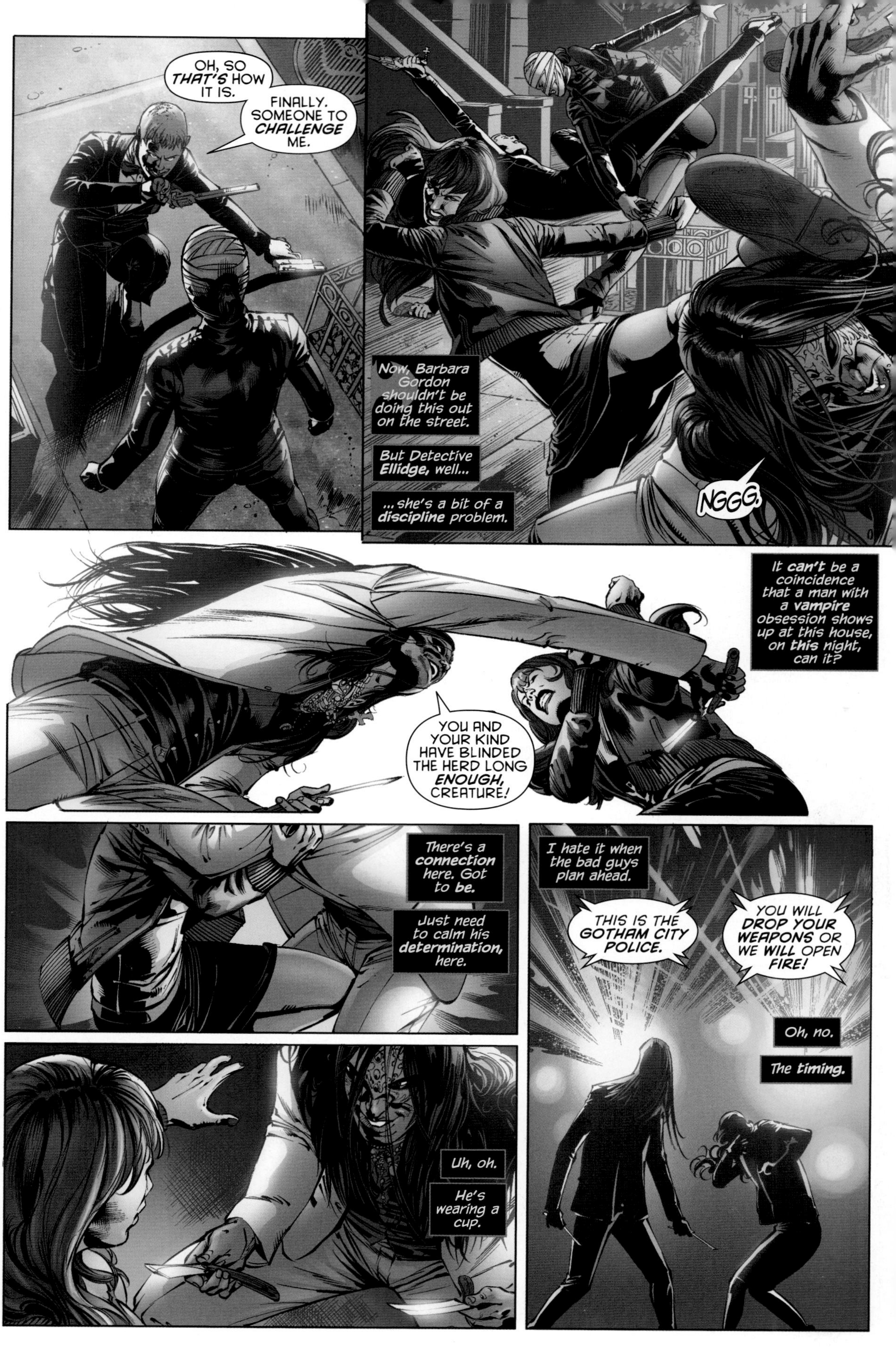

OH, SO *THAT'S* HOW IT IS.
FINALLY. SOMEONE TO *CHALLENGE* ME.
Now, Barbara Gordon shouldn't be doing this out on the street.
But Detective **Ellidge**, well...
...she's a bit of a **discipline** problem.
NGGG.
It **can't** be a coincidence that a man with a **vampire** obsession shows up at this house, on **this** night, can it?
YOU AND YOUR KIND HAVE BLINDED THE HERD LONG *ENOUGH*, CREATURE!
There's a **connection** here. Got to **be**.
Just need to calm his **determination**, here.
Uh, oh.
He's wearing a cup.
I hate it when the bad guys plan ahead.
THIS IS THE **GOTHAM CITY POLICE**.
YOU WILL **DROP YOUR WEAPONS** OR WE **WILL** OPEN **FIRE!**
Oh, no.
The **timing**.

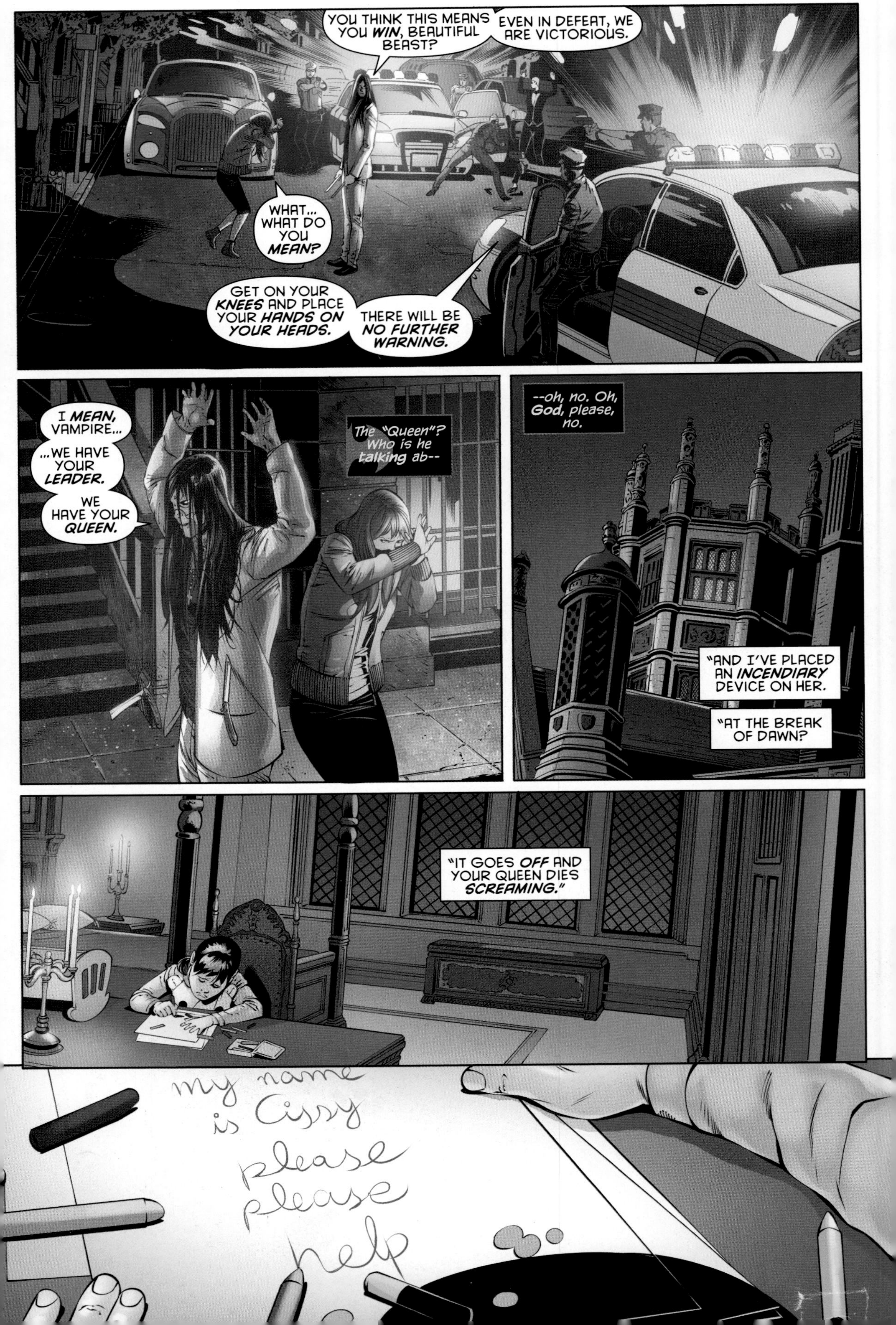
YOU THINK THIS MEANS YOU WIN, BEAUTIFUL BEAST?
EVEN IN DEFEAT, WE ARE VICTORIOUS.
WHAT... WHAT DO YOU MEAN?
GET ON YOUR KNEES AND PLACE YOUR HANDS ON YOUR HEADS.
THERE WILL BE NO FURTHER WARNING.
I MEAN, VAMPIRE...
...WE HAVE YOUR LEADER.
WE HAVE YOUR QUEEN.
The "Queen"? Who is he talking ab--
--oh, no. Oh, God, please, no.
"AND I'VE PLACED AN INCENDIARY DEVICE ON HER.
"AT THE BREAK OF DAWN?
"IT GOES OFF AND YOUR QUEEN DIES SCREAMING."
my name is Cissy please please help

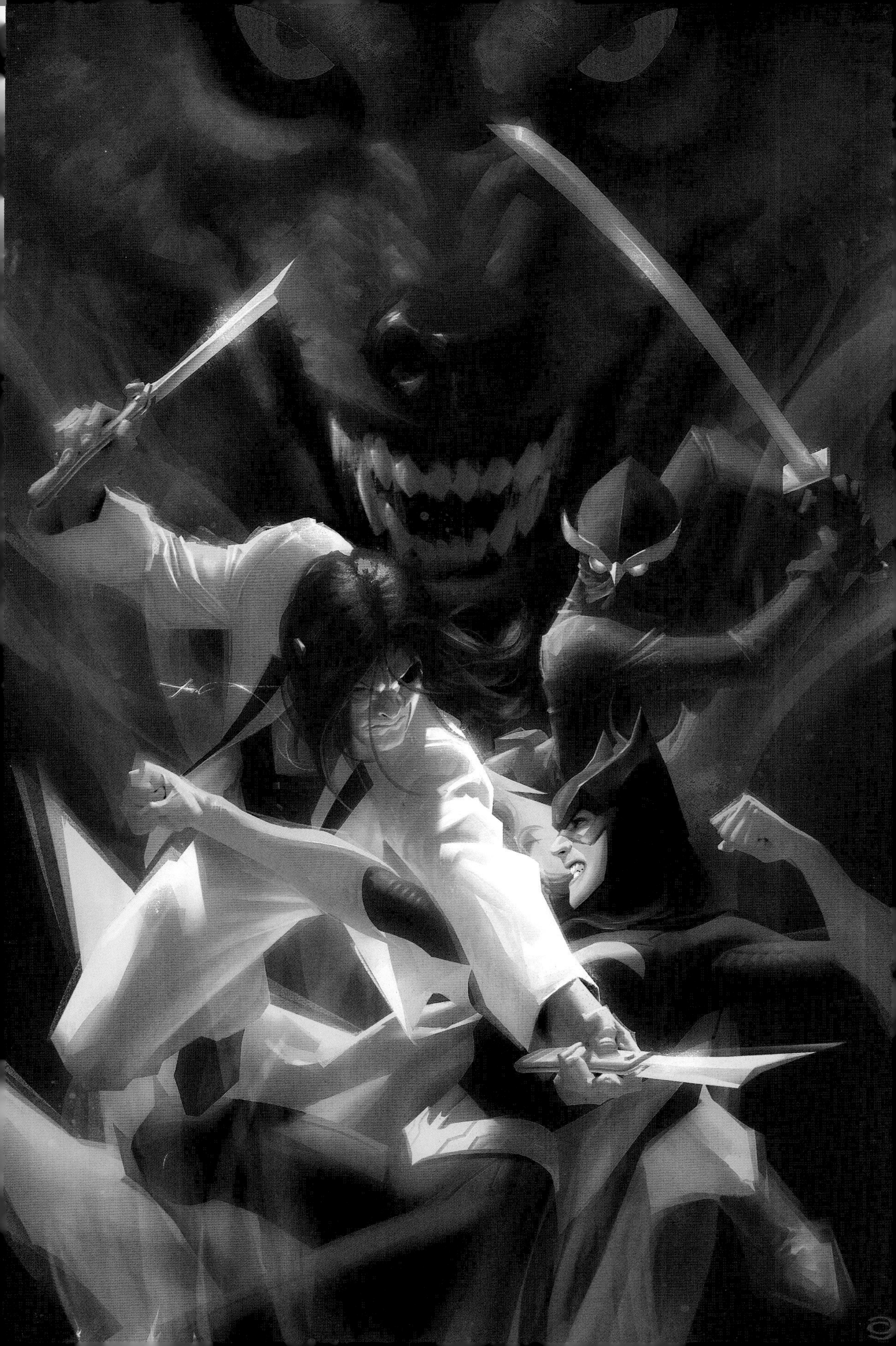

GAIL SIMONE writer **FERNANDO PASARIN** penciller **JONATHAN GLAPION** inker **BLOND** colorist **ALEX GARNER** cover artist

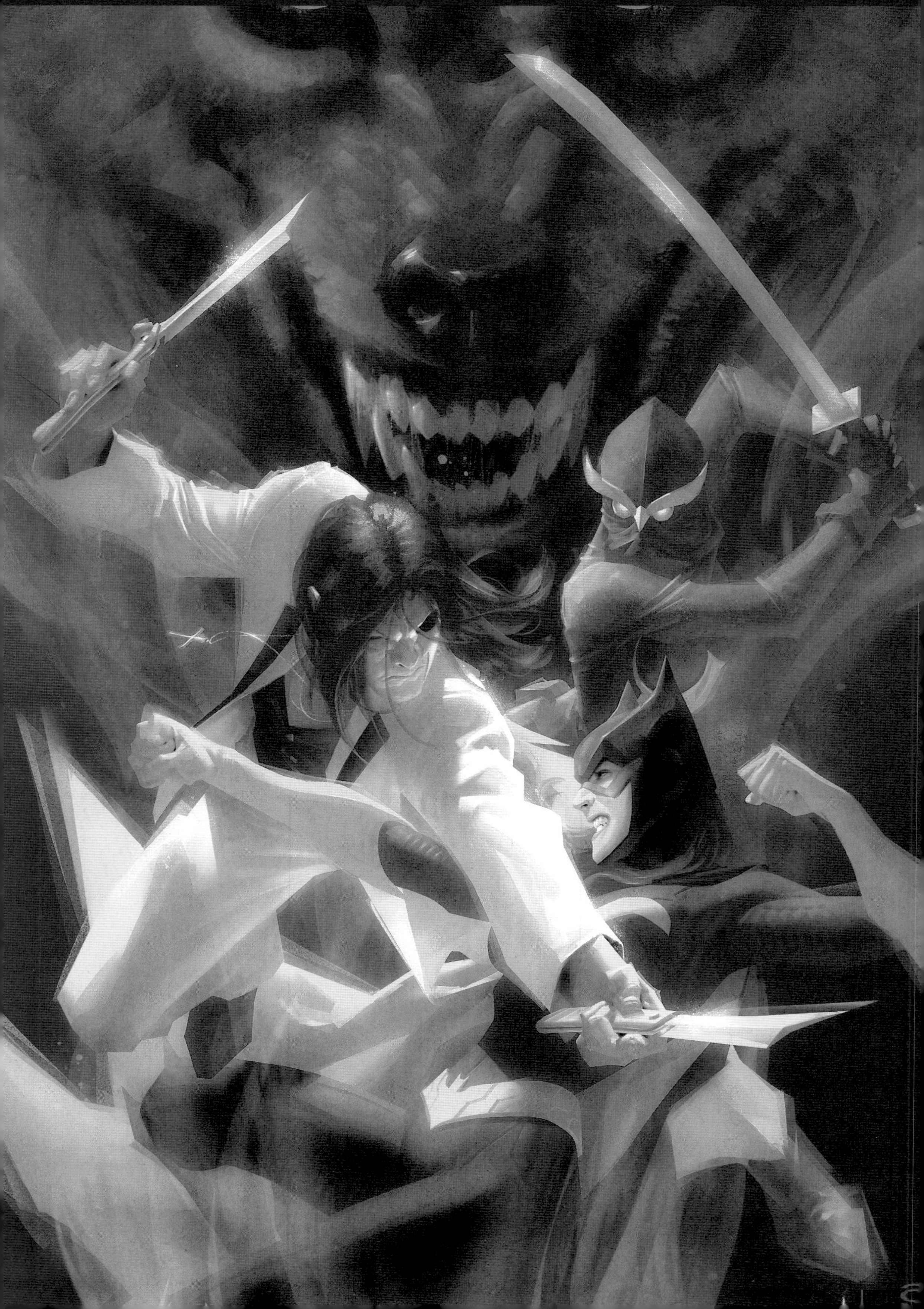

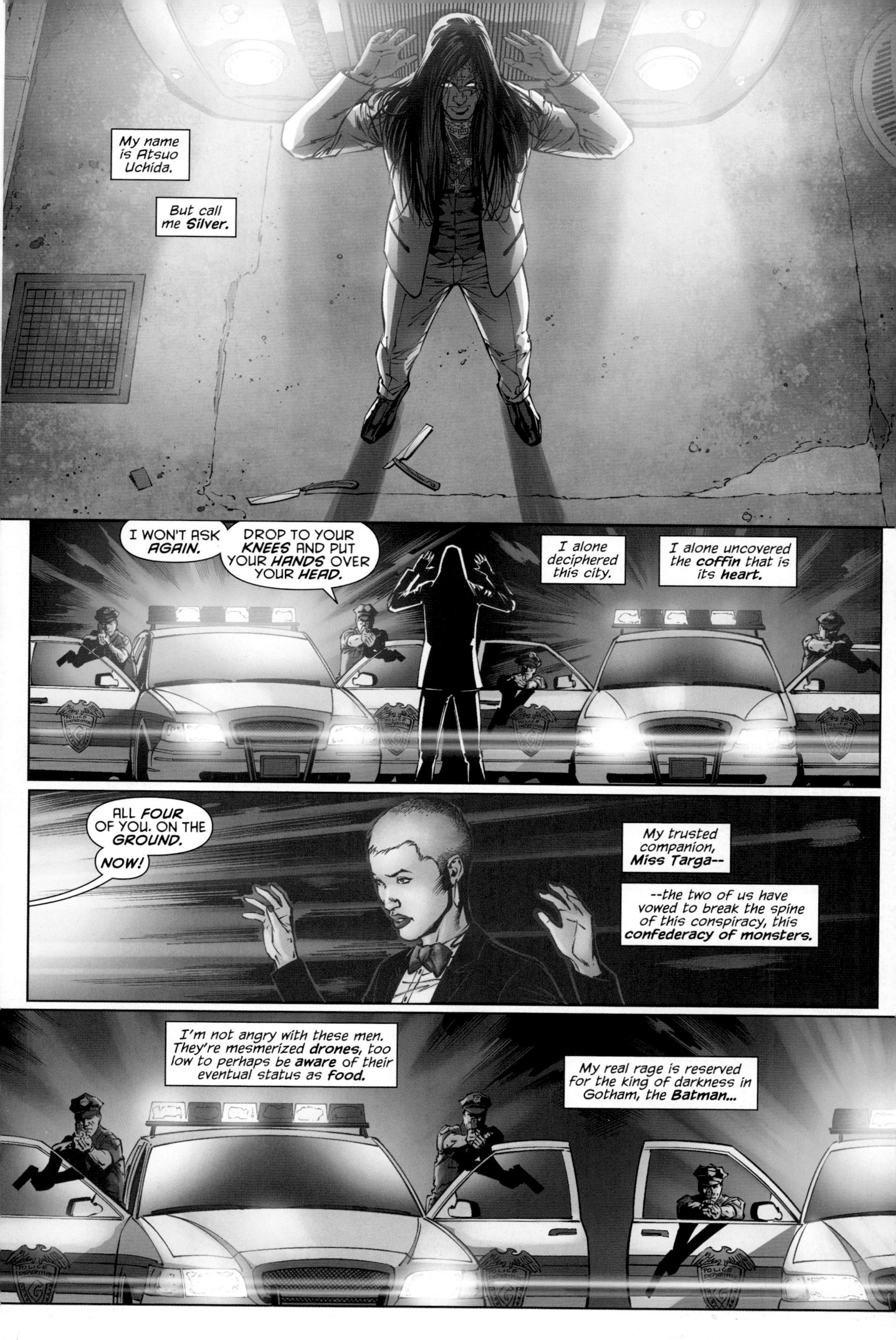
My name is Atsuo Uchida.
But call me Silver.
I WON'T ASK AGAIN.
DROP TO YOUR KNEES AND PUT YOUR HANDS OVER YOUR HEAD.
I alone deciphered this city.
I alone uncovered the coffin that is its heart.
ALL FOUR OF YOU. ON THE GROUND.
NOW!
My trusted companion, Miss Targa--
--the two of us have vowed to break the spine of this conspiracy, this confederacy of monsters.
I'm not angry with these men. They're mesmerized drones, too low to perhaps be aware of their eventual status as food.
My real rage is reserved for the king of darkness in Gotham, the Batman...

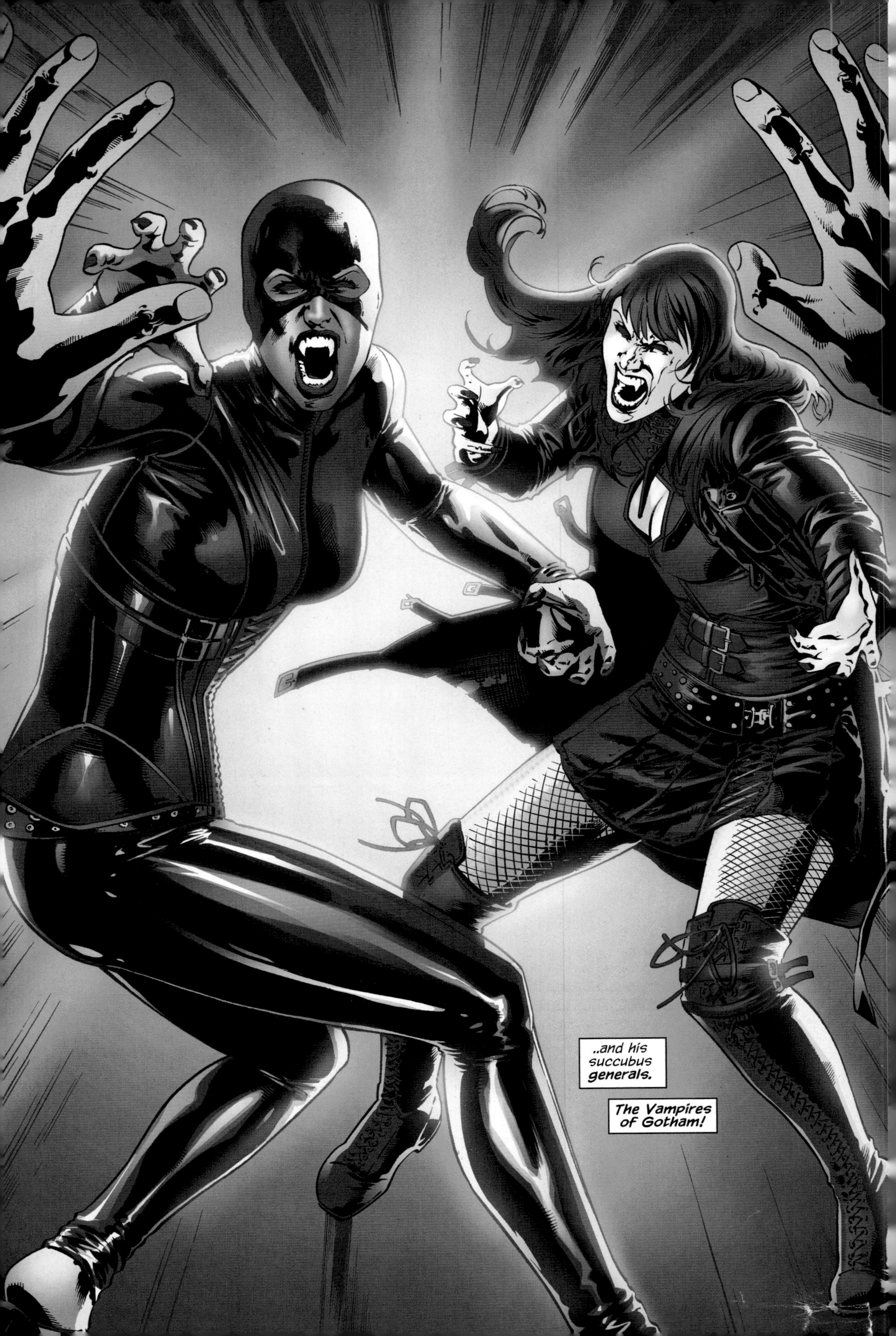
..and his succubus generals.
The Vampires of Gotham!

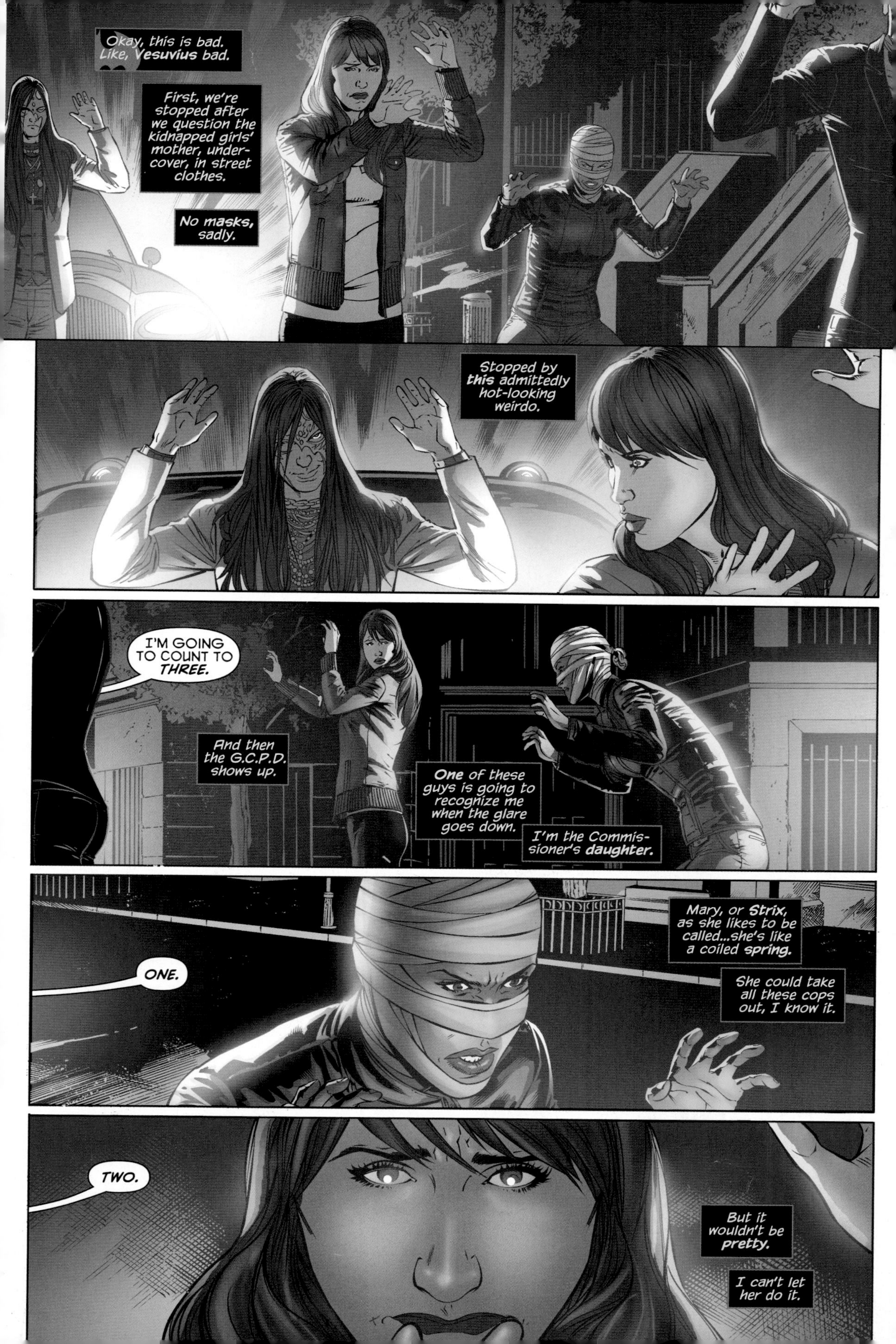

Okay, this is bad. Like, Vesuvius bad.
First, we're stopped after we question the kidnapped girls' mother, under-cover, in street clothes.
No masks, sadly.
Stopped by this admittedly hot-looking weirdo.
I'M GOING TO COUNT TO THREE.
And then the G.C.P.D. shows up.
One of these guys is going to recognize me when the glare goes down.
I'm the Commis-sioner's daughter.
ONE.
Mary, or Strix, as she likes to be called...she's like a coiled spring.
She could take all these cops out, I know it.
TWO.
But it wouldn't be pretty.
I can't let her do it.

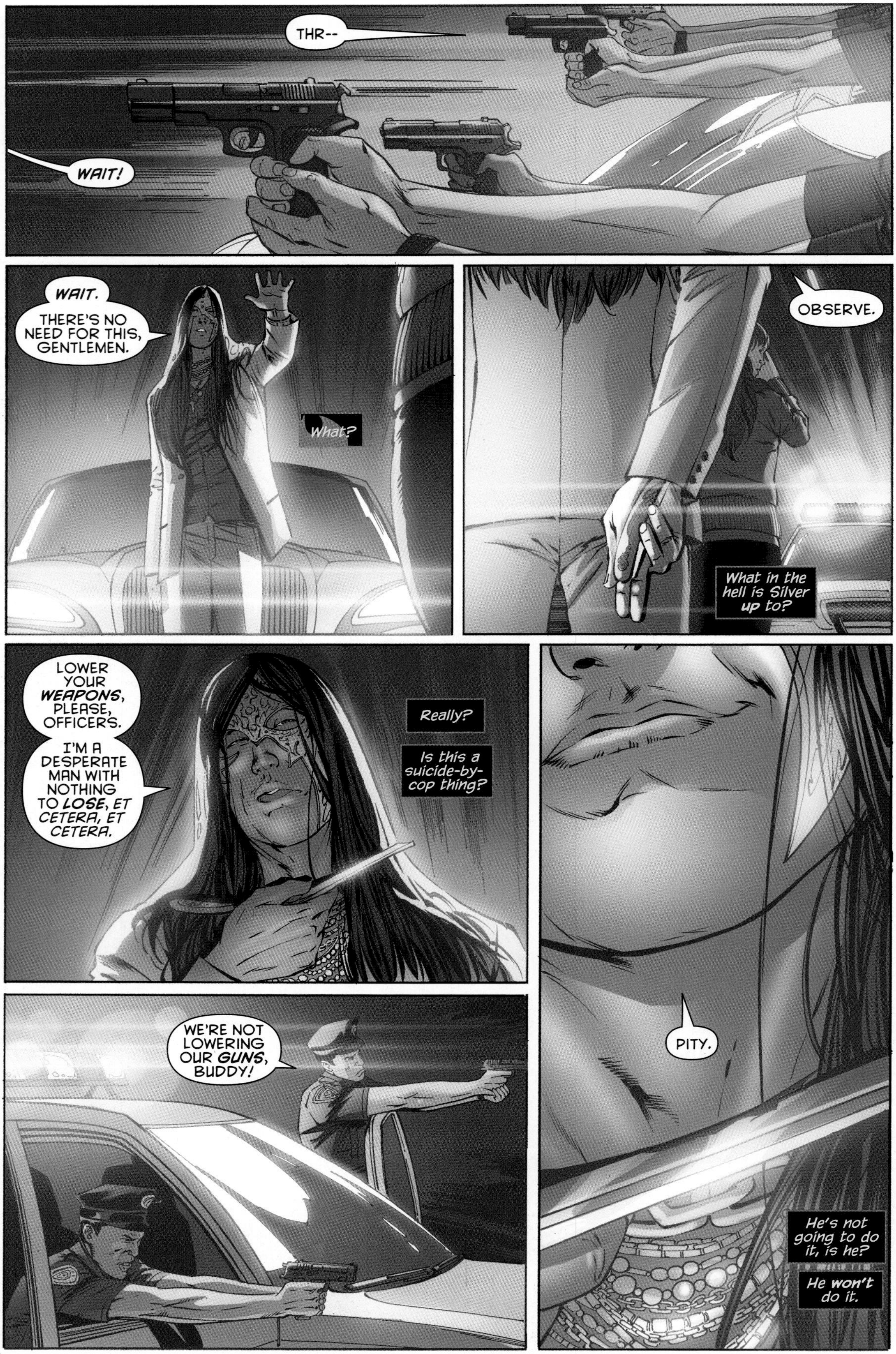
THR--
WAIT!
WAIT.
THERE'S NO NEED FOR THIS, GENTLEMEN.
What?
OBSERVE.
What in the hell is Silver up to?
LOWER YOUR WEAPONS, PLEASE, OFFICERS.
I'M A DESPERATE MAN WITH NOTHING TO LOSE, ET CETERA, ET CETERA.
Really?
Is this a suicide-by-cop thing?
WE'RE NOT LOWERING OUR GUNS, BUDDY!
PITY.
He's not going to do it, is he?
He won't do it.

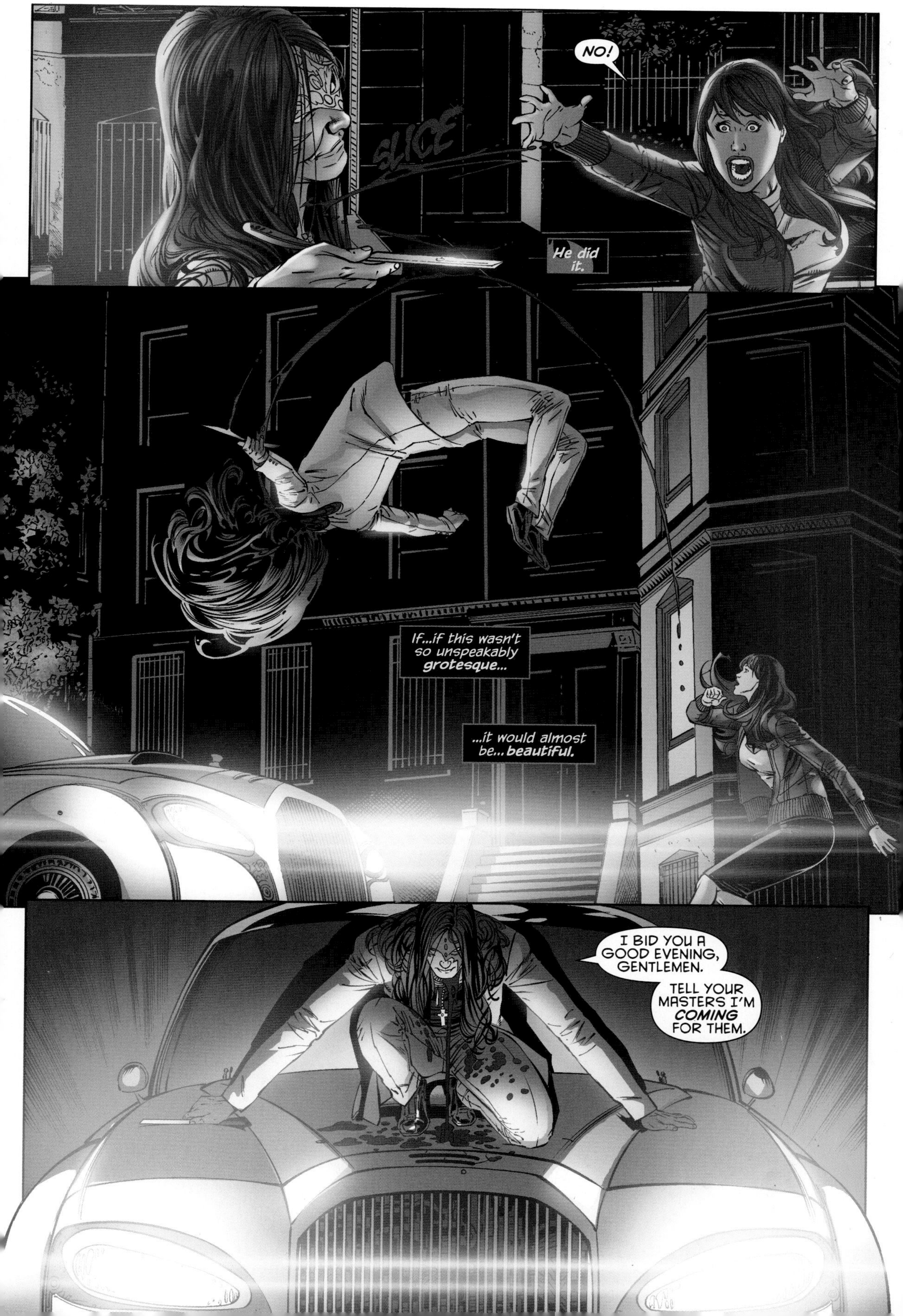
NO!
SLICE
He did it.
If...if this wasn't so unspeakably grotesque...
...it would almost be...beautiful.
I BID YOU A GOOD EVENING, GENTLEMEN.
TELL YOUR MASTERS I'M COMING FOR THEM.

Uh, oh.

KLI-KLAK

GET *DOWN!* EVERY-BODY, TAKE *COVER!*

BUDDA BUDDA BUDDA

Can't let this happen. *Even if it blows my cover.*

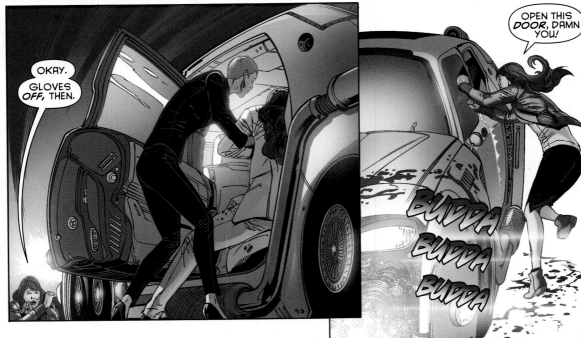

OKAY. GLOVES *OFF,* THEN.

OPEN THIS *DOOR,* DAMN YOU!

BUDDA BUDDA BUDDA

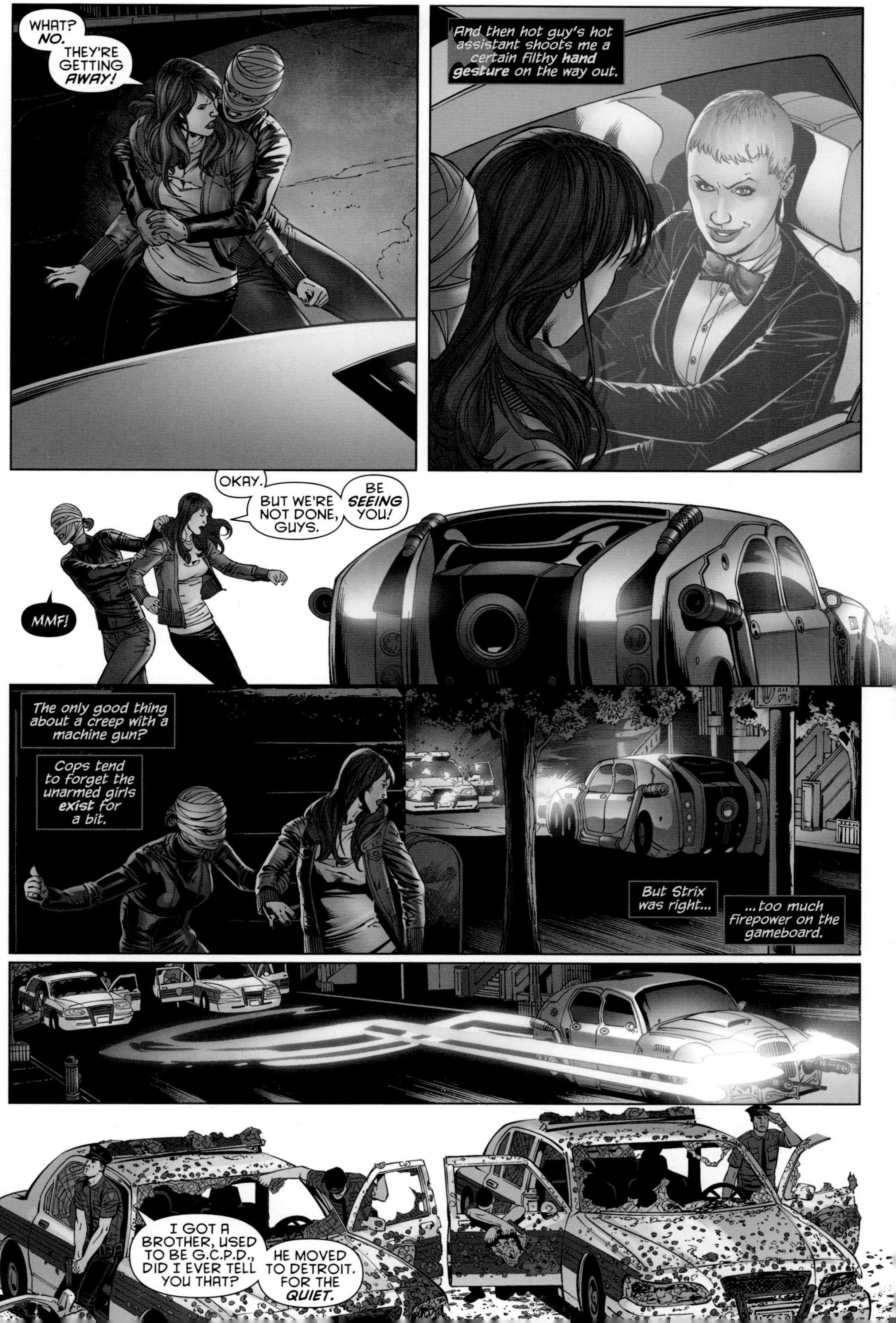
WHAT? NO. THEY'RE GETTING AWAY!
And then hot guy's hot assistant shoots me a certain filthy hand gesture on the way out.
OKAY.
BUT WE'RE NOT DONE, GUYS.
BE SEEING YOU!
MMF!
The only good thing about a creep with a machine gun?
Cops tend to forget the unarmed girls exist for a bit.
But Strix was right...
...too much firepower on the gameboard.
I GOT A BROTHER, USED TO BE G.C.P.D., DID I EVER TELL YOU THAT?
HE MOVED TO DETROIT. FOR THE QUIET.

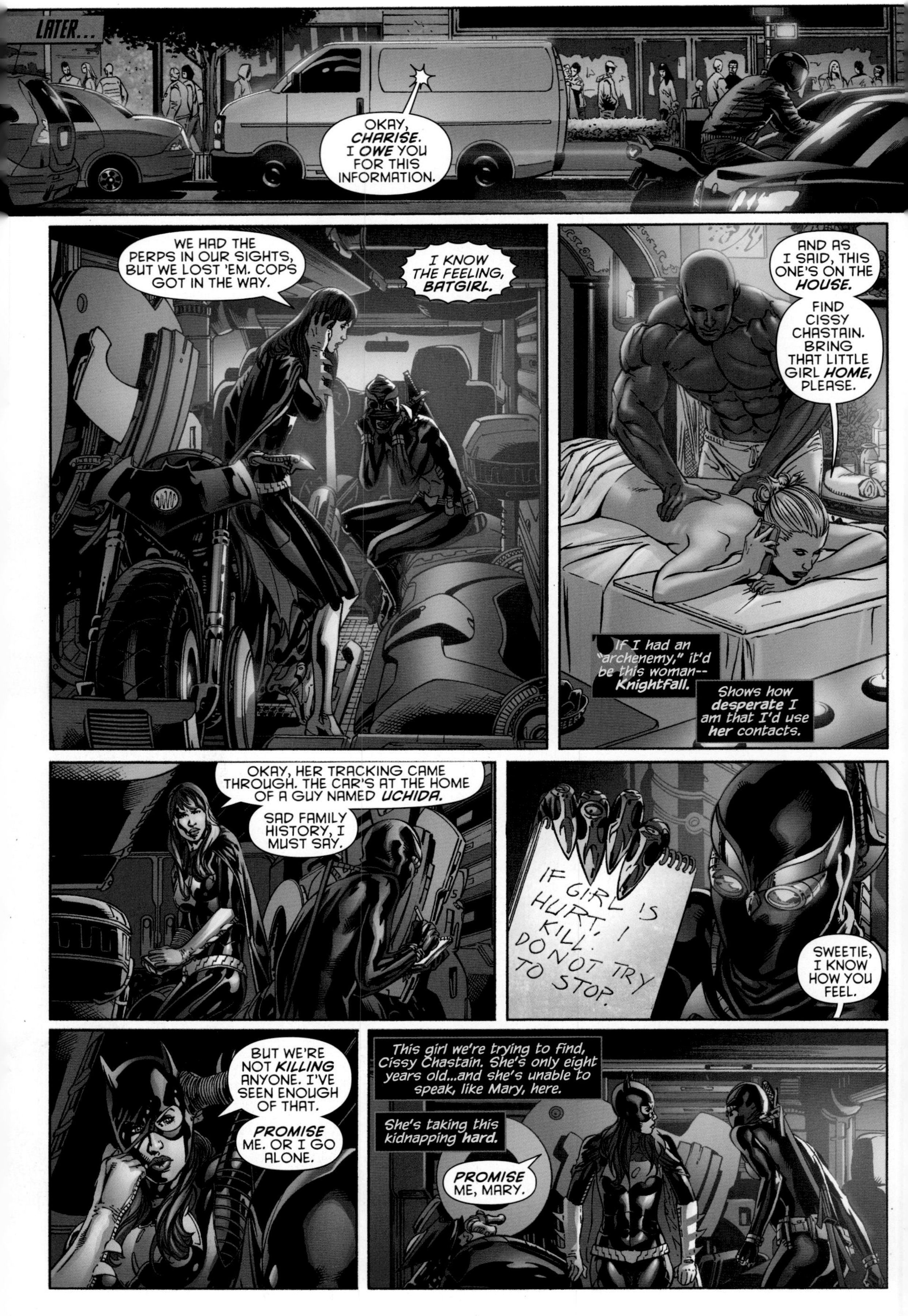
LATER...
OKAY, CHARISE. I OWE YOU FOR THIS INFORMATION.
WE HAD THE PERPS IN OUR SIGHTS, BUT WE LOST 'EM. COPS GOT IN THE WAY.
I KNOW THE FEELING, BATGIRL.
AND AS I SAID, THIS ONE'S ON THE HOUSE.
FIND CISSY CHASTAIN. BRING THAT LITTLE GIRL HOME, PLEASE.
If I had an "archenemy," it'd be this woman--Knightfall.
Shows how desperate I am that I'd use her contacts.
OKAY, HER TRACKING CAME THROUGH. THE CAR'S AT THE HOME OF A GUY NAMED UCHIDA.
SAD FAMILY HISTORY, I MUST SAY.
IF GIRL IS HURT. I KILL. DO NOT TRY TO STOP.
SWEETIE, I KNOW HOW YOU FEEL.
BUT WE'RE NOT KILLING ANYONE. I'VE SEEN ENOUGH OF THAT.
PROMISE ME. OR I GO ALONE.
This girl we're trying to find, Cissy Chastain. She's only eight years old...and she's unable to speak, like Mary, here.
She's taking this kidnapping hard.
PROMISE ME, MARY.

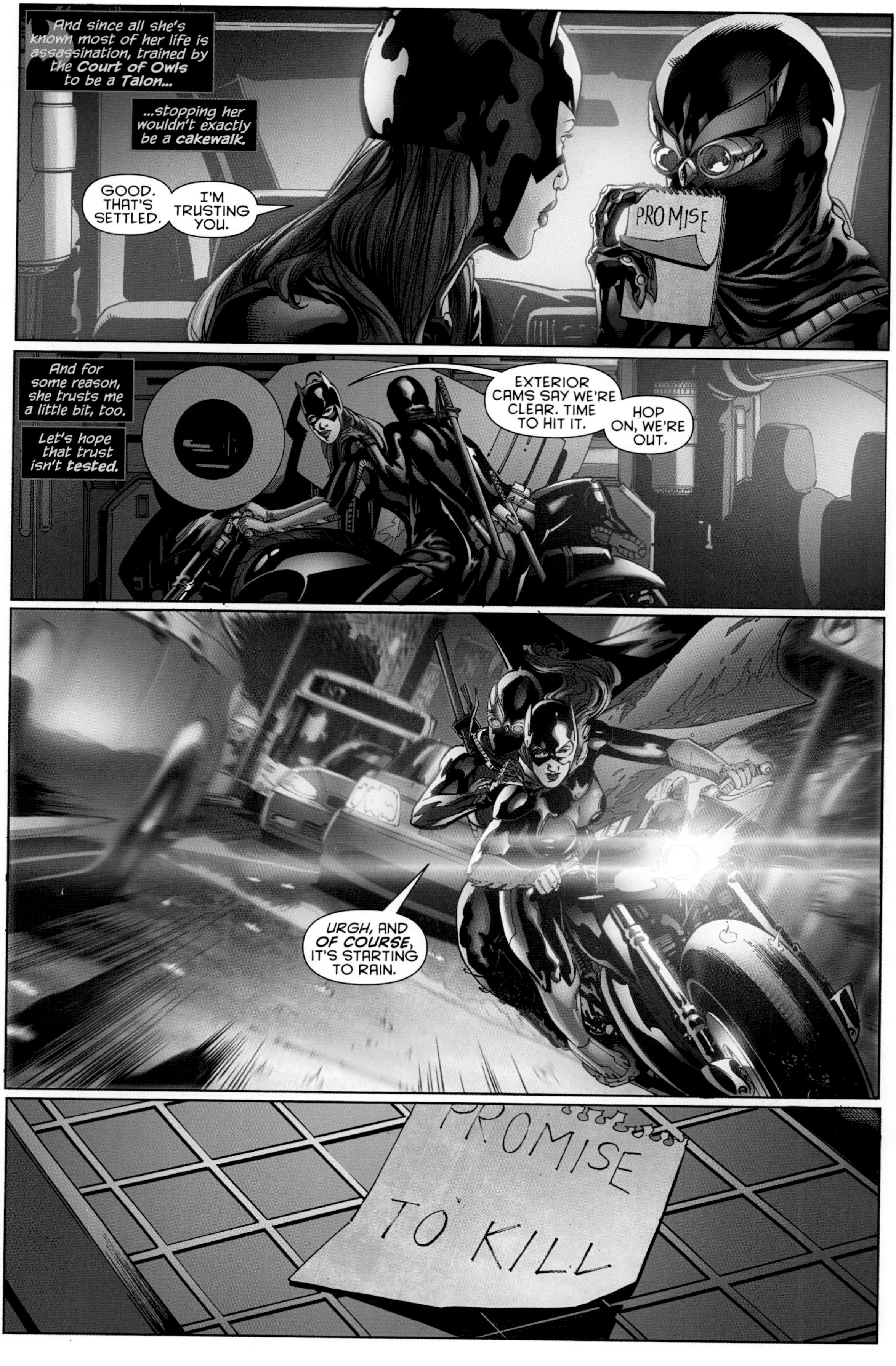

And since all she's known most of her life is assassination, trained by the Court of Owls to be a Talon...
...stopping her wouldn't exactly be a cakewalk.
GOOD. THAT'S SETTLED.
I'M TRUSTING YOU.
PROMISE
And for some reason, she trusts me a little bit, too.
Let's hope that trust isn't tested.
EXTERIOR CAMS SAY WE'RE CLEAR. TIME TO HIT IT.
HOP ON, WE'RE OUT.
URGH, AND OF COURSE, IT'S STARTING TO RAIN.
PROMISE TO KILL

THAT WAS RATHER A GRAND, DRAMATIC *GAMBIT*, WOULDN'T YOU SAY, *MISS TARGA?*

A DANGEROUS ONE, MASTER. YOU JUST *NICKED* THE BLOOD VESSELS AROUND THE THYROID GLAND. MASTERFUL. A BABY'S BREATH DEEPER AND YOU WOULD NEVER HAVE MADE IT HOME.

I CAN'T *LOSE* YOU, MR. UCHIDA.

OH... WELL...

...THIS IS AWKWARD.

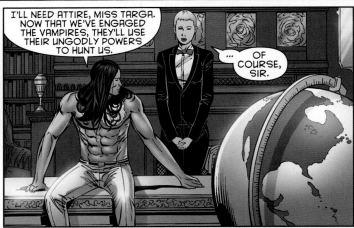

I'LL NEED ATTIRE, MISS TARGA. NOW THAT WE'VE ENGAGED THE VAMPIRES, THEY'LL USE THEIR UNGODLY POWERS TO HUNT US.

... OF COURSE, SIR.

YOU'LL NEED YOUR DRINK, SILVER.

ALL OF IT, PLEASE.

I HEARD THE CHILD CRYING, SIR. ARE YOU *CERTAIN* THAT--

IT'S NOT A *CHILD*, DEAR FRIEND.

THAT'S WHAT IT *WANTS* YOU TO BELIEVE.

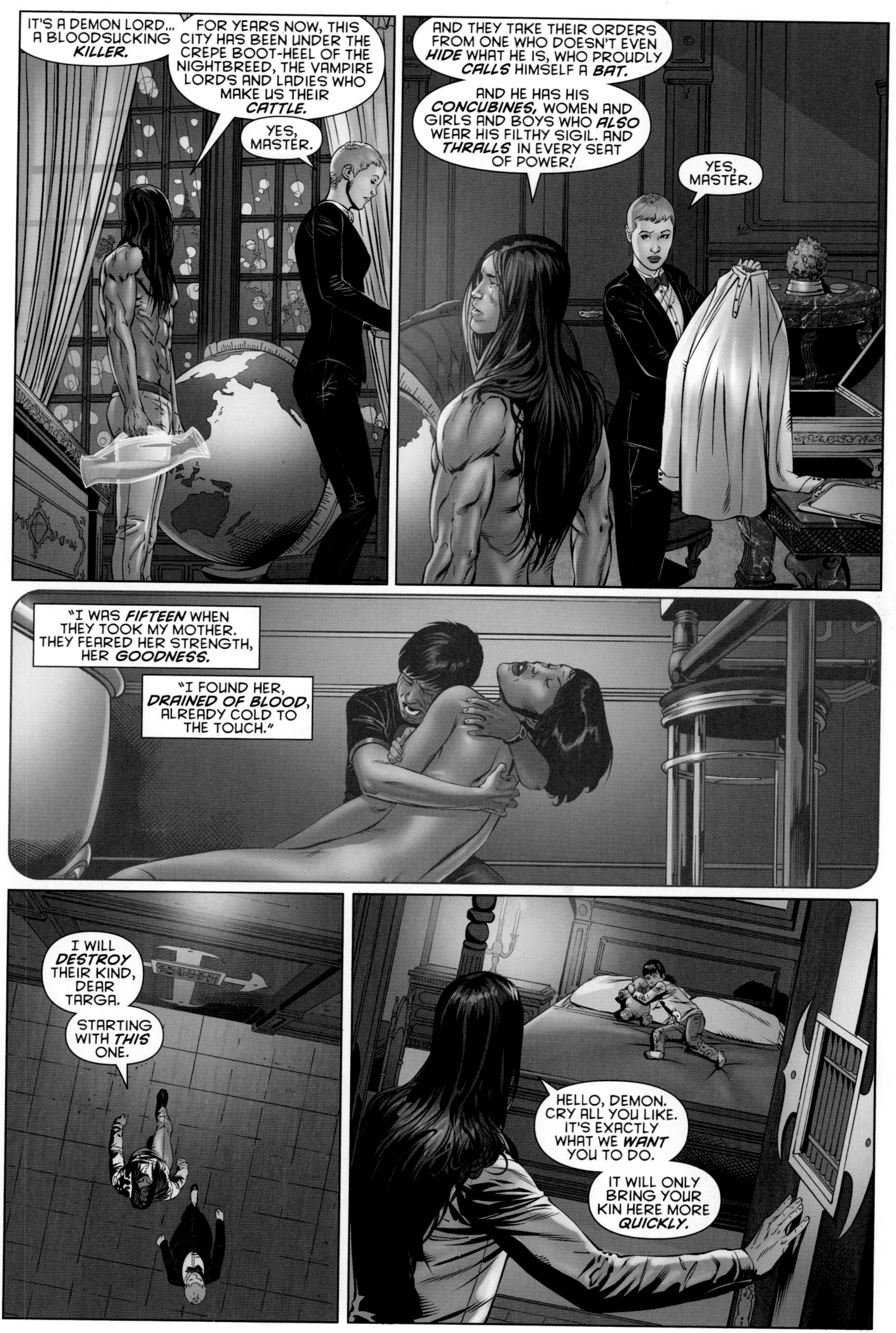
IT'S A DEMON LORD... A BLOODSUCKING KILLER.
FOR YEARS NOW, THIS CITY HAS BEEN UNDER THE CREPE BOOT-HEEL OF THE NIGHTBREED, THE VAMPIRE LORDS AND LADIES WHO MAKE US THEIR CATTLE.
YES, MASTER.
AND THEY TAKE THEIR ORDERS FROM ONE WHO DOESN'T EVEN HIDE WHAT HE IS, WHO PROUDLY CALLS HIMSELF A BAT.
AND HE HAS HIS CONCUBINES, WOMEN AND GIRLS AND BOYS WHO ALSO WEAR HIS FILTHY SIGIL. AND THRALLS IN EVERY SEAT OF POWER!
YES, MASTER.
"I WAS FIFTEEN WHEN THEY TOOK MY MOTHER. THEY FEARED HER STRENGTH, HER GOODNESS.
"I FOUND HER, DRAINED OF BLOOD, ALREADY COLD TO THE TOUCH."
I WILL DESTROY THEIR KIND, DEAR TARGA.
STARTING WITH THIS ONE.
HELLO, DEMON. CRY ALL YOU LIKE. IT'S EXACTLY WHAT WE WANT YOU TO DO.
IT WILL ONLY BRING YOUR KIN HERE MORE QUICKLY.

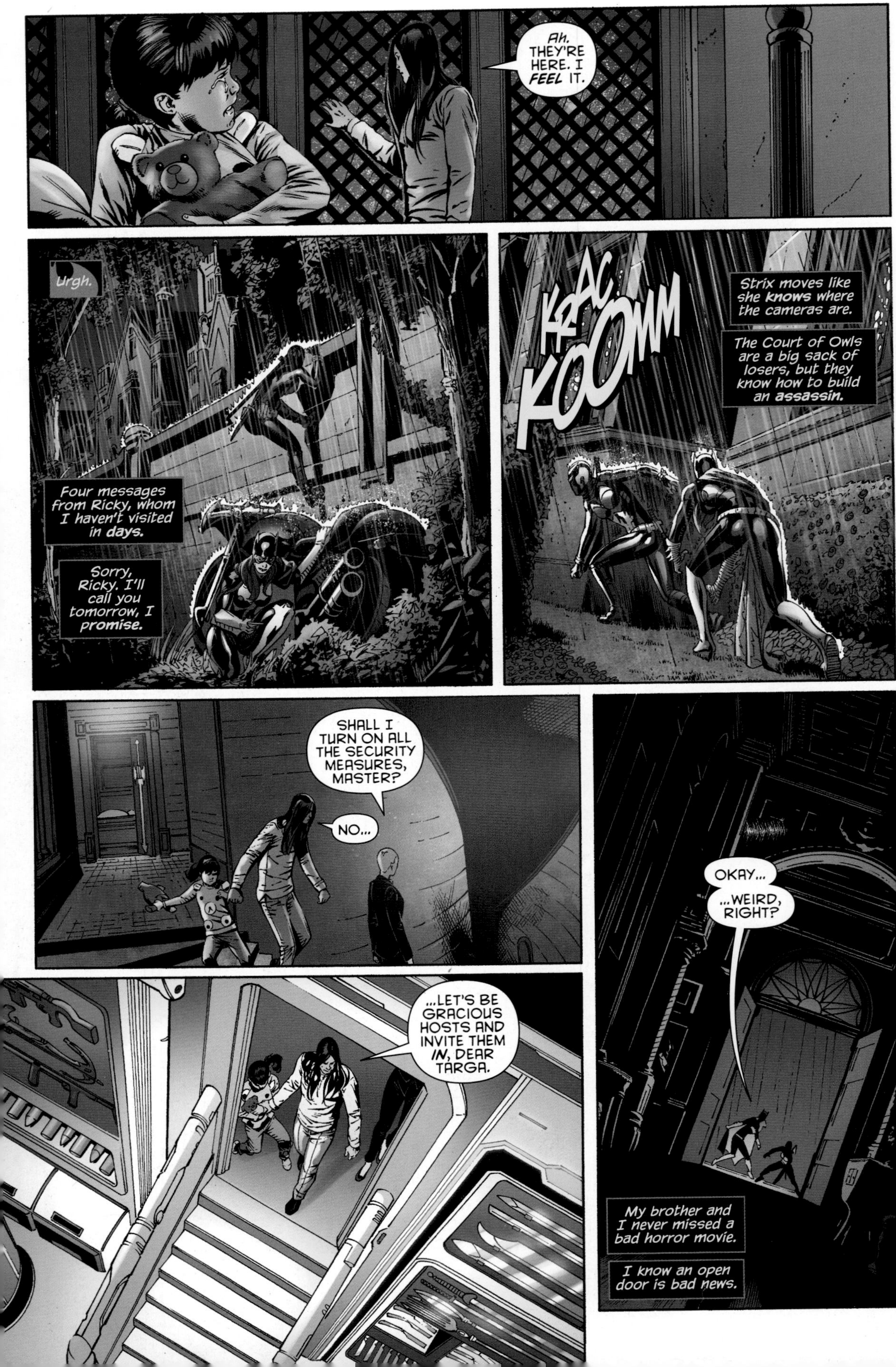

Ah. THEY'RE HERE. I FEEL IT.
Urgh.
Four messages from Ricky, whom I haven't visited in days.
Sorry, Ricky. I'll call you tomorrow, I promise.
KRAC KOOMM
Strix moves like she knows where the cameras are.
The Court of Owls are a big sack of losers, but they know how to build an assassin.
SHALL I TURN ON ALL THE SECURITY MEASURES, MASTER?
NO...
...LET'S BE GRACIOUS HOSTS AND INVITE THEM IN, DEAR TARGA.
OKAY...
...WEIRD, RIGHT?
My brother and I never missed a bad horror movie.
I know an open door is bad news.

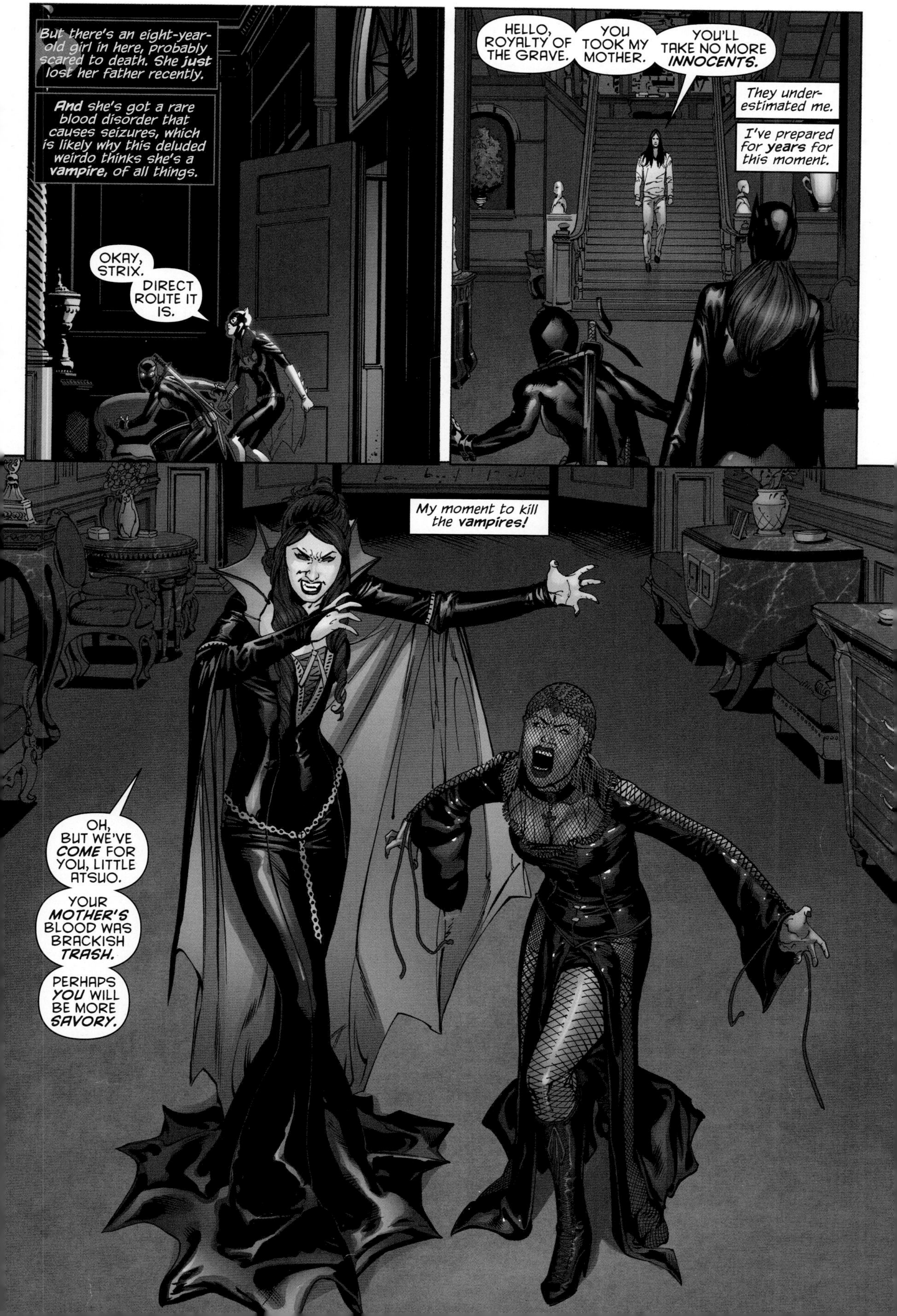

But there's an eight-year-old girl in here, probably scared to death. She just lost her father recently.
And she's got a rare blood disorder that causes seizures, which is likely why this deluded weirdo thinks she's a vampire, of all things.
OKAY, STRIX.
DIRECT ROUTE IT IS.
HELLO, ROYALTY OF THE GRAVE.
YOU TOOK MY MOTHER.
YOU'LL TAKE NO MORE INNOCENTS.
They under-estimated me.
I've prepared for years for this moment.
My moment to kill the vampires!
OH, BUT WE'VE COME FOR YOU, LITTLE ATSUO.
YOUR MOTHER'S BLOOD WAS BRACKISH TRASH.
PERHAPS YOU WILL BE MORE SAVORY.

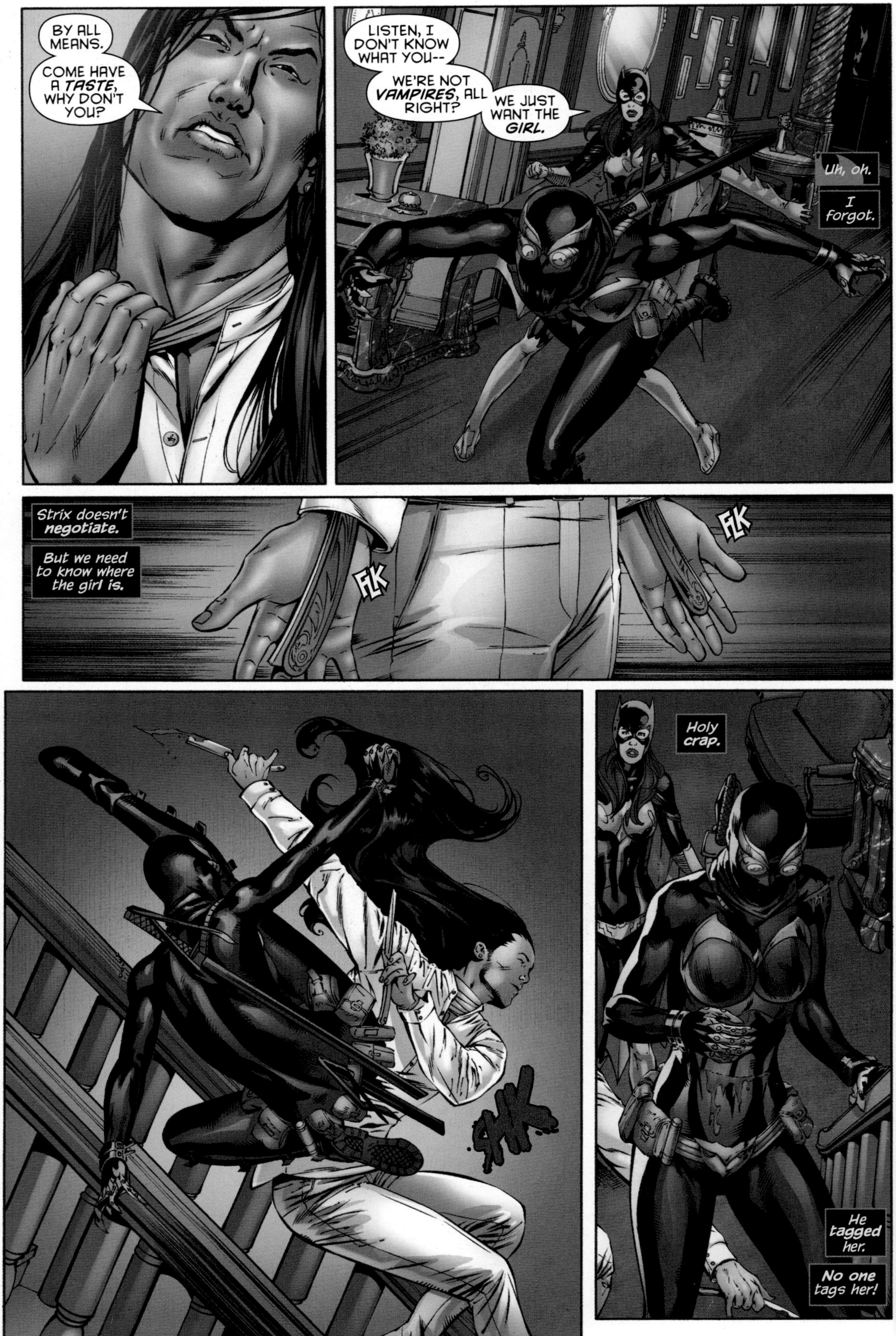
BY ALL MEANS.
COME HAVE A TASTE, WHY DON'T YOU?
LISTEN, I DON'T KNOW WHAT YOU--
WE'RE NOT VAMPIRES, ALL RIGHT?
WE JUST WANT THE GIRL.
Uh, oh.
I forgot.
Strix doesn't negotiate.
But we need to know where the girl is.
FLK
FLK
SHK
Holy crap.
He tagged her.
No one tags her!

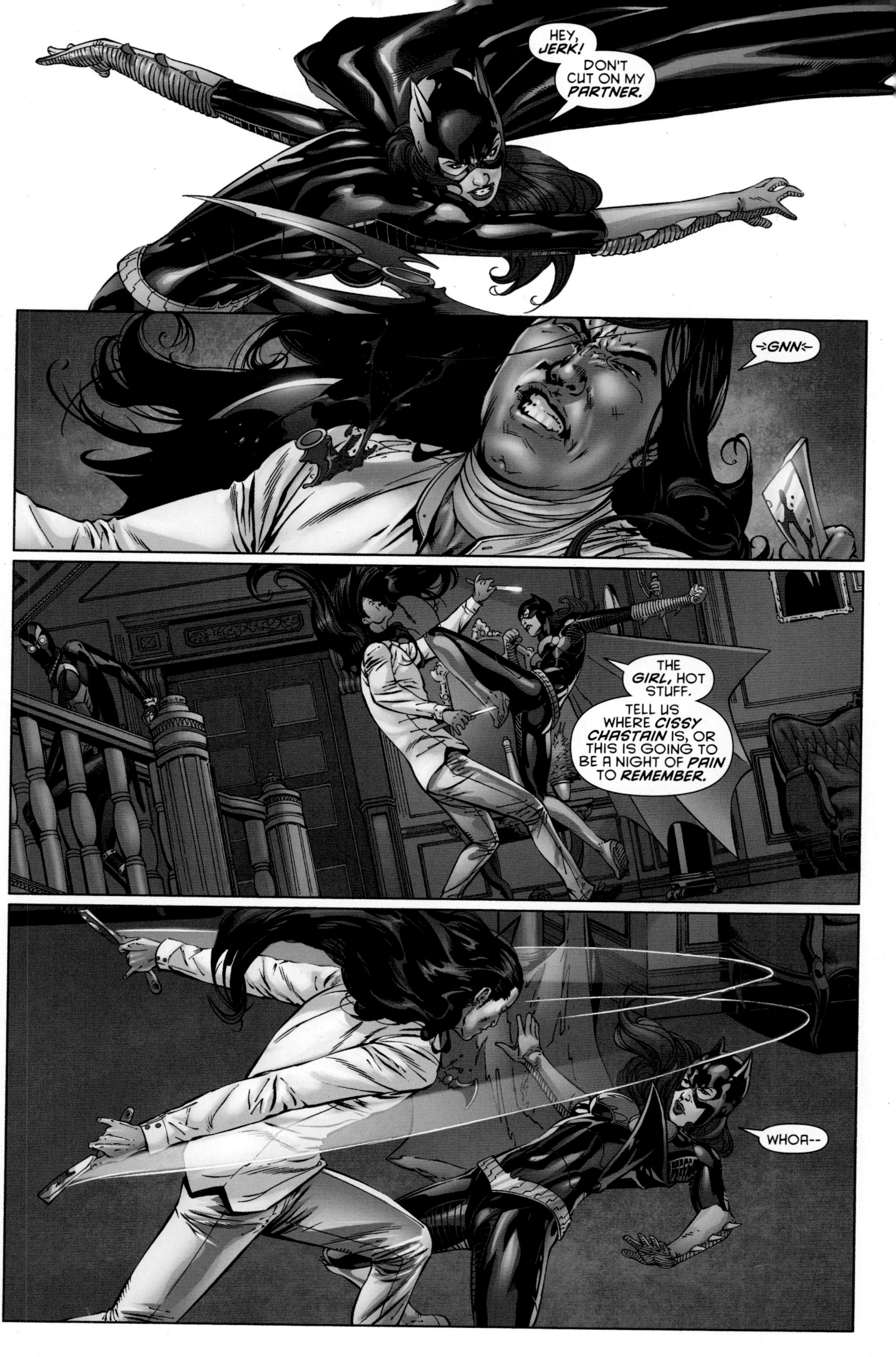
HEY, *JERK!* DON'T CUT ON MY *PARTNER.*
-GNN-
THE *GIRL,* HOT STUFF.
TELL US WHERE *CISSY CHASTAIN* IS, OR THIS IS GOING TO BE A NIGHT OF *PAIN* TO *REMEMBER.*
WHOA--

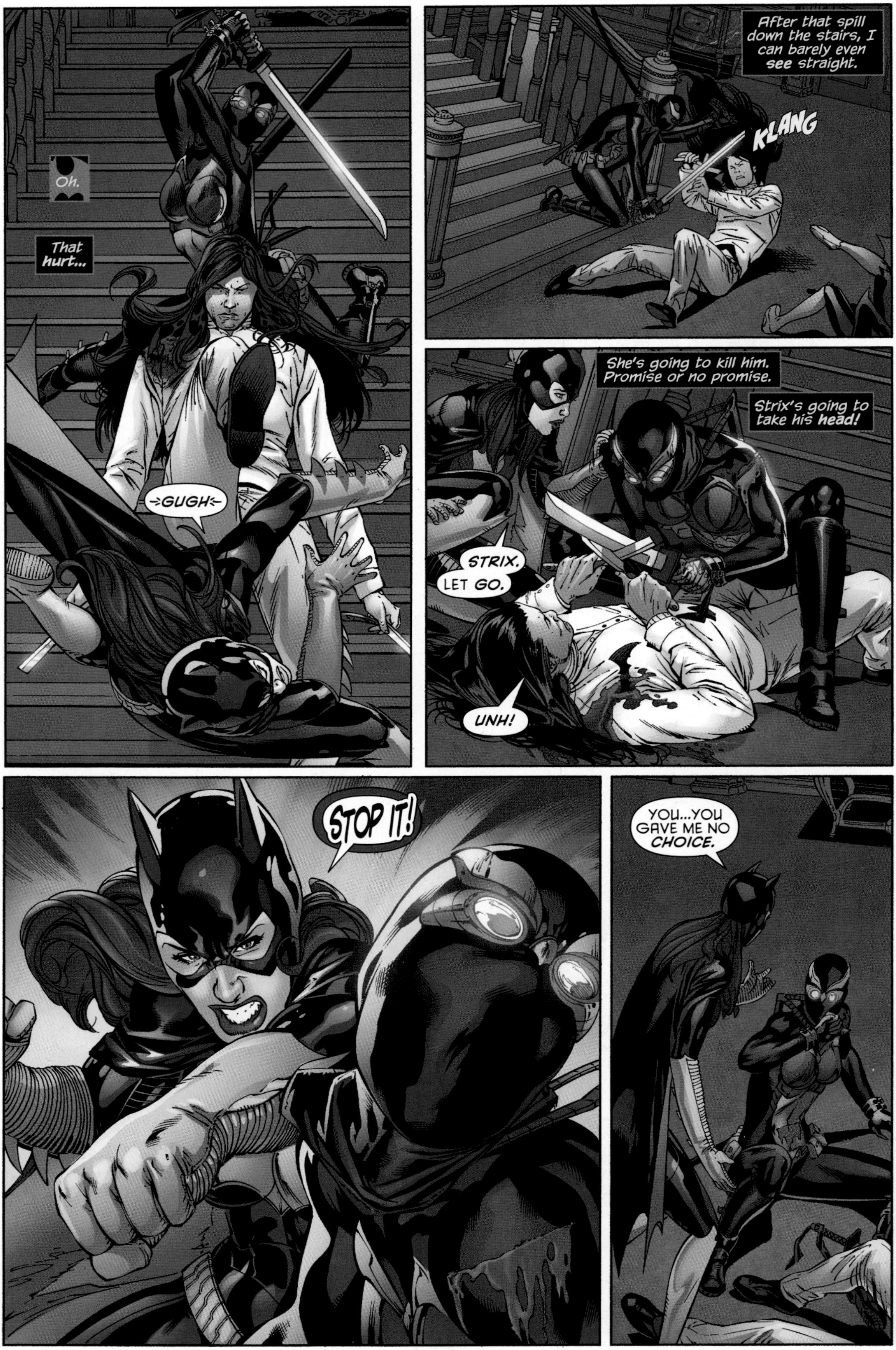
Oh.
That hurt...
GUGH
After that spill down the stairs, I can barely even see straight.
KLANG
She's going to kill him. Promise or no promise.
Strix's going to take his head!
STRIX. LET GO.
UNH!
STOP IT!
YOU...YOU GAVE ME NO CHOICE.

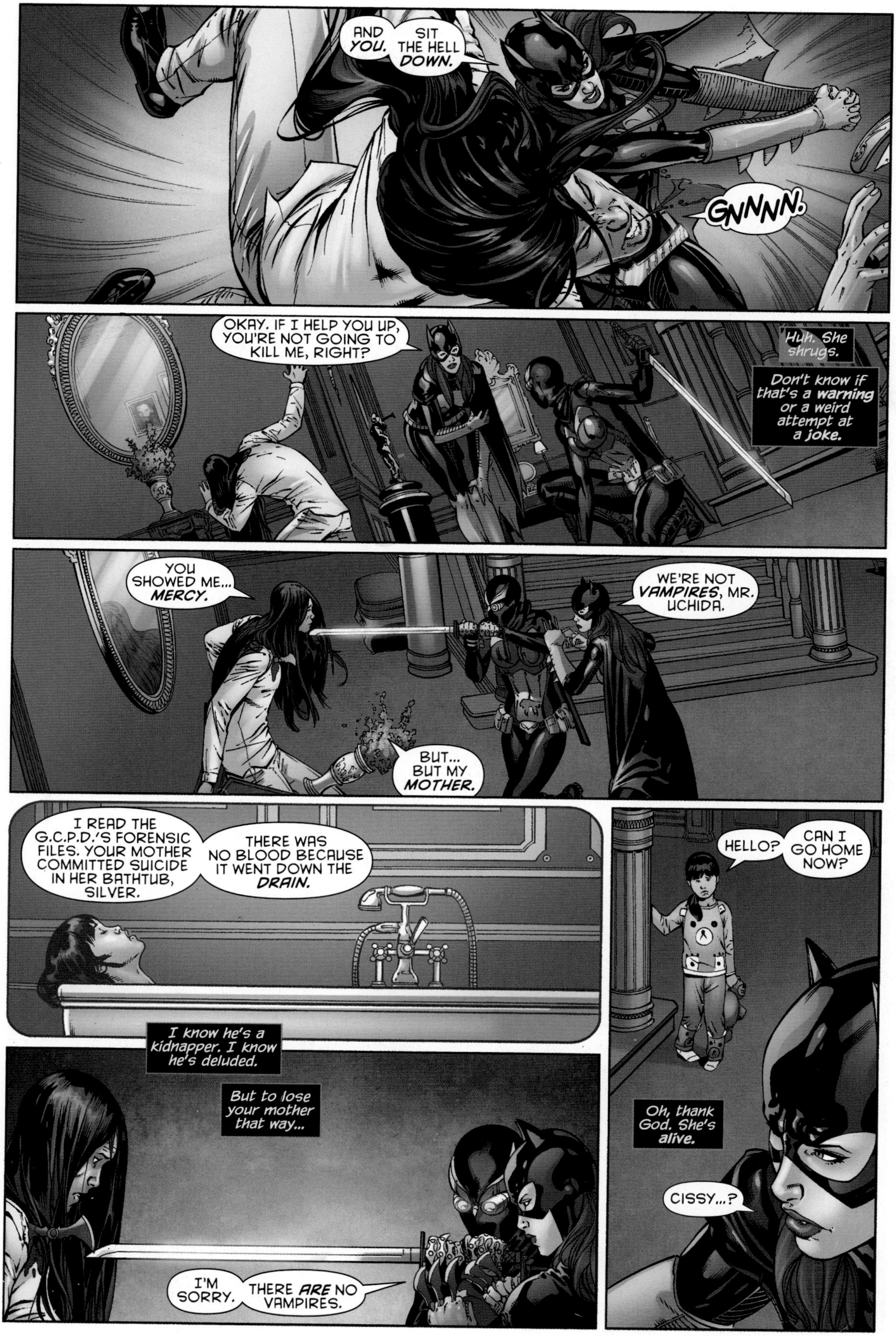
AND YOU. SIT THE HELL DOWN.
GNNNN.
OKAY. IF I HELP YOU UP, YOU'RE NOT GOING TO KILL ME, RIGHT?
Huh. She shrugs.
Don't know if that's a warning or a weird attempt at a joke.
YOU SHOWED ME... MERCY.
WE'RE NOT VAMPIRES, MR. UCHIDA.
BUT... BUT MY MOTHER.
I READ THE G.C.P.D.'S FORENSIC FILES. YOUR MOTHER COMMITTED SUICIDE IN HER BATHTUB, SILVER.
THERE WAS NO BLOOD BECAUSE IT WENT DOWN THE DRAIN.
I know he's a kidnapper. I know he's deluded.
But to lose your mother that way...
I'M SORRY.
THERE ARE NO VAMPIRES.
HELLO?
CAN I GO HOME NOW?
Oh, thank God. She's alive.
CISSY...?

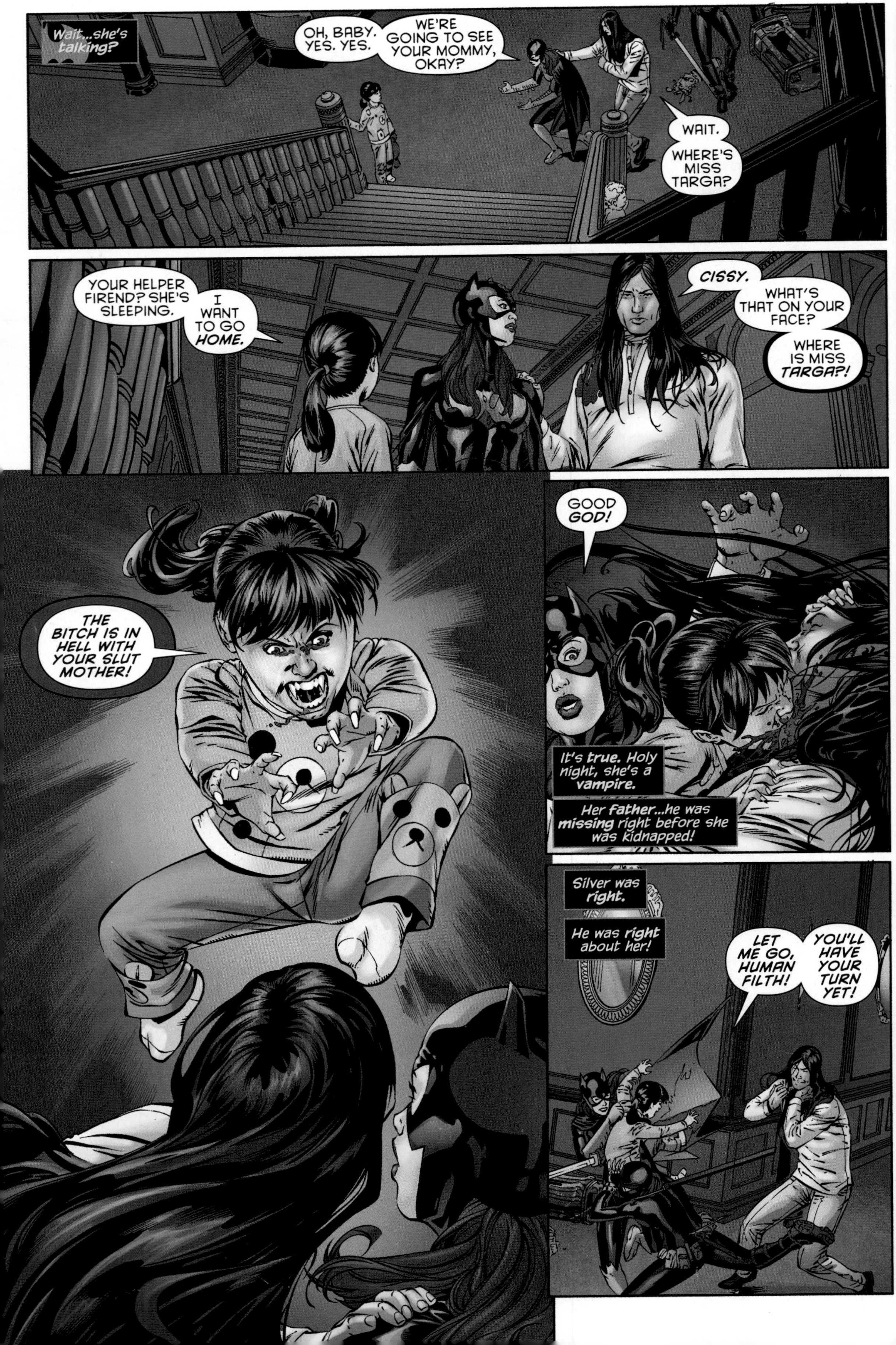
Wait...she's talking?
OH, BABY. YES. YES.
WE'RE GOING TO SEE YOUR MOMMY, OKAY?
WAIT. WHERE'S MISS TARGA?
YOUR HELPER FIREND? SHE'S SLEEPING.
I WANT TO GO HOME.
CISSY.
WHAT'S THAT ON YOUR FACE?
WHERE IS MISS TARGA?!
THE BITCH IS IN HELL WITH YOUR SLUT MOTHER!
GOOD GOD!
It's true. Holy night, she's a vampire.
Her father...he was missing right before she was kidnapped!
Silver was right.
He was right about her!
LET ME GO, HUMAN FILTH!
YOU'LL HAVE YOUR TURN YET!

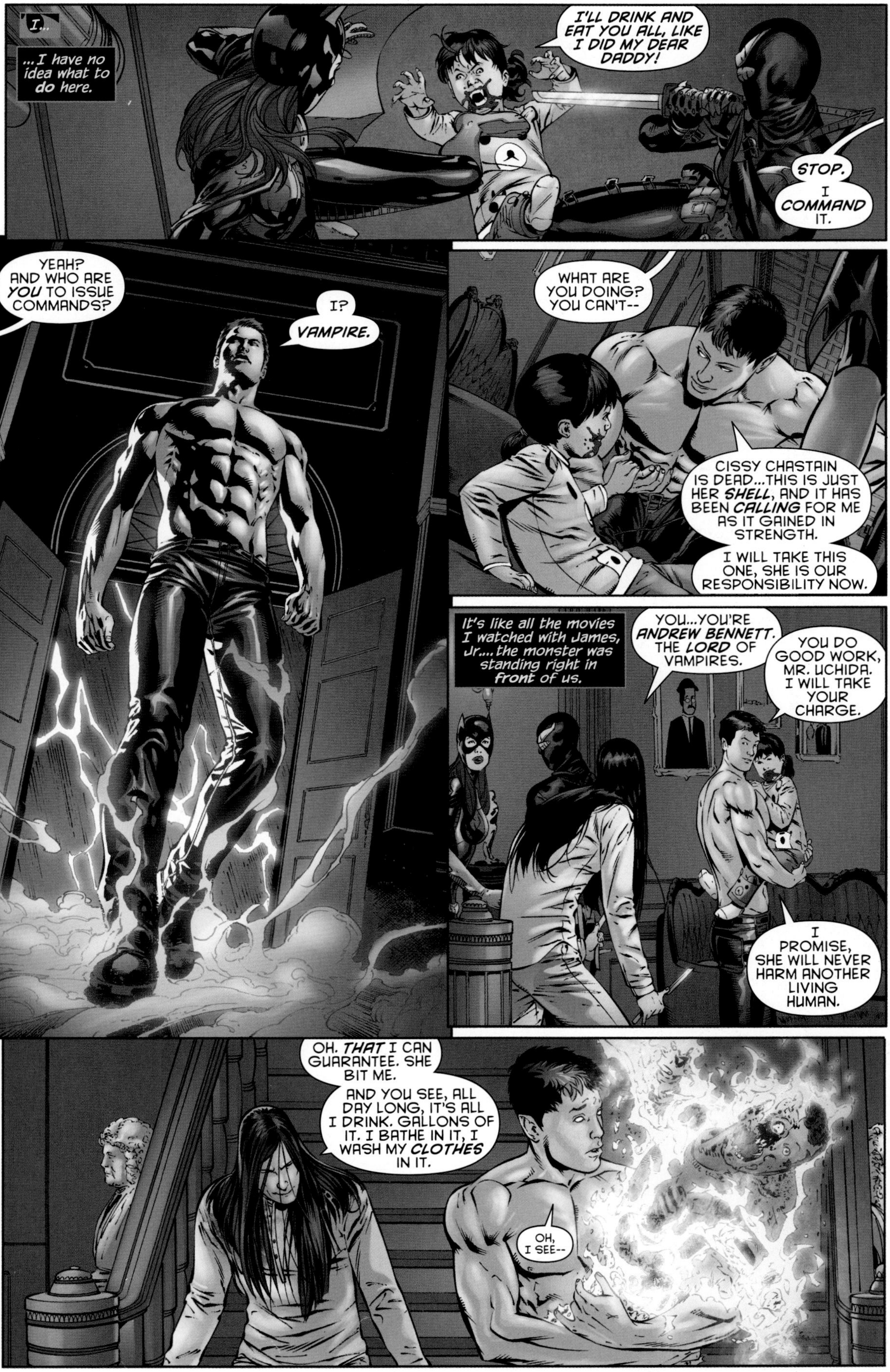
I...
...I have no idea what to do here.
I'LL DRINK AND EAT YOU ALL, LIKE I DID MY DEAR DADDY!
STOP. I COMMAND IT.
YEAH? AND WHO ARE YOU TO ISSUE COMMANDS?
I? VAMPIRE.
WHAT ARE YOU DOING? YOU CAN'T--
CISSY CHASTAIN IS DEAD...THIS IS JUST HER SHELL, AND IT HAS BEEN CALLING FOR ME AS IT GAINED IN STRENGTH.
I WILL TAKE THIS ONE, SHE IS OUR RESPONSIBILITY NOW.
It's like all the movies I watched with James, Jr.... the monster was standing right in front of us.
YOU...YOU'RE ANDREW BENNETT. THE LORD OF VAMPIRES.
YOU DO GOOD WORK, MR. UCHIDA. I WILL TAKE YOUR CHARGE.
I PROMISE, SHE WILL NEVER HARM ANOTHER LIVING HUMAN.
OH. THAT I CAN GUARANTEE. SHE BIT ME.
AND YOU SEE, ALL DAY LONG, IT'S ALL I DRINK. GALLONS OF IT. I BATHE IN IT, I WASH MY CLOTHES IN IT.
OH, I SEE--

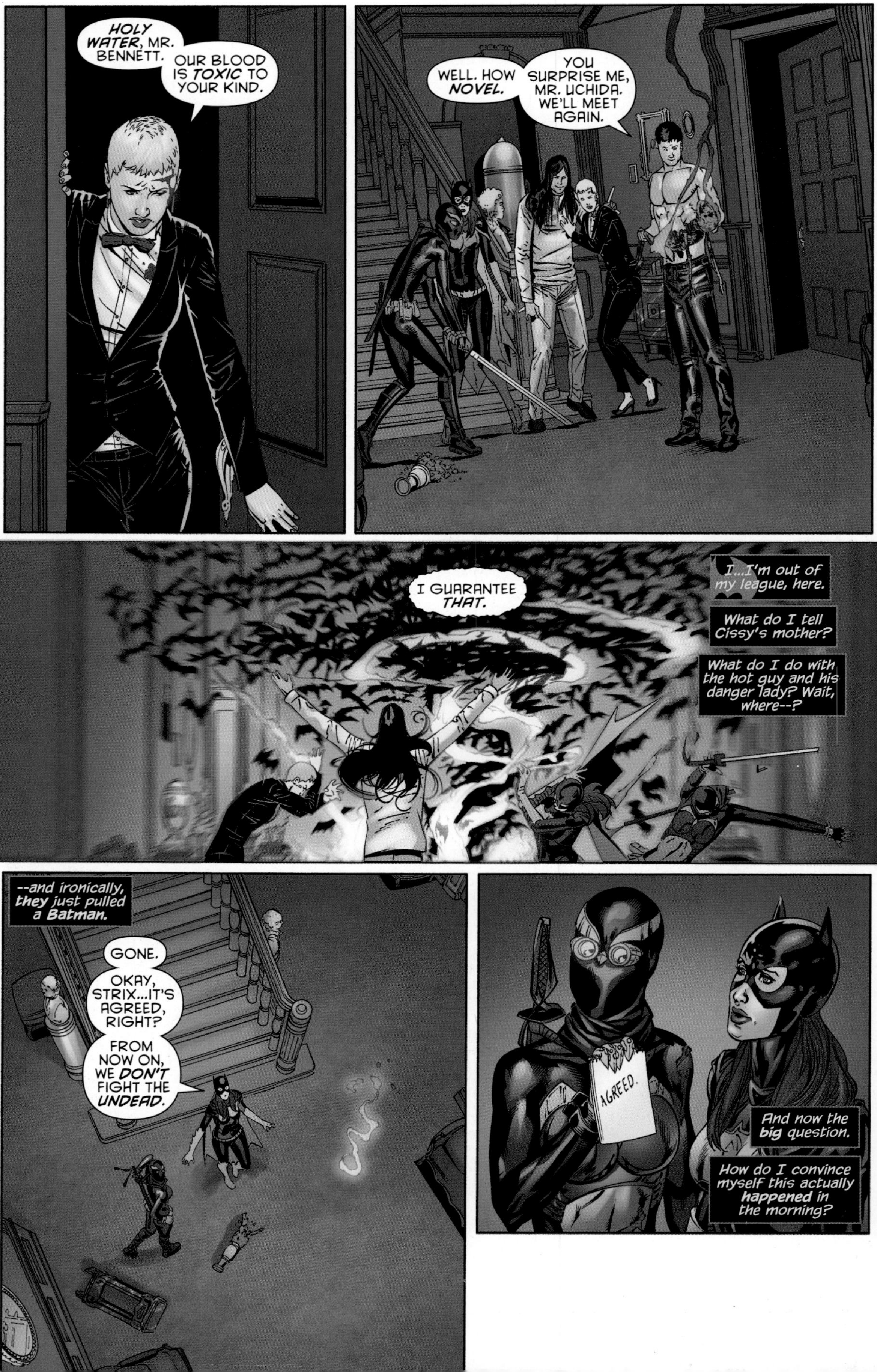
HOLY WATER, MR. BENNETT.
OUR BLOOD IS TOXIC TO YOUR KIND.
WELL. HOW NOVEL.
YOU SURPRISE ME, MR. UCHIDA. WE'LL MEET AGAIN.
I GUARANTEE THAT.
I...I'm out of my league, here.
What do I tell Cissy's mother?
What do I do with the hot guy and his danger lady? Wait, where--?
--and ironically, they just pulled a Batman.
GONE.
OKAY, STRIX...IT'S AGREED, RIGHT?
FROM NOW ON, WE DON'T FIGHT THE UNDEAD.
AGREED.
And now the big question.
How do I convince myself this actually happened in the morning?

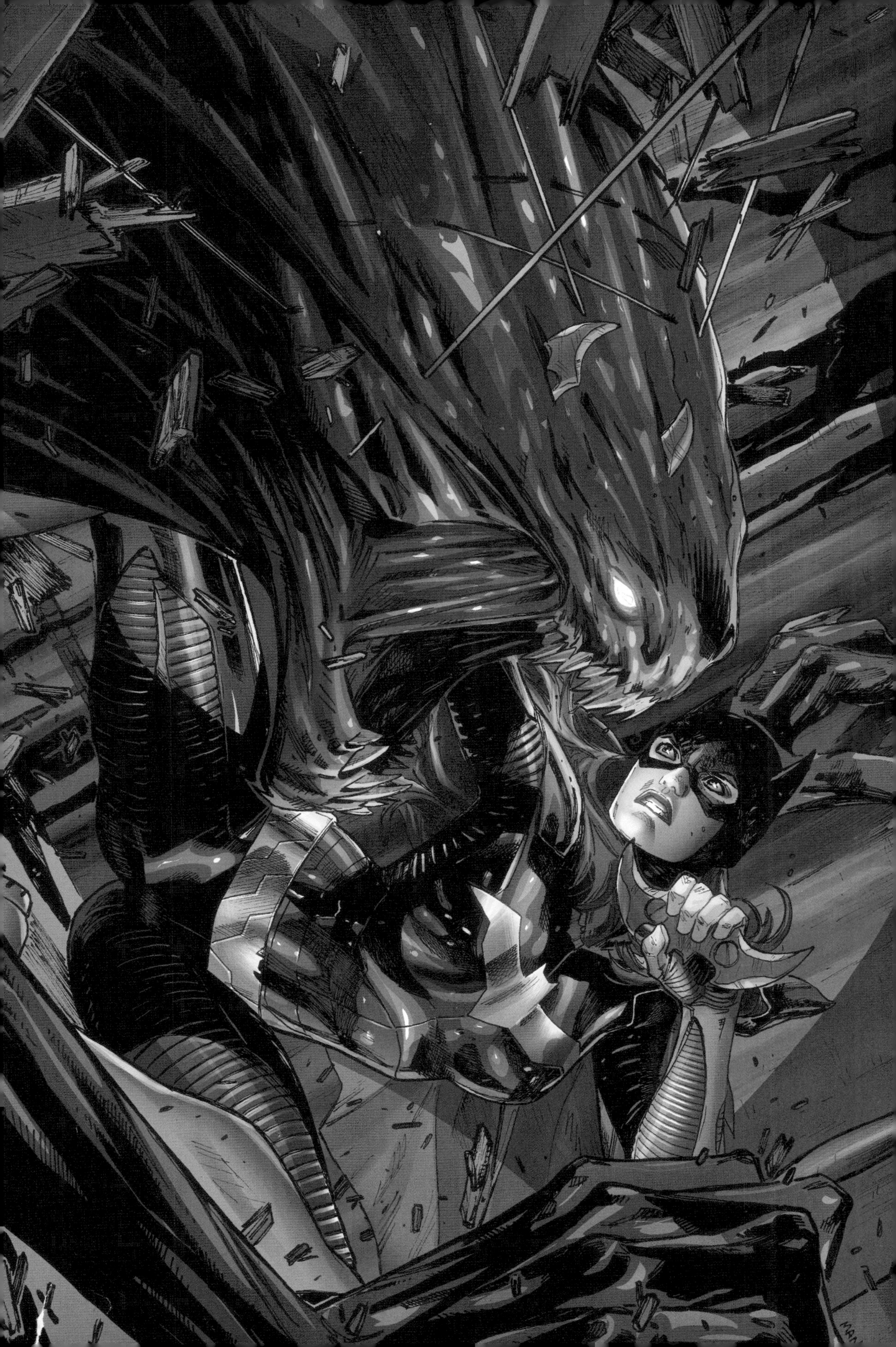

MARGUERITE BENNETT writer ROBERT GILL artist ROMULO FAJARDO, JR. colorist
CLAY MANN & PAUL MOUNTS cover artists

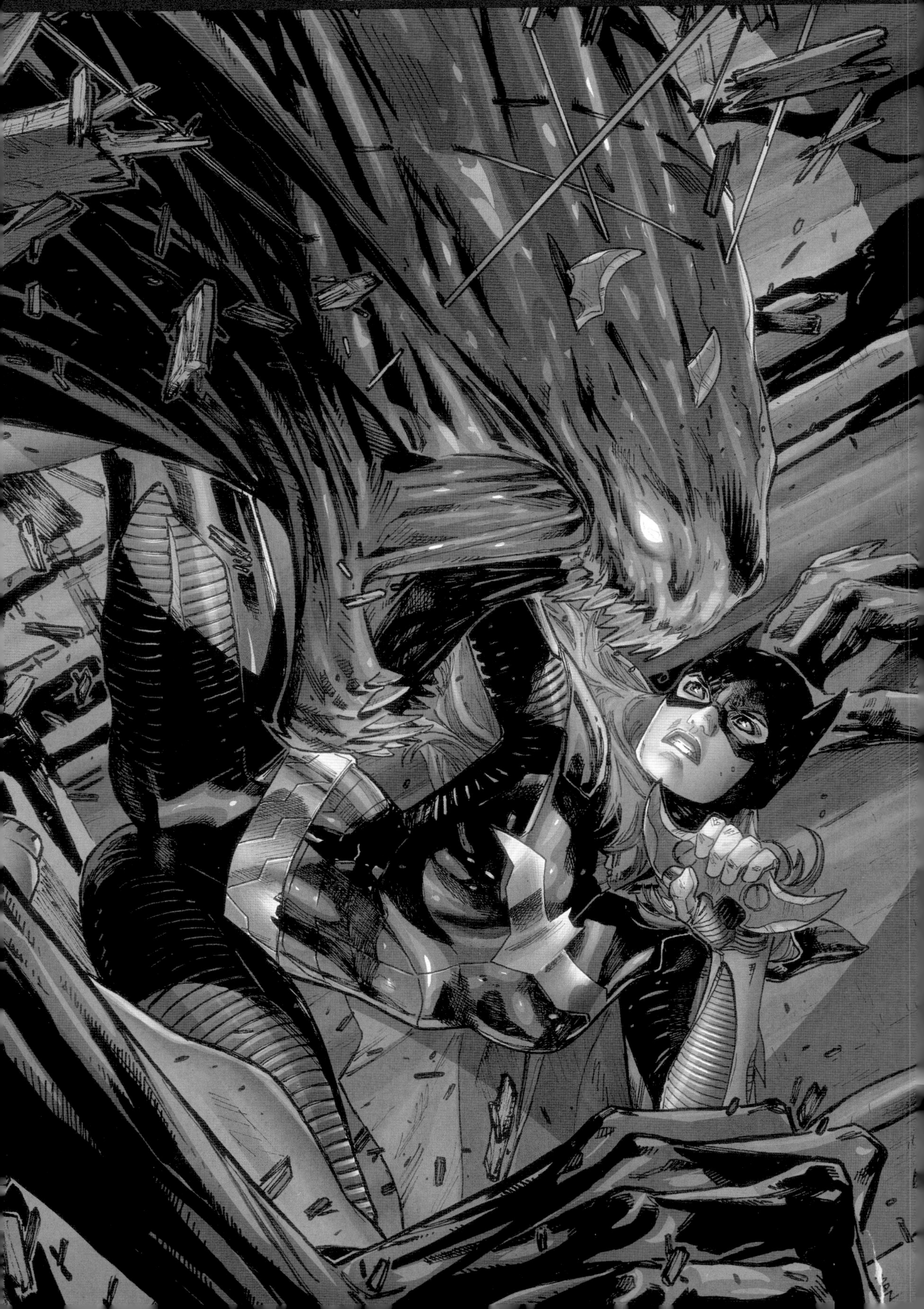

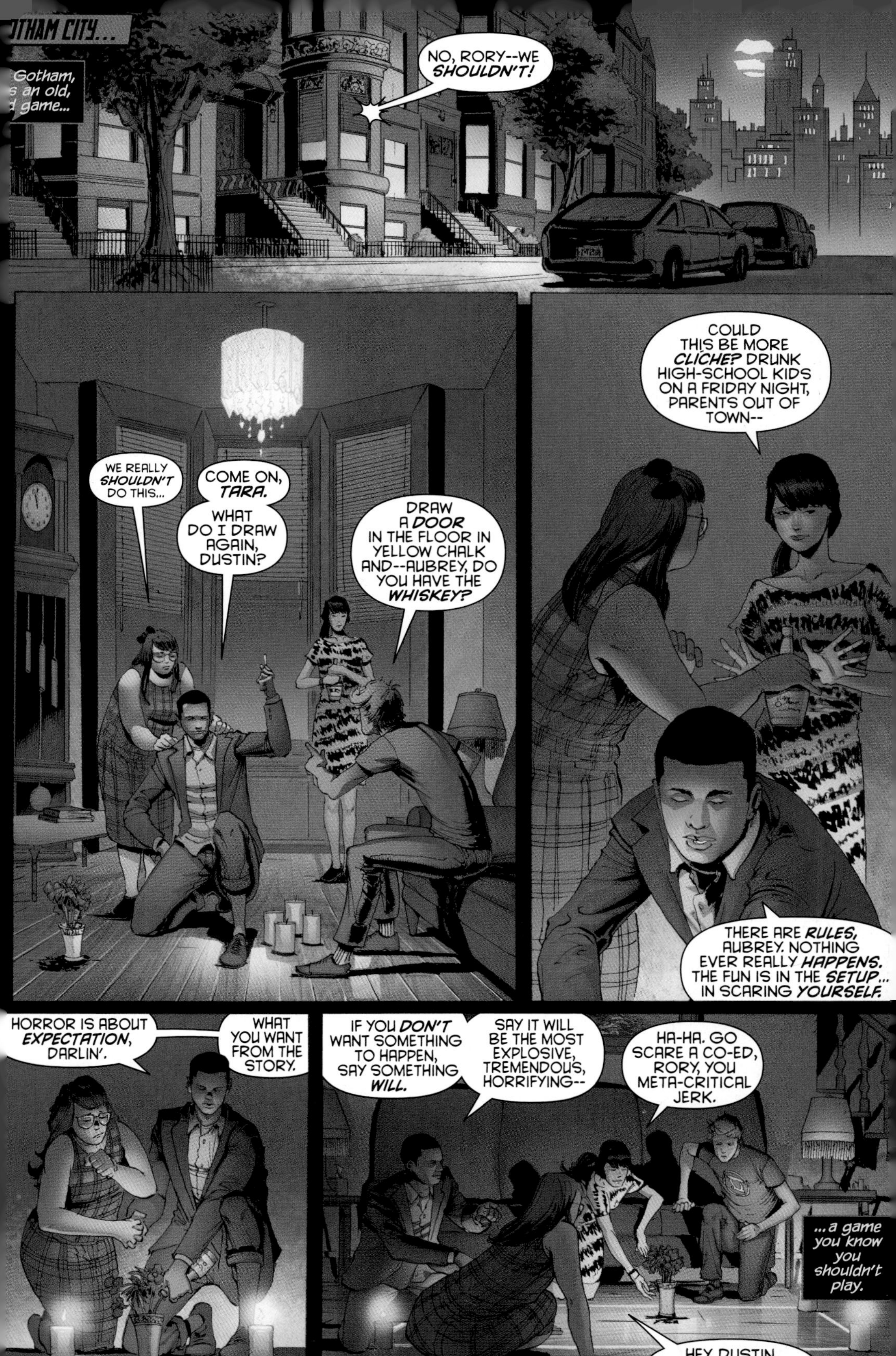

OTHAM CITY...
Gotham,
s an old,
d game...
NO, RORY--WE SHOULDN'T!
WE REALLY SHOULDN'T DO THIS...
COME ON, TARA.
WHAT DO I DRAW AGAIN, DUSTIN?
DRAW A DOOR IN THE FLOOR IN YELLOW CHALK AND--AUBREY, DO YOU HAVE THE WHISKEY?
COULD THIS BE MORE CLICHE? DRUNK HIGH-SCHOOL KIDS ON A FRIDAY NIGHT, PARENTS OUT OF TOWN--
THERE ARE RULES, AUBREY. NOTHING EVER REALLY HAPPENS. THE FUN IS IN THE SETUP... IN SCARING YOURSELF.
HORROR IS ABOUT EXPECTATION, DARLIN'.
WHAT YOU WANT FROM THE STORY.
IF YOU DON'T WANT SOMETHING TO HAPPEN, SAY SOMETHING WILL.
SAY IT WILL BE THE MOST EXPLOSIVE, TREMENDOUS, HORRIFYING--
HA-HA. GO SCARE A CO-ED, RORY, YOU META-CRITICAL JERK.
...a game you know you shouldn't play.
HEY, DUSTIN, WHAT'S THE NAME OF THIS GAME AGAIN?

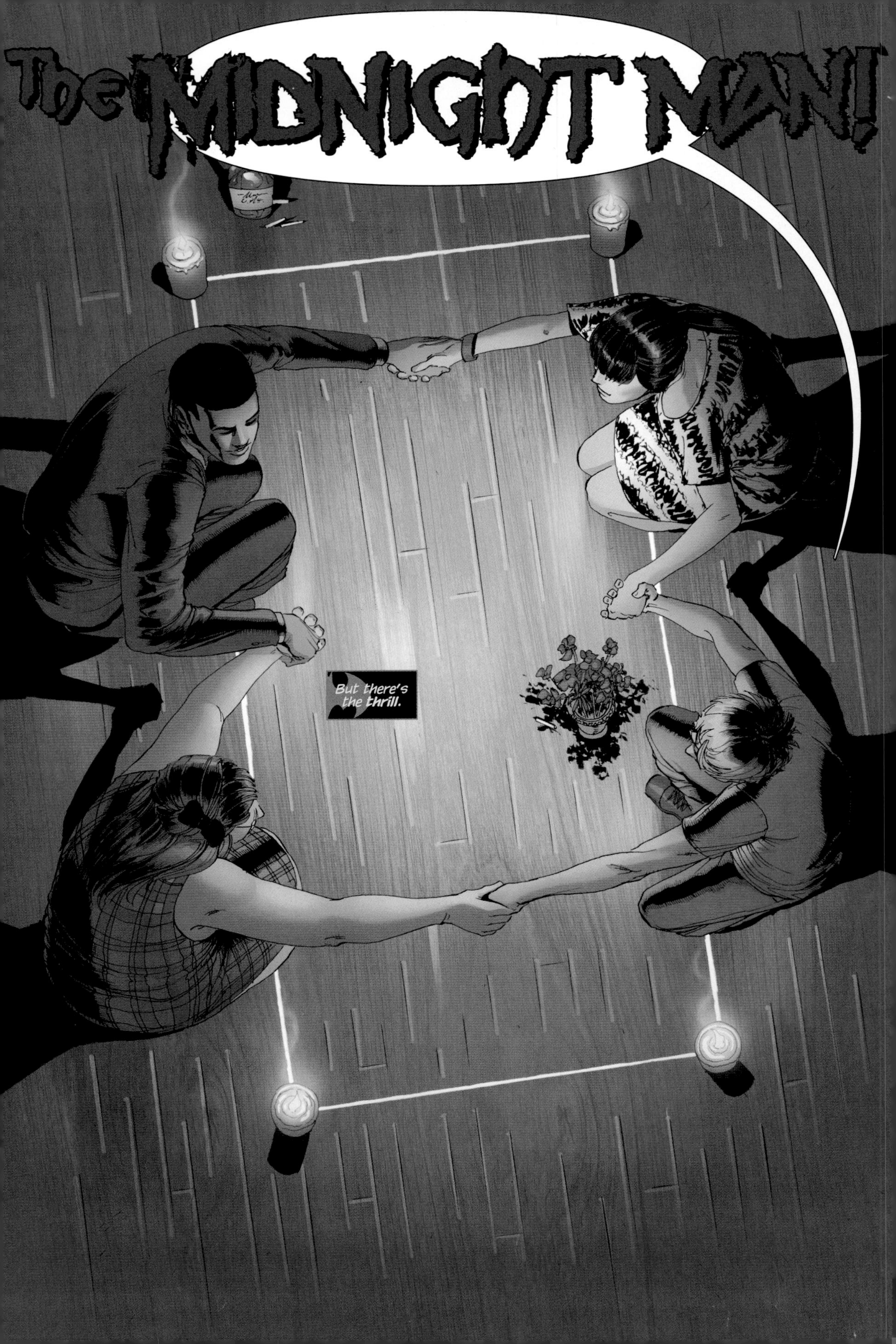
The MIDNIGHT MAN!
But there's the thrill.

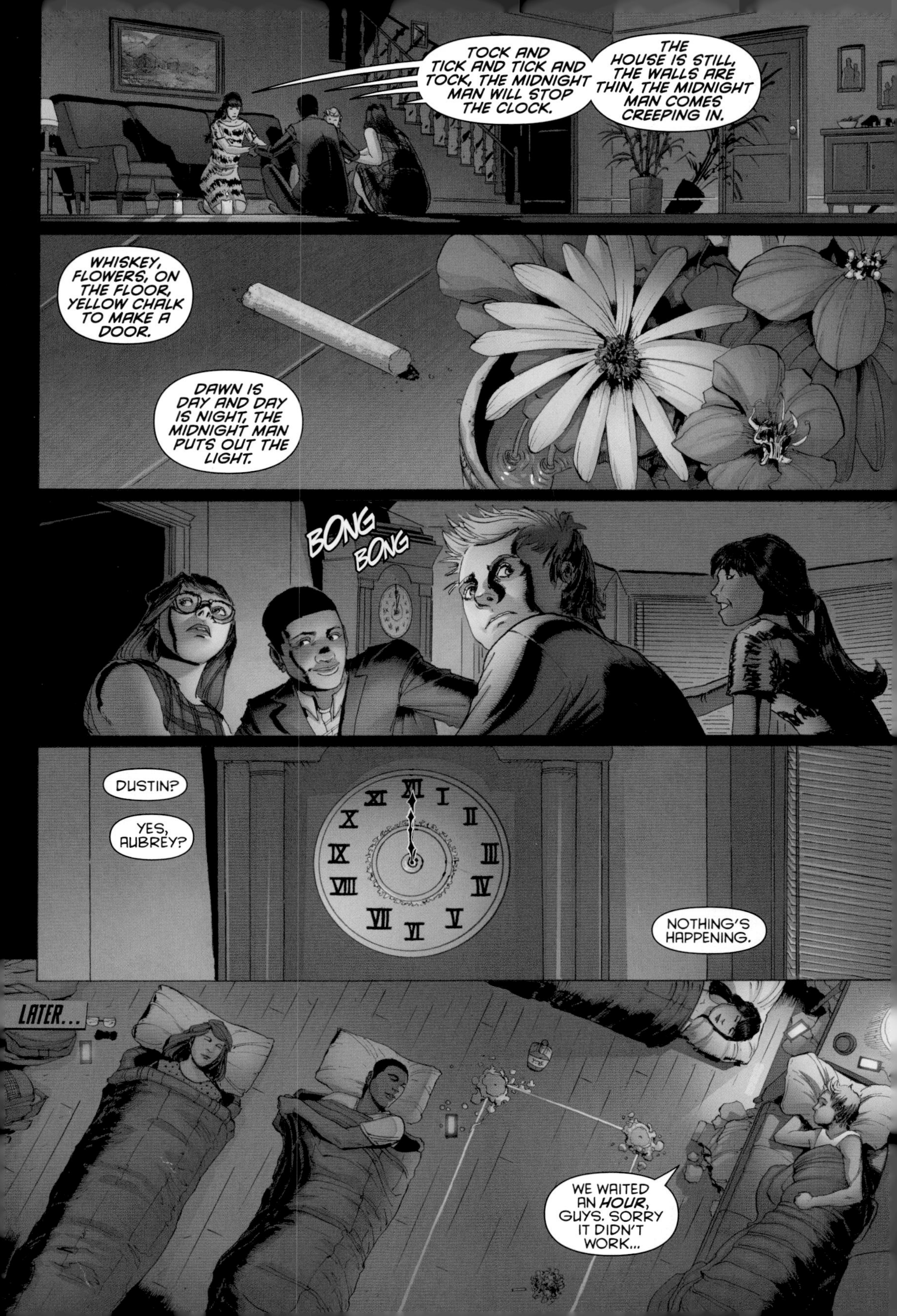
TOCK AND TICK AND TICK AND TOCK, THE MIDNIGHT MAN WILL STOP THE CLOCK.
THE HOUSE IS STILL, THE WALLS ARE THIN, THE MIDNIGHT MAN COMES CREEPING IN.
WHISKEY, FLOWERS, ON THE FLOOR, YELLOW CHALK TO MAKE A DOOR.
DAWN IS DAY AND DAY IS NIGHT, THE MIDNIGHT MAN PUTS OUT THE LIGHT.
BONG
BONG
DUSTIN?
YES, AUBREY?
NOTHING'S HAPPENING.
LATER...
WE WAITED AN *HOUR*, GUYS. SORRY IT DIDN'T WORK...

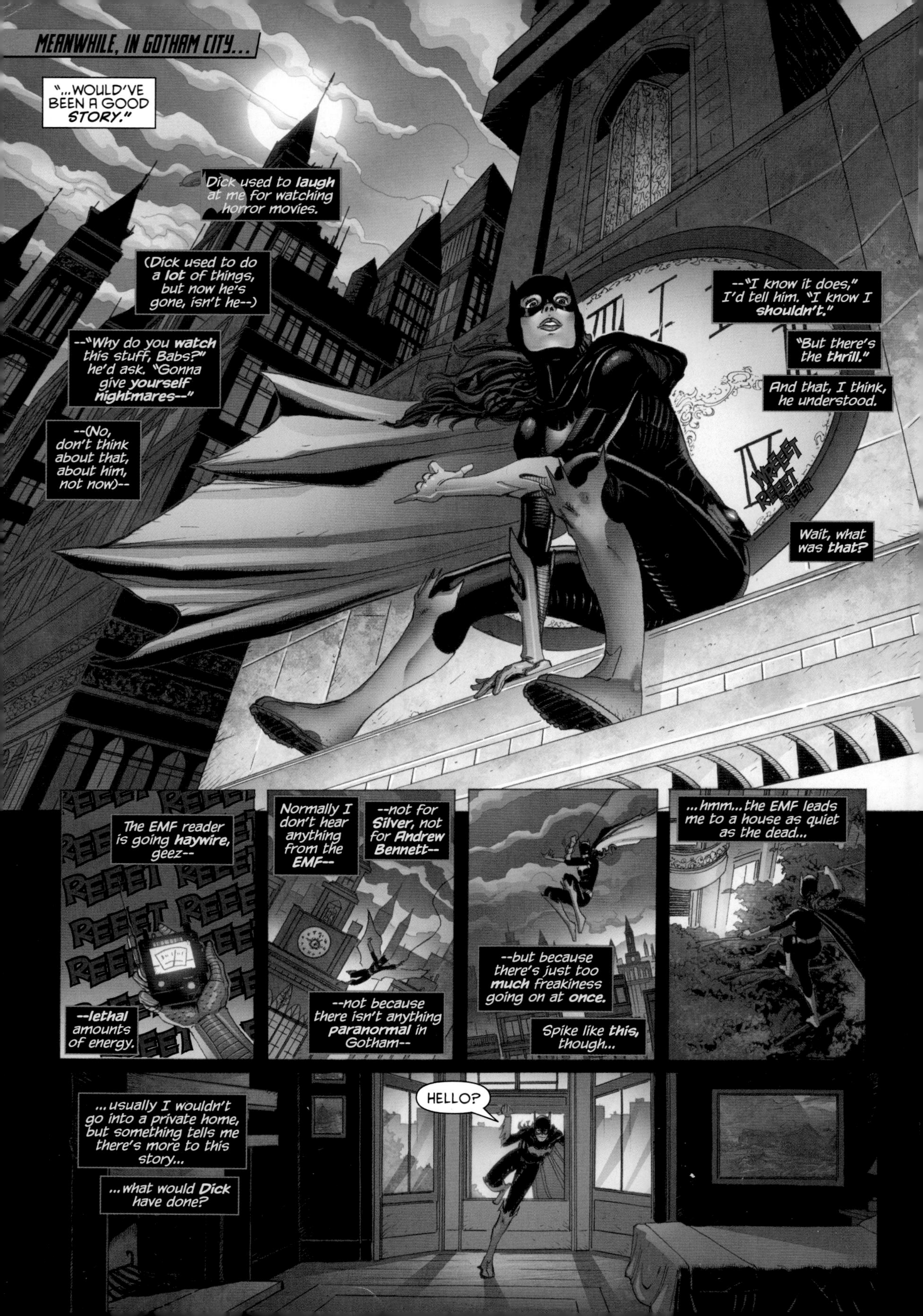

MEANWHILE, IN GOTHAM CITY...
"...WOULD'VE BEEN A GOOD STORY."
Dick used to laugh at me for watching horror movies.
(Dick used to do a lot of things, but now he's gone, isn't he--)
--"Why do you watch this stuff, Babs?" he'd ask. "Gonna give yourself nightmares--"
--(No, don't think about that, about him, not now)--
--"I know it does," I'd tell him. "I know I shouldn't."
"But there's the thrill."
And that, I think, he understood.
WREEET REEET REEET
Wait, what was that?
The EMF reader is going haywire, geez--
--lethal amounts of energy.
Normally I don't hear anything from the EMF--
--not for Silver, not for Andrew Bennett--
--not because there isn't anything paranormal in Gotham--
--but because there's just too much freakiness going on at once.
Spike like this, though...
...hmm...the EMF leads me to a house as quiet as the dead...
...usually I wouldn't go into a private home, but something tells me there's more to this story...
...what would Dick have done?
HELLO?

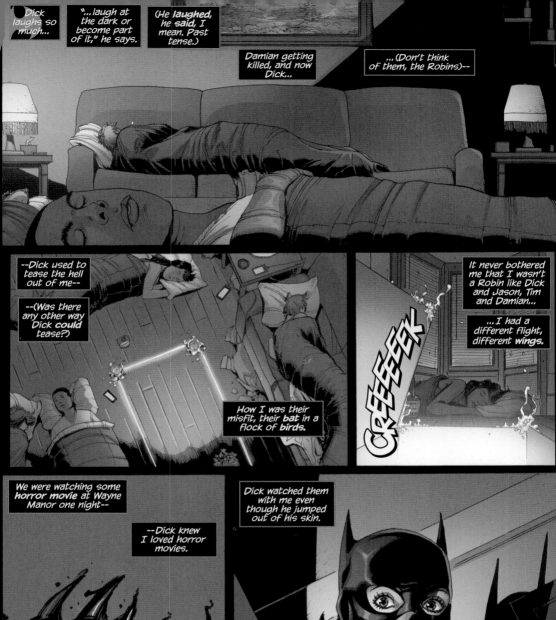

Dick laughs so much...

"...laugh at the dark or become part of it," he says.

(He *laughed*, he *said*, I mean. Past tense.)

Damian getting killed, and now Dick...

...(Don't think of them, the Robins)--

--Dick used to tease the hell out of me--

--(Was there any other way Dick *could* tease?)

How I was their misfit, their *bat* in a flock of *birds*.

It never bothered me that I wasn't a Robin like Dick and Jason, Tim and Damian...

...I had a *different* flight, different *wings*.

CREEEEEK

We were watching some *horror movie* at Wayne Manor one night--

--Dick knew I loved horror movies.

Dick watched them with me even though he jumped out of his skin.

He always told the same stupid *joke*--

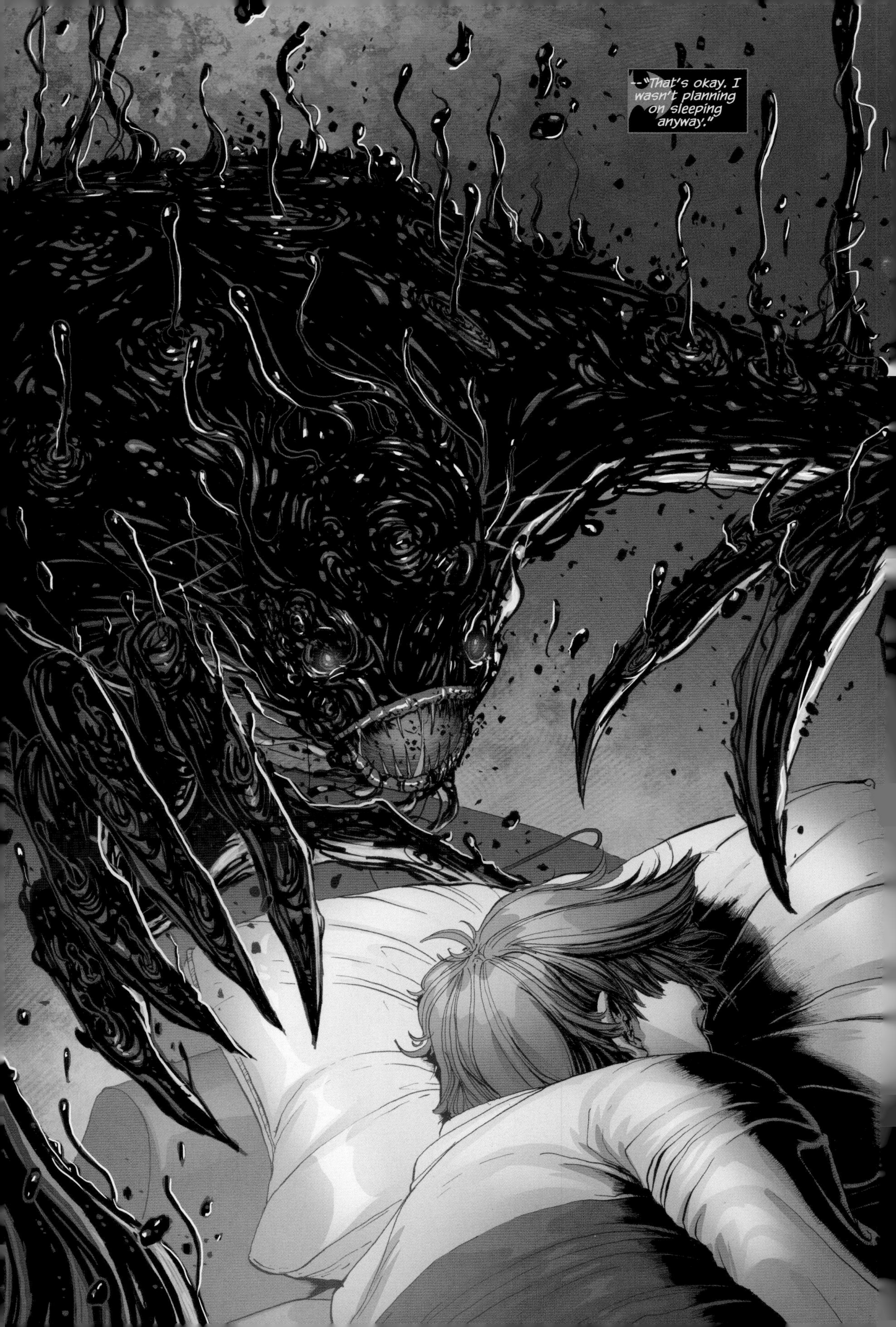
--"That's okay. I wasn't planning on sleeping anyway."

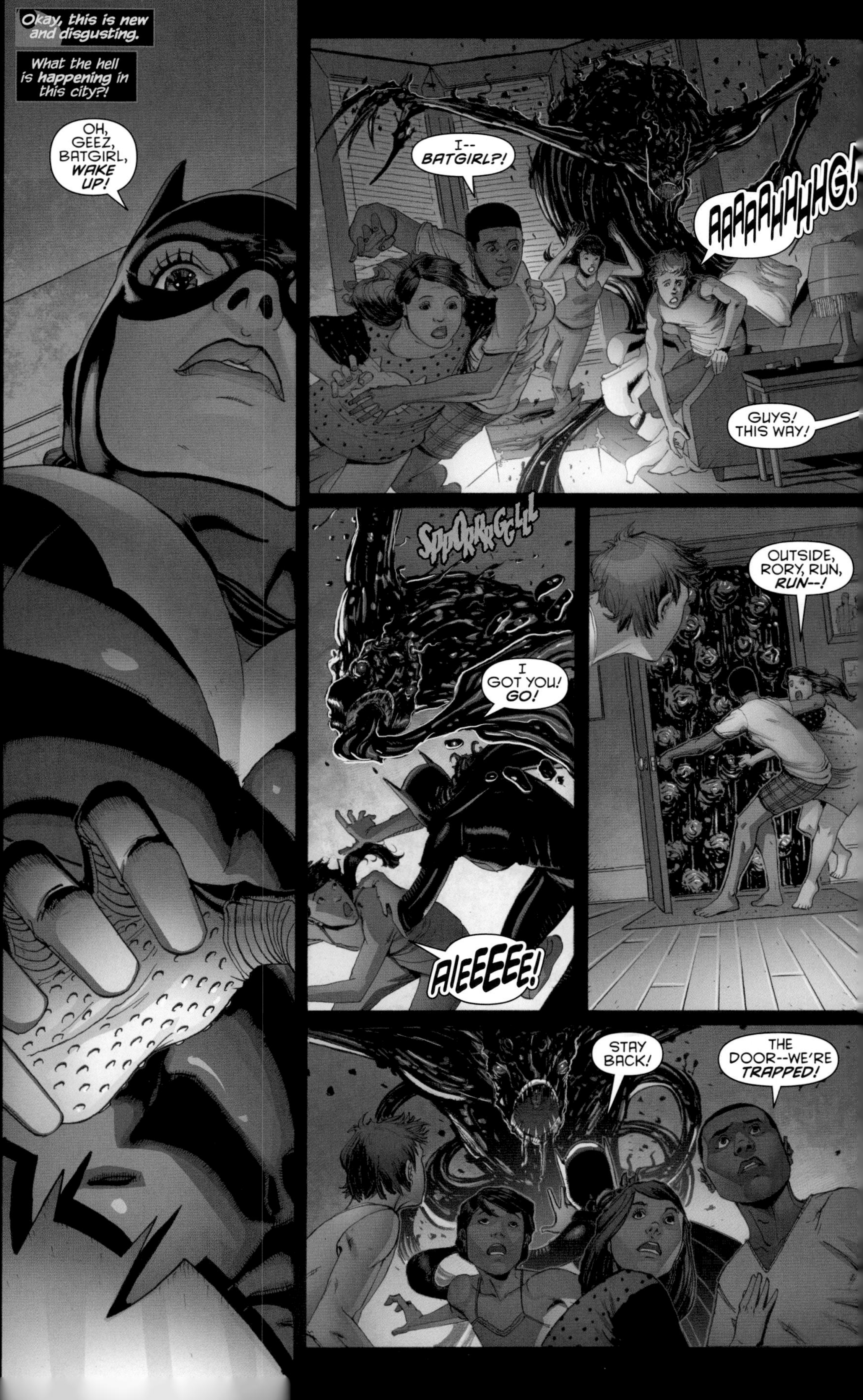
Okay, this is new and disgusting.
What the hell is happening in this city?!
OH, GEEZ, BATGIRL, WAKE UP!
I-- BATGIRL?!
AAAAAHHHHG!
GUYS! THIS WAY!
SPPORRRGGLLL
I GOT YOU! GO!
AIEEEEE!
OUTSIDE, RORY, RUN, RUN--!
STAY BACK!
THE DOOR--WE'RE TRAPPED!

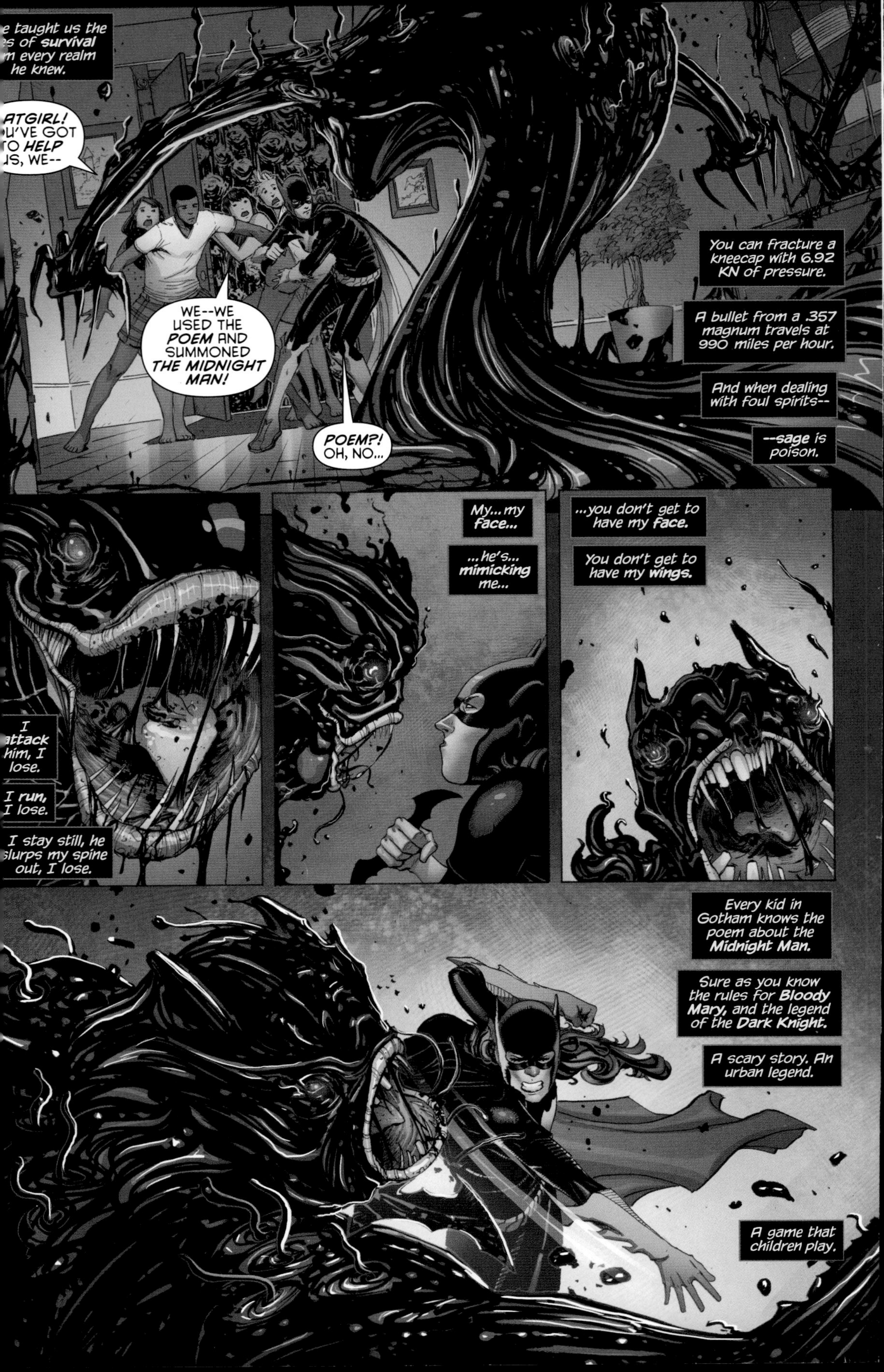

e taught us the
es of survival
m every realm
he knew.
ATGIRL!
U'VE GOT
TO HELP
US, WE--
WE--WE USED THE POEM AND SUMMONED THE MIDNIGHT MAN!
POEM?! OH, NO...
You can fracture a kneecap with 6.92 KN of pressure.
A bullet from a .357 magnum travels at 990 miles per hour.
And when dealing with foul spirits--
--sage is poison.
I attack him, I lose.
I run, I lose.
I stay still, he slurps my spine out, I lose.
My... my face...
...he's... mimicking me...
...you don't get to have my face.
You don't get to have my wings.
Every kid in Gotham knows the poem about the Midnight Man.
Sure as you know the rules for Bloody Mary, and the legend of the Dark Knight.
A scary story. An urban legend.
A game that children play.

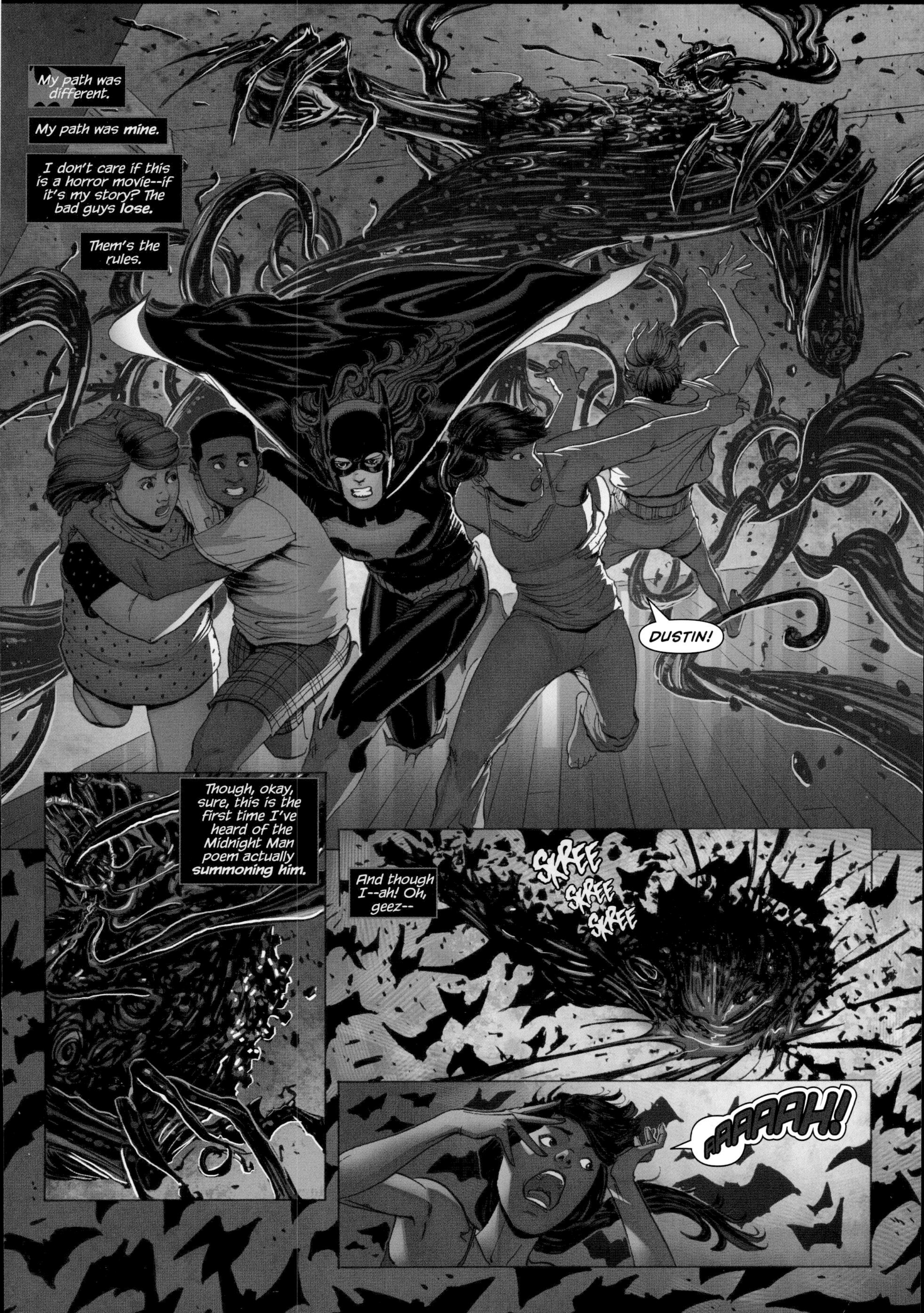

My path was different.
My path was mine.
I don't care if this is a horror movie--if it's my story? The bad guys lose.
Them's the rules.
DUSTIN!
Though, okay, sure, this is the first time I've heard of the Midnight Man poem actually summoning him.
And though I--ah! Oh, geez--
SKREE SKREE SKREE
AAAAAH!

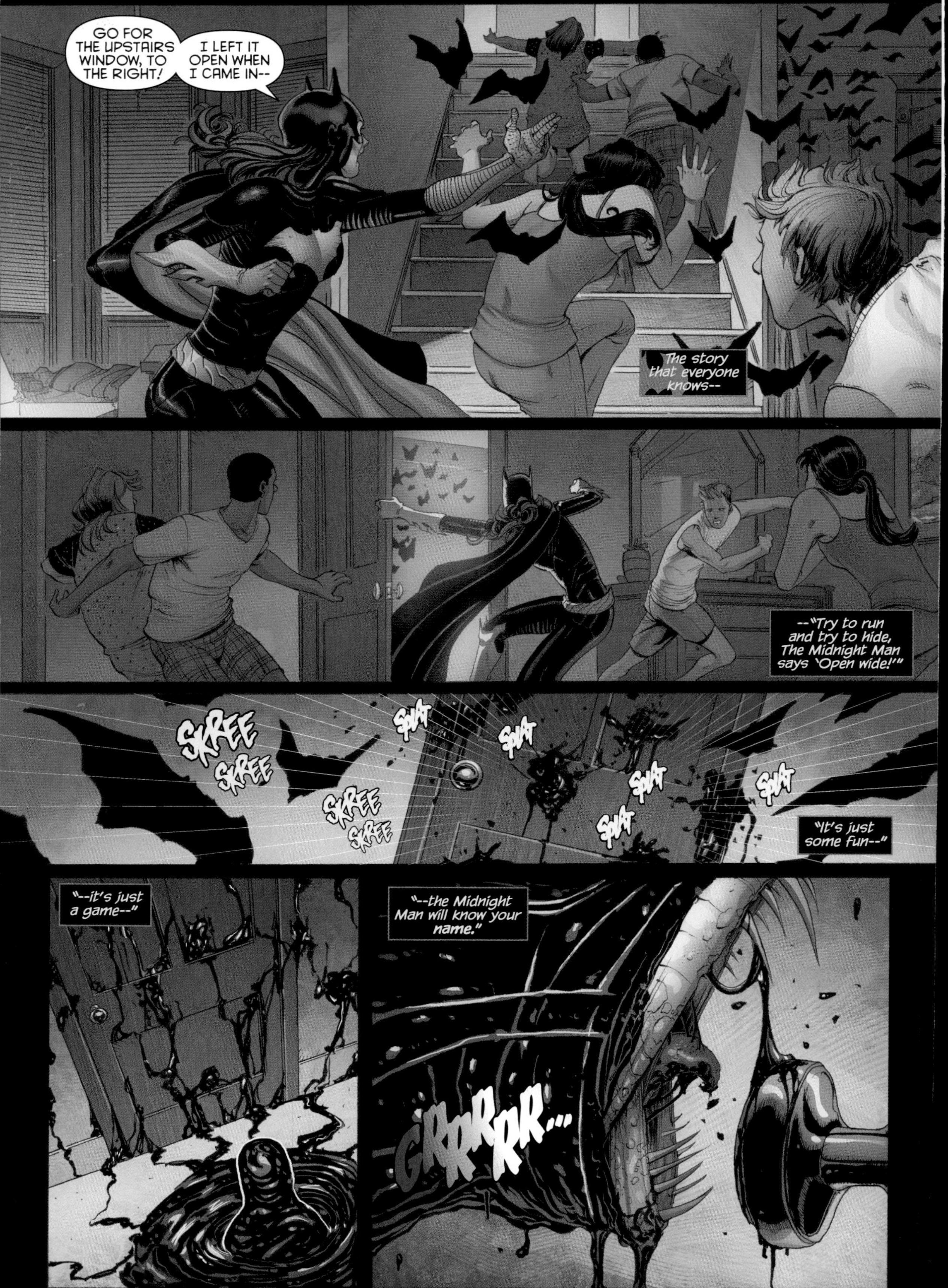
GO FOR THE UPSTAIRS WINDOW, TO THE RIGHT!
I LEFT IT OPEN WHEN I CAME IN--
The story that everyone knows--
--"Try to run and try to hide, The Midnight Man says 'Open wide!'"
SKREE
SKREE
SKREE
SKREE
SPLAT
SPLAT
SPLAT
SPLAT
SPLAT
"It's just some fun--"
"--it's just a game--"
"--the Midnight Man will know your name."
GRRRRR...

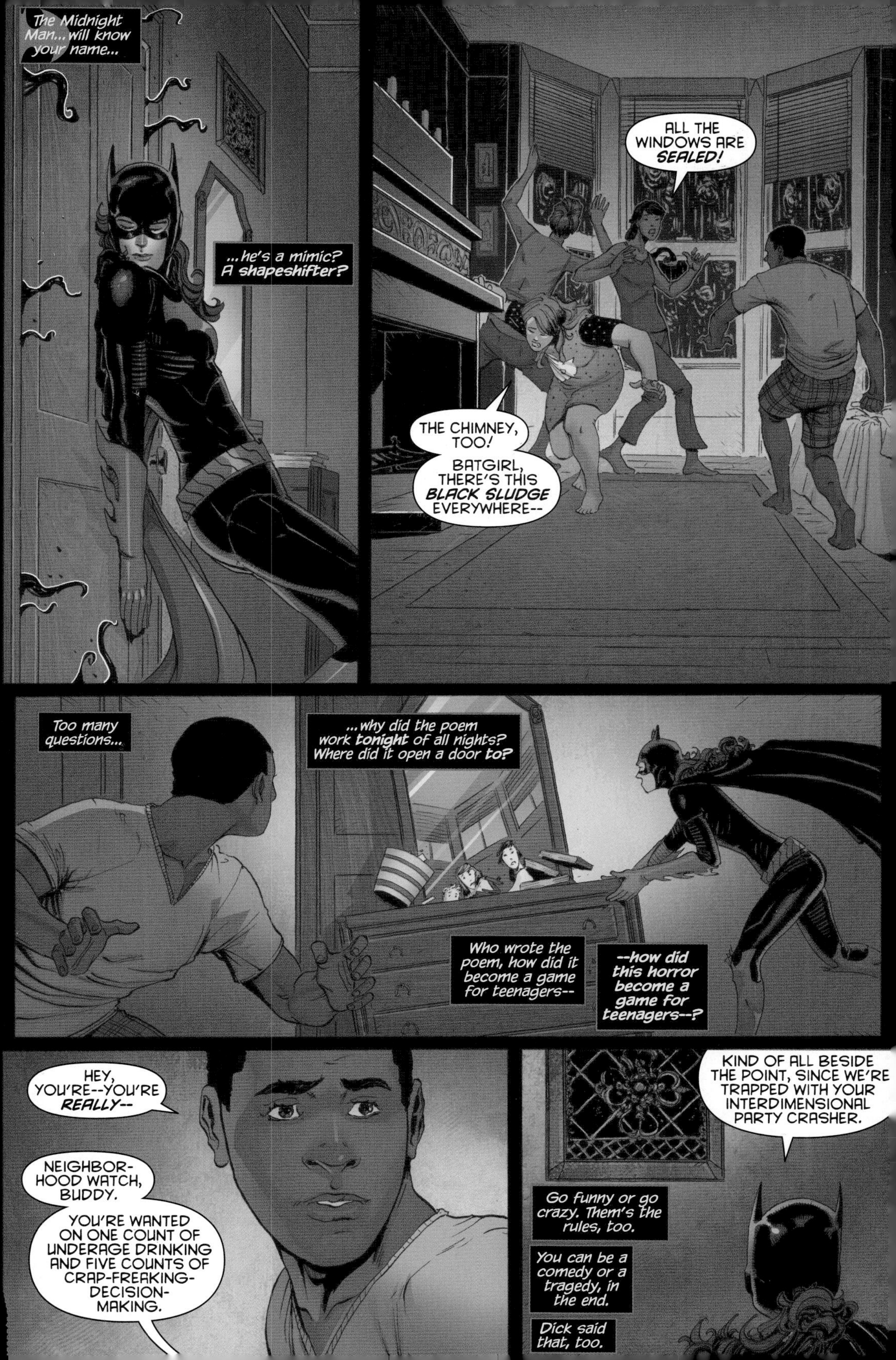
The Midnight Man... will know your name...
...he's a mimic? A shapeshifter?
ALL THE WINDOWS ARE SEALED!
THE CHIMNEY, TOO!
BATGIRL, THERE'S THIS BLACK SLUDGE EVERYWHERE--
Too many questions...
...why did the poem work tonight of all nights? Where did it open a door to?
Who wrote the poem, how did it become a game for teenagers--
--how did this horror become a game for teenagers--?
HEY, YOU'RE--YOU'RE REALLY--
NEIGHBOR-HOOD WATCH, BUDDY.
YOU'RE WANTED ON ONE COUNT OF UNDERAGE DRINKING AND FIVE COUNTS OF CRAP-FREAKING-DECISION-MAKING.
KIND OF ALL BESIDE THE POINT, SINCE WE'RE TRAPPED WITH YOUR INTERDIMENSIONAL PARTY CRASHER.
Go funny or go crazy. Them's the rules, too.
You can be a comedy or a tragedy, in the end.
Dick said that, too.

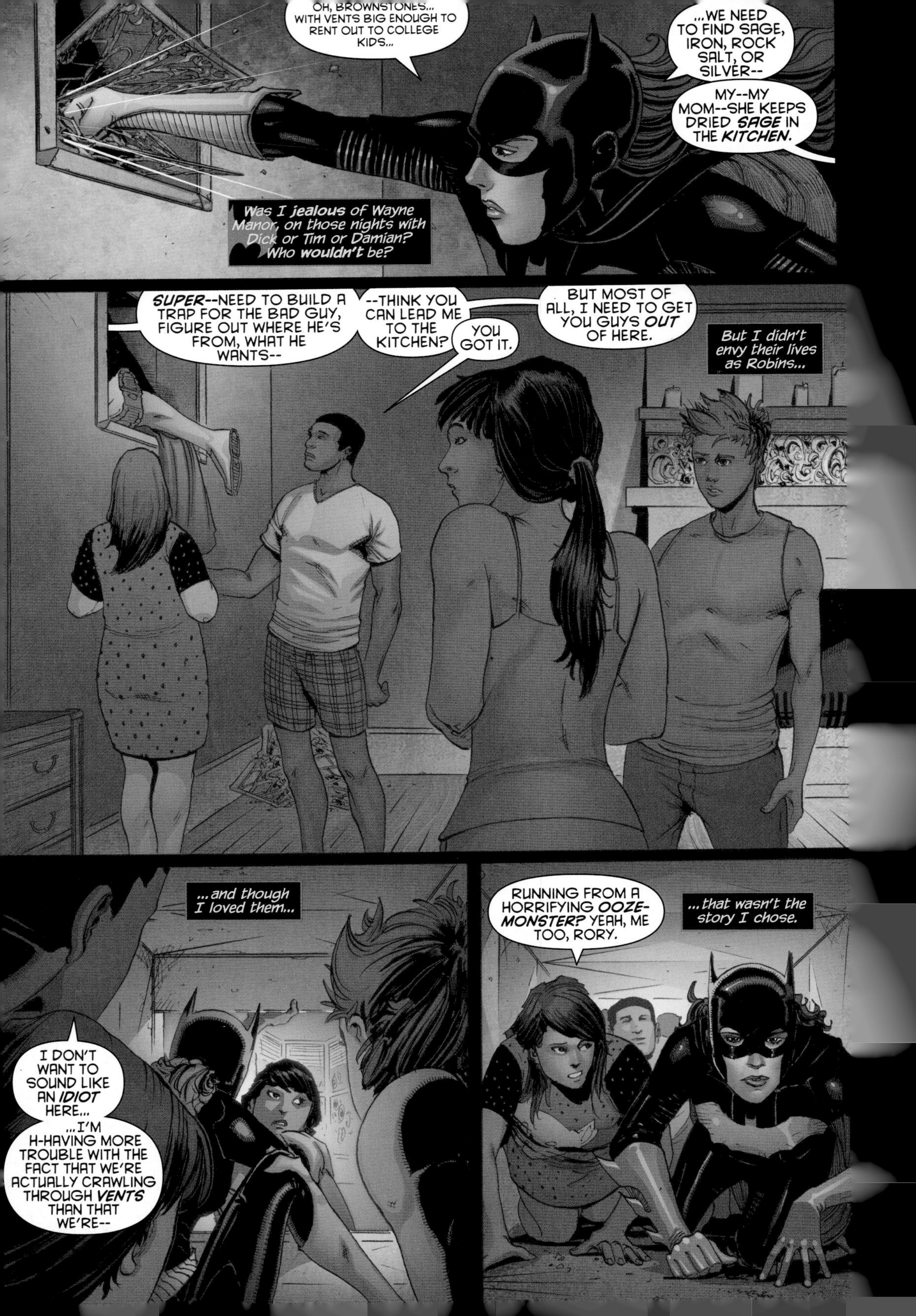
OH, BROWNSTONES... WITH VENTS BIG ENOUGH TO RENT OUT TO COLLEGE KIDS...
...WE NEED TO FIND SAGE, IRON, ROCK SALT, OR SILVER--
MY--MY MOM--SHE KEEPS DRIED SAGE IN THE KITCHEN.
Was I jealous of Wayne Manor, on those nights with Dick or Tim or Damian? Who wouldn't be?
SUPER--NEED TO BUILD A TRAP FOR THE BAD GUY, FIGURE OUT WHERE HE'S FROM, WHAT HE WANTS--
--THINK YOU CAN LEAD ME TO THE KITCHEN?
YOU GOT IT.
BUT MOST OF ALL, I NEED TO GET YOU GUYS OUT OF HERE.
But I didn't envy their lives as Robins...
...and though I loved them...
I DON'T WANT TO SOUND LIKE AN IDIOT HERE...
...I'M H-HAVING MORE TROUBLE WITH THE FACT THAT WE'RE ACTUALLY CRAWLING THROUGH VENTS THAN THAT WE'RE--
RUNNING FROM A HORRIFYING OOZE-MONSTER? YEAH, ME TOO, RORY.
...that wasn't the story I chose.

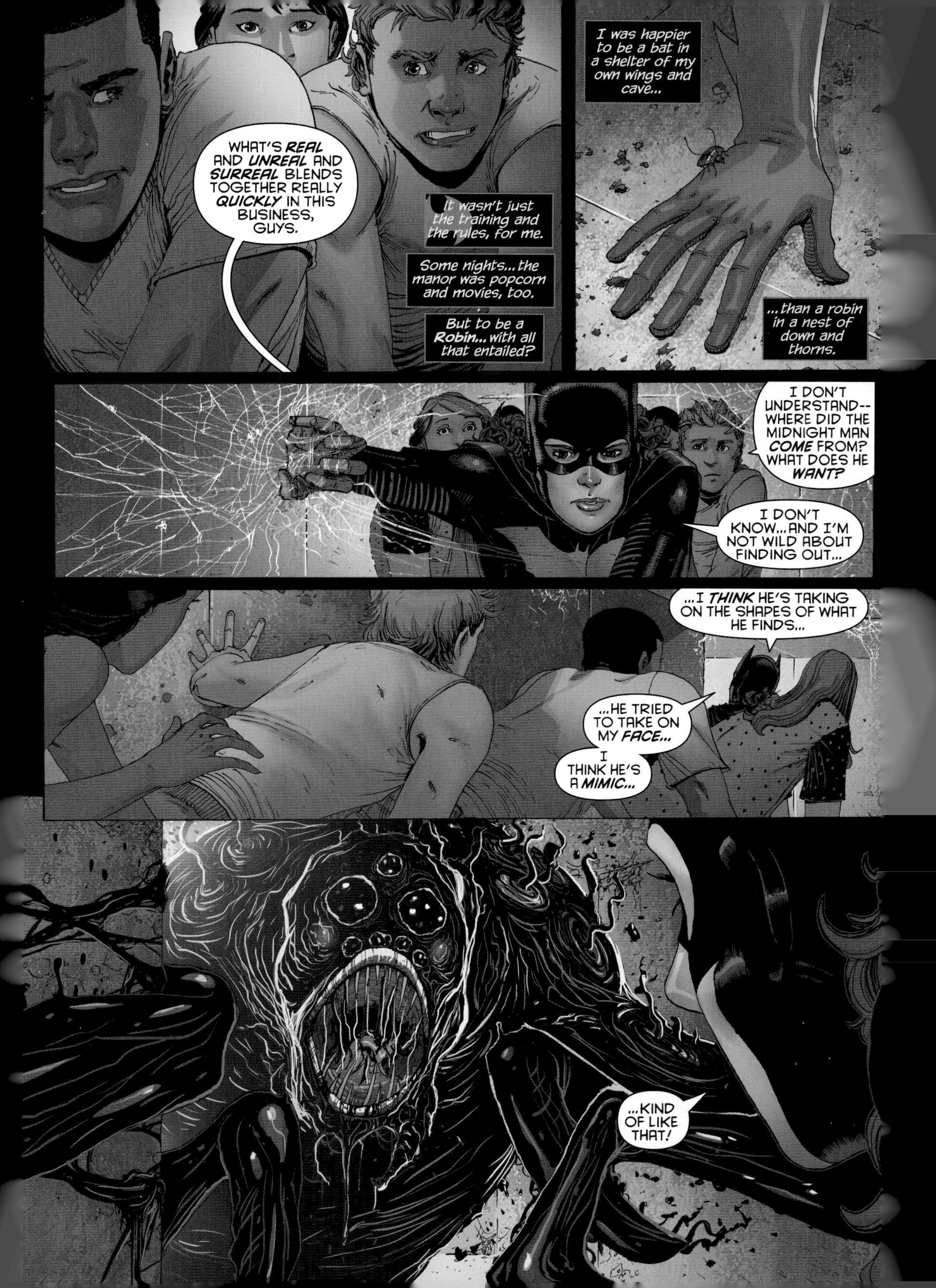
WHAT'S REAL AND UNREAL AND SURREAL BLENDS TOGETHER REALLY QUICKLY IN THIS BUSINESS, GUYS.
It wasn't just the training and the rules, for me.
Some nights... the manor was popcorn and movies, too.
But to be a Robin... with all that entailed?
I was happier to be a bat in a shelter of my own wings and cave...
...than a robin in a nest of down and thorns.
I DON'T UNDERSTAND-- WHERE DID THE MIDNIGHT MAN COME FROM? WHAT DOES HE WANT?
I DON'T KNOW... AND I'M NOT WILD ABOUT FINDING OUT...
...I THINK HE'S TAKING ON THE SHAPES OF WHAT HE FINDS...
...HE TRIED TO TAKE ON MY FACE...
I THINK HE'S A MIMIC...
...KIND OF LIKE THAT!

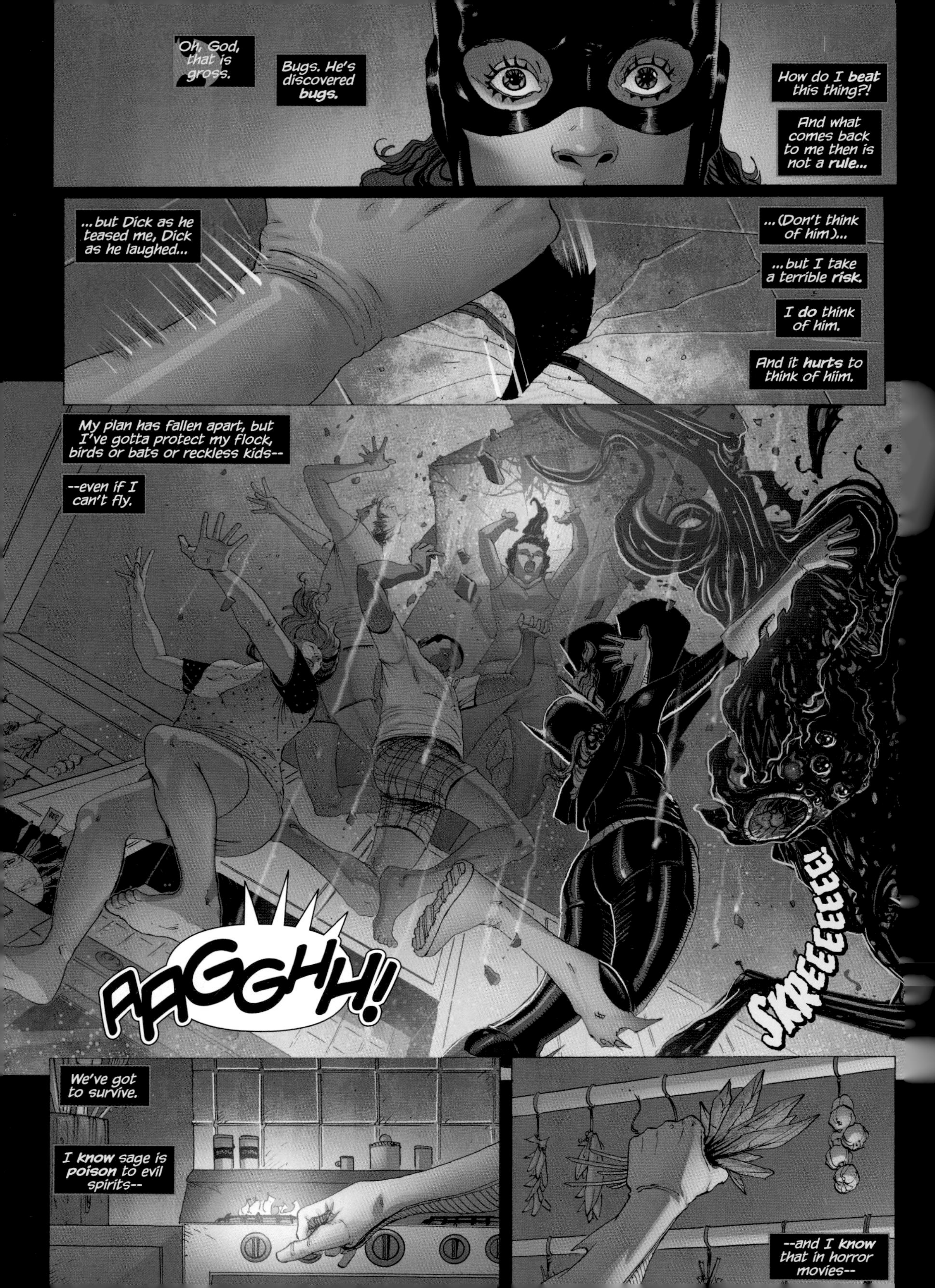
Oh, God, that is gross.
Bugs. He's discovered bugs.
How do I beat this thing?!
And what comes back to me then is not a rule...
...but Dick as he teased me, Dick as he laughed...
...(Don't think of him)...
...but I take a terrible risk.
I do think of him.
And it hurts to think of hiim.
My plan has fallen apart, but I've gotta protect my flock, birds or bats or reckless kids--
--even if I can't fly.
AAGGHH!
SKREEEEEEE!
We've got to survive.
I know sage is poison to evil spirits--
--and I know that in horror movies--

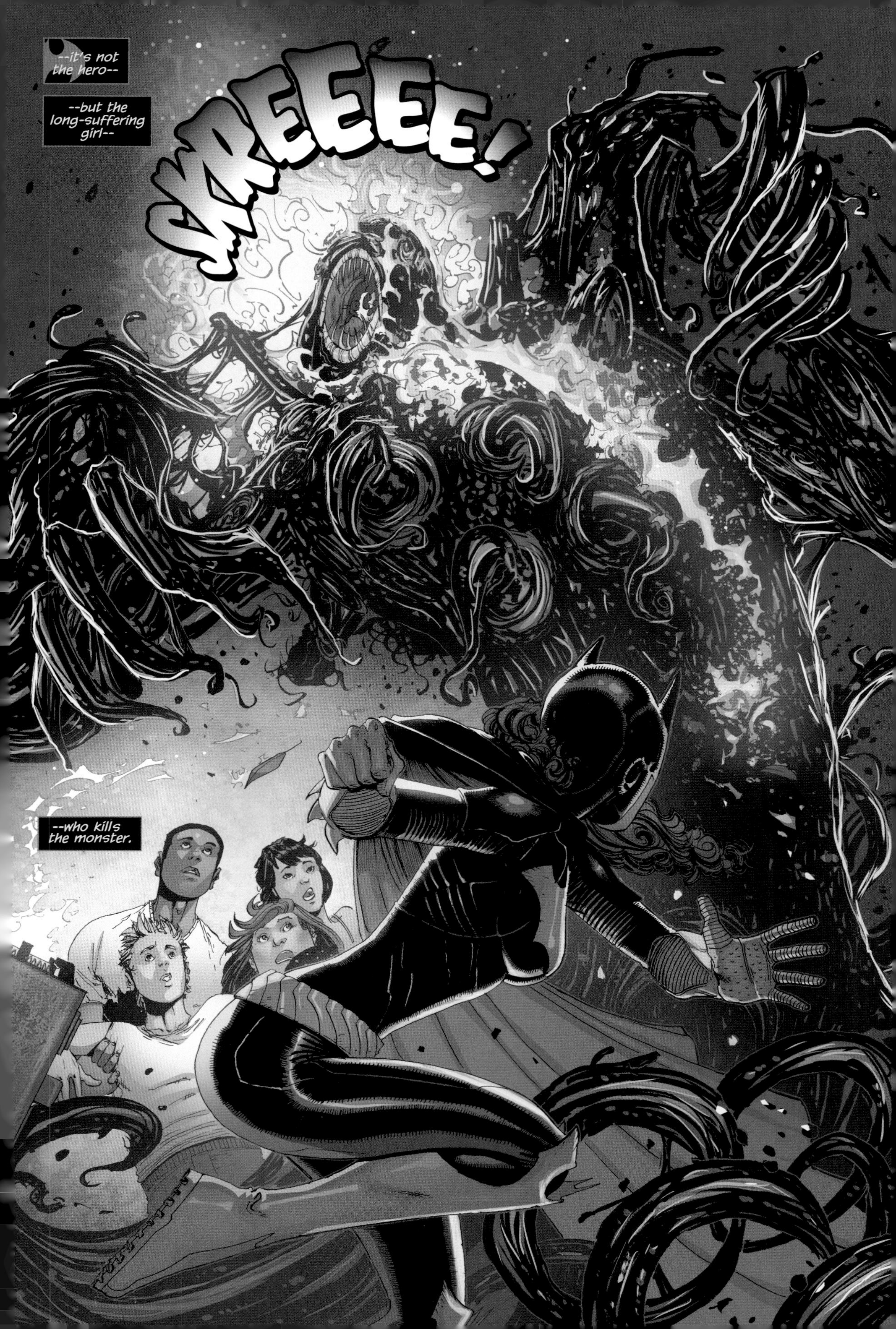
--it's not the hero--
--but the long-suffering girl--
SKREEEEE!
--who kills the monster.

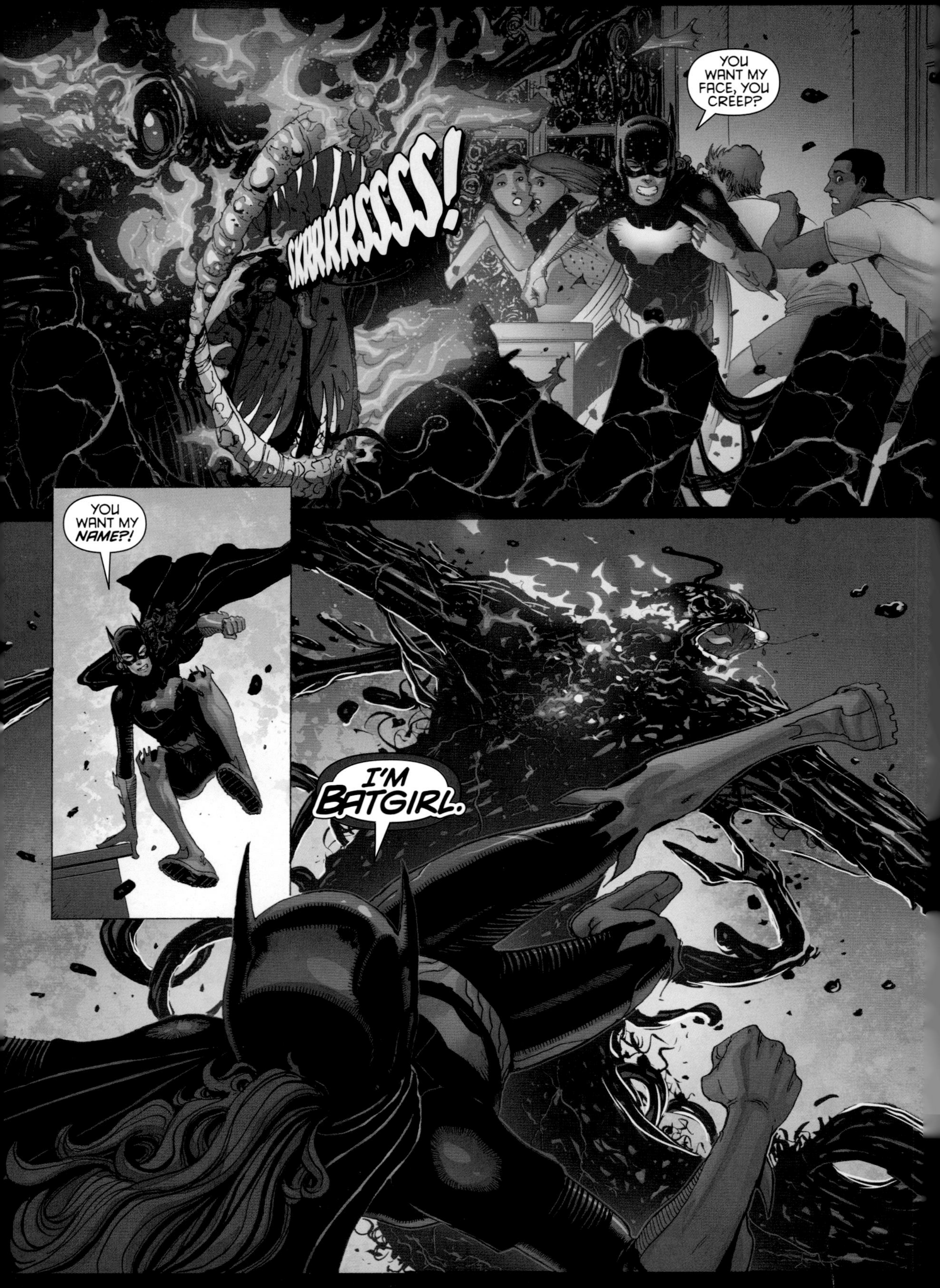

YOU WANT MY FACE, YOU CREEP?
SKRRRRSSSSS!
YOU WANT MY NAME?!
I'M BATGIRL.

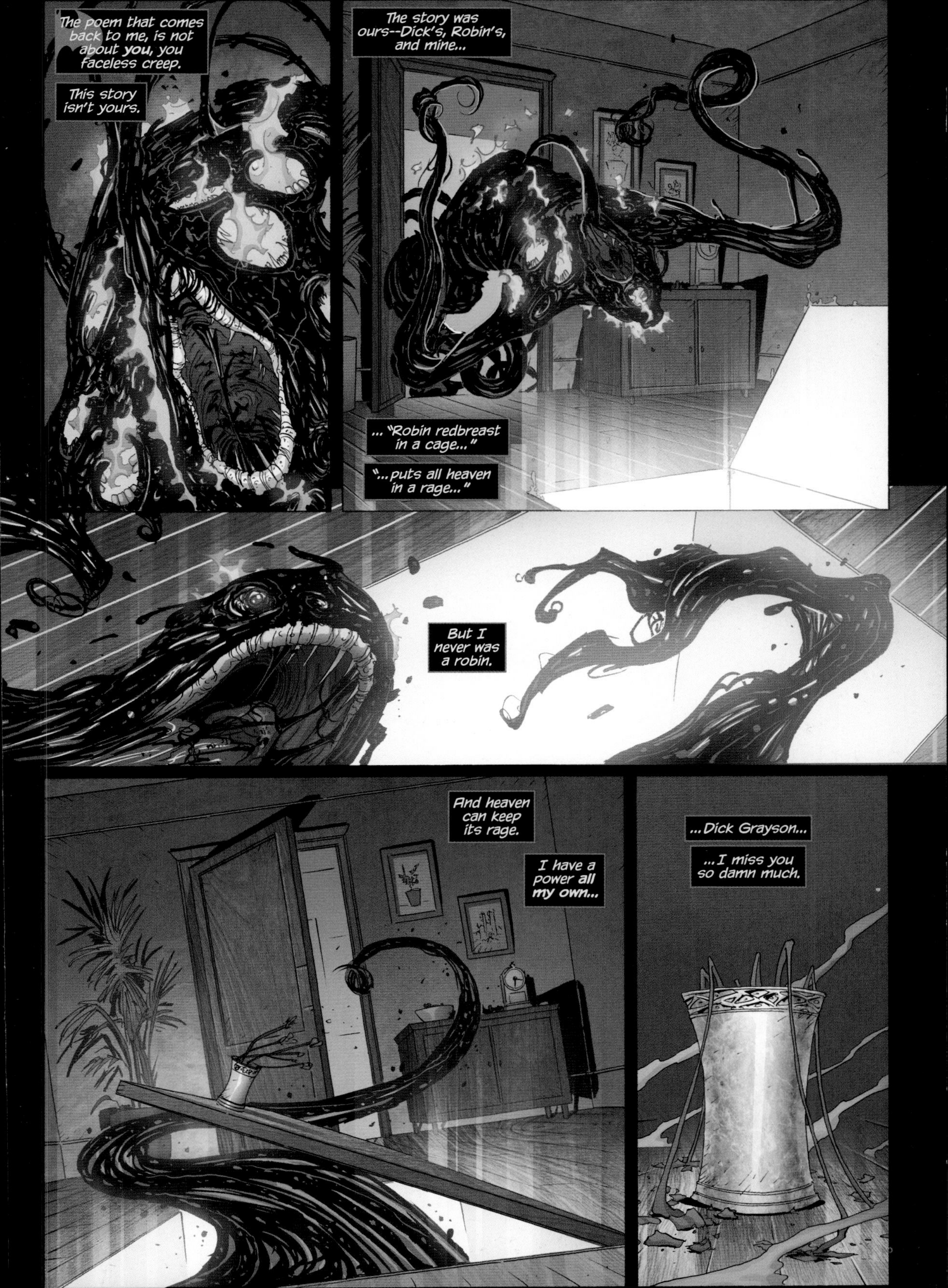
The poem that comes back to me, is not about **you**, you faceless creep.
This story isn't yours.
The story was ours--Dick's, Robin's, and mine...
..."Robin redbreast in a cage..."
"...puts all heaven in a rage..."
But I never was a robin.
And heaven can keep its rage.
I have a power **all my own...**
...Dick Grayson...
...I miss you so damn much.

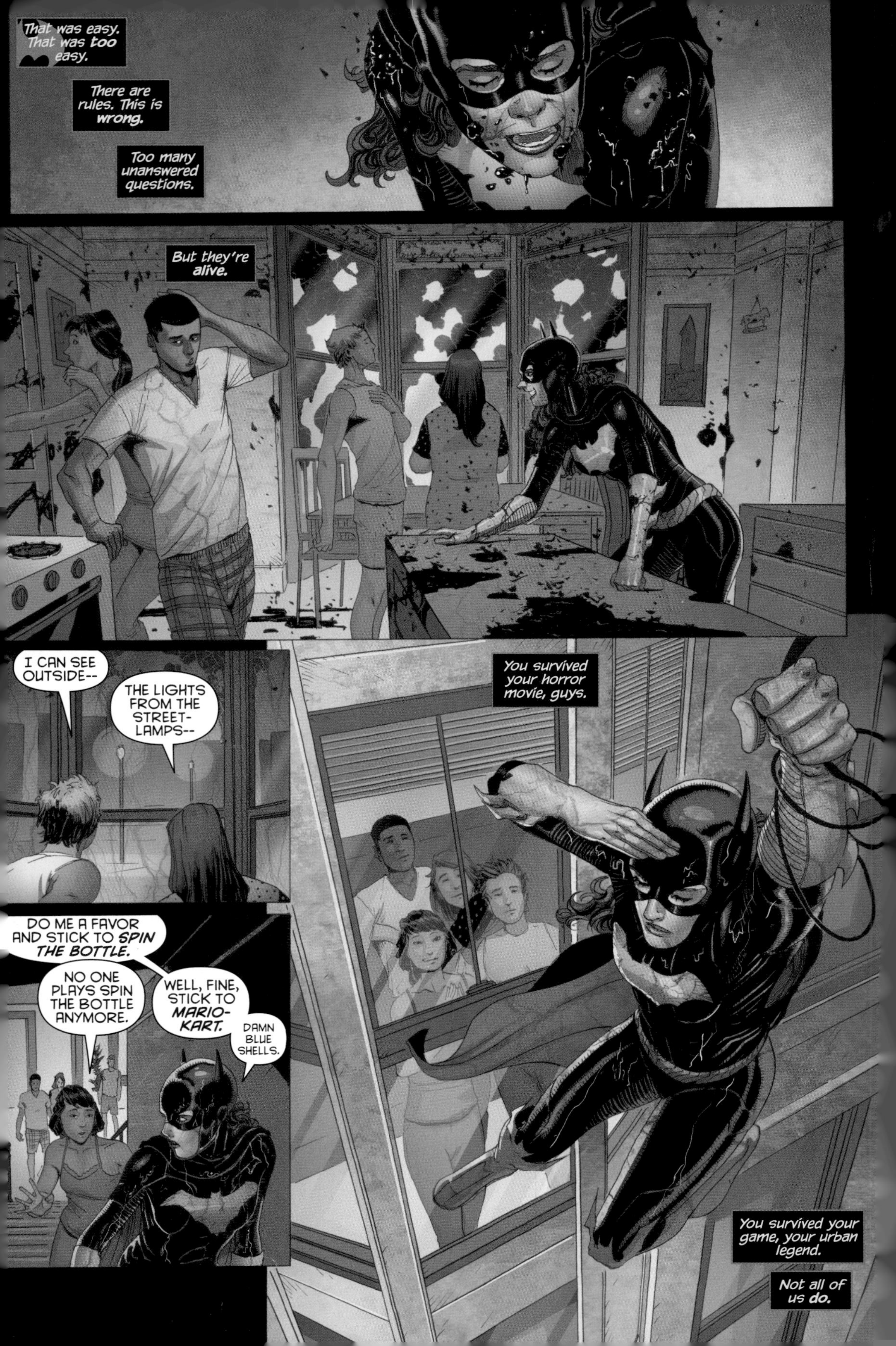
That was easy. That was too easy.
There are rules. This is wrong.
Too many unanswered questions.
But they're alive.
I CAN SEE OUTSIDE--
THE LIGHTS FROM THE STREET-LAMPS--
You survived your horror movie, guys.
DO ME A FAVOR AND STICK TO SPIN THE BOTTLE.
NO ONE PLAYS SPIN THE BOTTLE ANYMORE.
WELL, FINE, STICK TO MARIO-KART.
DAMN BLUE SHELLS.
You survived your game, your urban legend.
Not all of us do.

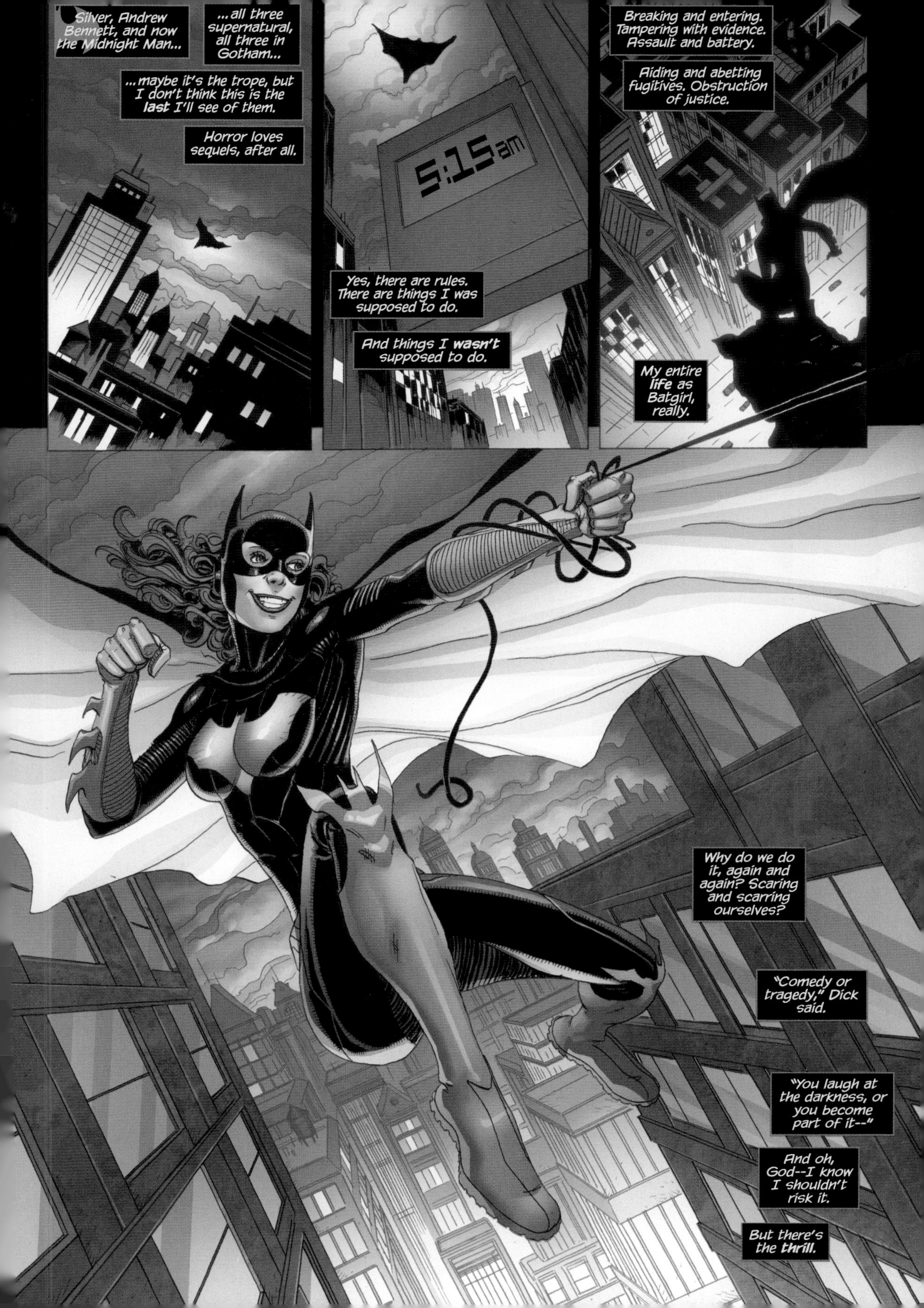

Silver, Andrew Bennett, and now the Midnight Man...
...all three supernatural, all three in Gotham...
...maybe it's the trope, but I don't think this is the last I'll see of them.
Horror loves sequels, after all.
5:15am
Yes, there are rules. There are things I was supposed to do.
And things I wasn't supposed to do.
Breaking and entering. Tampering with evidence. Assault and battery.
Aiding and abetting fugitives. Obstruction of justice.
My entire life as Batgirl, really.
Why do we do it, again and again? Scaring and scarring ourselves?
"Comedy or tragedy," Dick said.
"You laugh at the darkness, or you become part of it--"
And oh, God--I know I shouldn't risk it.
But there's the thrill.

LATER...
WHAT IS IT?
CAN YOU SMELL THAT?
YUCK--
IT'S LIKE SOMEBODY MIXED IN BOOZE AND...WHAT, CHALK? AND THESE LITTLE FLOWER BITS--
WHY WOULD SOMEONE PUT THAT CRAP IN OUR BARRELS?
DO WE NEED TO LOAD IN NEW PAINT?
TOO LATE. WE'VE ALREADY USED IT TO PAINT THE LINES FROM FRANKLIN TO WEST BROAD, AND DOWN OVER ON KIMBALL, TOO.
WEIRD, BUT IT'S ALL RIGHT. NO ONE WILL NOTICE ONCE IT DRIES.
"ALL THAT JUNK MIXED IN THE BARREL. IT AIN'T WORTH MENTIONING. SOMEONE JUST LOOKING FOR A THRILL."

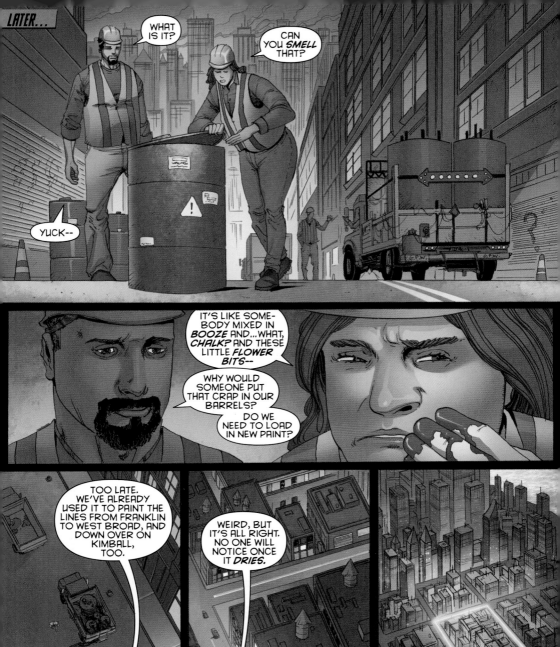

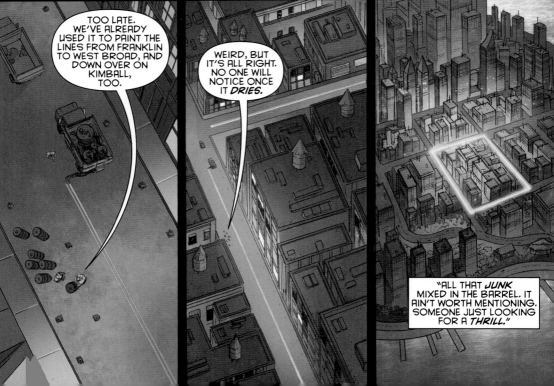

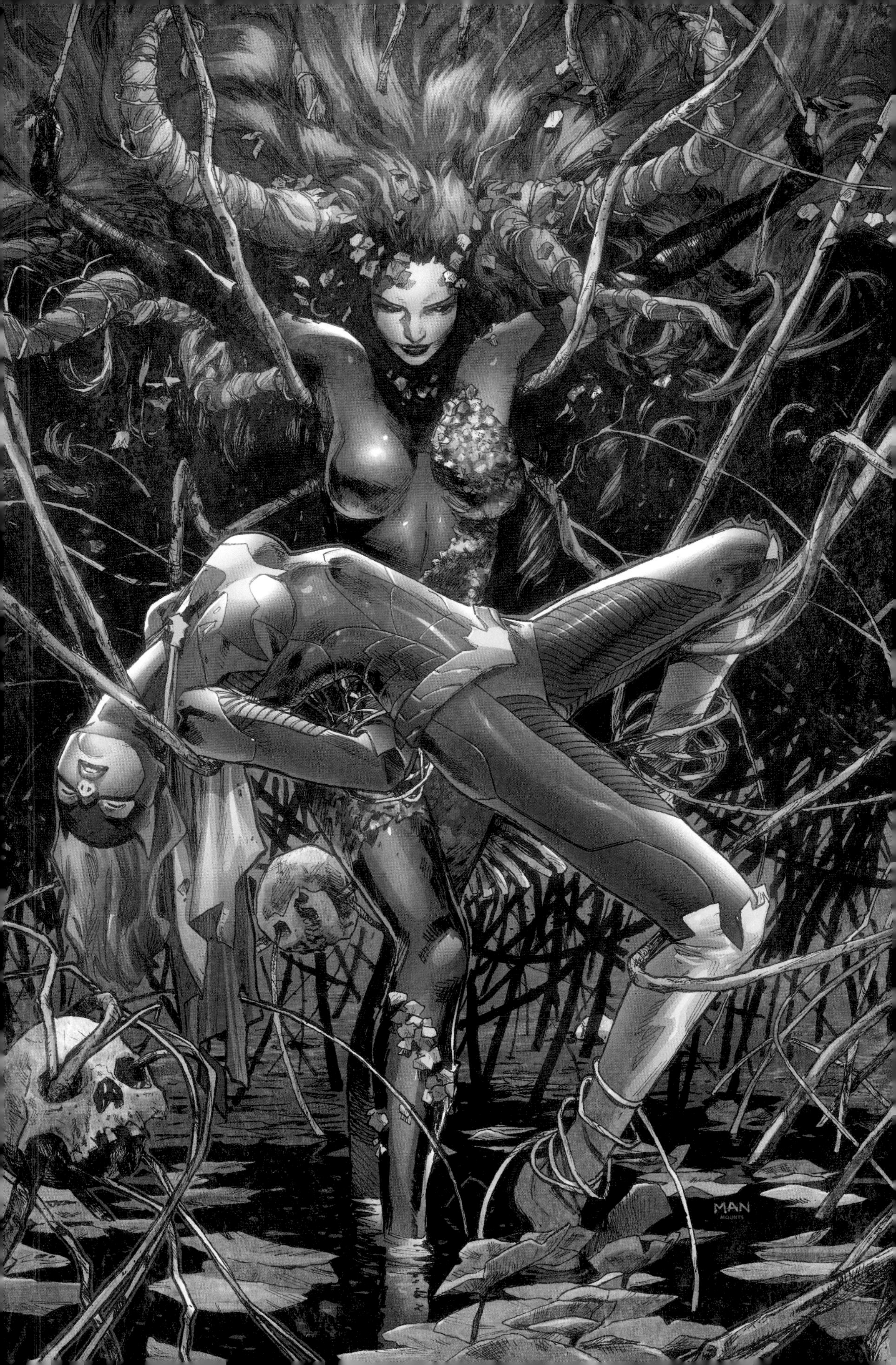
MAN
MOUNTS

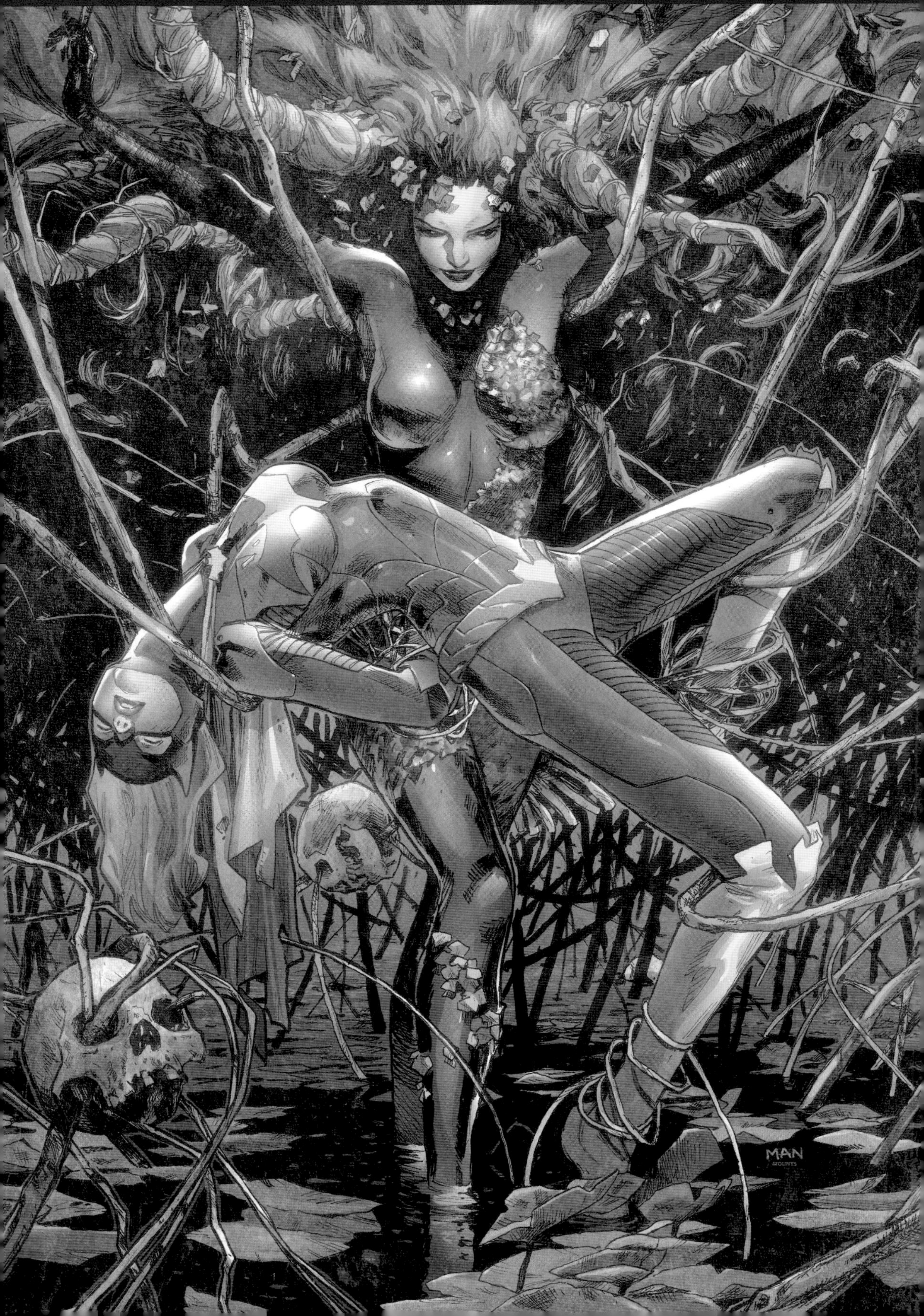
MAN
MOUNTS

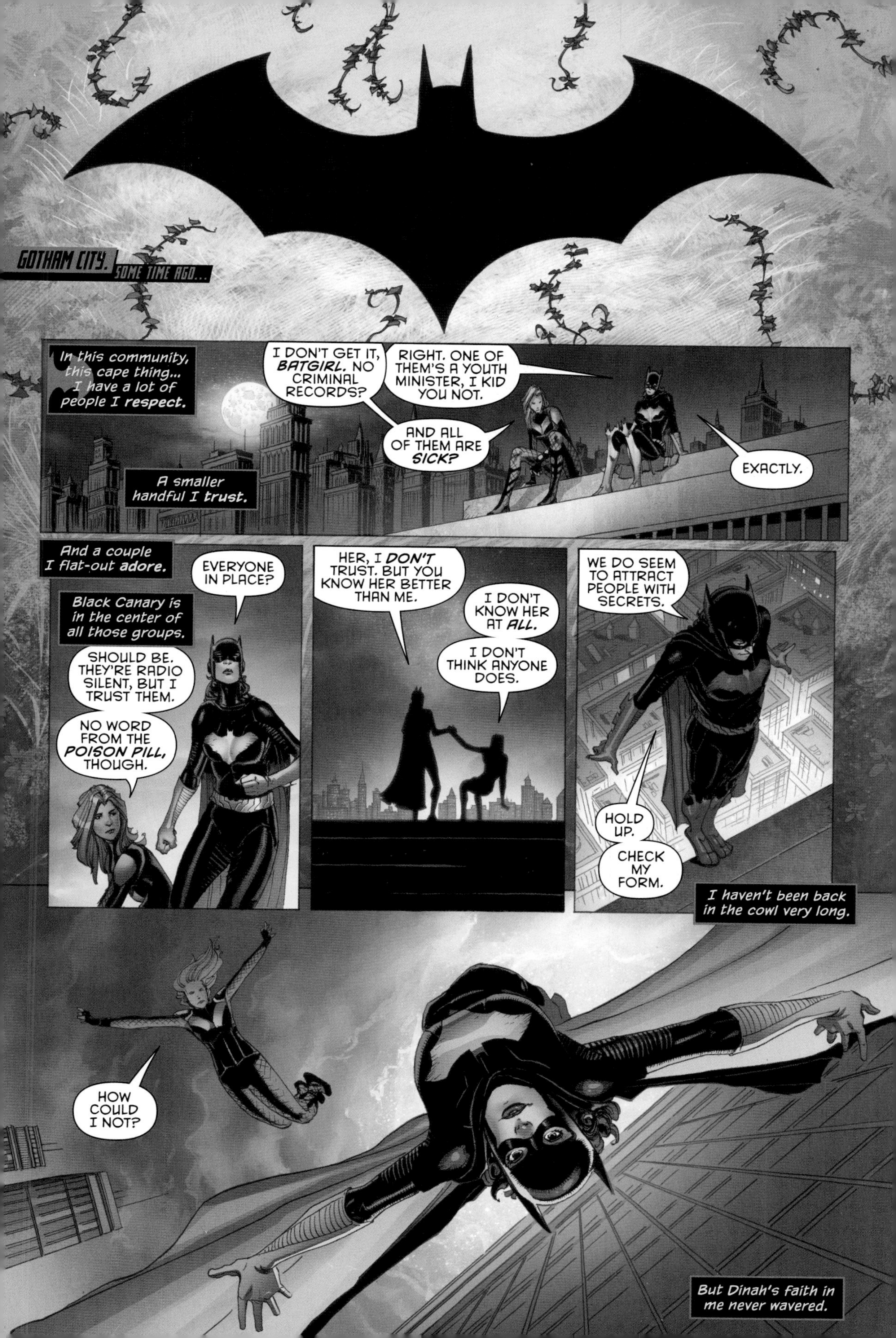
GOTHAM CITY.
SOME TIME AGO...
In this community, this cape thing... I have a lot of people I respect.
A smaller handful I trust.
I DON'T GET IT, BATGIRL. NO CRIMINAL RECORDS?
RIGHT. ONE OF THEM'S A YOUTH MINISTER, I KID YOU NOT.
AND ALL OF THEM ARE SICK?
EXACTLY.
And a couple I flat-out adore.
Black Canary is in the center of all those groups.
EVERYONE IN PLACE?
SHOULD BE. THEY'RE RADIO SILENT, BUT I TRUST THEM.
NO WORD FROM THE POISON PILL, THOUGH.
HER, I DON'T TRUST. BUT YOU KNOW HER BETTER THAN ME.
I DON'T KNOW HER AT ALL.
I DON'T THINK ANYONE DOES.
WE DO SEEM TO ATTRACT PEOPLE WITH SECRETS.
HOLD UP.
CHECK MY FORM.
I haven't been back in the cowl very long.
HOW COULD I NOT?
But Dinah's faith in me never wavered.

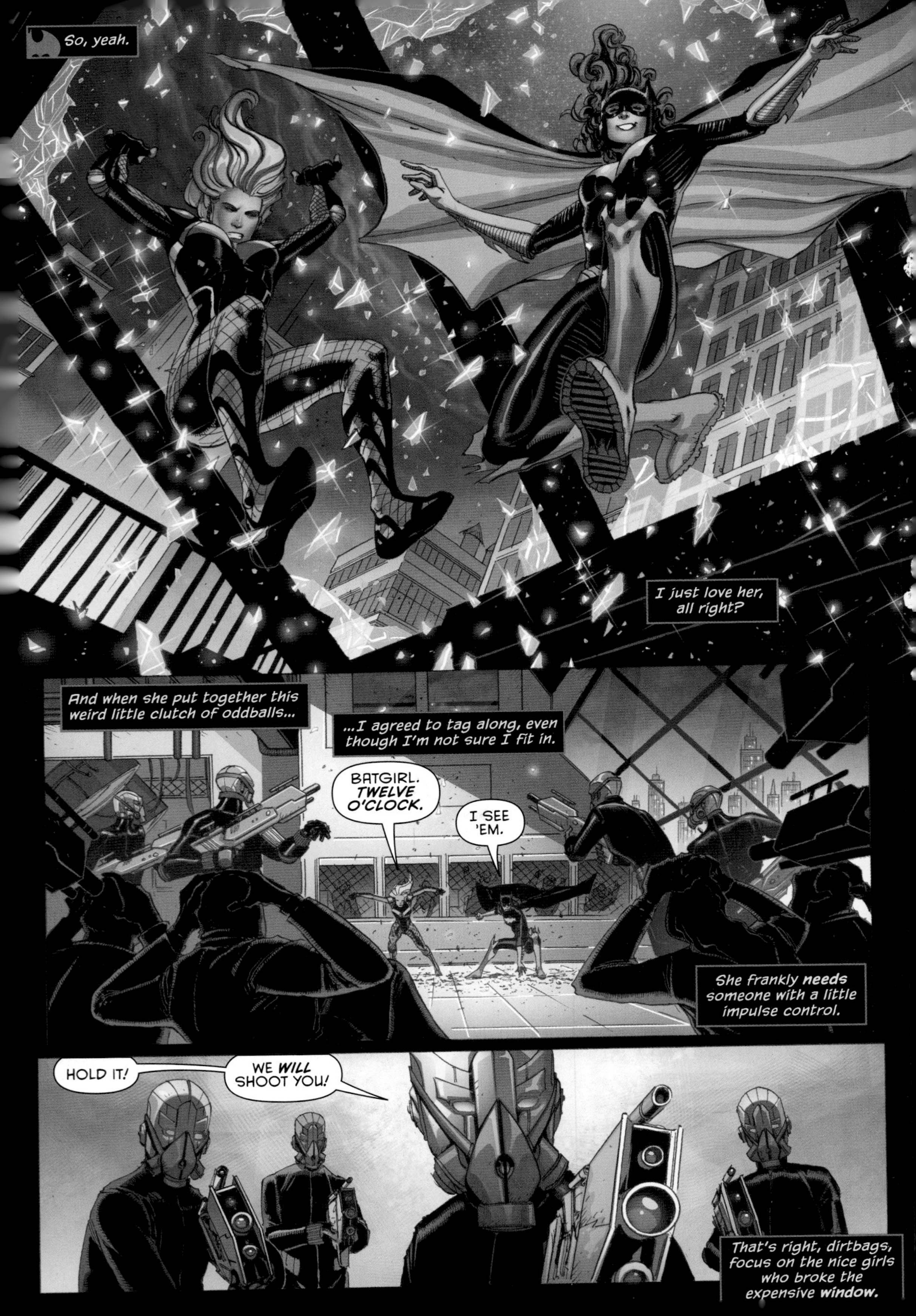
So, yeah.
I just love her, all right?
And when she put together this weird little clutch of oddballs...
...I agreed to tag along, even though I'm not sure I fit in.
BATGIRL. TWELVE O'CLOCK.
I SEE 'EM.
She frankly **needs** someone with a little impulse control.
HOLD IT!
WE **WILL** SHOOT YOU!
That's right, dirtbags, focus on the nice girls who broke the expensive **window**.

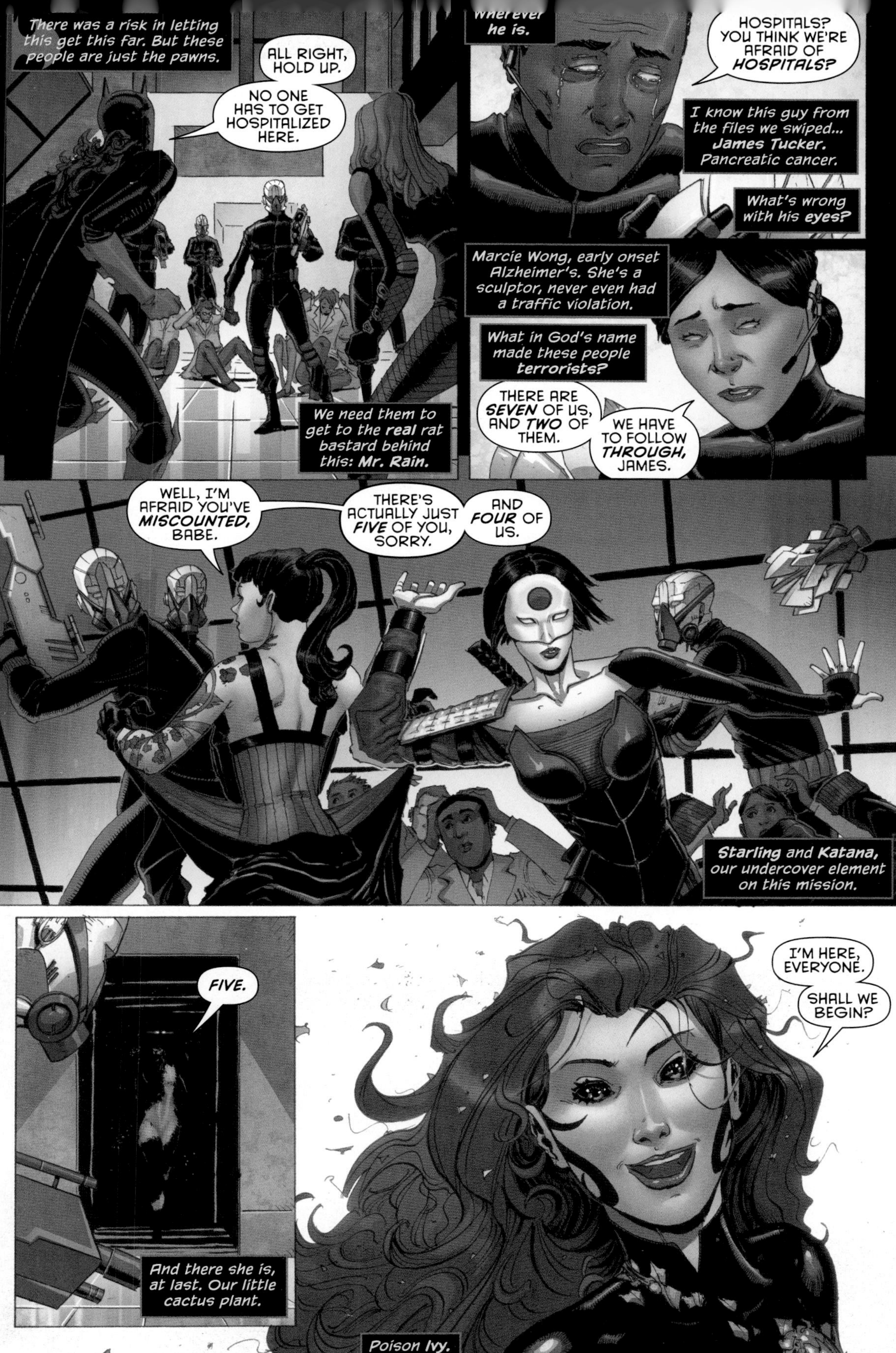

There was a risk in letting this get this far. But these people are just the pawns.
ALL RIGHT, HOLD UP.
NO ONE HAS TO GET HOSPITALIZED HERE.
We need them to get to the real rat bastard behind this: Mr. Rain.
Wherever he is.
HOSPITALS? YOU THINK WE'RE AFRAID OF HOSPITALS?
I know this guy from the files we swiped... James Tucker. Pancreatic cancer.
What's wrong with his eyes?
Marcie Wong, early onset Alzheimer's. She's a sculptor, never even had a traffic violation.
What in God's name made these people terrorists?
THERE ARE SEVEN OF US, AND TWO OF THEM.
WE HAVE TO FOLLOW THROUGH, JAMES.
WELL, I'M AFRAID YOU'VE MISCOUNTED, BABE.
THERE'S ACTUALLY JUST FIVE OF YOU, SORRY.
AND FOUR OF US.
Starling and Katana, our undercover element on this mission.
FIVE.
And there she is, at last. Our little cactus plant.
I'M HERE, EVERYONE.
SHALL WE BEGIN?
Poison Ivy.

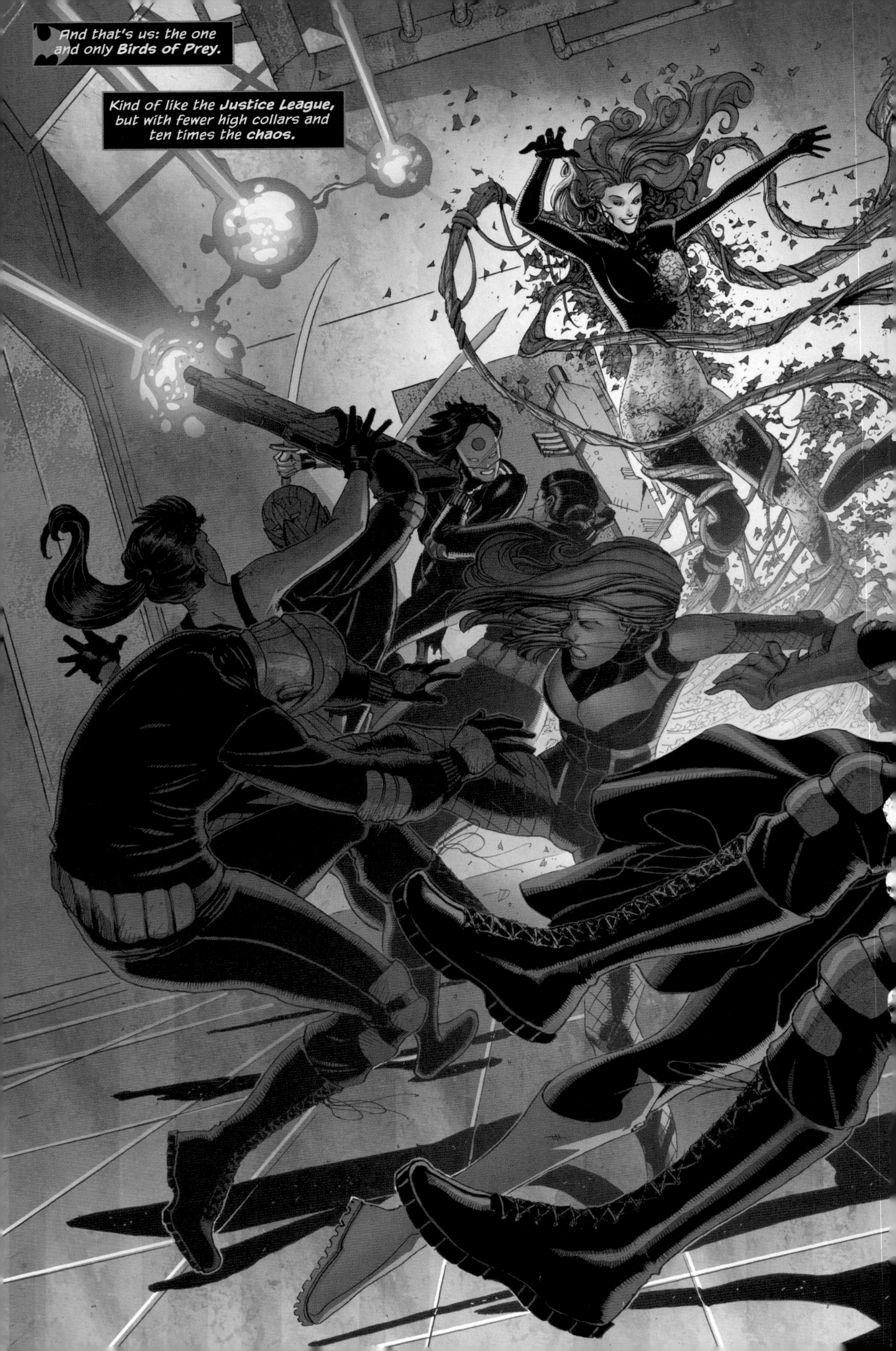
And that's us: the one and only Birds of Prey.
Kind of like the Justice League, but with fewer high collars and ten times the chaos.

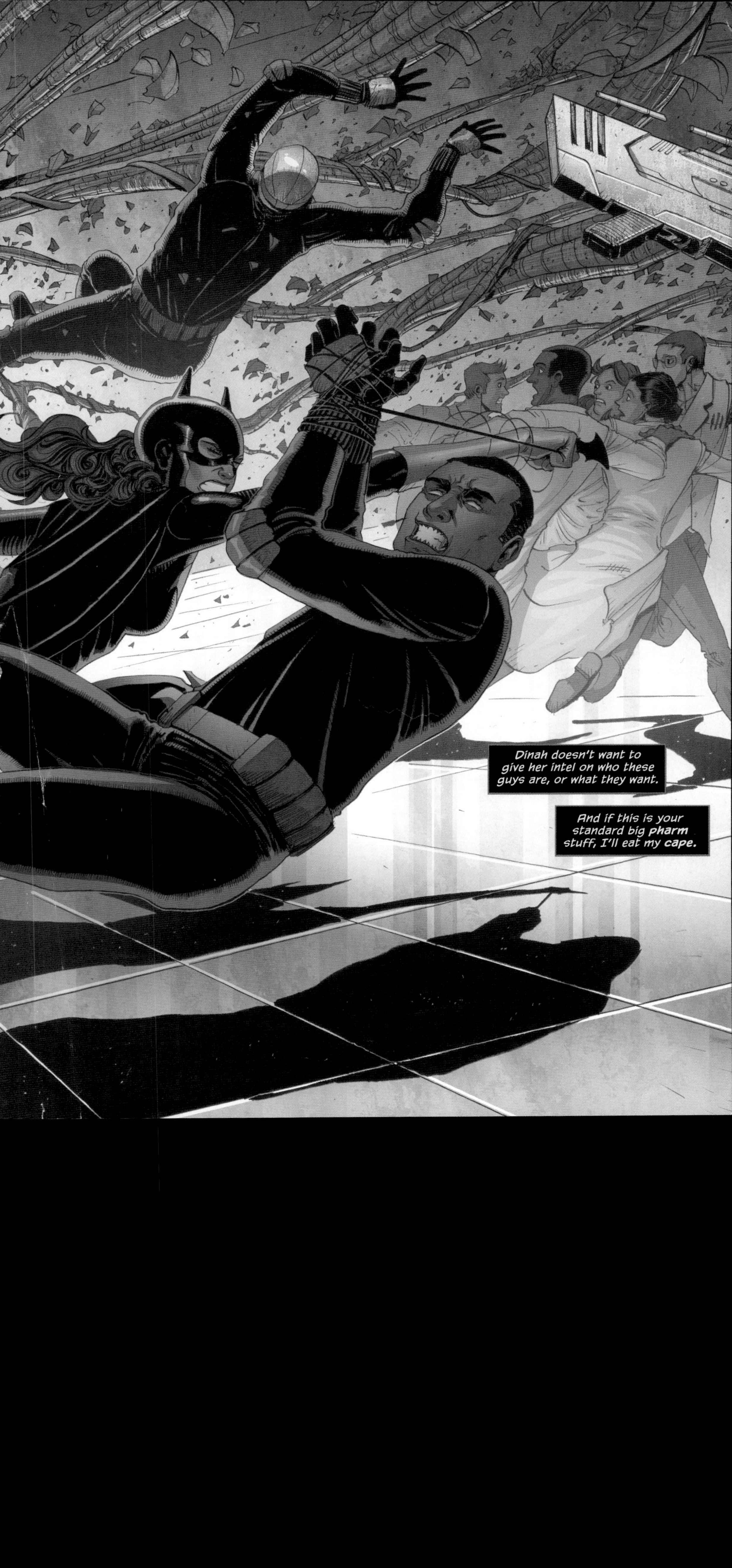
Dinah doesn't want to give her intel on who these guys are, or what they want.
And if this is your standard big **pharm** stuff, I'll eat my **cape.**

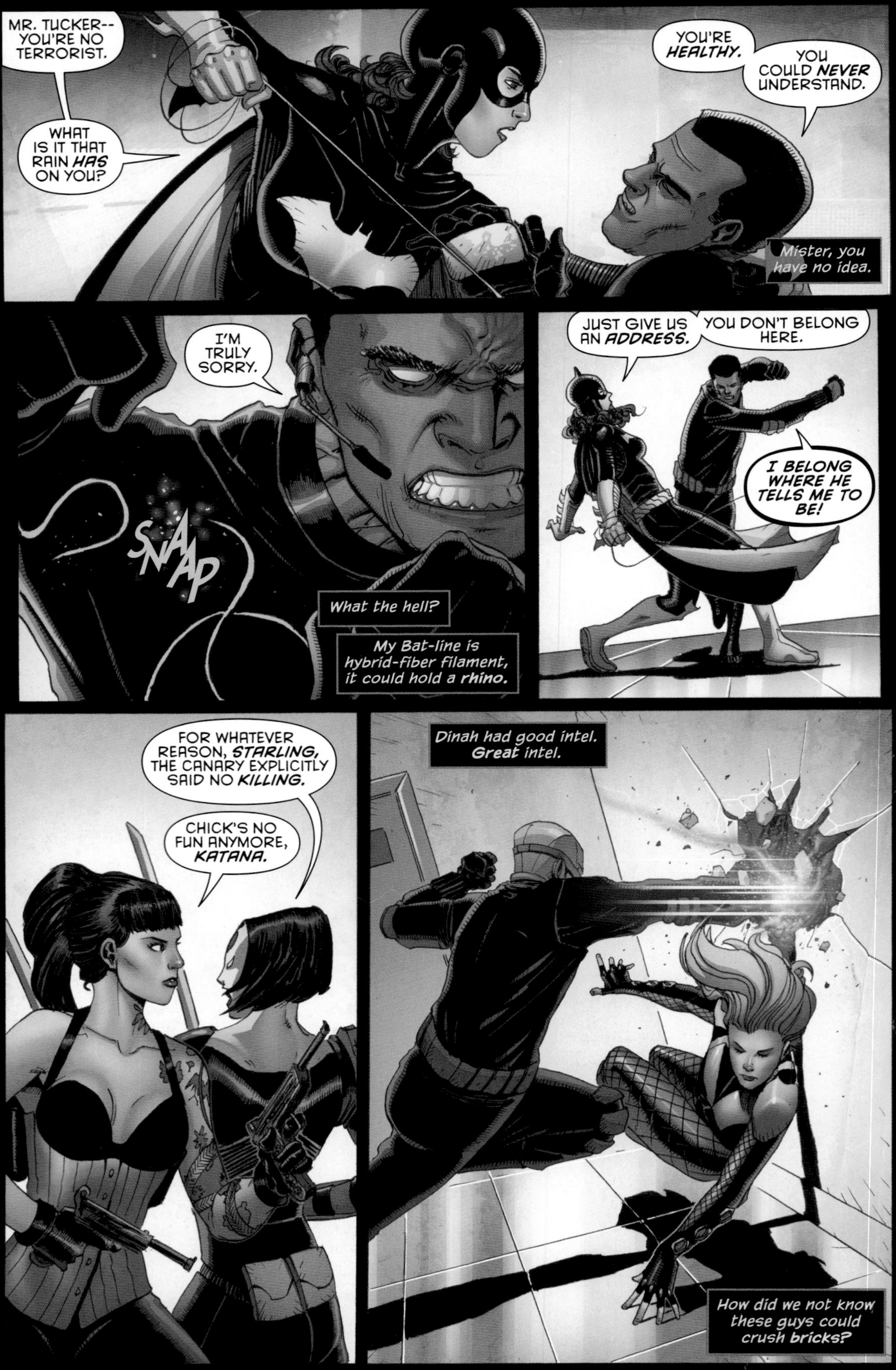
MR. TUCKER--YOU'RE NO TERRORIST.
WHAT IS IT THAT RAIN HAS ON YOU?
YOU'RE HEALTHY.
YOU COULD NEVER UNDERSTAND.
Mister, you have no idea.
I'M TRULY SORRY.
SNAAP
What the hell?
My Bat-line is hybrid-fiber filament, it could hold a rhino.
JUST GIVE US AN ADDRESS.
YOU DON'T BELONG HERE.
I BELONG WHERE HE TELLS ME TO BE!
FOR WHATEVER REASON, STARLING, THE CANARY EXPLICITLY SAID NO KILLING.
CHICK'S NO FUN ANYMORE, KATANA.
Dinah had good intel. Great intel.
How did we not know these guys could crush bricks?

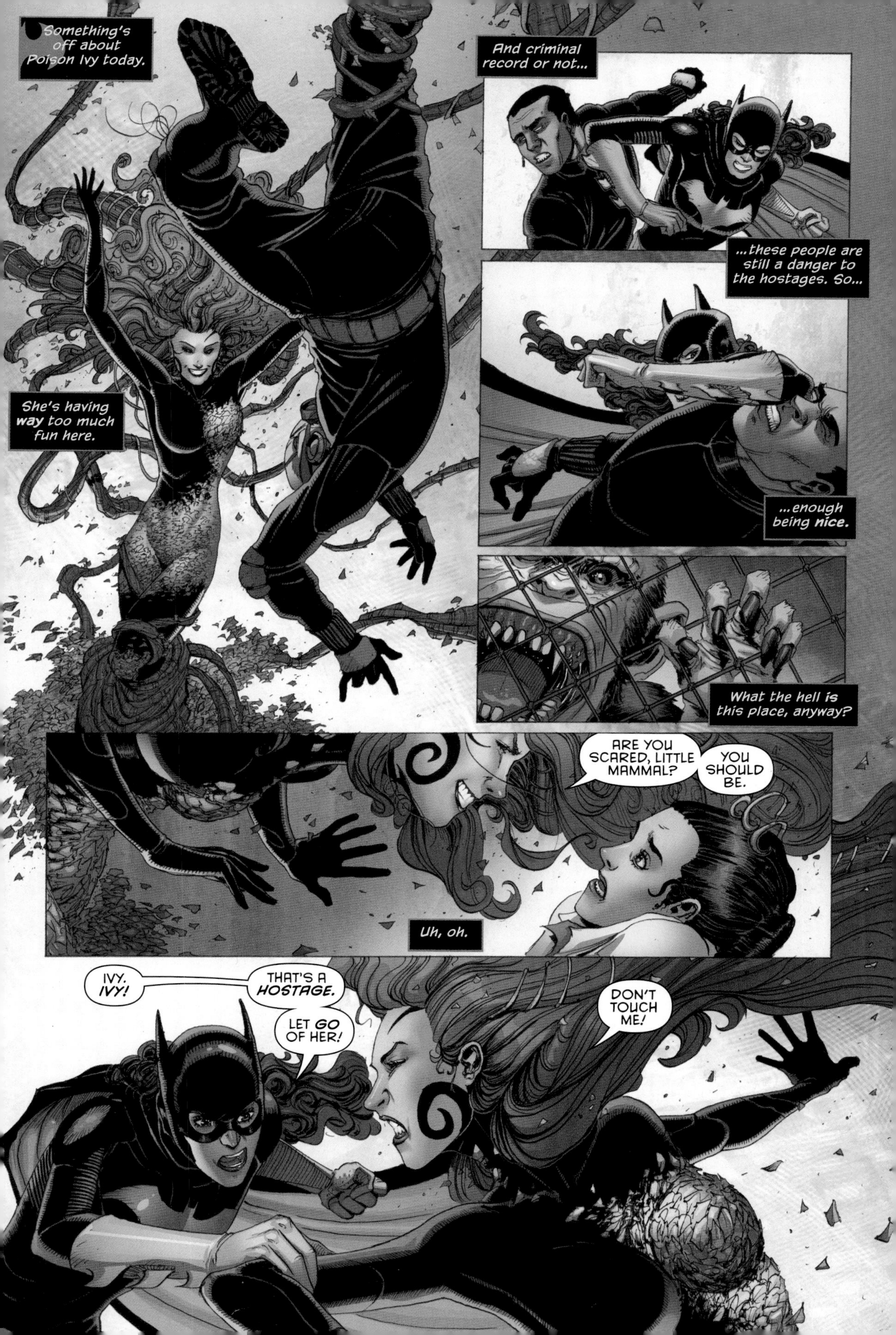
Something's off about Poison Ivy today.
And criminal record or not...
...these people are still a danger to the hostages. So...
...enough being nice.
What the hell is this place, anyway?
She's having way too much fun here.
ARE YOU SCARED, LITTLE MAMMAL?
YOU SHOULD BE.
Uh, oh.
IVY. IVY!
THAT'S A HOSTAGE.
LET GO OF HER!
DON'T TOUCH ME!

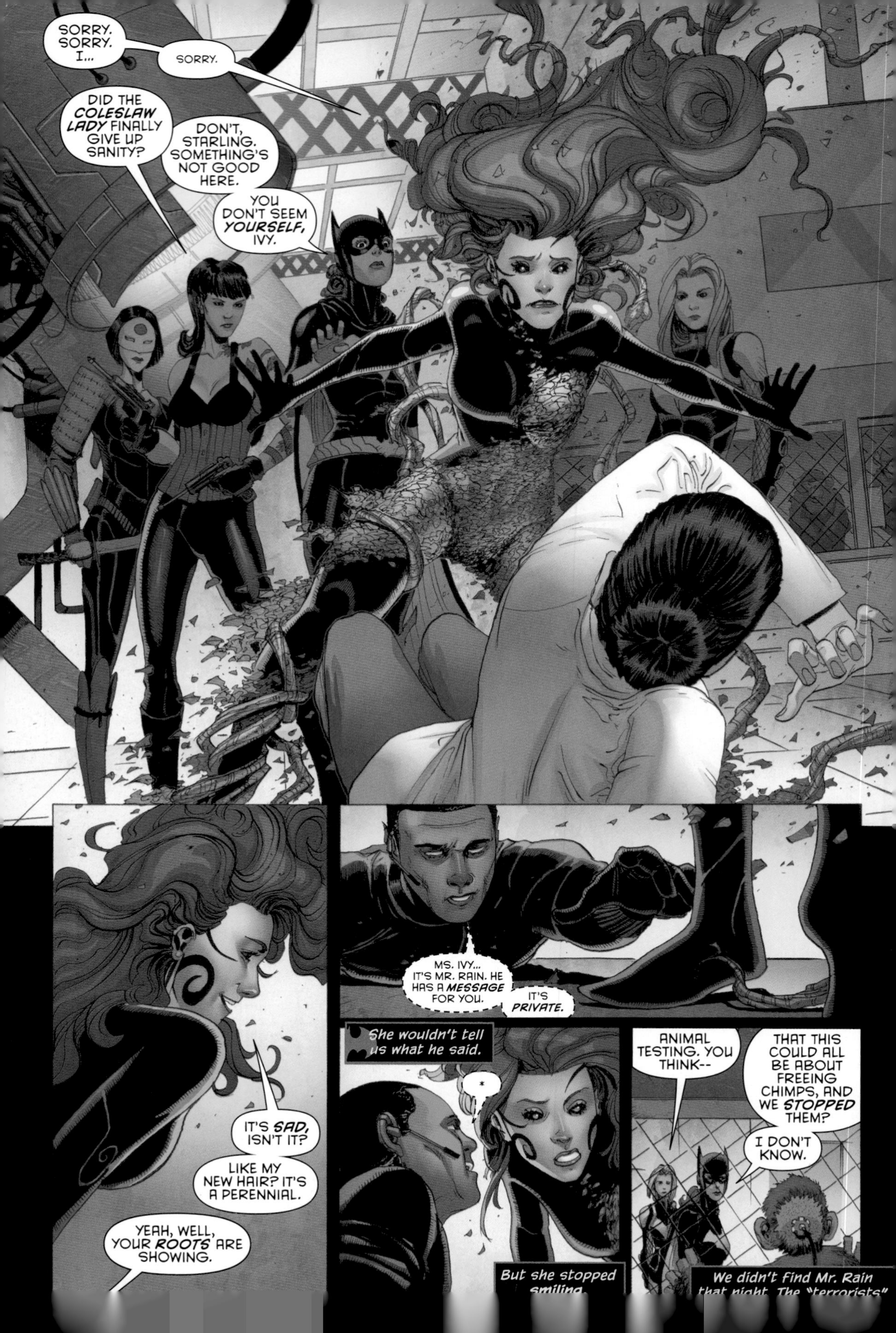
SORRY. SORRY. I...
SORRY.
DID THE COLESLAW LADY FINALLY GIVE UP SANITY?
DON'T, STARLING. SOMETHING'S NOT GOOD HERE.
YOU DON'T SEEM YOURSELF, IVY.
IT'S SAD, ISN'T IT?
LIKE MY NEW HAIR? IT'S A PERENNIAL.
YEAH, WELL, YOUR ROOTS ARE SHOWING.
MS. IVY... IT'S MR. RAIN. HE HAS A MESSAGE FOR YOU.
IT'S PRIVATE.
She wouldn't tell us what he said.
*
But she stopped smiling.
ANIMAL TESTING. YOU THINK--
THAT THIS COULD ALL BE ABOUT FREEING CHIMPS, AND WE STOPPED THEM?
I DON'T KNOW.
We didn't find Mr. Rain that night. The "terrorists"

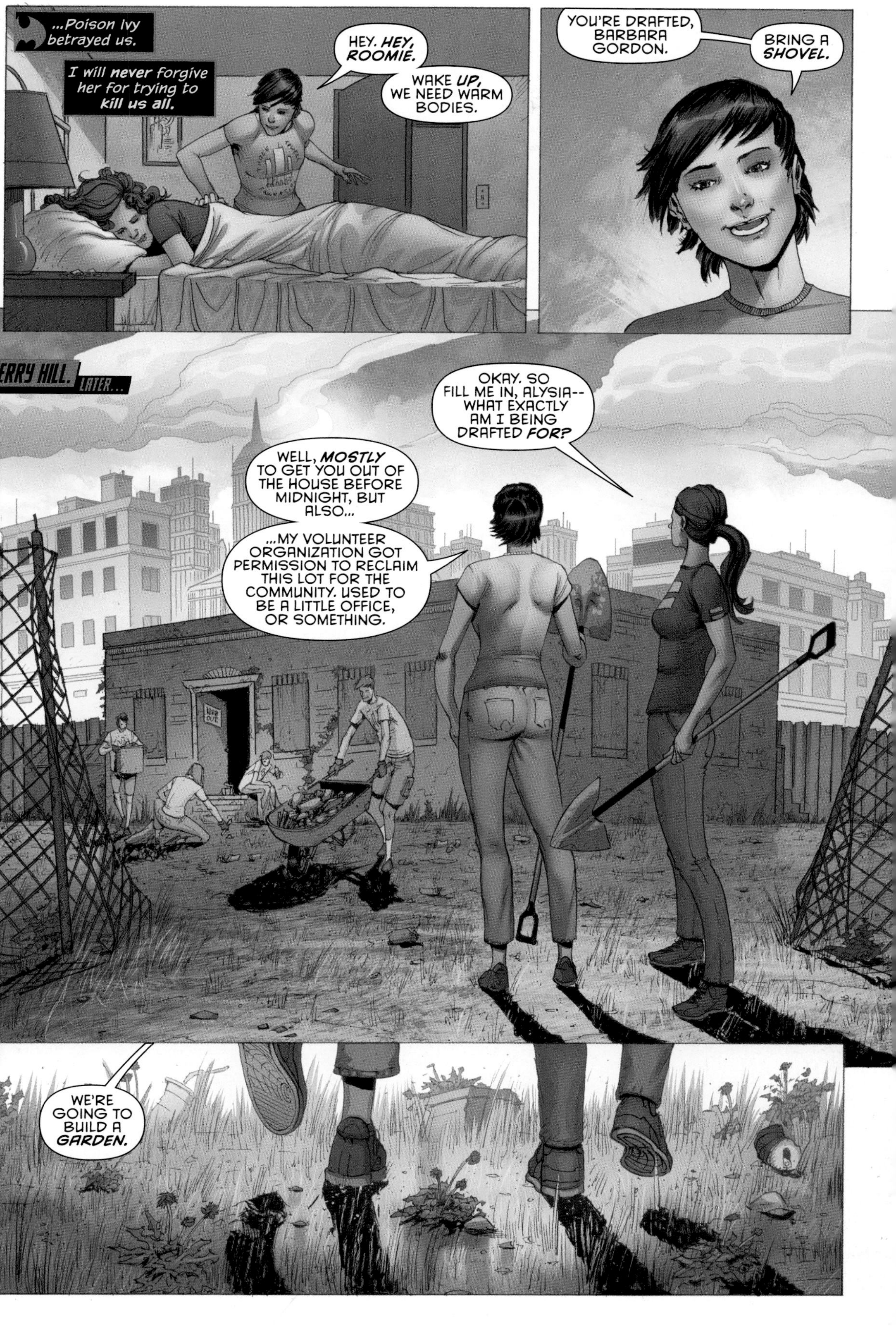

...Poison Ivy betrayed us.
I will never forgive her for trying to kill us all.
HEY. HEY, ROOMIE.
WAKE UP, WE NEED WARM BODIES.
YOU'RE DRAFTED, BARBARA GORDON.
BRING A SHOVEL.
CHERRY HILL. LATER...
OKAY. SO FILL ME IN, ALYSIA-- WHAT EXACTLY AM I BEING DRAFTED FOR?
WELL, MOSTLY TO GET YOU OUT OF THE HOUSE BEFORE MIDNIGHT, BUT ALSO...
...MY VOLUNTEER ORGANIZATION GOT PERMISSION TO RECLAIM THIS LOT FOR THE COMMUNITY. USED TO BE A LITTLE OFFICE, OR SOMETHING.
WE'RE GOING TO BUILD A GARDEN.

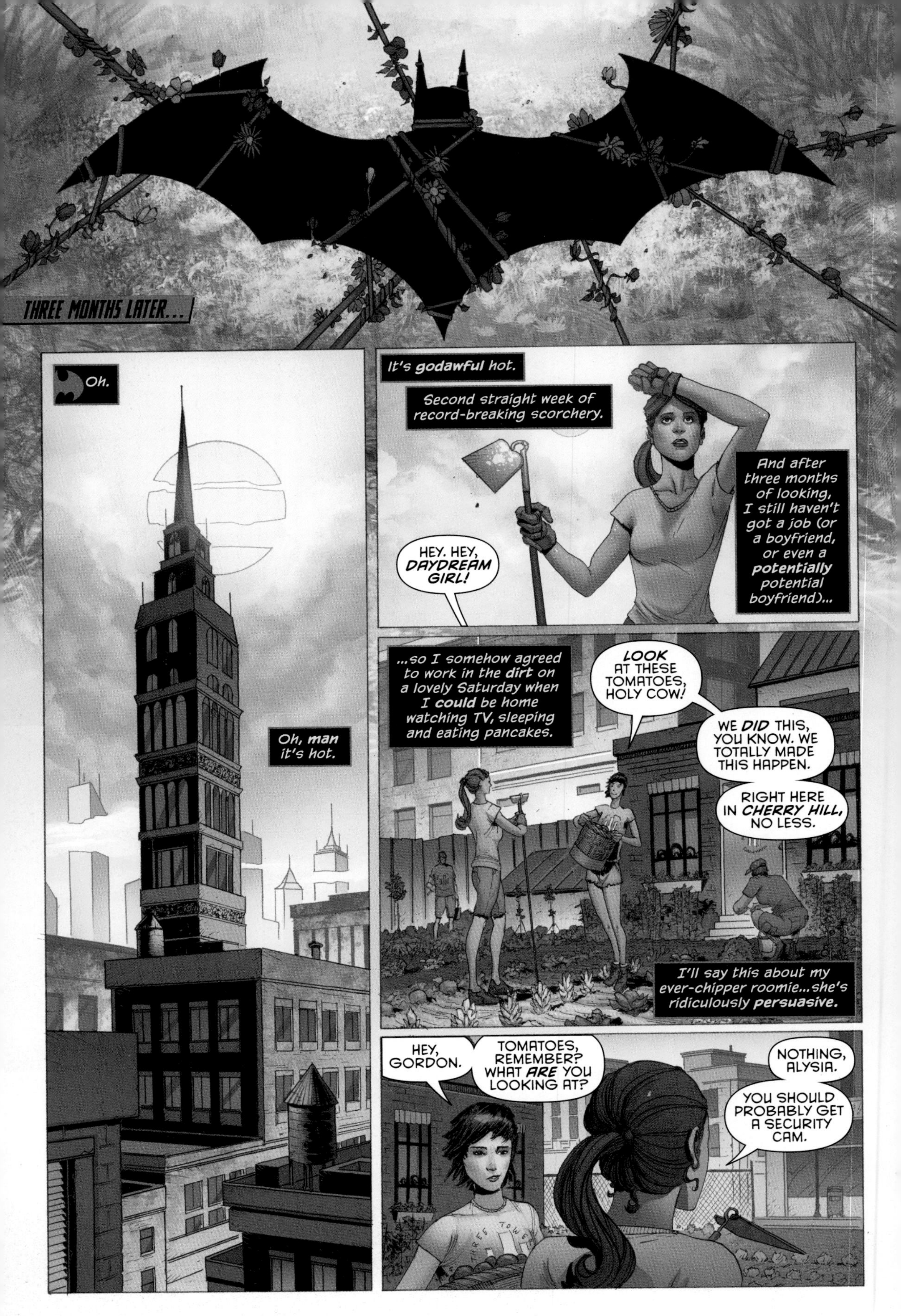

THREE MONTHS LATER...
Oh.
Oh, man it's hot.
It's godawful hot.
Second straight week of record-breaking scorchery.
And after three months of looking, I still haven't got a job (or a boyfriend, or even a potentially potential boyfriend)...
HEY. HEY, DAYDREAM GIRL!
...so I somehow agreed to work in the dirt on a lovely Saturday when I could be home watching TV, sleeping and eating pancakes.
LOOK AT THESE TOMATOES, HOLY COW!
WE DID THIS, YOU KNOW. WE TOTALLY MADE THIS HAPPEN.
RIGHT HERE IN CHERRY HILL, NO LESS.
I'll say this about my ever-chipper roomie...she's ridiculously persuasive.
HEY, GORDON.
TOMATOES, REMEMBER? WHAT ARE YOU LOOKING AT?
NOTHING, ALYSIA.
YOU SHOULD PROBABLY GET A SECURITY CAM.

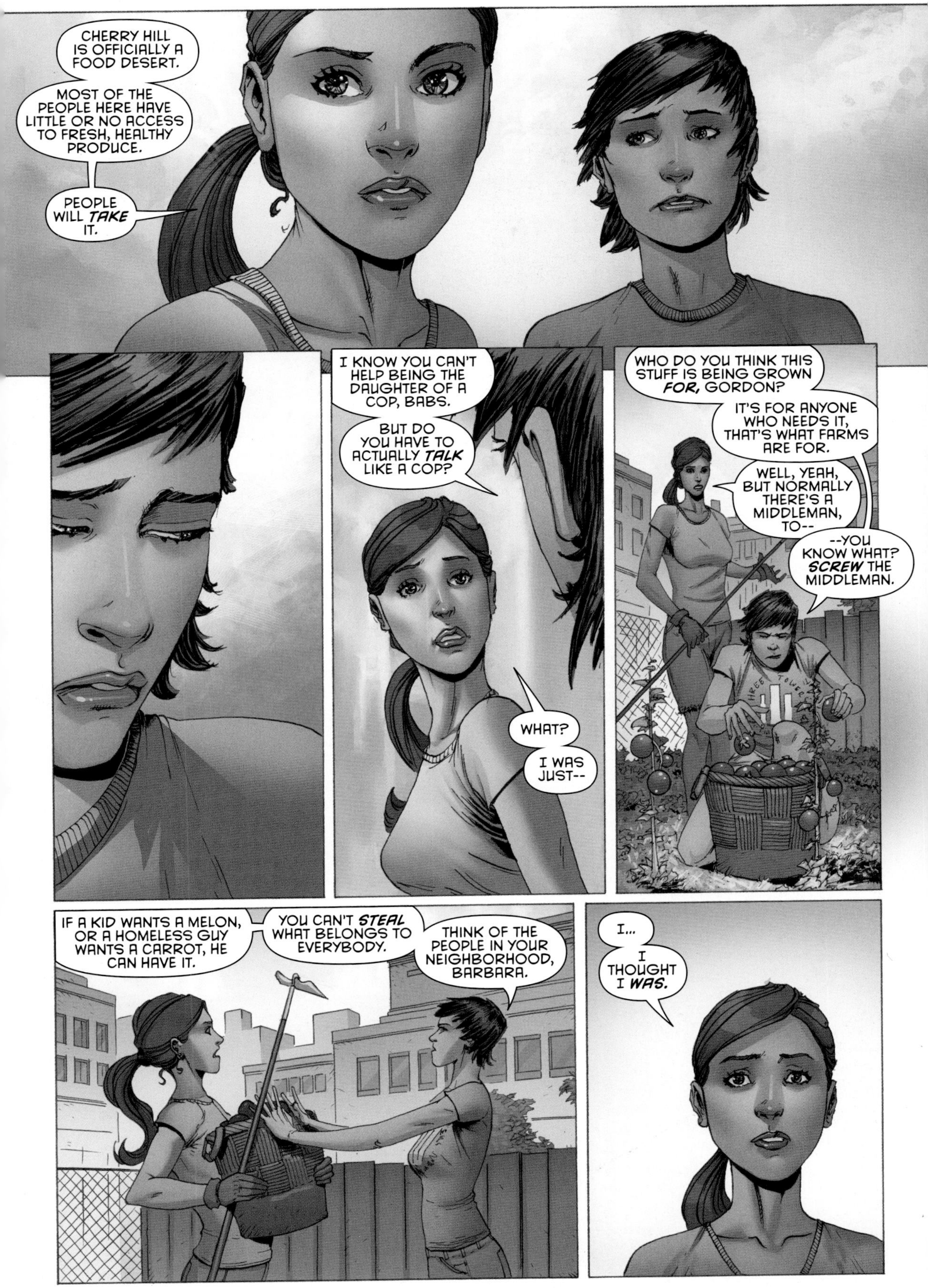
CHERRY HILL IS OFFICIALLY A FOOD DESERT.
MOST OF THE PEOPLE HERE HAVE LITTLE OR NO ACCESS TO FRESH, HEALTHY PRODUCE.
PEOPLE WILL *TAKE* IT.
I KNOW YOU CAN'T HELP BEING THE DAUGHTER OF A COP, BABS.
BUT DO YOU HAVE TO ACTUALLY *TALK* LIKE A COP?
WHAT?
I WAS JUST--
WHO DO YOU THINK THIS STUFF IS BEING GROWN *FOR,* GORDON?
IT'S FOR ANYONE WHO NEEDS IT, THAT'S WHAT FARMS ARE FOR.
WELL, YEAH, BUT NORMALLY THERE'S A MIDDLEMAN, TO--
--YOU KNOW WHAT? *SCREW* THE MIDDLEMAN.
IF A KID WANTS A MELON, OR A HOMELESS GUY WANTS A CARROT, HE CAN HAVE IT.
YOU CAN'T *STEAL* WHAT BELONGS TO EVERYBODY.
THINK OF THE PEOPLE IN YOUR NEIGHBORHOOD, BARBARA.
I...
I THOUGHT I *WAS.*

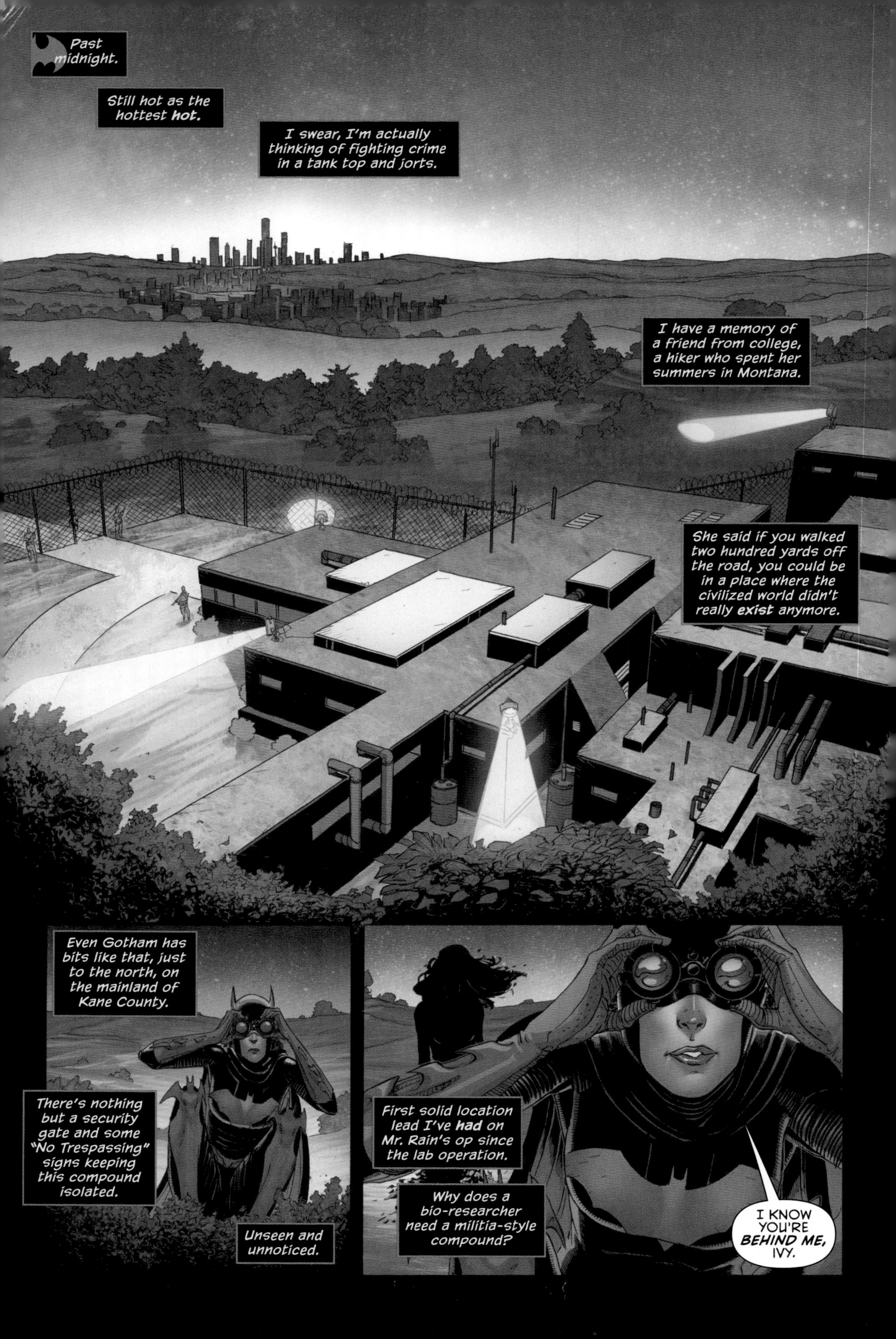
Past midnight.
Still hot as the hottest hot.
I swear, I'm actually thinking of fighting crime in a tank top and jorts.
I have a memory of a friend from college, a hiker who spent her summers in Montana.
She said if you walked two hundred yards off the road, you could be in a place where the civilized world didn't really exist anymore.
Even Gotham has bits like that, just to the north, on the mainland of Kane County.
There's nothing but a security gate and some "No Trespassing" signs keeping this compound isolated.
Unseen and unnoticed.
First solid location lead I've had on Mr. Rain's op since the lab operation.
Why does a bio-researcher need a militia-style compound?
I KNOW YOU'RE BEHIND ME, IVY.

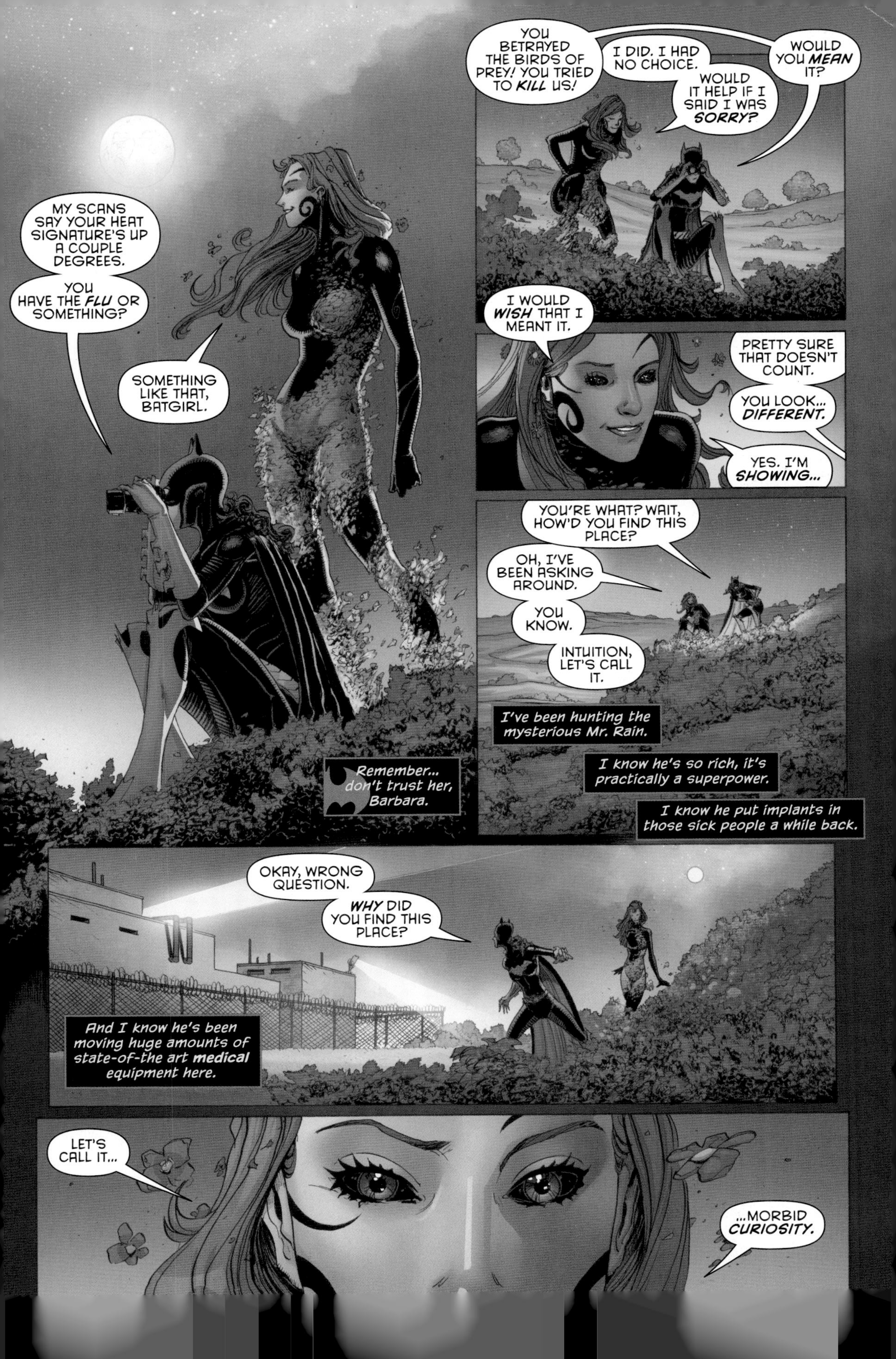

MY SCANS SAY YOUR HEAT SIGNATURE'S UP A COUPLE DEGREES.
YOU HAVE THE FLU OR SOMETHING?
SOMETHING LIKE THAT, BATGIRL.
Remember... don't trust her, Barbara.
YOU BETRAYED THE BIRDS OF PREY! YOU TRIED TO KILL US!
I DID. I HAD NO CHOICE.
WOULD IT HELP IF I SAID I WAS SORRY?
WOULD YOU MEAN IT?
I WOULD WISH THAT I MEANT IT.
PRETTY SURE THAT DOESN'T COUNT.
YOU LOOK... DIFFERENT.
YES. I'M SHOWING...
YOU'RE WHAT? WAIT, HOW'D YOU FIND THIS PLACE?
OH, I'VE BEEN ASKING AROUND.
YOU KNOW.
INTUITION, LET'S CALL IT.
I've been hunting the mysterious Mr. Rain.
I know he's so rich, it's practically a superpower.
I know he put implants in those sick people a while back.
OKAY, WRONG QUESTION.
WHY DID YOU FIND THIS PLACE?
And I know he's been moving huge amounts of state-of-the art medical equipment here.
LET'S CALL IT...
...MORBID CURIOSITY.

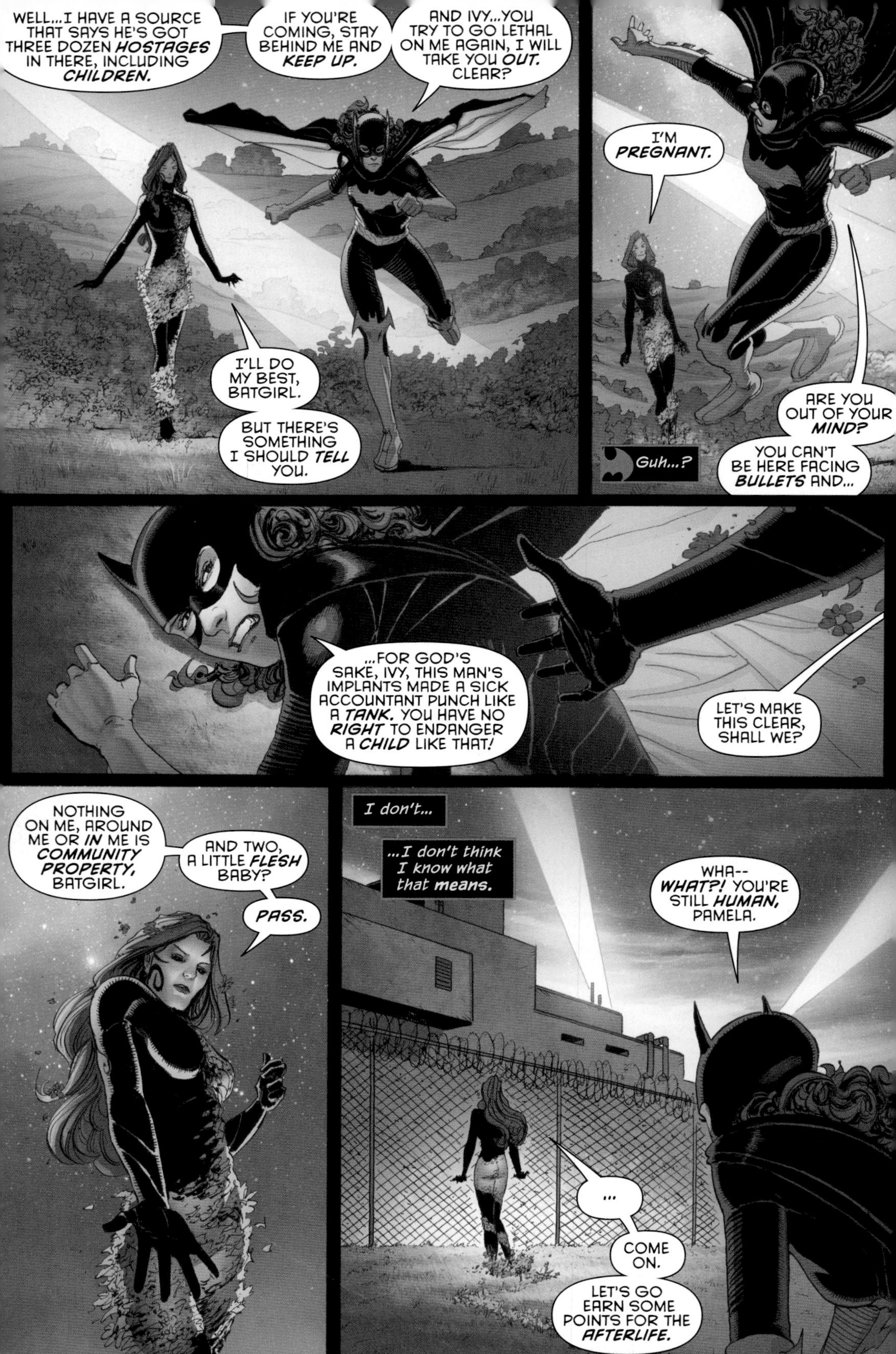

WELL...I HAVE A SOURCE THAT SAYS HE'S GOT THREE DOZEN HOSTAGES IN THERE, INCLUDING CHILDREN.
IF YOU'RE COMING, STAY BEHIND ME AND KEEP UP.
AND IVY...YOU TRY TO GO LETHAL ON ME AGAIN, I WILL TAKE YOU OUT. CLEAR?
I'LL DO MY BEST, BATGIRL.
BUT THERE'S SOMETHING I SHOULD TELL YOU.
I'M PREGNANT.
Guh...?
ARE YOU OUT OF YOUR MIND?
YOU CAN'T BE HERE FACING BULLETS AND...
...FOR GOD'S SAKE, IVY, THIS MAN'S IMPLANTS MADE A SICK ACCOUNTANT PUNCH LIKE A TANK. YOU HAVE NO RIGHT TO ENDANGER A CHILD LIKE THAT!
LET'S MAKE THIS CLEAR, SHALL WE?
NOTHING ON ME, AROUND ME OR IN ME IS COMMUNITY PROPERTY, BATGIRL.
AND TWO, A LITTLE FLESH BABY?
PASS.
I don't...
...I don't think I know what that means.
WHA-- WHAT?! YOU'RE STILL HUMAN, PAMELA.
...
COME ON.
LET'S GO EARN SOME POINTS FOR THE AFTERLIFE.

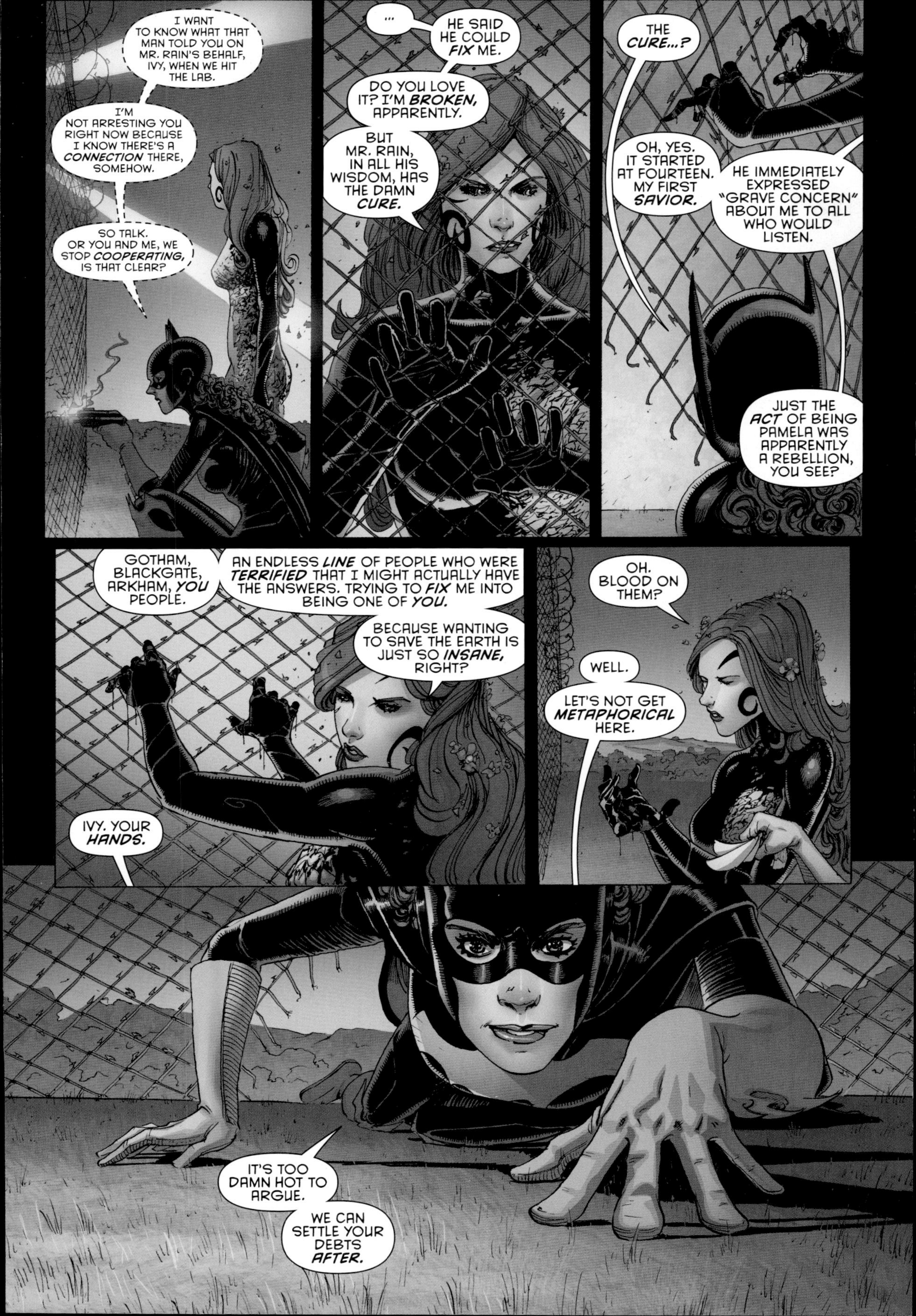

I WANT TO KNOW WHAT THAT MAN TOLD YOU ON MR. RAIN'S BEHALF, IVY, WHEN WE HIT THE LAB.
I'M NOT ARRESTING YOU RIGHT NOW BECAUSE I KNOW THERE'S A CONNECTION THERE, SOMEHOW.
SO TALK. OR YOU AND ME, WE STOP COOPERATING, IS THAT CLEAR?
...
HE SAID HE COULD FIX ME.
DO YOU LOVE IT? I'M BROKEN, APPARENTLY.
BUT MR. RAIN, IN ALL HIS WISDOM, HAS THE DAMN CURE.
THE CURE...?
OH, YES. IT STARTED AT FOURTEEN. MY FIRST SAVIOR.
HE IMMEDIATELY EXPRESSED "GRAVE CONCERN" ABOUT ME TO ALL WHO WOULD LISTEN.
JUST THE ACT OF BEING PAMELA WAS APPARENTLY A REBELLION, YOU SEE?
GOTHAM, BLACKGATE, ARKHAM, YOU PEOPLE.
AN ENDLESS LINE OF PEOPLE WHO WERE TERRIFIED THAT I MIGHT ACTUALLY HAVE THE ANSWERS. TRYING TO FIX ME INTO BEING ONE OF YOU.
BECAUSE WANTING TO SAVE THE EARTH IS JUST SO INSANE, RIGHT?
IVY. YOUR HANDS.
OH. BLOOD ON THEM?
WELL.
LET'S NOT GET METAPHORICAL HERE.
IT'S TOO DAMN HOT TO ARGUE.
WE CAN SETTLE YOUR DEBTS AFTER.

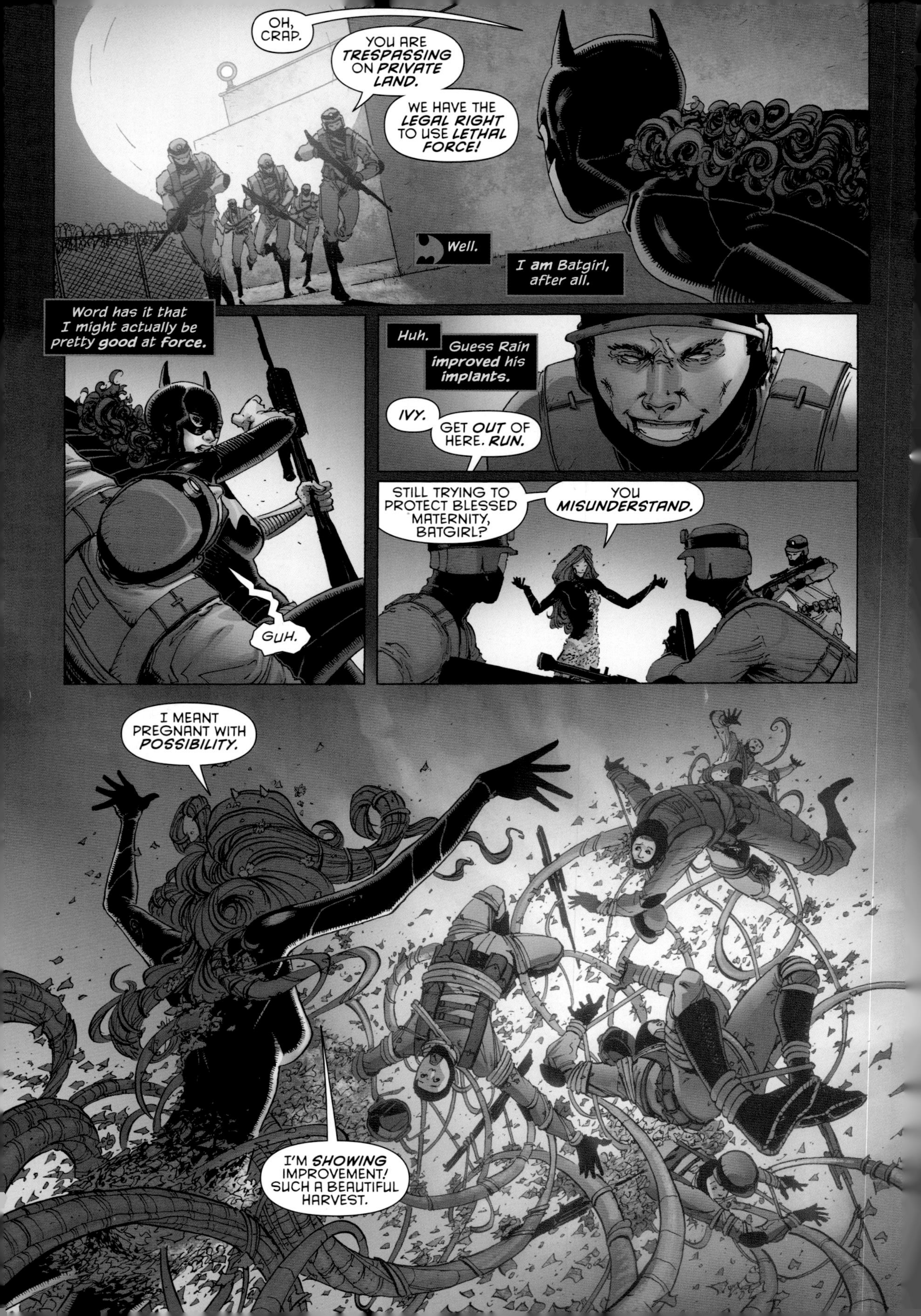

OH, CRAP.
YOU ARE TRESPASSING ON PRIVATE LAND.
WE HAVE THE LEGAL RIGHT TO USE LETHAL FORCE!
Well.
I am Batgirl, after all.
Word has it that I might actually be pretty good at force.
GUH.
Huh.
Guess Rain improved his implants.
IVY.
GET OUT OF HERE. RUN.
STILL TRYING TO PROTECT BLESSED MATERNITY, BATGIRL?
YOU MISUNDERSTAND.
I MEANT PREGNANT WITH POSSIBILITY.
I'M SHOWING IMPROVEMENT! SUCH A BEAUTIFUL HARVEST.

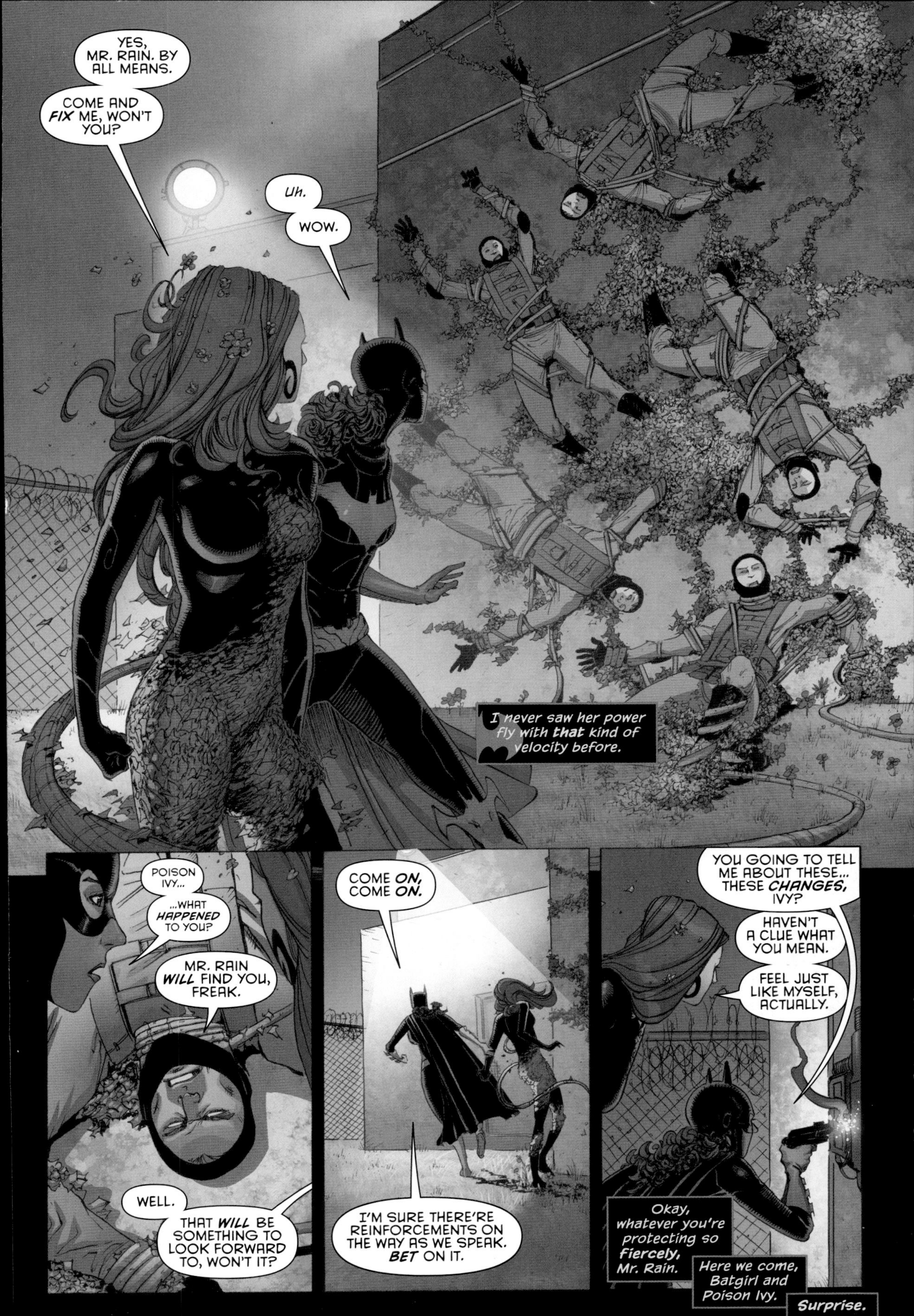
YES, MR. RAIN. BY ALL MEANS.
COME AND FIX ME, WON'T YOU?
Uh.
WOW.
I never saw her power fly with that kind of velocity before.
POISON IVY...
...WHAT HAPPENED TO YOU?
MR. RAIN WILL FIND YOU, FREAK.
WELL.
THAT WILL BE SOMETHING TO LOOK FORWARD TO, WON'T IT?
COME ON, COME ON.
I'M SURE THERE'RE REINFORCEMENTS ON THE WAY AS WE SPEAK. BET ON IT.
YOU GOING TO TELL ME ABOUT THESE... THESE CHANGES, IVY?
HAVEN'T A CLUE WHAT YOU MEAN.
FEEL JUST LIKE MYSELF, ACTUALLY.
Okay, whatever you're protecting so fiercely, Mr. Rain.
Here we come, Batgirl and Poison Ivy.
Surprise.

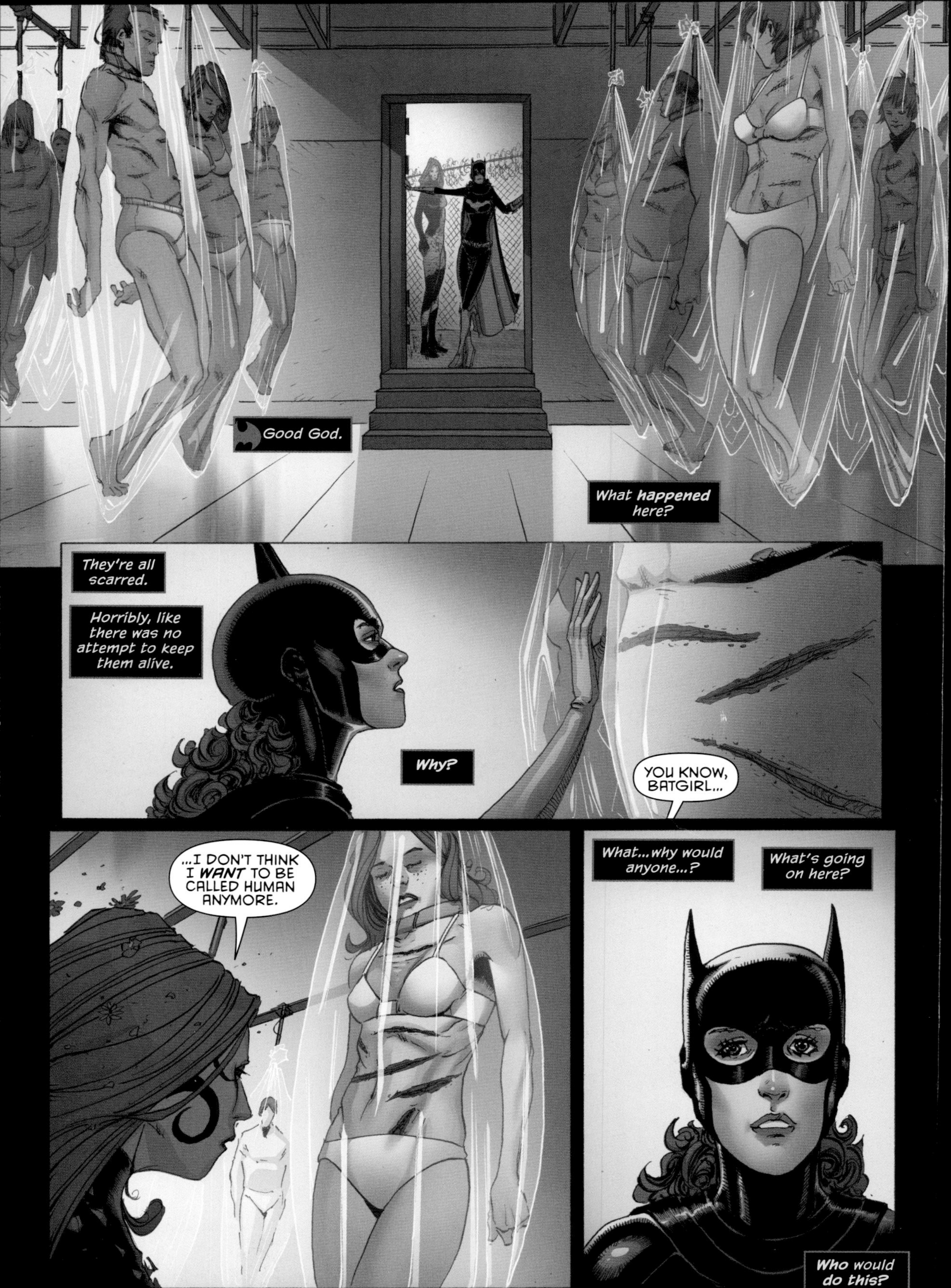
Good God.
What happened here?
They're all scarred.
Horribly, like there was no attempt to keep them alive.
Why?
YOU KNOW, BATGIRL...
...I DON'T THINK I WANT TO BE CALLED HUMAN ANYMORE.
What...why would anyone...?
What's going on here?
Who would do this?

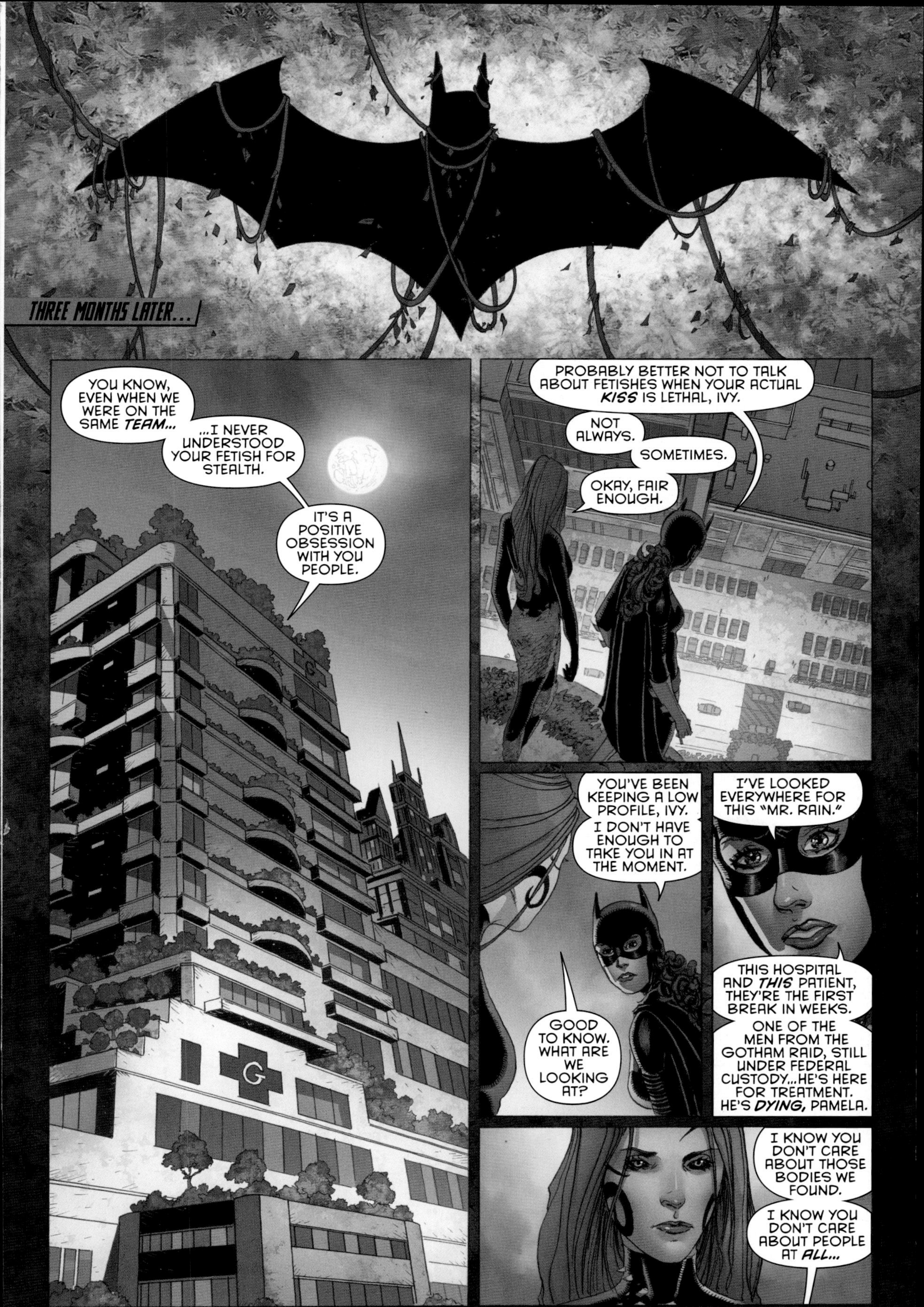
THREE MONTHS LATER...
YOU KNOW, EVEN WHEN WE WERE ON THE SAME TEAM...
...I NEVER UNDERSTOOD YOUR FETISH FOR STEALTH.
IT'S A POSITIVE OBSESSION WITH YOU PEOPLE.
PROBABLY BETTER NOT TO TALK ABOUT FETISHES WHEN YOUR ACTUAL KISS IS LETHAL, IVY.
NOT ALWAYS.
SOMETIMES.
OKAY, FAIR ENOUGH.
YOU'VE BEEN KEEPING A LOW PROFILE, IVY.
I DON'T HAVE ENOUGH TO TAKE YOU IN AT THE MOMENT.
GOOD TO KNOW. WHAT ARE WE LOOKING AT?
I'VE LOOKED EVERYWHERE FOR THIS "MR. RAIN."
THIS HOSPITAL AND THIS PATIENT, THEY'RE THE FIRST BREAK IN WEEKS.
ONE OF THE MEN FROM THE GOTHAM RAID, STILL UNDER FEDERAL CUSTODY...HE'S HERE FOR TREATMENT. HE'S DYING, PAMELA.
I KNOW YOU DON'T CARE ABOUT THOSE BODIES WE FOUND.
I KNOW YOU DON'T CARE ABOUT PEOPLE AT ALL...

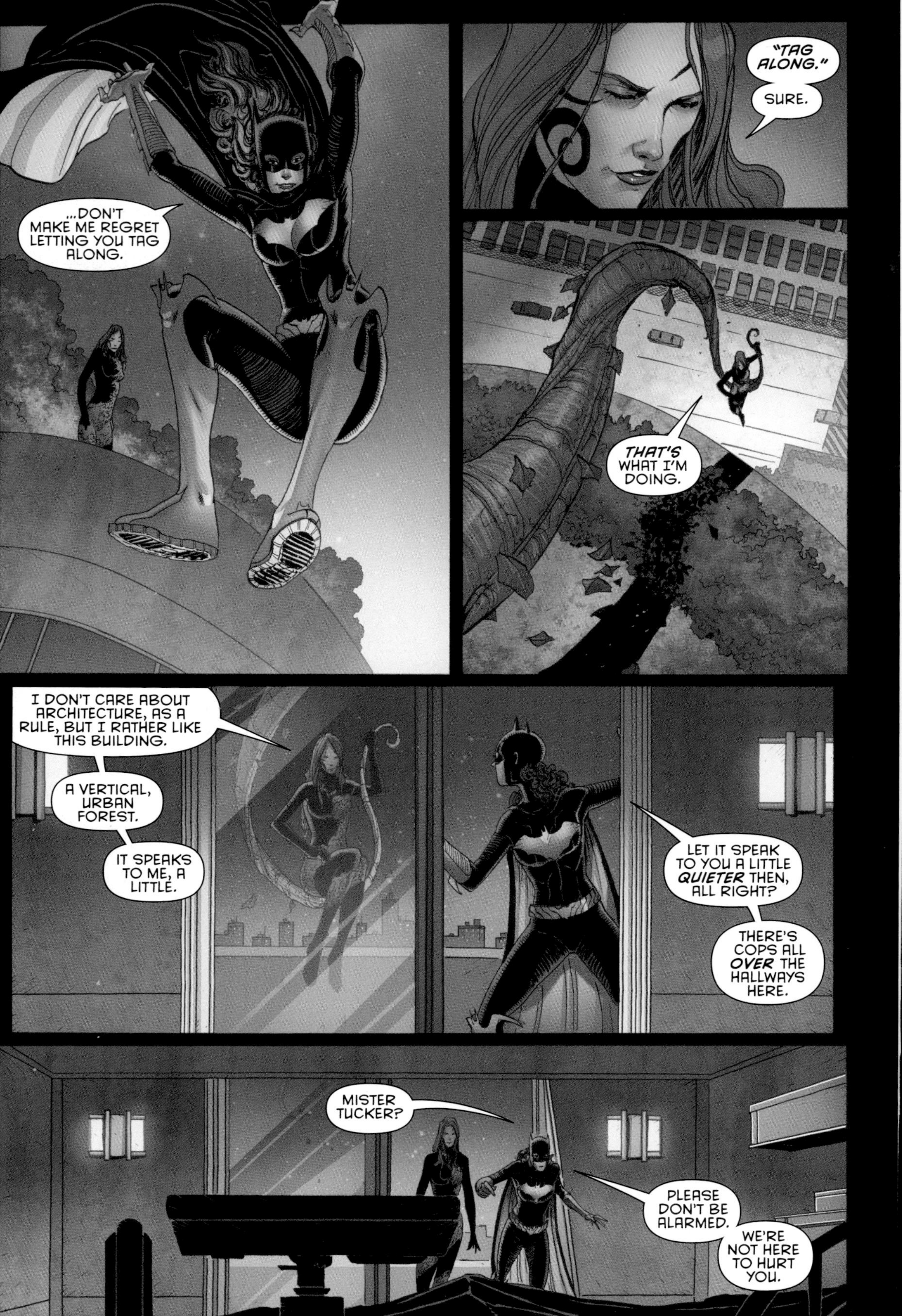
...DON'T MAKE ME REGRET LETTING YOU TAG ALONG.
"TAG ALONG."
SURE.
THAT'S WHAT I'M DOING.
I DON'T CARE ABOUT ARCHITECTURE, AS A RULE, BUT I RATHER LIKE THIS BUILDING.
A VERTICAL, URBAN FOREST.
IT SPEAKS TO ME, A LITTLE.
LET IT SPEAK TO YOU A LITTLE QUIETER THEN, ALL RIGHT?
THERE'S COPS ALL OVER THE HALLWAYS HERE.
MISTER TUCKER?
PLEASE DON'T BE ALARMED.
WE'RE NOT HERE TO HURT YOU.

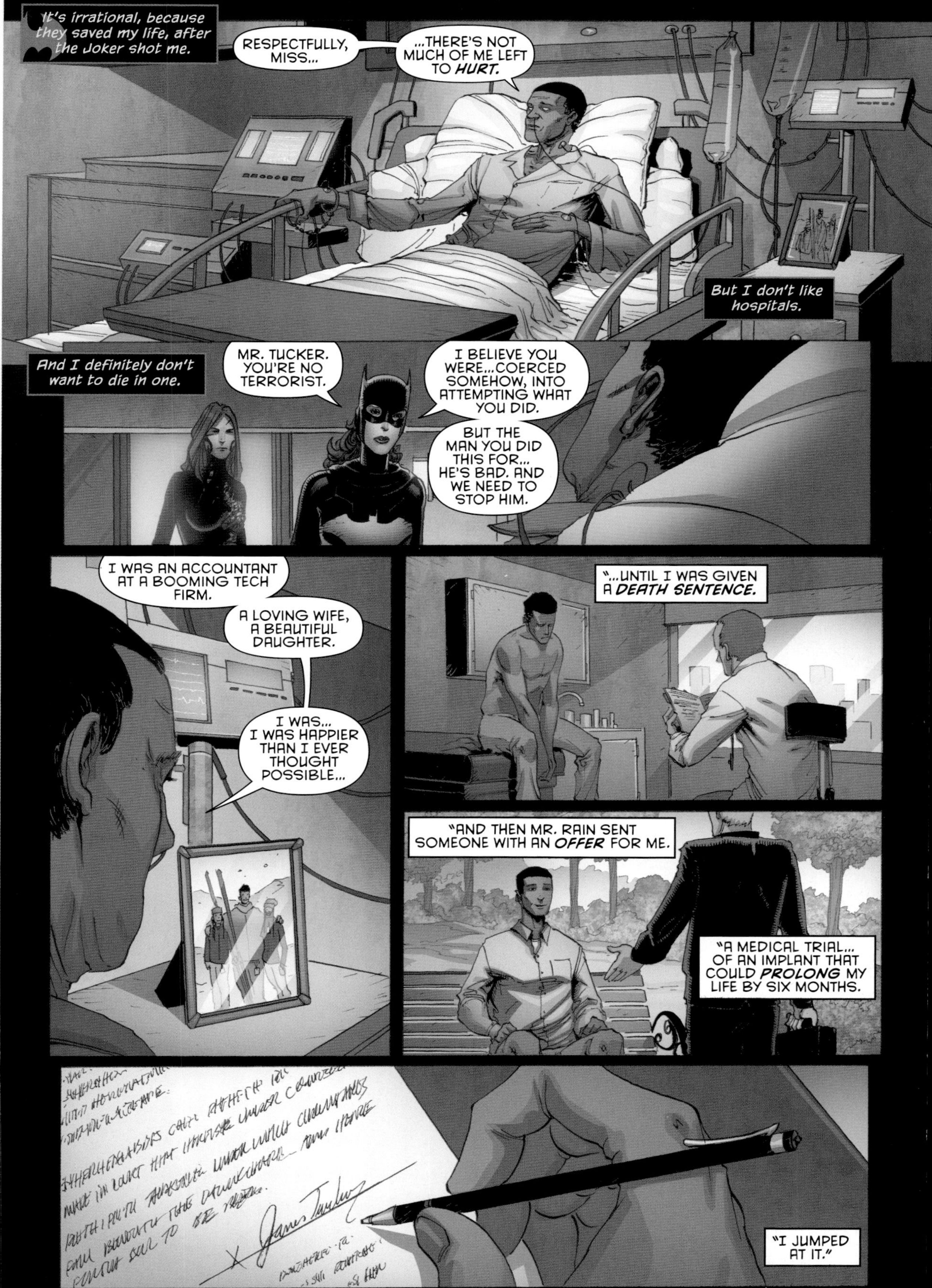
It's irrational, because they saved my life, after the Joker shot me.
RESPECTFULLY, MISS...
...THERE'S NOT MUCH OF ME LEFT TO HURT.
But I don't like hospitals.
And I definitely don't want to die in one.
MR. TUCKER. YOU'RE NO TERRORIST.
I BELIEVE YOU WERE...COERCED SOMEHOW, INTO ATTEMPTING WHAT YOU DID.
BUT THE MAN YOU DID THIS FOR... HE'S BAD. AND WE NEED TO STOP HIM.
I WAS AN ACCOUNTANT AT A BOOMING TECH FIRM.
A LOVING WIFE, A BEAUTIFUL DAUGHTER.
I WAS... I WAS HAPPIER THAN I EVER THOUGHT POSSIBLE...
"...UNTIL I WAS GIVEN A DEATH SENTENCE.
"AND THEN MR. RAIN SENT SOMEONE WITH AN OFFER FOR ME.
"A MEDICAL TRIAL... OF AN IMPLANT THAT COULD PROLONG MY LIFE BY SIX MONTHS.
"I JUMPED AT IT."

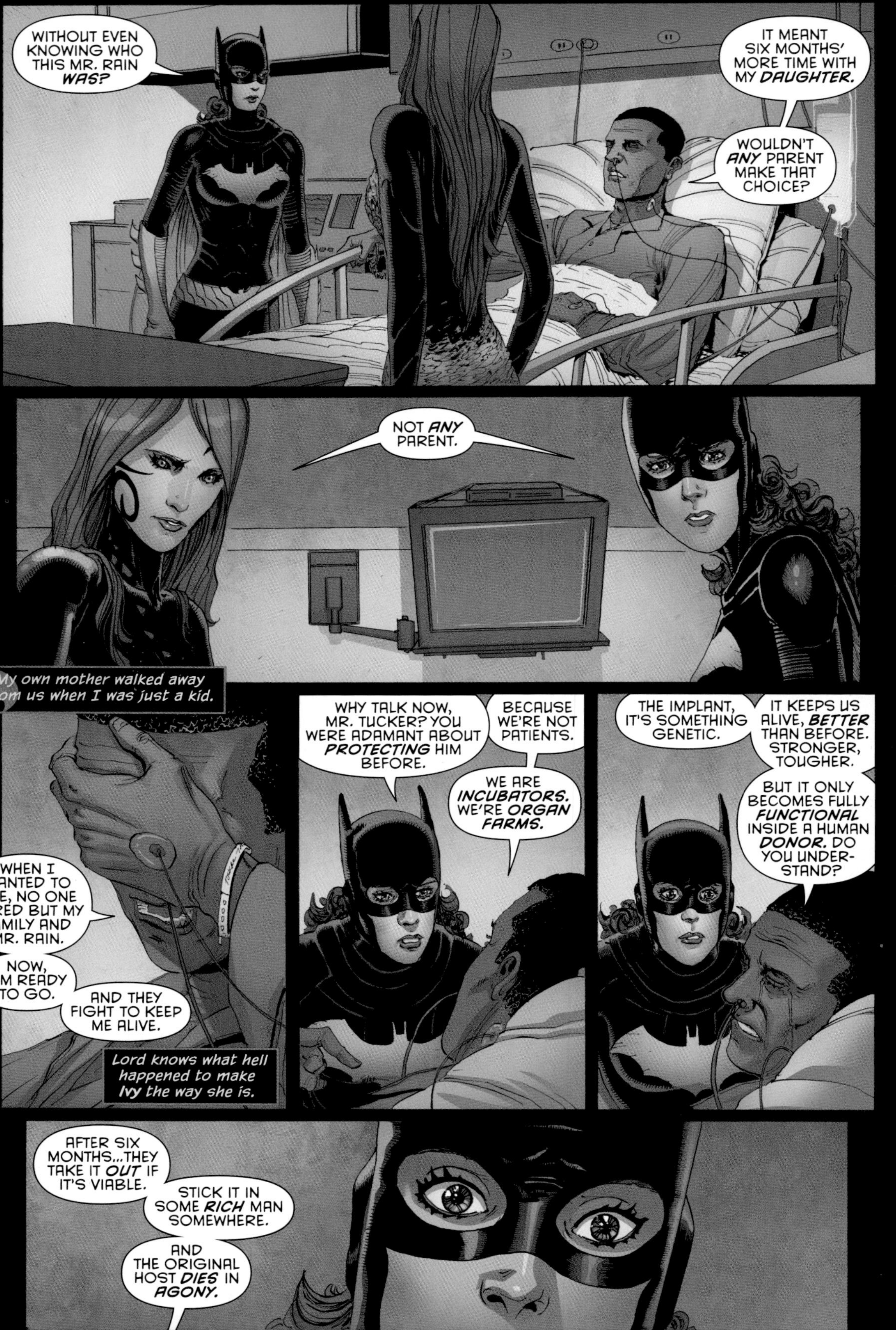
WITHOUT EVEN KNOWING WHO THIS MR. RAIN WAS?
IT MEANT SIX MONTHS' MORE TIME WITH MY DAUGHTER.
WOULDN'T ANY PARENT MAKE THAT CHOICE?
NOT ANY PARENT.
My own mother walked away from us when I was just a kid.
WHEN I WANTED TO LIVE, NO ONE CARED BUT MY FAMILY AND MR. RAIN.
NOW, I'M READY TO GO.
AND THEY FIGHT TO KEEP ME ALIVE.
Lord knows what hell happened to make Ivy the way she is.
WHY TALK NOW, MR. TUCKER? YOU WERE ADAMANT ABOUT PROTECTING HIM BEFORE.
BECAUSE WE'RE NOT PATIENTS.
WE ARE INCUBATORS. WE'RE ORGAN FARMS.
THE IMPLANT, IT'S SOMETHING GENETIC.
IT KEEPS US ALIVE, BETTER THAN BEFORE. STRONGER, TOUGHER.
BUT IT ONLY BECOMES FULLY FUNCTIONAL INSIDE A HUMAN DONOR. DO YOU UNDERSTAND?
AFTER SIX MONTHS...THEY TAKE IT OUT IF IT'S VIABLE.
STICK IT IN SOME RICH MAN SOMEWHERE.
AND THE ORIGINAL HOST DIES IN AGONY.

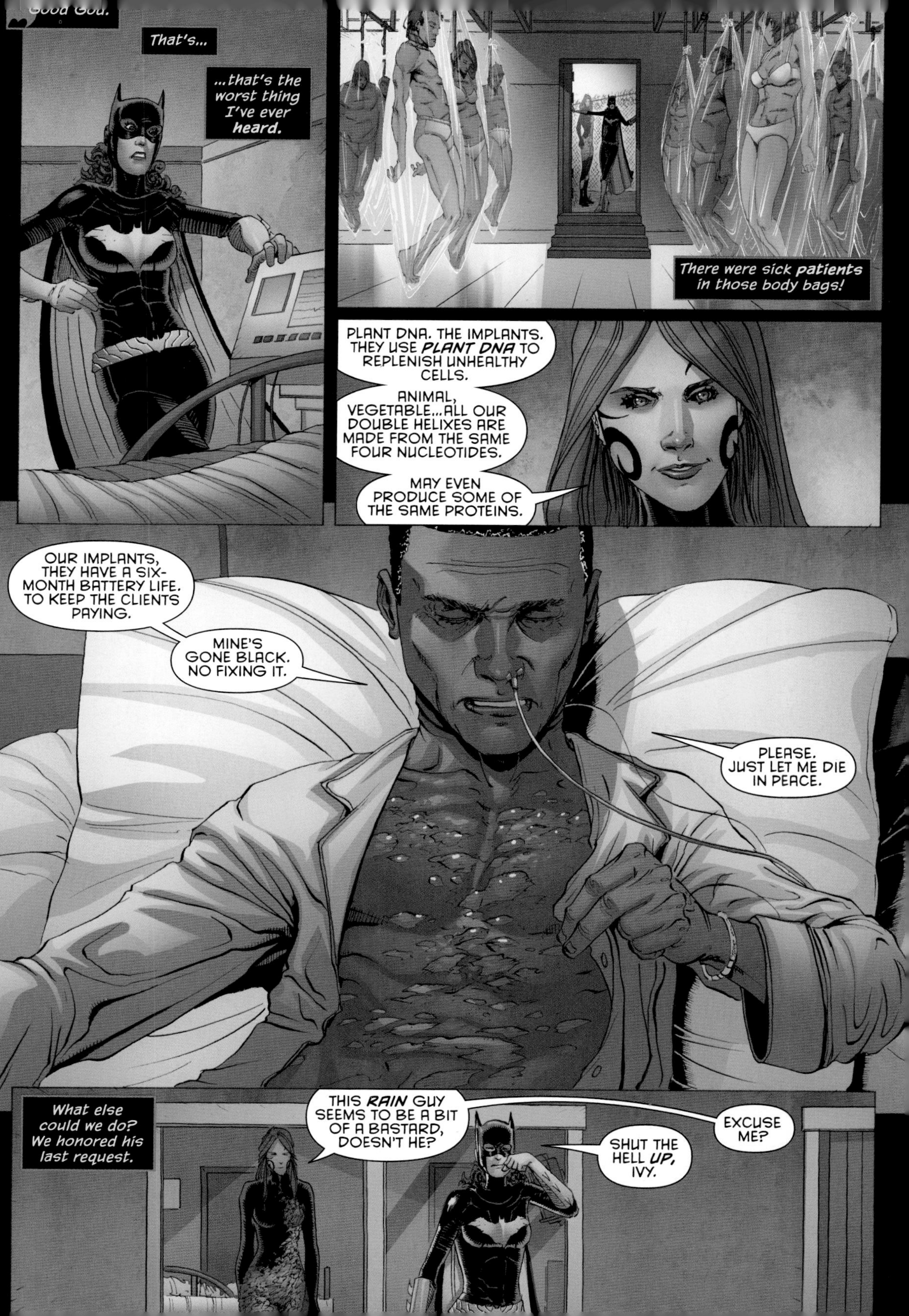
Good God.
That's...
...that's the worst thing I've ever heard.
There were sick patients in those body bags!
PLANT DNA. THE IMPLANTS. THEY USE PLANT DNA TO REPLENISH UNHEALTHY CELLS.
ANIMAL, VEGETABLE...ALL OUR DOUBLE HELIXES ARE MADE FROM THE SAME FOUR NUCLEOTIDES.
MAY EVEN PRODUCE SOME OF THE SAME PROTEINS.
OUR IMPLANTS, THEY HAVE A SIX-MONTH BATTERY LIFE. TO KEEP THE CLIENTS PAYING.
MINE'S GONE BLACK. NO FIXING IT.
PLEASE. JUST LET ME DIE IN PEACE.
What else could we do? We honored his last request.
THIS RAIN GUY SEEMS TO BE A BIT OF A BASTARD, DOESN'T HE?
EXCUSE ME?
SHUT THE HELL UP, IVY.

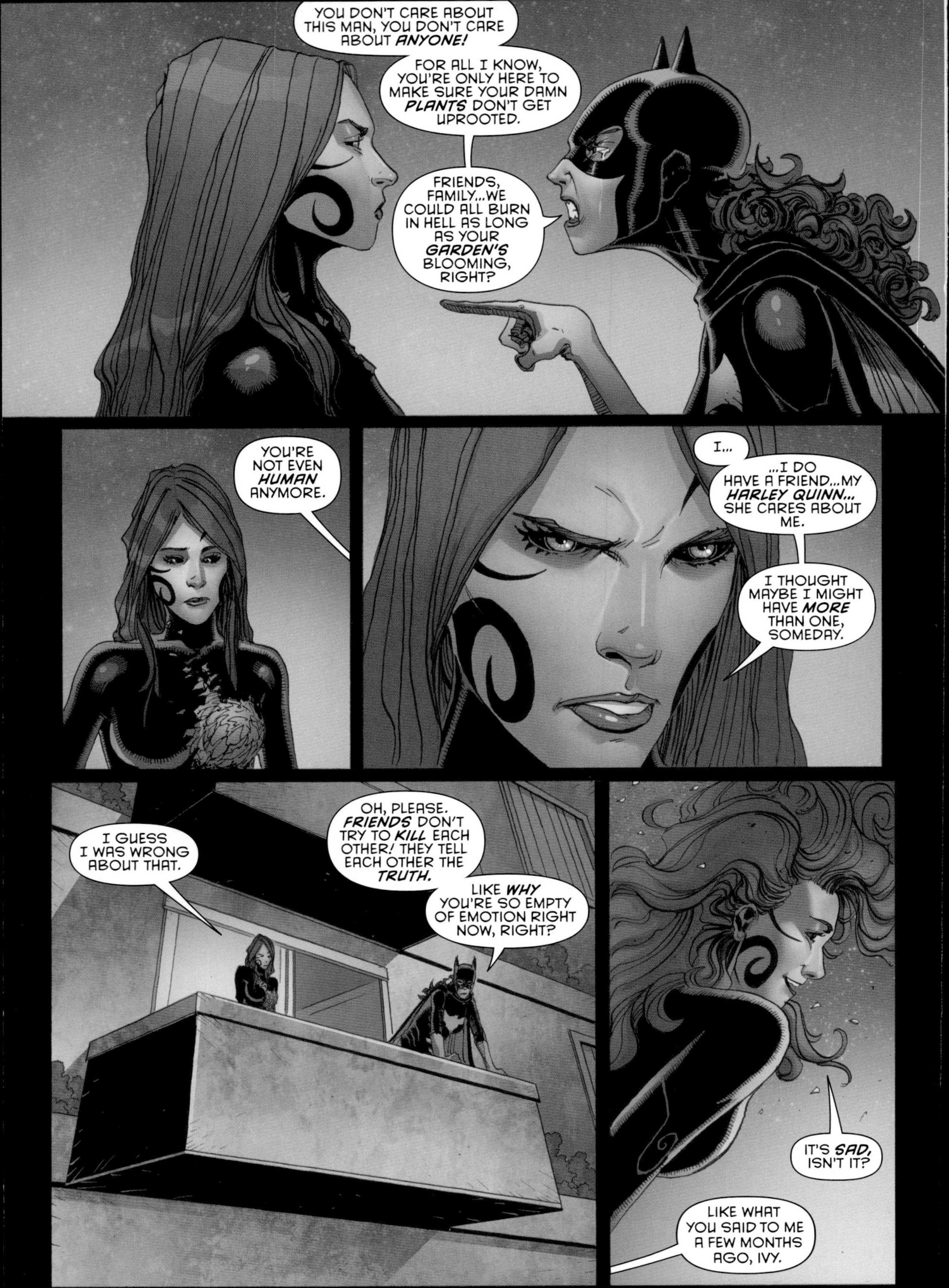

YOU DON'T CARE ABOUT THIS MAN, YOU DON'T CARE ABOUT ANYONE!
FOR ALL I KNOW, YOU'RE ONLY HERE TO MAKE SURE YOUR DAMN PLANTS DON'T GET UPROOTED.
FRIENDS, FAMILY...WE COULD ALL BURN IN HELL AS LONG AS YOUR GARDEN'S BLOOMING, RIGHT?
YOU'RE NOT EVEN HUMAN ANYMORE.
I...
...I DO HAVE A FRIEND...MY HARLEY QUINN... SHE CARES ABOUT ME.
I THOUGHT MAYBE I MIGHT HAVE MORE THAN ONE, SOMEDAY.
I GUESS I WAS WRONG ABOUT THAT.
OH, PLEASE. FRIENDS DON'T TRY TO KILL EACH OTHER! THEY TELL EACH OTHER THE TRUTH.
LIKE WHY YOU'RE SO EMPTY OF EMOTION RIGHT NOW, RIGHT?
IT'S SAD, ISN'T IT?
LIKE WHAT YOU SAID TO ME A FEW MONTHS AGO, IVY.

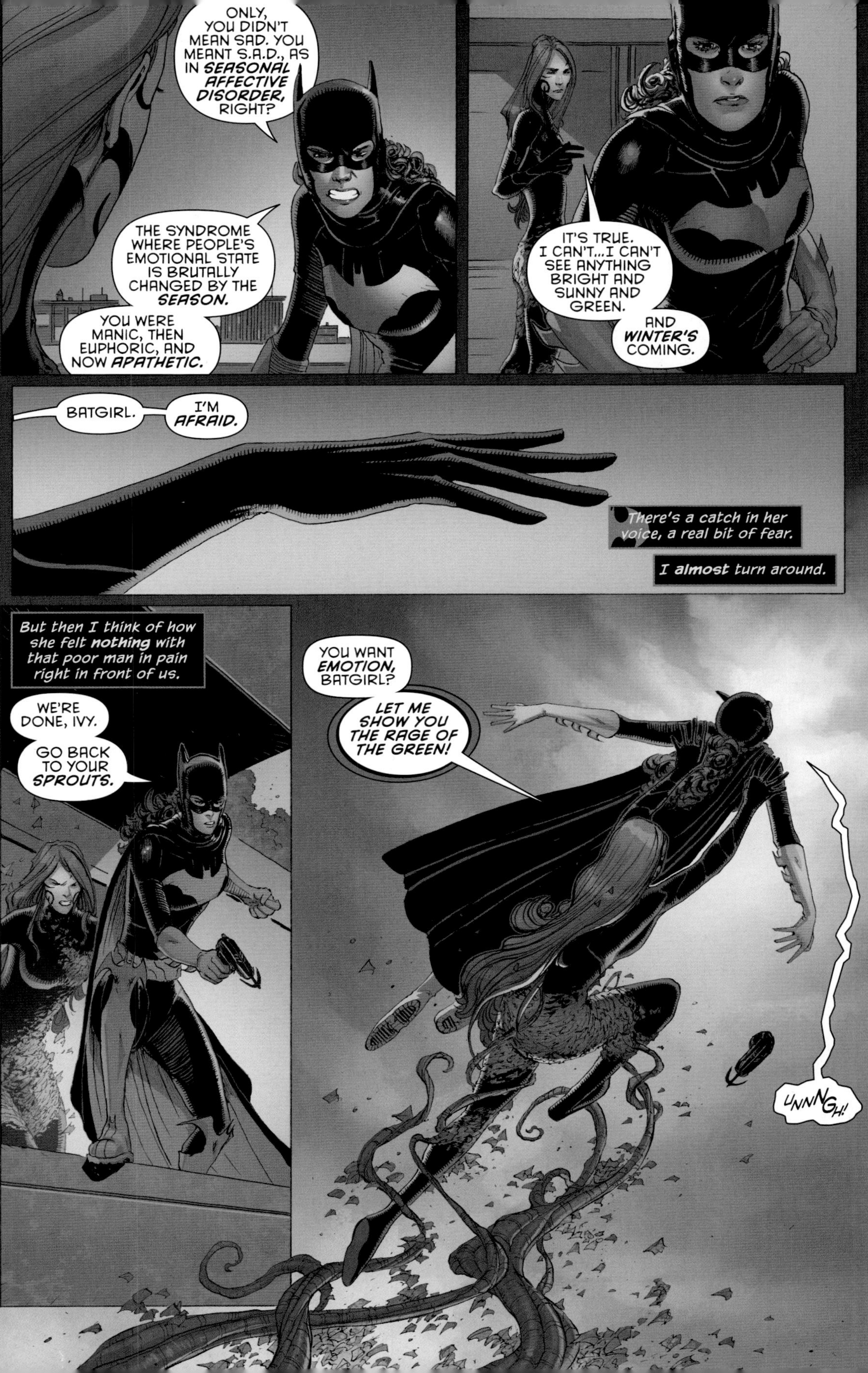

ONLY, YOU DIDN'T MEAN SAD. YOU MEANT S.A.D., AS IN SEASONAL AFFECTIVE DISORDER, RIGHT?
THE SYNDROME WHERE PEOPLE'S EMOTIONAL STATE IS BRUTALLY CHANGED BY THE SEASON.
YOU WERE MANIC, THEN EUPHORIC, AND NOW APATHETIC.
IT'S TRUE. I CAN'T...I CAN'T SEE ANYTHING BRIGHT AND SUNNY AND GREEN.
AND WINTER'S COMING.
BATGIRL.
I'M AFRAID.
There's a catch in her voice, a real bit of fear.
I almost turn around.
But then I think of how she felt nothing with that poor man in pain right in front of us.
WE'RE DONE, IVY.
GO BACK TO YOUR SPROUTS.
YOU WANT EMOTION, BATGIRL?
LET ME SHOW YOU THE RAGE OF THE GREEN!
UNNNGH!

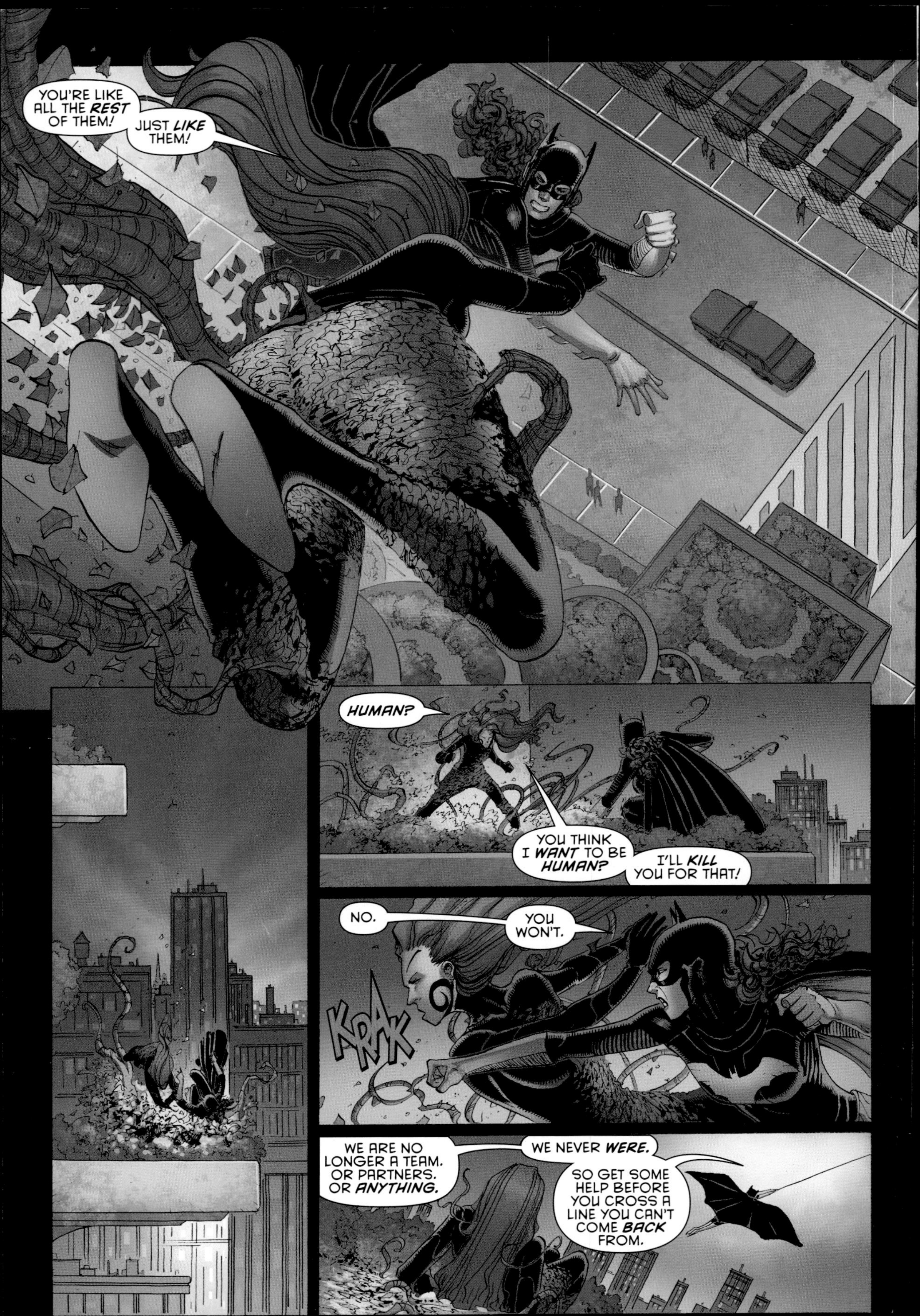

YOU'RE LIKE ALL THE REST OF THEM!
JUST LIKE THEM!
HUMAN?
YOU THINK I WANT TO BE HUMAN?
I'LL KILL YOU FOR THAT!
NO.
YOU WON'T.
KRAK
WE ARE NO LONGER A TEAM. OR PARTNERS. OR ANYTHING.
WE NEVER WERE.
SO GET SOME HELP BEFORE YOU CROSS A LINE YOU CAN'T COME BACK FROM.

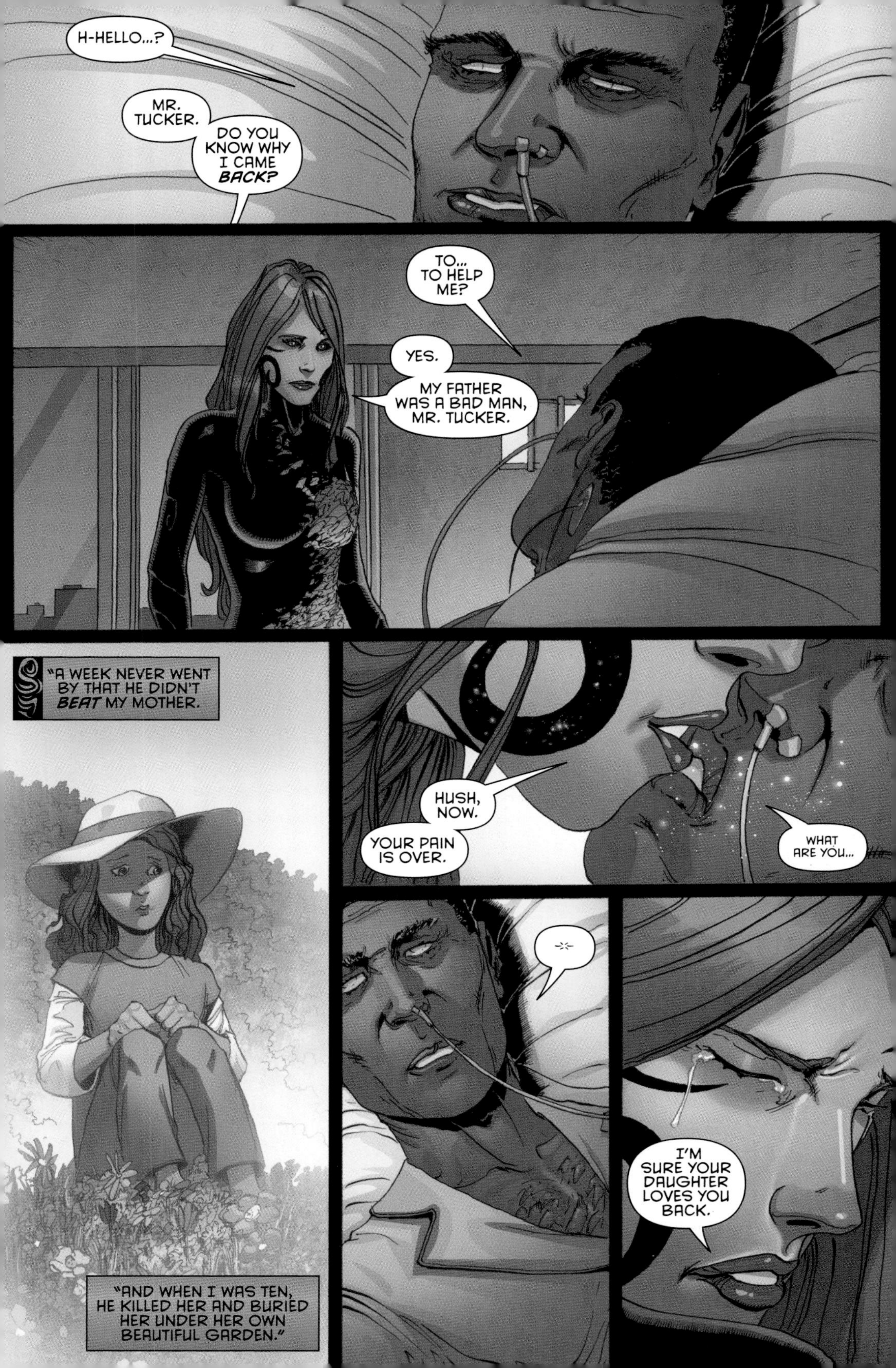
H-HELLO...?
MR. TUCKER.
DO YOU KNOW WHY I CAME *BACK?*
TO... TO HELP ME?
YES.
MY FATHER WAS A BAD MAN, MR. TUCKER.
"A WEEK NEVER WENT BY THAT HE DIDN'T *BEAT* MY MOTHER.
"AND WHEN I WAS TEN, HE KILLED HER AND BURIED HER UNDER HER OWN BEAUTIFUL GARDEN."
HUSH, NOW.
YOUR PAIN IS OVER.
WHAT ARE YOU...
I'M SURE YOUR DAUGHTER LOVES YOU BACK.

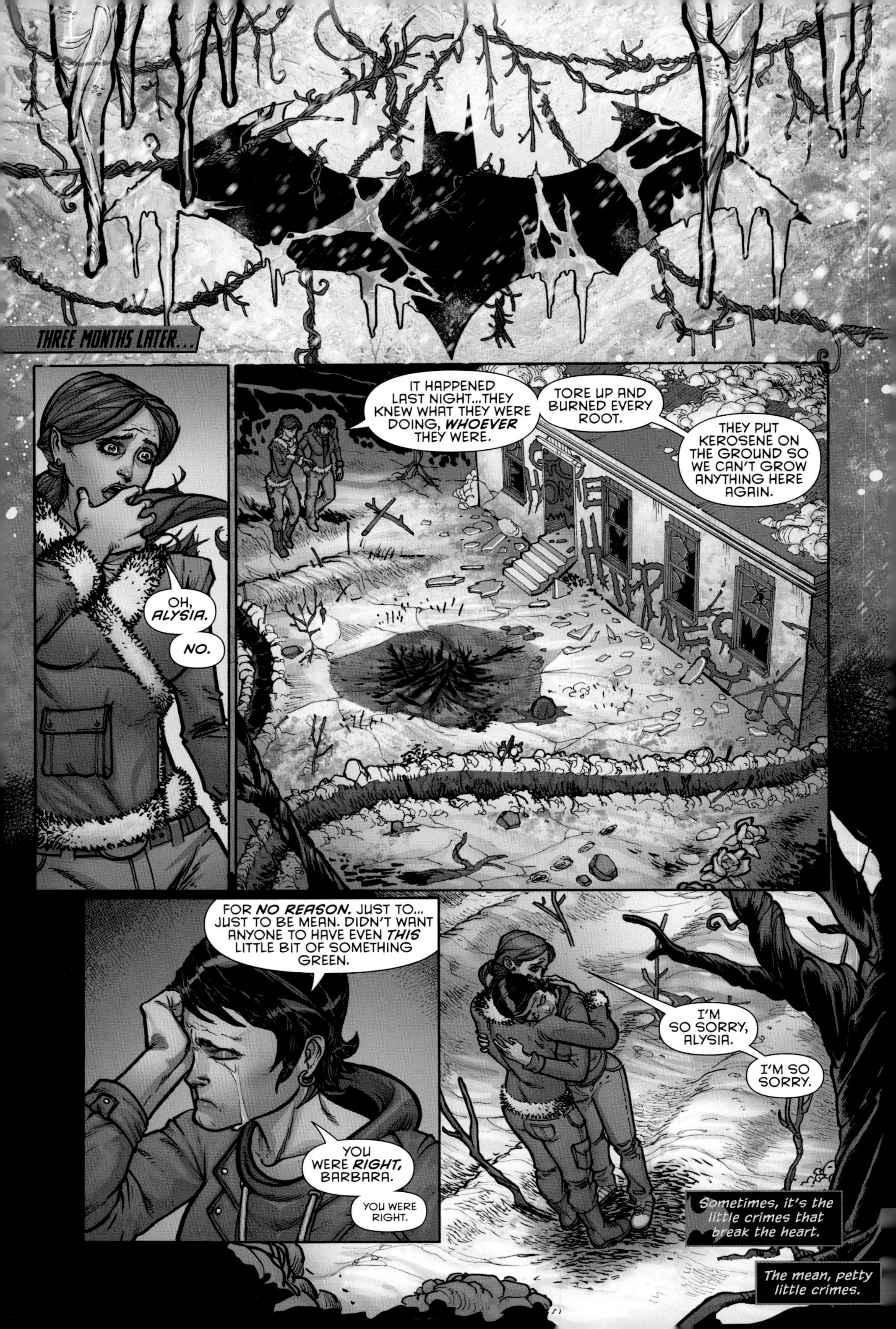
THREE MONTHS LATER...
OH, ALYSIA.
NO.
IT HAPPENED LAST NIGHT...THEY KNEW WHAT THEY WERE DOING, WHOEVER THEY WERE.
TORE UP AND BURNED EVERY ROOT.
THEY PUT KEROSENE ON THE GROUND SO WE CAN'T GROW ANYTHING HERE AGAIN.
FOR NO REASON. JUST TO... JUST TO BE MEAN. DIDN'T WANT ANYONE TO HAVE EVEN THIS LITTLE BIT OF SOMETHING GREEN.
YOU WERE RIGHT, BARBARA.
YOU WERE RIGHT.
I'M SO SORRY, ALYSIA.
I'M SO SORRY.
Sometimes, it's the little crimes that break the heart.
The mean, petty little crimes.

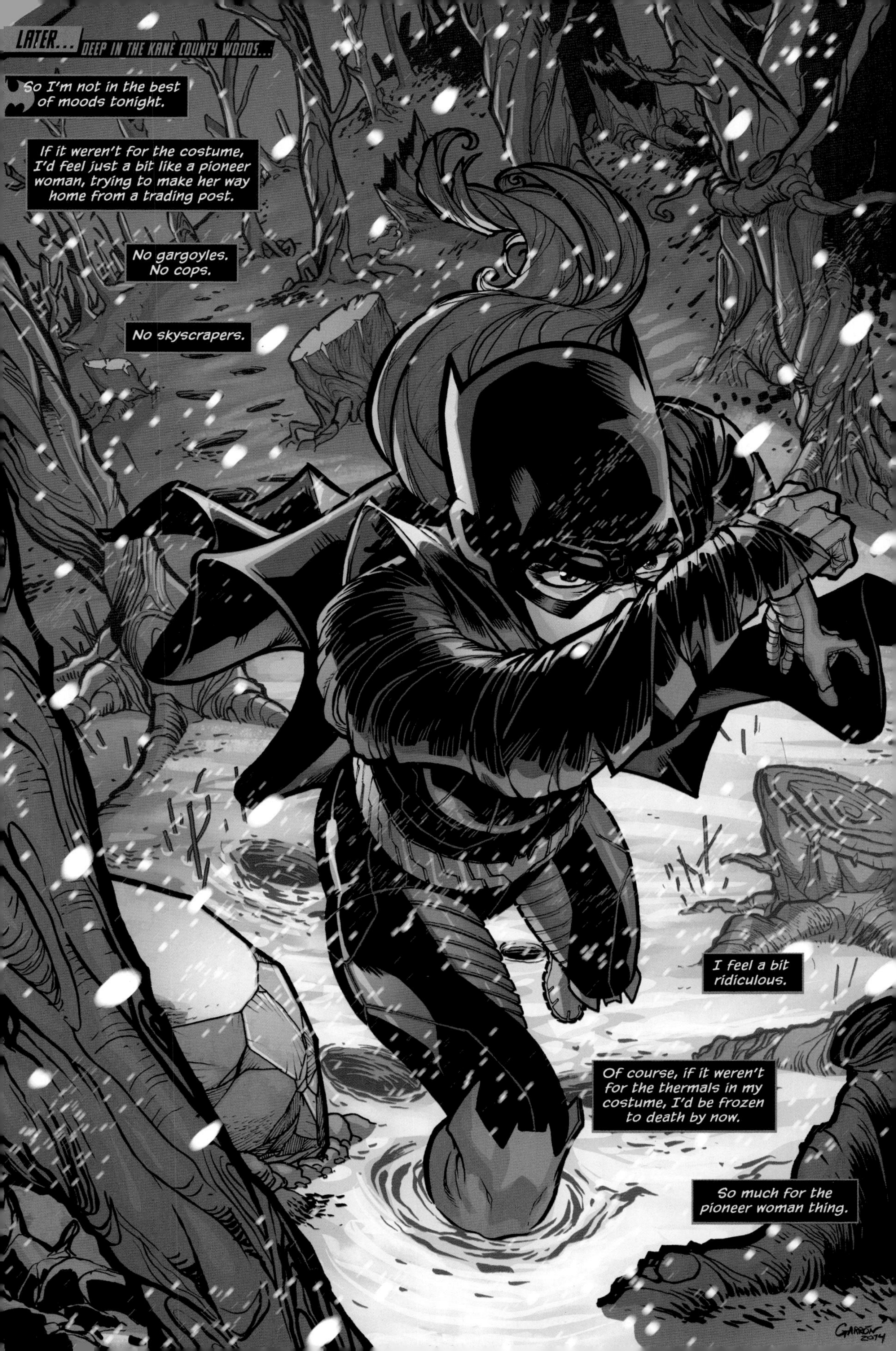
LATER...
DEEP IN THE KANE COUNTY WOODS...
So I'm not in the best of moods tonight.
If it weren't for the costume, I'd feel just a bit like a pioneer woman, trying to make her way home from a trading post.
No gargoyles. No cops.
No skyscrapers.
I feel a bit ridiculous.
Of course, if it weren't for the thermals in my costume, I'd be frozen to death by now.
So much for the pioneer woman thing.
GARRÓN 2014

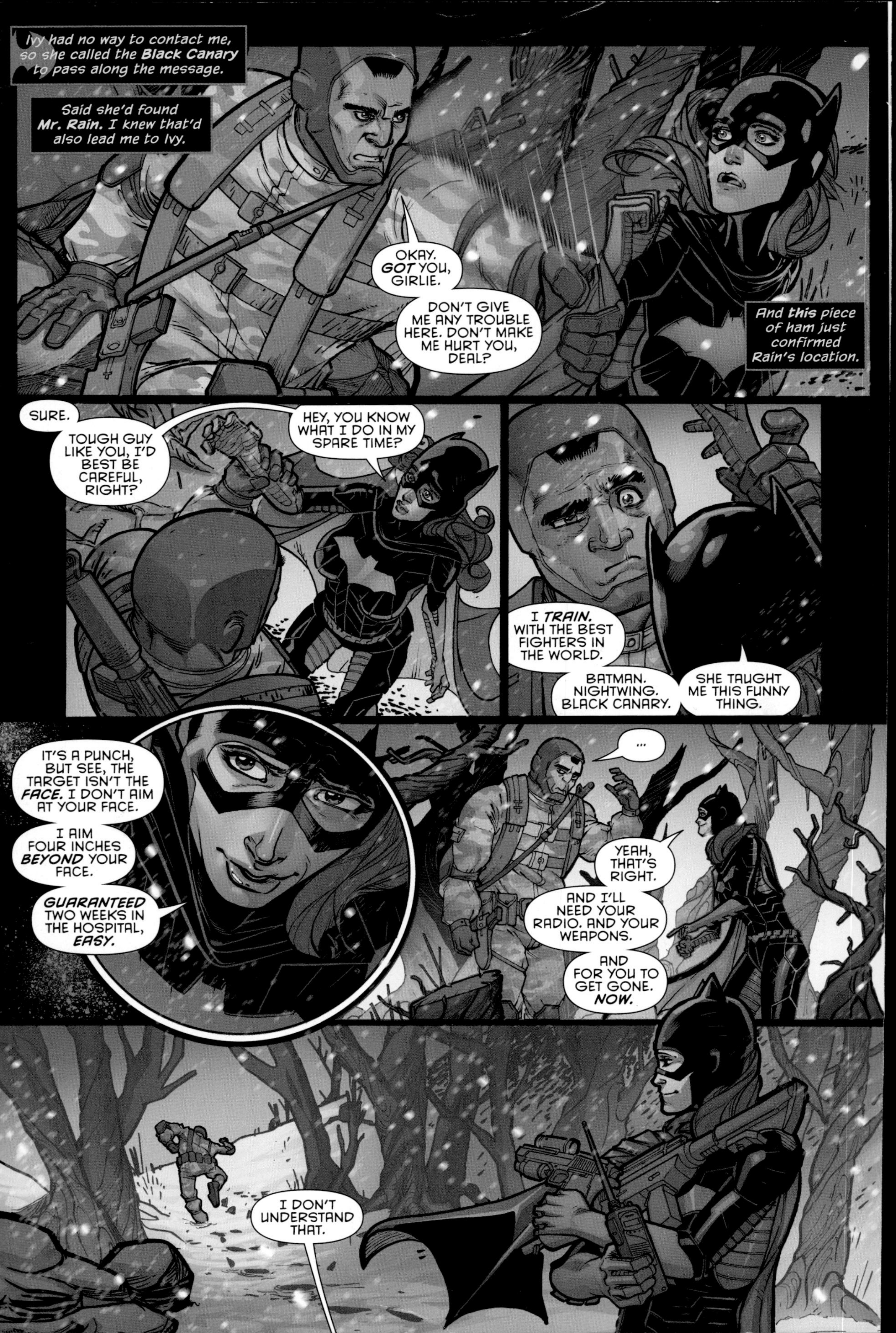
Ivy had no way to contact me, so she called the Black Canary to pass along the message.
Said she'd found Mr. Rain. I knew that'd also lead me to Ivy.
OKAY. GOT YOU, GIRLIE.
DON'T GIVE ME ANY TROUBLE HERE. DON'T MAKE ME HURT YOU, DEAL?
And this piece of ham just confirmed Rain's location.
SURE.
TOUGH GUY LIKE YOU, I'D BEST BE CAREFUL, RIGHT?
HEY, YOU KNOW WHAT I DO IN MY SPARE TIME?
I TRAIN. WITH THE BEST FIGHTERS IN THE WORLD.
BATMAN. NIGHTWING. BLACK CANARY.
SHE TAUGHT ME THIS FUNNY THING.
IT'S A PUNCH, BUT SEE, THE TARGET ISN'T THE FACE. I DON'T AIM AT YOUR FACE.
I AIM FOUR INCHES BEYOND YOUR FACE.
GUARANTEED TWO WEEKS IN THE HOSPITAL, EASY.
...
YEAH, THAT'S RIGHT.
AND I'LL NEED YOUR RADIO. AND YOUR WEAPONS.
AND FOR YOU TO GET GONE. NOW.
I DON'T UNDERSTAND THAT.

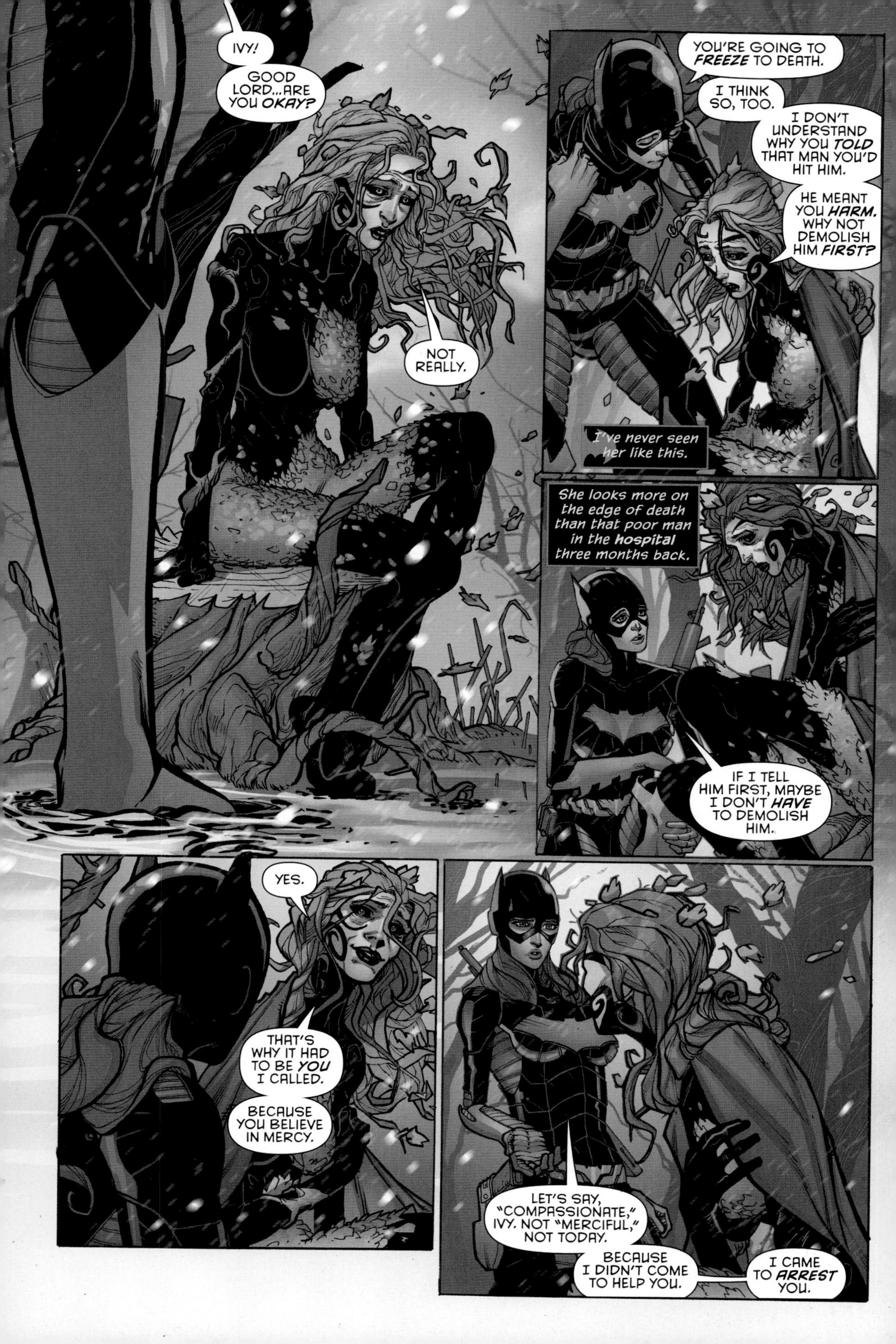

IVY!
GOOD LORD...ARE YOU *OKAY?*
NOT REALLY.
YOU'RE GOING TO *FREEZE* TO DEATH.
I THINK SO, TOO.
I DON'T UNDERSTAND WHY YOU *TOLD* THAT MAN YOU'D HIT HIM.
HE MEANT YOU *HARM.* WHY NOT DEMOLISH HIM *FIRST?*
I've never seen her like this.
She looks more on the edge of death than that poor man in the **hospital** three months back.
IF I TELL HIM FIRST, MAYBE I DON'T *HAVE* TO DEMOLISH HIM.
YES.
THAT'S WHY IT HAD TO BE *YOU* I CALLED.
BECAUSE YOU BELIEVE IN MERCY.
LET'S SAY, "COMPASSIONATE," IVY. NOT "MERCIFUL," NOT TODAY.
BECAUSE I DIDN'T COME TO HELP YOU.
I CAME TO *ARREST* YOU.

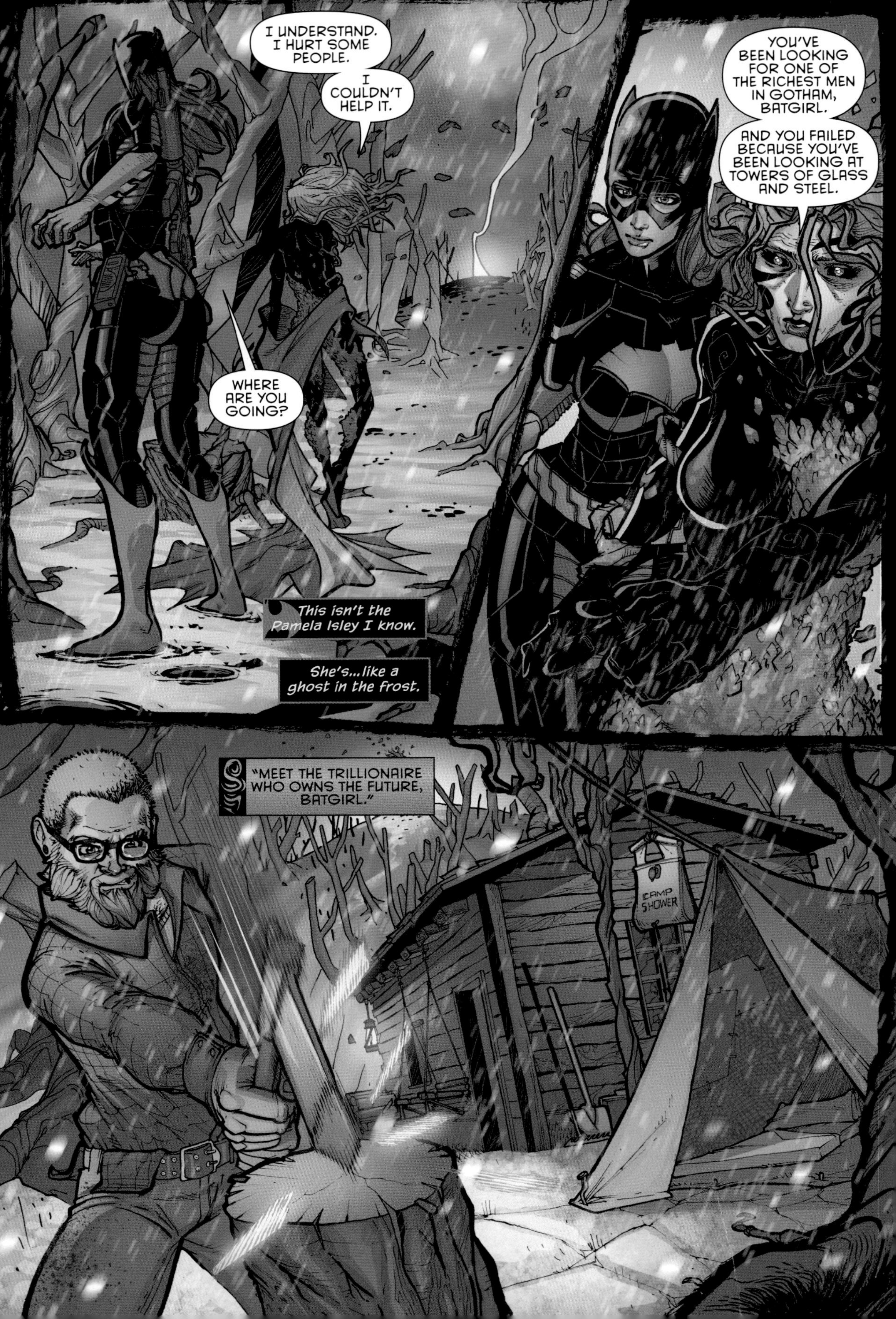

I UNDERSTAND. I HURT SOME PEOPLE.
I COULDN'T HELP IT.
WHERE ARE YOU GOING?
This isn't the Pamela Isley I know.
She's...like a ghost in the frost.
YOU'VE BEEN LOOKING FOR ONE OF THE RICHEST MEN IN GOTHAM, BATGIRL.
AND YOU FAILED BECAUSE YOU'VE BEEN LOOKING AT TOWERS OF GLASS AND STEEL.
"MEET THE TRILLIONAIRE WHO OWNS THE FUTURE, BATGIRL."
CAMP SHOWER

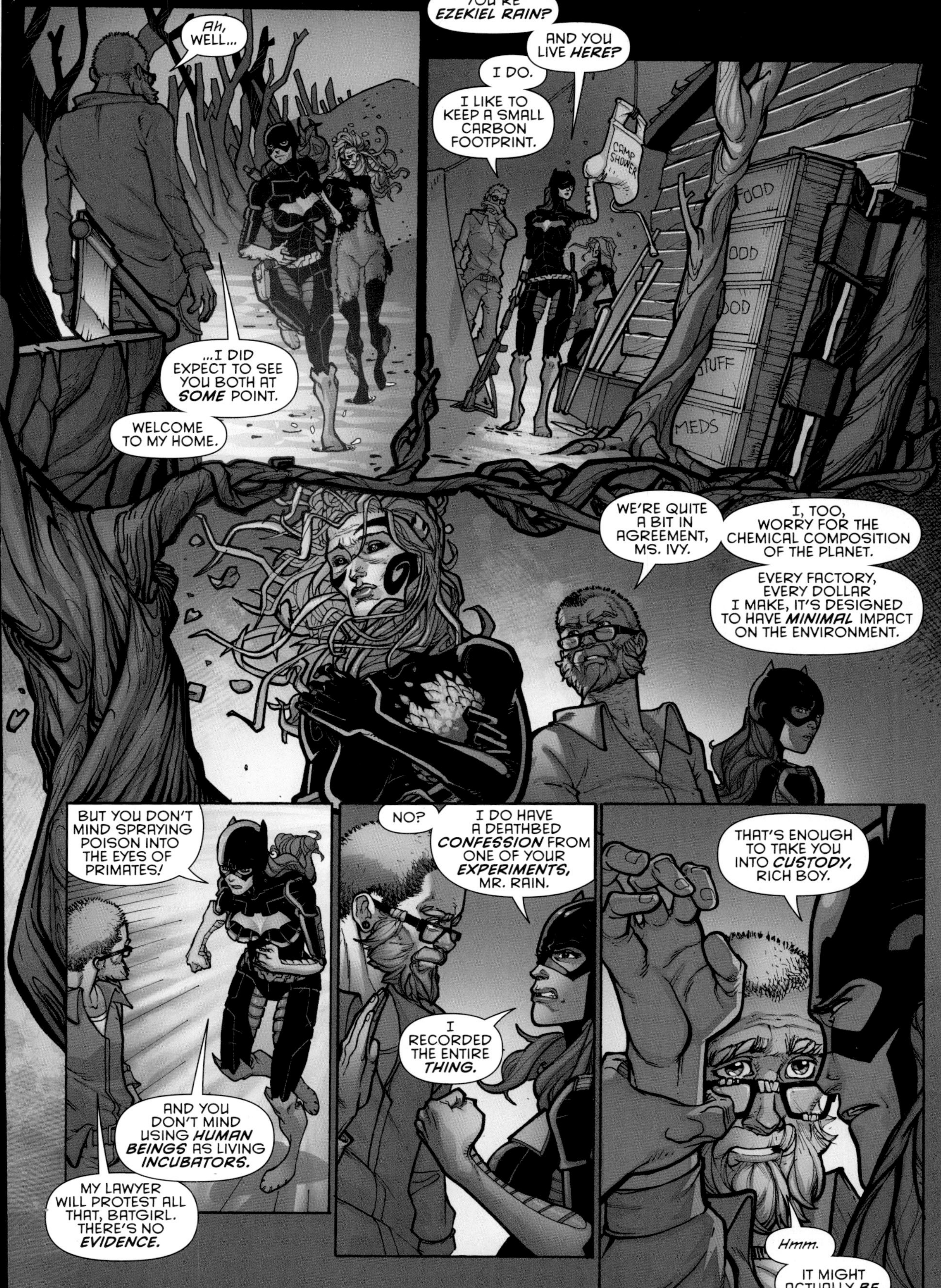
Ah, WELL...
...I DID EXPECT TO SEE YOU BOTH AT SOME POINT.
WELCOME TO MY HOME.
YOU'RE EZEKIEL RAIN?
AND YOU LIVE HERE?
I DO.
I LIKE TO KEEP A SMALL CARBON FOOTPRINT.
CAMP SHOWER
OOD
OOD
OOD
STUFF
MEDS
WE'RE QUITE A BIT IN AGREEMENT, MS. IVY.
I, TOO, WORRY FOR THE CHEMICAL COMPOSITION OF THE PLANET.
EVERY FACTORY, EVERY DOLLAR I MAKE, IT'S DESIGNED TO HAVE MINIMAL IMPACT ON THE ENVIRONMENT.
BUT YOU DON'T MIND SPRAYING POISON INTO THE EYES OF PRIMATES!
AND YOU DON'T MIND USING HUMAN BEINGS AS LIVING INCUBATORS.
MY LAWYER WILL PROTEST ALL THAT, BATGIRL. THERE'S NO EVIDENCE.
NO?
I DO HAVE A DEATHBED CONFESSION FROM ONE OF YOUR EXPERIMENTS, MR. RAIN.
I RECORDED THE ENTIRE THING.
THAT'S ENOUGH TO TAKE YOU INTO CUSTODY, RICH BOY.
Hmm.
IT MIGHT ACTUALLY BE.

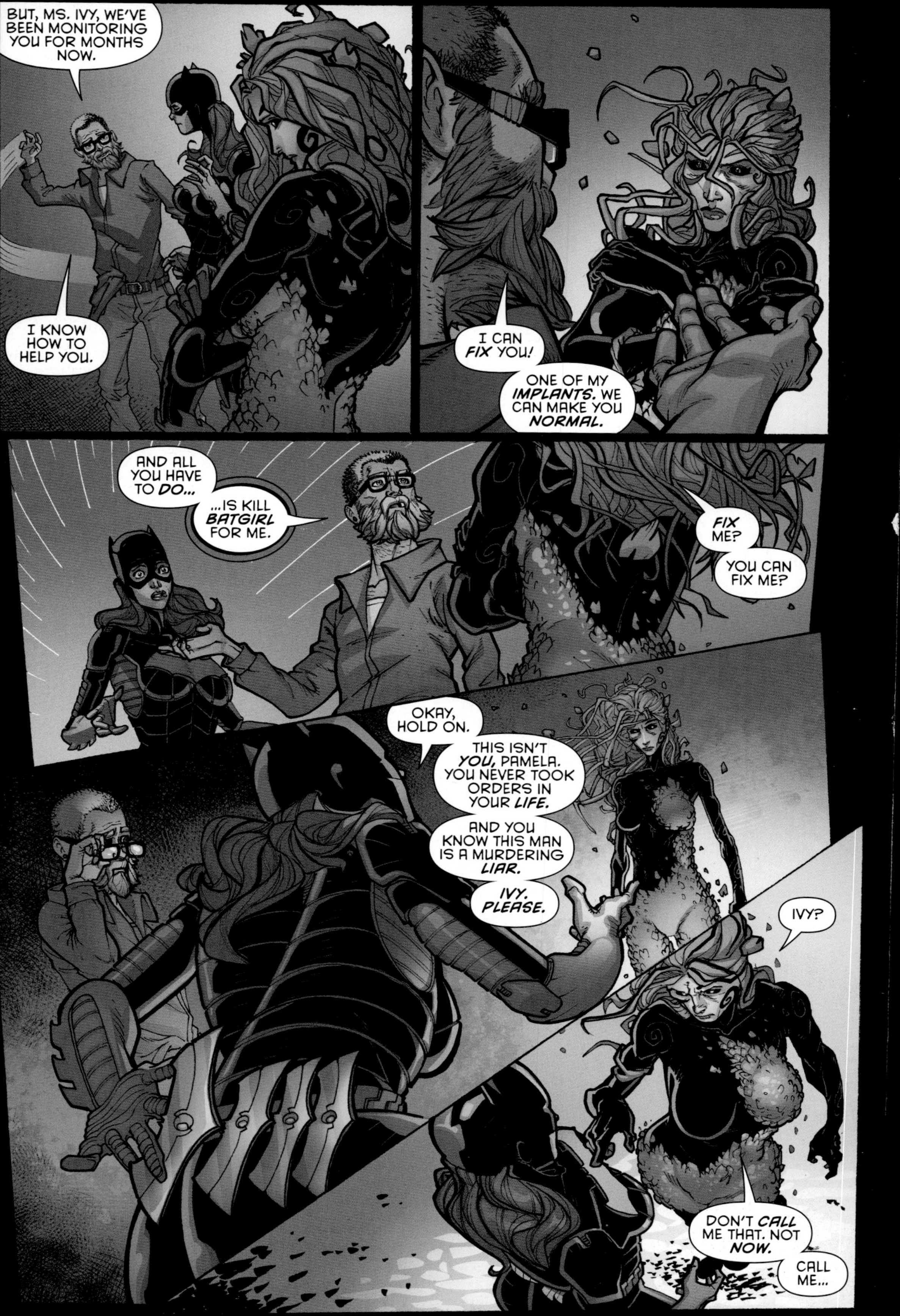
BUT, MS. IVY, WE'VE BEEN MONITORING YOU FOR MONTHS NOW.
I KNOW HOW TO HELP YOU.
I CAN FIX YOU!
ONE OF MY IMPLANTS. WE CAN MAKE YOU NORMAL.
AND ALL YOU HAVE TO DO...
...IS KILL BATGIRL FOR ME.
FIX ME?
YOU CAN FIX ME?
OKAY, HOLD ON.
THIS ISN'T YOU, PAMELA. YOU NEVER TOOK ORDERS IN YOUR LIFE.
AND YOU KNOW THIS MAN IS A MURDERING LIAR.
IVY. PLEASE.
IVY?
DON'T CALL ME THAT. NOT NOW.
CALL ME...

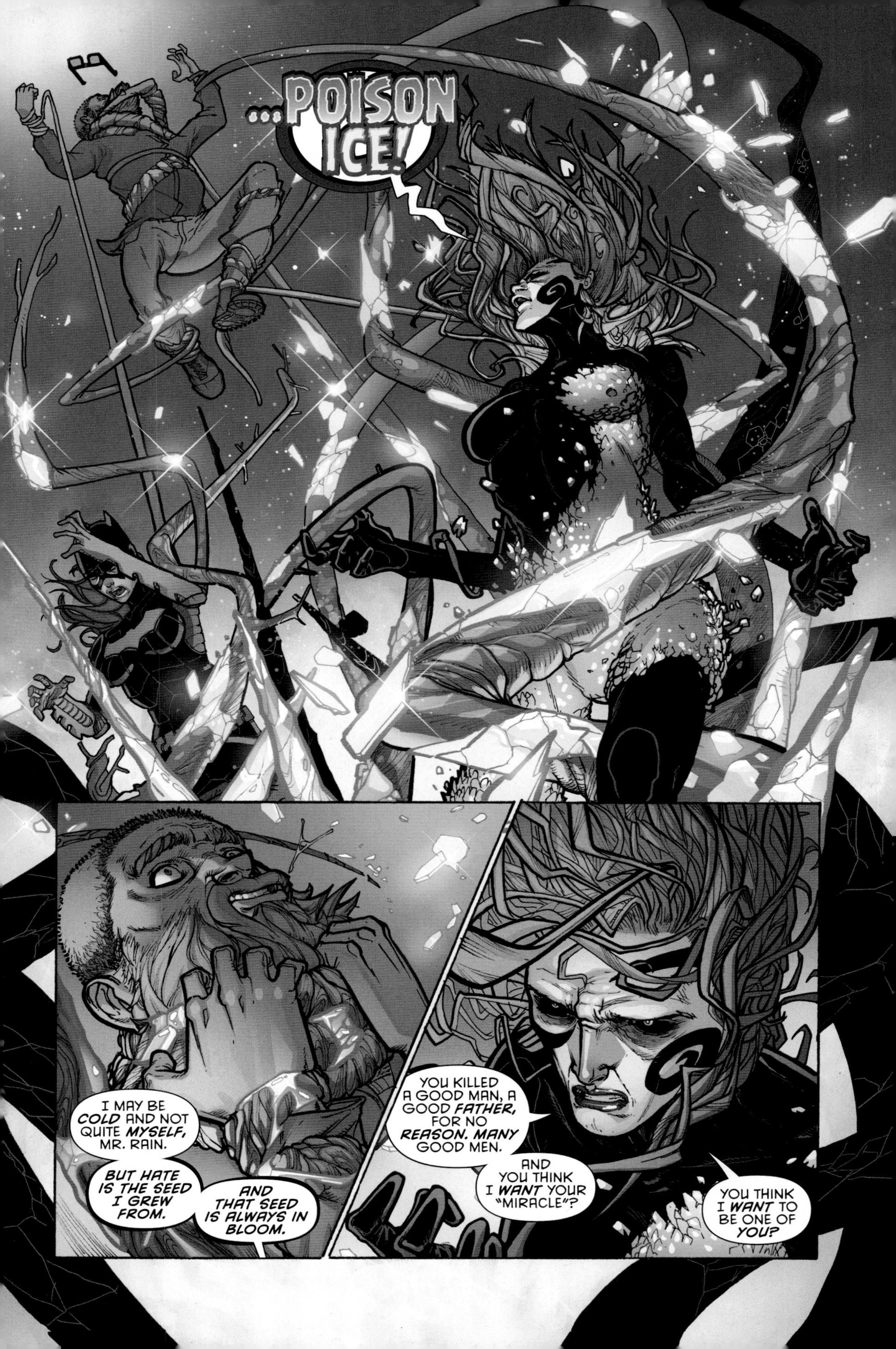
...POISON ICE!
I MAY BE COLD AND NOT QUITE MYSELF, MR. RAIN.
BUT HATE IS THE SEED I GREW FROM.
AND THAT SEED IS ALWAYS IN BLOOM.
YOU KILLED A GOOD MAN, A GOOD FATHER, FOR NO REASON. MANY GOOD MEN.
AND YOU THINK I WANT YOUR "MIRACLE"?
YOU THINK I WANT TO BE ONE OF YOU?

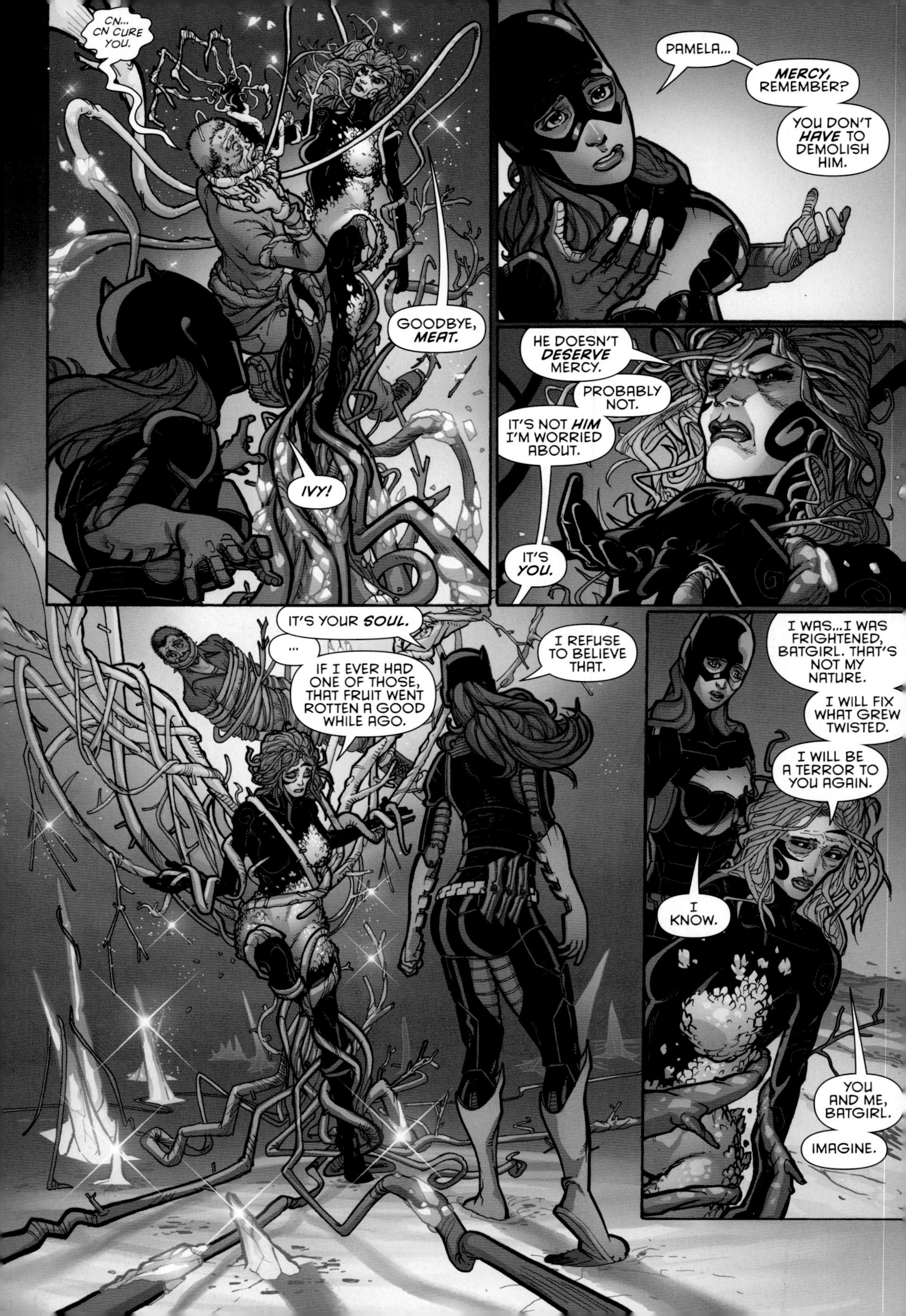

CN... CN CURE YOU.
GOODBYE, MEAT.
IVY!
PAMELA...
MERCY, REMEMBER?
YOU DON'T HAVE TO DEMOLISH HIM.
HE DOESN'T DESERVE MERCY.
PROBABLY NOT.
IT'S NOT HIM I'M WORRIED ABOUT.
IT'S YOU.
IT'S YOUR SOUL.
...
IF I EVER HAD ONE OF THOSE, THAT FRUIT WENT ROTTEN A GOOD WHILE AGO.
I REFUSE TO BELIEVE THAT.
I WAS...I WAS FRIGHTENED, BATGIRL. THAT'S NOT MY NATURE.
I WILL FIX WHAT GREW TWISTED.
I WILL BE A TERROR TO YOU AGAIN.
I KNOW.
YOU AND ME, BATGIRL.
IMAGINE.

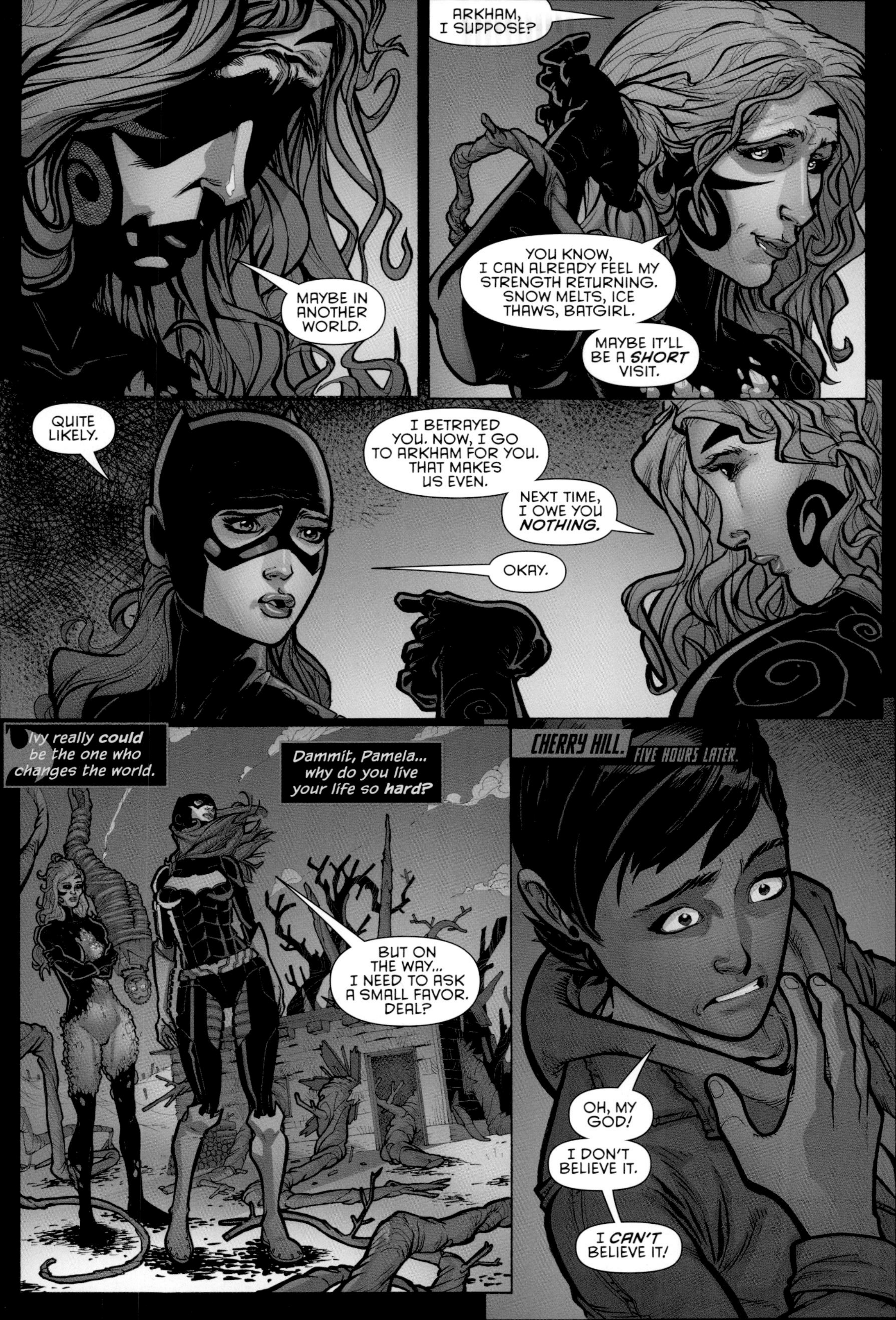
ARKHAM, I SUPPOSE?
MAYBE IN ANOTHER WORLD.
YOU KNOW, I CAN ALREADY FEEL MY STRENGTH RETURNING. SNOW MELTS, ICE THAWS, BATGIRL.
MAYBE IT'LL BE A SHORT VISIT.
QUITE LIKELY.
I BETRAYED YOU. NOW, I GO TO ARKHAM FOR YOU. THAT MAKES US EVEN.
NEXT TIME, I OWE YOU NOTHING.
OKAY.
Ivy really could be the one who changes the world.
Dammit, Pamela... why do you live your life so hard?
BUT ON THE WAY... I NEED TO ASK A SMALL FAVOR. DEAL?
CHERRY HILL.
FIVE HOURS LATER.
OH, MY GOD!
I DON'T BELIEVE IT.
I CAN'T BELIEVE IT!

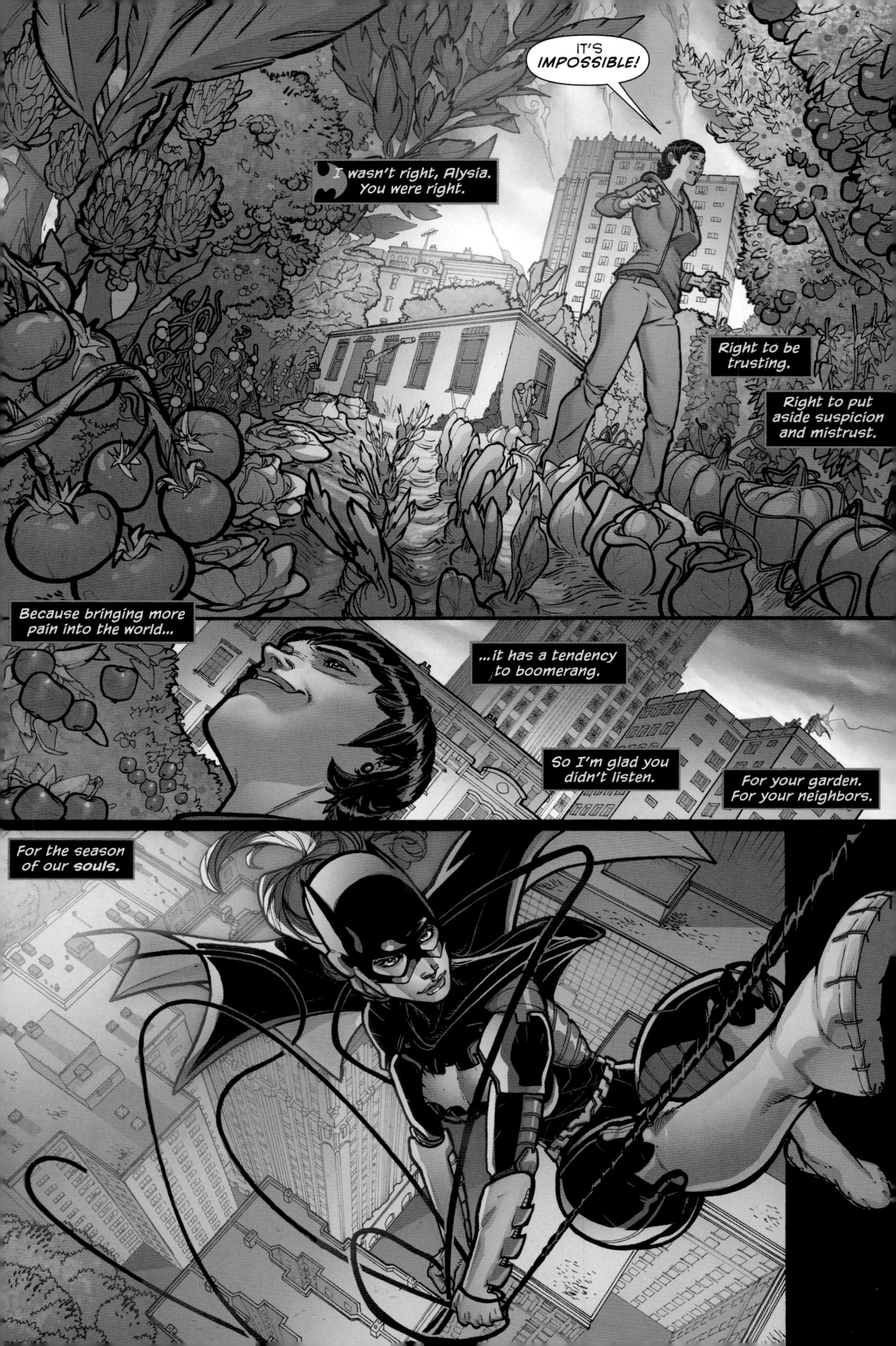
IT'S IMPOSSIBLE!
I wasn't right, Alysia. You were right.
Right to be trusting.
Right to put aside suspicion and mistrust.
Because bringing more pain into the world...
...it has a tendency to boomerang.
So I'm glad you didn't listen.
For your garden. For your neighbors.
For the season of our souls.

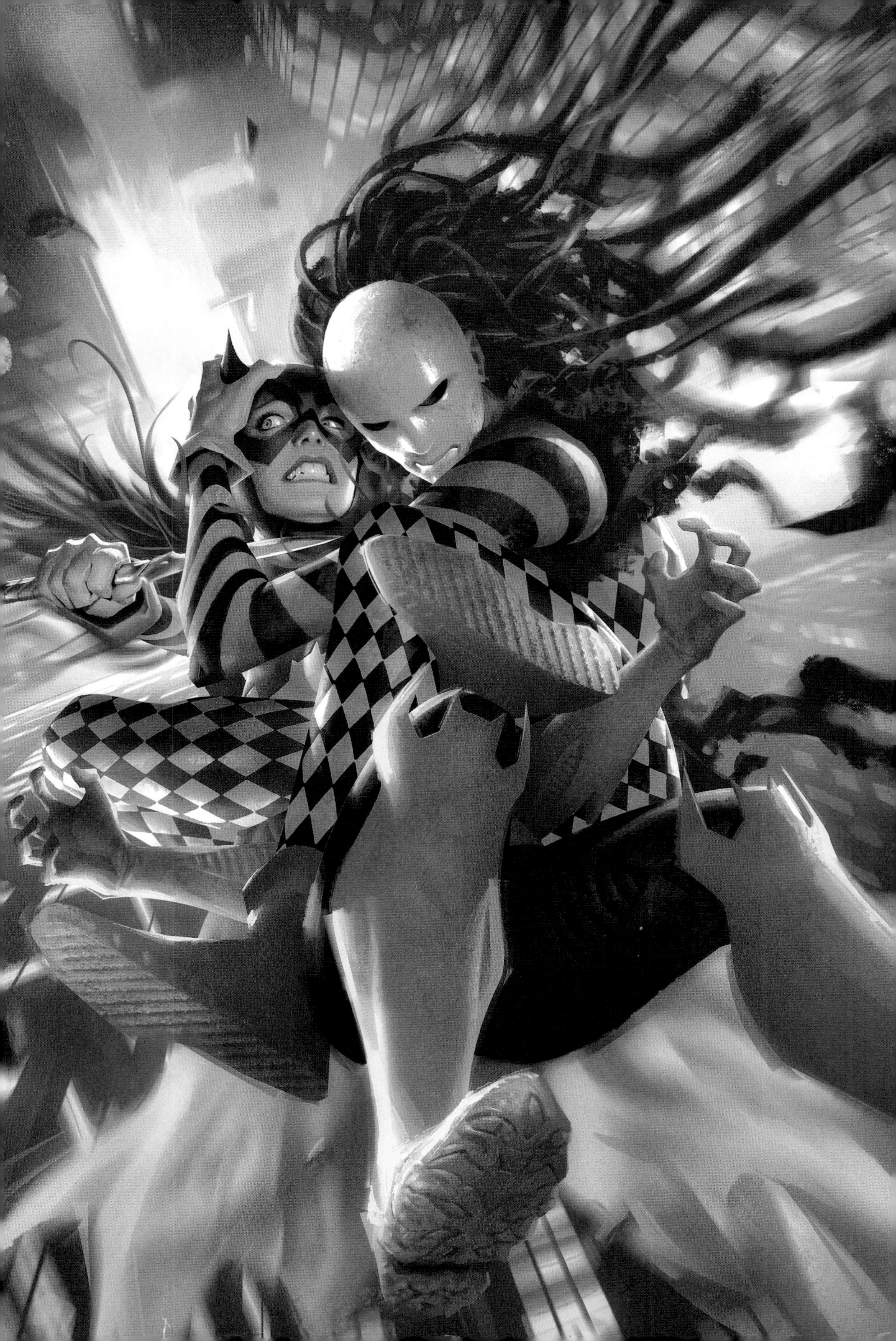

GAIL SIMONE writer FERNANDO PASARIN penciller JONATHAN GLAPION inker BLOND colorist ALEX GARNER cover artist

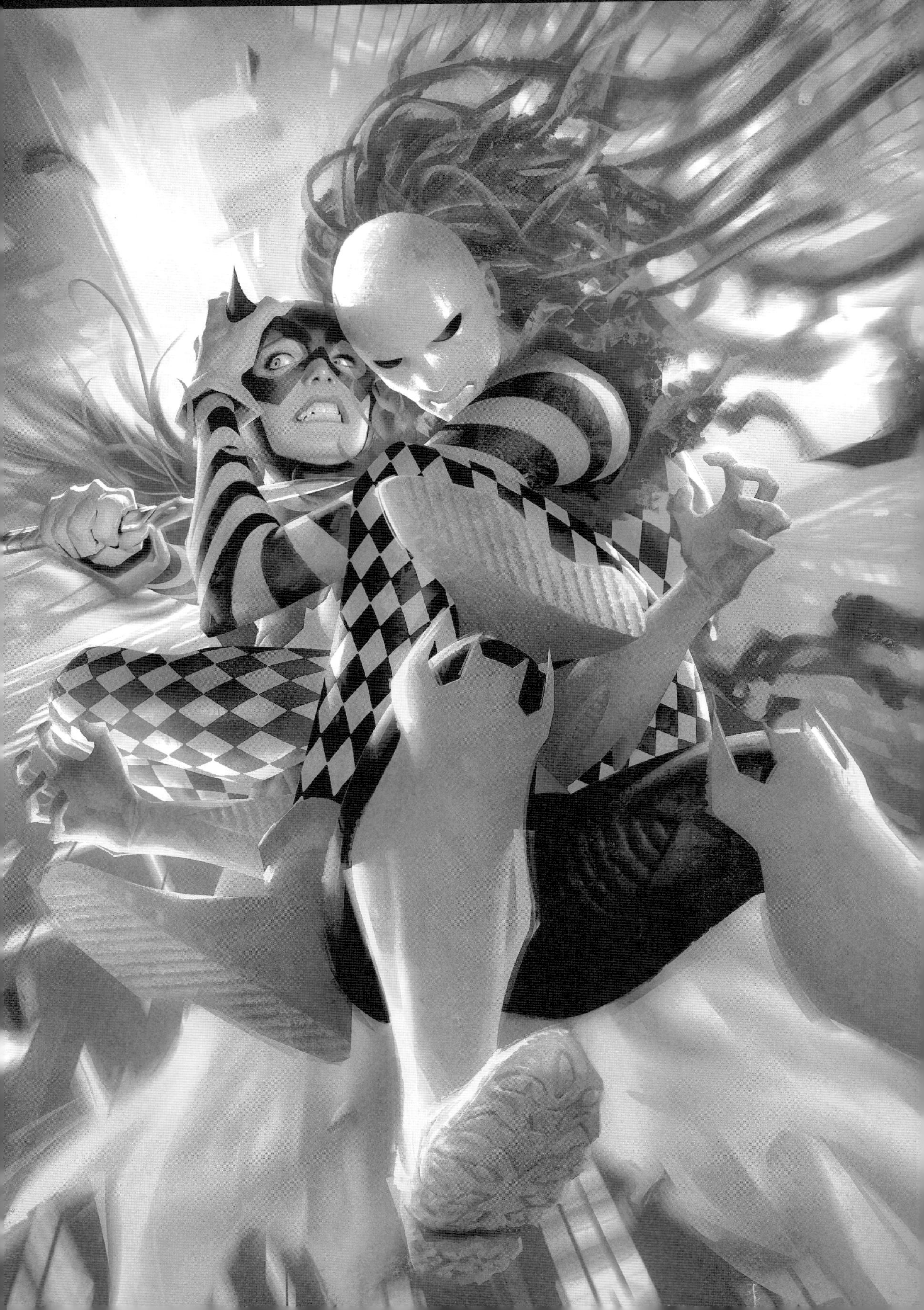

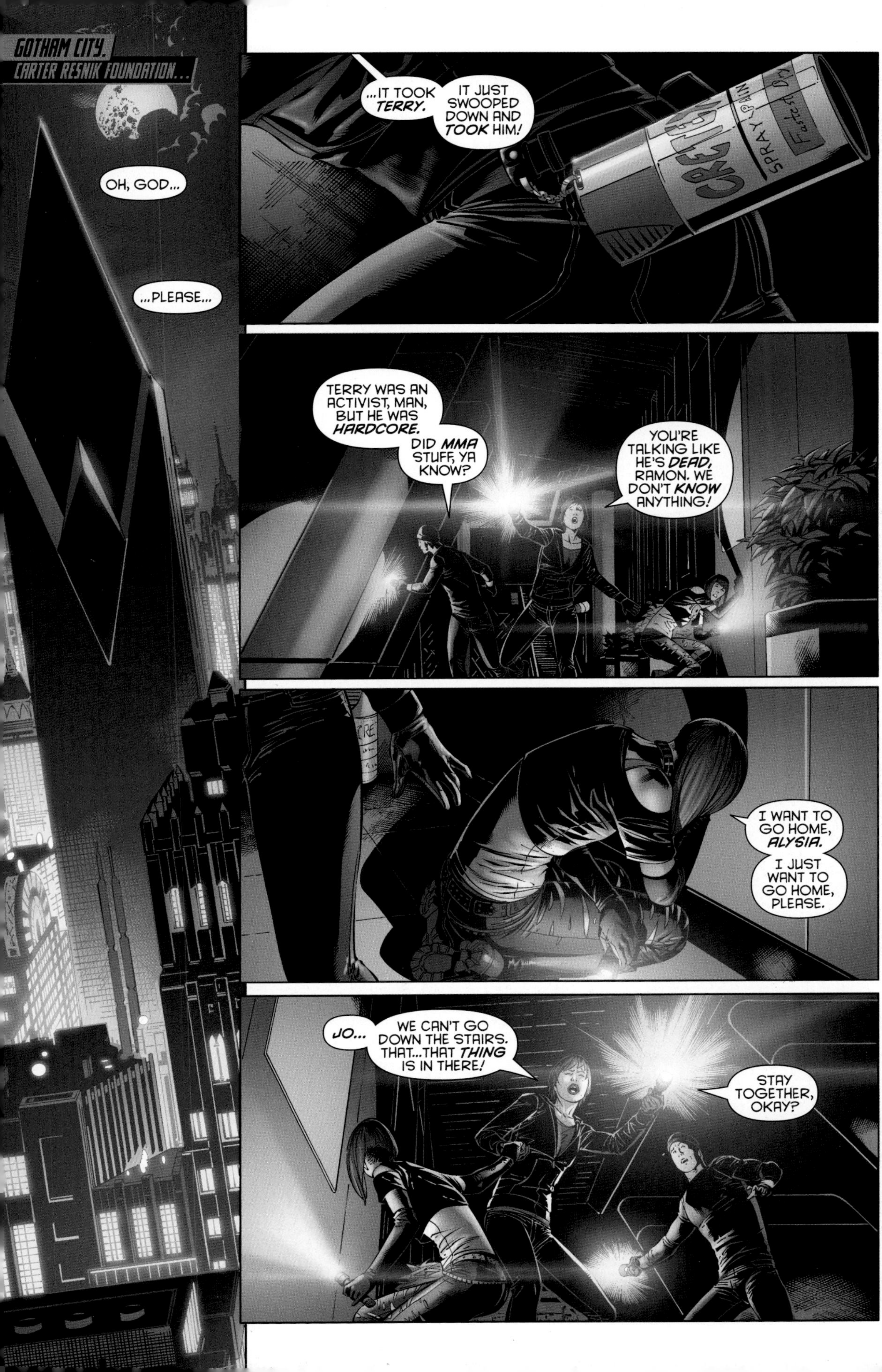
GOTHAM CITY.
CARTER RESNIK FOUNDATION...
OH, GOD...
...PLEASE...
...IT TOOK TERRY.
IT JUST SWOOPED DOWN AND TOOK HIM!
CRE
SPRAY PAINT
Fastest Dry
TERRY WAS AN ACTIVIST, MAN, BUT HE WAS HARDCORE.
DID MMA STUFF, YA KNOW?
YOU'RE TALKING LIKE HE'S DEAD, RAMON. WE DON'T KNOW ANYTHING!
I WANT TO GO HOME, ALYSIA.
I JUST WANT TO GO HOME, PLEASE.
JO...
WE CAN'T GO DOWN THE STAIRS. THAT...THAT THING IS IN THERE!
STAY TOGETHER, OKAY?

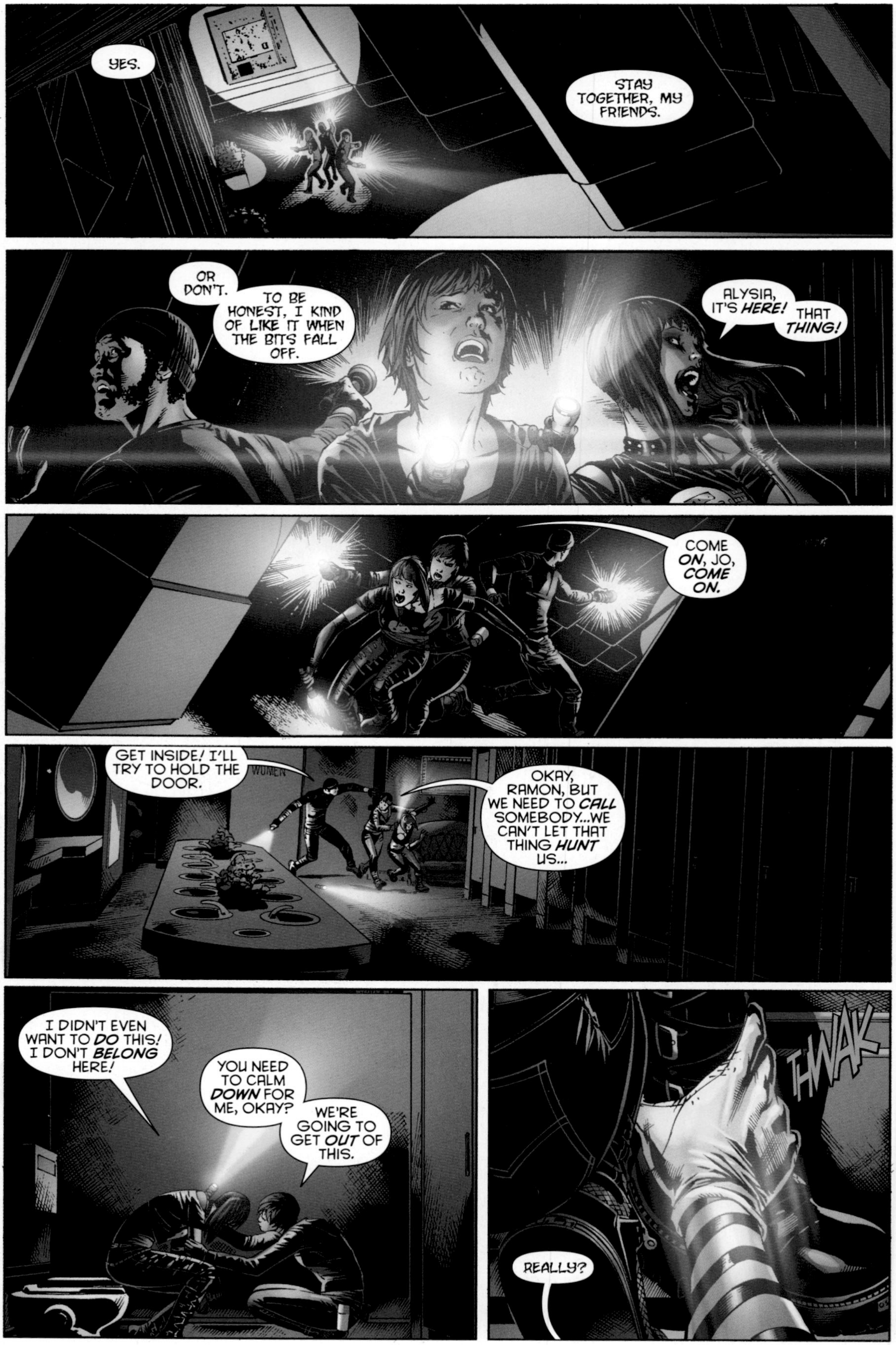
YES.
STAY TOGETHER, MY FRIENDS.
OR DON'T.
TO BE HONEST, I KIND OF LIKE IT WHEN THE BITS FALL OFF.
ALYSIA, IT'S HERE! THAT THING!
COME ON, JO, COME ON.
GET INSIDE! I'LL TRY TO HOLD THE DOOR.
WOMEN
OKAY, RAMON, BUT WE NEED TO CALL SOMEBODY...WE CAN'T LET THAT THING HUNT US...
I DIDN'T EVEN WANT TO DO THIS! I DON'T BELONG HERE!
YOU NEED TO CALM DOWN FOR ME, OKAY?
WE'RE GOING TO GET OUT OF THIS.
THWAK
REALLY?

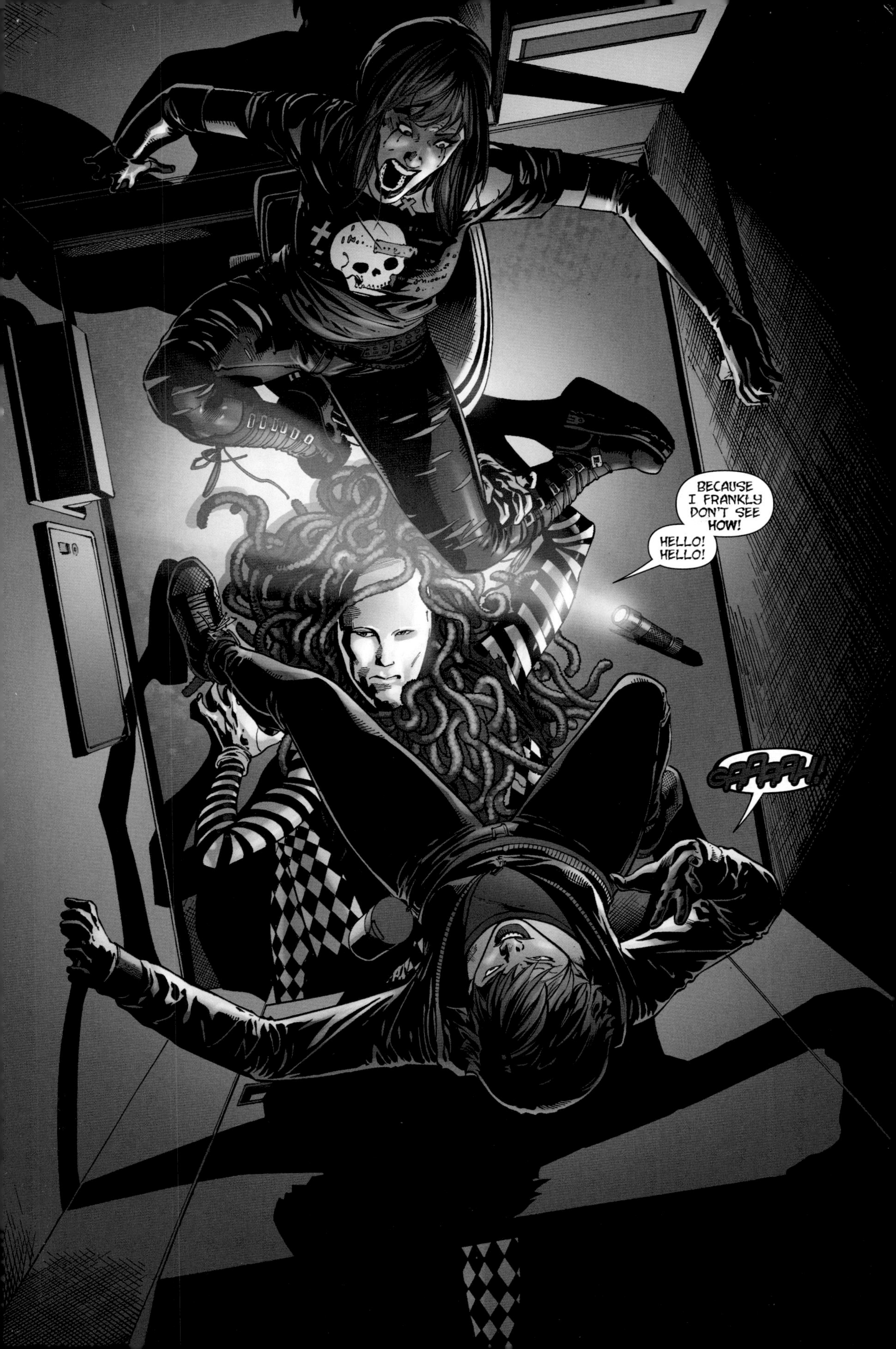
BECAUSE I FRANKLY DON'T SEE HOW!
HELLO! HELLO!
GAAAAH!

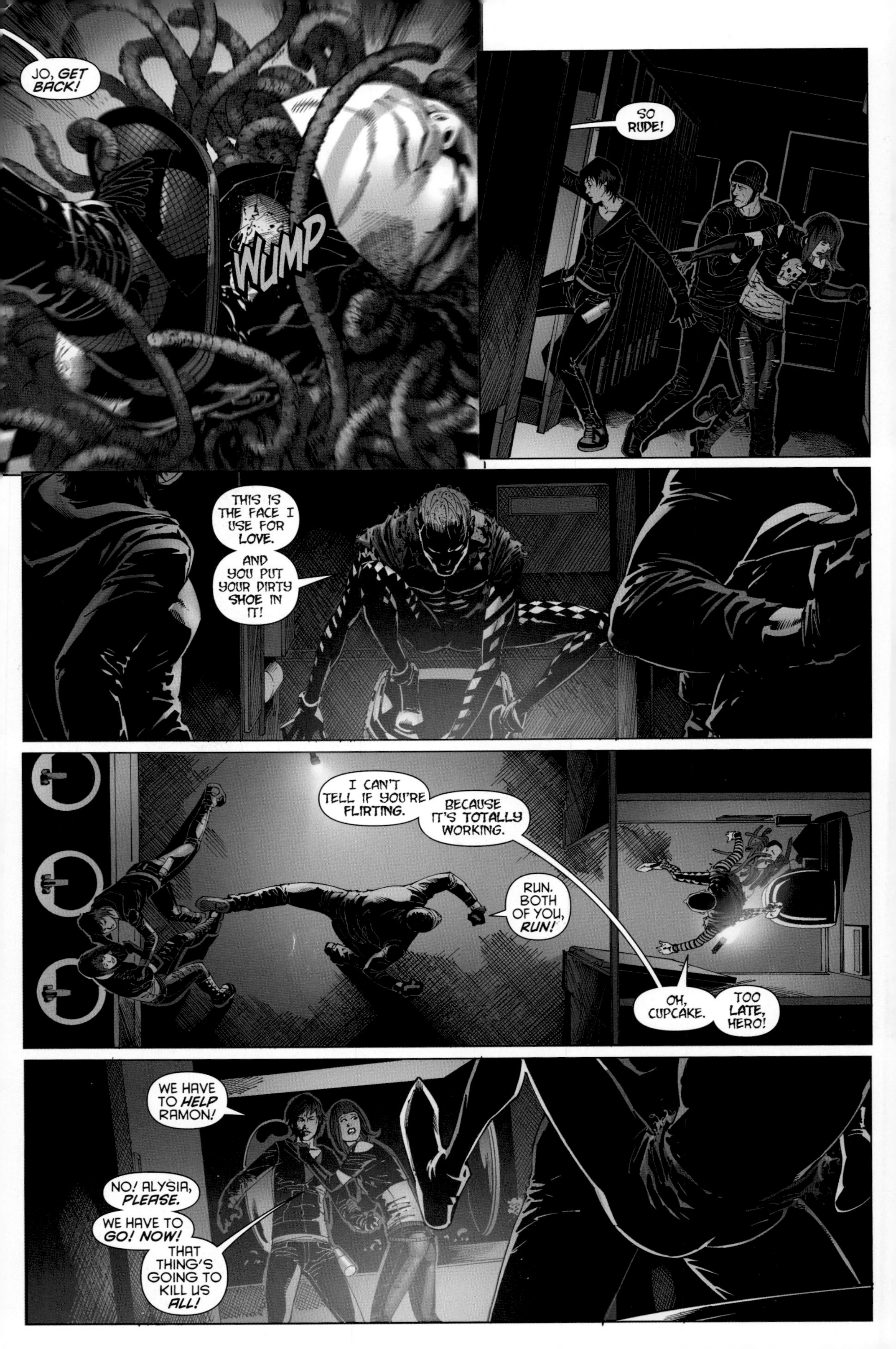
JO, GET BACK!
WUMP
SO RUDE!
THIS IS THE FACE I USE FOR LOVE.
AND YOU PUT YOUR DIRTY SHOE IN IT!
I CAN'T TELL IF YOU'RE FLIRTING.
BECAUSE IT'S TOTALLY WORKING.
RUN. BOTH OF YOU, RUN!
OH, CUPCAKE.
TOO LATE, HERO!
WE HAVE TO HELP RAMON!
NO! ALYSIA, PLEASE.
WE HAVE TO GO! NOW!
THAT THING'S GOING TO KILL US ALL!

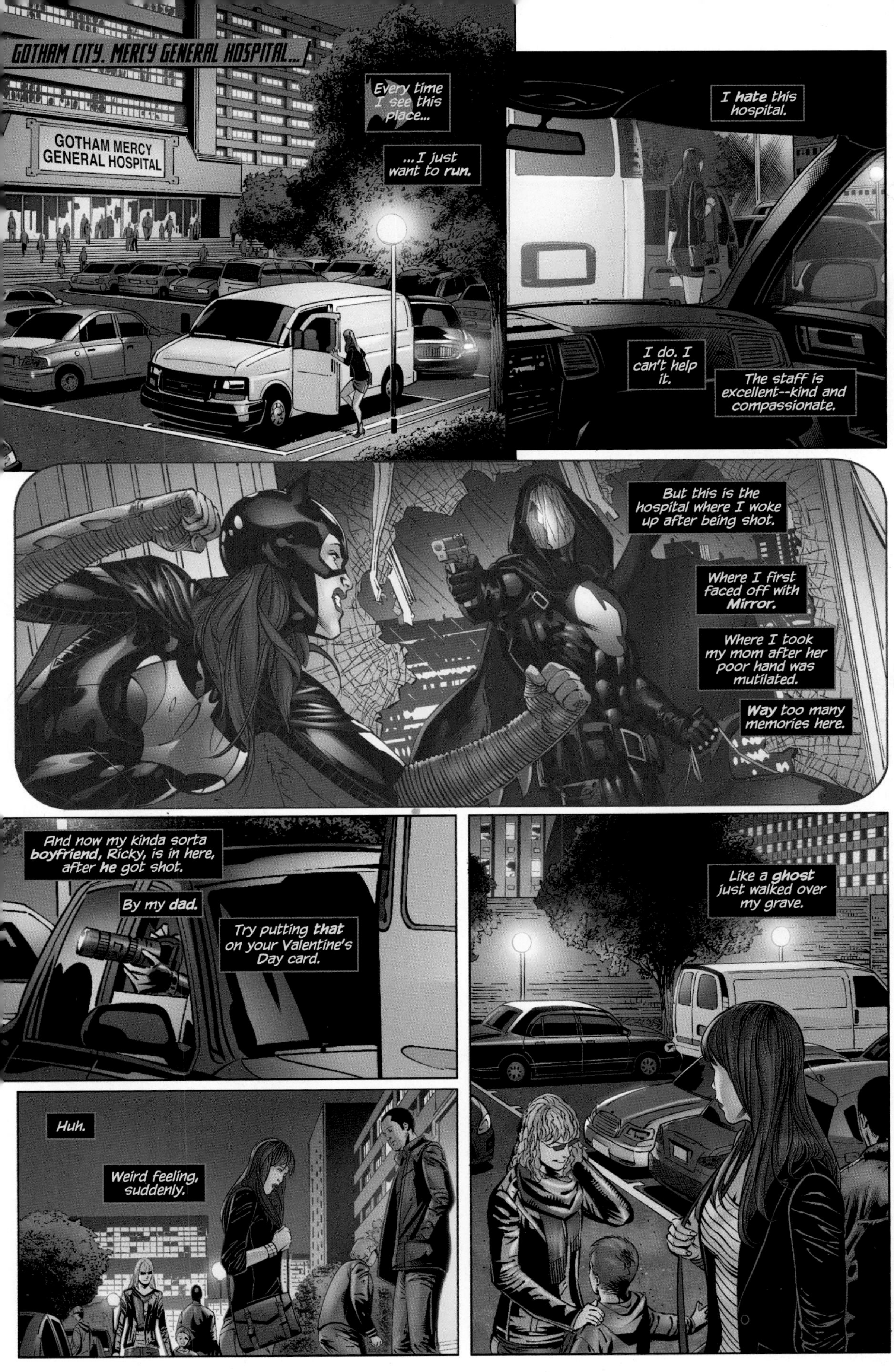
GOTHAM CITY. MERCY GENERAL HOSPITAL...
GOTHAM MERCY GENERAL HOSPITAL
Every time I see this place...
...I just want to run.
I hate this hospital.
I do. I can't help it.
The staff is excellent--kind and compassionate.
But this is the hospital where I woke up after being shot.
Where I first faced off with Mirror.
Where I took my mom after her poor hand was mutilated.
Way too many memories here.
And now my kinda sorta boyfriend, Ricky, is in here, after he got shot.
By my dad.
Try putting that on your Valentine's Day card.
Huh.
Weird feeling, suddenly.
Like a ghost just walked over my grave.

Gotta be this place. It's spooking me.

Or maybe I'm just getting paranoid.

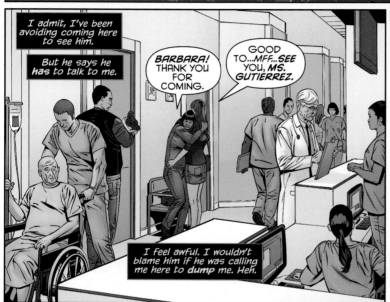

I admit, I've been avoiding coming here to see him.

But he says he *has* to talk to me.

BARBARA! THANK YOU FOR COMING.

GOOD TO...MFF...*SEE* YOU, *MS. GUTIERREZ.*

I feel awful. I wouldn't blame him if he was calling me here to *dump* me. Heh.

Oh, man. What if he's calling me here to *dump* me?

HE'LL BE *SO* GLAD TO SEE YOU.

I MADE YOU THESE TAMALES...I KNOW YOU LIKE THEM, AND YOU'RE GETTING SO *SKINNY*, BARBARA.

WELL. SINCE YOU *INSIST.*

One thing Ms. Gutierrez and my mom have in common...they turn food into an antidote.

For pretty much *anything.*

I'M... SORRY I'VE BEEN *AWAY...*

GO *IN*, GO *IN.*

He looks good. He looks...like Ricky.

Urgh. I really *am* a terrible girlfriend.

RICKY...?

I have no idea what to say.

UPTOWN!

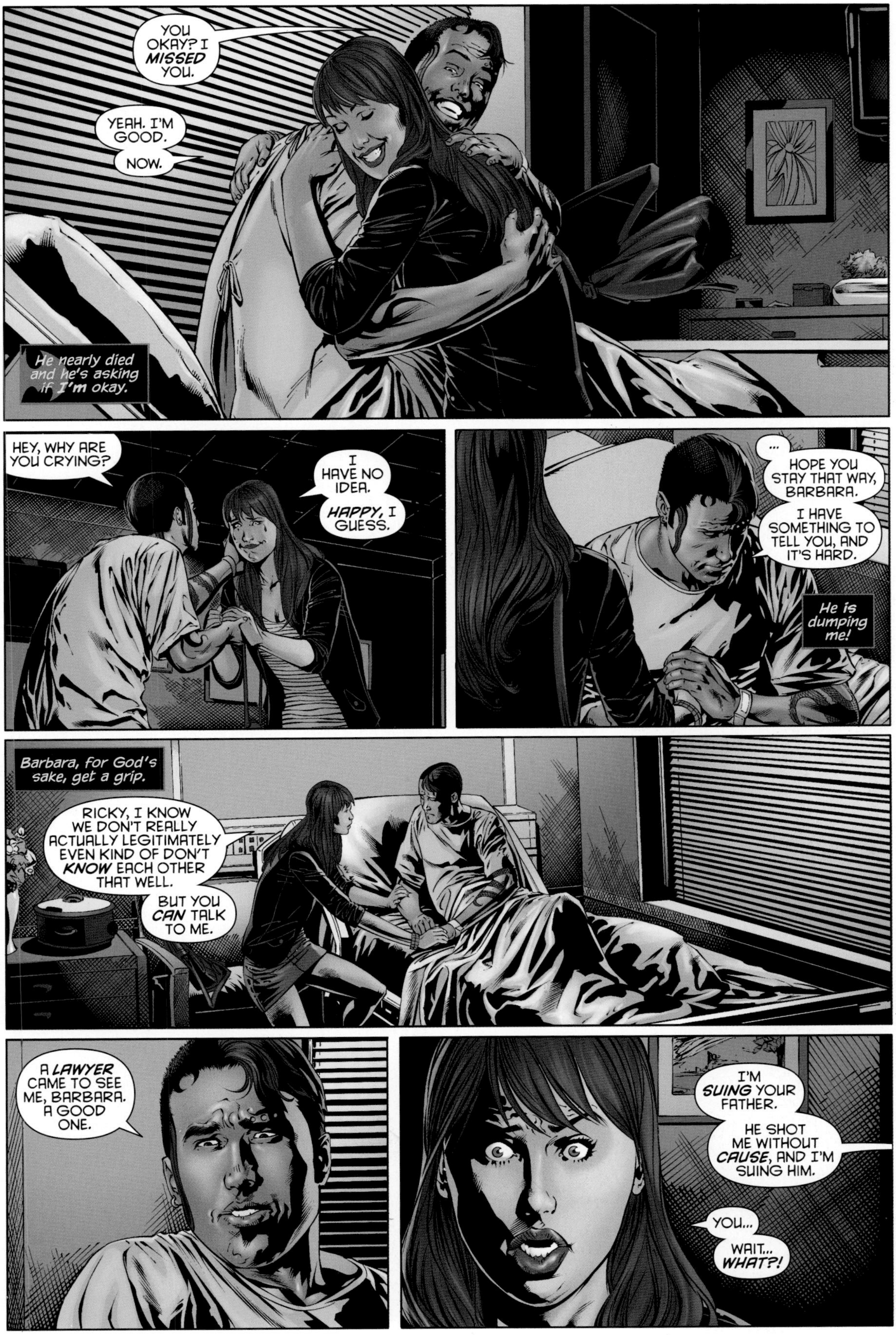
YOU OKAY? I *MISSED* YOU.
YEAH. I'M GOOD.
NOW.
He nearly died and he's asking if *I'm* okay.
HEY, WHY ARE YOU CRYING?
I HAVE NO IDEA.
HAPPY, I GUESS.
...
HOPE YOU STAY THAT WAY, BARBARA.
I HAVE SOMETHING TO TELL YOU, AND IT'S HARD.
He is dumping me!
Barbara, for God's sake, get a grip.
RICKY, I KNOW WE DON'T REALLY ACTUALLY LEGITIMATELY EVEN KIND OF DON'T *KNOW* EACH OTHER THAT WELL.
BUT YOU *CAN* TALK TO ME.
A *LAWYER* CAME TO SEE ME, BARBARA. A GOOD ONE.
I'M *SUING* YOUR FATHER.
HE SHOT ME WITHOUT *CAUSE,* AND I'M SUING HIM.
YOU...
WAIT... *WHAT?!*

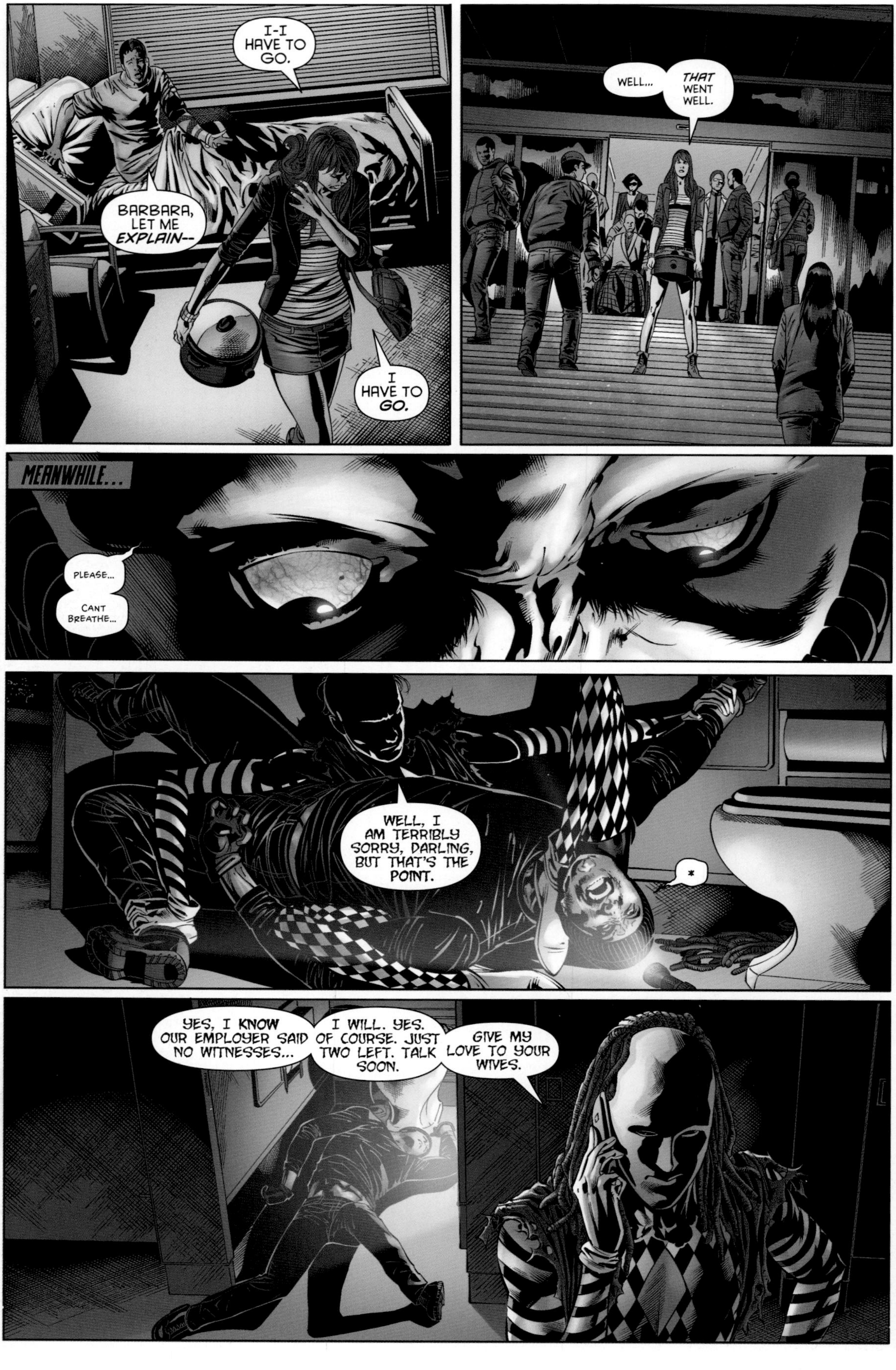
I-I HAVE TO GO.
BARBARA, LET ME EXPLAIN--
I HAVE TO GO.
WELL...
THAT WENT WELL.
MEANWHILE...
PLEASE...
CANT BREATHE...
WELL, I AM TERRIBLY SORRY, DARLING, BUT THAT'S THE POINT.
*
YES, I KNOW OUR EMPLOYER SAID NO WITNESSES...
I WILL. YES. OF COURSE. JUST TWO LEFT. TALK SOON.
GIVE MY LOVE TO YOUR WIVES.

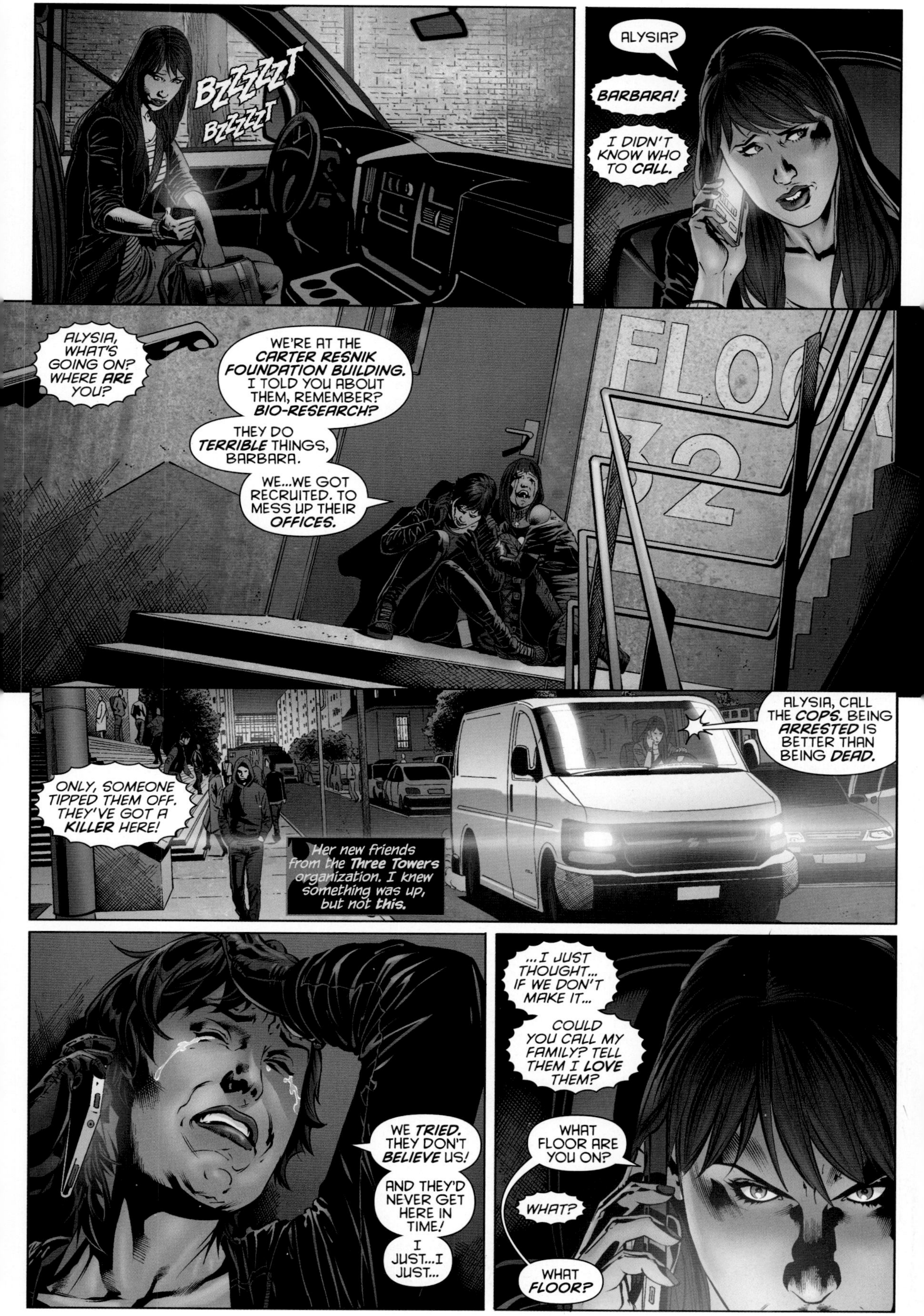
BZZZZZZT
BZZZZZT
ALYSIA?
BARBARA!
I DIDN'T KNOW WHO TO CALL.
ALYSIA, WHAT'S GOING ON? WHERE ARE YOU?
WE'RE AT THE CARTER RESNIK FOUNDATION BUILDING. I TOLD YOU ABOUT THEM, REMEMBER? BIO-RESEARCH?
THEY DO TERRIBLE THINGS, BARBARA.
WE...WE GOT RECRUITED. TO MESS UP THEIR OFFICES.
FLOOR 32
ONLY, SOMEONE TIPPED THEM OFF. THEY'VE GOT A KILLER HERE!
Her new friends from the Three Towers organization. I knew something was up, but not this.
ALYSIA, CALL THE COPS. BEING ARRESTED IS BETTER THAN BEING DEAD.
WE TRIED. THEY DON'T BELIEVE US!
AND THEY'D NEVER GET HERE IN TIME!
I JUST...I JUST...
...I JUST THOUGHT... IF WE DON'T MAKE IT...
COULD YOU CALL MY FAMILY? TELL THEM I LOVE THEM?
WHAT FLOOR ARE YOU ON?
WHAT?
WHAT FLOOR?

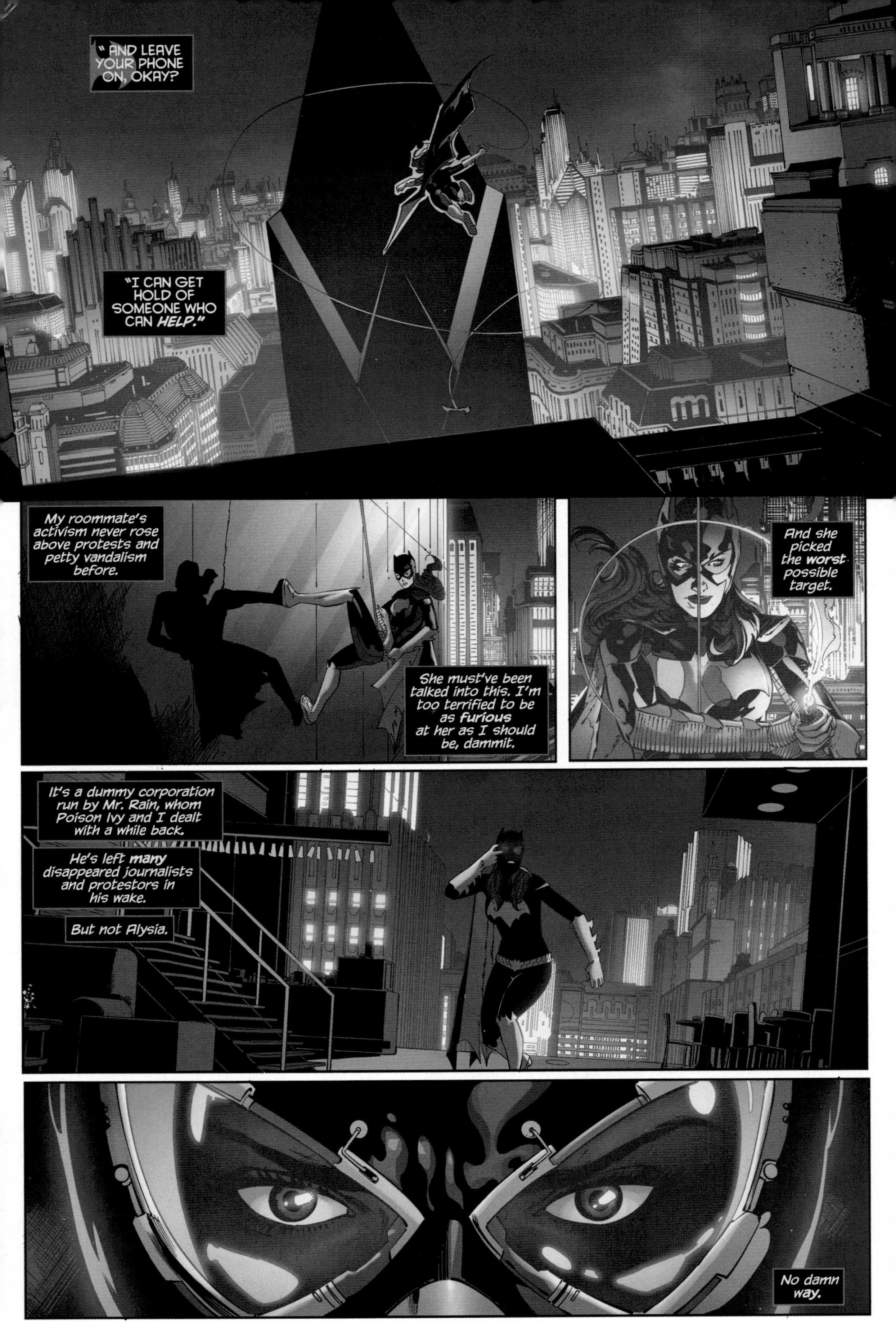
"AND LEAVE YOUR PHONE ON, OKAY?
"I CAN GET HOLD OF SOMEONE WHO CAN HELP."
My roommate's activism never rose above protests and petty vandalism before.
She must've been talked into this. I'm too terrified to be as furious at her as I should be, dammit.
And she picked the worst possible target.
It's a dummy corporation run by Mr. Rain, whom Poison Ivy and I dealt with a while back.
He's left many disappeared journalists and protestors in his wake.
But not Alysia.
No damn way.

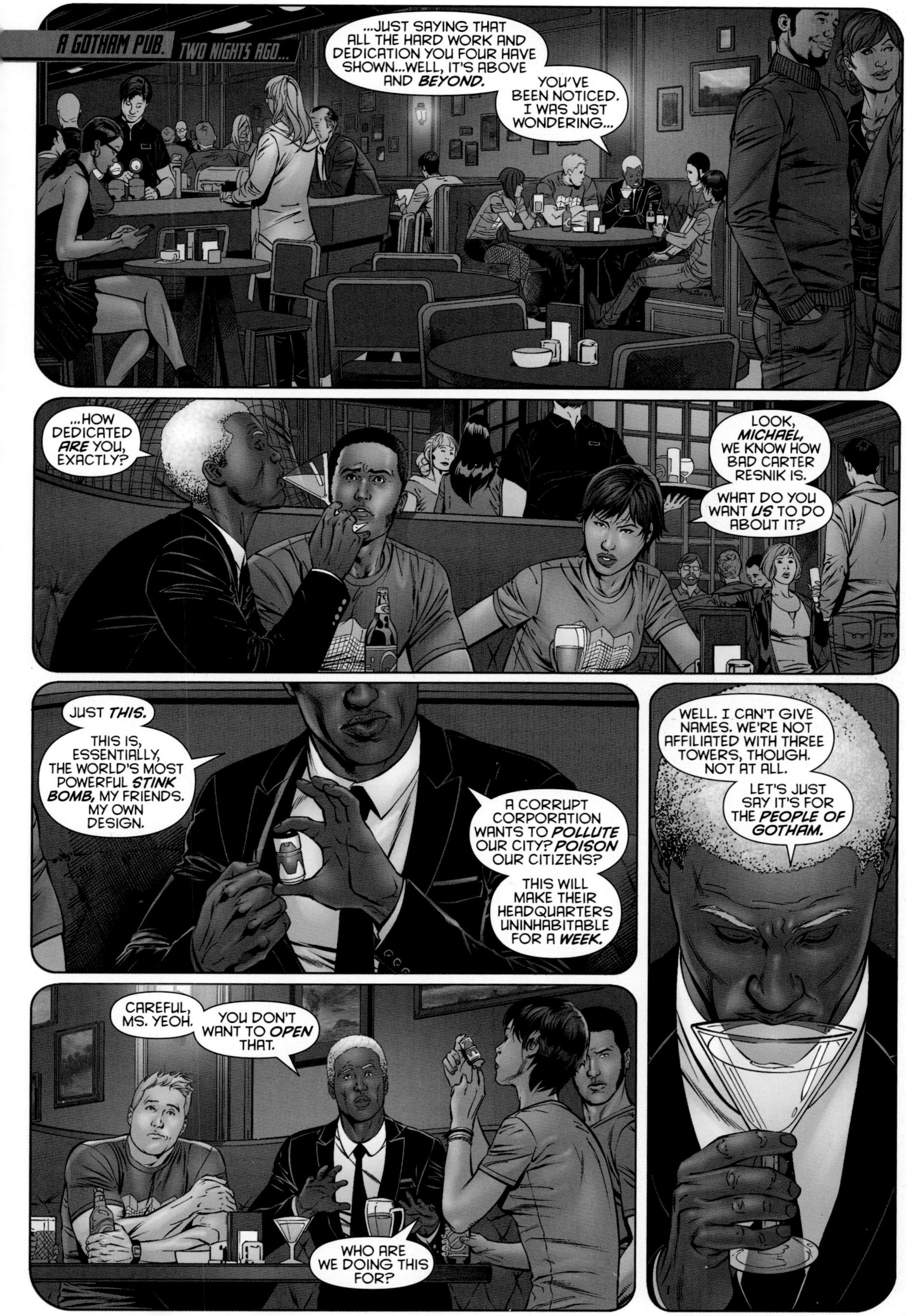
A GOTHAM PUB. TWO NIGHTS AGO...
...JUST SAYING THAT ALL THE HARD WORK AND DEDICATION YOU FOUR HAVE SHOWN...WELL, IT'S ABOVE AND BEYOND.
YOU'VE BEEN NOTICED. I WAS JUST WONDERING...
...HOW DEDICATED ARE YOU, EXACTLY?
LOOK, MICHAEL, WE KNOW HOW BAD CARTER RESNIK IS.
WHAT DO YOU WANT US TO DO ABOUT IT?
JUST THIS.
THIS IS, ESSENTIALLY, THE WORLD'S MOST POWERFUL STINK BOMB, MY FRIENDS. MY OWN DESIGN.
A CORRUPT CORPORATION WANTS TO POLLUTE OUR CITY? POISON OUR CITIZENS?
THIS WILL MAKE THEIR HEADQUARTERS UNINHABITABLE FOR A WEEK.
CAREFUL, MS. YEOH.
YOU DON'T WANT TO OPEN THAT.
WHO ARE WE DOING THIS FOR?
WELL. I CAN'T GIVE NAMES. WE'RE NOT AFFILIATED WITH THREE TOWERS, THOUGH. NOT AT ALL.
LET'S JUST SAY IT'S FOR THE PEOPLE OF GOTHAM.

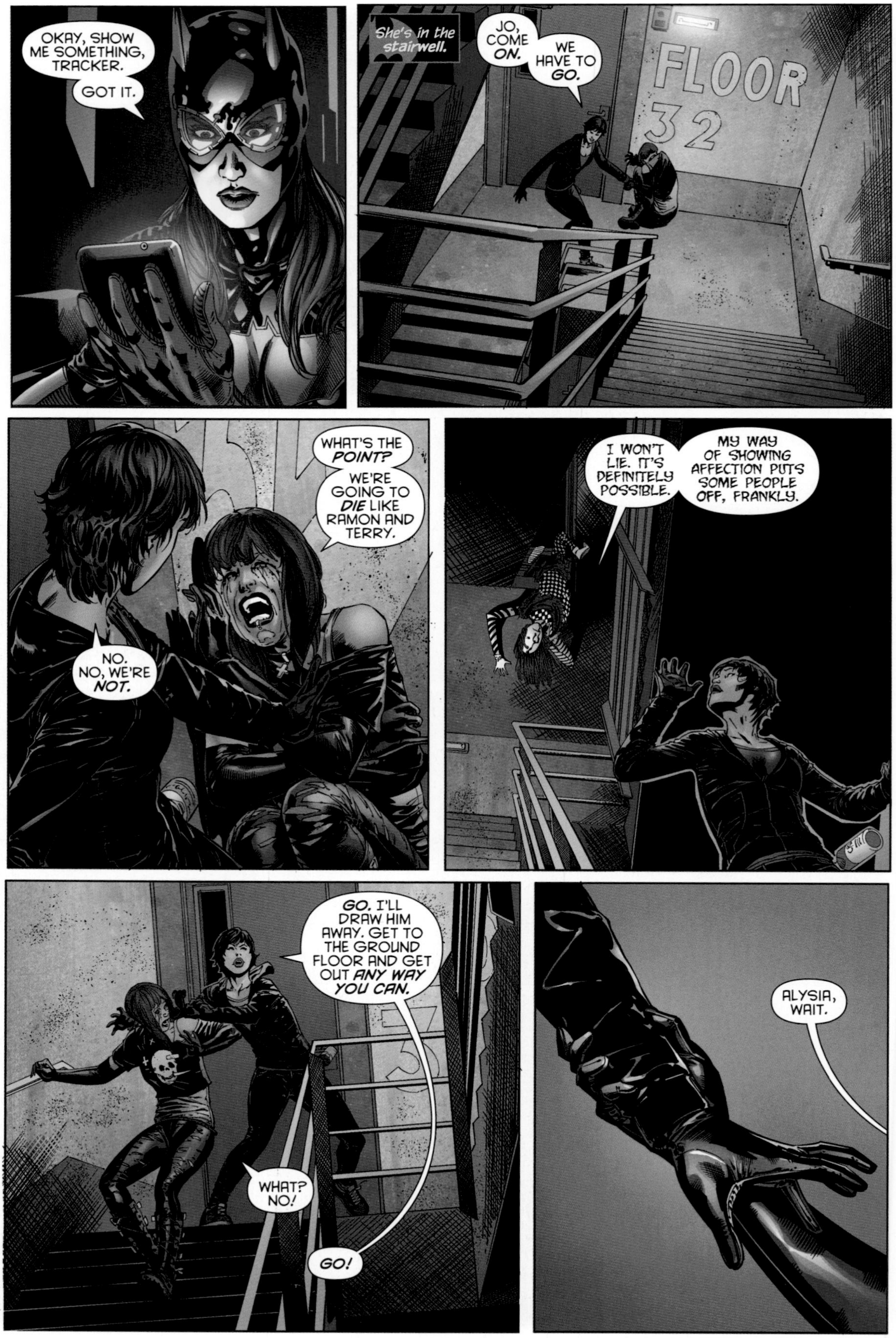
OKAY, SHOW ME SOMETHING, TRACKER.
GOT IT.
She's in the stairwell.
JO, COME ON.
WE HAVE TO GO.
FLOOR 32
WHAT'S THE POINT?
WE'RE GOING TO DIE LIKE RAMON AND TERRY.
NO. NO, WE'RE NOT.
I WON'T LIE. IT'S DEFINITELY POSSIBLE.
MY WAY OF SHOWING AFFECTION PUTS SOME PEOPLE OFF, FRANKLY.
GO. I'LL DRAW HIM AWAY. GET TO THE GROUND FLOOR AND GET OUT ANY WAY YOU CAN.
WHAT? NO!
GO!
ALYSIA, WAIT.

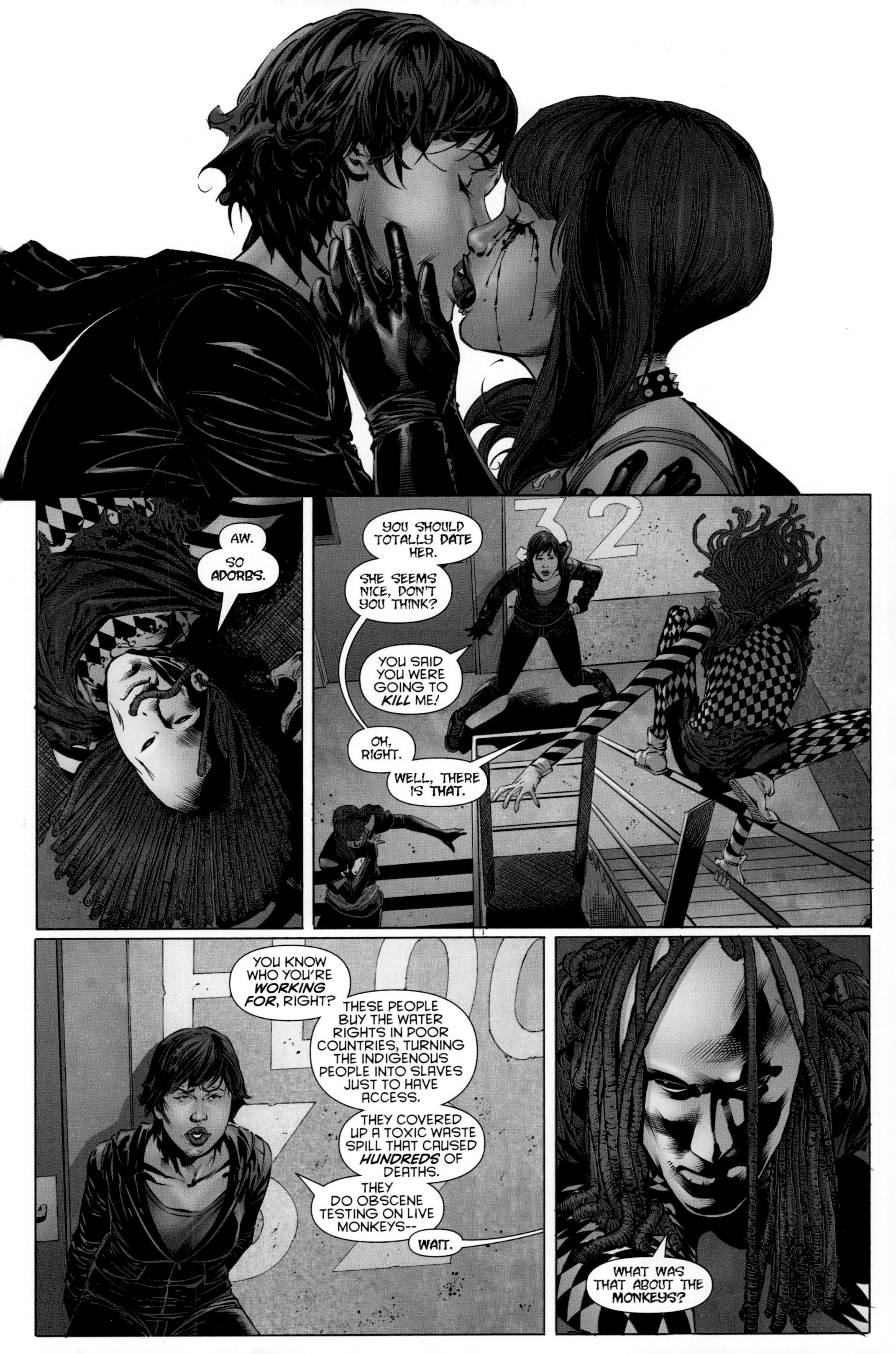
AW.
SO ADORBS.
YOU SHOULD TOTALLY DATE HER.
SHE SEEMS NICE, DON'T YOU THINK?
YOU SAID YOU WERE GOING TO KILL ME!
OH, RIGHT.
WELL, THERE IS THAT.
32
YOU KNOW WHO YOU'RE WORKING FOR, RIGHT?
THESE PEOPLE BUY THE WATER RIGHTS IN POOR COUNTRIES, TURNING THE INDIGENOUS PEOPLE INTO SLAVES JUST TO HAVE ACCESS.
THEY COVERED UP A TOXIC WASTE SPILL THAT CAUSED HUNDREDS OF DEATHS.
THEY DO OBSCENE TESTING ON LIVE MONKEYS--
WAIT.
WHAT WAS THAT ABOUT THE MONKEYS?

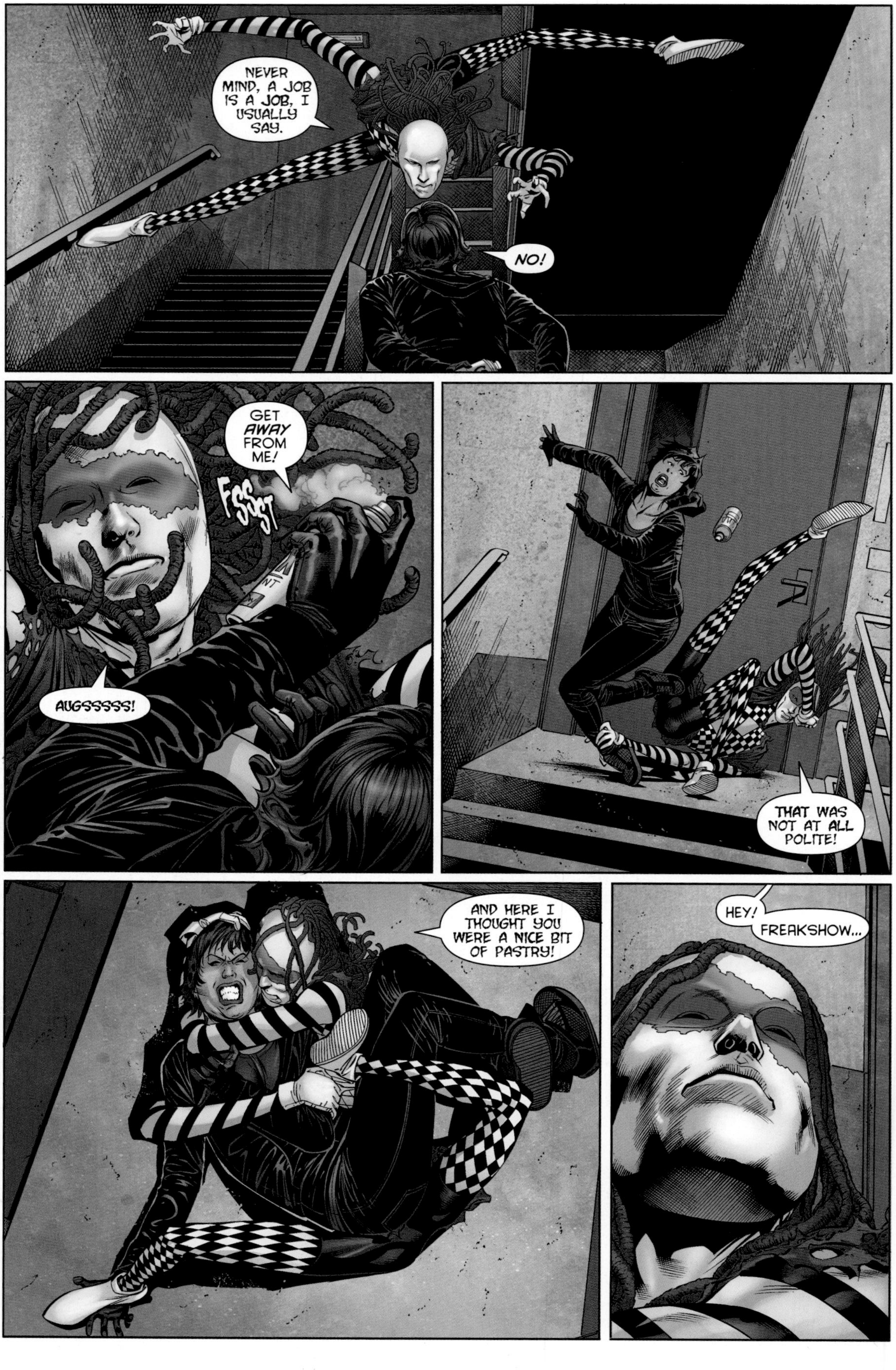

NEVER MIND, A JOB IS A JOB, I USUALLY SAY.
NO!
GET AWAY FROM ME!
FSSST
AUGSSSSS!
THAT WAS NOT AT ALL POLITE!
AND HERE I THOUGHT YOU WERE A NICE BIT OF PASTRY!
HEY!
FREAKSHOW...

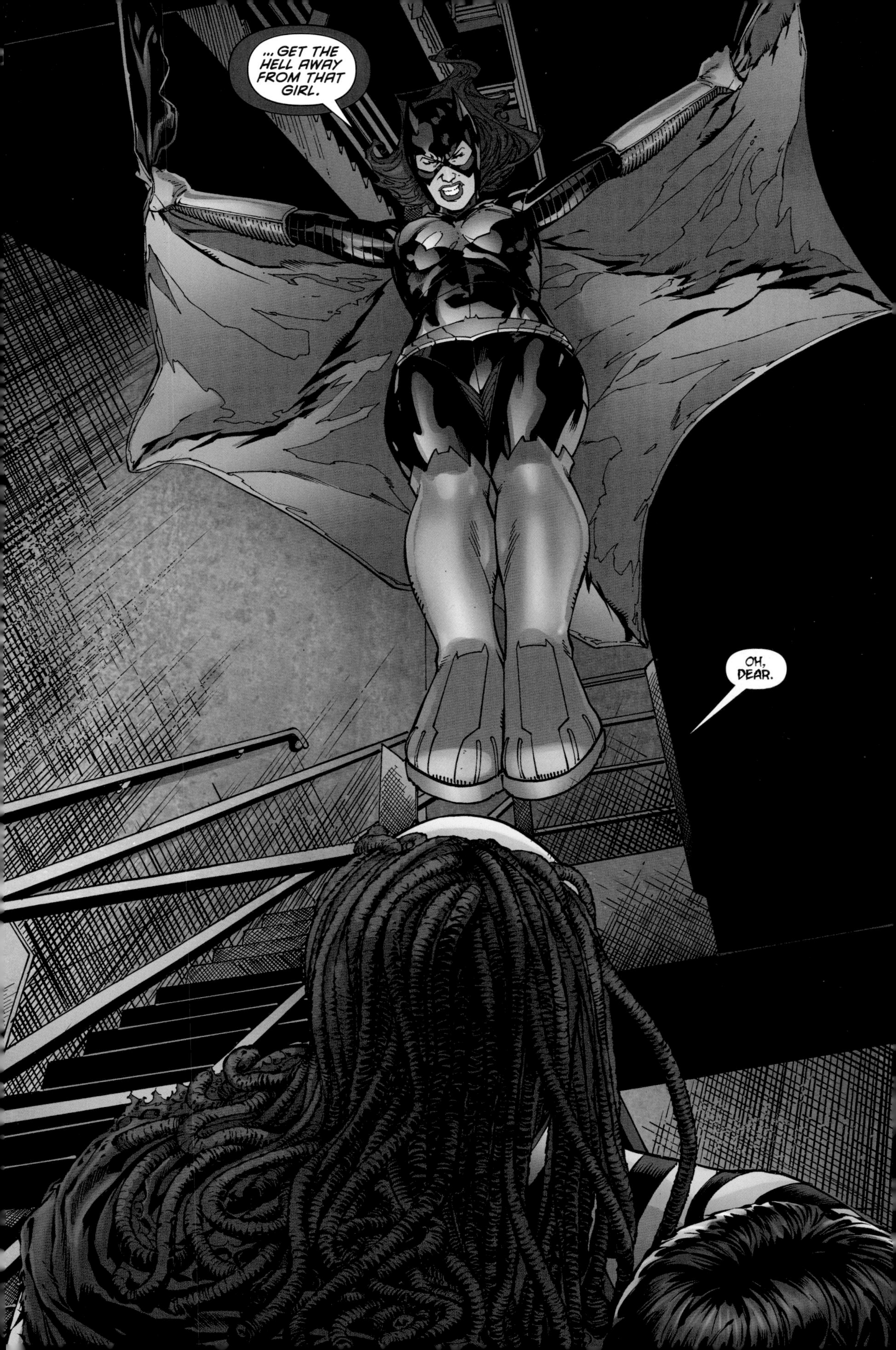
...GET THE HELL AWAY FROM THAT GIRL.
OH, DEAR.

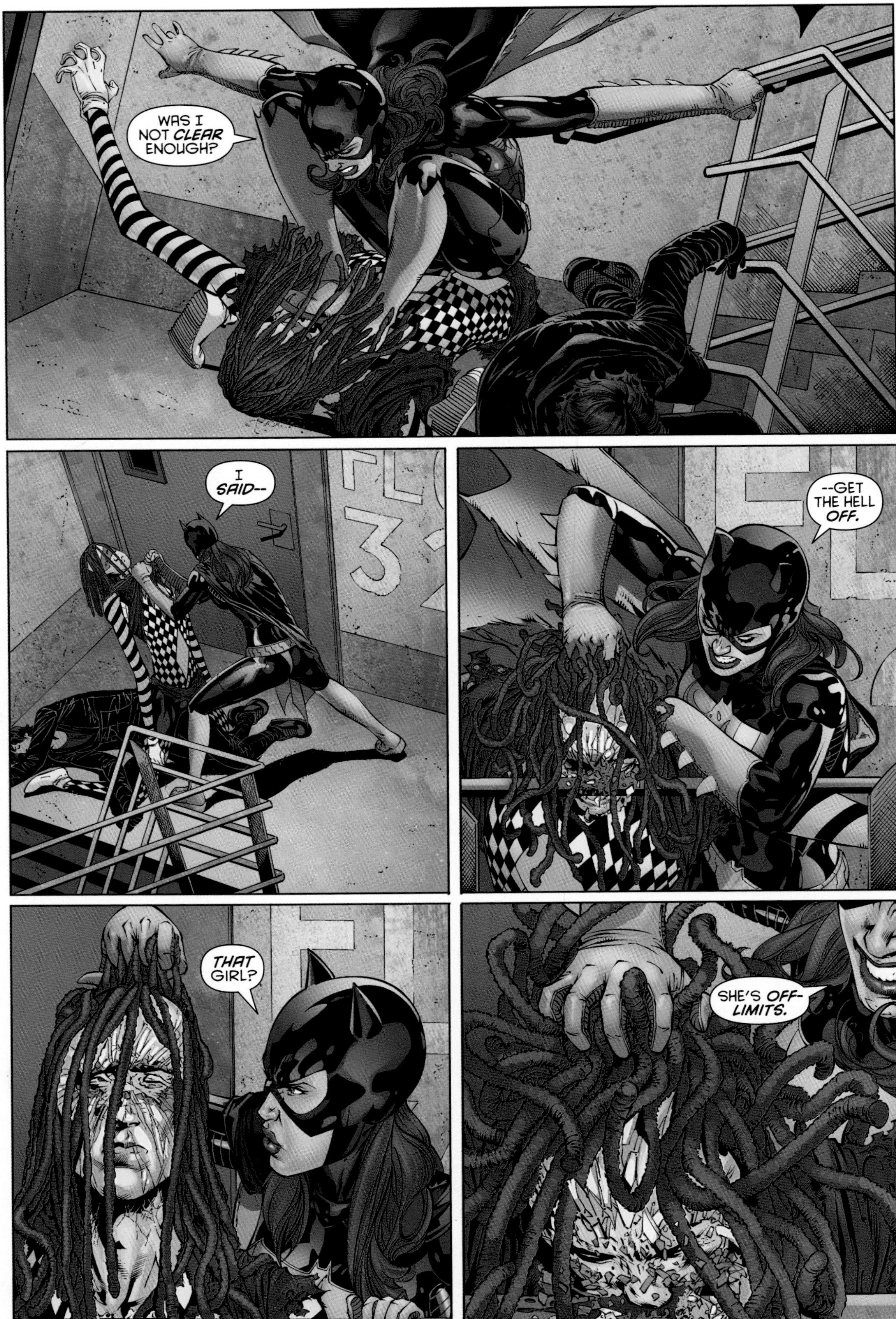
WAS I NOT *CLEAR* ENOUGH?
I *SAID*--
--GET THE HELL *OFF.*
THAT GIRL?
SHE'S *OFF-LIMITS.*

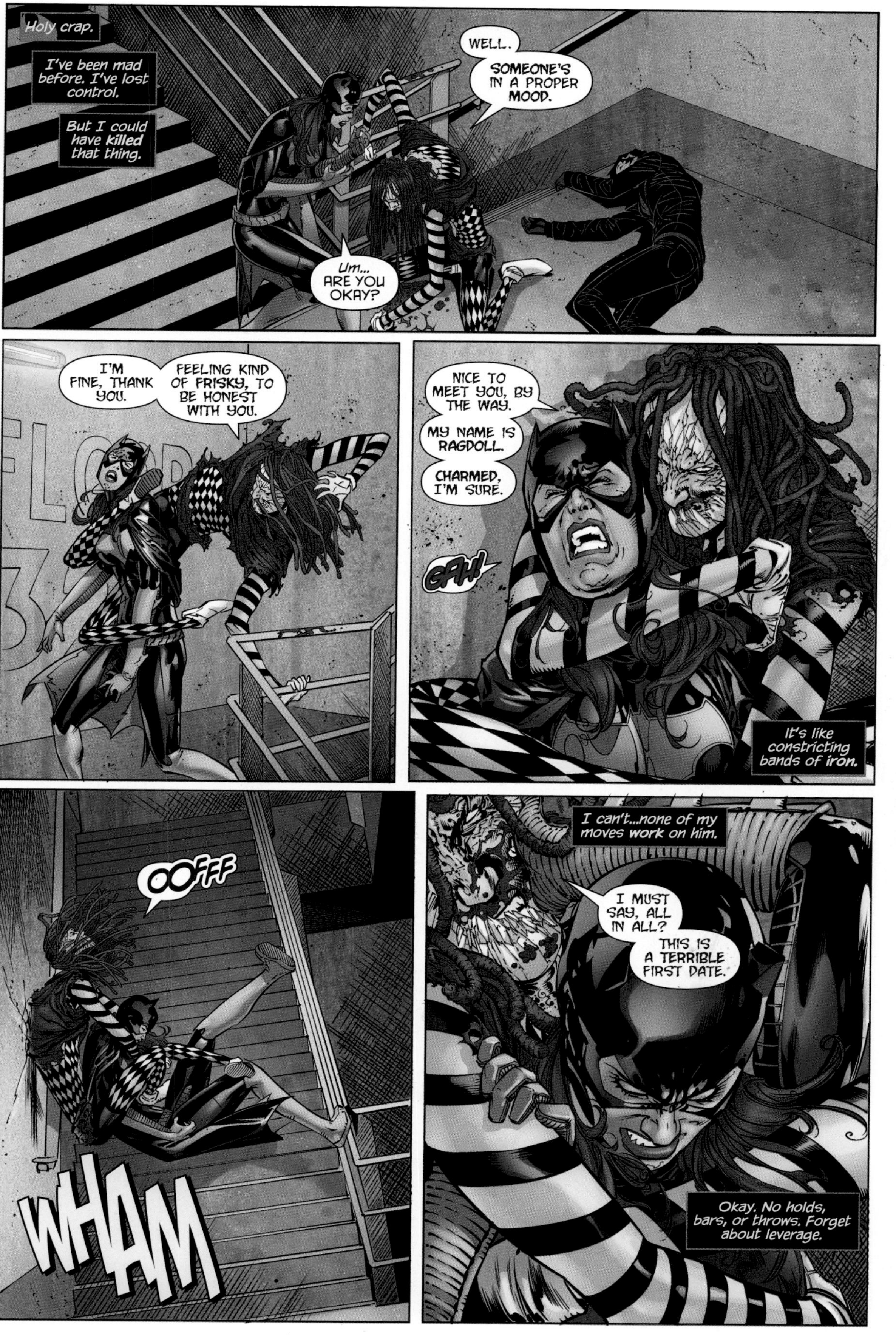
Holy crap.
I've been mad before. I've lost control.
But I could have killed that thing.
WELL.
SOMEONE'S IN A PROPER MOOD.
Um... ARE YOU OKAY?
I'M FINE, THANK YOU.
FEELING KIND OF FRISKY, TO BE HONEST WITH YOU.
NICE TO MEET YOU, BY THE WAY.
MY NAME IS RAGDOLL.
CHARMED, I'M SURE.
GAH!
It's like constricting bands of iron.
OOFFF
WHAM
I can't...none of my moves work on him.
I MUST SAY, ALL IN ALL?
THIS IS A TERRIBLE FIRST DATE.
Okay. No holds, bars, or throws. Forget about leverage.

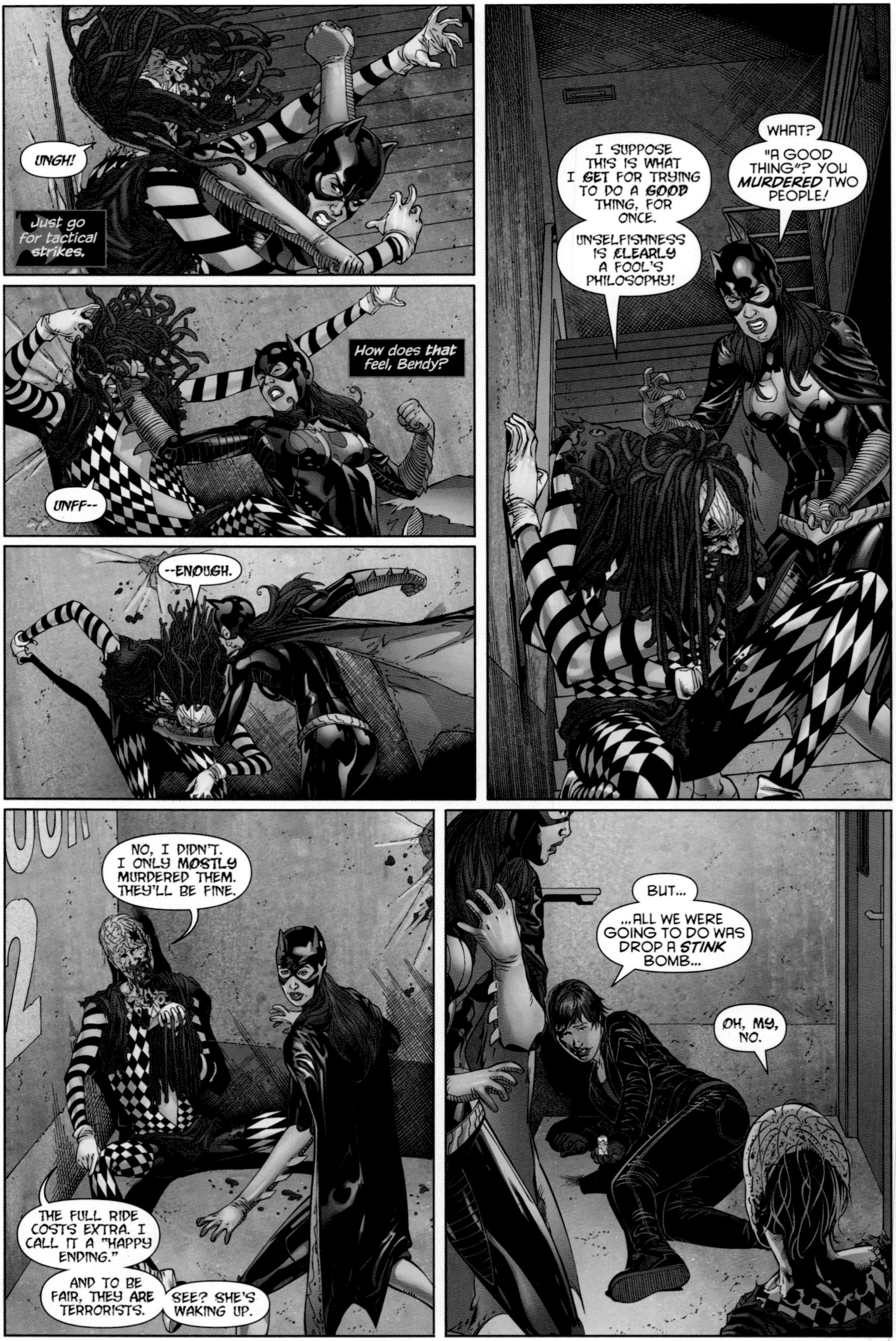
UNGH!
Just go for tactical strikes.
How does that feel, Bendy?
UNFF--
--ENOUGH.
I SUPPOSE THIS IS WHAT I GET FOR TRYING TO DO A GOOD THING, FOR ONCE.
UNSELFISHNESS IS CLEARLY A FOOL'S PHILOSOPHY!
WHAT?
"A GOOD THING"? YOU MURDERED TWO PEOPLE!
NO, I DIDN'T. I ONLY MOSTLY MURDERED THEM. THEY'LL BE FINE.
THE FULL RIDE COSTS EXTRA. I CALL IT A "HAPPY ENDING."
AND TO BE FAIR, THEY ARE TERRORISTS.
SEE? SHE'S WAKING UP.
BUT...
...ALL WE WERE GOING TO DO WAS DROP A STINK BOMB...
OH, MY, NO.

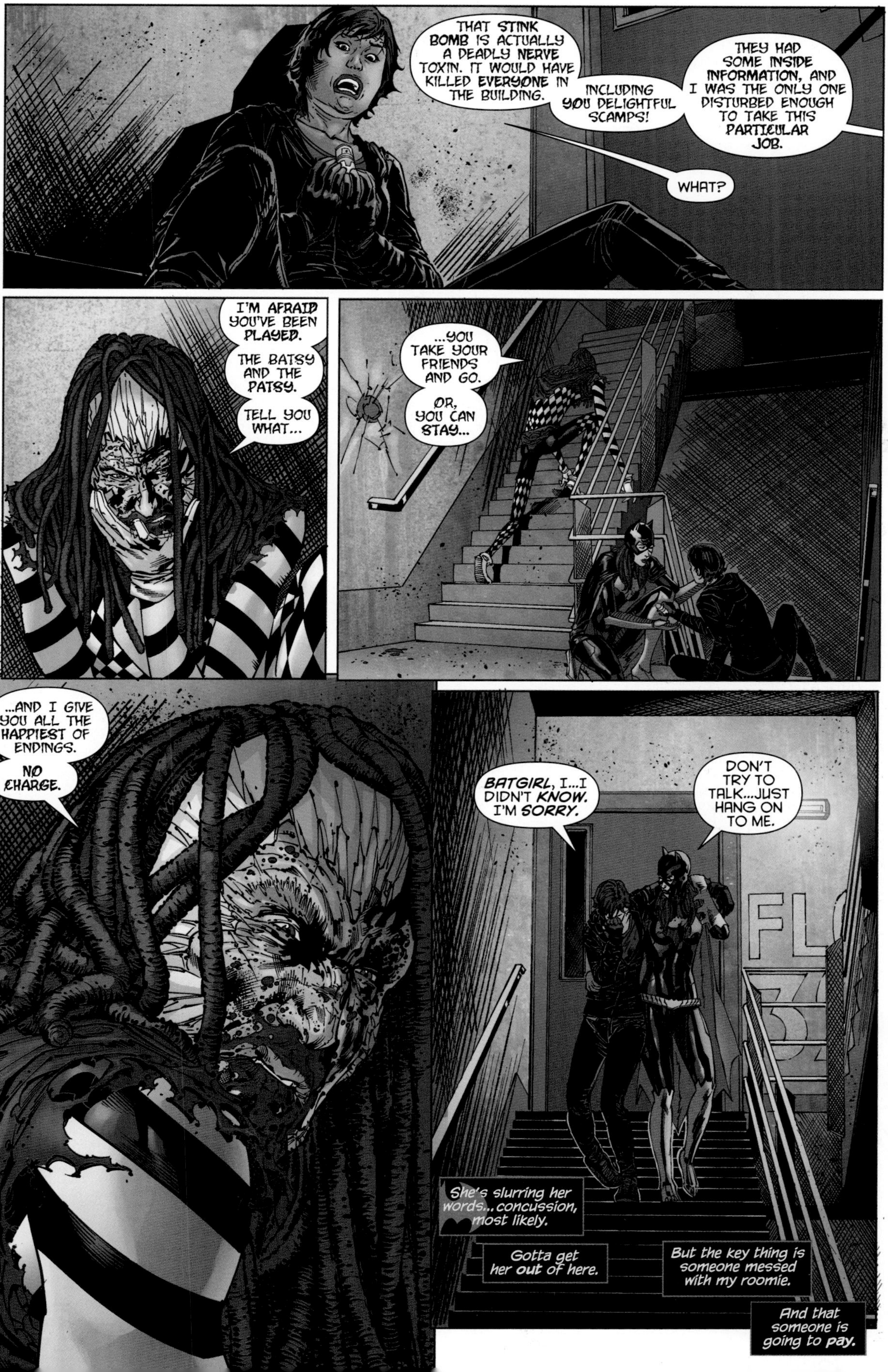
THAT STINK BOMB IS ACTUALLY A DEADLY NERVE TOXIN. IT WOULD HAVE KILLED EVERYONE IN THE BUILDING.
INCLUDING YOU DELIGHTFUL SCAMPS!
THEY HAD SOME INSIDE INFORMATION, AND I WAS THE ONLY ONE DISTURBED ENOUGH TO TAKE THIS PARTICULAR JOB.
WHAT?
I'M AFRAID YOU'VE BEEN PLAYED.
THE BATSY AND THE PATSY.
TELL YOU WHAT...
...YOU TAKE YOUR FRIENDS AND GO.
OR, YOU CAN STAY...
...AND I GIVE YOU ALL THE HAPPIEST OF ENDINGS.
NO CHARGE.
BATGIRL, I...I DIDN'T KNOW. I'M SORRY.
DON'T TRY TO TALK...JUST HANG ON TO ME.
She's slurring her words...concussion, most likely.
Gotta get her out of here.
But the key thing is someone messed with my roomie.
And that someone is going to pay.

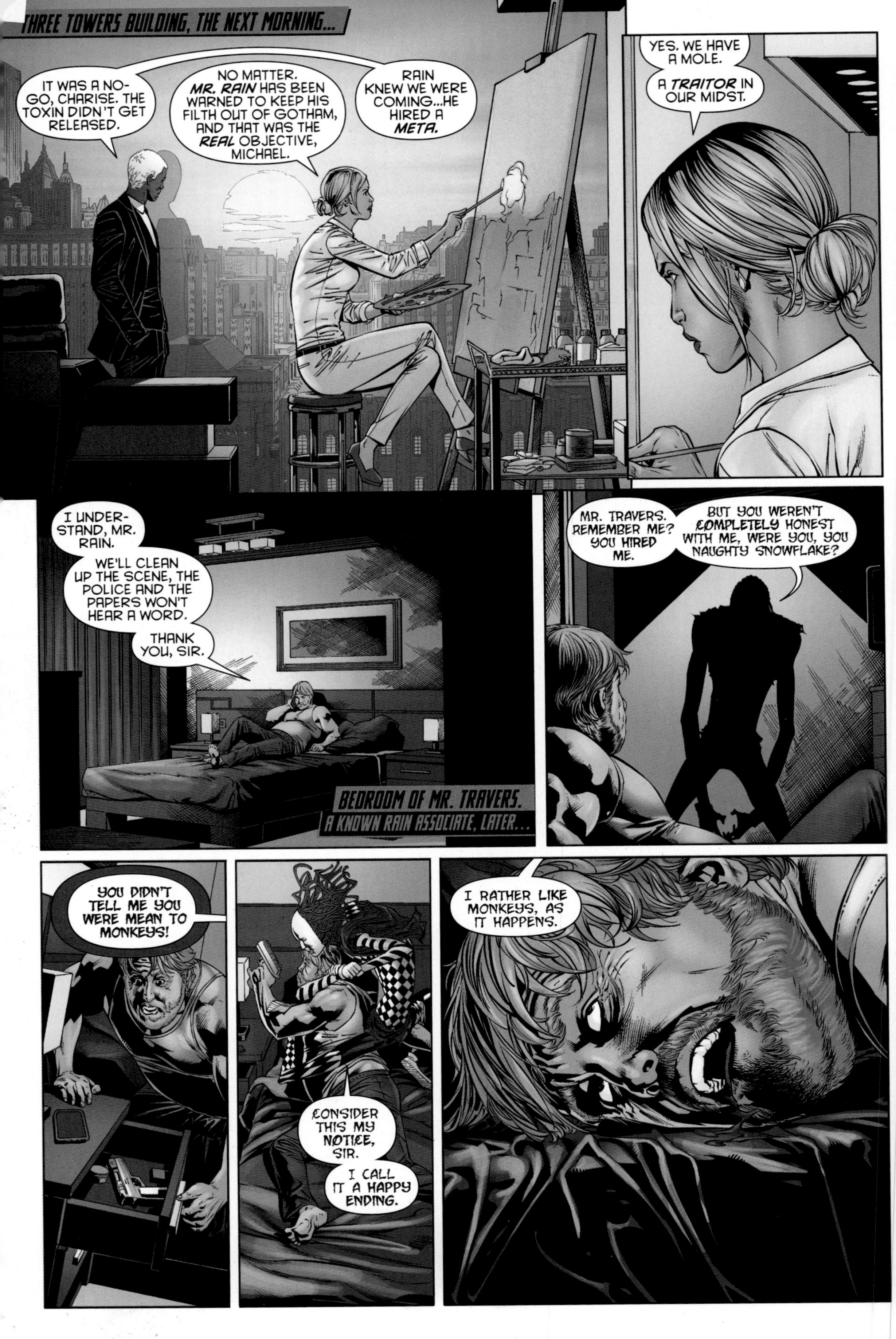
THREE TOWERS BUILDING, THE NEXT MORNING...
IT WAS A NO-GO, CHARISE. THE TOXIN DIDN'T GET RELEASED.
NO MATTER. MR. RAIN HAS BEEN WARNED TO KEEP HIS FILTH OUT OF GOTHAM, AND THAT WAS THE REAL OBJECTIVE, MICHAEL.
RAIN KNEW WE WERE COMING...HE HIRED A META.
YES. WE HAVE A MOLE.
A TRAITOR IN OUR MIDST.
I UNDERSTAND, MR. RAIN.
WE'LL CLEAN UP THE SCENE, THE POLICE AND THE PAPERS WON'T HEAR A WORD.
THANK YOU, SIR.
BEDROOM OF MR. TRAVERS. A KNOWN RAIN ASSOCIATE, LATER...
MR. TRAVERS. REMEMBER ME? YOU HIRED ME.
BUT YOU WEREN'T COMPLETELY HONEST WITH ME, WERE YOU, YOU NAUGHTY SNOWFLAKE?
YOU DIDN'T TELL ME YOU WERE MEAN TO MONKEYS!
CONSIDER THIS MY NOTICE, SIR.
I CALL IT A HAPPY ENDING.
I RATHER LIKE MONKEYS, AS IT HAPPENS.

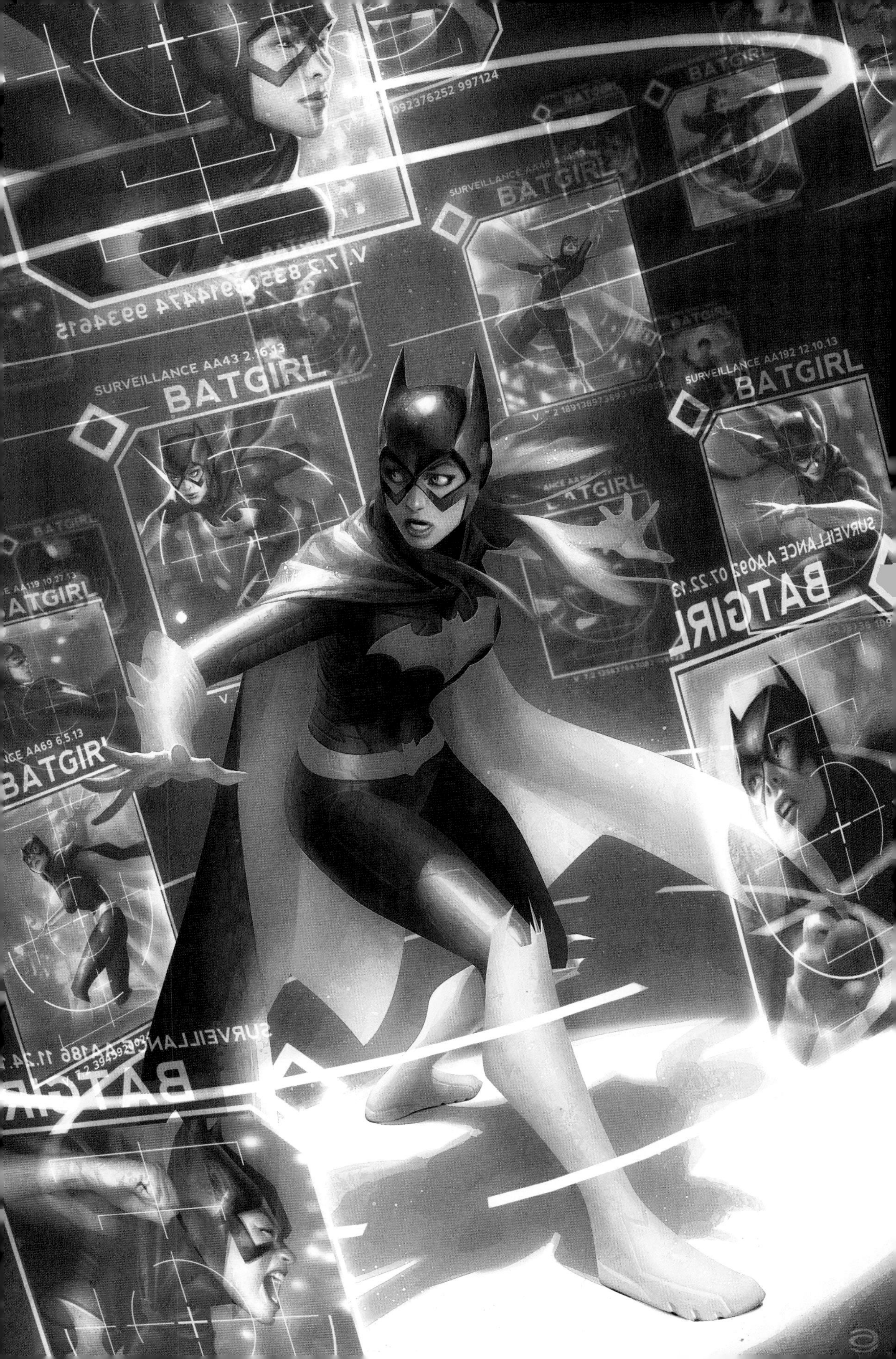
SURVEILLANCE AA48 4.4.13
BATGIRL
SURVEILLANCE AA43 2.16.13
BATGIRL
SURVEILLANCE AA192 12.10.13
BATGIRL
BATGIRL
BATGIRL
BATGIRL

DEADLINE PART ONE: THE RAZORS UNDER THE FLOORBOARDS

GAIL SIMONE writer **FERNANDO PASARIN** penciller **JONATHAN GLAPION** inker **BLOND** colorist **ALEX GARNER** cover artist

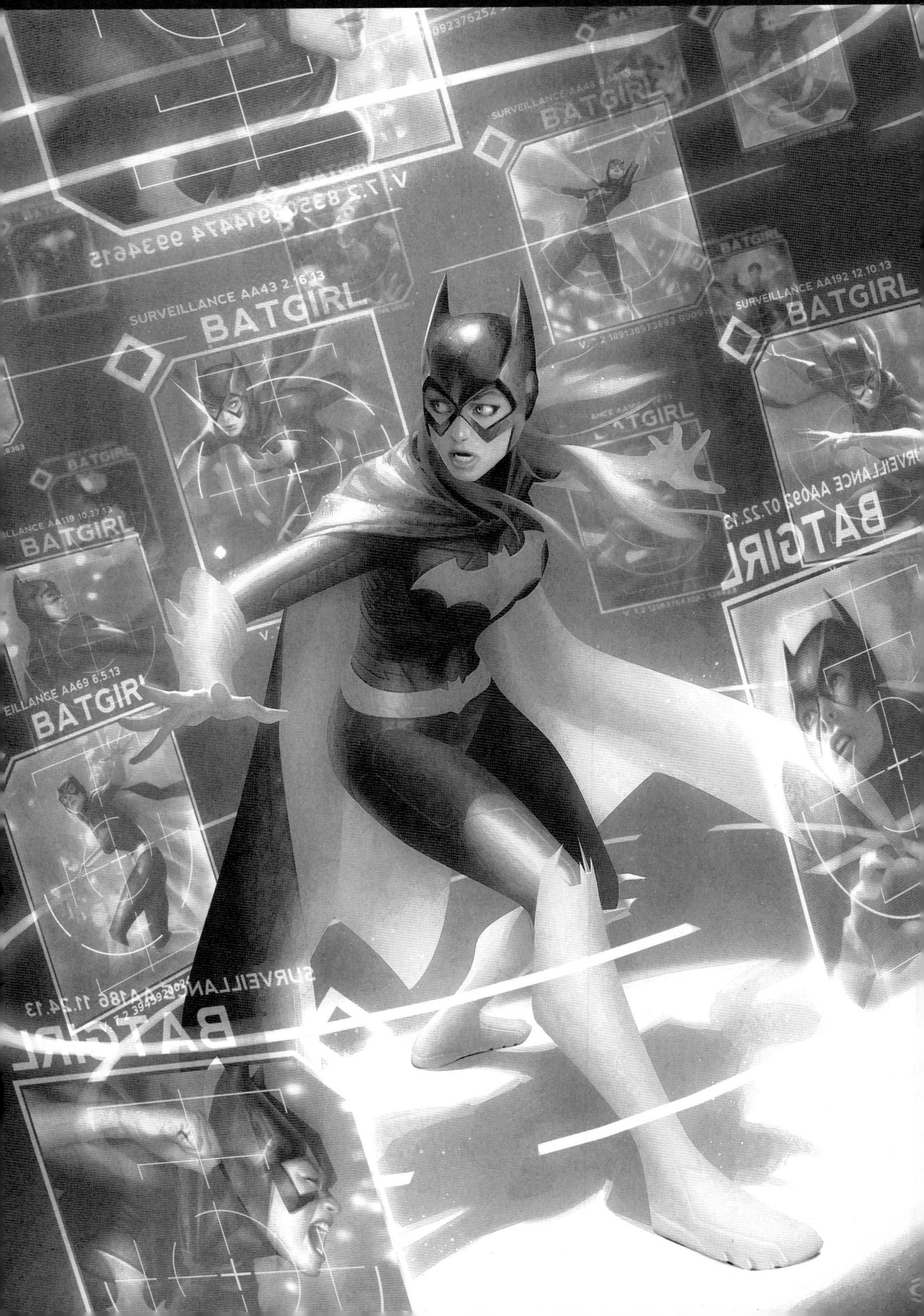

SURVEILLANCE AA43 2.16.13
BATGIRL
SURVEILLANCE AA192 12.10.13
BATGIRL
SURVEILLANCE AA119 10.27.13
BATGIRL
SURVEILLANCE AA69 6.5.13
BATGIRL
BATGIRL

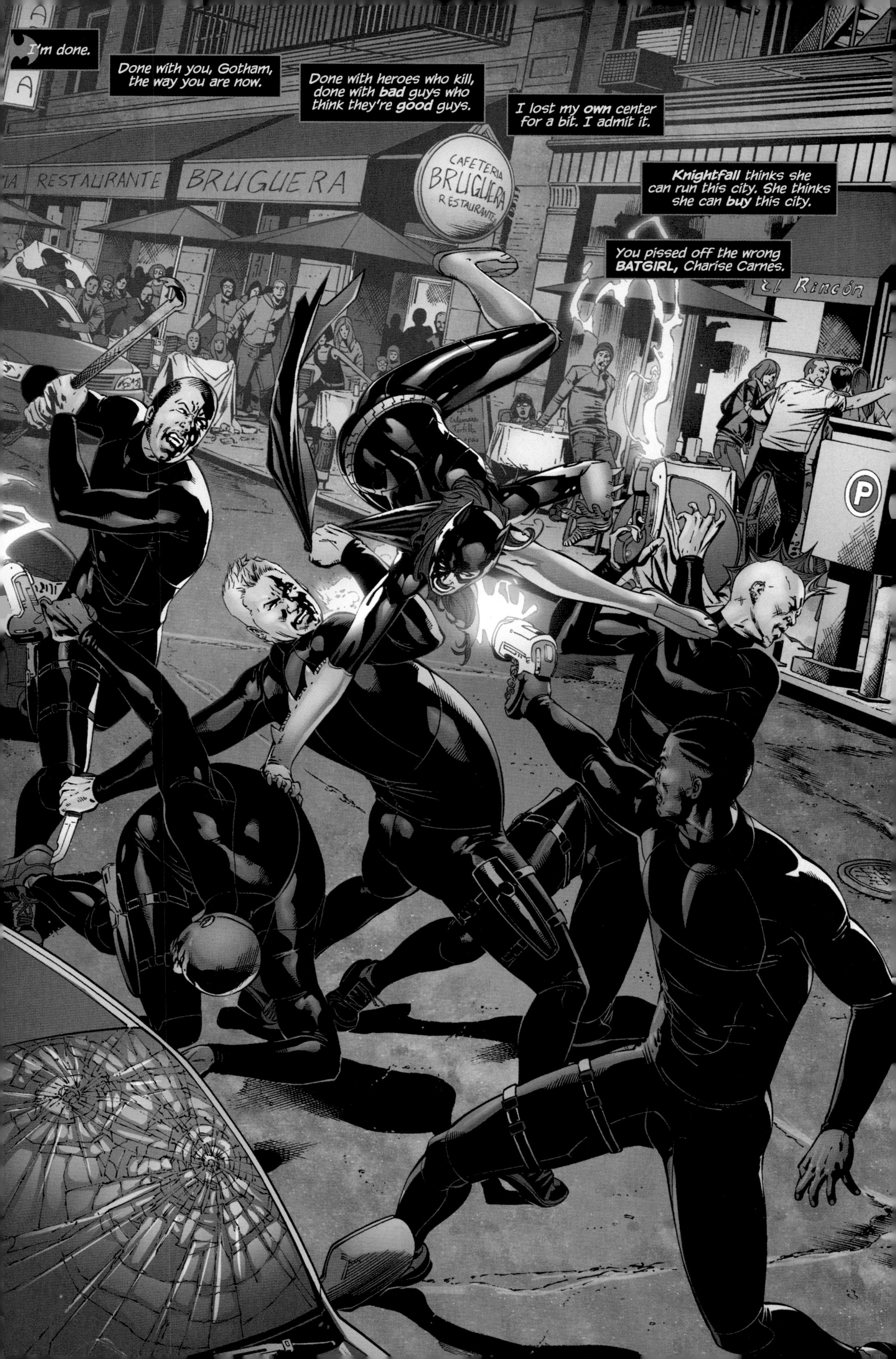

I'm done.
Done with you, Gotham, the way you are now.
Done with heroes who kill, done with **bad** guys who think they're **good** guys.
I lost my **own** center for a bit. I admit it.
Knightfall thinks she can run this city. She thinks she can **buy** this city.
You pissed off the wrong **BATGIRL**, Charise Carnes.
RESTAURANTE
BRUGUERA
CAFETERIA BRUGUERA RESTAURANTE
El Rincón

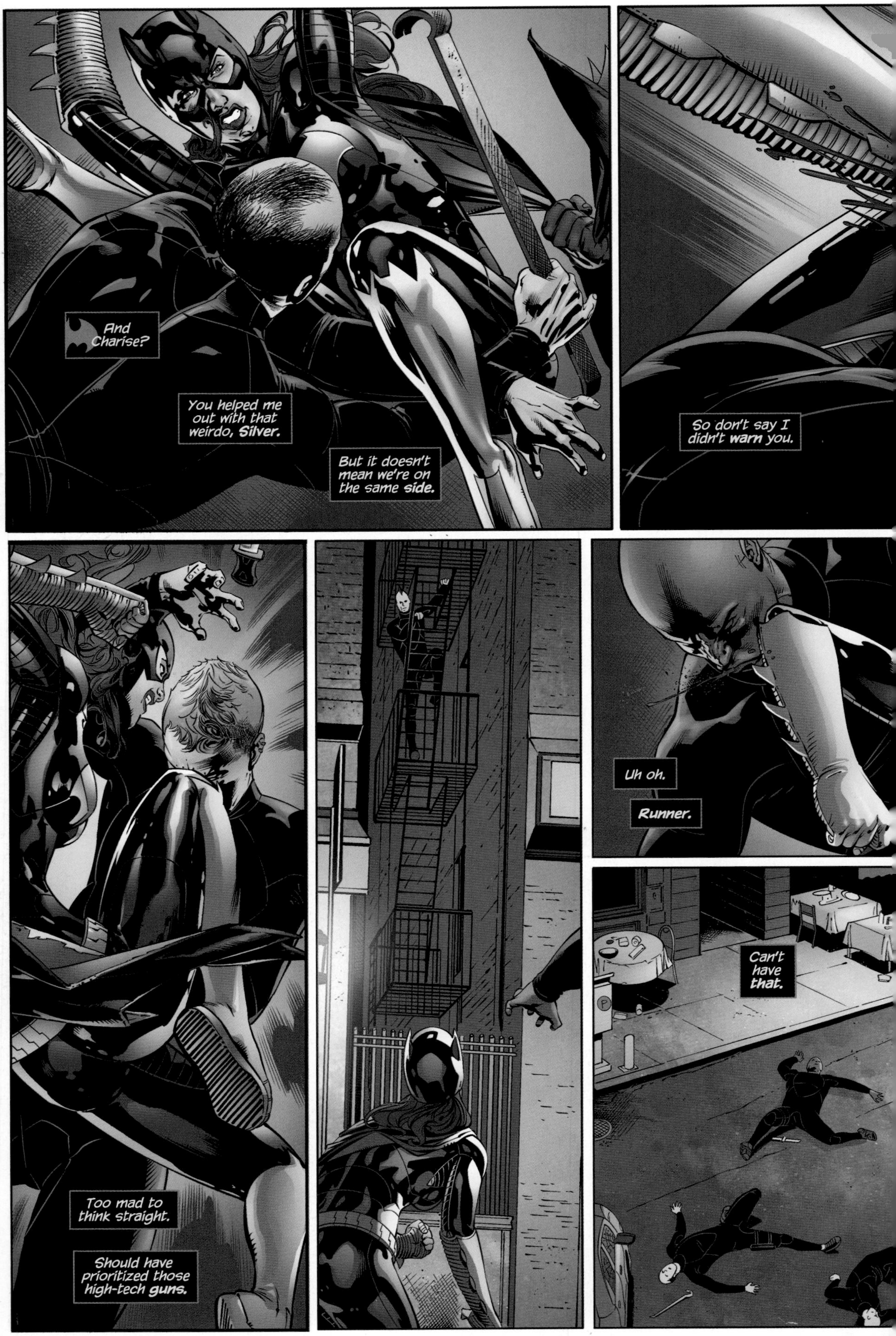
And Charise?
You helped me out with that weirdo, Silver.
But it doesn't mean we're on the same side.
So don't say I didn't warn you.
Too mad to think straight.
Should have prioritized those high-tech guns.
Uh oh.
Runner.
Can't have that.

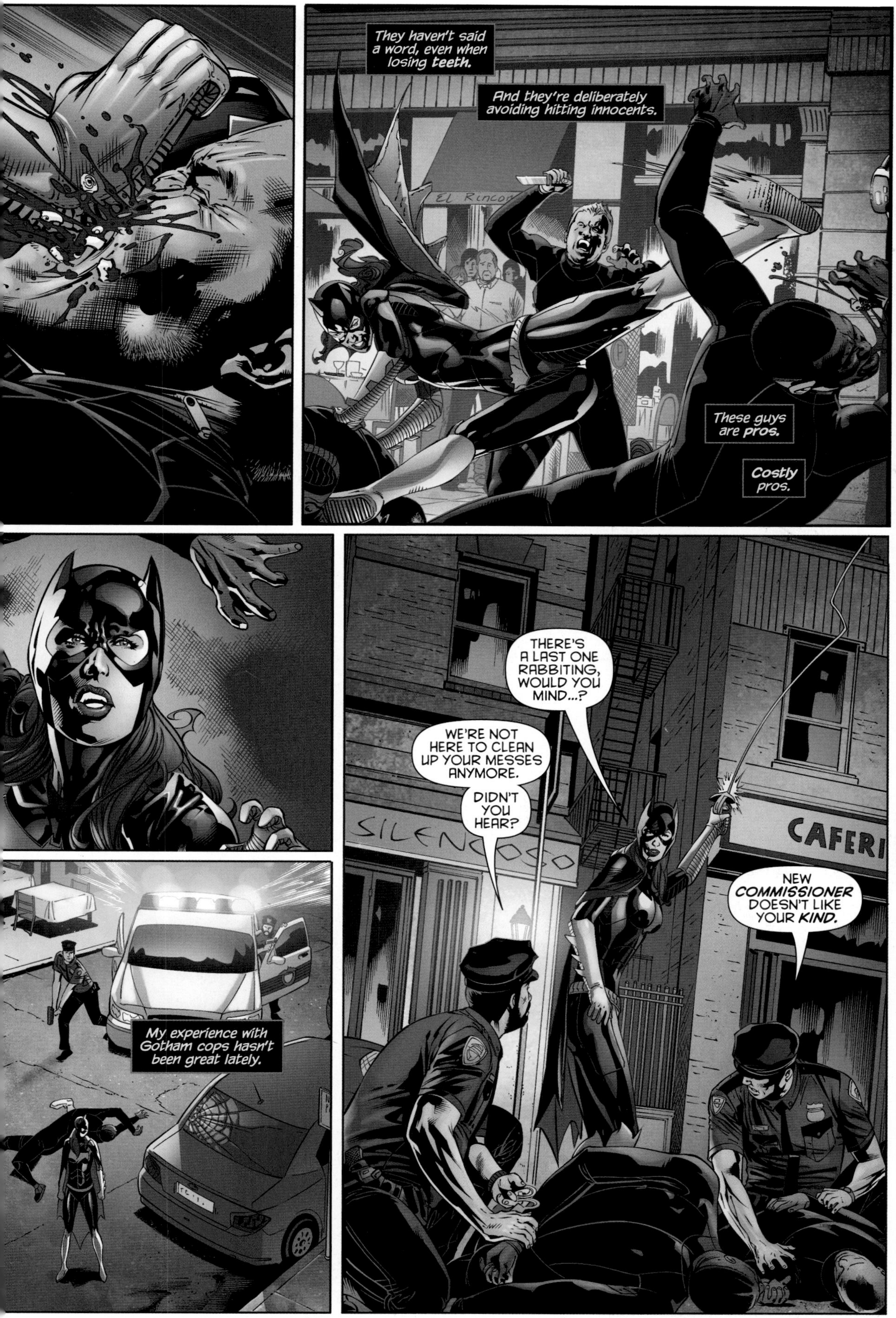

They haven't said a word, even when losing teeth.
And they're deliberately avoiding hitting innocents.
El Rincon
These guys are pros.
Costly pros.
My experience with Gotham cops hasn't been great lately.
THERE'S A LAST ONE RABBITING, WOULD YOU MIND...?
WE'RE NOT HERE TO CLEAN UP YOUR MESSES ANYMORE.
DIDN'T YOU HEAR?
NEW COMMISSIONER DOESN'T LIKE YOUR KIND.
SILENCIOSO
CAFERI

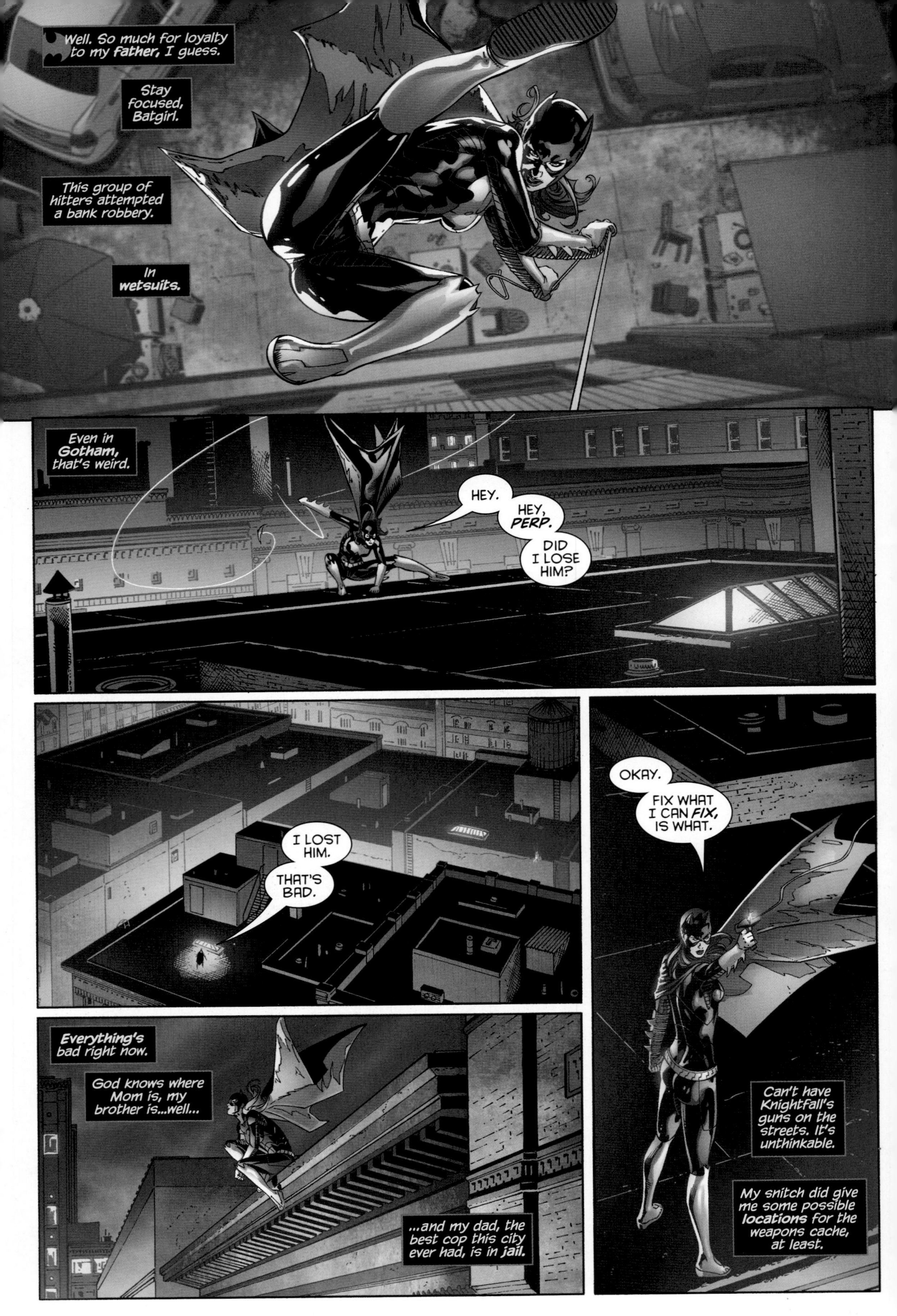
Well. So much for loyalty to my father, I guess.
Stay focused, Batgirl.
This group of hitters attempted a bank robbery.
In wetsuits.
Even in Gotham, that's weird.
HEY.
HEY, PERP.
DID I LOSE HIM?
I LOST HIM.
THAT'S BAD.
OKAY.
FIX WHAT I CAN FIX, IS WHAT.
Everything's bad right now.
God knows where Mom is, my brother is...well...
...and my dad, the best cop this city ever had, is in jail.
Can't have Knightfall's guns on the streets. It's unthinkable.
My snitch did give me some possible locations for the weapons cache, at least.

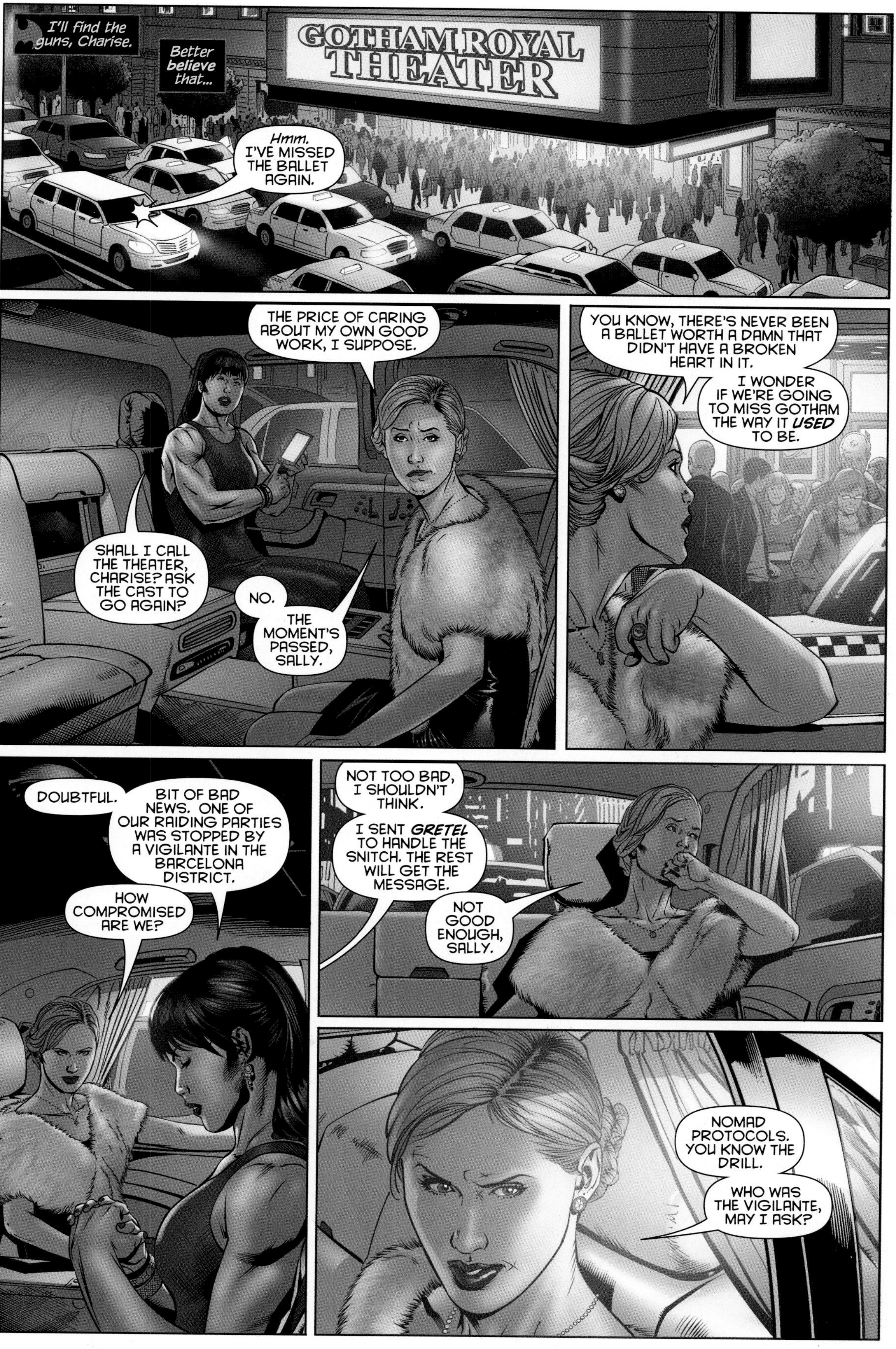
I'll find the guns, Charise.
Better believe that...
GOTHAM ROYAL THEATER
Hmm. I'VE MISSED THE BALLET AGAIN.
THE PRICE OF CARING ABOUT MY OWN GOOD WORK, I SUPPOSE.
SHALL I CALL THE THEATER, CHARISE? ASK THE CAST TO GO AGAIN?
NO.
THE MOMENT'S PASSED, SALLY.
YOU KNOW, THERE'S NEVER BEEN A BALLET WORTH A DAMN THAT DIDN'T HAVE A BROKEN HEART IN IT.
I WONDER IF WE'RE GOING TO MISS GOTHAM THE WAY IT USED TO BE.
DOUBTFUL.
BIT OF BAD NEWS. ONE OF OUR RAIDING PARTIES WAS STOPPED BY A VIGILANTE IN THE BARCELONA DISTRICT.
HOW COMPROMISED ARE WE?
NOT TOO BAD, I SHOULDN'T THINK.
I SENT GRETEL TO HANDLE THE SNITCH. THE REST WILL GET THE MESSAGE.
NOT GOOD ENOUGH, SALLY.
NOMAD PROTOCOLS. YOU KNOW THE DRILL.
WHO WAS THE VIGILANTE, MAY I ASK?

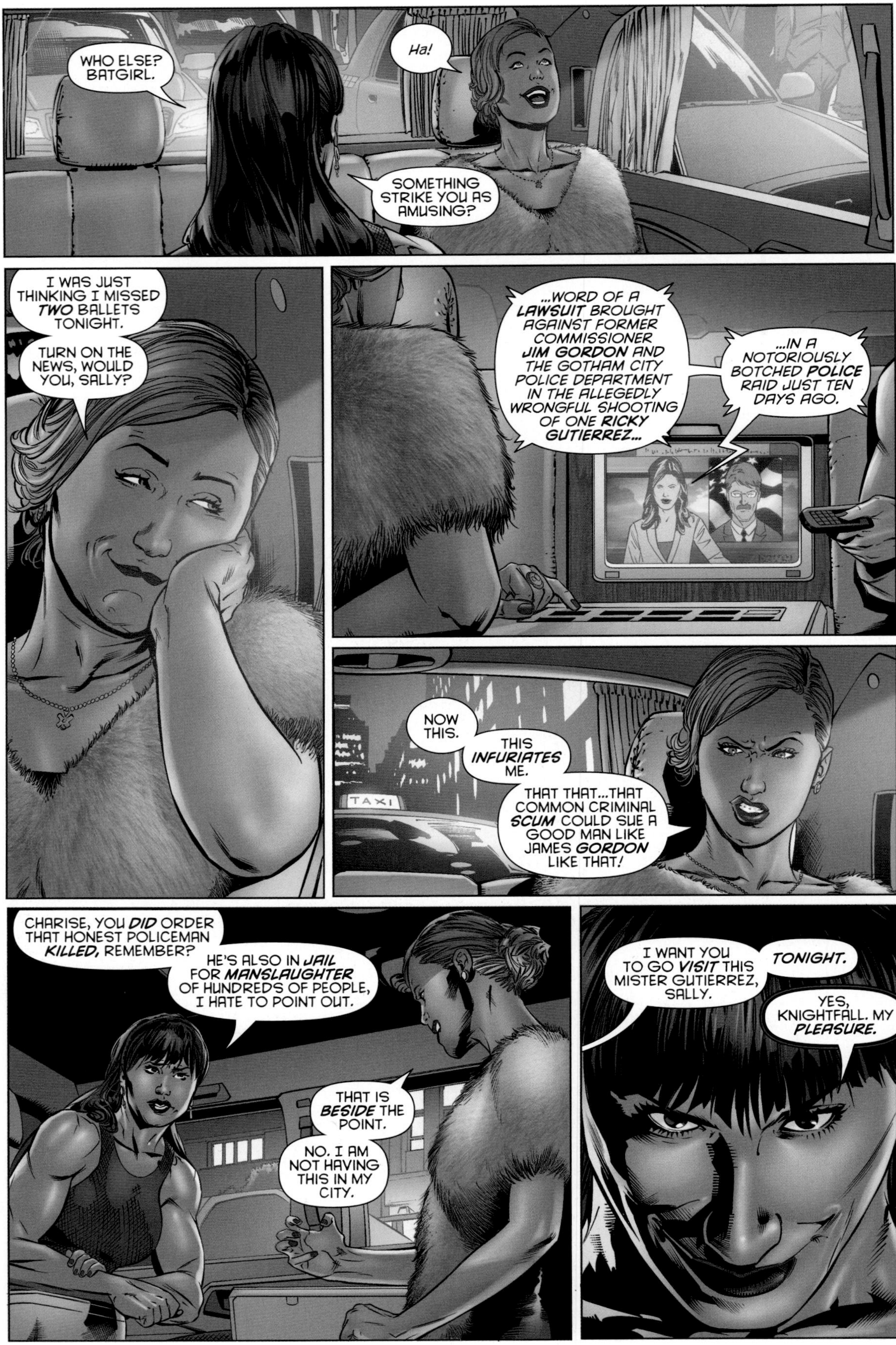
WHO ELSE? BATGIRL.
Ha!
SOMETHING STRIKE YOU AS AMUSING?
I WAS JUST THINKING I MISSED TWO BALLETS TONIGHT.
TURN ON THE NEWS, WOULD YOU, SALLY?
...WORD OF A LAWSUIT BROUGHT AGAINST FORMER COMMISSIONER JIM GORDON AND THE GOTHAM CITY POLICE DEPARTMENT IN THE ALLEGEDLY WRONGFUL SHOOTING OF ONE RICKY GUTIERREZ...
...IN A NOTORIOUSLY BOTCHED POLICE RAID JUST TEN DAYS AGO.
NOW THIS.
THIS INFURIATES ME.
THAT THAT...THAT COMMON CRIMINAL SCUM COULD SUE A GOOD MAN LIKE JAMES GORDON LIKE THAT!
TAXI
CHARISE, YOU DID ORDER THAT HONEST POLICEMAN KILLED, REMEMBER?
HE'S ALSO IN JAIL FOR MANSLAUGHTER OF HUNDREDS OF PEOPLE, I HATE TO POINT OUT.
THAT IS BESIDE THE POINT.
NO. I AM NOT HAVING THIS IN MY CITY.
I WANT YOU TO GO VISIT THIS MISTER GUTIERREZ, SALLY.
TONIGHT.
YES, KNIGHTFALL. MY PLEASURE.

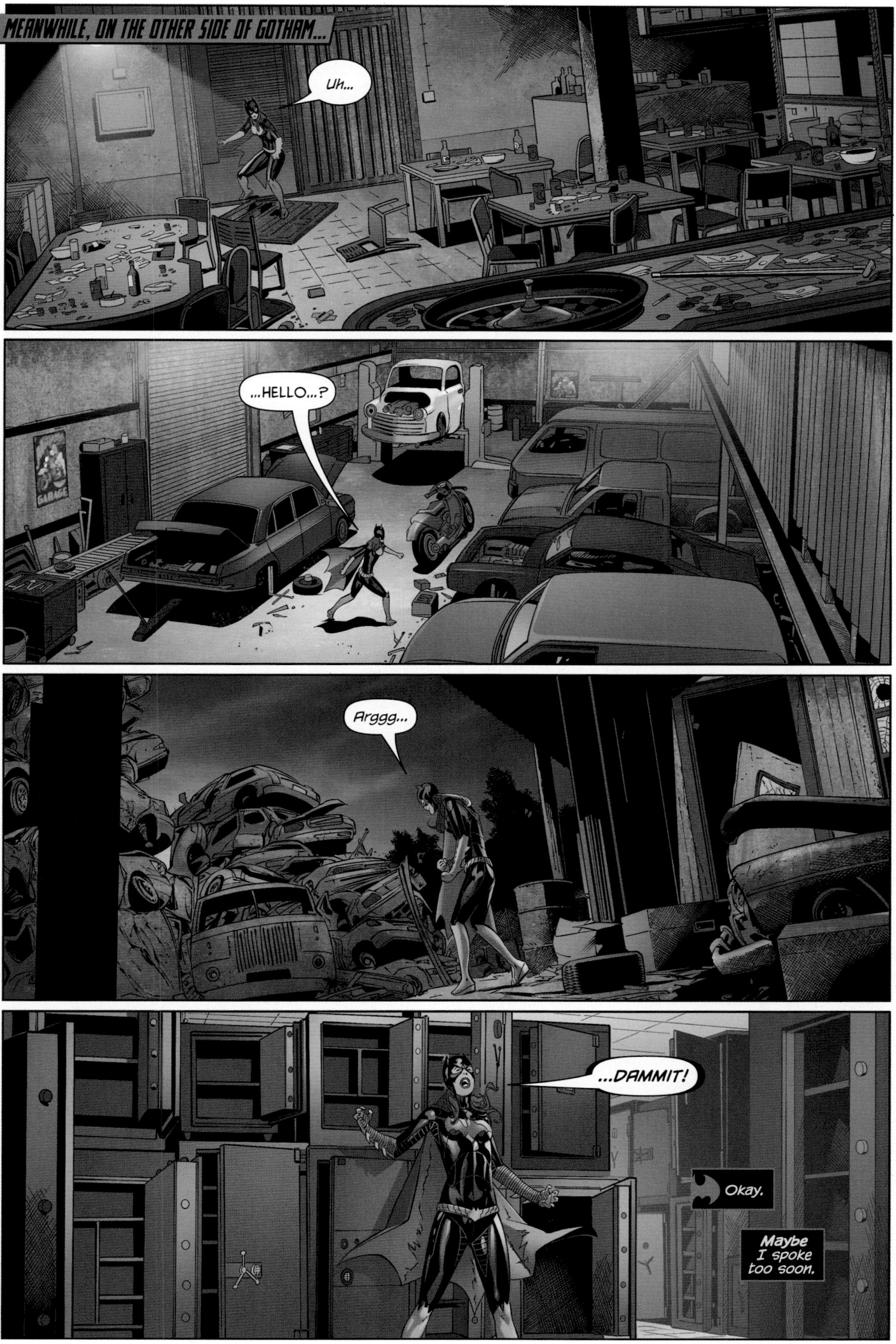
MEANWHILE, ON THE OTHER SIDE OF GOTHAM...
Uh...
...HELLO...?
Arggg...
...DAMMIT!
Okay.
Maybe I spoke too soon.

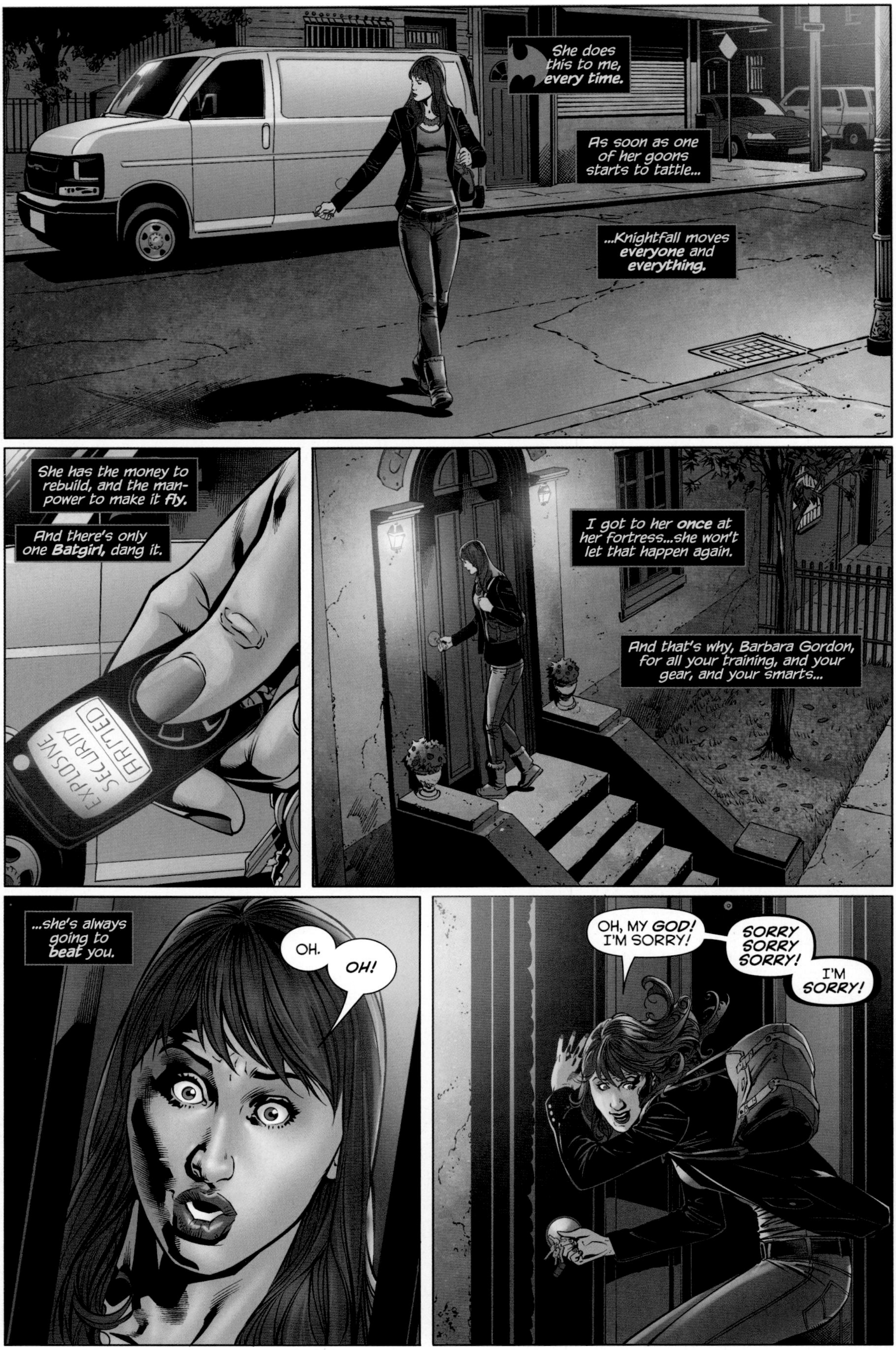
She does this to me, every time.
As soon as one of her goons starts to tattle...
...Knightfall moves everyone and everything.
She has the money to rebuild, and the man-power to make it fly.
And there's only one Batgirl, dang it.
EXPLOSIVE SECURITY ARMED
I got to her once at her fortress...she won't let that happen again.
And that's why, Barbara Gordon, for all your training, and your gear, and your smarts...
...she's always going to beat you.
OH.
OH!
OH, MY GOD! I'M SORRY!
SORRY SORRY SORRY!
I'M SORRY!

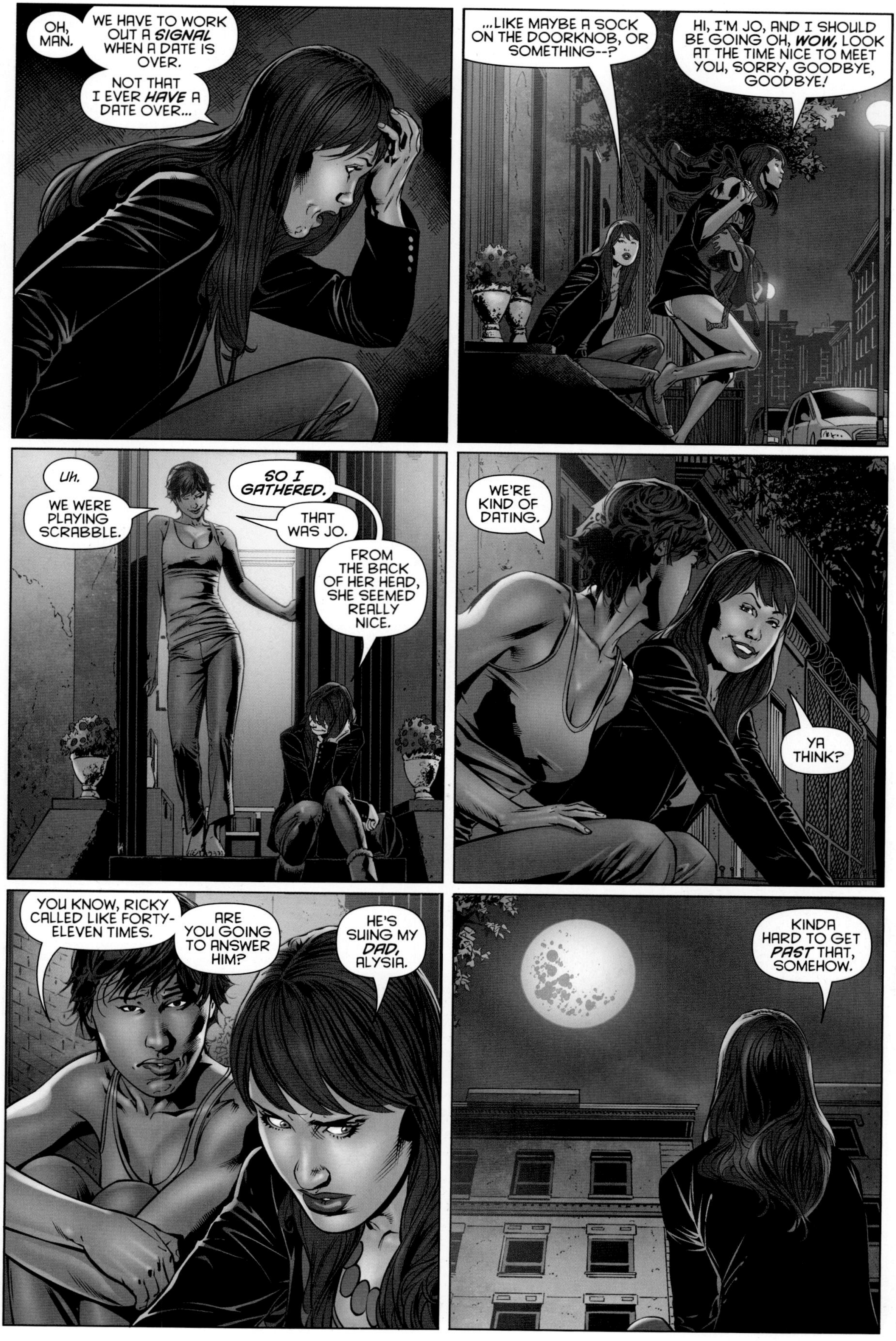
OH, MAN.
WE HAVE TO WORK OUT A SIGNAL WHEN A DATE IS OVER.
NOT THAT I EVER HAVE A DATE OVER...
...LIKE MAYBE A SOCK ON THE DOORKNOB, OR SOMETHING--?
HI, I'M JO, AND I SHOULD BE GOING OH, WOW, LOOK AT THE TIME NICE TO MEET YOU, SORRY, GOODBYE, GOODBYE!
Uh.
WE WERE PLAYING SCRABBLE.
SO I GATHERED.
THAT WAS JO.
FROM THE BACK OF HER HEAD, SHE SEEMED REALLY NICE.
WE'RE KIND OF DATING.
YA THINK?
YOU KNOW, RICKY CALLED LIKE FORTY-ELEVEN TIMES.
ARE YOU GOING TO ANSWER HIM?
HE'S SUING MY DAD, ALYSIA.
KINDA HARD TO GET PAST THAT, SOMEHOW.

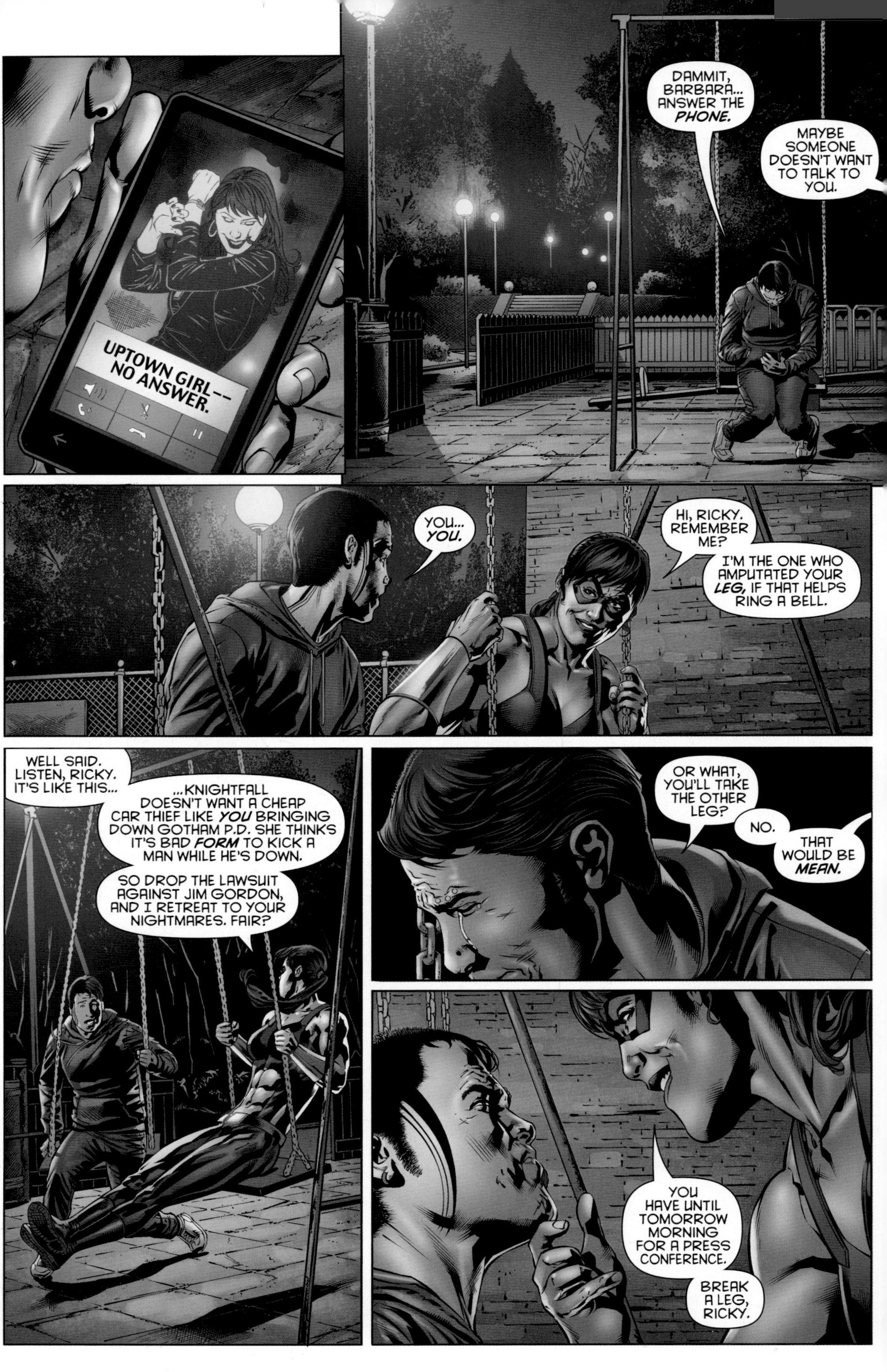
UPTOWN GIRL-- NO ANSWER.
DAMMIT, BARBARA... ANSWER THE *PHONE.*
MAYBE SOMEONE DOESN'T WANT TO TALK TO YOU.
YOU... *YOU.*
HI, RICKY. REMEMBER ME?
I'M THE ONE WHO AMPUTATED YOUR *LEG,* IF THAT HELPS RING A BELL.
WELL SAID. LISTEN, RICKY. IT'S LIKE THIS...
...KNIGHTFALL DOESN'T WANT A CHEAP CAR THIEF LIKE *YOU* BRINGING DOWN GOTHAM P.D. SHE THINKS IT'S BAD *FORM* TO KICK A MAN WHILE HE'S DOWN.
SO DROP THE LAWSUIT AGAINST JIM GORDON, AND I RETREAT TO YOUR NIGHTMARES. FAIR?
OR WHAT, YOU'LL TAKE THE OTHER LEG?
NO.
THAT WOULD BE *MEAN.*
YOU HAVE UNTIL TOMORROW MORNING FOR A PRESS CONFERENCE.
BREAK A LEG, RICKY.

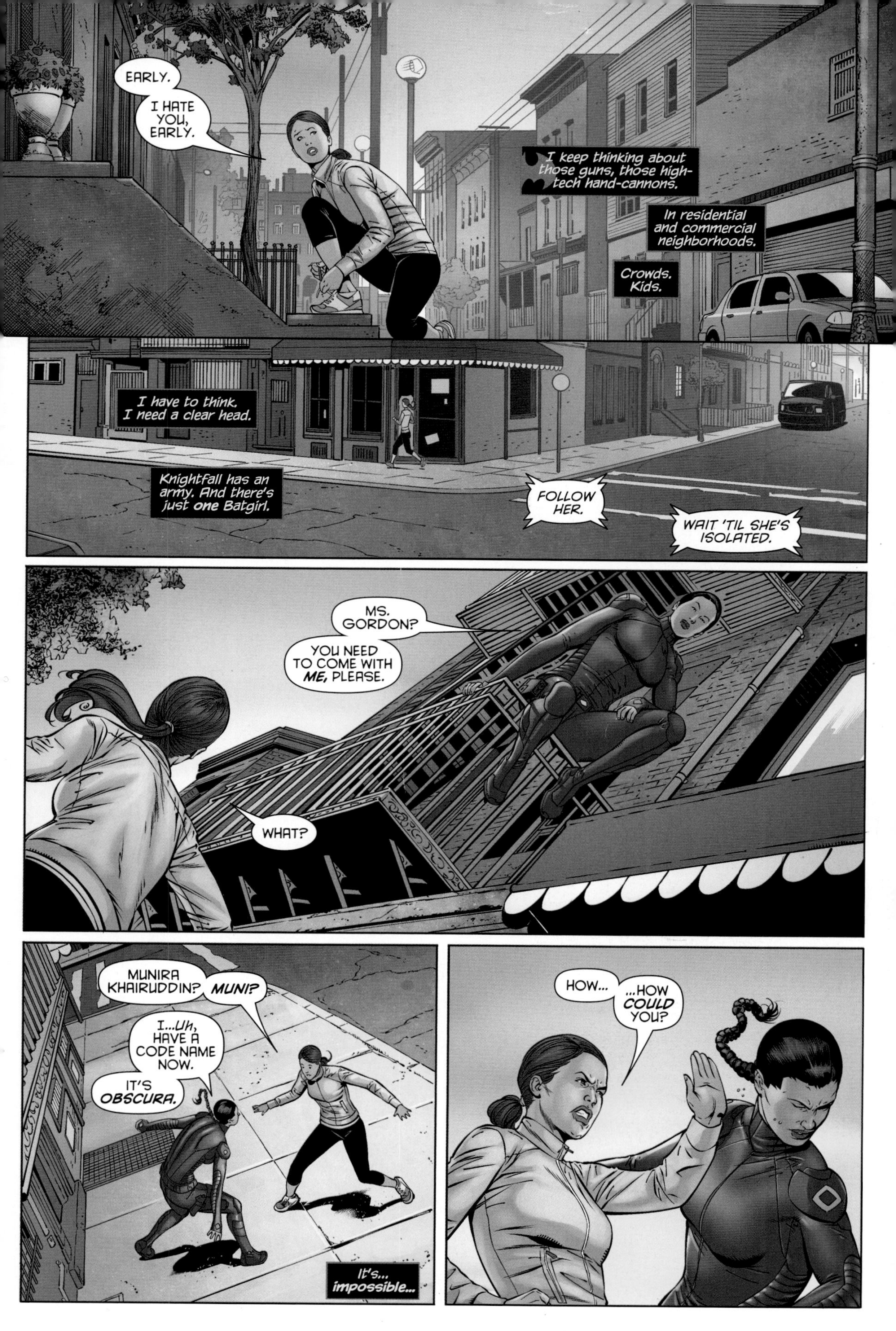
EARLY.
I HATE YOU, EARLY.
I keep thinking about those guns, those high-tech hand-cannons.
In residential and commercial neighborhoods.
Crowds. Kids.
I have to think. I need a clear head.
Knightfall has an army. And there's just one Batgirl.
FOLLOW HER.
WAIT 'TIL SHE'S ISOLATED.
MS. GORDON?
YOU NEED TO COME WITH ME, PLEASE.
WHAT?
MUNIRA KHAIRUDDIN? MUNI?
I...UH, HAVE A CODE NAME NOW.
IT'S OBSCURA.
It's... impossible...
HOW...
...HOW COULD YOU?

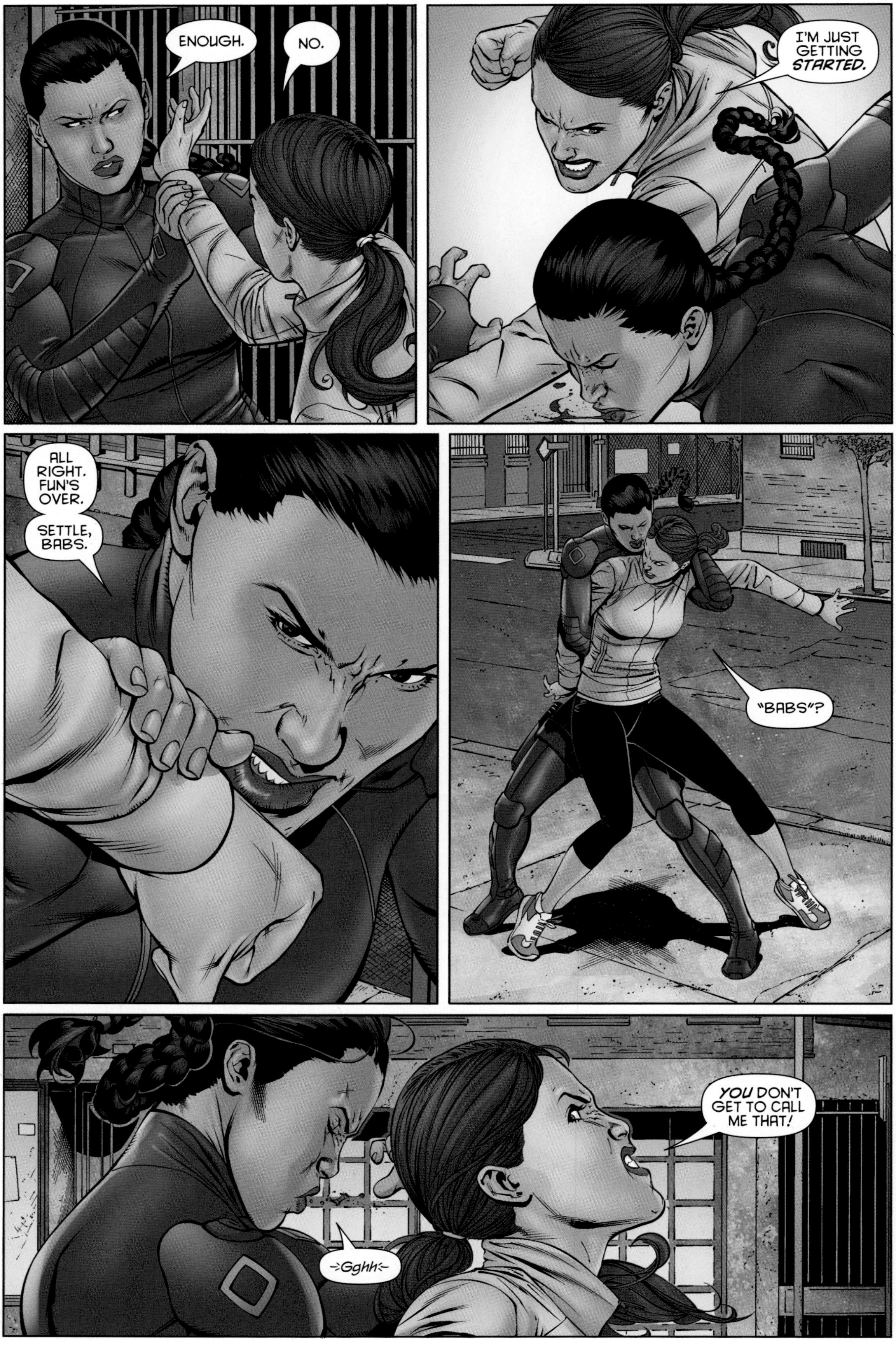
ENOUGH.
NO.
I'M JUST GETTING STARTED.
ALL RIGHT. FUN'S OVER.
SETTLE, BABS.
"BABS"?
YOU DON'T GET TO CALL ME THAT!
Gghh

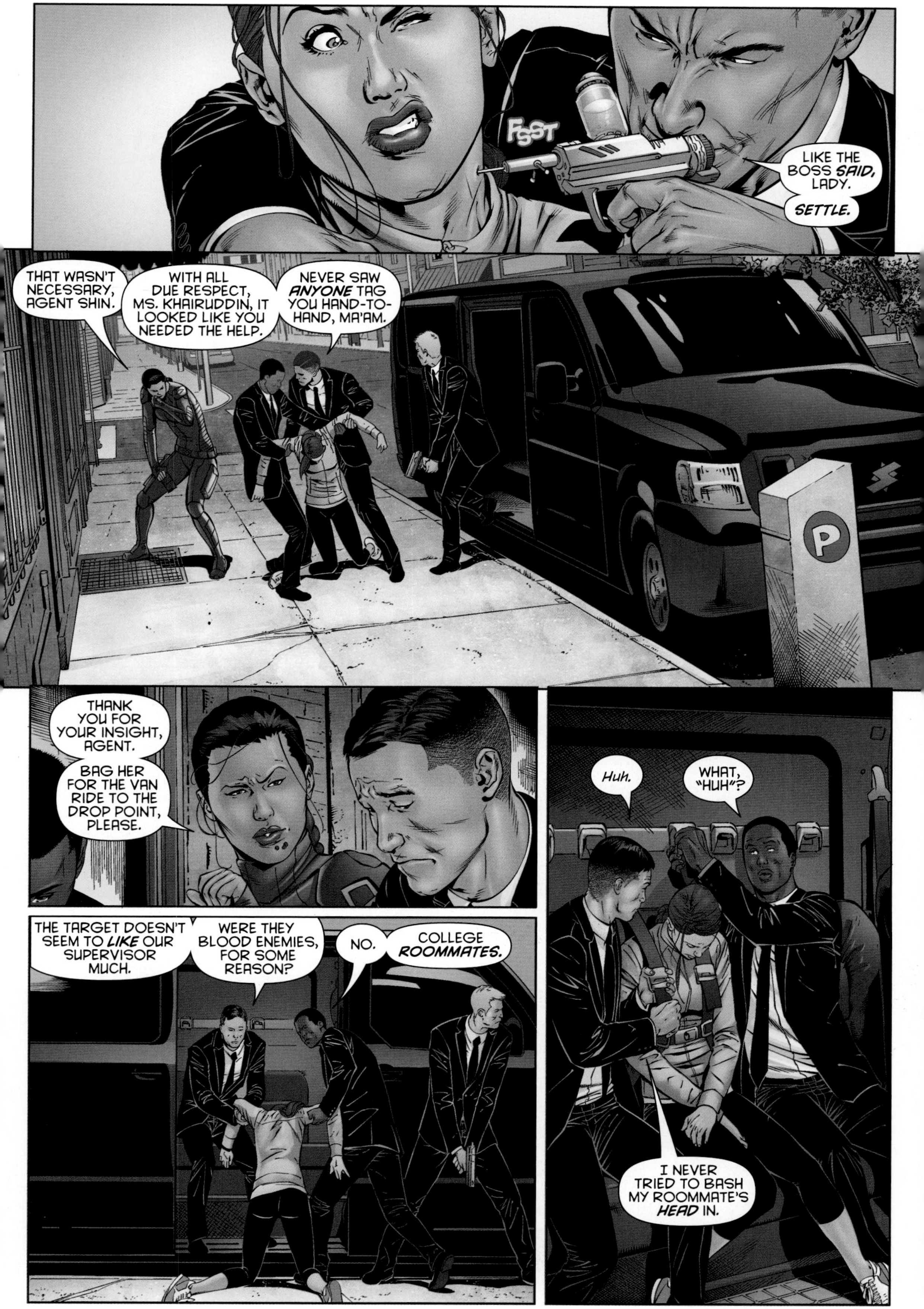
FSST
LIKE THE BOSS SAID, LADY.
SETTLE.
THAT WASN'T NECESSARY, AGENT SHIN.
WITH ALL DUE RESPECT, MS. KHAIRUDDIN, IT LOOKED LIKE YOU NEEDED THE HELP.
NEVER SAW ANYONE TAG YOU HAND-TO-HAND, MA'AM.
THANK YOU FOR YOUR INSIGHT, AGENT.
BAG HER FOR THE VAN RIDE TO THE DROP POINT, PLEASE.
THE TARGET DOESN'T SEEM TO LIKE OUR SUPERVISOR MUCH.
WERE THEY BLOOD ENEMIES, FOR SOME REASON?
NO.
COLLEGE ROOMMATES.
Huh.
WHAT, "HUH"?
I NEVER TRIED TO BASH MY ROOMMATE'S HEAD IN.

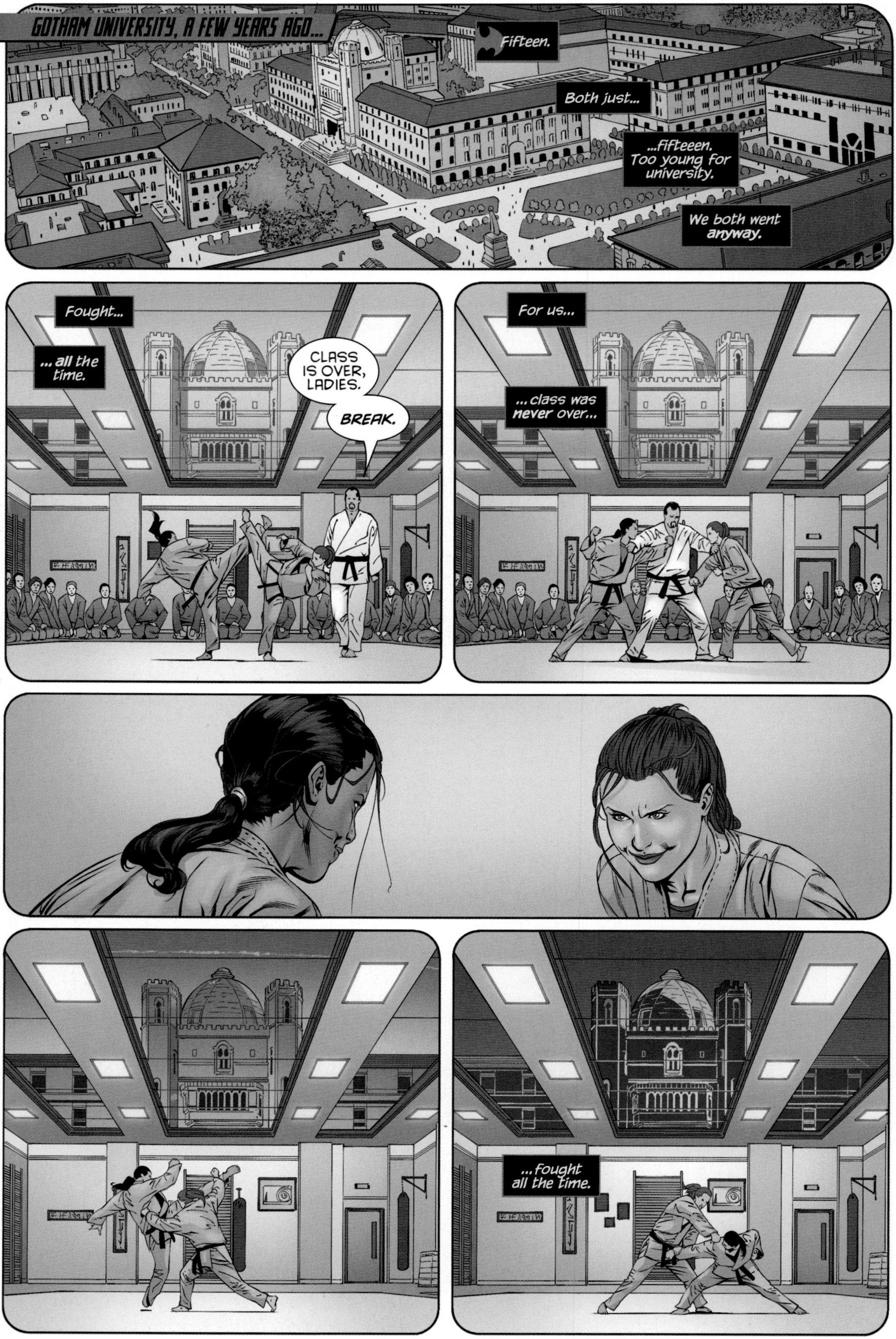
GOTHAM UNIVERSITY, A FEW YEARS AGO...
Fifteen.
Both just...
...fifteeen. Too young for university.
We both went anyway.
Fought...
...all the time.
CLASS IS OVER, LADIES.
BREAK.
For us...
...class was never over...
...fought all the time.

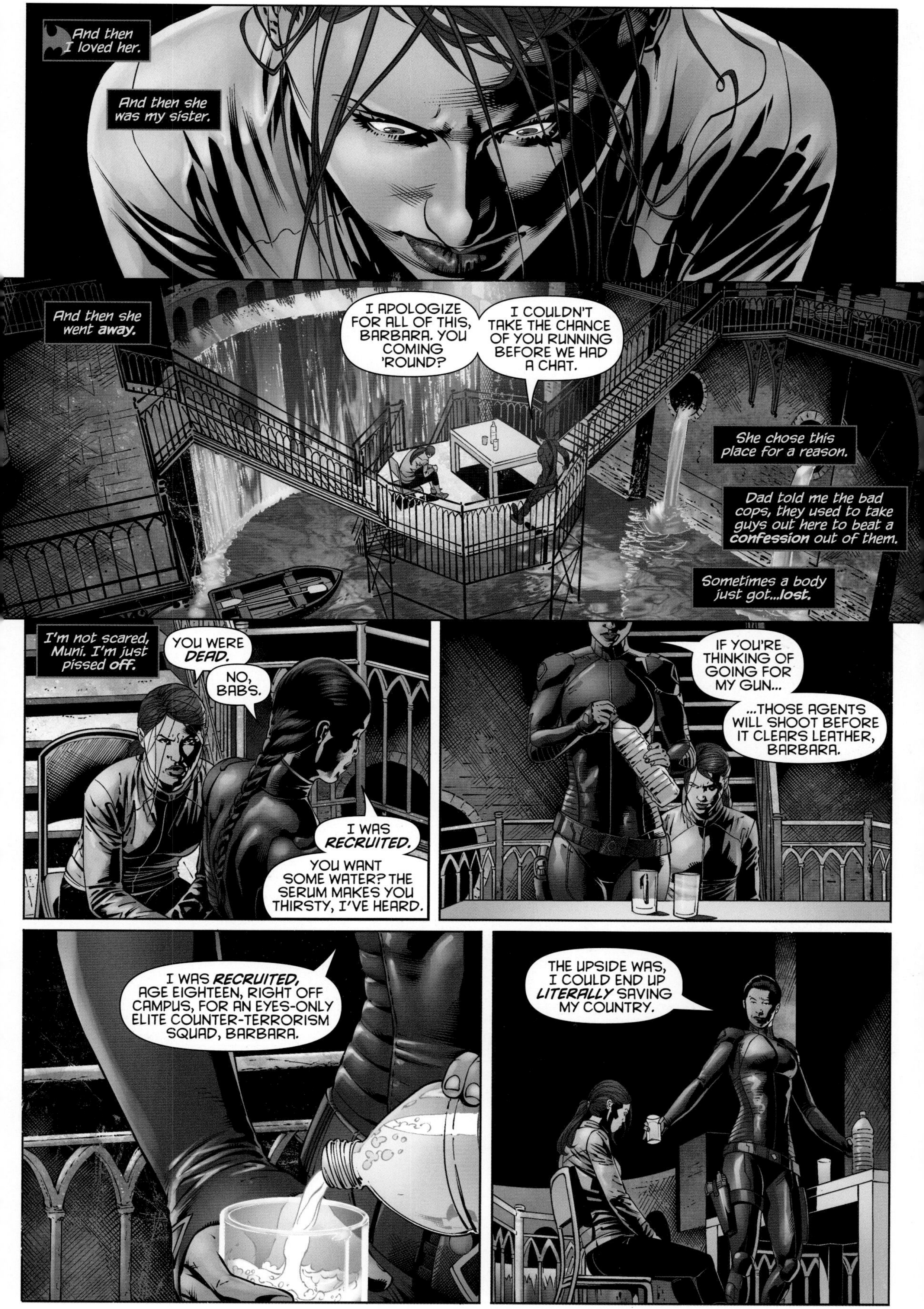
And then I loved her.
And then she was my sister.
And then she went away.
I APOLOGIZE FOR ALL OF THIS, BARBARA. YOU COMING 'ROUND?
I COULDN'T TAKE THE CHANCE OF YOU RUNNING BEFORE WE HAD A CHAT.
She chose this place for a reason.
Dad told me the bad cops, they used to take guys out here to beat a confession out of them.
Sometimes a body just got...lost.
I'm not scared, Muni. I'm just pissed off.
YOU WERE DEAD.
NO, BABS.
I WAS RECRUITED.
YOU WANT SOME WATER? THE SERUM MAKES YOU THIRSTY, I'VE HEARD.
IF YOU'RE THINKING OF GOING FOR MY GUN...
...THOSE AGENTS WILL SHOOT BEFORE IT CLEARS LEATHER, BARBARA.
I WAS RECRUITED, AGE EIGHTEEN, RIGHT OFF CAMPUS, FOR AN EYES-ONLY ELITE COUNTER-TERRORISM SQUAD, BARBARA.
THE UPSIDE WAS, I COULD END UP LITERALLY SAVING MY COUNTRY.

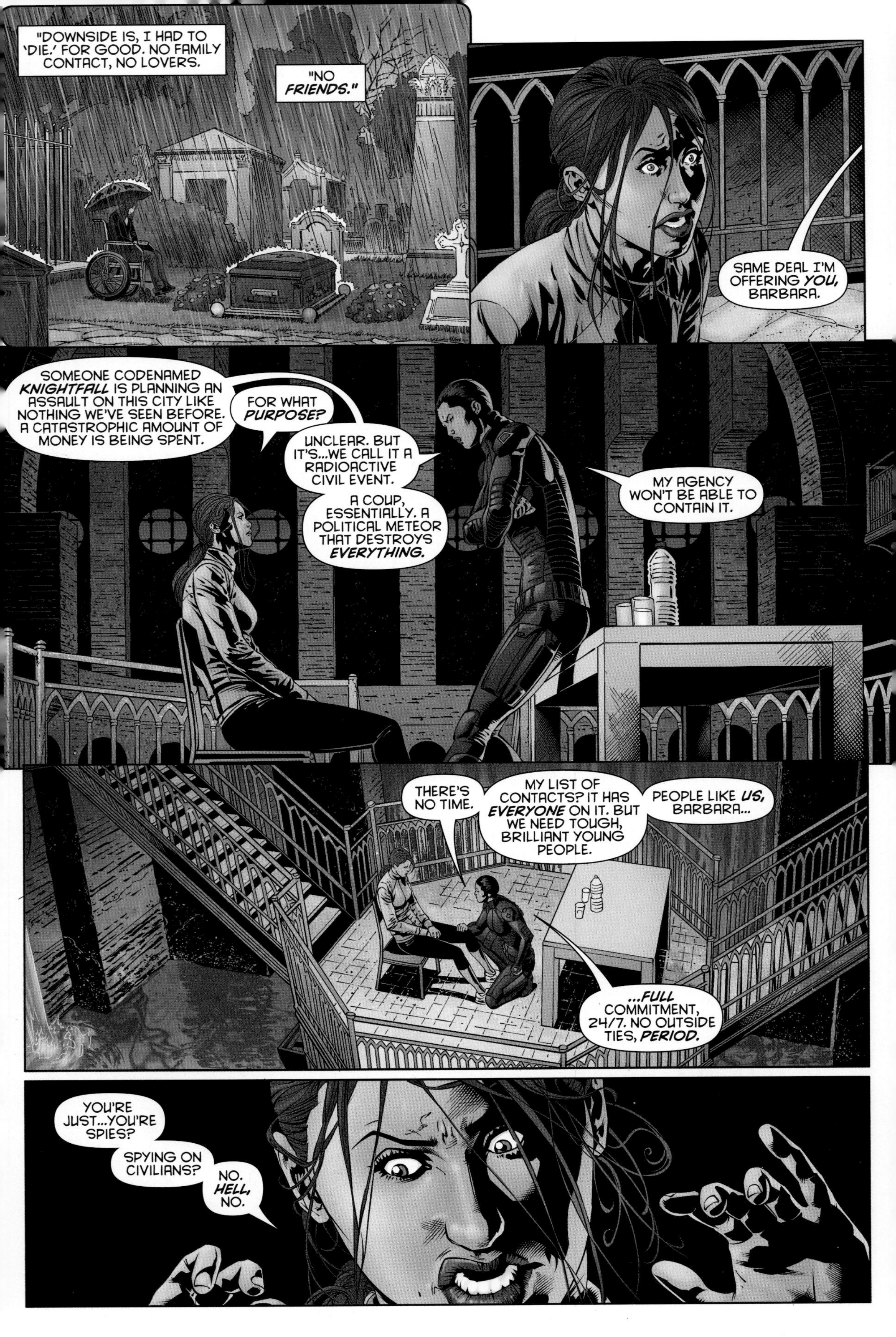
"DOWNSIDE IS, I HAD TO 'DIE.' FOR GOOD. NO FAMILY CONTACT, NO LOVERS.
"NO FRIENDS."
SAME DEAL I'M OFFERING YOU, BARBARA.
SOMEONE CODENAMED KNIGHTFALL IS PLANNING AN ASSAULT ON THIS CITY LIKE NOTHING WE'VE SEEN BEFORE. A CATASTROPHIC AMOUNT OF MONEY IS BEING SPENT.
FOR WHAT PURPOSE?
UNCLEAR. BUT IT'S...WE CALL IT A RADIOACTIVE CIVIL EVENT.
A COUP, ESSENTIALLY. A POLITICAL METEOR THAT DESTROYS EVERYTHING.
MY AGENCY WON'T BE ABLE TO CONTAIN IT.
THERE'S NO TIME.
MY LIST OF CONTACTS? IT HAS EVERYONE ON IT. BUT WE NEED TOUGH, BRILLIANT YOUNG PEOPLE.
PEOPLE LIKE US, BARBARA...
...FULL COMMITMENT, 24/7. NO OUTSIDE TIES, PERIOD.
YOU'RE JUST...YOU'RE SPIES?
SPYING ON CIVILIANS?
NO. HELL, NO.

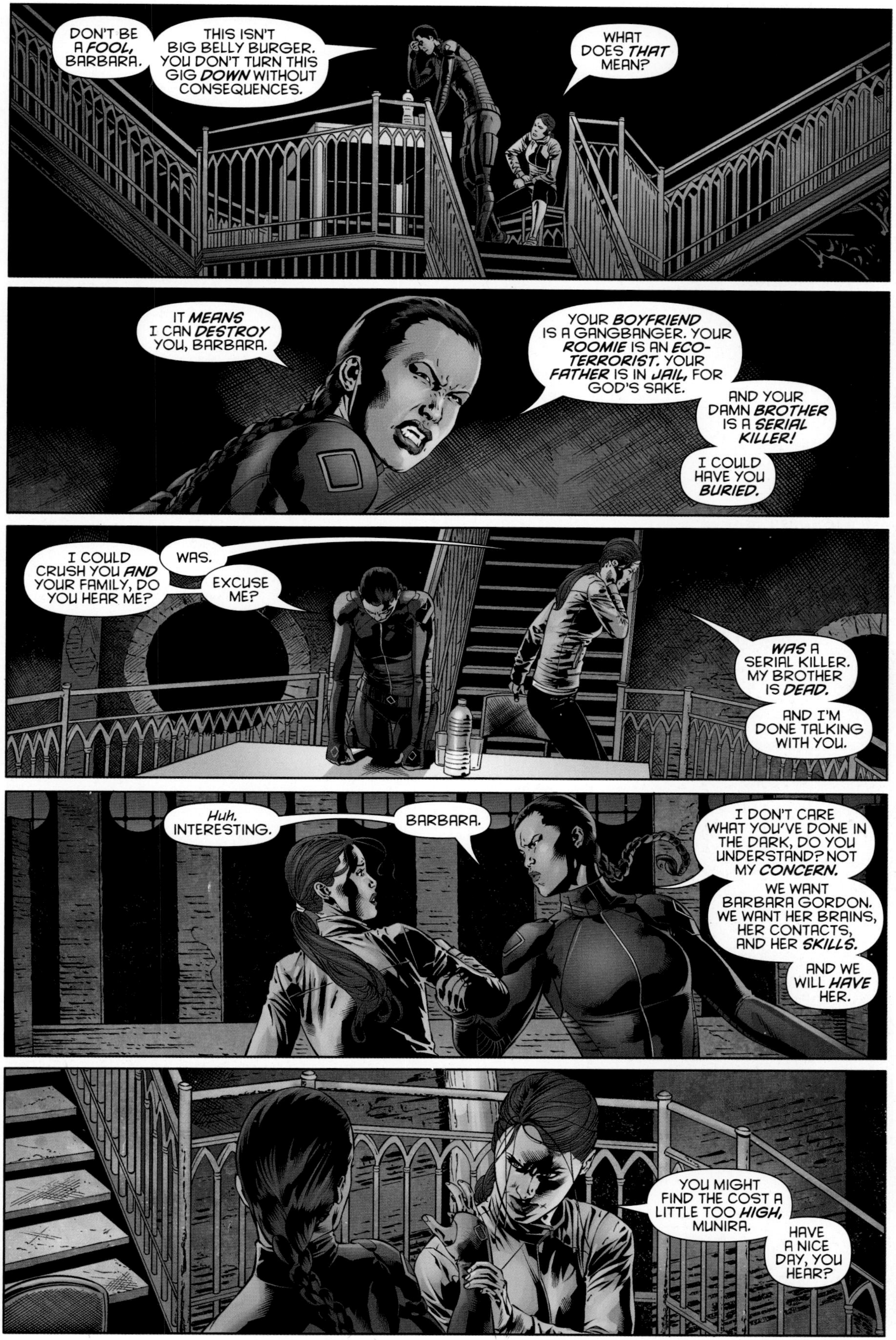
DON'T BE A *FOOL,* BARBARA.
THIS ISN'T BIG BELLY BURGER. YOU DON'T TURN THIS GIG *DOWN* WITHOUT CONSEQUENCES.
WHAT DOES *THAT* MEAN?
IT *MEANS* I CAN *DESTROY* YOU, BARBARA.
YOUR *BOYFRIEND* IS A GANGBANGER. YOUR *ROOMIE* IS AN *ECO-TERRORIST.* YOUR *FATHER* IS IN *JAIL,* FOR GOD'S SAKE.
AND YOUR DAMN *BROTHER* IS A *SERIAL KILLER!*
I COULD HAVE YOU *BURIED.*
I COULD CRUSH YOU *AND* YOUR FAMILY, DO YOU HEAR ME?
WAS.
EXCUSE ME?
WAS A SERIAL KILLER. MY BROTHER IS *DEAD.*
AND I'M DONE TALKING WITH YOU.
Huh. INTERESTING.
BARBARA.
I DON'T CARE WHAT YOU'VE DONE IN THE DARK, DO YOU UNDERSTAND? NOT MY *CONCERN.*
WE WANT BARBARA GORDON. WE WANT HER BRAINS, HER CONTACTS, AND HER *SKILLS.*
AND WE WILL *HAVE* HER.
YOU MIGHT FIND THE COST A LITTLE TOO *HIGH,* MUNIRA.
HAVE A NICE DAY, YOU HEAR?

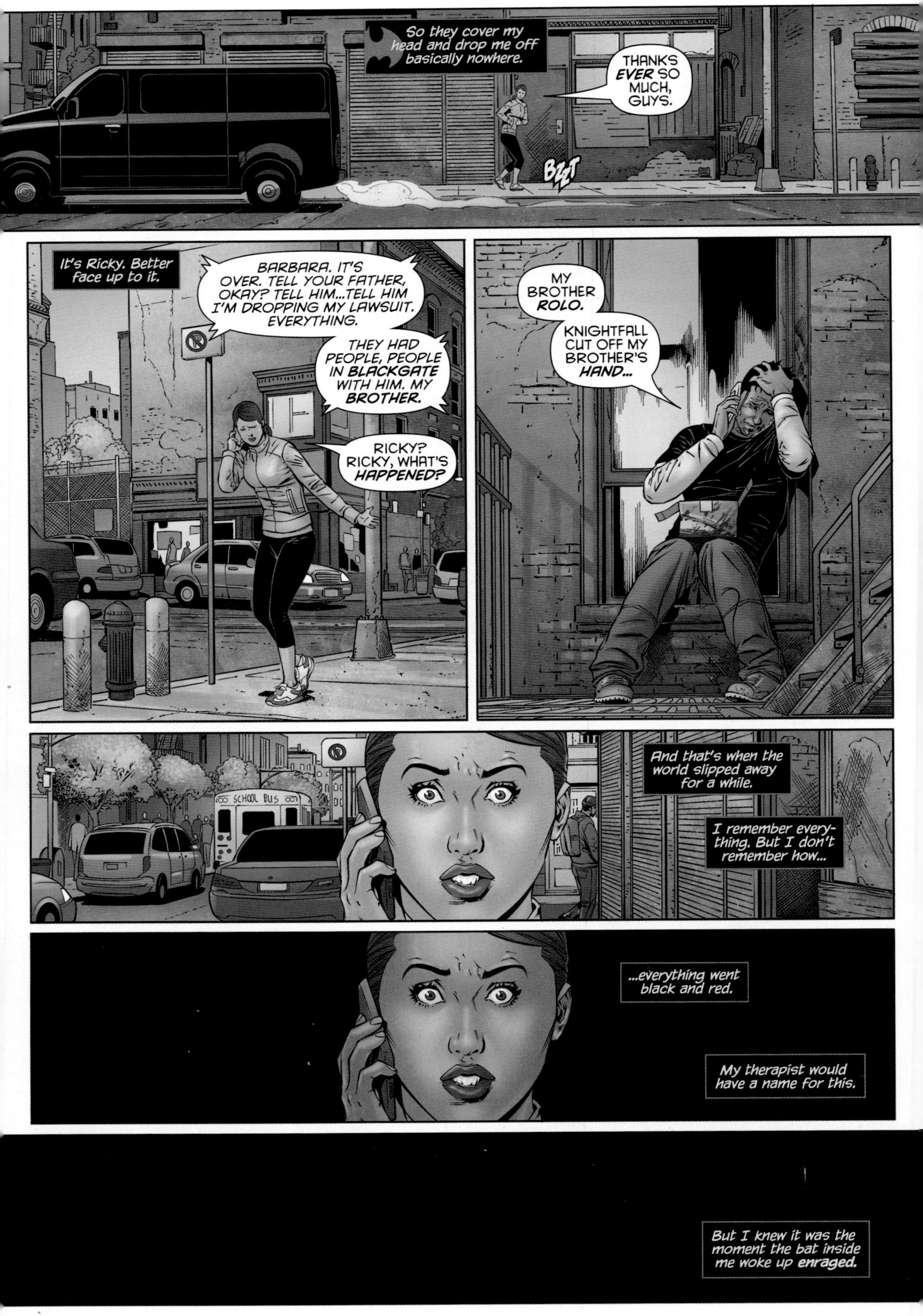
So they cover my head and drop me off basically nowhere.
THANKS EVER SO MUCH, GUYS.
BZZT
It's Ricky. Better face up to it.
BARBARA. IT'S OVER. TELL YOUR FATHER, OKAY? TELL HIM...TELL HIM I'M DROPPING MY LAWSUIT. EVERYTHING.
THEY HAD PEOPLE, PEOPLE IN BLACKGATE WITH HIM. MY BROTHER.
RICKY? RICKY, WHAT'S HAPPENED?
MY BROTHER ROLO.
KNIGHTFALL CUT OFF MY BROTHER'S HAND...
SCHOOL BUS
And that's when the world slipped away for a while.
I remember everything. But I don't remember how...
...everything went black and red.
My therapist would have a name for this.
But I knew it was the moment the bat inside me woke up enraged.

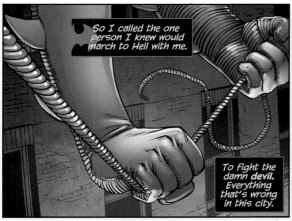

So I called the one person I knew would march to Hell with me.

To fight the damn *devil*. Everything that's wrong in this city.

NICE *ENTRANCE*, RED.

And because she is who she is, she showed.

The one and only *Black Canary.*

I'M IN. OF COURSE I'M IN.

LISTEN, LAST TIME YOU FACED THIS WOMAN YOU NEARLY GOT STABBED TO DEATH, AND THAT WAS *WITH* BACKUP.

KNIGHTFALL AND THE DISGRACED WILL BE *READY* THIS TIME.

EVERY TIME I SHUT DOWN AN OPERATION, SHE MOVES EVERYTHING AND EVERYONE. I CAN'T...

...I CAN'T GET TRACTION. AND I CAN'T LET HER *SLIDE* ANYMORE.

IT MIGHT BE A SUICIDE RUN.

IT'S NOT THE BEST ODDS, I'LL GRANT YOU.

MAYBE I CAN HELP?

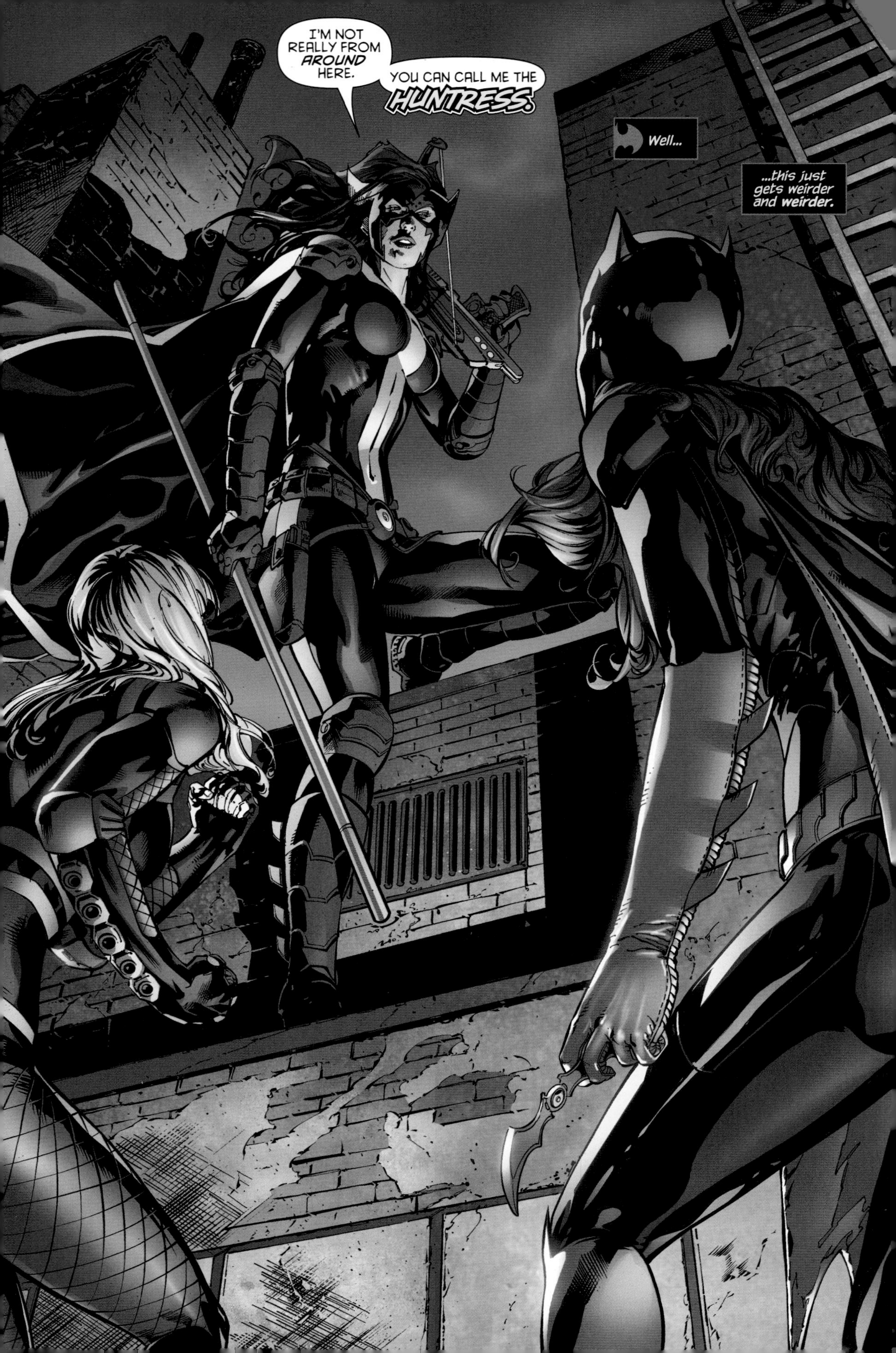
I'M NOT REALLY FROM AROUND HERE.
YOU CAN CALL ME THE HUNTRESS.
Well...
...this just gets weirder and weirder.

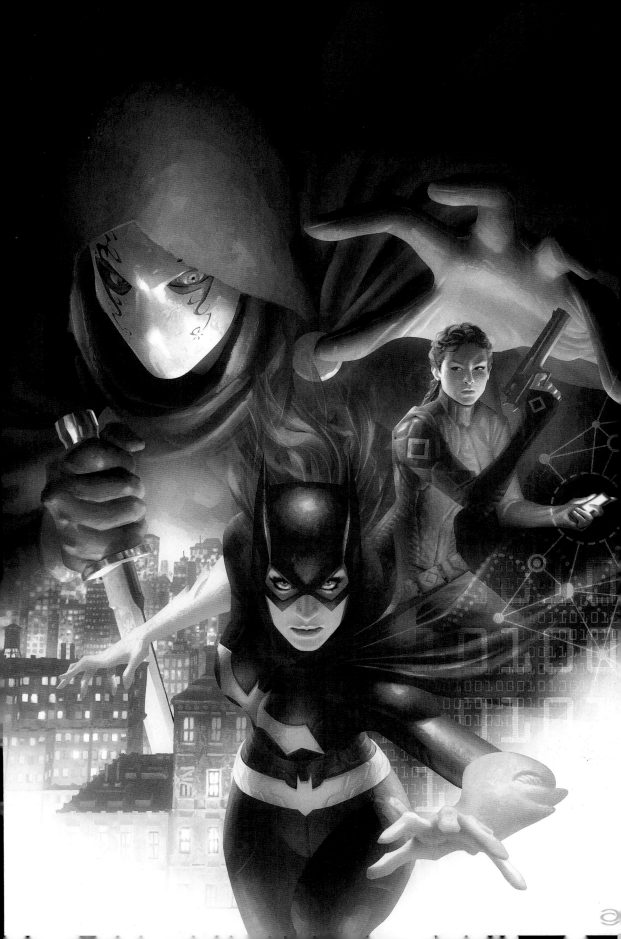

GAIL SIMONE writer **FERNANDO PASARIN** penciller **JONATHAN GLAPION** **MATT RYAN** inkers **BLOND** colorist **ALEX GARNER** cover artist

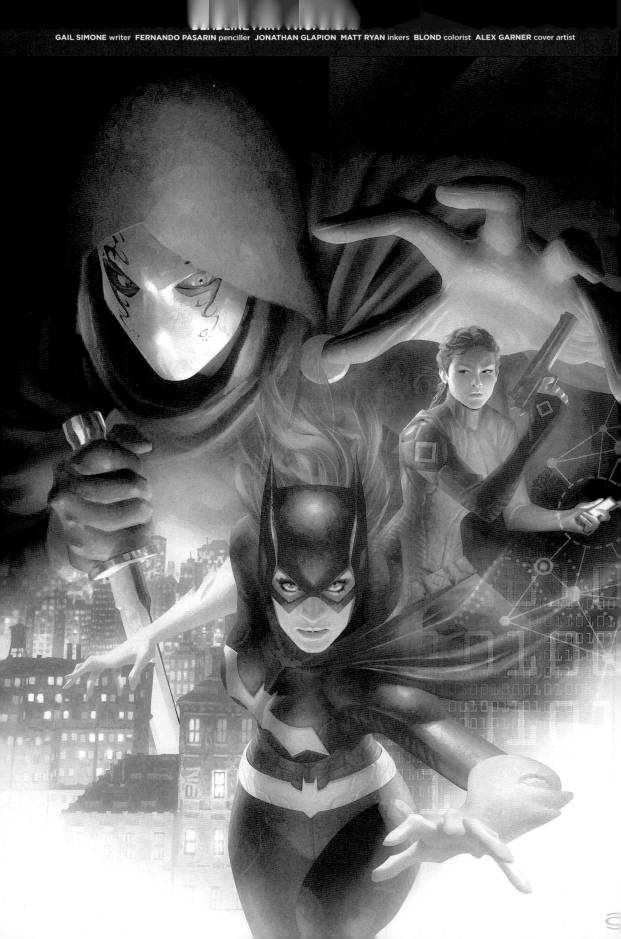

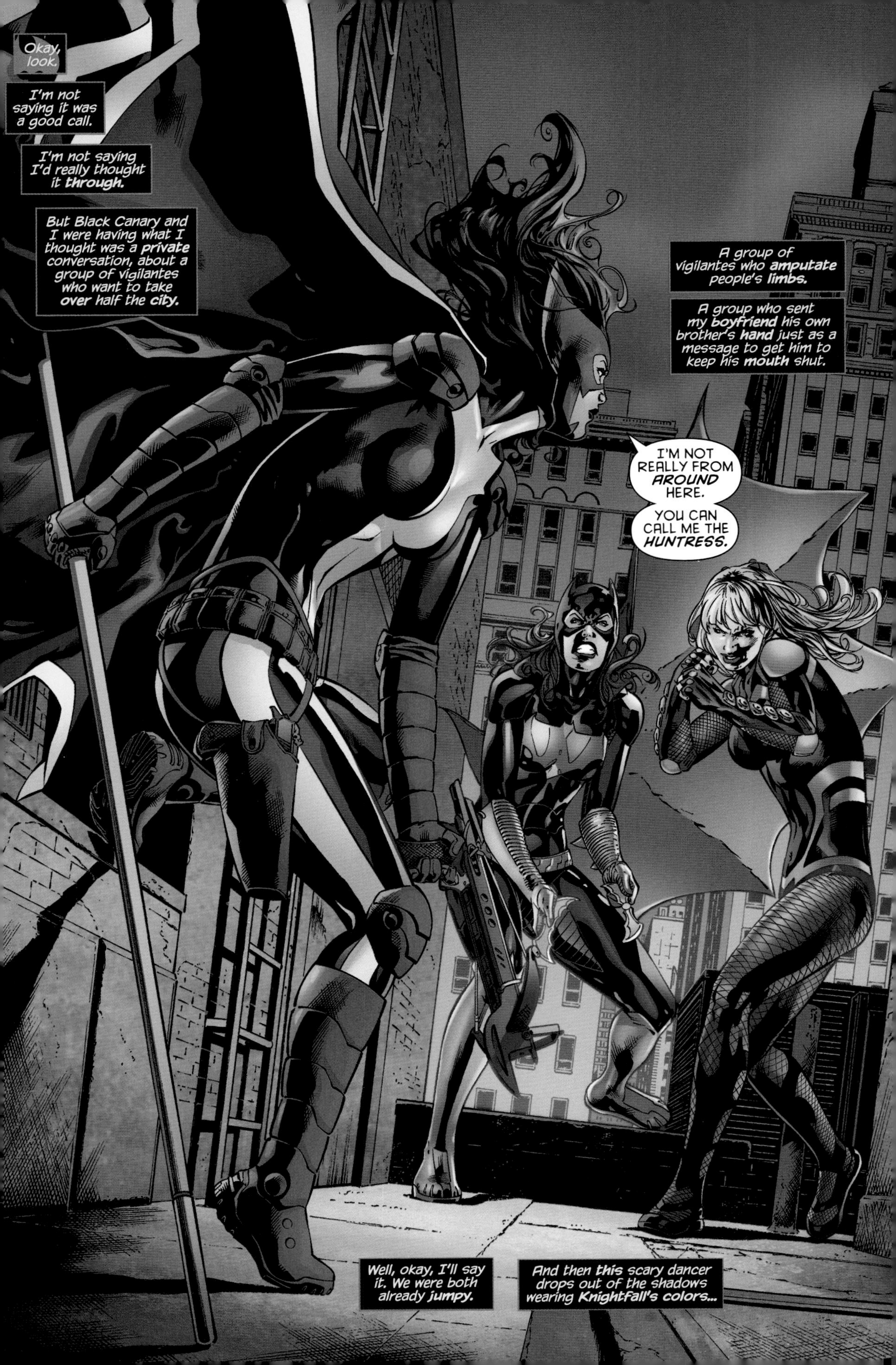
Okay, look.
I'm not saying it was a good call.
I'm not saying I'd really thought it through.
But Black Canary and I were having what I thought was a private conversation, about a group of vigilantes who want to take over half the city.
A group of vigilantes who amputate people's limbs.
A group who sent my boyfriend his own brother's hand just as a message to get him to keep his mouth shut.
I'M NOT REALLY FROM AROUND HERE.
YOU CAN CALL ME THE HUNTRESS.
Well, okay, I'll say it. We were both already jumpy.
And then this scary dancer drops out of the shadows wearing Knightfall's colors...

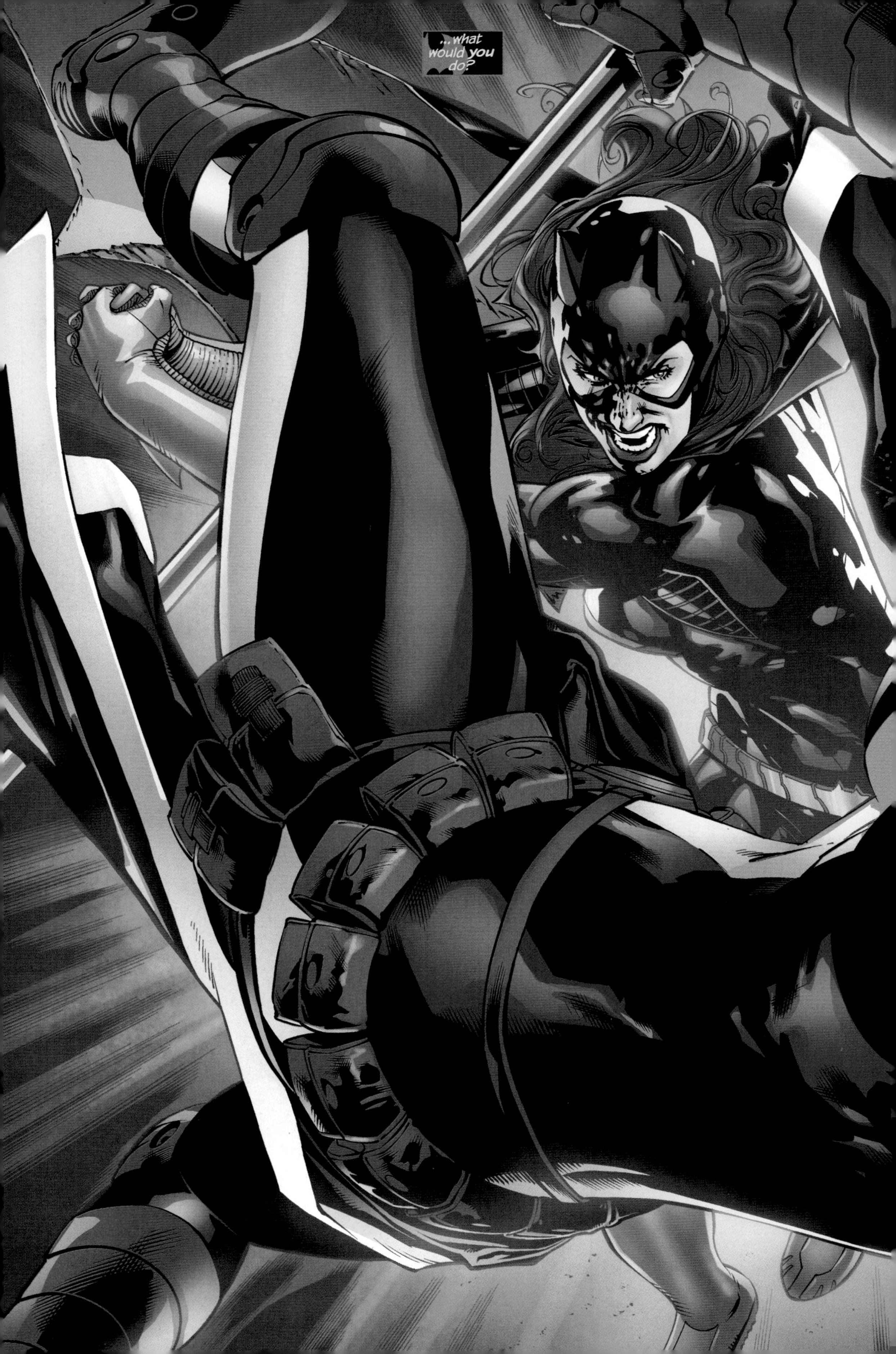
...what would you do?

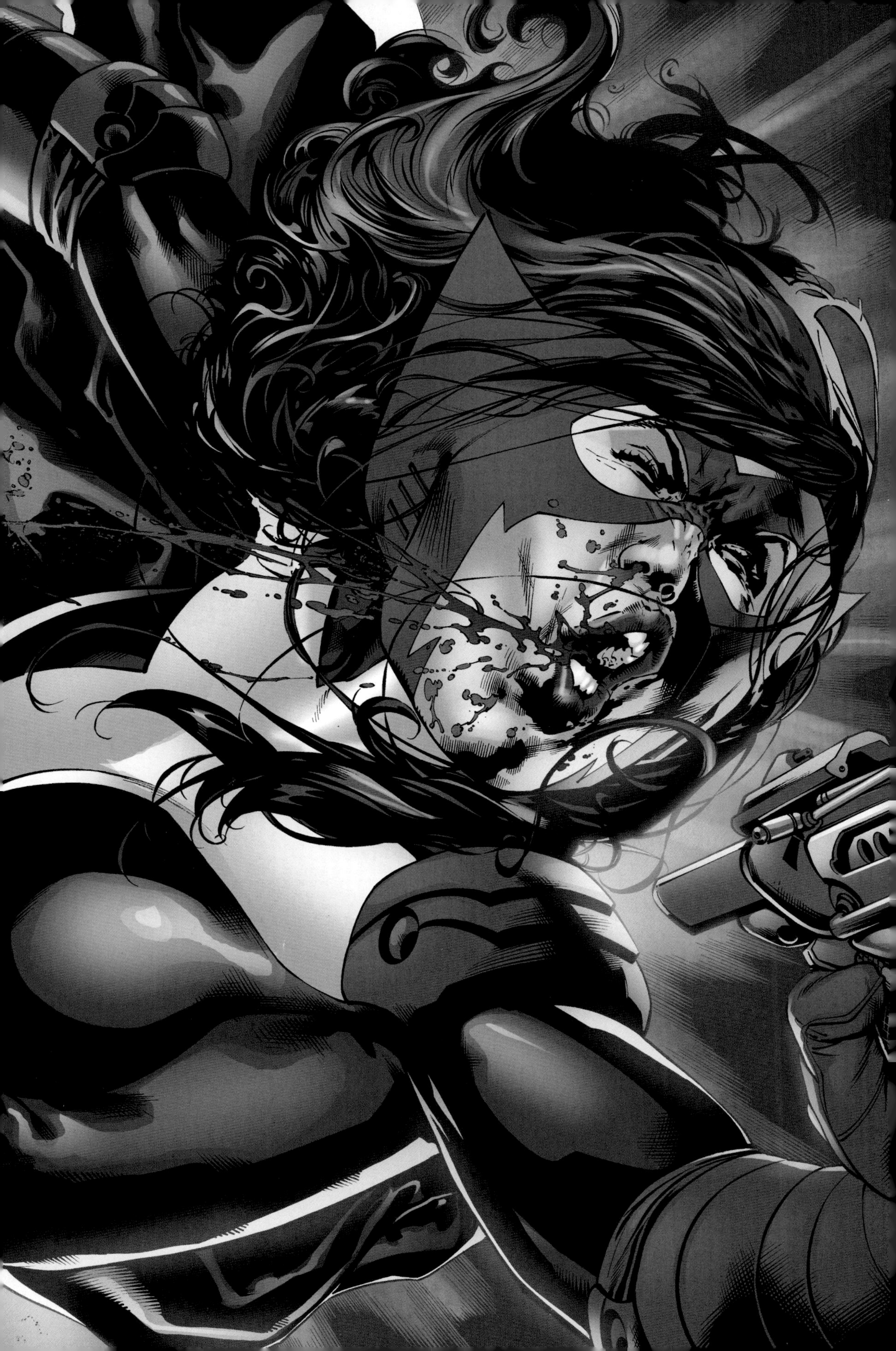

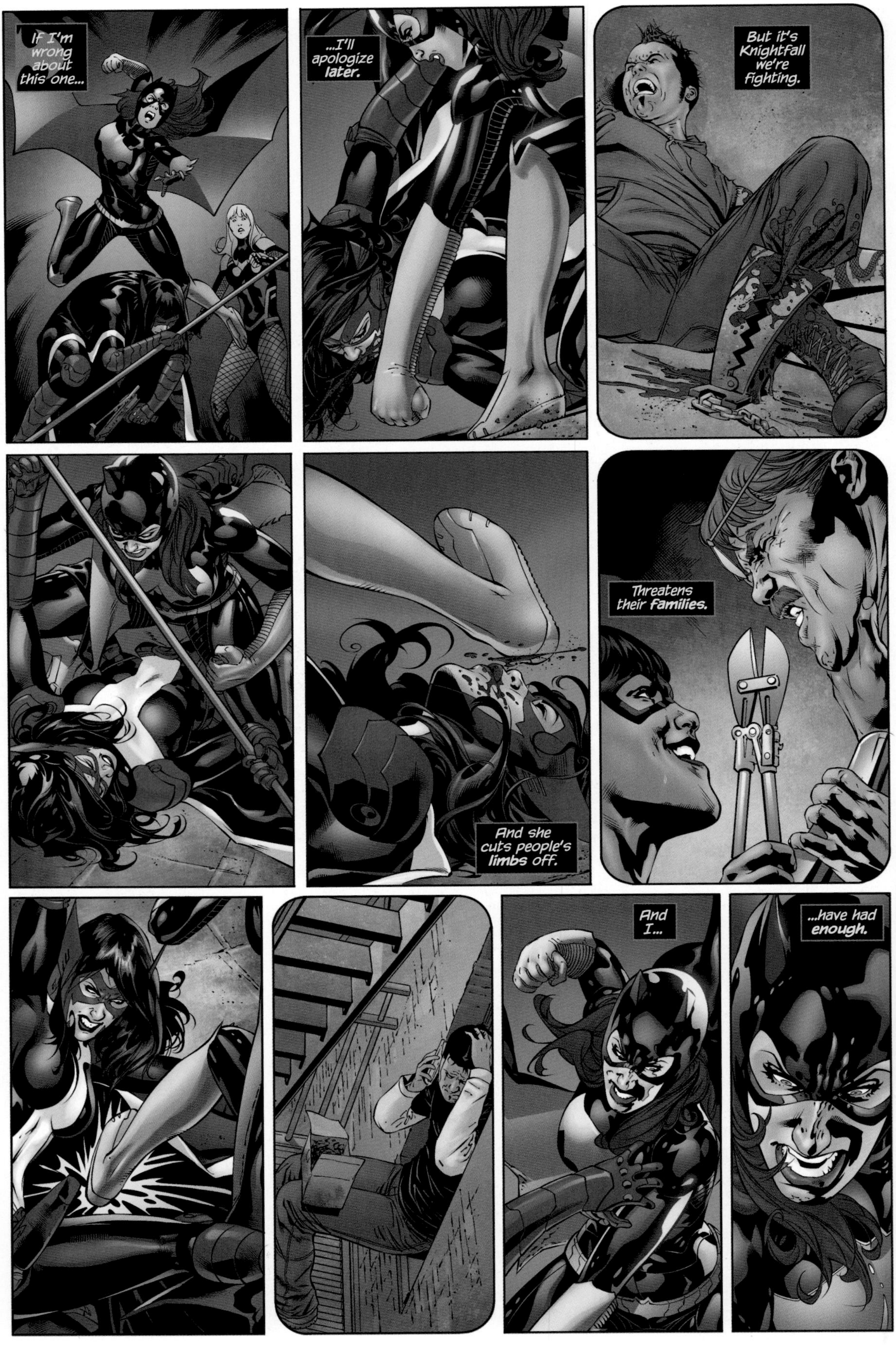
If I'm wrong about this one...
...I'll apologize later.
But it's Knightfall we're fighting.
And she cuts people's limbs off.
Threatens their families.
And I...
...have had enough.

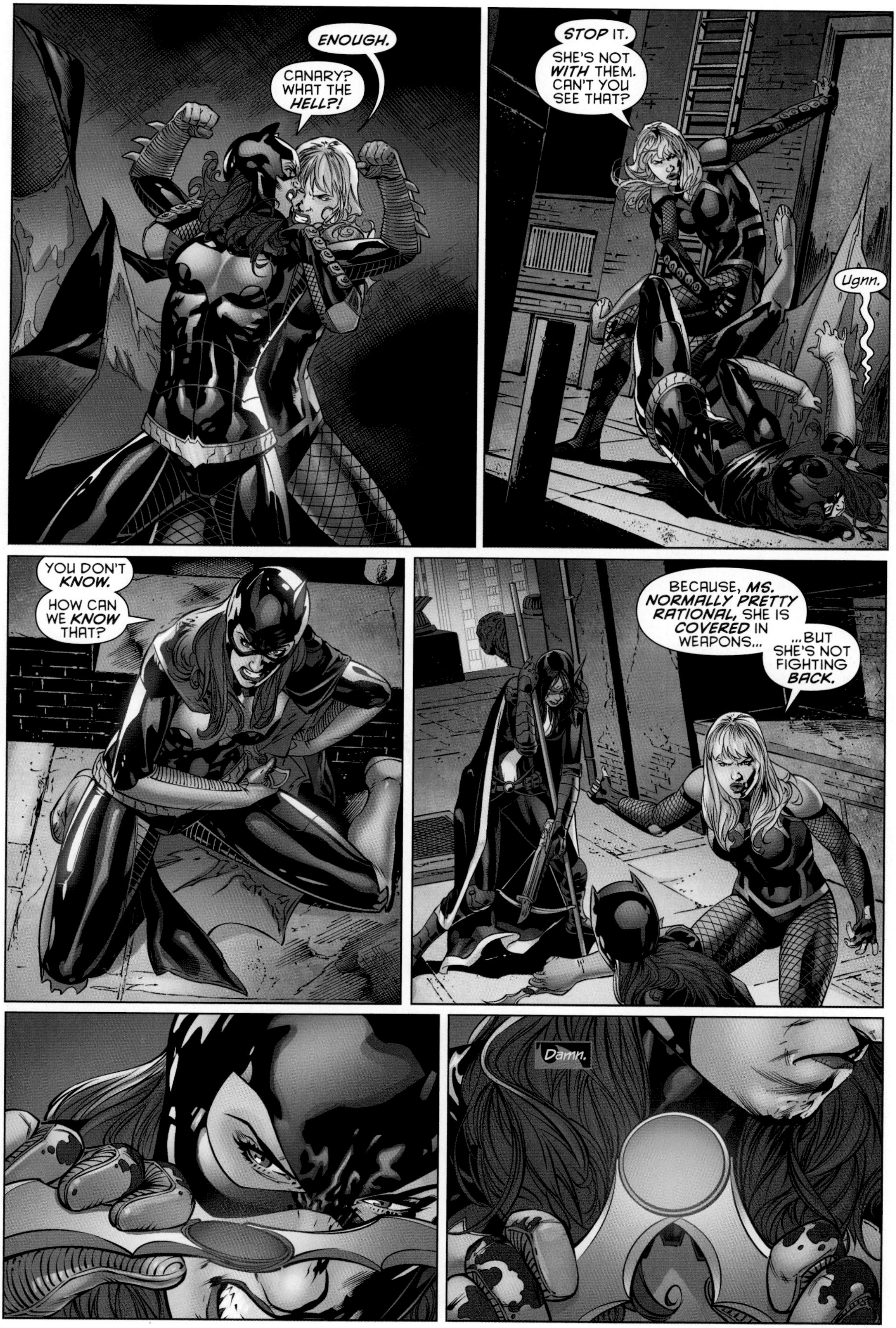
ENOUGH.
CANARY? WHAT THE HELL?!
STOP IT.
SHE'S NOT WITH THEM. CAN'T YOU SEE THAT?
Ugnn.
YOU DON'T KNOW.
HOW CAN WE KNOW THAT?
BECAUSE, MS. NORMALLY PRETTY RATIONAL, SHE IS COVERED IN WEAPONS...
...BUT SHE'S NOT FIGHTING BACK.
Damn.

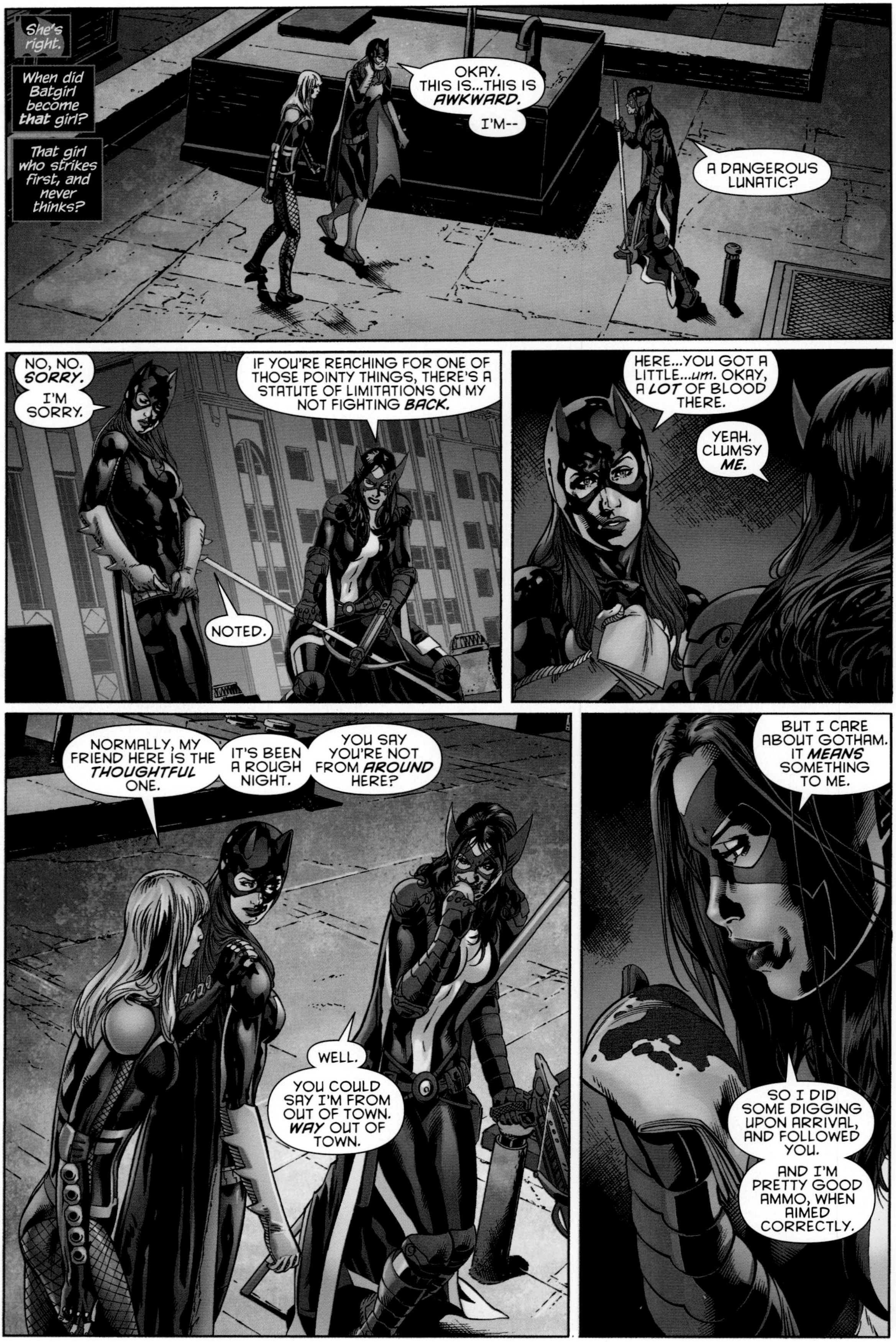
She's right.
When did Batgirl become *that* girl?--
That girl who strikes first, and never thinks?
OKAY. THIS IS...THIS IS AWKWARD.
I'M--
A DANGEROUS LUNATIC?
NO, NO. SORRY.
I'M SORRY.
IF YOU'RE REACHING FOR ONE OF THOSE POINTY THINGS, THERE'S A STATUTE OF LIMITATIONS ON MY NOT FIGHTING BACK.
NOTED.
HERE...YOU GOT A LITTLE...um. OKAY, A LOT OF BLOOD THERE.
YEAH. CLUMSY ME.
NORMALLY, MY FRIEND HERE IS THE THOUGHTFUL ONE.
IT'S BEEN A ROUGH NIGHT.
YOU SAY YOU'RE NOT FROM AROUND HERE?
WELL.
YOU COULD SAY I'M FROM OUT OF TOWN. WAY OUT OF TOWN.
BUT I CARE ABOUT GOTHAM. IT MEANS SOMETHING TO ME.
SO I DID SOME DIGGING UPON ARRIVAL, AND FOLLOWED YOU.
AND I'M PRETTY GOOD AMMO, WHEN AIMED CORRECTLY.

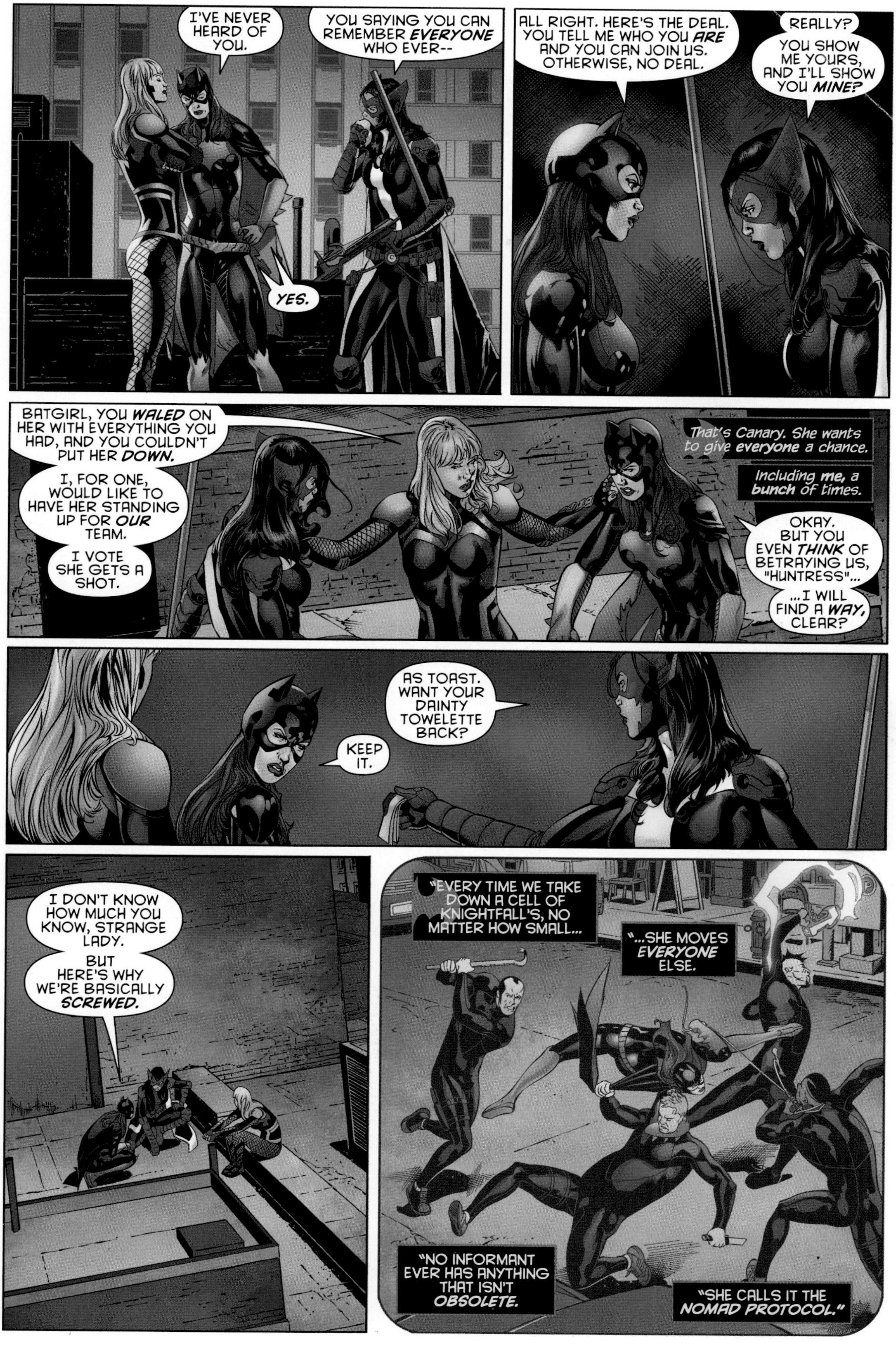

I'VE NEVER HEARD OF YOU.
YOU SAYING YOU CAN REMEMBER EVERYONE WHO EVER--
YES.
ALL RIGHT. HERE'S THE DEAL. YOU TELL ME WHO YOU ARE AND YOU CAN JOIN US. OTHERWISE, NO DEAL.
REALLY?
YOU SHOW ME YOURS, AND I'LL SHOW YOU MINE?
BATGIRL, YOU WALED ON HER WITH EVERYTHING YOU HAD, AND YOU COULDN'T PUT HER DOWN.
I, FOR ONE, WOULD LIKE TO HAVE HER STANDING UP FOR OUR TEAM.
I VOTE SHE GETS A SHOT.
That's Canary. She wants to give everyone a chance.
Including me, a bunch of times.
OKAY. BUT YOU EVEN THINK OF BETRAYING US, "HUNTRESS"...
...I WILL FIND A WAY, CLEAR?
AS TOAST. WANT YOUR DAINTY TOWELETTE BACK?
KEEP IT.
I DON'T KNOW HOW MUCH YOU KNOW, STRANGE LADY.
BUT HERE'S WHY WE'RE BASICALLY SCREWED.
"EVERY TIME WE TAKE DOWN A CELL OF KNIGHTFALL'S, NO MATTER HOW SMALL...
"...SHE MOVES EVERYONE ELSE.
"NO INFORMANT EVER HAS ANYTHING THAT ISN'T OBSOLETE.
"SHE CALLS IT THE NOMAD PROTOCOL."

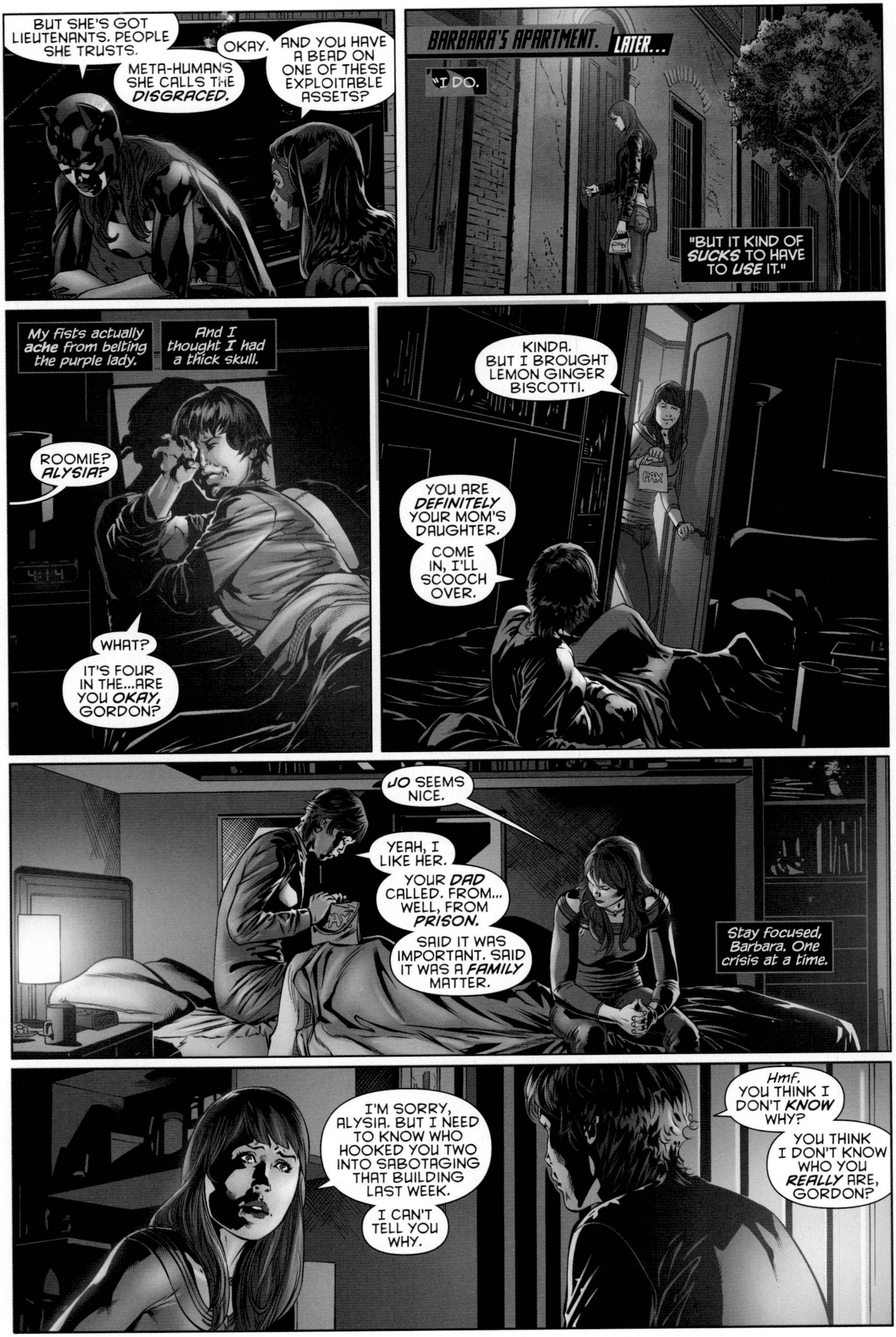

BUT SHE'S GOT LIEUTENANTS. PEOPLE SHE TRUSTS.
META-HUMANS SHE CALLS THE DISGRACED.
OKAY.
AND YOU HAVE A BEAD ON ONE OF THESE EXPLOITABLE ASSETS?
BARBARA'S APARTMENT. LATER...
"I DO.
"BUT IT KIND OF SUCKS TO HAVE TO USE IT."
My fists actually ache from belting the purple lady.
And I thought I had a thick skull.
ROOMIE? ALYSIA?
WHAT?
IT'S FOUR IN THE...ARE YOU OKAY, GORDON?
KINDA. BUT I BROUGHT LEMON GINGER BISCOTTI.
YOU ARE DEFINITELY YOUR MOM'S DAUGHTER.
COME IN, I'LL SCOOCH OVER.
JO SEEMS NICE.
YEAH, I LIKE HER.
YOUR DAD CALLED. FROM... WELL, FROM PRISON.
SAID IT WAS IMPORTANT. SAID IT WAS A FAMILY MATTER.
Stay focused, Barbara. One crisis at a time.
I'M SORRY, ALYSIA. BUT I NEED TO KNOW WHO HOOKED YOU TWO INTO SABOTAGING THAT BUILDING LAST WEEK.
I CAN'T TELL YOU WHY.
Hmf. YOU THINK I DON'T KNOW WHY?
YOU THINK I DON'T KNOW WHO YOU REALLY ARE, GORDON?

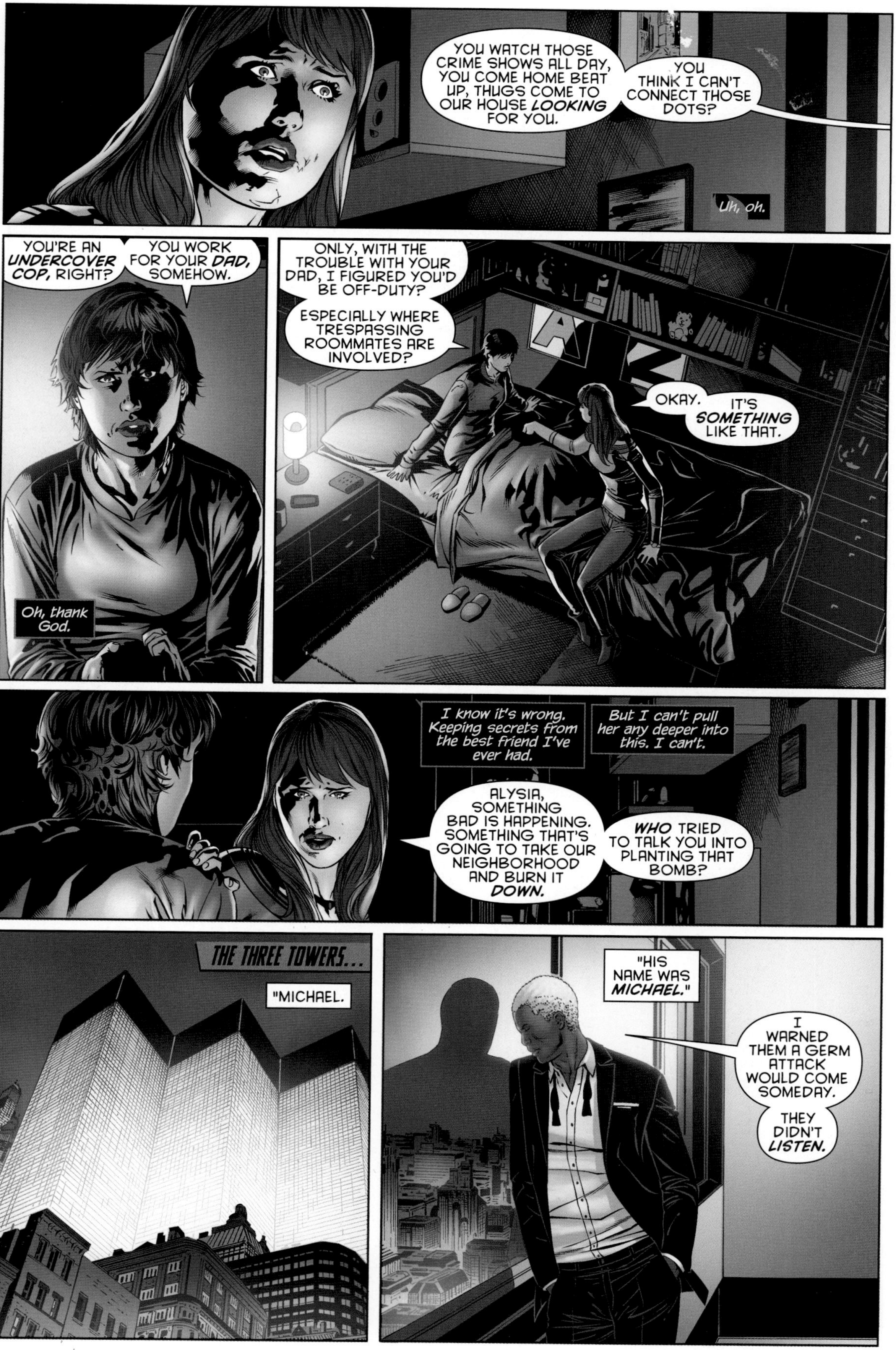
YOU WATCH THOSE CRIME SHOWS ALL DAY, YOU COME HOME BEAT UP, THUGS COME TO OUR HOUSE LOOKING FOR YOU.
YOU THINK I CAN'T CONNECT THOSE DOTS?
Uh, oh.
YOU'RE AN UNDERCOVER COP, RIGHT?
YOU WORK FOR YOUR DAD, SOMEHOW.
Oh, thank God.
ONLY, WITH THE TROUBLE WITH YOUR DAD, I FIGURED YOU'D BE OFF-DUTY?
ESPECIALLY WHERE TRESPASSING ROOMMATES ARE INVOLVED?
OKAY.
IT'S SOMETHING LIKE THAT.
I know it's wrong. Keeping secrets from the best friend I've ever had.
But I can't pull her any deeper into this. I can't.
ALYSIA, SOMETHING BAD IS HAPPENING. SOMETHING THAT'S GOING TO TAKE OUR NEIGHBORHOOD AND BURN IT DOWN.
WHO TRIED TO TALK YOU INTO PLANTING THAT BOMB?
THE THREE TOWERS...
"MICHAEL.
"HIS NAME WAS MICHAEL."
I WARNED THEM A GERM ATTACK WOULD COME SOMEDAY.
THEY DIDN'T LISTEN.

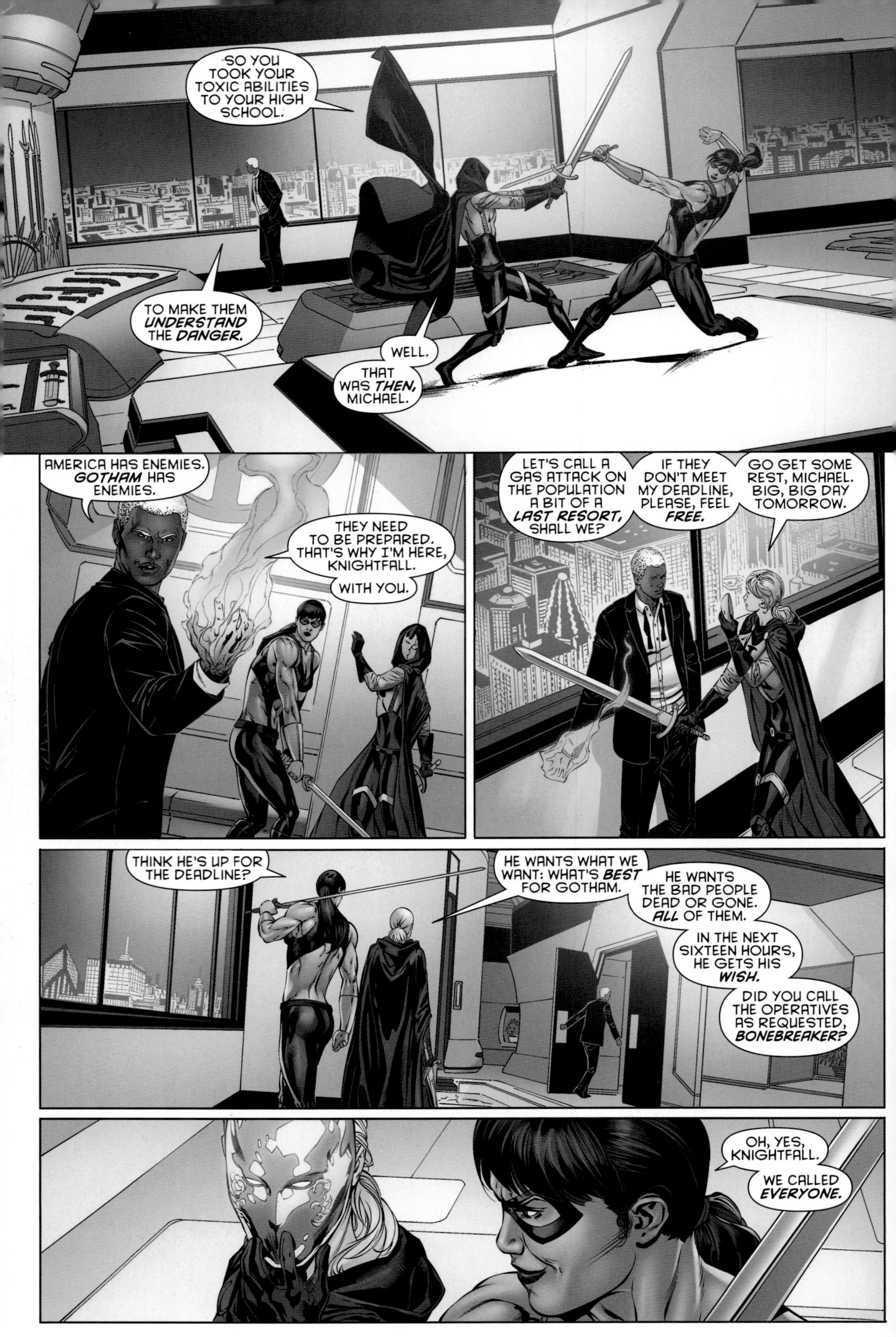
SO YOU TOOK YOUR TOXIC ABILITIES TO YOUR HIGH SCHOOL.
TO MAKE THEM *UNDERSTAND* THE *DANGER.*
WELL.
THAT WAS *THEN,* MICHAEL.
AMERICA HAS ENEMIES. *GOTHAM* HAS ENEMIES.
THEY NEED TO BE PREPARED. THAT'S WHY I'M HERE, KNIGHTFALL.
WITH YOU.
LET'S CALL A GAS ATTACK ON THE POPULATION A BIT OF A *LAST RESORT,* SHALL WE?
IF THEY DON'T MEET MY DEADLINE, PLEASE, FEEL *FREE.*
GO GET SOME REST, MICHAEL. BIG, BIG DAY TOMORROW.
THINK HE'S UP FOR THE DEADLINE?
HE WANTS WHAT WE WANT: WHAT'S *BEST* FOR GOTHAM.
HE WANTS THE BAD PEOPLE DEAD OR GONE. *ALL* OF THEM.
IN THE NEXT SIXTEEN HOURS, HE GETS HIS *WISH.*
DID YOU CALL THE OPERATIVES AS REQUESTED, *BONEBREAKER?*
OH, YES, KNIGHTFALL.
WE CALLED *EVERYONE.*

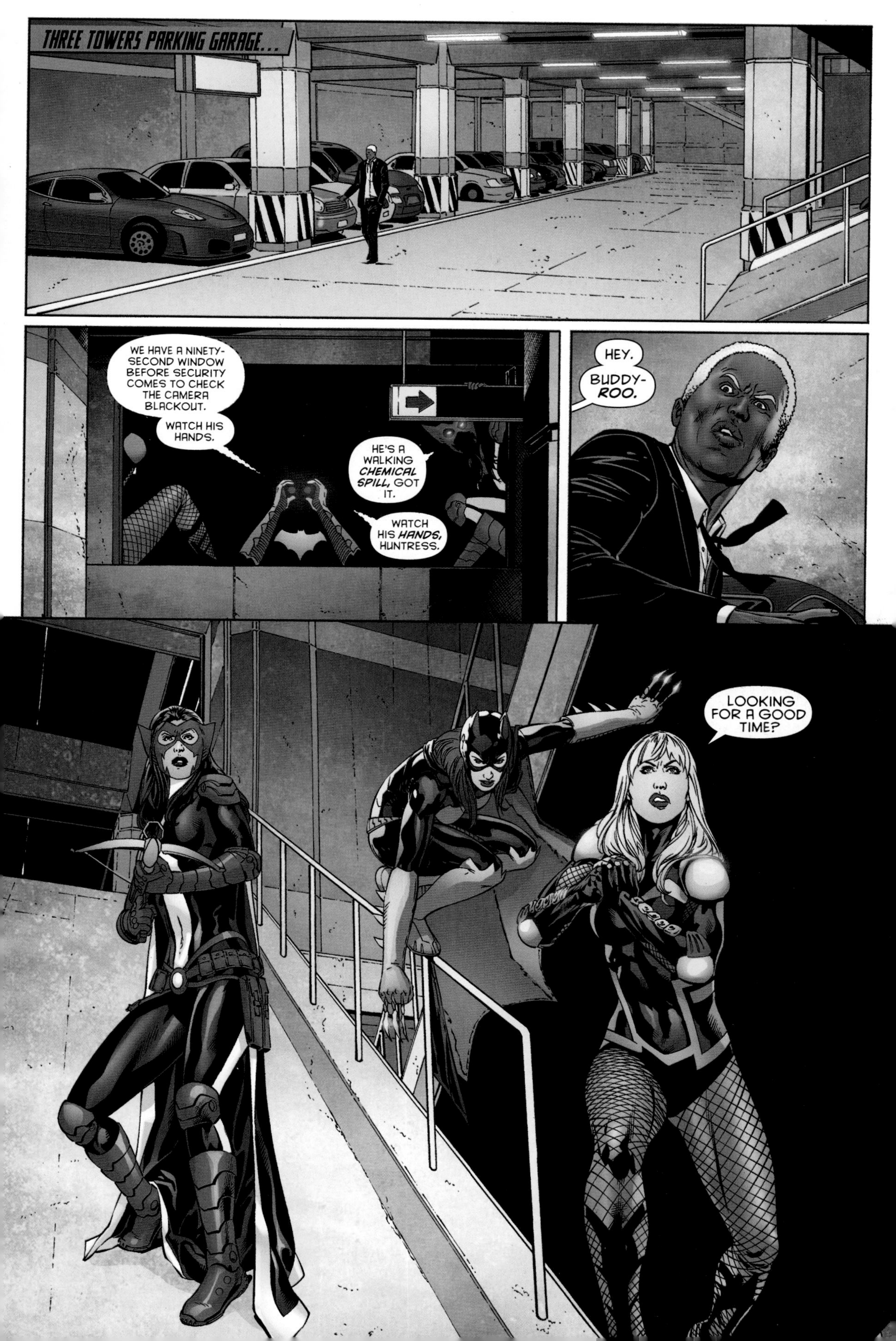
THREE TOWERS PARKING GARAGE...
WE HAVE A NINETY-SECOND WINDOW BEFORE SECURITY COMES TO CHECK THE CAMERA BLACKOUT.
WATCH HIS HANDS.
HE'S A WALKING *CHEMICAL SPILL*, GOT IT.
WATCH HIS *HANDS*, HUNTRESS.
HEY. BUDDY-*ROO*.
LOOKING FOR A GOOD TIME?

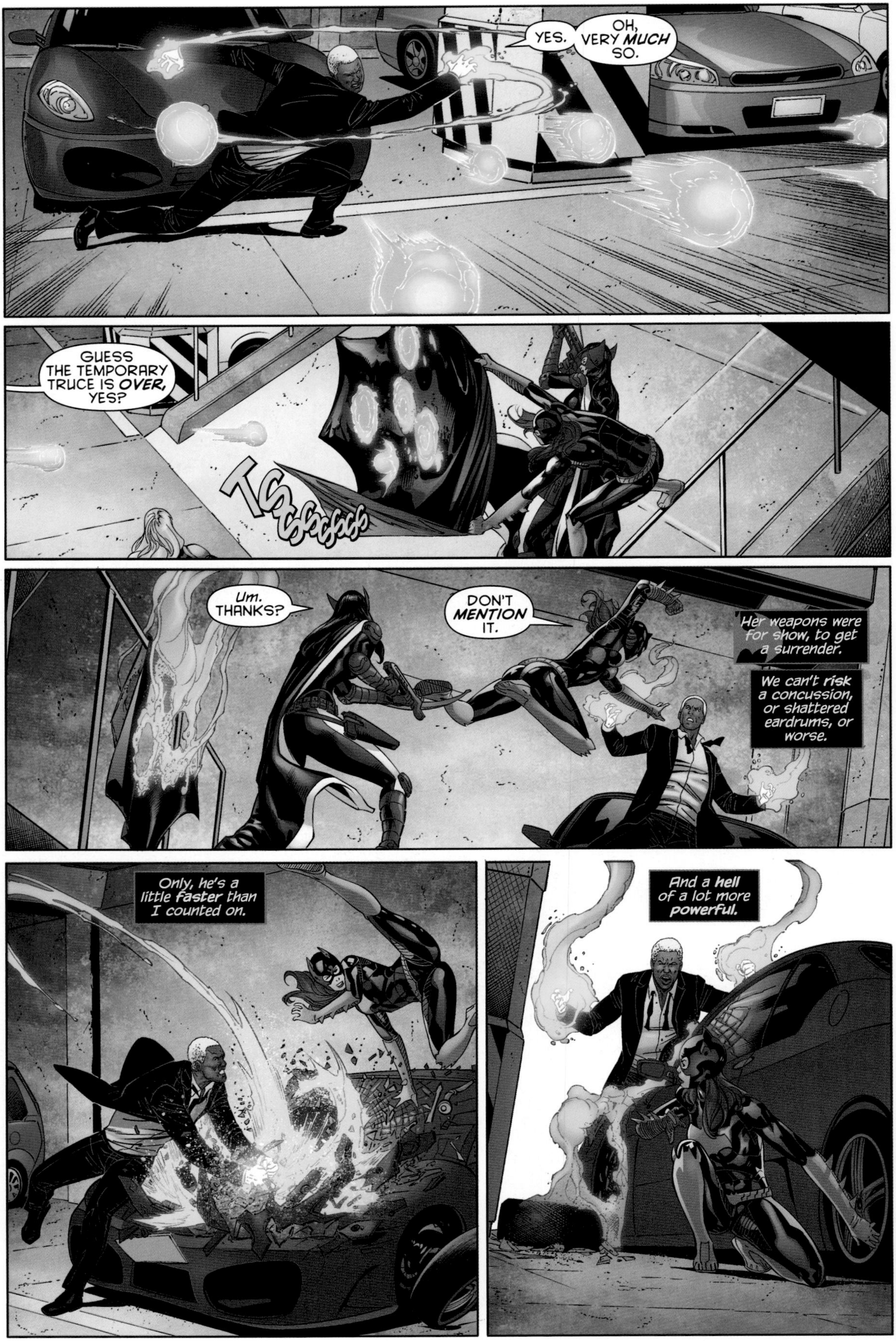
YES.
OH, VERY MUCH SO.
GUESS THE TEMPORARY TRUCE IS OVER, YES?
TSSSSSSSS
Um. THANKS?
DON'T MENTION IT.
Her weapons were for show, to get a surrender.
We can't risk a concussion, or shattered eardrums, or worse.
Only, he's a little faster than I counted on.
And a hell of a lot more powerful.

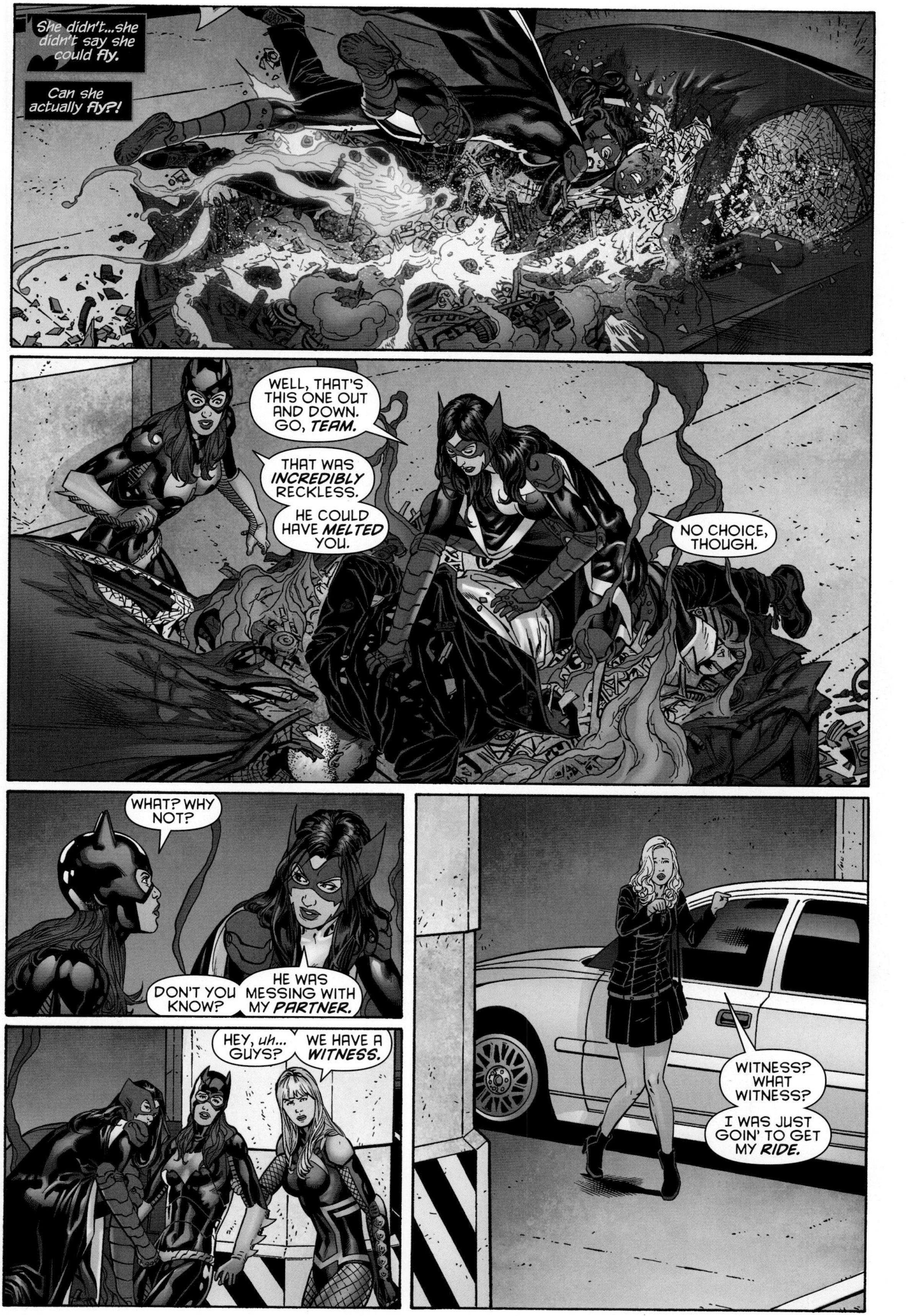
She didn't...she didn't say she could fly.
Can she actually fly?!
WELL, THAT'S THIS ONE OUT AND DOWN. GO, TEAM.
THAT WAS INCREDIBLY RECKLESS.
HE COULD HAVE MELTED YOU.
NO CHOICE, THOUGH.
WHAT? WHY NOT?
DON'T YOU KNOW?
HE WAS MESSING WITH MY PARTNER.
HEY, uh... GUYS?
WE HAVE A WITNESS.
WITNESS? WHAT WITNESS?
I WAS JUST GOIN' TO GET MY RIDE.

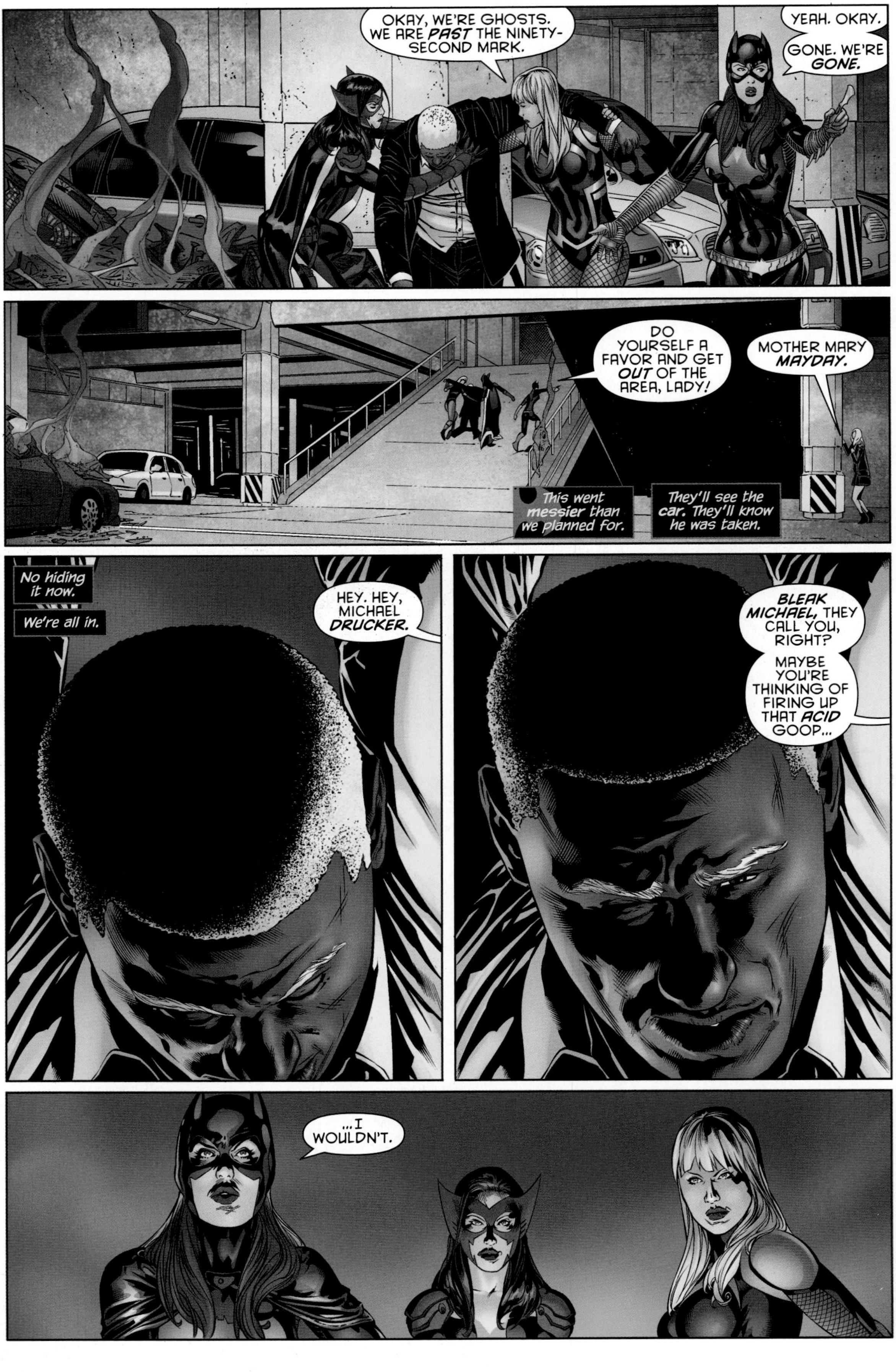
OKAY, WE'RE GHOSTS. WE ARE PAST THE NINETY-SECOND MARK.
YEAH. OKAY.
GONE. WE'RE GONE.
DO YOURSELF A FAVOR AND GET OUT OF THE AREA, LADY!
MOTHER MARY MAYDAY.
This went messier than we planned for.
They'll see the car. They'll know he was taken.
No hiding it now.
We're all in.
HEY. HEY, MICHAEL DRUCKER.
BLEAK MICHAEL, THEY CALL YOU, RIGHT?
MAYBE YOU'RE THINKING OF FIRING UP THAT ACID GOOP...
...I WOULDN'T.

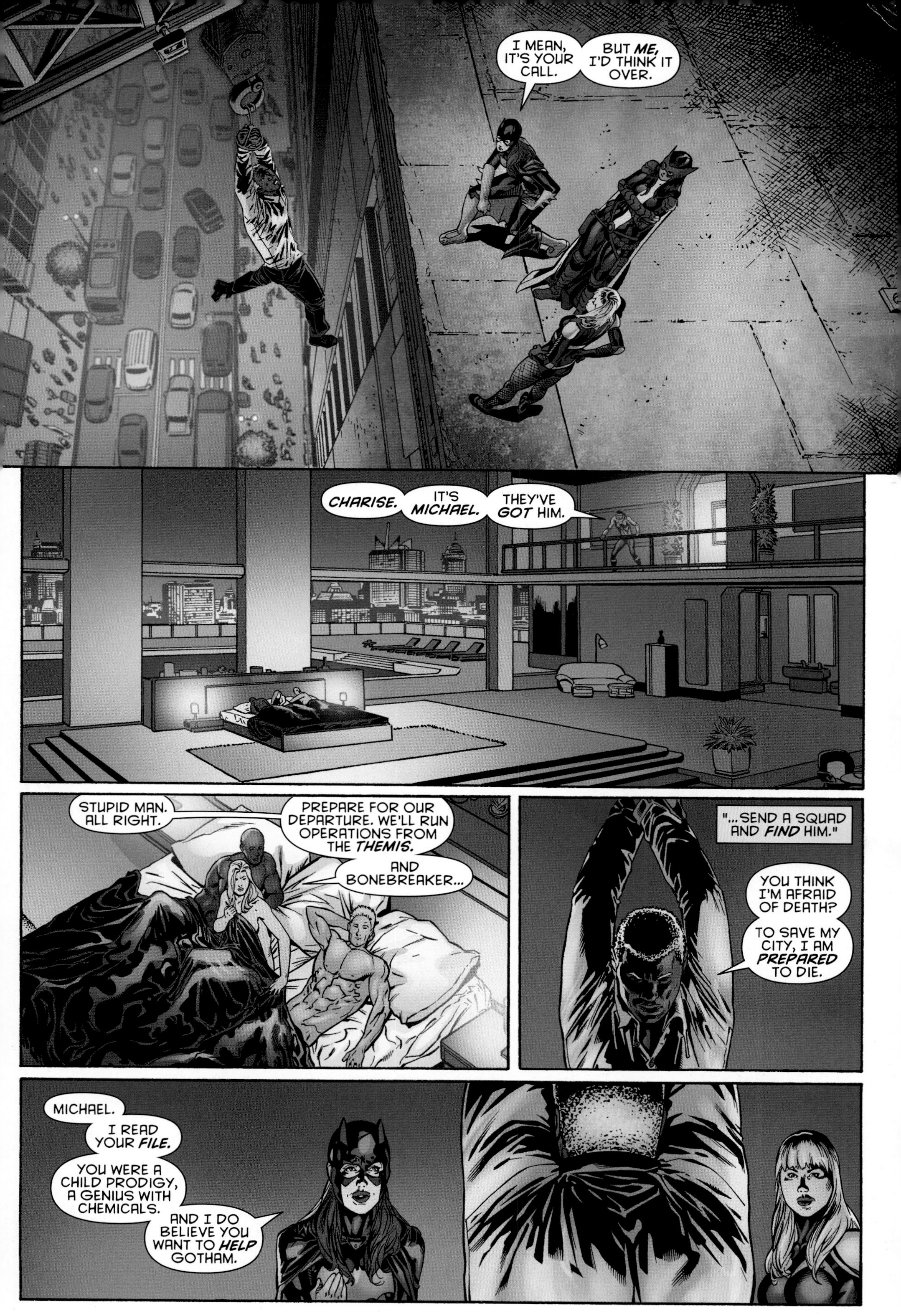
I MEAN, IT'S YOUR CALL.
BUT ME, I'D THINK IT OVER.
CHARISE.
IT'S MICHAEL.
THEY'VE GOT HIM.
STUPID MAN. ALL RIGHT.
PREPARE FOR OUR DEPARTURE. WE'LL RUN OPERATIONS FROM THE THEMIS.
AND BONEBREAKER...
"...SEND A SQUAD AND FIND HIM."
YOU THINK I'M AFRAID OF DEATH?
TO SAVE MY CITY, I AM PREPARED TO DIE.
MICHAEL.
I READ YOUR FILE.
YOU WERE A CHILD PRODIGY, A GENIUS WITH CHEMICALS.
AND I DO BELIEVE YOU WANT TO HELP GOTHAM.

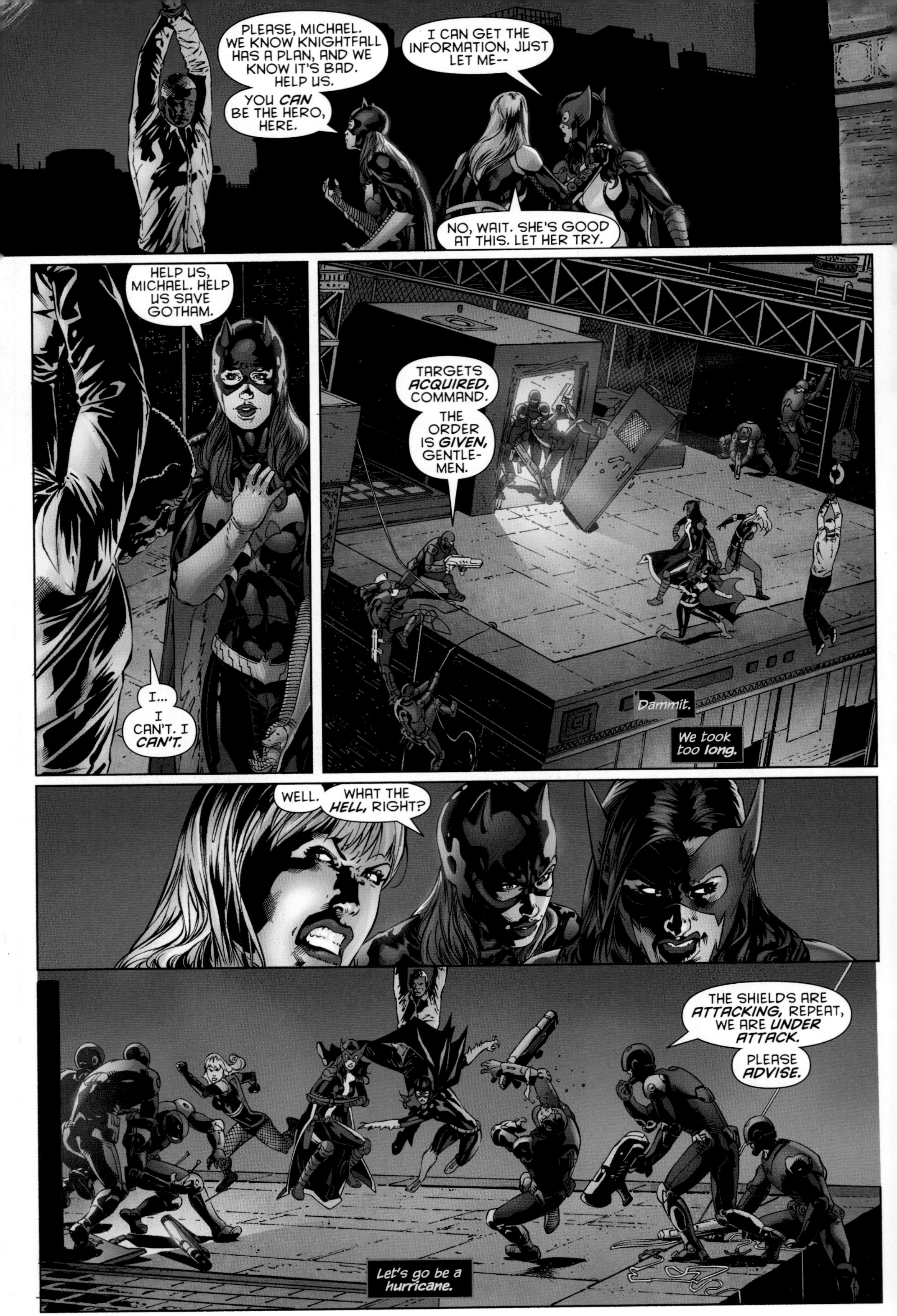

PLEASE, MICHAEL. WE KNOW KNIGHTFALL HAS A PLAN, AND WE KNOW IT'S BAD. HELP US.
YOU CAN BE THE HERO, HERE.
I CAN GET THE INFORMATION, JUST LET ME--
NO, WAIT. SHE'S GOOD AT THIS. LET HER TRY.
HELP US, MICHAEL. HELP US SAVE GOTHAM.
I... I CAN'T. I CAN'T.
TARGETS ACQUIRED, COMMAND.
THE ORDER IS GIVEN, GENTLE-MEN.
Dammit.
We took too long.
WELL.
WHAT THE HELL, RIGHT?
THE SHIELDS ARE ATTACKING, REPEAT, WE ARE UNDER ATTACK.
PLEASE ADVISE.
Let's go be a hurricane.

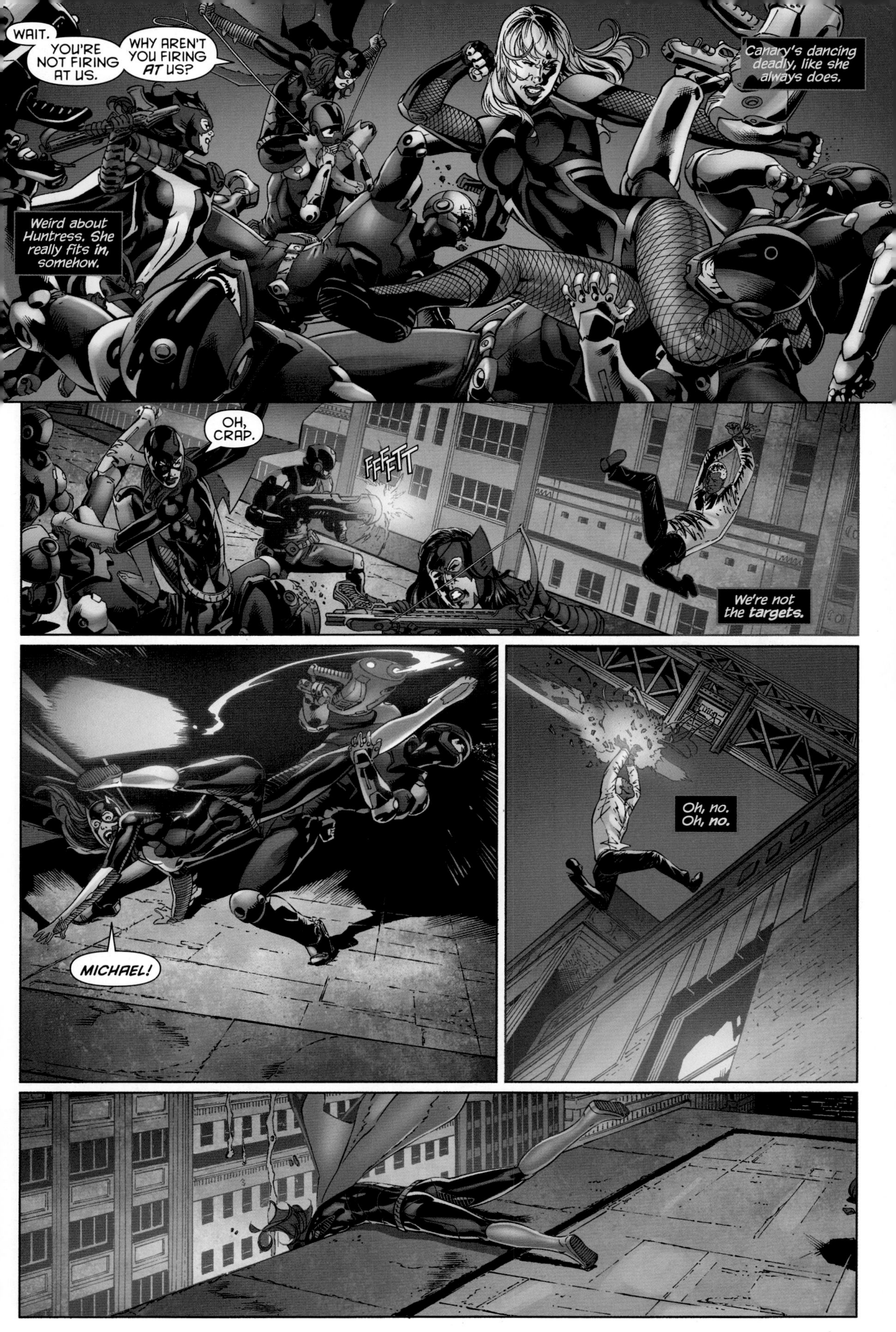
WAIT. YOU'RE NOT FIRING AT US.
WHY AREN'T YOU FIRING AT US?
Canary's dancing deadly, like she always does.
Weird about Huntress. She really fits in, somehow.
OH, CRAP.
FFFFTT
We're not the targets.
MICHAEL!
Oh, no. Oh, no.

Guh.
HANG *ON.*

I COULD... I COULD *BURN* YOU RIGHT NOW.

THEN I *BURN.*
HANG *ON.*

OKAY. OKAY, BATGIRL.
WE GOT HIM.

THANK GOD.

SHE'S GOT A *DEADLINE. MIDNIGHT TONIGHT...* FIFTEEN AND A HALF HOURS.

EVERY CRIMINAL LEAVES CHERRY HILL.

OR THEY *DIE.*

THAT...THAT'S *IMPOSSIBLE.*

OH, IT'S *VERY* POSSIBLE. IT'S ALREADY IN *MOTION.*

SHE'S HIRED MERCS FROM ALL OVER THE *WORLD.* IT'S AN *ARMY.*

WE'LL STOP HER. WE'LL STORM THE *BUILDING.*

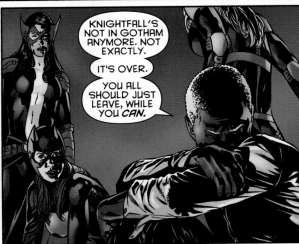

KNIGHTFALL'S NOT IN GOTHAM ANYMORE. NOT EXACTLY.

IT'S OVER.

YOU ALL SHOULD JUST LEAVE, WHILE YOU *CAN.*

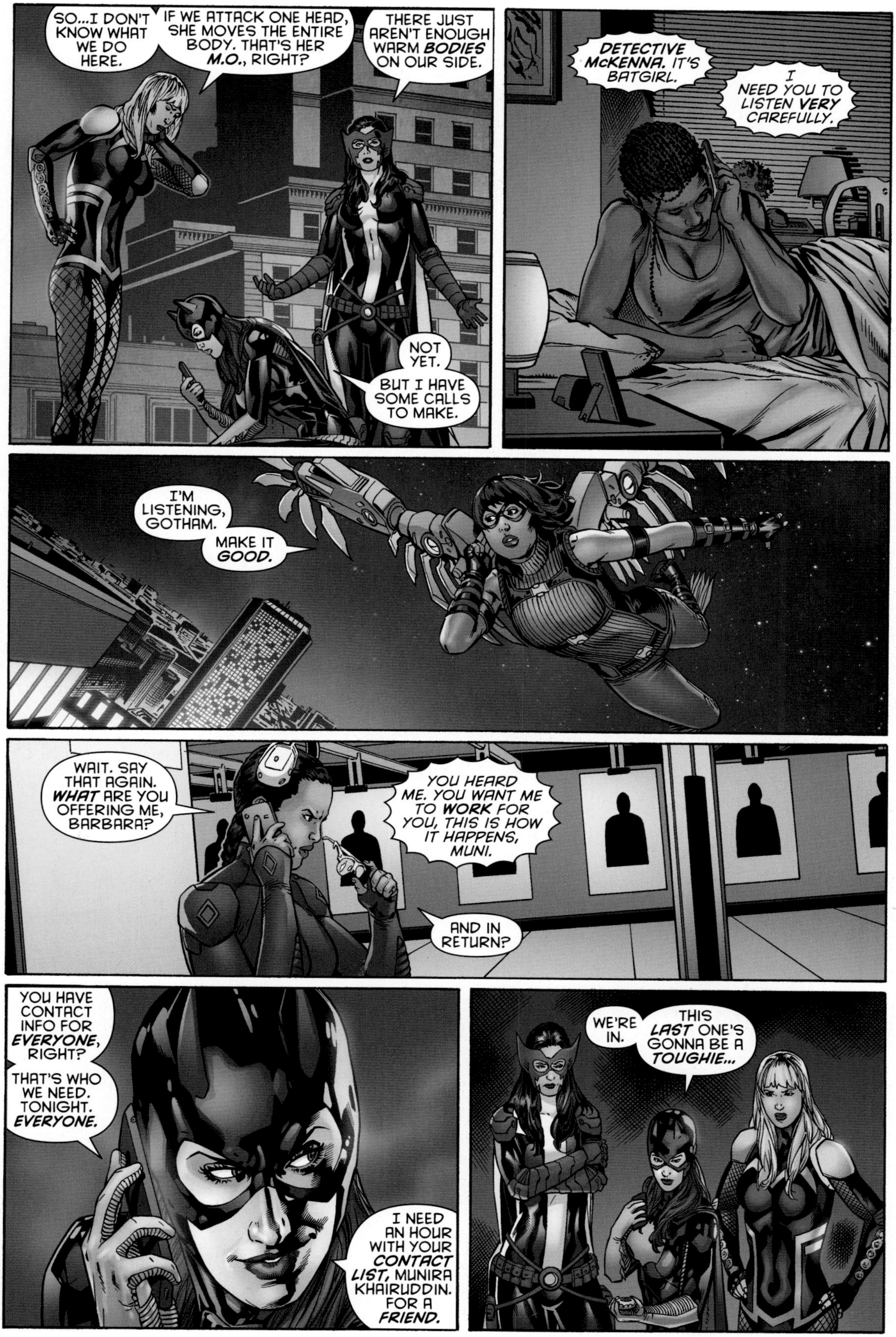
SO...I DON'T KNOW WHAT WE DO HERE.
IF WE ATTACK ONE HEAD, SHE MOVES THE ENTIRE BODY. THAT'S HER M.O., RIGHT?
THERE JUST AREN'T ENOUGH WARM BODIES ON OUR SIDE.
NOT YET.
BUT I HAVE SOME CALLS TO MAKE.
DETECTIVE McKENNA. IT'S BATGIRL.
I NEED YOU TO LISTEN VERY CAREFULLY.
I'M LISTENING, GOTHAM.
MAKE IT GOOD.
WAIT. SAY THAT AGAIN. WHAT ARE YOU OFFERING ME, BARBARA?
YOU HEARD ME. YOU WANT ME TO WORK FOR YOU, THIS IS HOW IT HAPPENS, MUNI.
AND IN RETURN?
YOU HAVE CONTACT INFO FOR EVERYONE, RIGHT?
THAT'S WHO WE NEED. TONIGHT. EVERYONE.
I NEED AN HOUR WITH YOUR CONTACT LIST, MUNIRA KHAIRUDDIN. FOR A FRIEND.
WE'RE IN.
THIS LAST ONE'S GONNA BE A TOUGHIE...

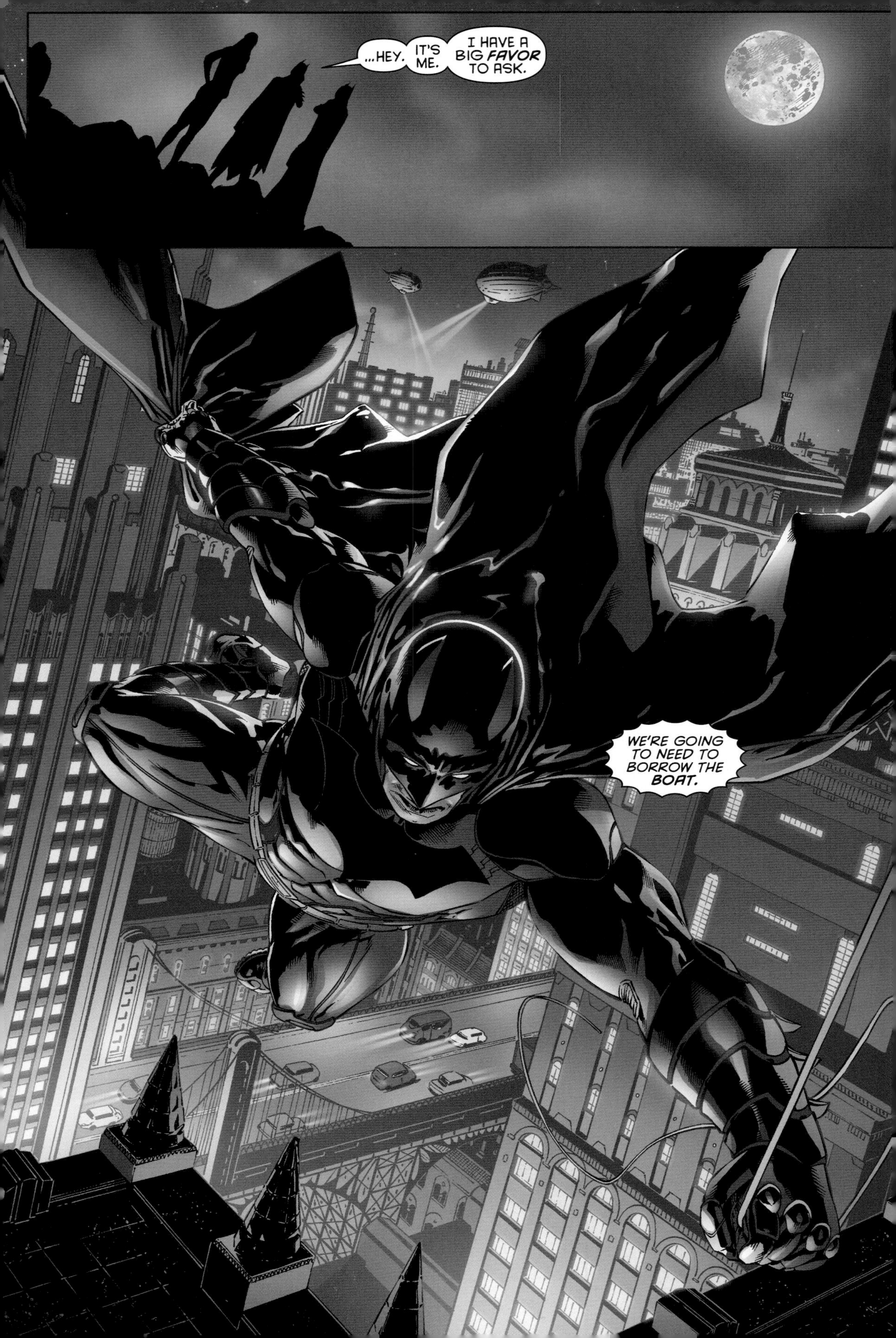
...HEY.
IT'S ME.
I HAVE A BIG FAVOR TO ASK.
WE'RE GOING TO NEED TO BORROW THE BOAT.

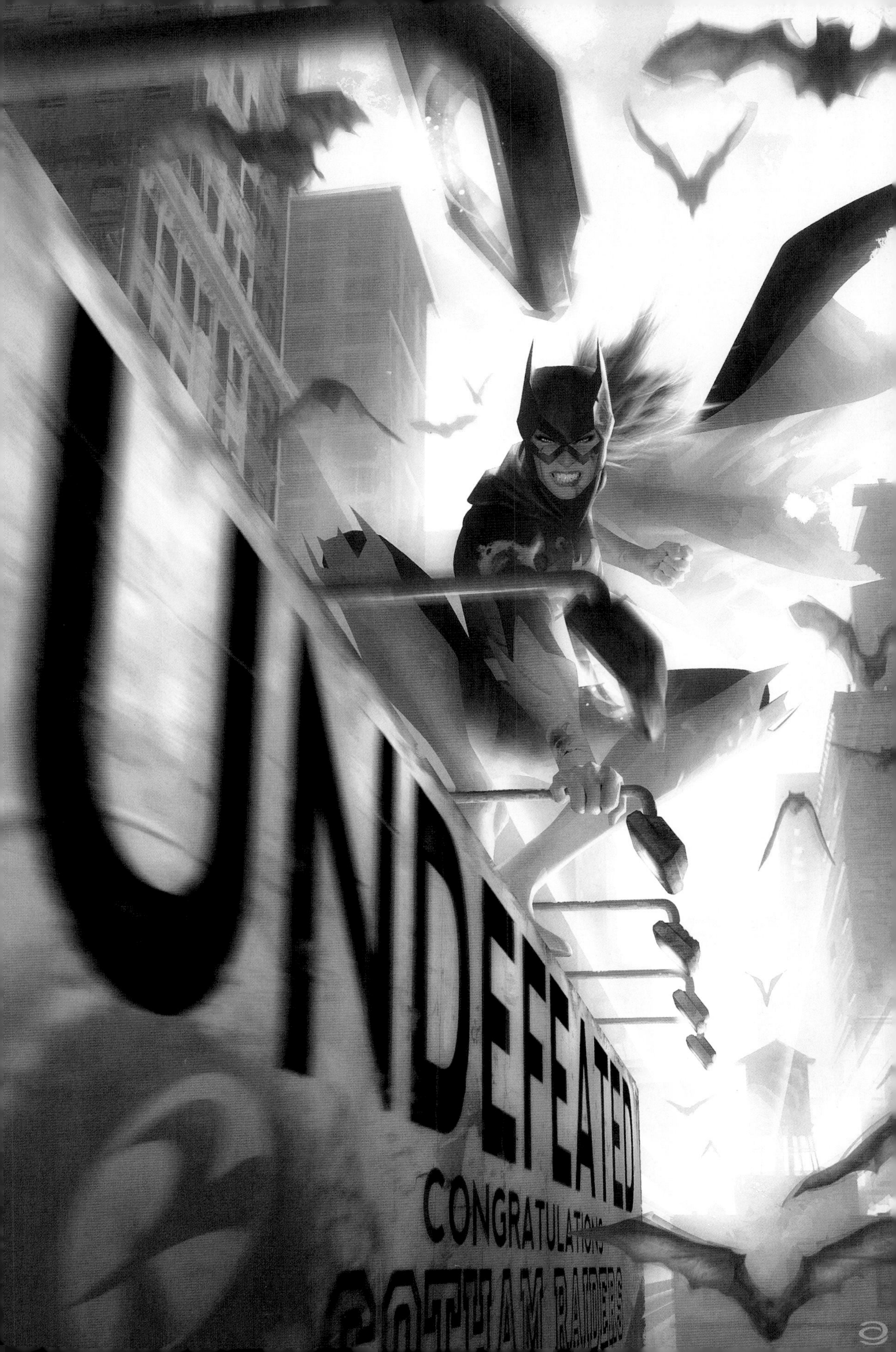
UNDEFEATED
CONGRATULATIONS
GOTHAM RAIDERS

DEADLINE PART THREE: CRASH AND BURN

GAIL SIMONE writer FERNANDO PASARIN penciller JONATHAN GLAPION MATT RYAN inkers BLOND colorist ALEX GARNER cover artist

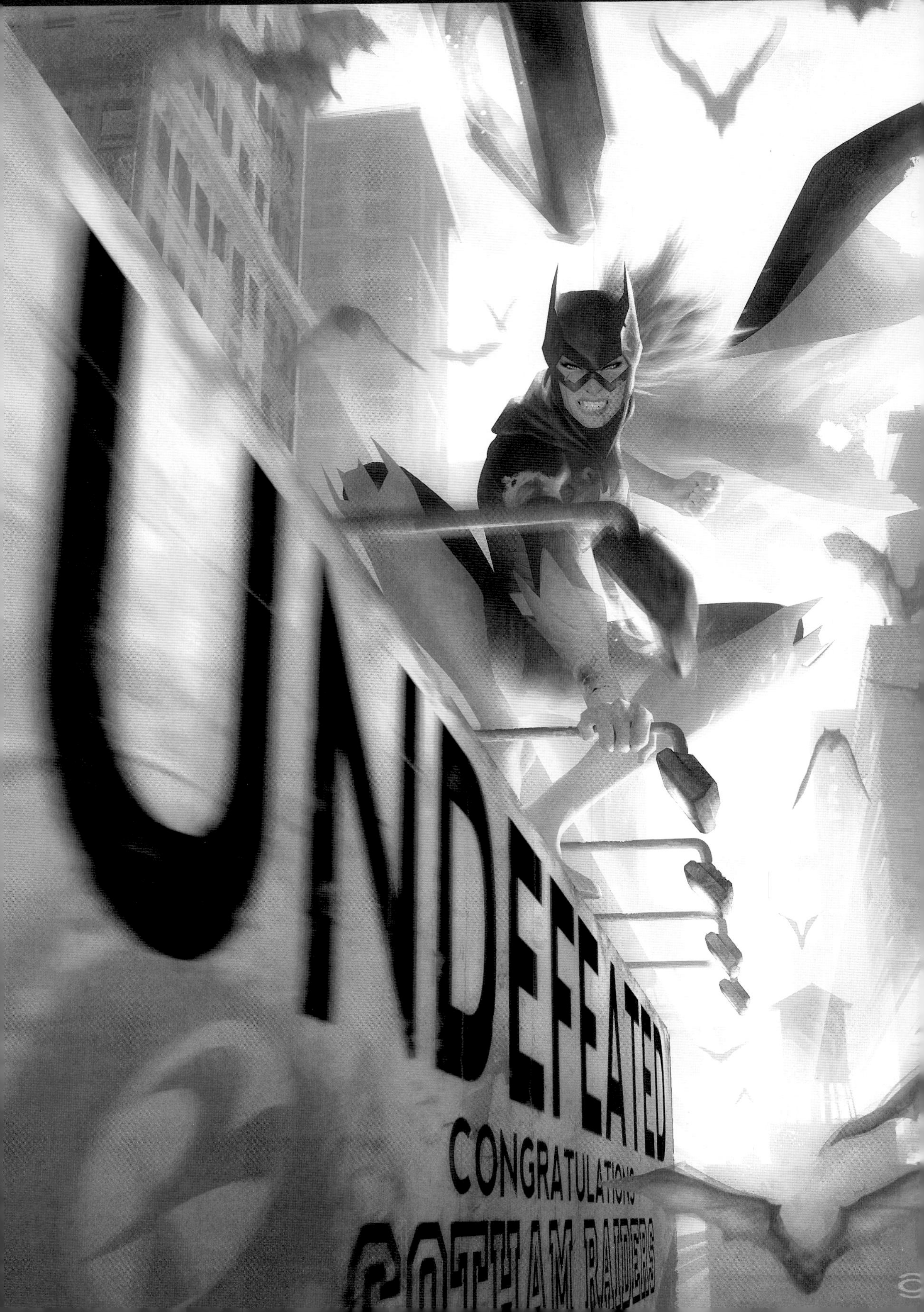
UNDEFEATED
CONGRATULATIONS
GOTHAM RAIDERS

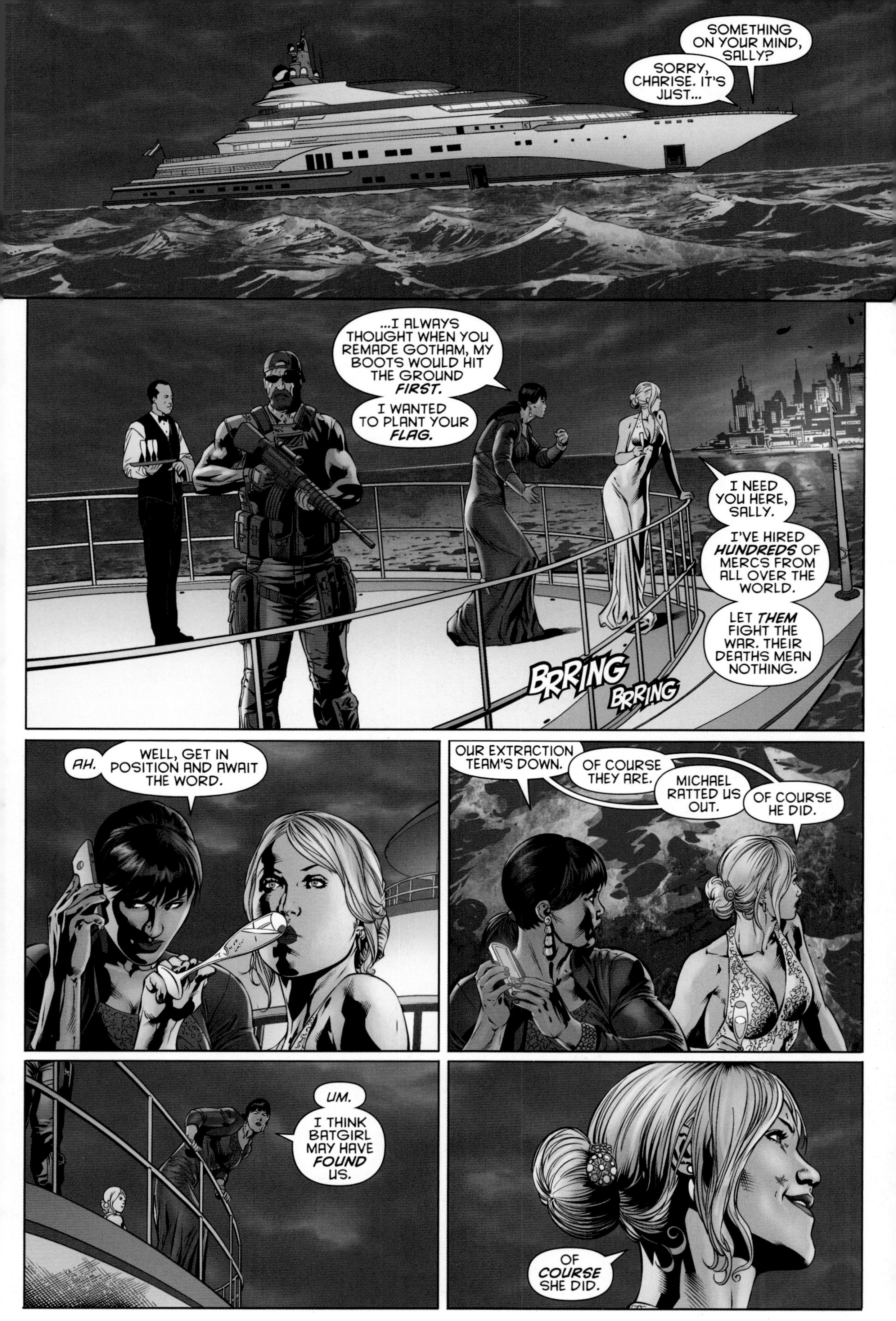
SOMETHING ON YOUR MIND, SALLY?
SORRY, CHARISE. IT'S JUST...
...I ALWAYS THOUGHT WHEN YOU REMADE GOTHAM, MY BOOTS WOULD HIT THE GROUND FIRST.
I WANTED TO PLANT YOUR FLAG.
I NEED YOU HERE, SALLY.
I'VE HIRED HUNDREDS OF MERCS FROM ALL OVER THE WORLD.
LET THEM FIGHT THE WAR. THEIR DEATHS MEAN NOTHING.
BRRING BRRING
AH.
WELL, GET IN POSITION AND AWAIT THE WORD.
OUR EXTRACTION TEAM'S DOWN.
OF COURSE THEY ARE.
MICHAEL RATTED US OUT.
OF COURSE HE DID.
UM.
I THINK BATGIRL MAY HAVE FOUND US.
OF COURSE SHE DID.

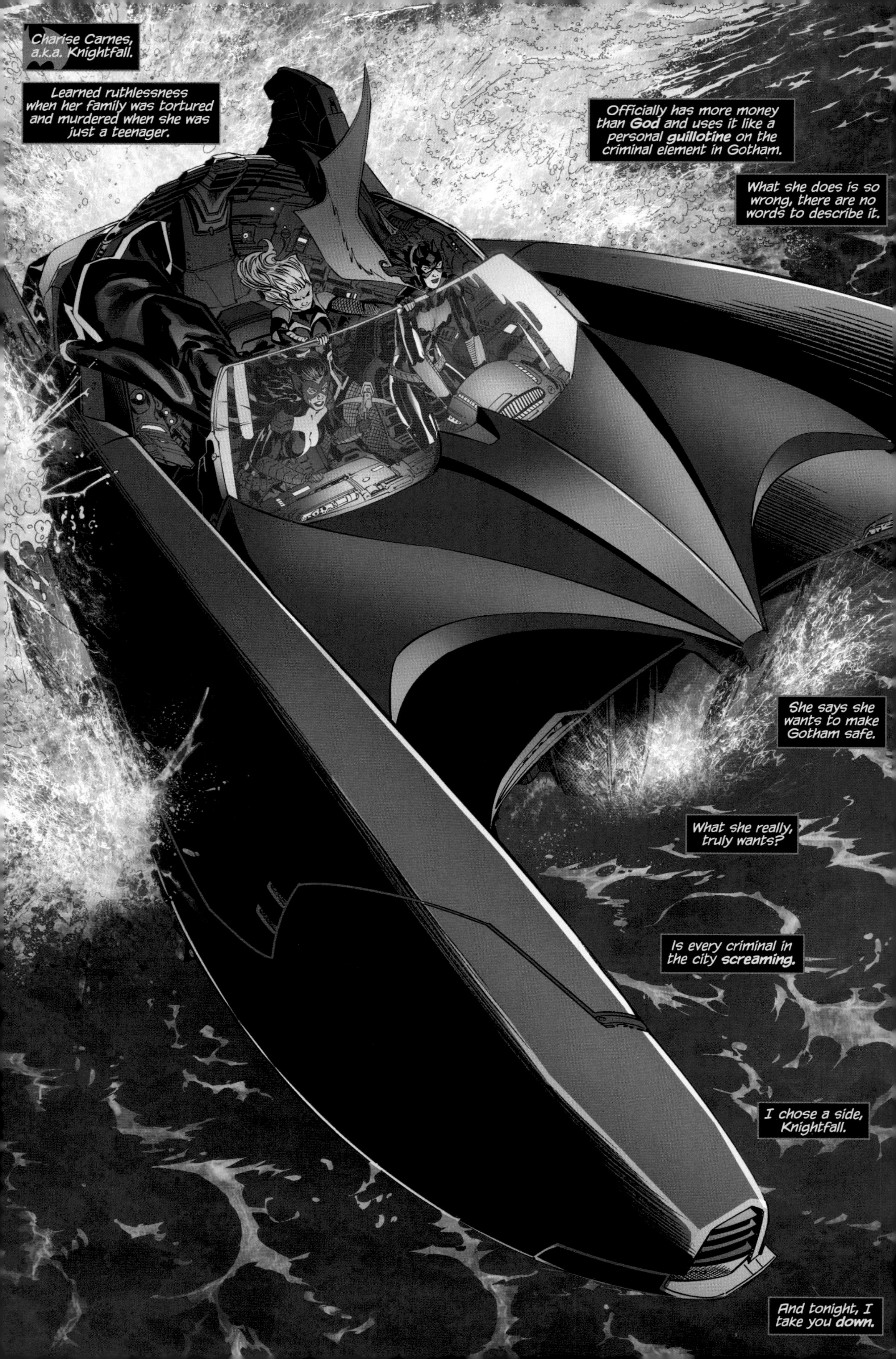

Charise Carnes, a.k.a. Knightfall.
Learned ruthlessness when her family was tortured and murdered when she was just a teenager.
Officially has more money than **God** and uses it like a personal **guillotine** on the criminal element in Gotham.
What she does is so wrong, there are no words to describe it.
She says she wants to make Gotham safe.
What she really, truly wants?
Is every criminal in the city **screaming.**
I chose a side, Knightfall.
And tonight, I take you **down.**

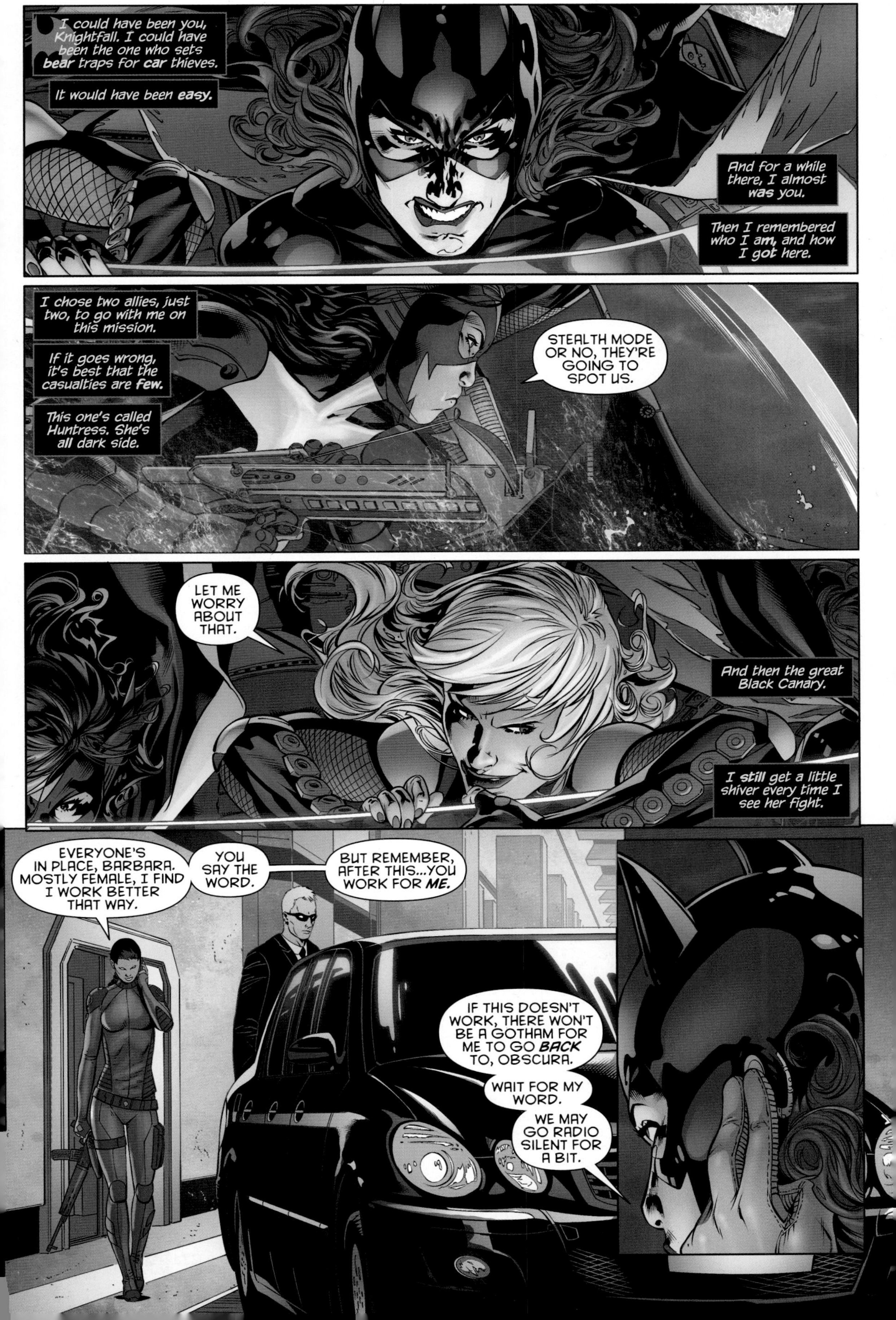
I could have been you, Knightfall. I could have been the one who sets bear traps for car thieves.
It would have been easy.
And for a while there, I almost was you.
Then I remembered who I am, and how I got here.
I chose two allies, just two, to go with me on this mission.
If it goes wrong, it's best that the casualties are few.
This one's called Huntress. She's all dark side.
STEALTH MODE OR NO, THEY'RE GOING TO SPOT US.
LET ME WORRY ABOUT THAT.
And then the great Black Canary.
I still get a little shiver every time I see her fight.
EVERYONE'S IN PLACE, BARBARA. MOSTLY FEMALE, I FIND I WORK BETTER THAT WAY.
YOU SAY THE WORD.
BUT REMEMBER, AFTER THIS...YOU WORK FOR ME.
IF THIS DOESN'T WORK, THERE WON'T BE A GOTHAM FOR ME TO GO BACK TO, OBSCURA.
WAIT FOR MY WORD.
WE MAY GO RADIO SILENT FOR A BIT.

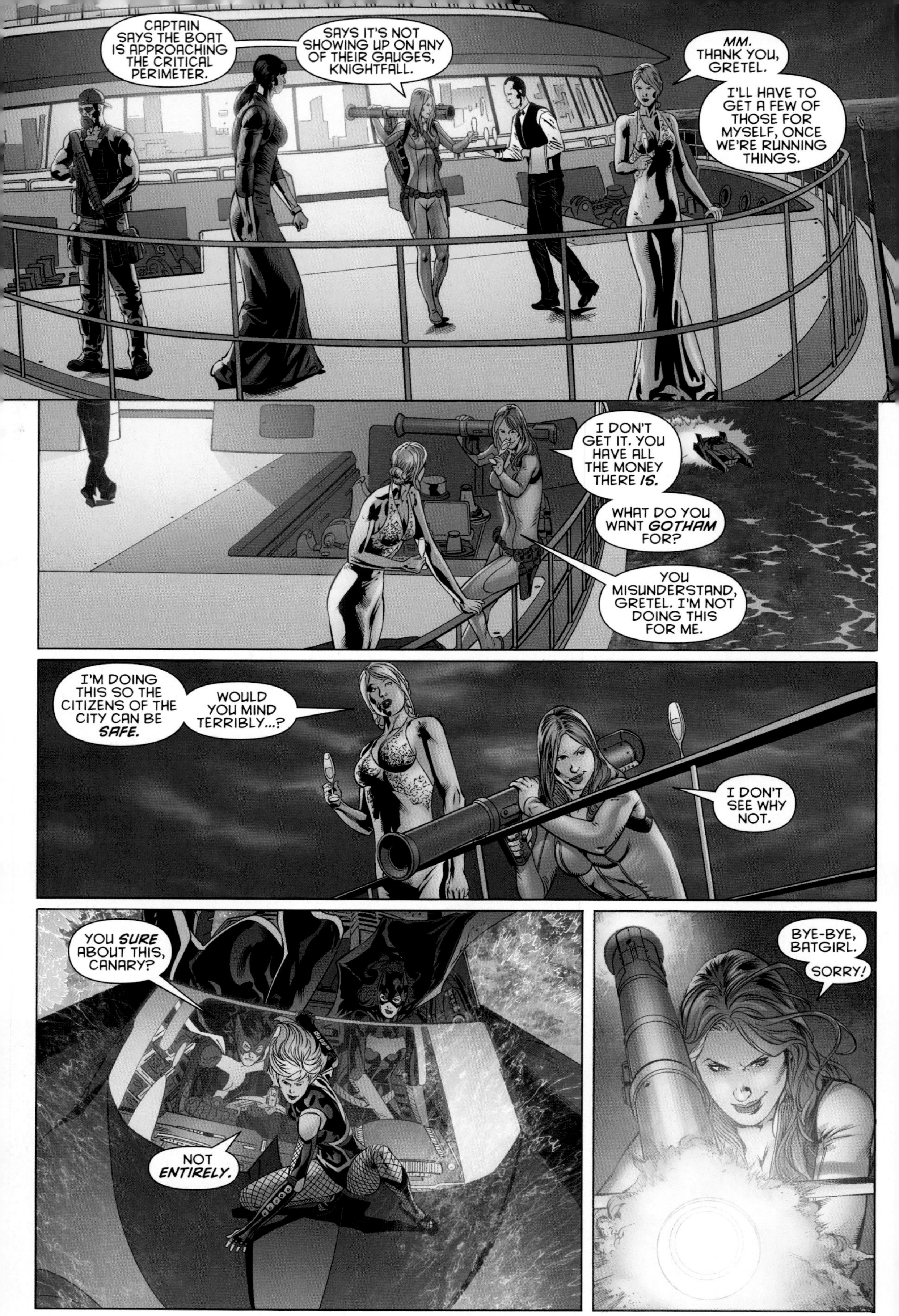
CAPTAIN SAYS THE BOAT IS APPROACHING THE CRITICAL PERIMETER.
SAYS IT'S NOT SHOWING UP ON ANY OF THEIR GAUGES, KNIGHTFALL.
MM. THANK YOU, GRETEL.
I'LL HAVE TO GET A FEW OF THOSE FOR MYSELF, ONCE WE'RE RUNNING THINGS.
I DON'T GET IT. YOU HAVE ALL THE MONEY THERE IS.
WHAT DO YOU WANT GOTHAM FOR?
YOU MISUNDERSTAND, GRETEL. I'M NOT DOING THIS FOR ME.
I'M DOING THIS SO THE CITIZENS OF THE CITY CAN BE SAFE.
WOULD YOU MIND TERRIBLY...?
I DON'T SEE WHY NOT.
YOU SURE ABOUT THIS, CANARY?
NOT ENTIRELY.
BYE-BYE, BATGIRL.
SORRY!

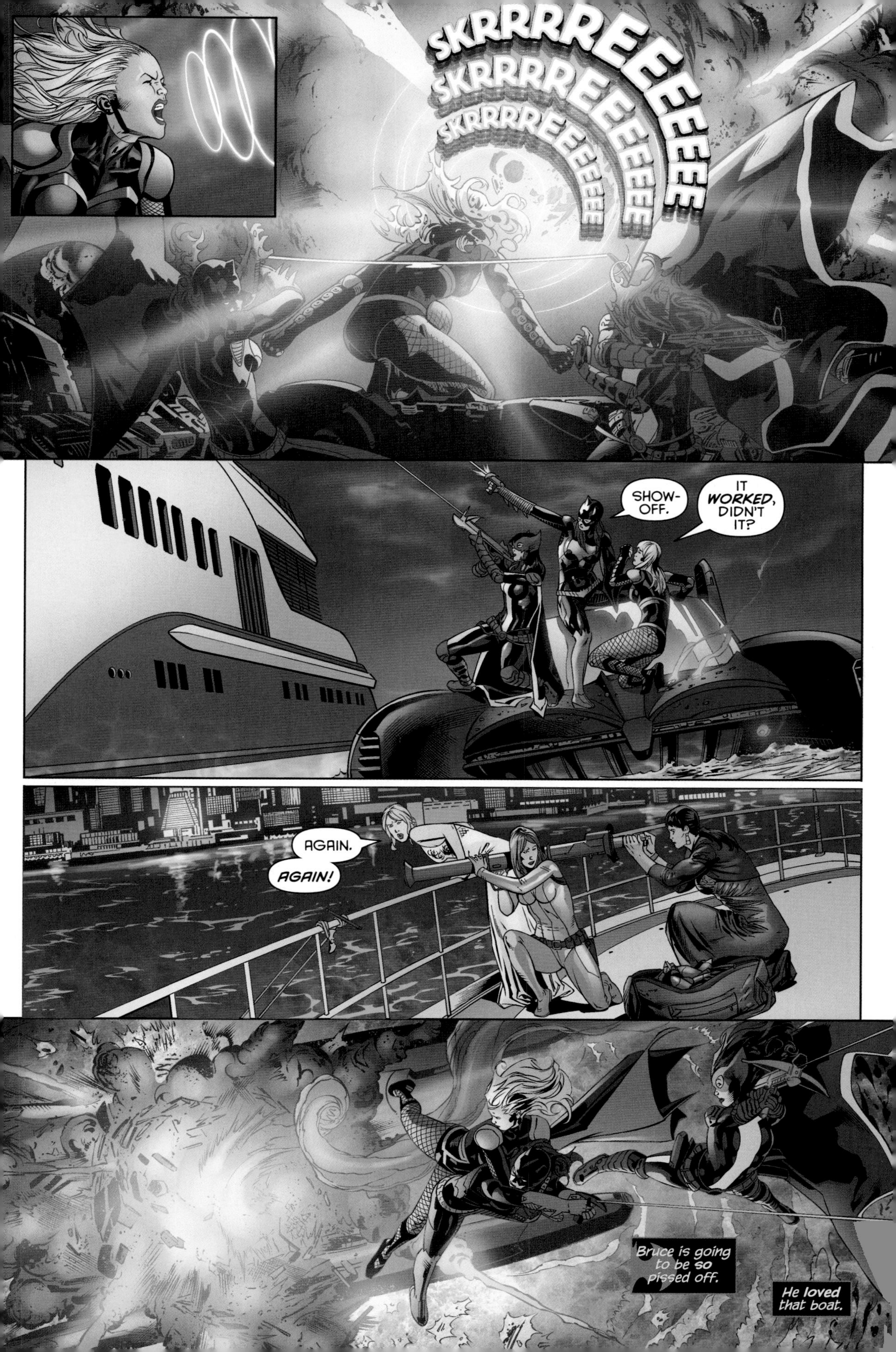
SKRRRREEEEEEE
SKRRRREEEEEEEE
SKRRRREEEEEEEE
SHOW-OFF.
IT WORKED, DIDN'T IT?
AGAIN.
AGAIN!
Bruce is going to be so pissed off.
He loved that boat.

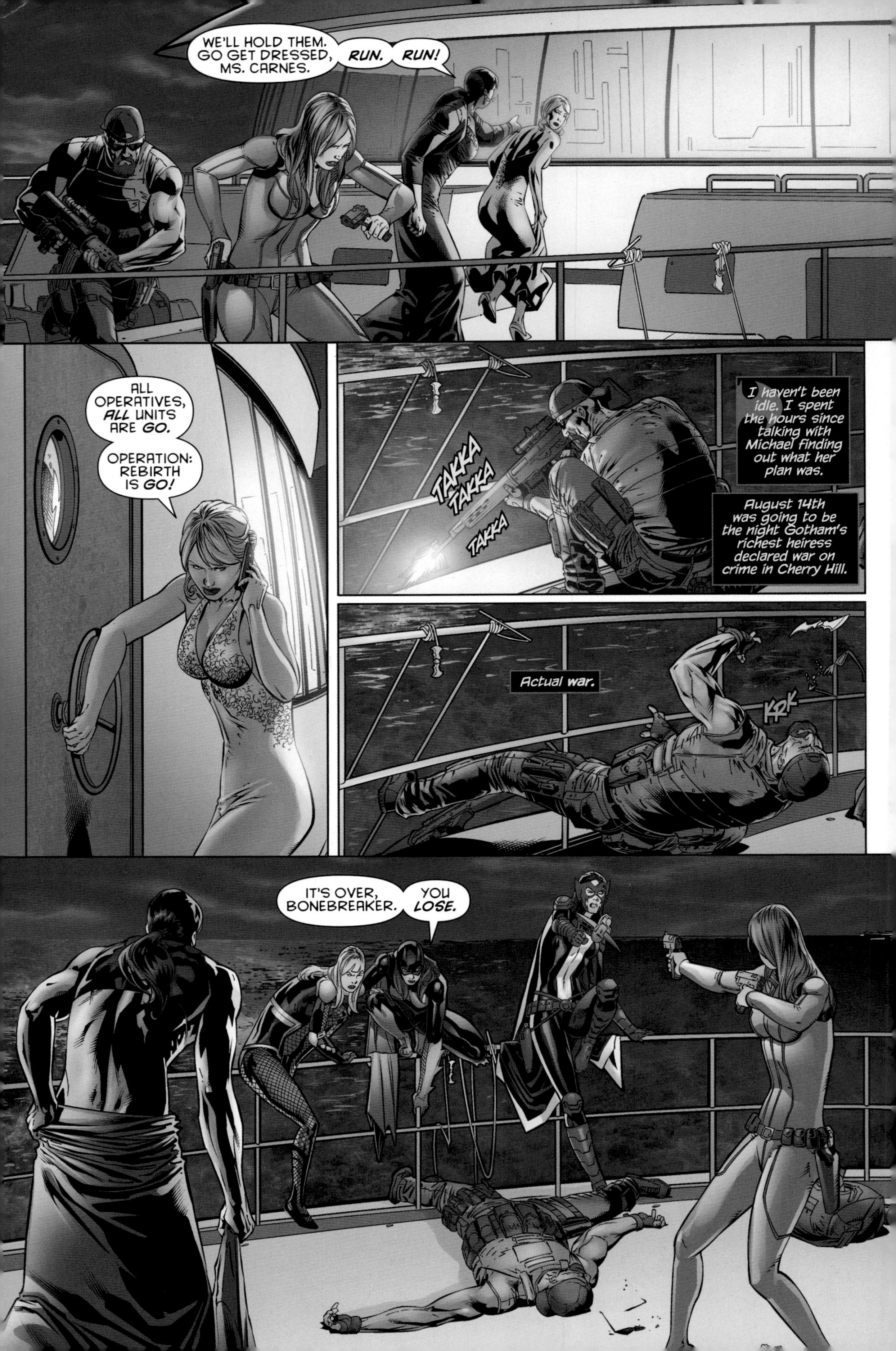

WE'LL HOLD THEM. GO GET DRESSED, MS. CARNES.
RUN.
RUN!
ALL OPERATIVES, ALL UNITS ARE GO.
OPERATION: REBIRTH IS GO!
TAKKA TAKKA
TAKKA
I haven't been idle. I spent the hours since talking with Michael finding out what her plan was.
August 14th was going to be the night Gotham's richest heiress declared war on crime in Cherry Hill.
Actual war.
KRK
IT'S OVER, BONEBREAKER.
YOU LOSE.

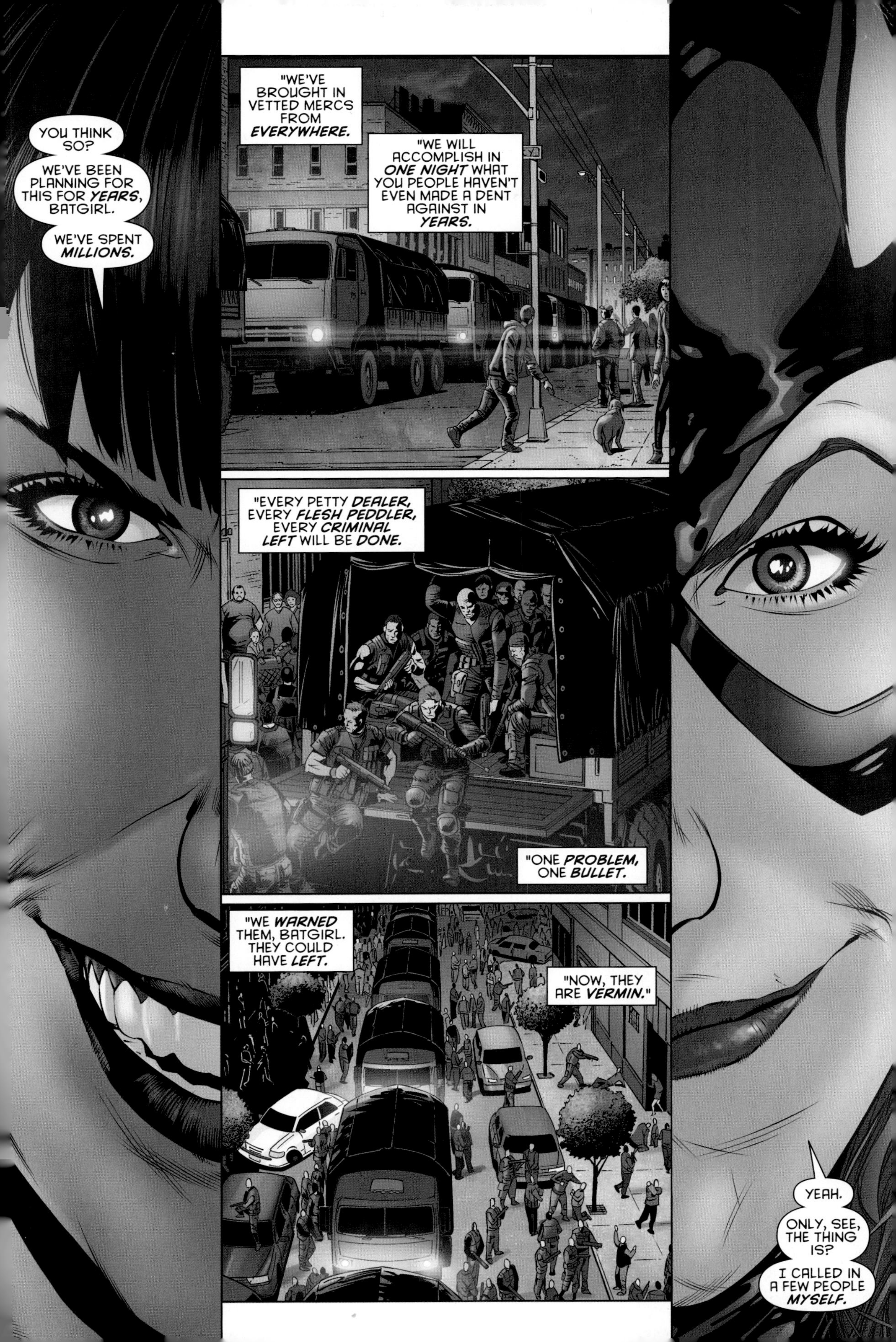
YOU THINK SO?
WE'VE BEEN PLANNING FOR THIS FOR YEARS, BATGIRL.
WE'VE SPENT MILLIONS.
"WE'VE BROUGHT IN VETTED MERCS FROM EVERYWHERE.
"WE WILL ACCOMPLISH IN ONE NIGHT WHAT YOU PEOPLE HAVEN'T EVEN MADE A DENT AGAINST IN YEARS.
"EVERY PETTY DEALER, EVERY FLESH PEDDLER, EVERY CRIMINAL LEFT WILL BE DONE.
"ONE PROBLEM, ONE BULLET.
"WE WARNED THEM, BATGIRL. THEY COULD HAVE LEFT.
"NOW, THEY ARE VERMIN."
YEAH.
ONLY, SEE, THE THING IS?
I CALLED IN A FEW PEOPLE MYSELF.

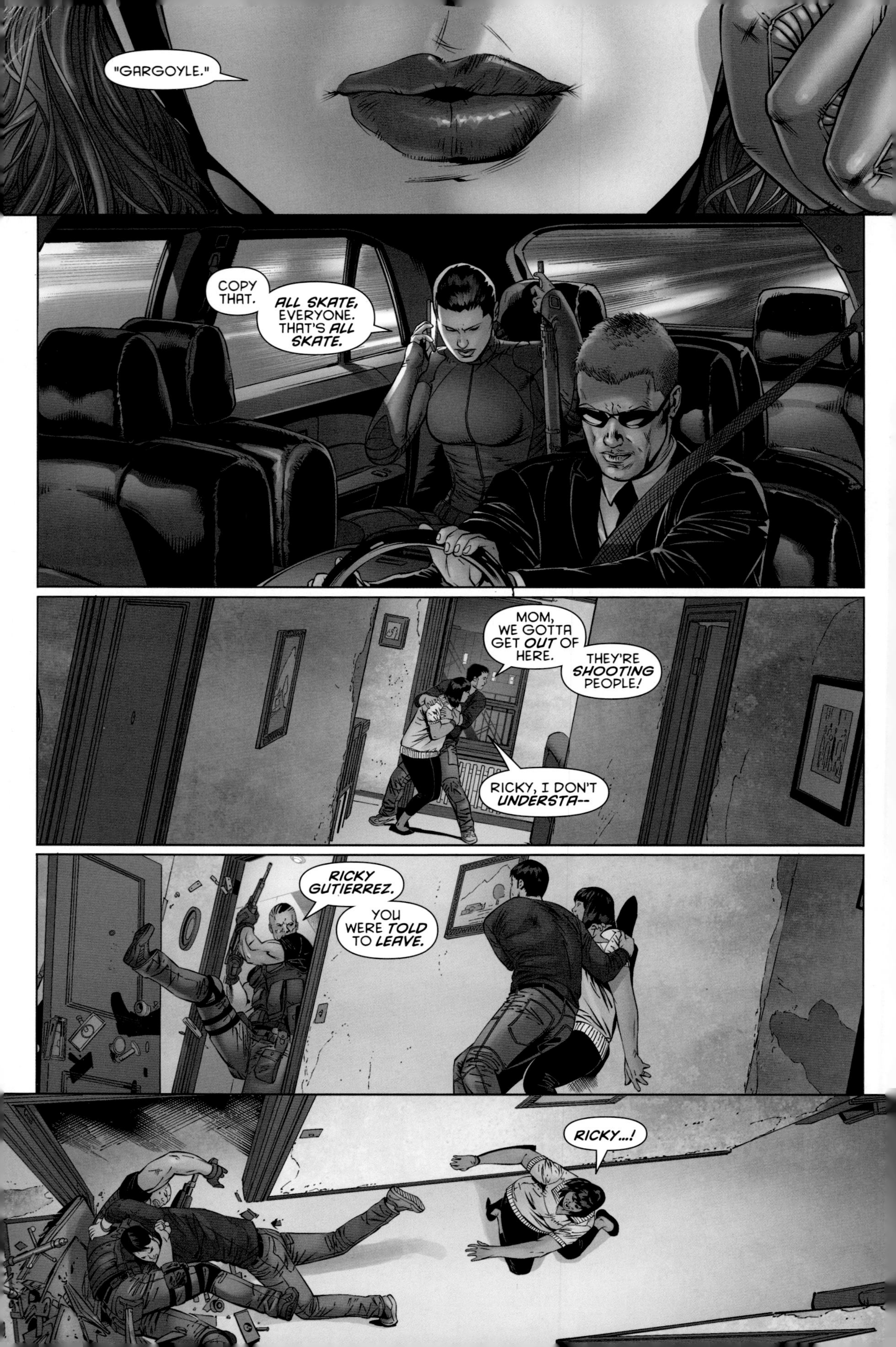
"GARGOYLE."
COPY THAT.
ALL SKATE, EVERYONE. THAT'S *ALL SKATE.*
MOM, WE GOTTA GET *OUT* OF HERE.
THEY'RE *SHOOTING* PEOPLE!
RICKY, I DON'T *UNDERSTA--*
RICKY GUTIERREZ.
YOU WERE *TOLD* TO *LEAVE.*
RICKY...!

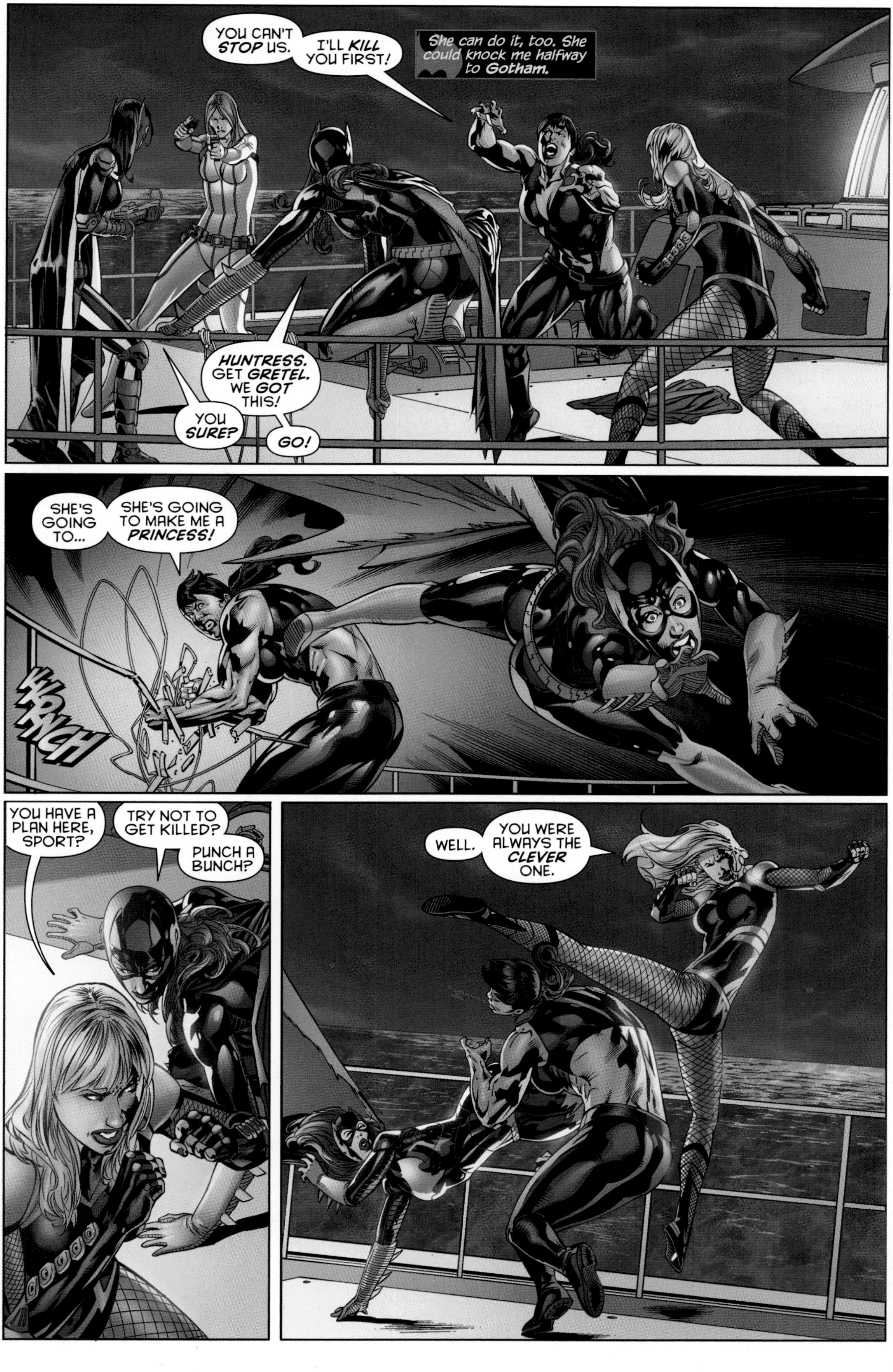
YOU CAN'T STOP US.
I'LL KILL YOU FIRST!
She can do it, too. She could knock me halfway to Gotham.
HUNTRESS. GET GRETEL. WE GOT THIS!
YOU SURE?
GO!
SHE'S GOING TO...
SHE'S GOING TO MAKE ME A PRINCESS!
KRNCH
YOU HAVE A PLAN HERE, SPORT?
TRY NOT TO GET KILLED?
PUNCH A BUNCH?
WELL.
YOU WERE ALWAYS THE CLEVER ONE.

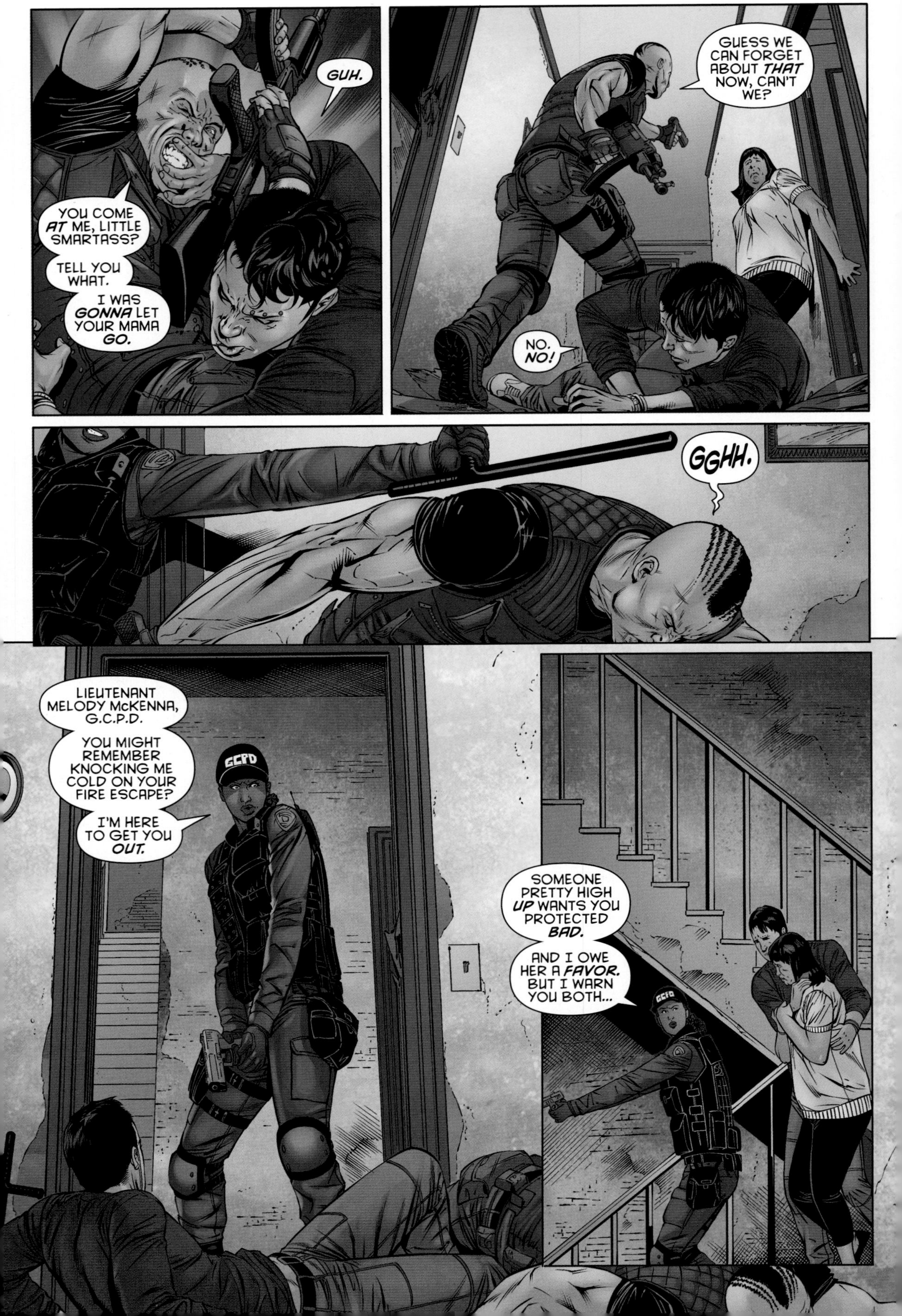
GUH.
YOU COME AT ME, LITTLE SMARTASS?
TELL YOU WHAT.
I WAS GONNA LET YOUR MAMA GO.
GUESS WE CAN FORGET ABOUT THAT NOW, CAN'T WE?
NO. NO!
GGHH.
LIEUTENANT MELODY McKENNA, G.C.P.D.
YOU MIGHT REMEMBER KNOCKING ME COLD ON YOUR FIRE ESCAPE?
I'M HERE TO GET YOU OUT.
SOMEONE PRETTY HIGH UP WANTS YOU PROTECTED BAD.
AND I OWE HER A FAVOR. BUT I WARN YOU BOTH...

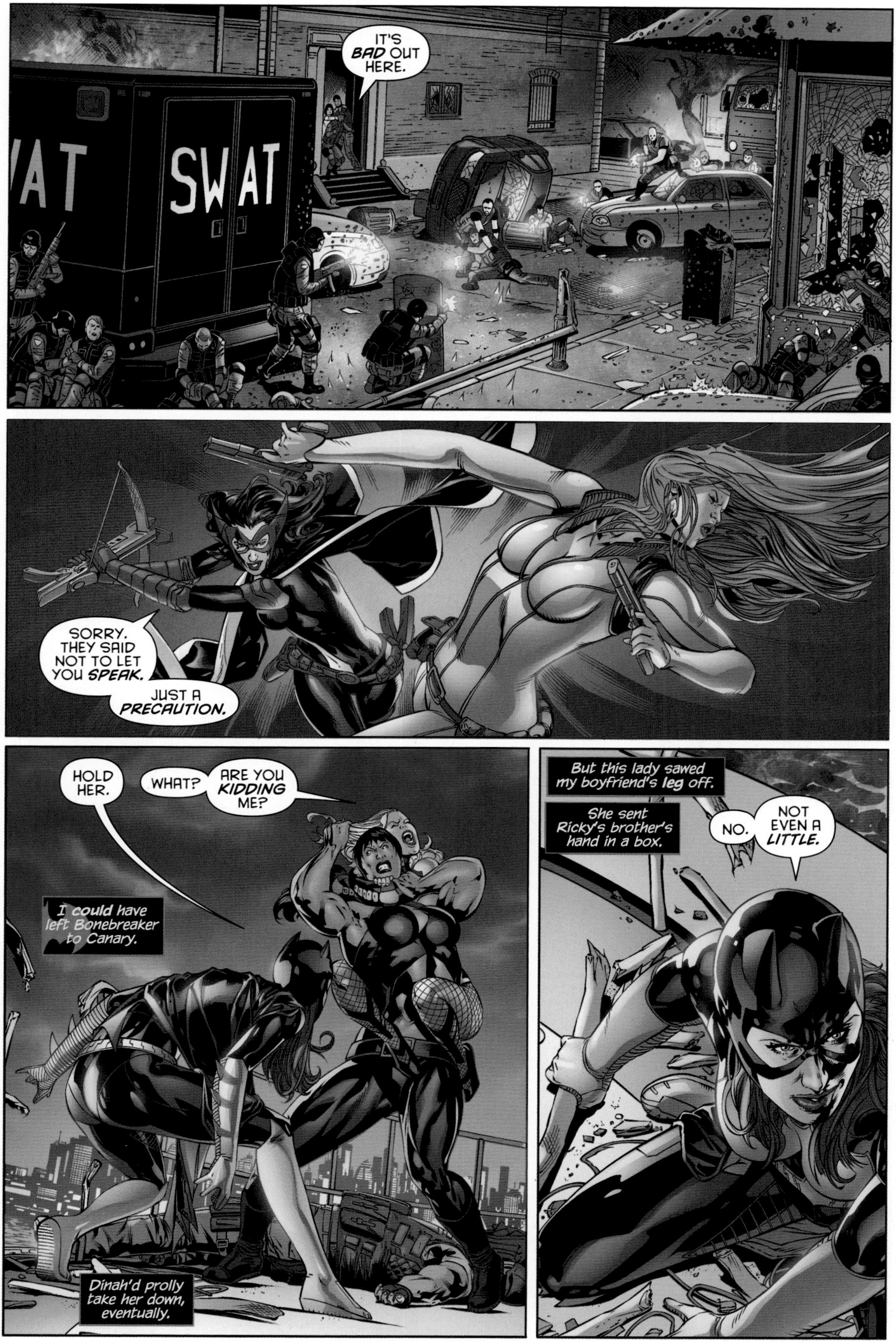
IT'S BAD OUT HERE.
SORRY. THEY SAID NOT TO LET YOU SPEAK.
JUST A PRECAUTION.
HOLD HER.
WHAT?
ARE YOU KIDDING ME?
I could have left Bonebreaker to Canary.
Dinah'd prolly take her down, eventually.
But this lady sawed my boyfriend's leg off.
She sent Ricky's brother's hand in a box.
NO.
NOT EVEN A LITTLE.
SWAT
SWAT

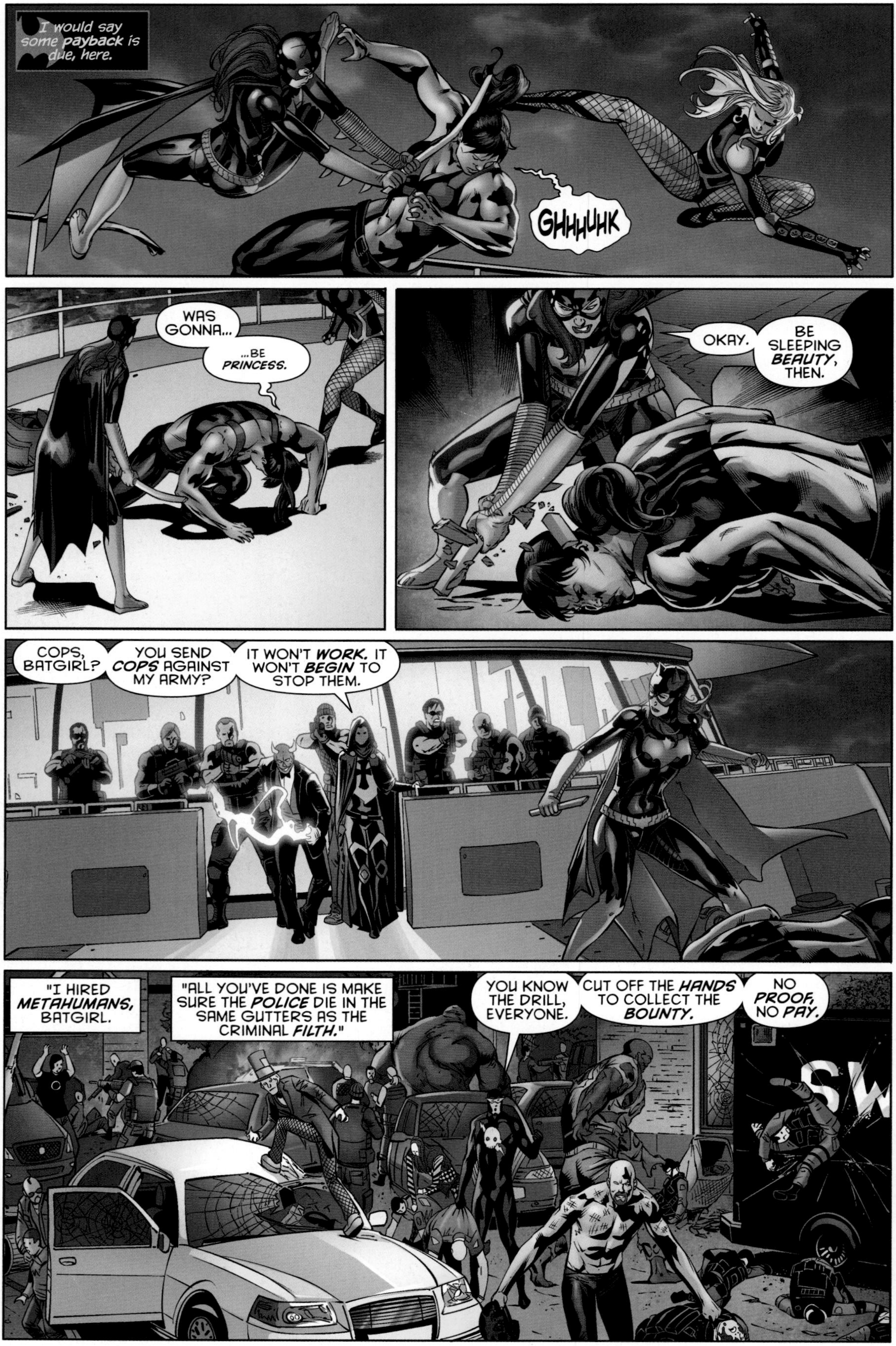
I would say some payback is due, here.
GHHHUHK
WAS GONNA...
...BE PRINCESS.
OKAY.
BE SLEEPING BEAUTY, THEN.
COPS, BATGIRL?
YOU SEND COPS AGAINST MY ARMY?
IT WON'T WORK. IT WON'T BEGIN TO STOP THEM.
"I HIRED METAHUMANS, BATGIRL.
"ALL YOU'VE DONE IS MAKE SURE THE POLICE DIE IN THE SAME GUTTERS AS THE CRIMINAL FILTH."
YOU KNOW THE DRILL, EVERYONE.
CUT OFF THE HANDS TO COLLECT THE BOUNTY.
NO PROOF, NO PAY.

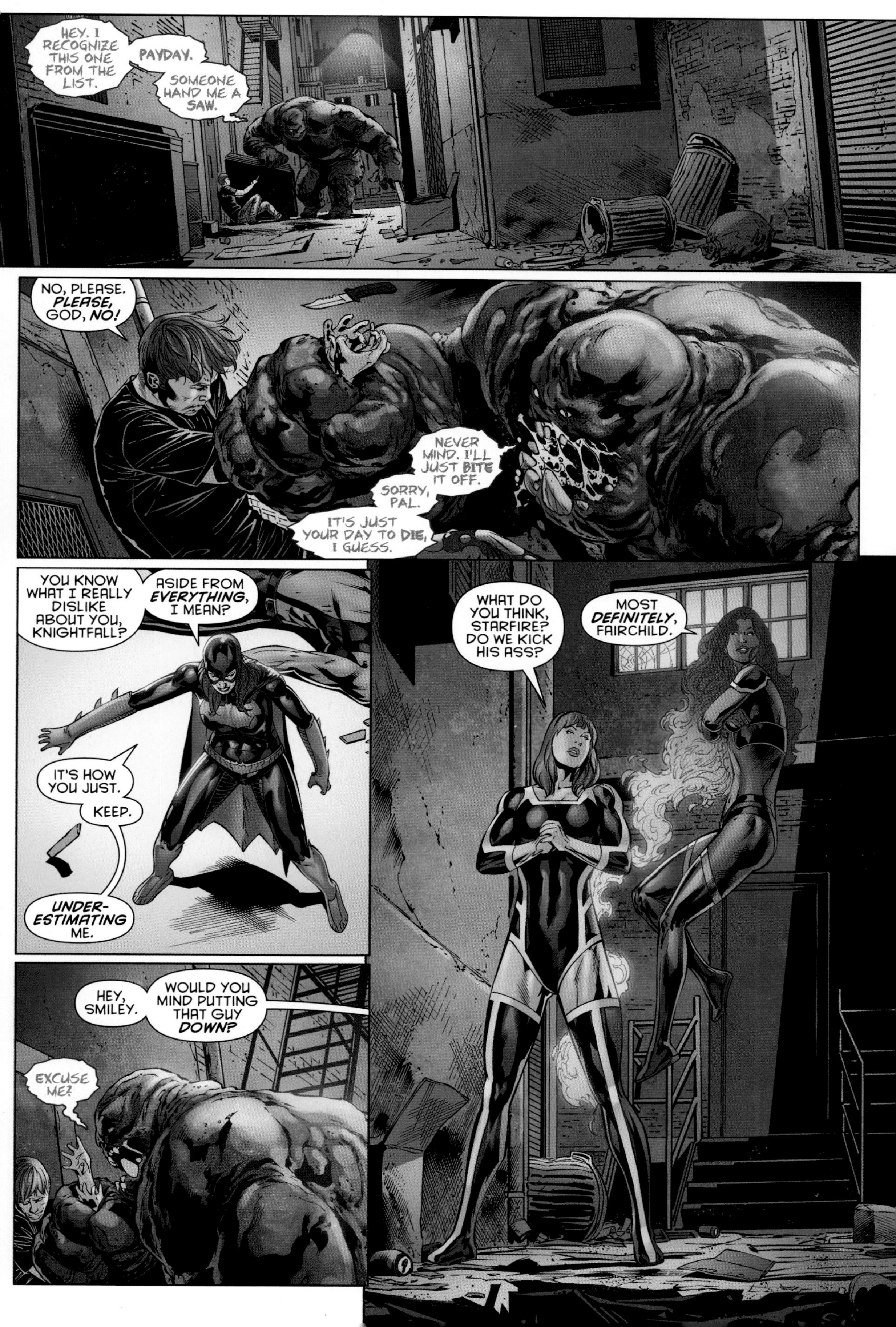
HEY. I RECOGNIZE THIS ONE FROM THE LIST.
PAYDAY.
SOMEONE HAND ME A SAW.
NO, PLEASE. PLEASE, GOD, NO!
NEVER MIND. I'LL JUST BITE IT OFF.
SORRY, PAL.
IT'S JUST YOUR DAY TO DIE, I GUESS.
YOU KNOW WHAT I REALLY DISLIKE ABOUT YOU, KNIGHTFALL?
ASIDE FROM EVERYTHING, I MEAN?
IT'S HOW YOU JUST.
KEEP.
UNDER-ESTIMATING ME.
HEY, SMILEY.
WOULD YOU MIND PUTTING THAT GUY DOWN?
EXCUSE ME?
WHAT DO YOU THINK, STARFIRE? DO WE KICK HIS ASS?
MOST DEFINITELY, FAIRCHILD.

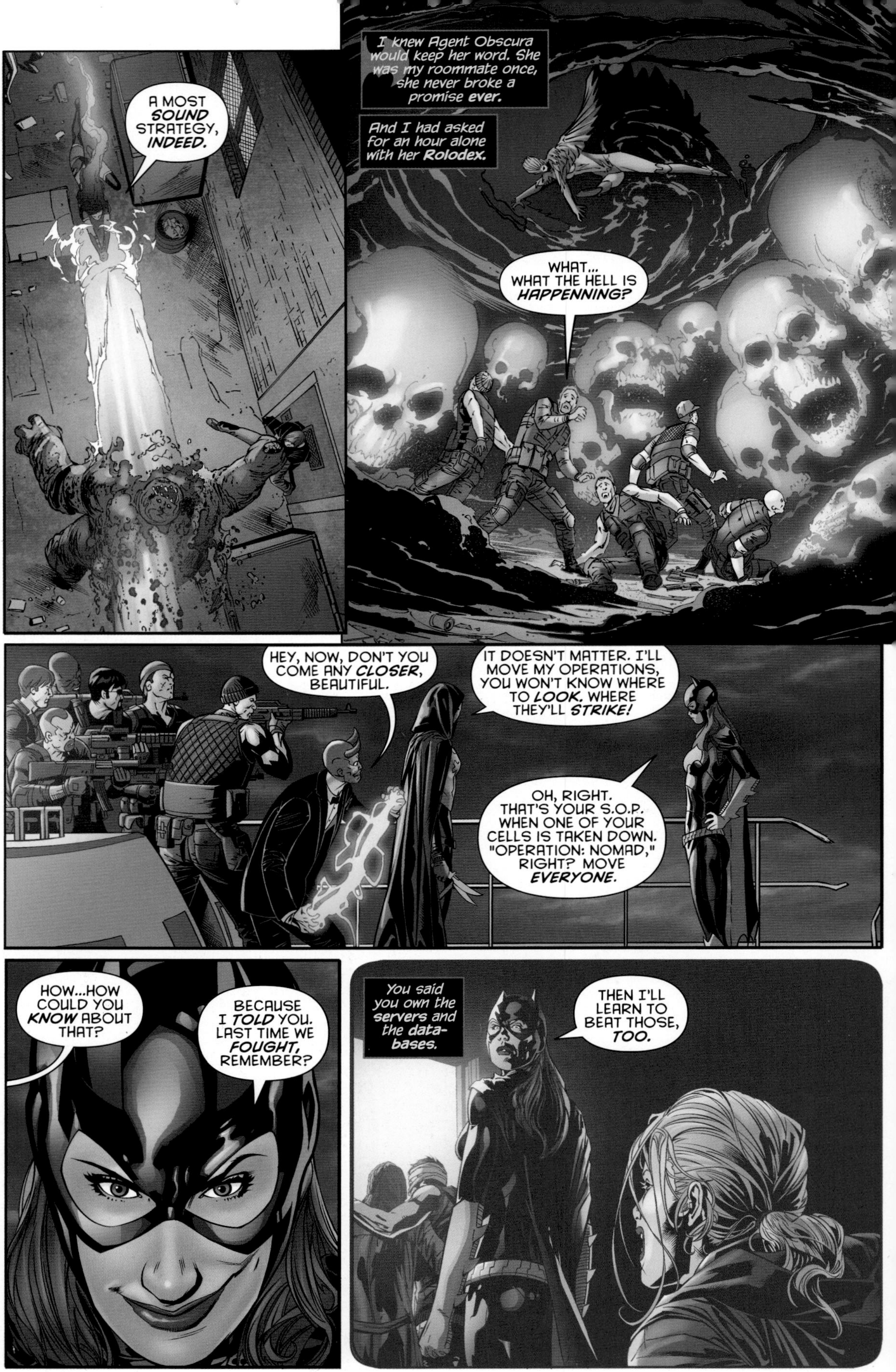
A MOST SOUND STRATEGY, INDEED.
I knew Agent Obscura would keep her word. She was my roommate once, she never broke a promise ever.
And I had asked for an hour alone with her Rolodex.
WHAT... WHAT THE HELL IS HAPPENNING?
HEY, NOW, DON'T YOU COME ANY CLOSER, BEAUTIFUL.
IT DOESN'T MATTER. I'LL MOVE MY OPERATIONS, YOU WON'T KNOW WHERE TO LOOK. WHERE THEY'LL STRIKE!
OH, RIGHT. THAT'S YOUR S.O.P. WHEN ONE OF YOUR CELLS IS TAKEN DOWN. "OPERATION: NOMAD," RIGHT? MOVE EVERYONE.
HOW...HOW COULD YOU KNOW ABOUT THAT?
BECAUSE I TOLD YOU. LAST TIME WE FOUGHT, REMEMBER?
You said you own the servers and the data-bases.
THEN I'LL LEARN TO BEAT THOSE, TOO.

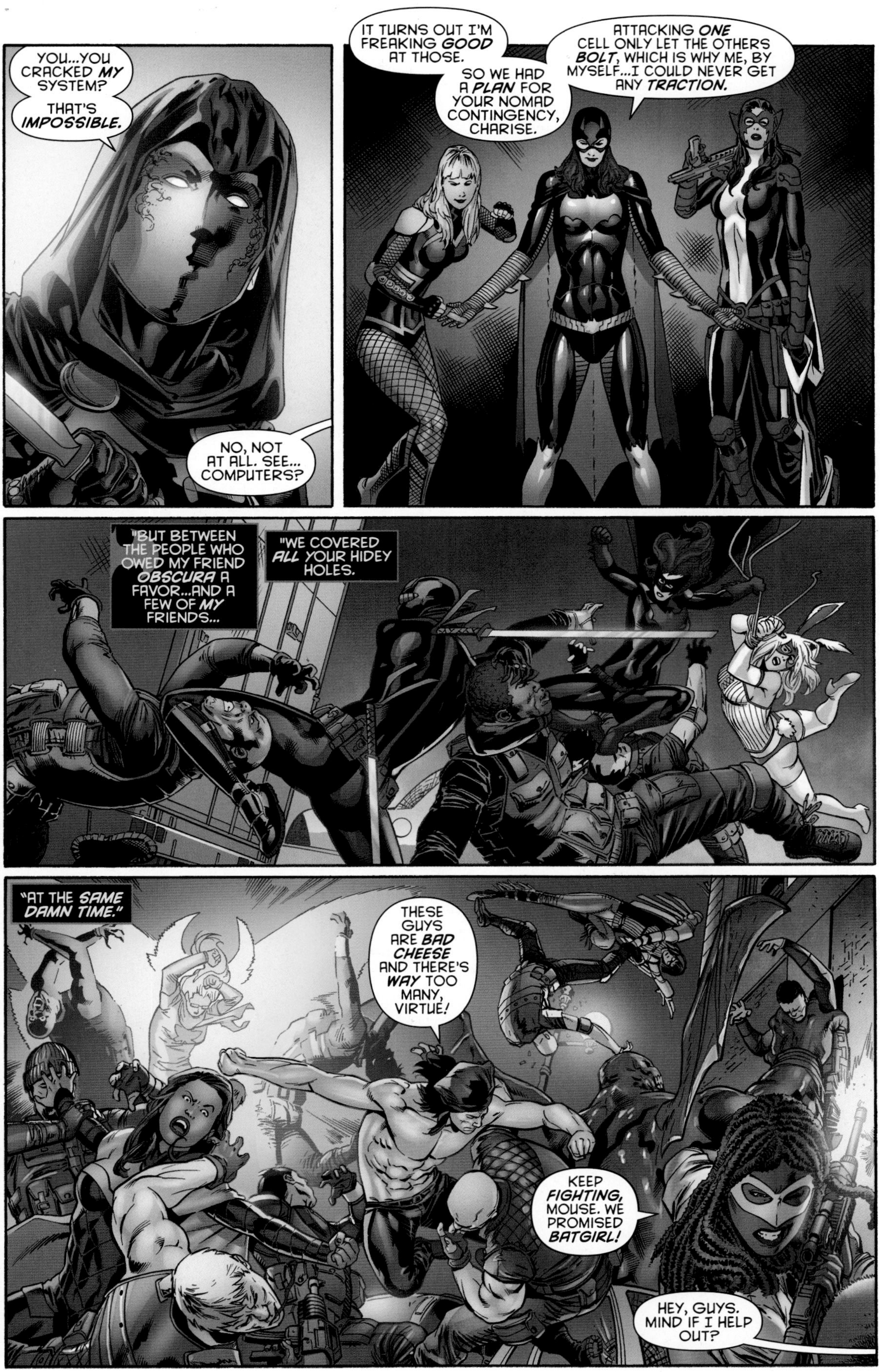
YOU...YOU CRACKED MY SYSTEM?
THAT'S IMPOSSIBLE.
NO, NOT AT ALL. SEE... COMPUTERS?
IT TURNS OUT I'M FREAKING GOOD AT THOSE.
SO WE HAD A PLAN FOR YOUR NOMAD CONTINGENCY, CHARISE.
ATTACKING ONE CELL ONLY LET THE OTHERS BOLT, WHICH IS WHY ME, BY MYSELF...I COULD NEVER GET ANY TRACTION.
"BUT BETWEEN THE PEOPLE WHO OWED MY FRIEND OBSCURA A FAVOR...AND A FEW OF MY FRIENDS...
"WE COVERED ALL YOUR HIDEY HOLES.
"AT THE SAME DAMN TIME."
THESE GUYS ARE BAD CHEESE AND THERE'S WAY TOO MANY, VIRTUE!
KEEP FIGHTING, MOUSE. WE PROMISED BATGIRL!
HEY, GUYS. MIND IF I HELP OUT?

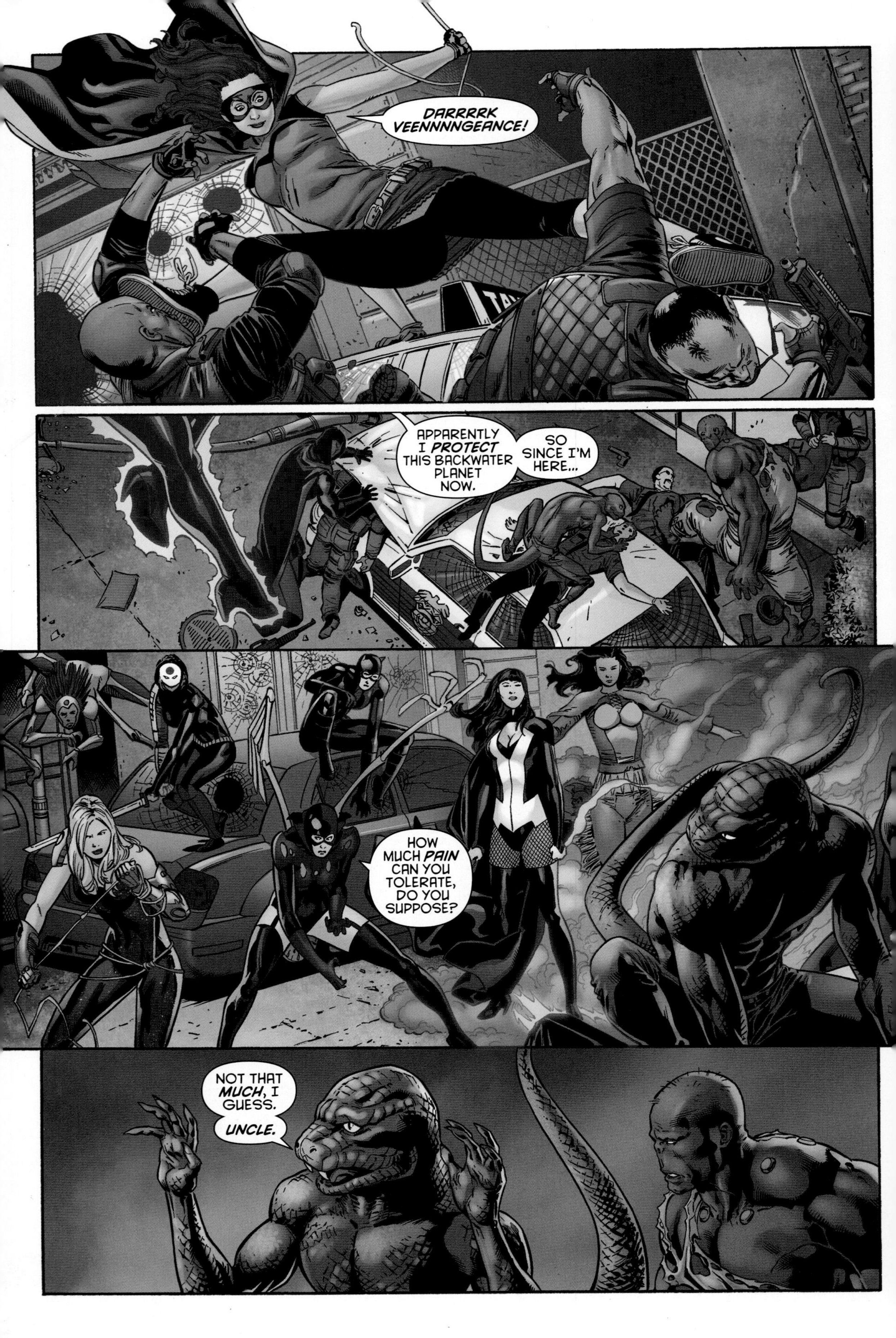
DARRRRK VEENNNNGEANCE!
APPARENTLY I PROTECT THIS BACKWATER PLANET NOW.
SO SINCE I'M HERE...
HOW MUCH PAIN CAN YOU TOLERATE, DO YOU SUPPOSE?
NOT THAT MUCH, I GUESS.
UNCLE.

Okay. I once beat Knightfall within an inch of her life and it only made her *mad*.

Time to use the *big* guns.

HANG ON, I HAVE SOMETHING TO SHOW YOU, CHARISE.

LOOK *OUT.* SHE'S GOING FOR A *WEAPON!*

OH, SHUT *UP,* GROTESQUE. NO ONE WAS *TALKING* TO YOU.

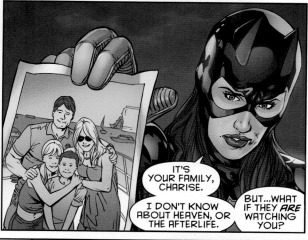

IT'S YOUR FAMILY, CHARISE.

I DON'T KNOW ABOUT HEAVEN, OR THE AFTERLIFE.

BUT...WHAT IF THEY *ARE* WATCHING YOU?

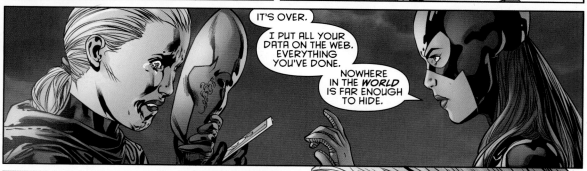

IT'S OVER.

I PUT ALL YOUR DATA ON THE WEB. EVERYTHING YOU'VE DONE.

NOWHERE IN THE *WORLD* IS FAR ENOUGH TO HIDE.

I THOUGHT, I THOUGHT WE WOULD...

I DON'T WANT TO FIGHT YOU, CHARISE.

I DON'T THINK YOU TRULY *KNOW* WHAT YOU'VE DONE.

YOU NEED HELP.

I WANT TO BELIEVE.

I'M SO TIRED.

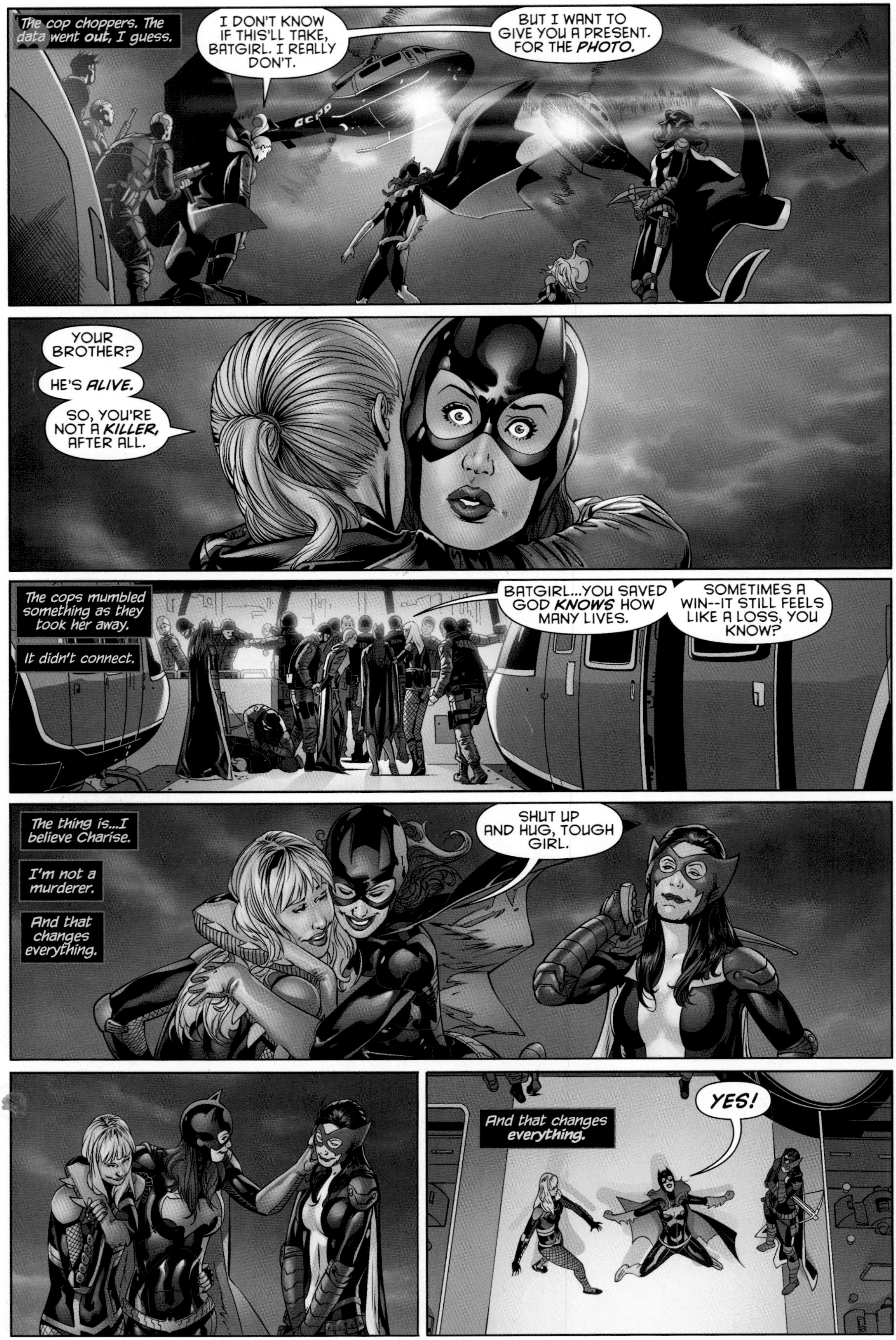
The cop choppers. The data went out, I guess.
I DON'T KNOW IF THIS'LL TAKE, BATGIRL. I REALLY DON'T.
BUT I WANT TO GIVE YOU A PRESENT. FOR THE PHOTO.
YOUR BROTHER?
HE'S ALIVE.
SO, YOU'RE NOT A KILLER, AFTER ALL.
The cops mumbled something as they took her away.
It didn't connect.
BATGIRL...YOU SAVED GOD KNOWS HOW MANY LIVES.
SOMETIMES A WIN--IT STILL FEELS LIKE A LOSS, YOU KNOW?
The thing is...I believe Charise.
I'm not a murderer.
And that changes everything.
SHUT UP AND HUG, TOUGH GIRL.
And that changes everything.
YES!

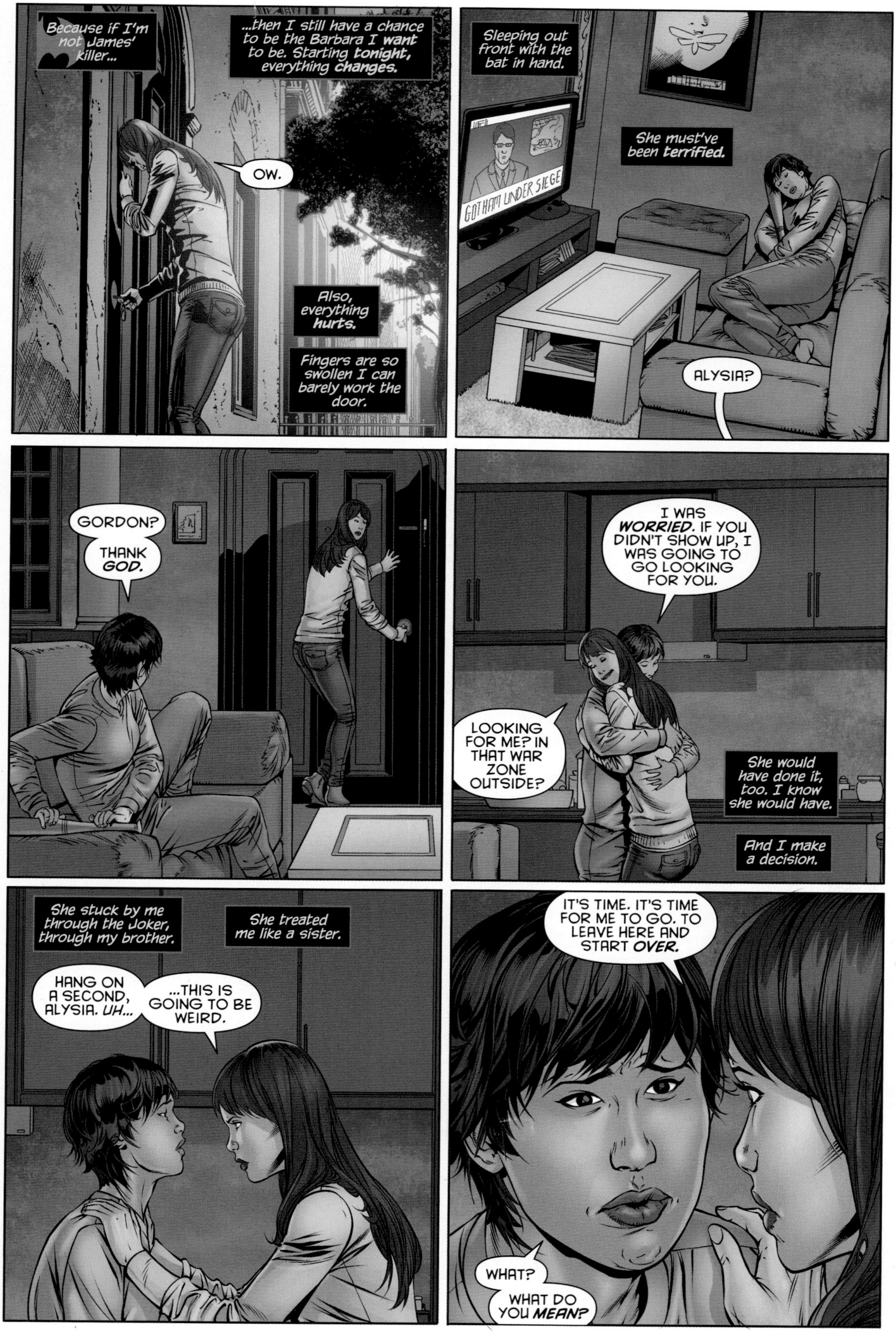
Because if I'm not James' killer...
...then I still have a chance to be the Barbara I want to be. Starting tonight, everything changes.
OW.
Also, everything hurts.
Fingers are so swollen I can barely work the door.
Sleeping out front with the bat in hand.
GOTHAM UNDER SIEGE
She must've been terrified.
ALYSIA?
GORDON?
THANK GOD.
I WAS WORRIED. IF YOU DIDN'T SHOW UP, I WAS GOING TO GO LOOKING FOR YOU.
LOOKING FOR ME? IN THAT WAR ZONE OUTSIDE?
She would have done it, too. I know she would have.
And I make a decision.
She stuck by me through the Joker, through my brother.
She treated me like a sister.
HANG ON A SECOND, ALYSIA. UH...
...THIS IS GOING TO BE WEIRD.
IT'S TIME. IT'S TIME FOR ME TO GO. TO LEAVE HERE AND START OVER.
WHAT?
WHAT DO YOU MEAN?

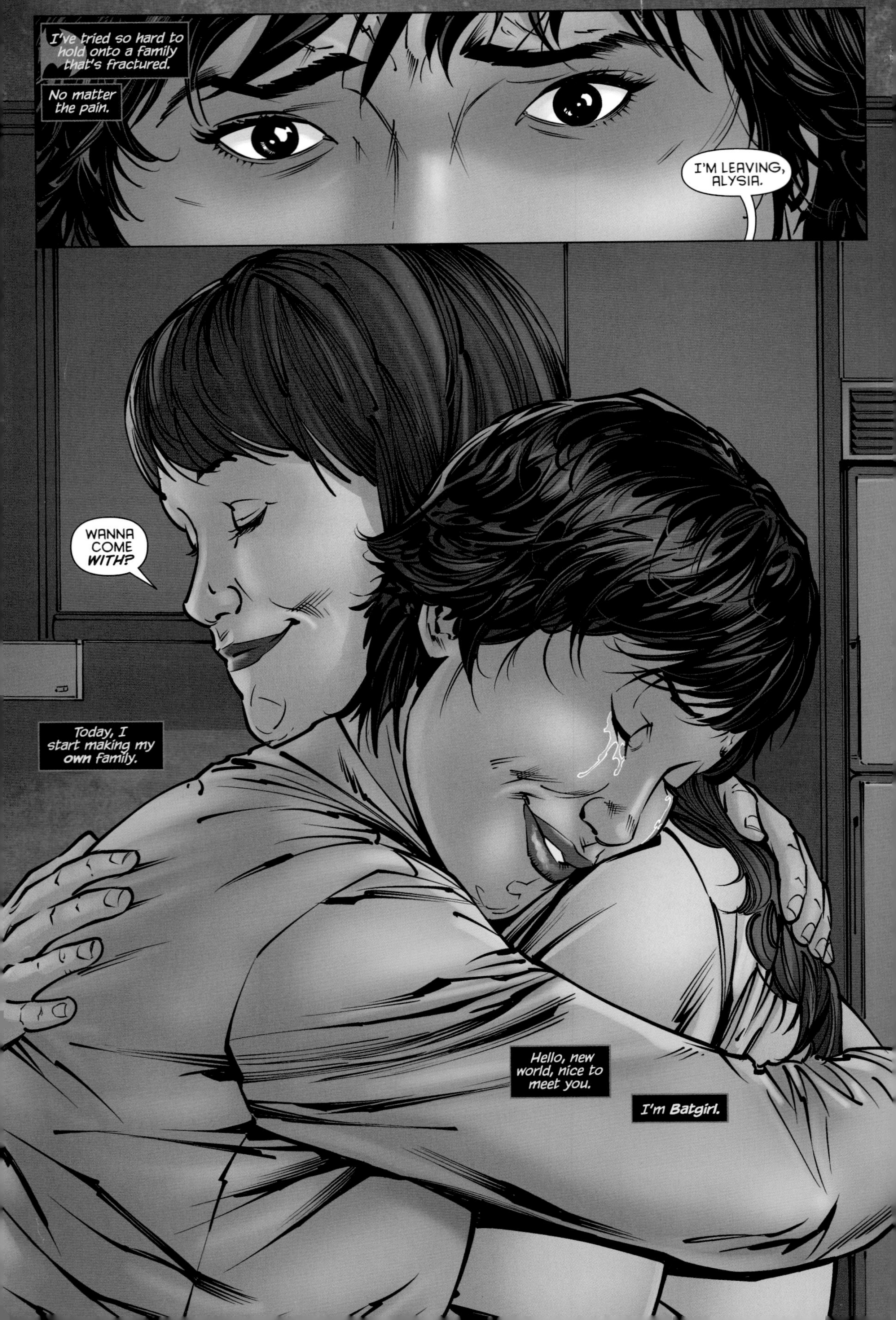
I've tried so hard to hold onto a family that's fractured.
No matter the pain.
I'M LEAVING, ALYSIA.
WANNA COME WITH?
Today, I start making my own family.
Hello, new world, nice to meet you.
I'm Batgirl.

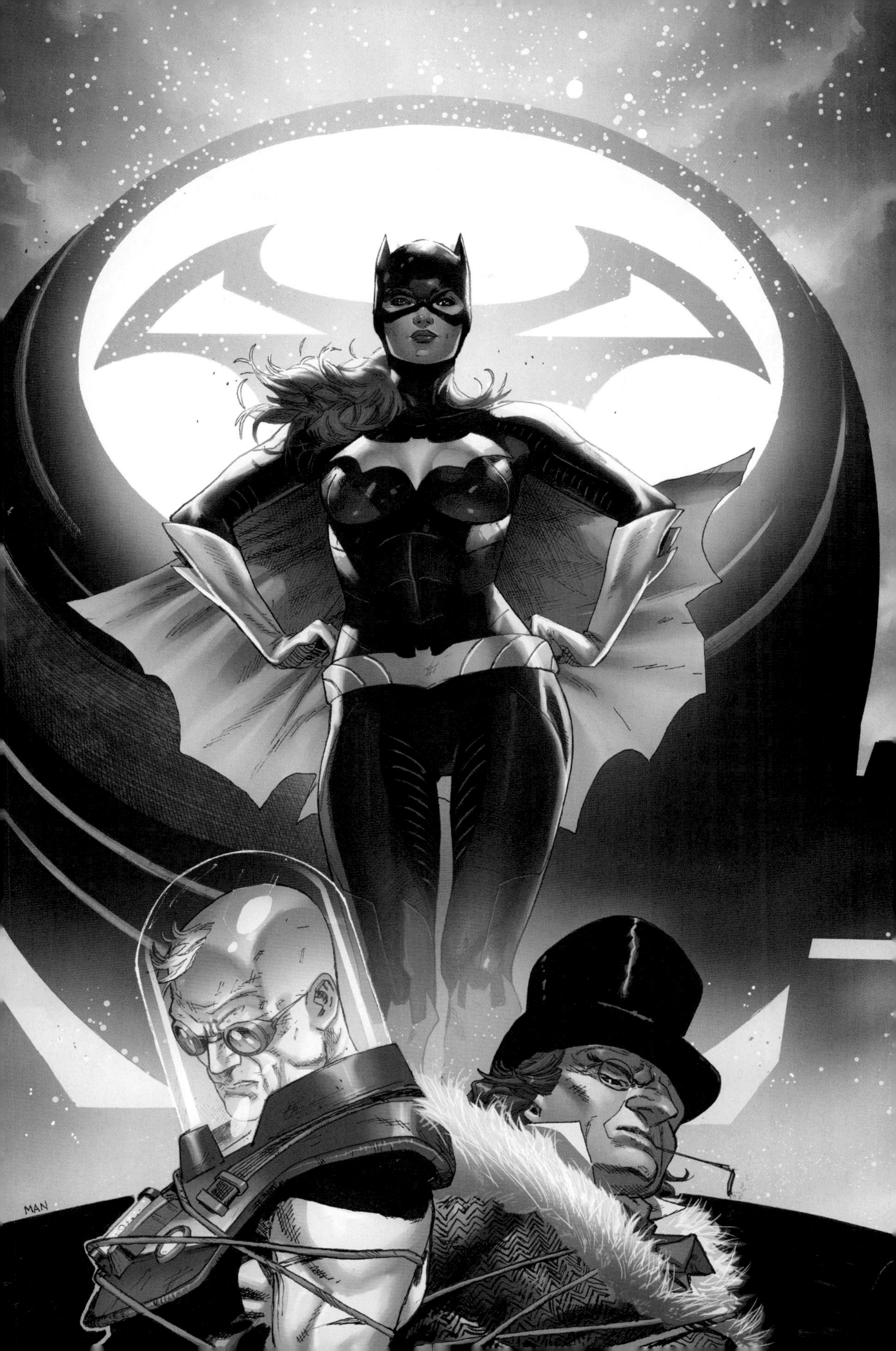
MAN

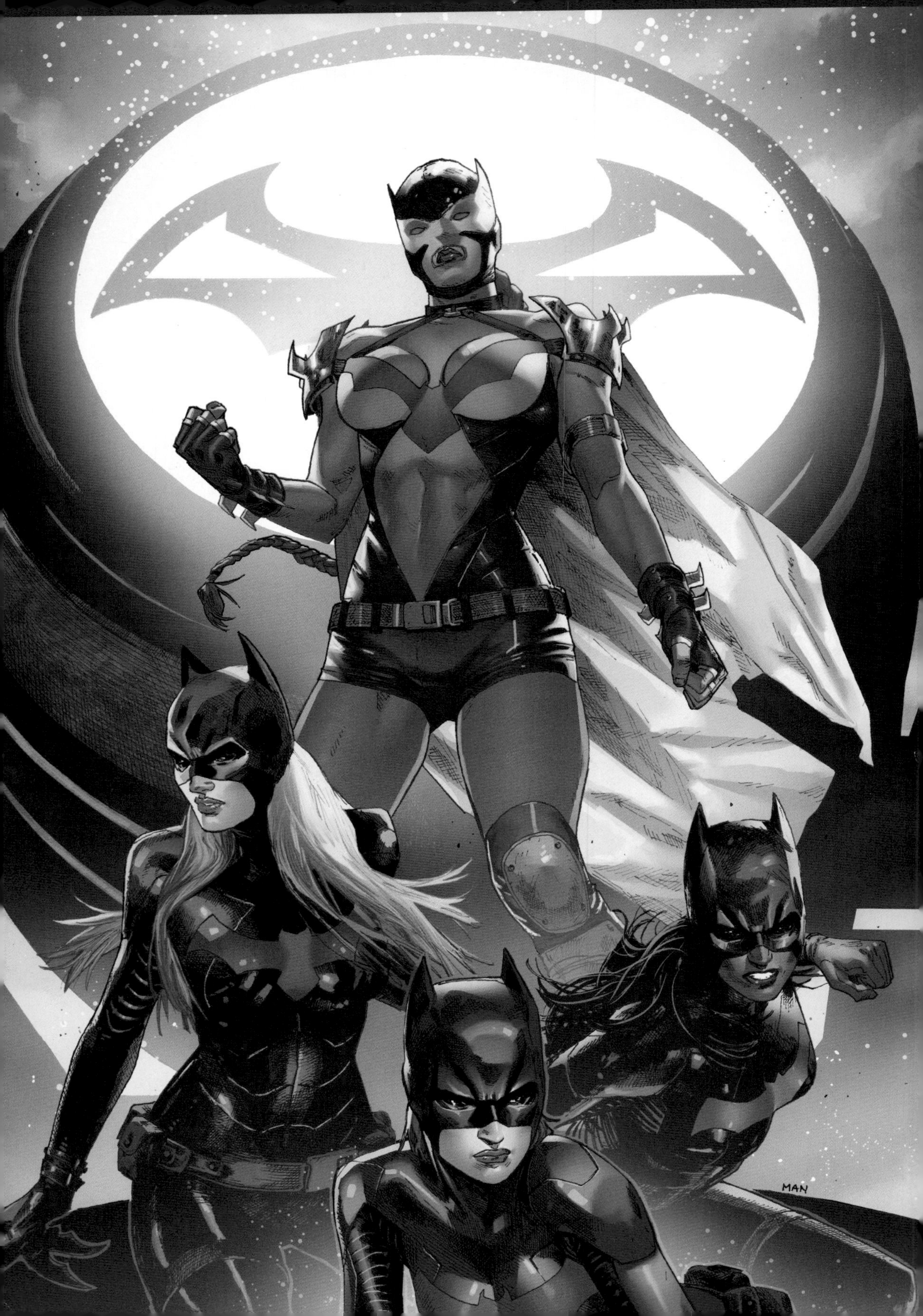
MAN

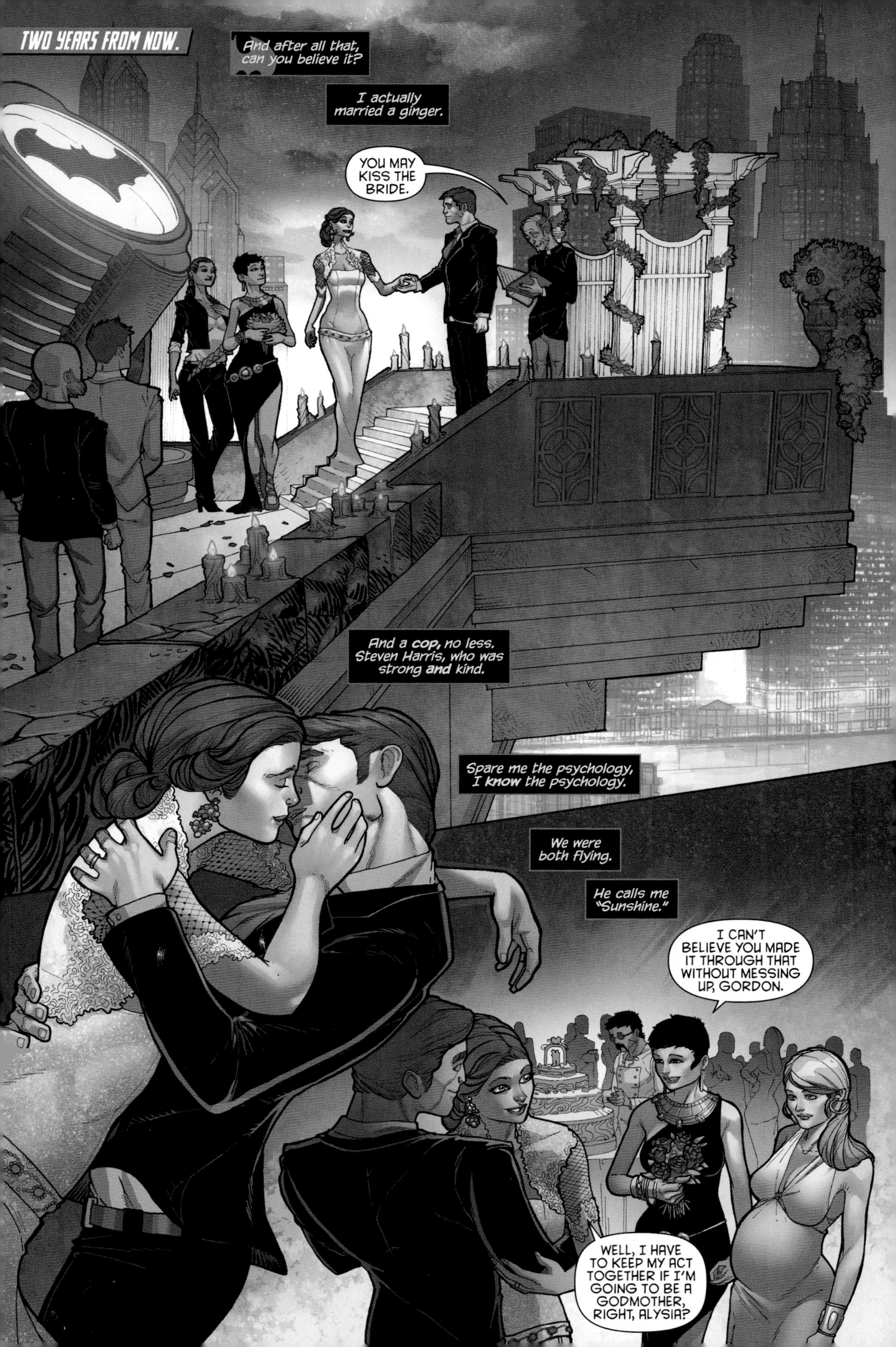
TWO YEARS FROM NOW.
And after all that, can you believe it?
I actually married a ginger.
YOU MAY KISS THE BRIDE.
And a cop, no less. Steven Harris, who was strong and kind.
Spare me the psychology, I know the psychology.
We were both flying.
He calls me "Sunshine."
I CAN'T BELIEVE YOU MADE IT THROUGH THAT WITHOUT MESSING UP, GORDON.
WELL, I HAVE TO KEEP MY ACT TOGETHER IF I'M GOING TO BE A GODMOTHER, RIGHT, ALYSIA?

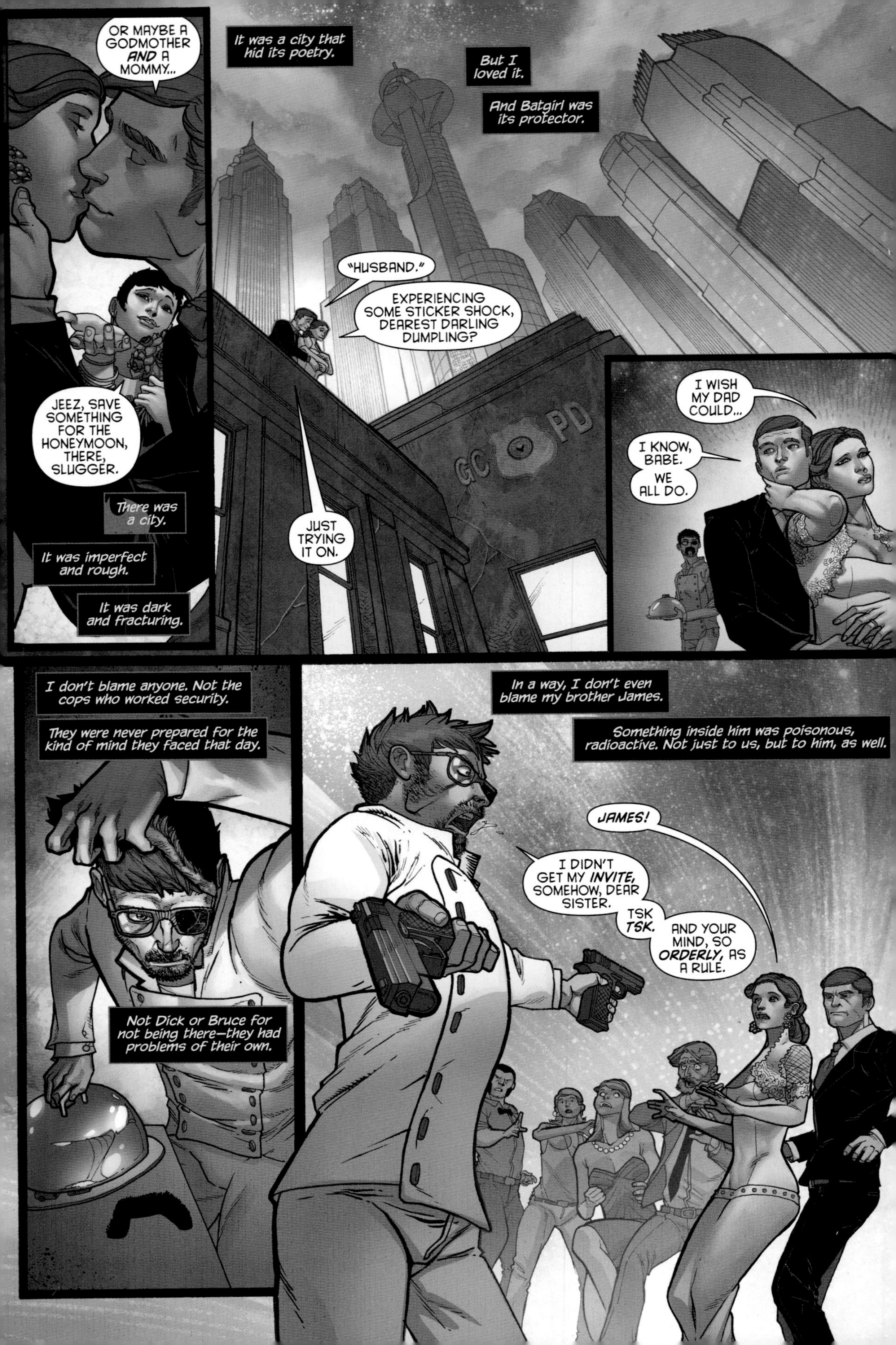
OR MAYBE A GODMOTHER AND A MOMMY...
JEEZ, SAVE SOMETHING FOR THE HONEYMOON, THERE, SLUGGER.
There was a city.
It was imperfect and rough.
It was dark and fracturing.
It was a city that hid its poetry.
But I loved it.
And Batgirl was its protector.
"HUSBAND."
EXPERIENCING SOME STICKER SHOCK, DEAREST DARLING DUMPLING?
JUST TRYING IT ON.
GC PD
I WISH MY DAD COULD...
I KNOW, BABE.
WE ALL DO.
I don't blame anyone. Not the cops who worked security.
They were never prepared for the kind of mind they faced that day.
Not Dick or Bruce for not being there—they had problems of their own.
In a way, I don't even blame my brother James.
Something inside him was poisonous, radioactive. Not just to us, but to him, as well.
JAMES!
I DIDN'T GET MY INVITE, SOMEHOW, DEAR SISTER.
TSK TSK.
AND YOUR MIND, SO ORDERLY, AS A RULE.

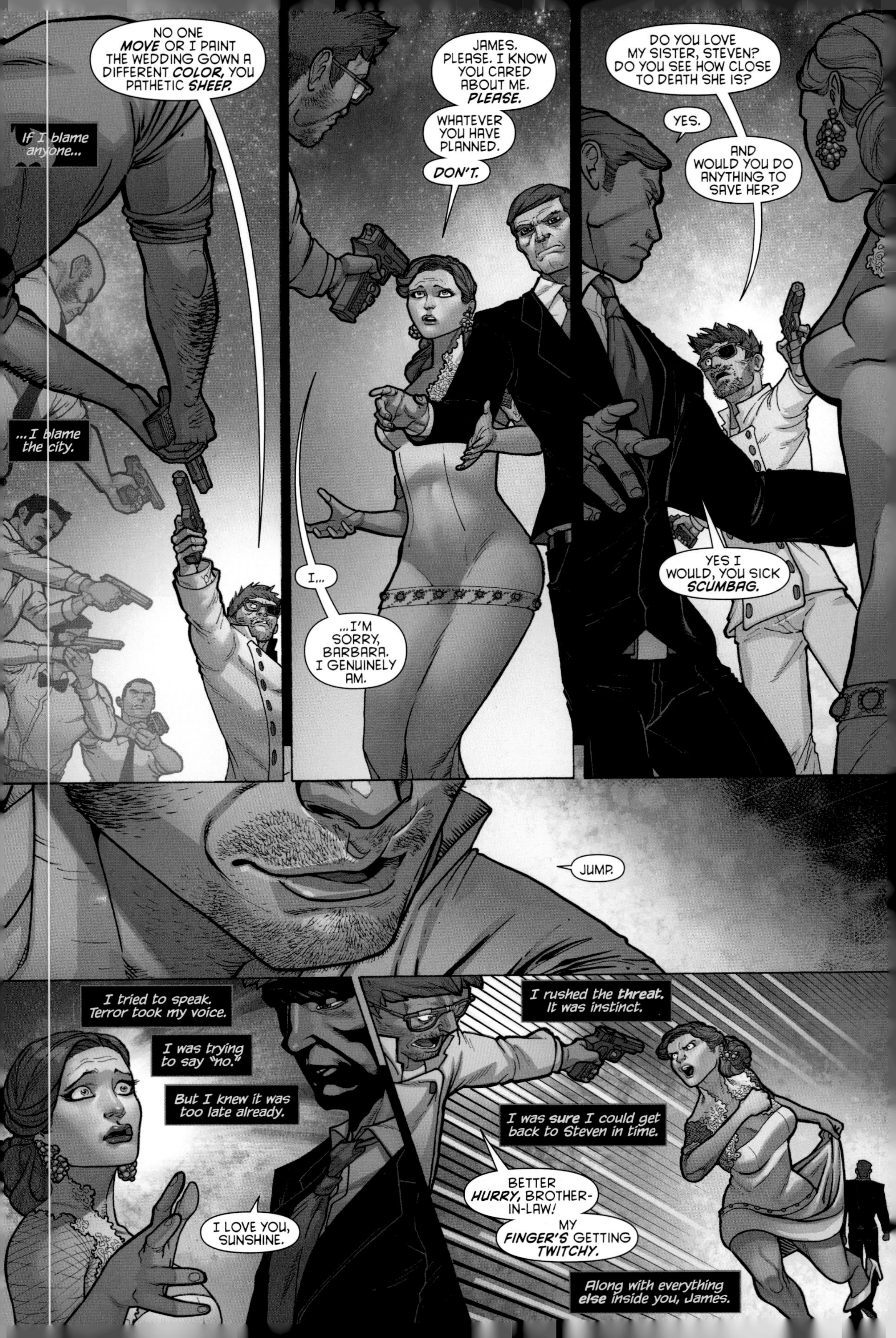
NO ONE MOVE OR I PAINT THE WEDDING GOWN A DIFFERENT COLOR, YOU PATHETIC SHEEP.
If I blame anyone...
...I blame the city.
JAMES. PLEASE. I KNOW YOU CARED ABOUT ME. PLEASE.
WHATEVER YOU HAVE PLANNED.
DON'T.
I...
...I'M SORRY, BARBARA. I GENUINELY AM.
DO YOU LOVE MY SISTER, STEVEN? DO YOU SEE HOW CLOSE TO DEATH SHE IS?
YES.
AND WOULD YOU DO ANYTHING TO SAVE HER?
YES I WOULD, YOU SICK SCUMBAG.
JUMP.
I tried to speak. Terror took my voice.
I was trying to say "no."
But I knew it was too late already.
I LOVE YOU, SUNSHINE.
I rushed the threat. It was instinct.
I was sure I could get back to Steven in time.
BETTER HURRY, BROTHER-IN-LAW!
MY FINGER'S GETTING TWITCHY.
Along with everything else inside you, James.

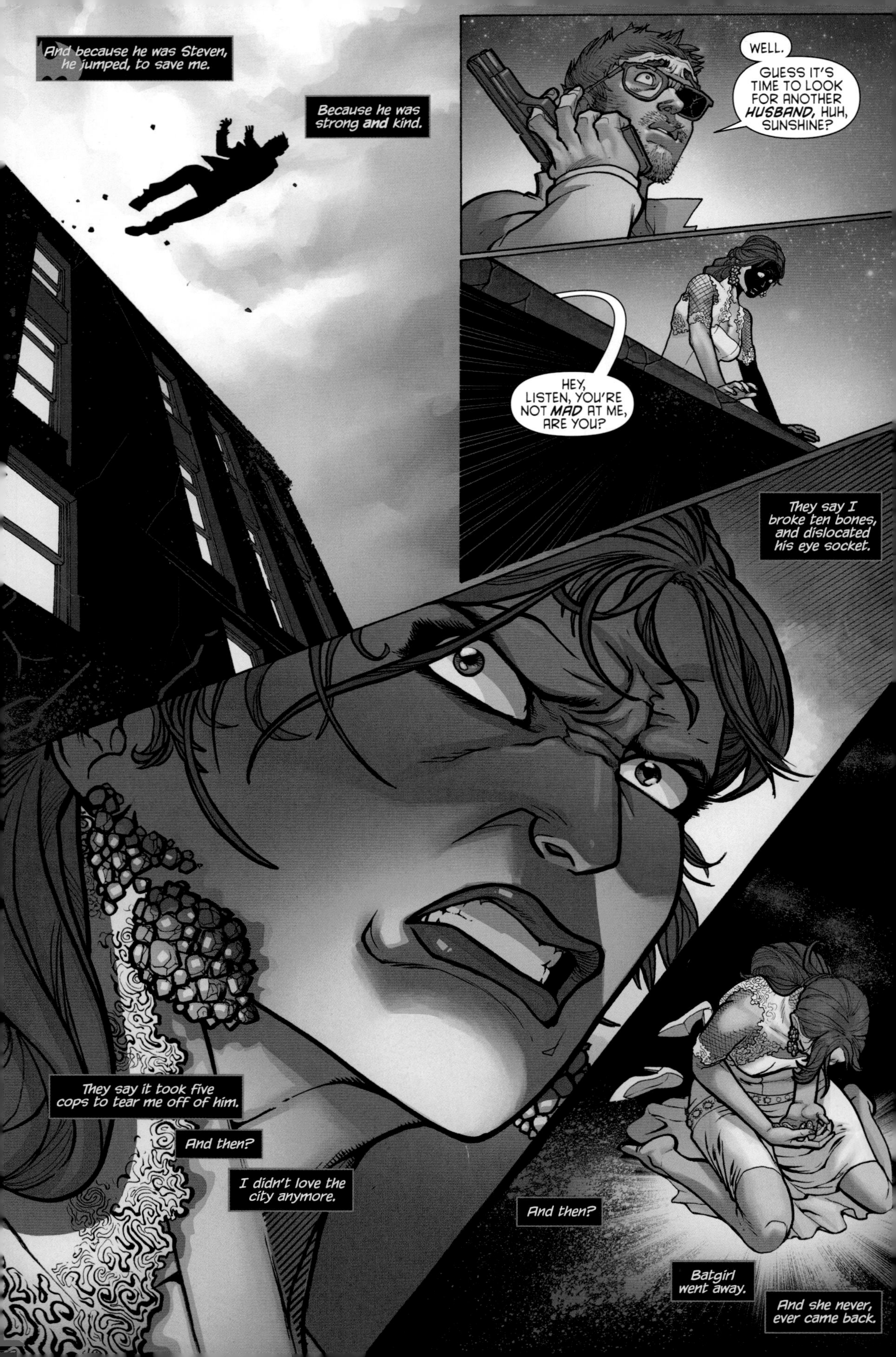
And because he was Steven, he jumped, to save me.
Because he was strong and kind.
WELL.
GUESS IT'S TIME TO LOOK FOR ANOTHER HUSBAND, HUH, SUNSHINE?
HEY, LISTEN, YOU'RE NOT MAD AT ME, ARE YOU?
They say I broke ten bones, and dislocated his eye socket.
They say it took five cops to tear me off of him.
And then?
I didn't love the city anymore.
And then?
Batgirl went away.
And she never, ever came back.

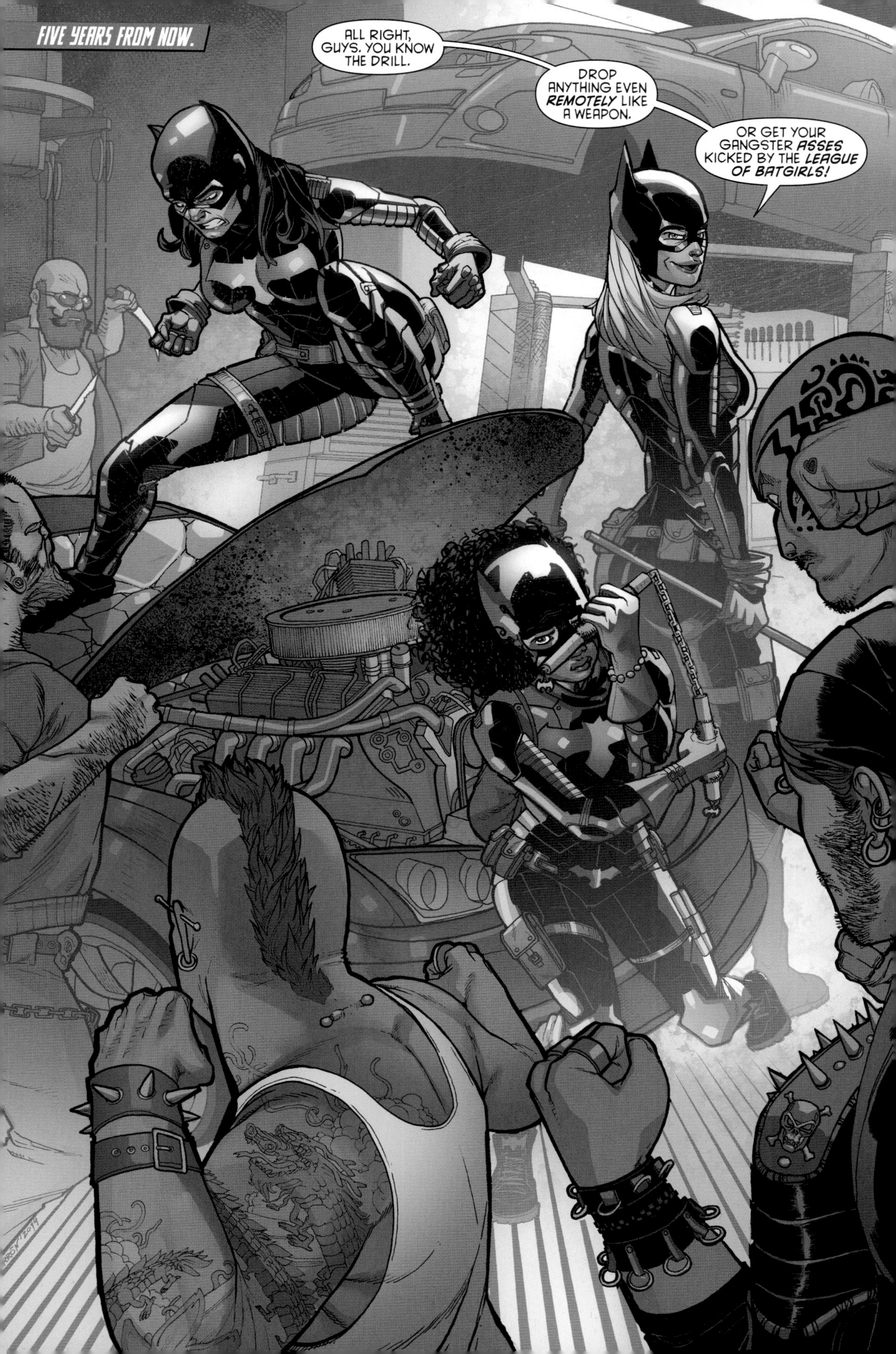
FIVE YEARS FROM NOW.
ALL RIGHT, GUYS. YOU KNOW THE DRILL.
DROP ANYTHING EVEN REMOTELY LIKE A WEAPON.
OR GET YOUR GANGSTER ASSES KICKED BY THE LEAGUE OF BATGIRLS!

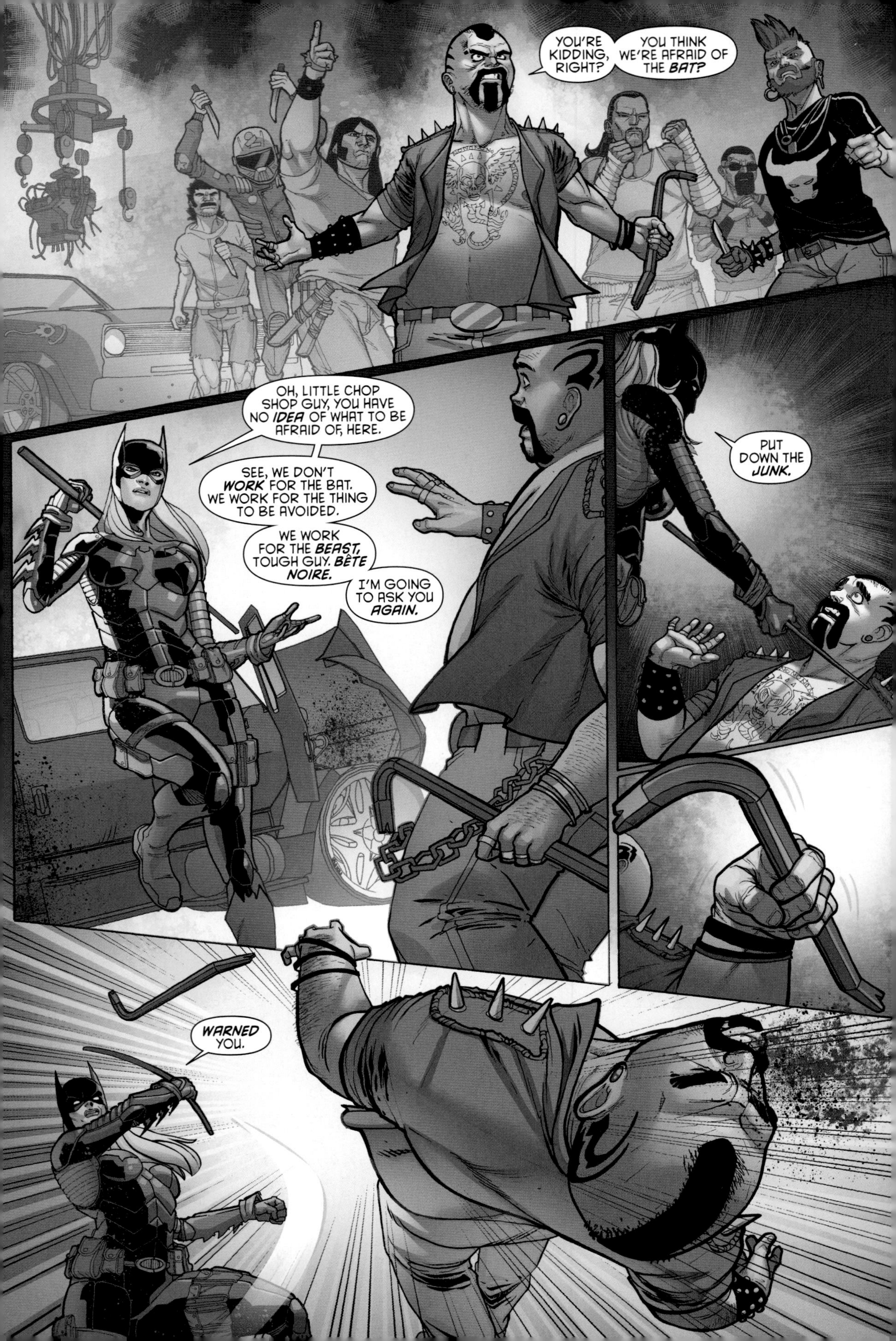
YOU'RE KIDDING, RIGHT?
YOU THINK WE'RE AFRAID OF THE BAT?
OH, LITTLE CHOP SHOP GUY, YOU HAVE NO IDEA OF WHAT TO BE AFRAID OF, HERE.
SEE, WE DON'T WORK FOR THE BAT. WE WORK FOR THE THING TO BE AVOIDED.
WE WORK FOR THE BEAST, TOUGH GUY. BÊTE NOIRE.
I'M GOING TO ASK YOU AGAIN.
PUT DOWN THE JUNK.
WARNED YOU.

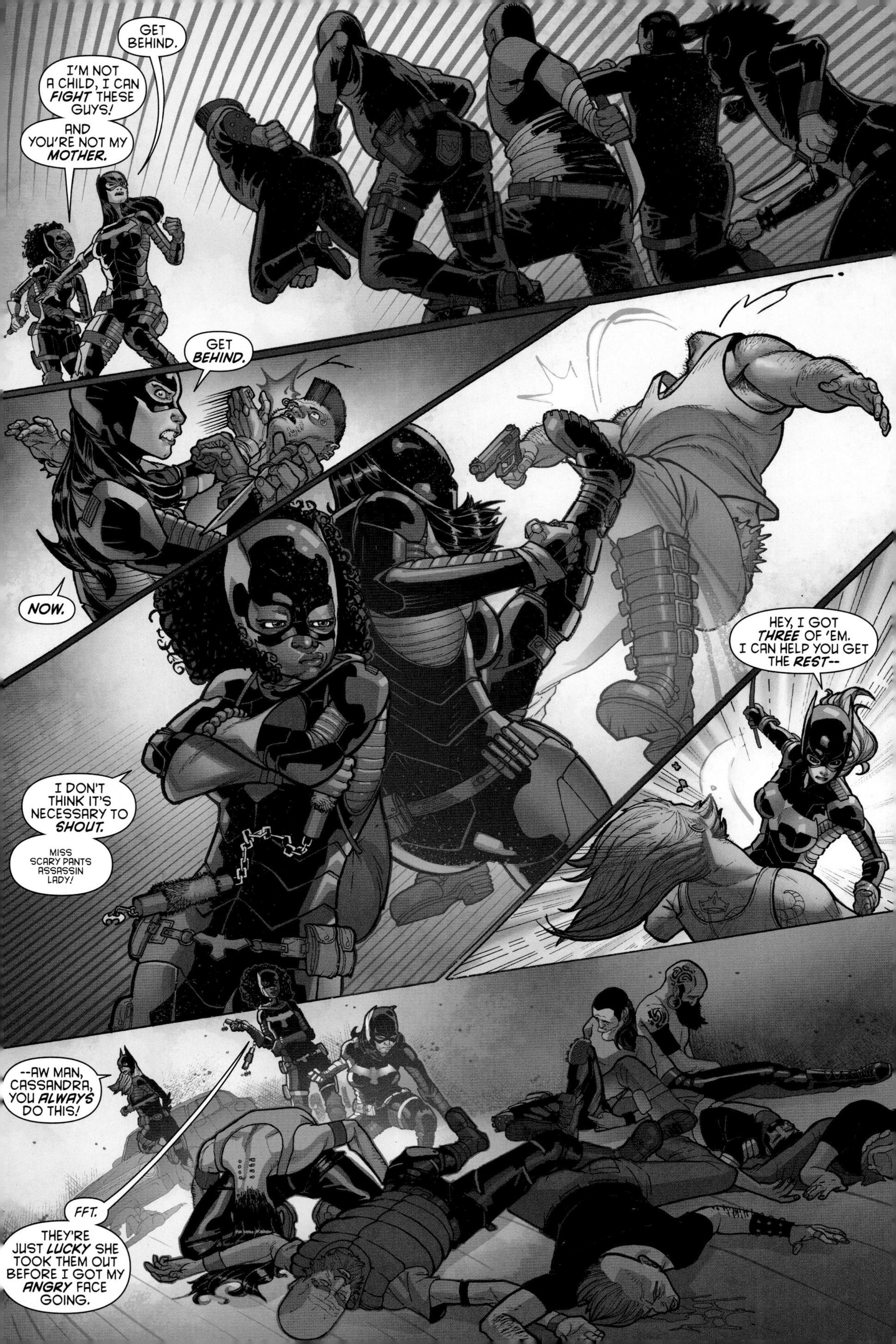
GET BEHIND.
I'M NOT A CHILD, I CAN FIGHT THESE GUYS!
AND YOU'RE NOT MY MOTHER.
GET BEHIND.
NOW.
I DON'T THINK IT'S NECESSARY TO SHOUT.
MISS SCARY PANTS ASSASSIN LADY!
HEY, I GOT THREE OF 'EM. I CAN HELP YOU GET THE REST--
--AW MAN, CASSANDRA, YOU ALWAYS DO THIS!
FFT.
THEY'RE JUST LUCKY SHE TOOK THEM OUT BEFORE I GOT MY ANGRY FACE GOING.

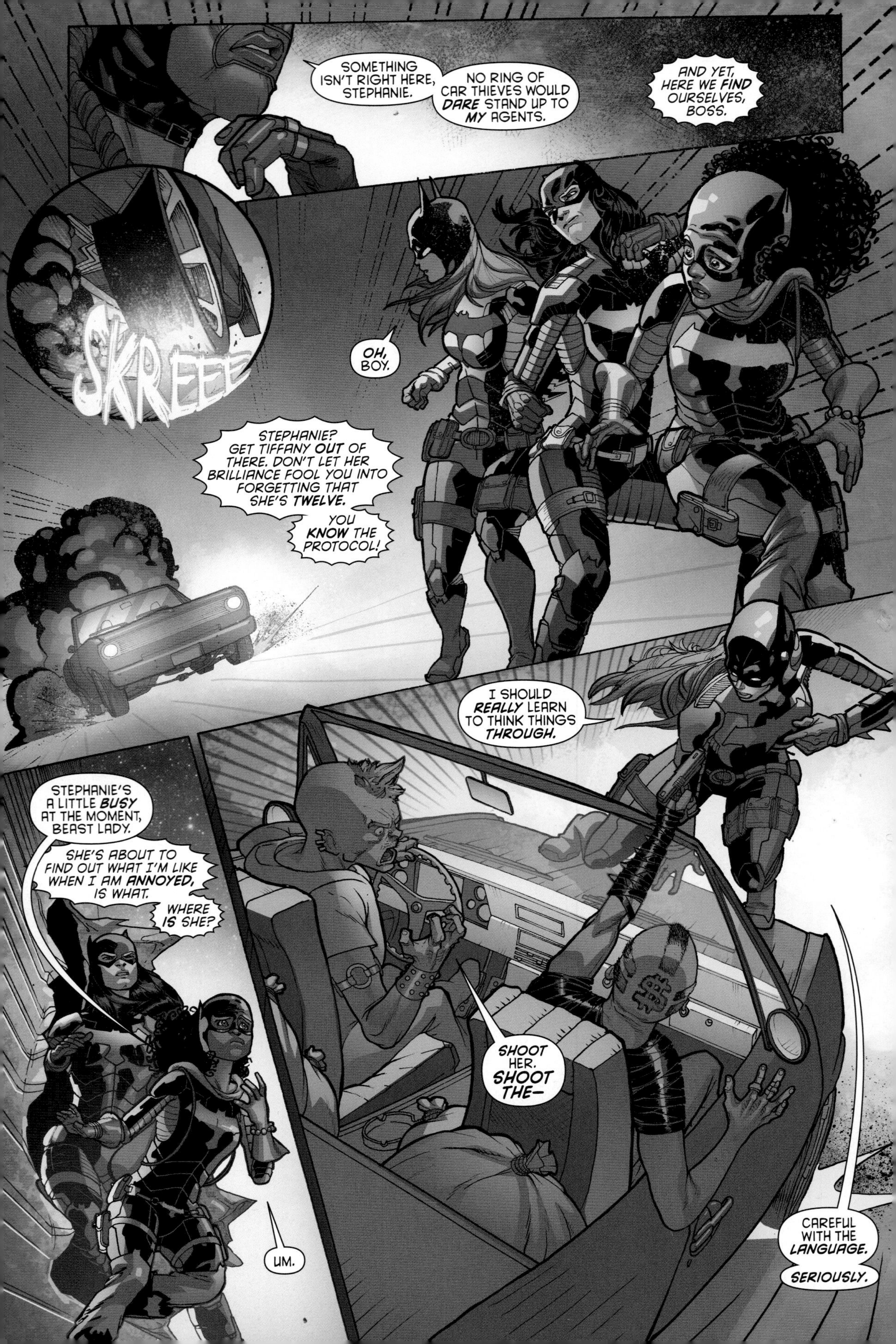
SOMETHING ISN'T RIGHT HERE, STEPHANIE.
NO RING OF CAR THIEVES WOULD **DARE** STAND UP TO **MY** AGENTS.
AND YET, HERE WE **FIND** OURSELVES, BOSS.
SKREEE
OH, BOY.
STEPHANIE? GET TIFFANY **OUT** OF THERE. DON'T LET HER BRILLIANCE FOOL YOU INTO FORGETTING THAT SHE'S **TWELVE.**
YOU **KNOW** THE PROTOCOL!
I SHOULD **REALLY** LEARN TO THINK THINGS **THROUGH.**
STEPHANIE'S A LITTLE **BUSY** AT THE MOMENT, BEAST LADY.
SHE'S ABOUT TO FIND OUT WHAT I'M LIKE WHEN I AM **ANNOYED,** IS WHAT.
WHERE **IS** SHE?
SHOOT HER. **SHOOT THE—**
UM.
CAREFUL WITH THE **LANGUAGE.**
SERIOUSLY.

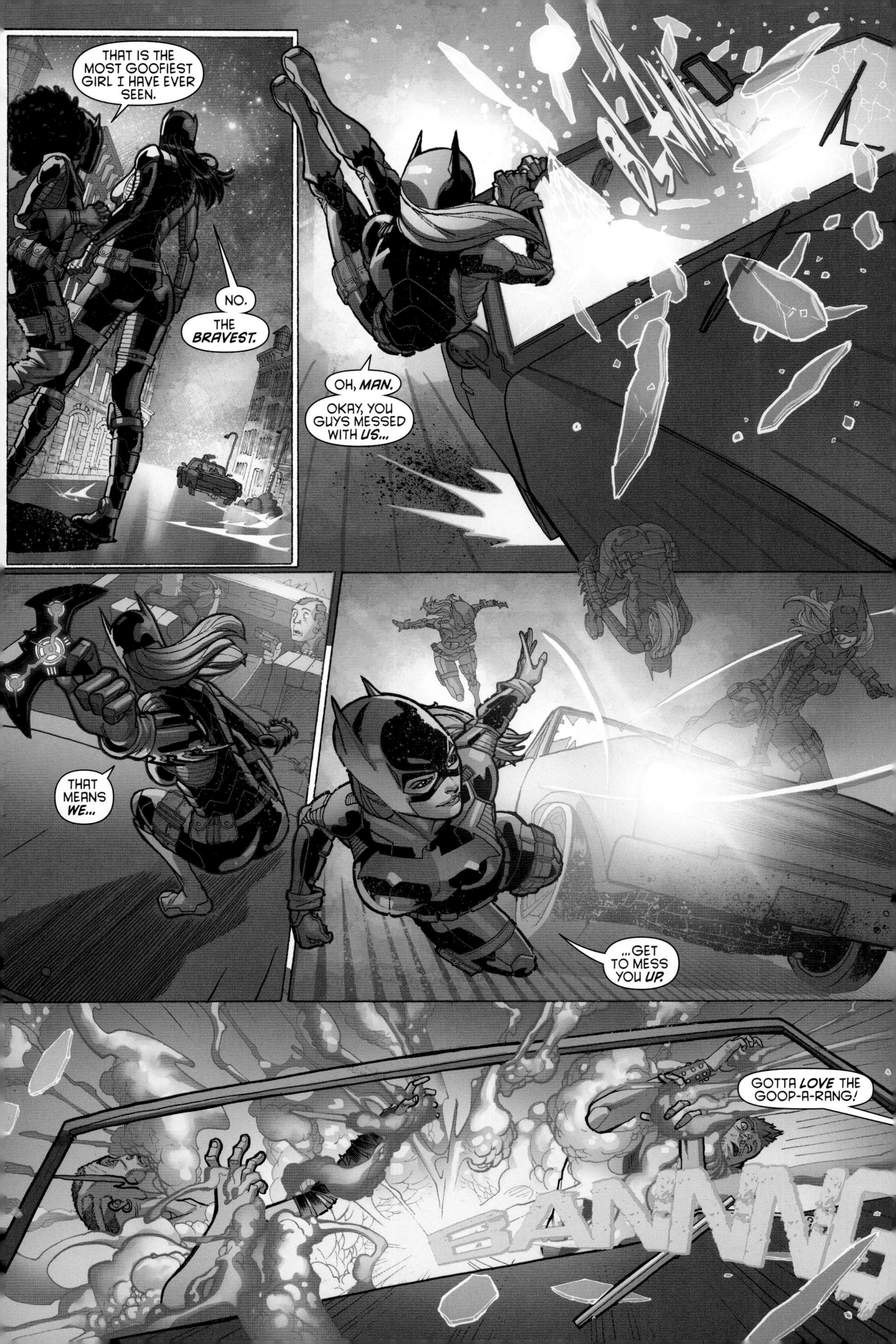
THAT IS THE MOST GOOFIEST GIRL I HAVE EVER SEEN.
NO. THE BRAVEST.
OH, MAN.
OKAY, YOU GUYS MESSED WITH US...
THAT MEANS WE...
...GET TO MESS YOU UP.
GOTTA LOVE THE GOOP-A-RANG!

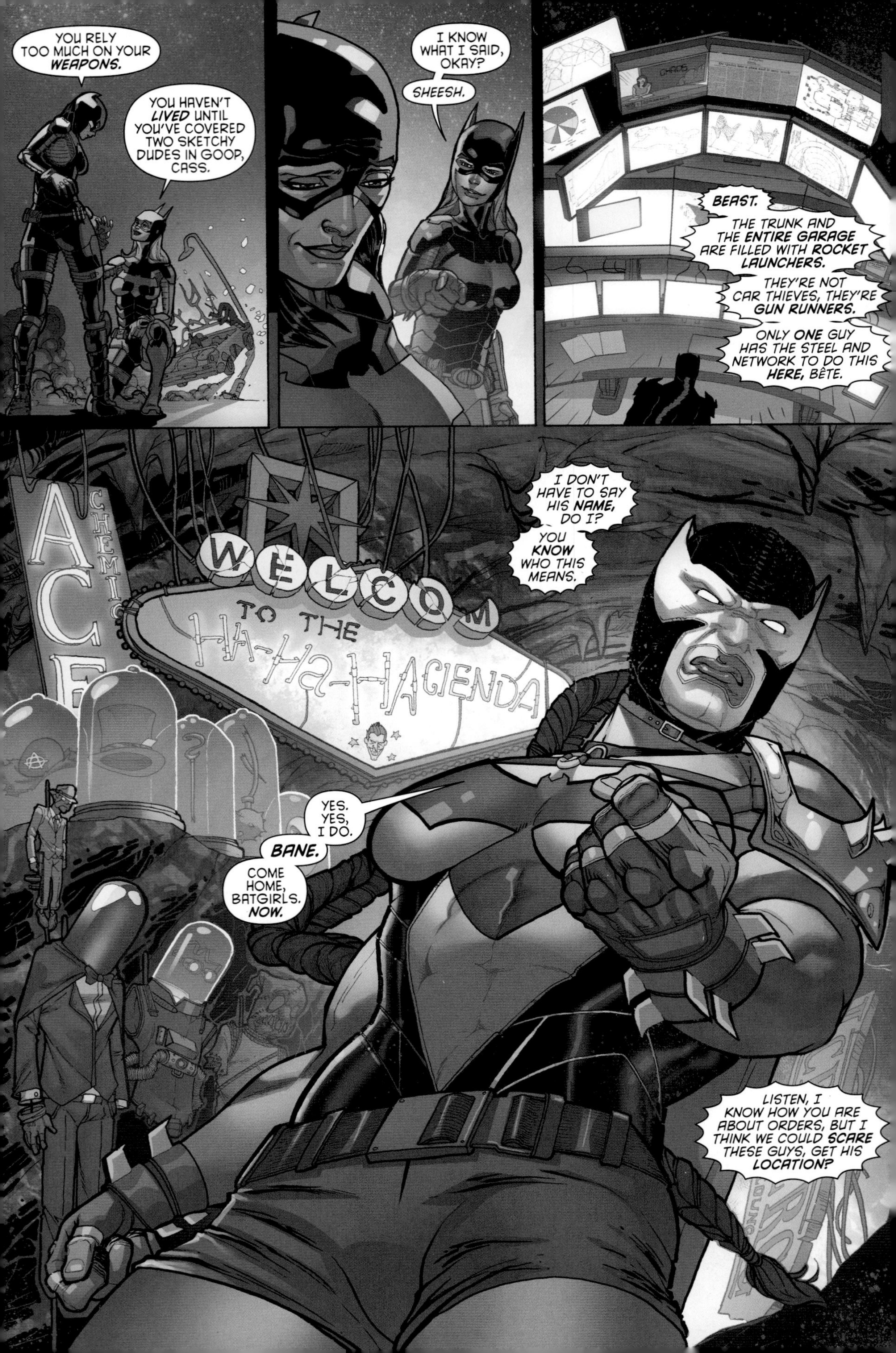
YOU RELY TOO MUCH ON YOUR WEAPONS.
YOU HAVEN'T LIVED UNTIL YOU'VE COVERED TWO SKETCHY DUDES IN GOOP, CASS.
I KNOW WHAT I SAID, OKAY?
SHEESH.
CHAOS
BEAST.
THE TRUNK AND THE ENTIRE GARAGE ARE FILLED WITH ROCKET LAUNCHERS.
THEY'RE NOT CAR THIEVES, THEY'RE GUN RUNNERS.
ONLY ONE GUY HAS THE STEEL AND NETWORK TO DO THIS HERE, BÊTE.
ACE CHEMIC
WELCOM TO THE HA-HA-HACIENDA
I DON'T HAVE TO SAY HIS NAME, DO I?
YOU KNOW WHO THIS MEANS.
YES. YES, I DO.
BANE.
COME HOME, BATGIRLS. NOW.
LISTEN, I KNOW HOW YOU ARE ABOUT ORDERS, BUT I THINK WE COULD SCARE THESE GUYS, GET HIS LOCATION?

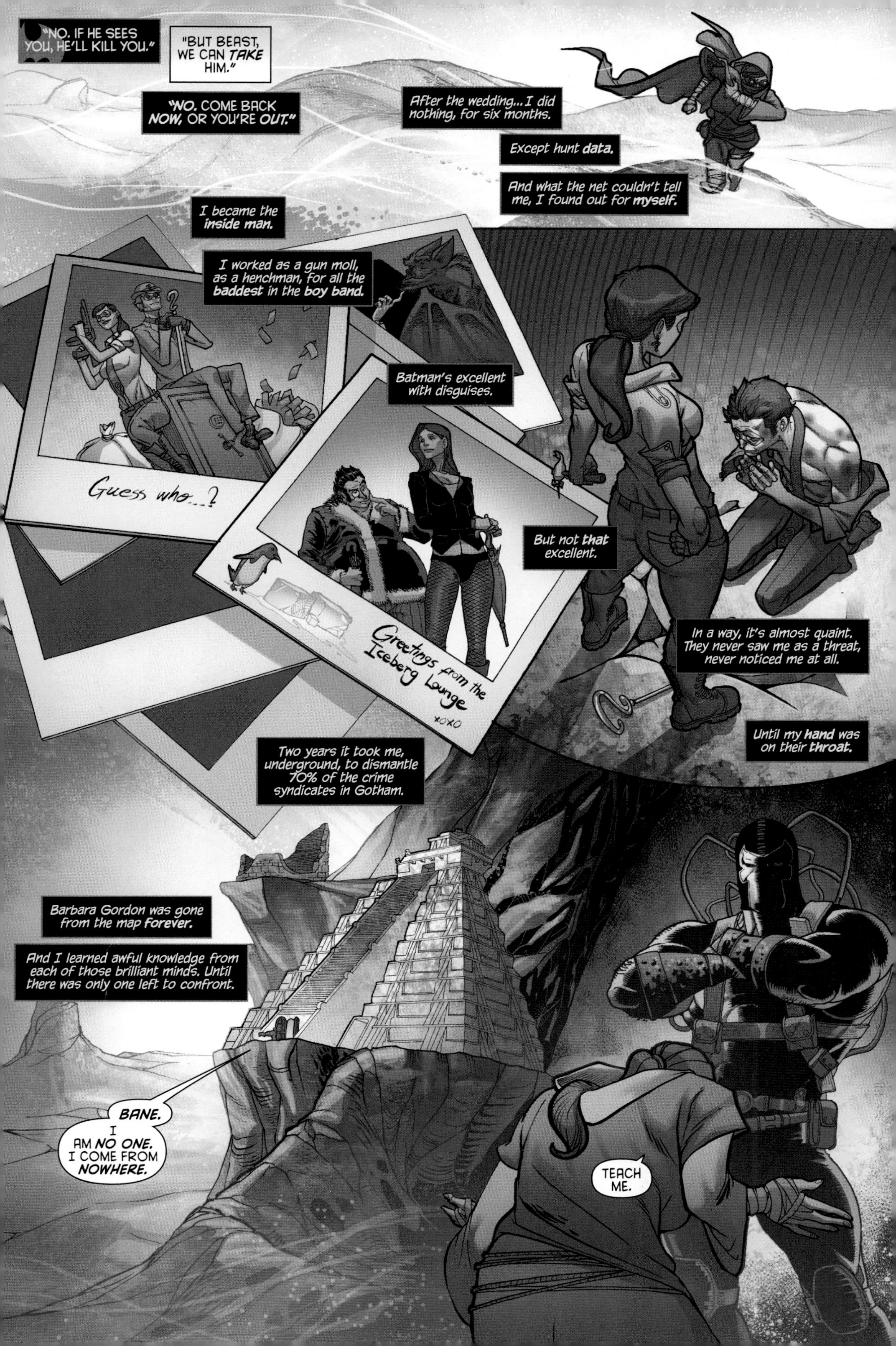
"NO. IF HE SEES YOU, HE'LL KILL YOU."
"BUT BEAST, WE CAN TAKE HIM."
"NO. COME BACK NOW, OR YOU'RE OUT."
After the wedding... I did nothing, for six months.
Except hunt data.
And what the net couldn't tell me, I found out for myself.
I became the inside man.
I worked as a gun moll, as a henchman, for all the baddest in the boy band.
Guess who...?
Batman's excellent with disguises.
But not that excellent.
Greetings from the Iceberg Lounge
xoxo
In a way, it's almost quaint. They never saw me as a threat, never noticed me at all.
Until my hand was on their throat.
Two years it took me, underground, to dismantle 70% of the crime syndicates in Gotham.
Barbara Gordon was gone from the map forever.
And I learned awful knowledge from each of those brilliant minds. Until there was only one left to confront.
BANE. I AM NO ONE. I COME FROM NOWHERE.
TEACH ME.

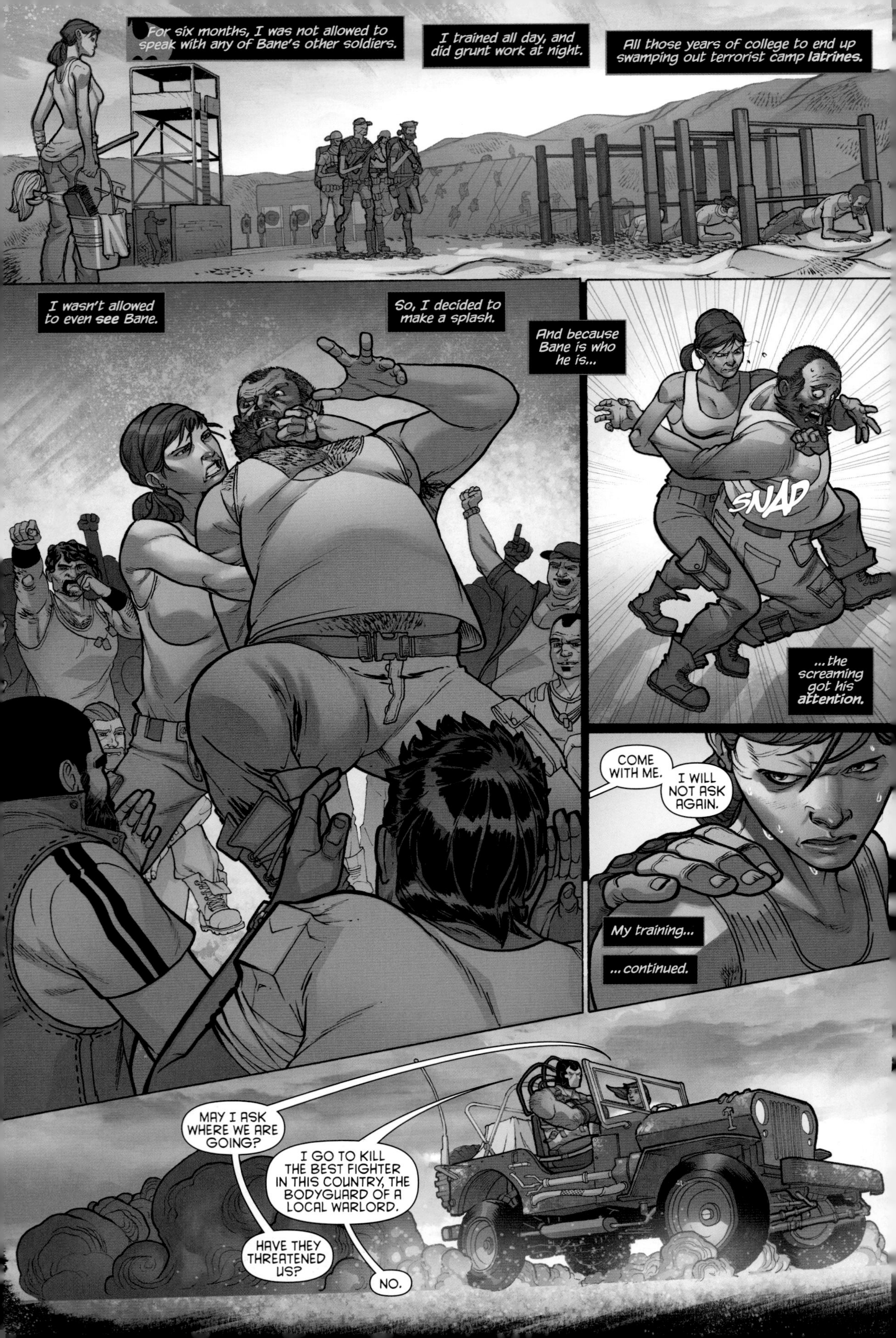

For six months, I was not allowed to speak with any of Bane's other soldiers.
I trained all day, and did grunt work at night.
All those years of college to end up swamping out terrorist camp latrines.
I wasn't allowed to even see Bane.
So, I decided to make a splash.
And because Bane is who he is...
SNAP
...the screaming got his attention.
COME WITH ME.
I WILL NOT ASK AGAIN.
My training...
...continued.
MAY I ASK WHERE WE ARE GOING?
I GO TO KILL THE BEST FIGHTER IN THIS COUNTRY, THE BODYGUARD OF A LOCAL WARLORD.
HAVE THEY THREATENED US?
NO.

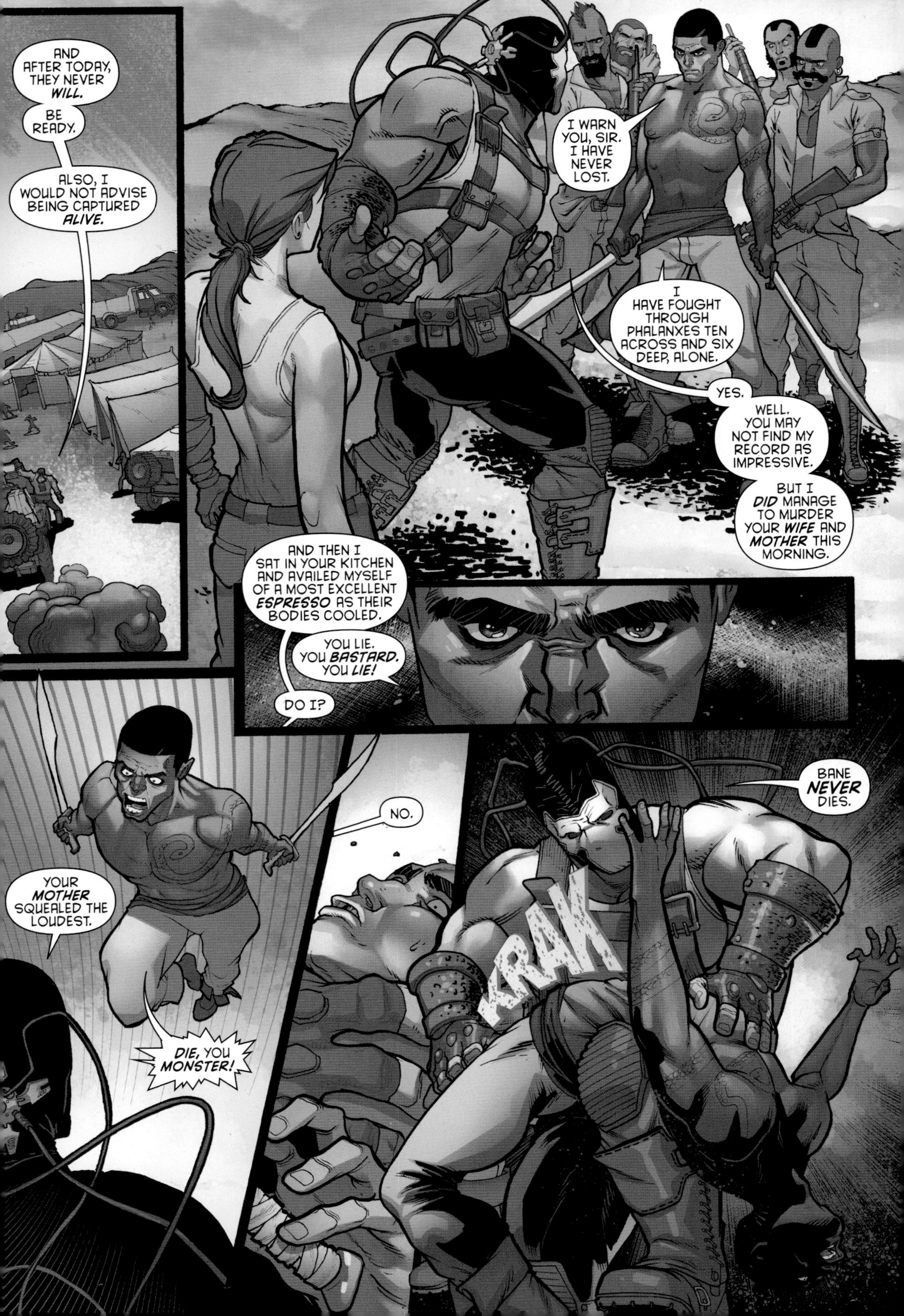
AND AFTER TODAY, THEY NEVER WILL.
BE READY.
ALSO, I WOULD NOT ADVISE BEING CAPTURED ALIVE.
I WARN YOU, SIR. I HAVE NEVER LOST.
I HAVE FOUGHT THROUGH PHALANXES TEN ACROSS AND SIX DEEP, ALONE.
YES.
WELL. YOU MAY NOT FIND MY RECORD AS IMPRESSIVE.
BUT I DID MANAGE TO MURDER YOUR WIFE AND MOTHER THIS MORNING.
AND THEN I SAT IN YOUR KITCHEN AND AVAILED MYSELF OF A MOST EXCELLENT ESPRESSO AS THEIR BODIES COOLED.
YOU LIE. YOU BASTARD. YOU LIE!
DO I?
YOUR MOTHER SQUEALED THE LOUDEST.
DIE, YOU MONSTER!
NO.
KRAK
BANE NEVER DIES.

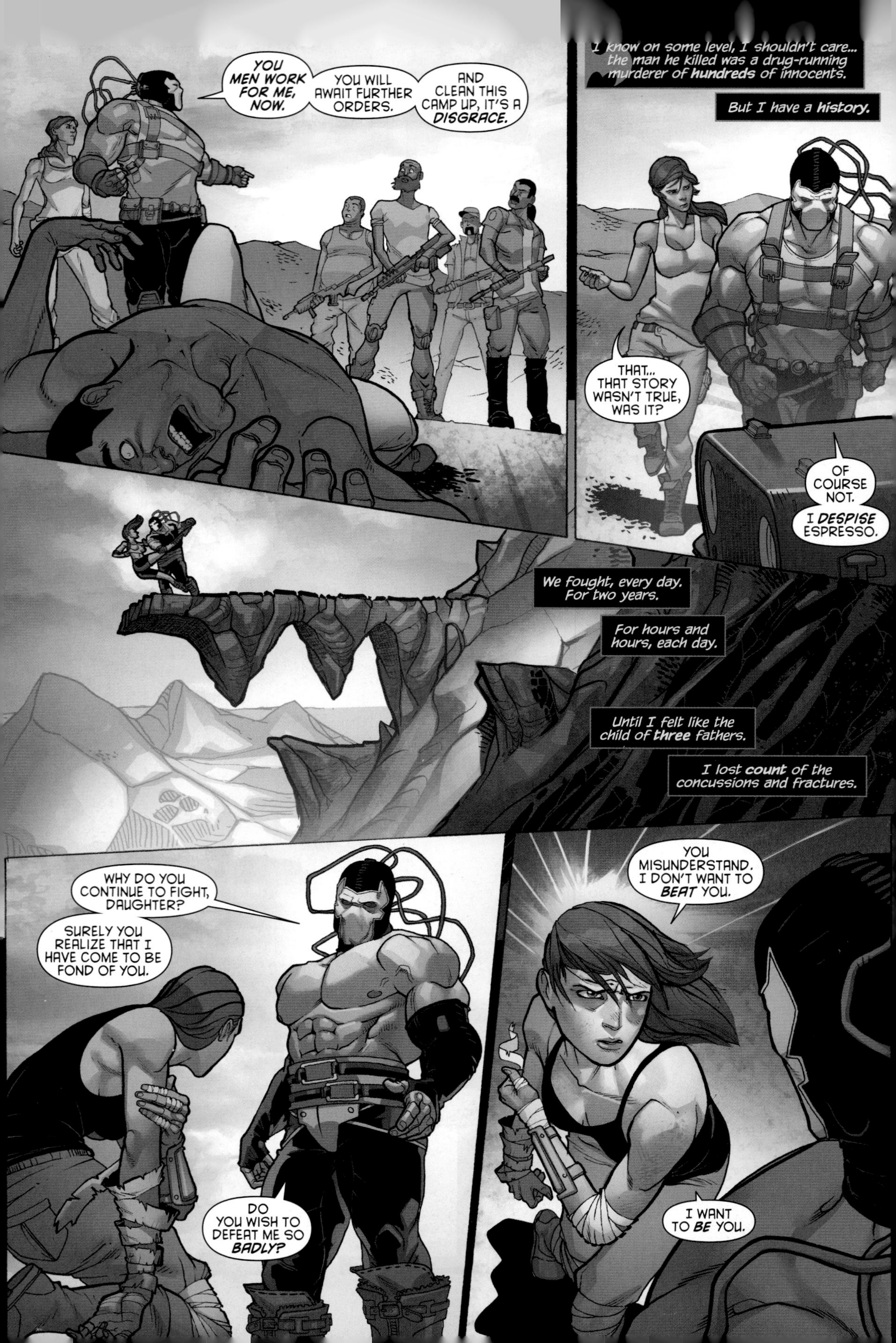
YOU MEN WORK FOR ME, NOW.
YOU WILL AWAIT FURTHER ORDERS.
AND CLEAN THIS CAMP UP, IT'S A DISGRACE.
I know on some level, I shouldn't care... the man he killed was a drug-running murderer of hundreds of innocents.
But I have a history.
THAT... THAT STORY WASN'T TRUE, WAS IT?
OF COURSE NOT.
I DESPISE ESPRESSO.
We fought, every day. For two years.
For hours and hours, each day.
Until I felt like the child of three fathers.
I lost count of the concussions and fractures.
WHY DO YOU CONTINUE TO FIGHT, DAUGHTER?
SURELY YOU REALIZE THAT I HAVE COME TO BE FOND OF YOU.
DO YOU WISH TO DEFEAT ME SO BADLY?
YOU MISUNDERSTAND. I DON'T WANT TO BEAT YOU.
I WANT TO BE YOU.

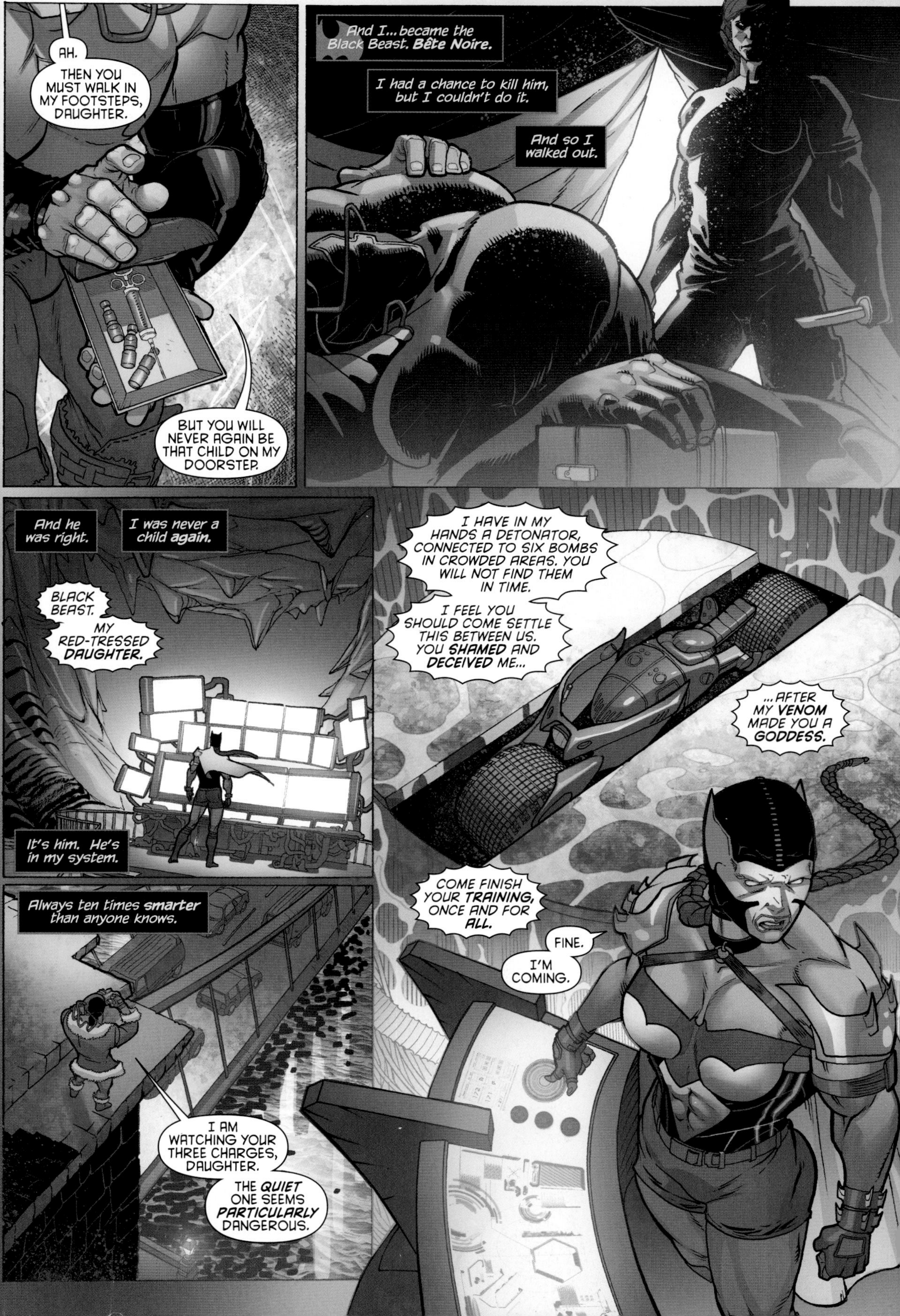
AH.
THEN YOU MUST WALK IN MY FOOTSTEPS, DAUGHTER.
BUT YOU WILL NEVER AGAIN BE THAT CHILD ON MY DOORSTEP.
And I...became the Black Beast. Bête Noire.
I had a chance to kill him, but I couldn't do it.
And so I walked out.
And he was right.
I was never a child again.
BLACK BEAST.
MY RED-TRESSED DAUGHTER.
It's him. He's in my system.
I HAVE IN MY HANDS A DETONATOR, CONNECTED TO SIX BOMBS IN CROWDED AREAS. YOU WILL NOT FIND THEM IN TIME.
I FEEL YOU SHOULD COME SETTLE THIS BETWEEN US. YOU SHAMED AND DECEIVED ME...
...AFTER MY VENOM MADE YOU A GODDESS.
Always ten times smarter than anyone knows.
I AM WATCHING YOUR THREE CHARGES, DAUGHTER.
THE QUIET ONE SEEMS PARTICULARLY DANGEROUS.
COME FINISH YOUR TRAINING, ONCE AND FOR ALL.
FINE.
I'M COMING.

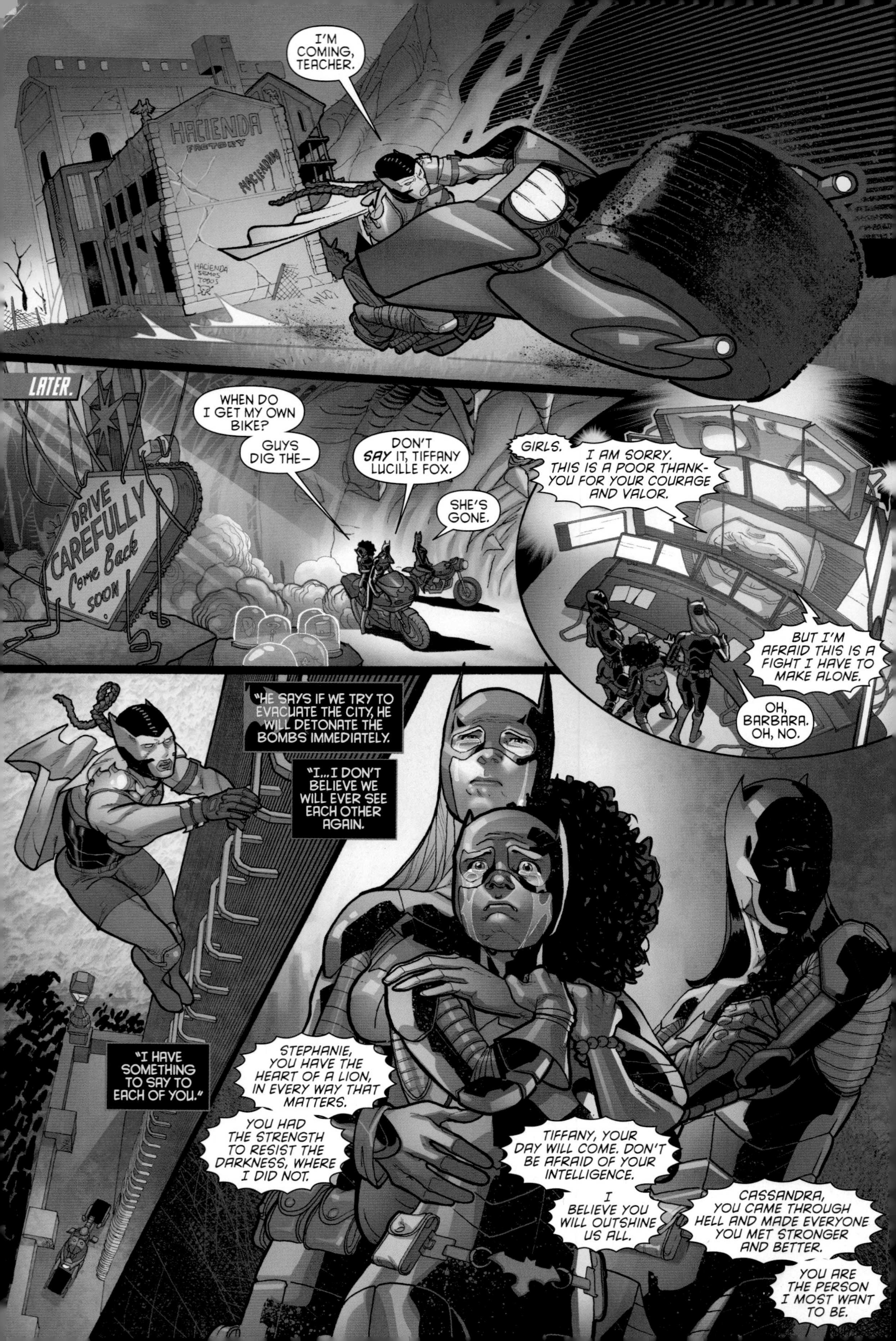
I'M COMING, TEACHER.
HACIENDA FACTORY
HACIENDA SEMOS TODOS
LATER.
WHEN DO I GET MY OWN BIKE?
GUYS DIG THE—
DON'T SAY IT, TIFFANY LUCILLE FOX.
SHE'S GONE.
DRIVE CAREFULLY Come Back SOON
GIRLS.
I AM SORRY. THIS IS A POOR THANK-YOU FOR YOUR COURAGE AND VALOR.
BUT I'M AFRAID THIS IS A FIGHT I HAVE TO MAKE ALONE.
OH, BARBARA. OH, NO.
"HE SAYS IF WE TRY TO EVACUATE THE CITY, HE WILL DETONATE THE BOMBS IMMEDIATELY.
"I...I DON'T BELIEVE WE WILL EVER SEE EACH OTHER AGAIN.
"I HAVE SOMETHING TO SAY TO EACH OF YOU."
STEPHANIE, YOU HAVE THE HEART OF A LION, IN EVERY WAY THAT MATTERS.
YOU HAD THE STRENGTH TO RESIST THE DARKNESS, WHERE I DID NOT.
TIFFANY, YOUR DAY WILL COME. DON'T BE AFRAID OF YOUR INTELLIGENCE.
I BELIEVE YOU WILL OUTSHINE US ALL.
CASSANDRA, YOU CAME THROUGH HELL AND MADE EVERYONE YOU MET STRONGER AND BETTER.
YOU ARE THE PERSON I MOST WANT TO BE.

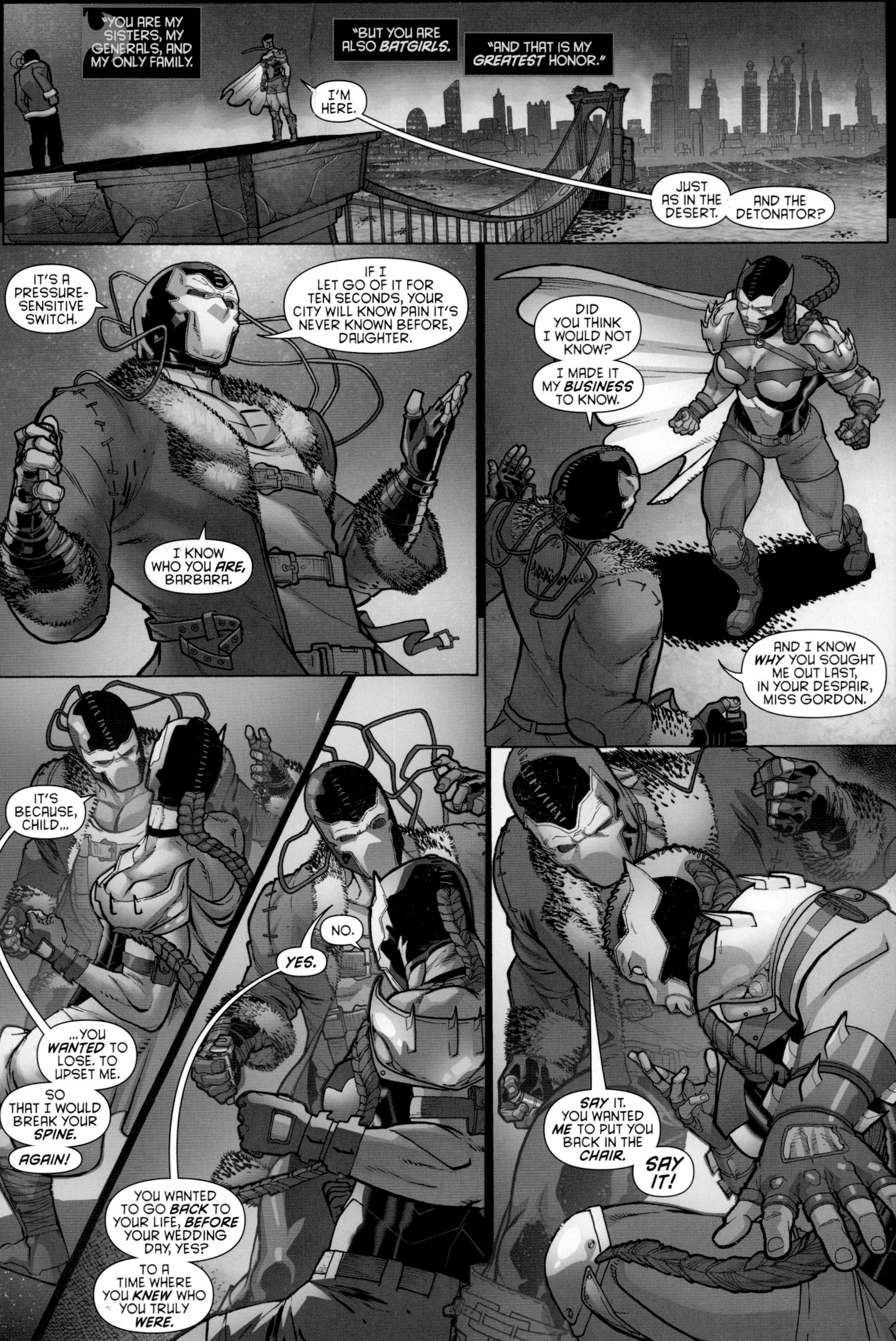
"YOU ARE MY SISTERS, MY GENERALS, AND MY ONLY FAMILY.
"BUT YOU ARE ALSO BATGIRLS.
"AND THAT IS MY GREATEST HONOR."
I'M HERE.
JUST AS IN THE DESERT.
AND THE DETONATOR?
IT'S A PRESSURE-SENSITIVE SWITCH.
IF I LET GO OF IT FOR TEN SECONDS, YOUR CITY WILL KNOW PAIN IT'S NEVER KNOWN BEFORE, DAUGHTER.
I KNOW WHO YOU ARE, BARBARA.
DID YOU THINK I WOULD NOT KNOW?
I MADE IT MY BUSINESS TO KNOW.
AND I KNOW WHY YOU SOUGHT ME OUT LAST, IN YOUR DESPAIR, MISS GORDON.
IT'S BECAUSE, CHILD...
...YOU WANTED TO LOSE. TO UPSET ME.
SO THAT I WOULD BREAK YOUR SPINE.
AGAIN!
NO.
YES.
YOU WANTED TO GO BACK TO YOUR LIFE, BEFORE YOUR WEDDING DAY, YES?
TO A TIME WHERE YOU KNEW WHO YOU TRULY WERE.
SAY IT. YOU WANTED ME TO PUT YOU BACK IN THE CHAIR.
SAY IT!

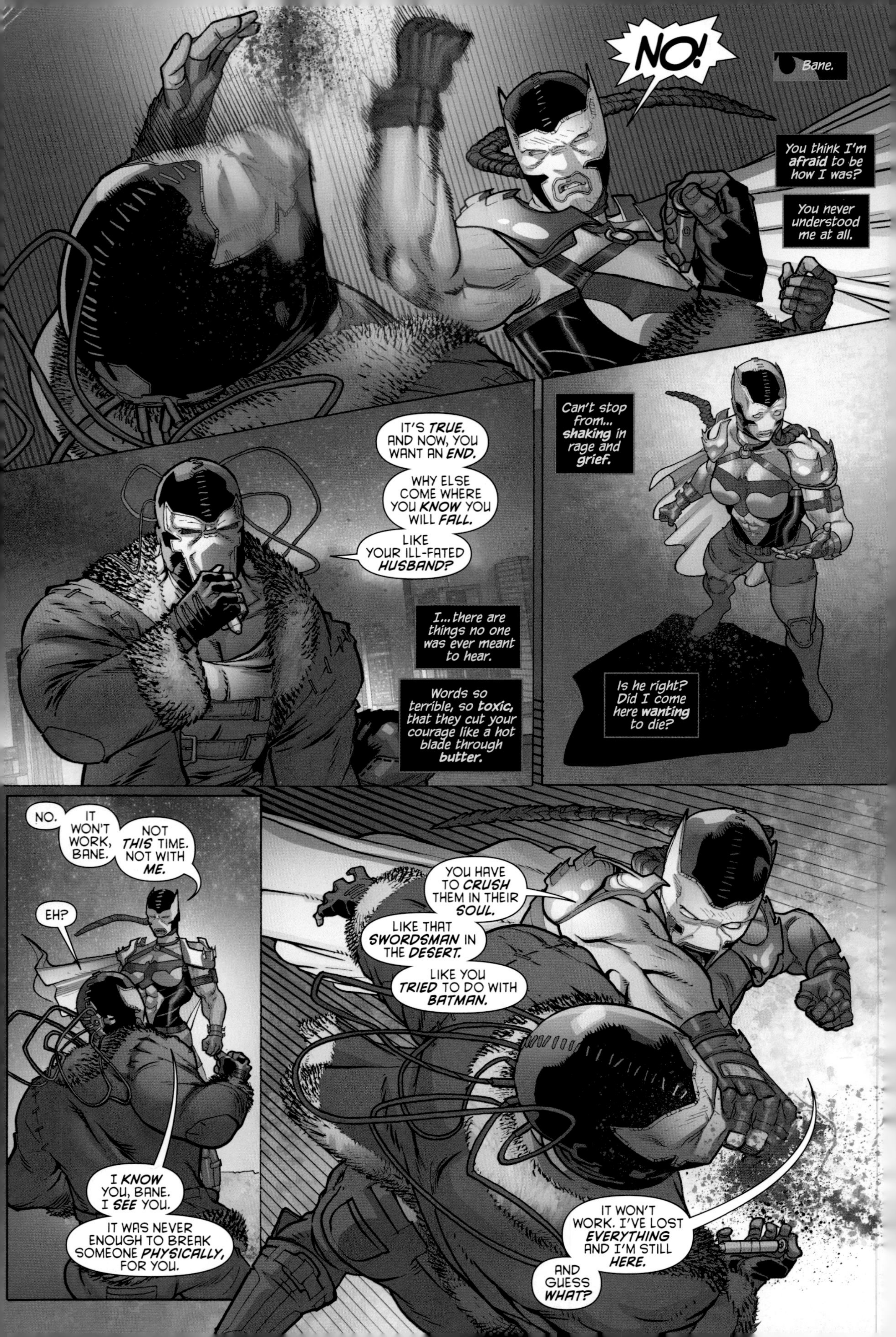
NO!
Bane.
You think I'm afraid to be how I was?
You never understood me at all.
IT'S TRUE. AND NOW, YOU WANT AN END.
WHY ELSE COME WHERE YOU KNOW YOU WILL FALL.
LIKE YOUR ILL-FATED HUSBAND?
I... there are things no one was ever meant to hear.
Words so terrible, so toxic, that they cut your courage like a hot blade through butter.
Can't stop from... shaking in rage and grief.
Is he right? Did I come here wanting to die?
NO.
IT WON'T WORK, BANE.
NOT THIS TIME. NOT WITH ME.
EH?
I KNOW YOU, BANE. I SEE YOU.
IT WAS NEVER ENOUGH TO BREAK SOMEONE PHYSICALLY, FOR YOU.
YOU HAVE TO CRUSH THEM IN THEIR SOUL.
LIKE THAT SWORDSMAN IN THE DESERT.
LIKE YOU TRIED TO DO WITH BATMAN.
IT WON'T WORK. I'VE LOST EVERYTHING AND I'M STILL HERE.
AND GUESS WHAT?

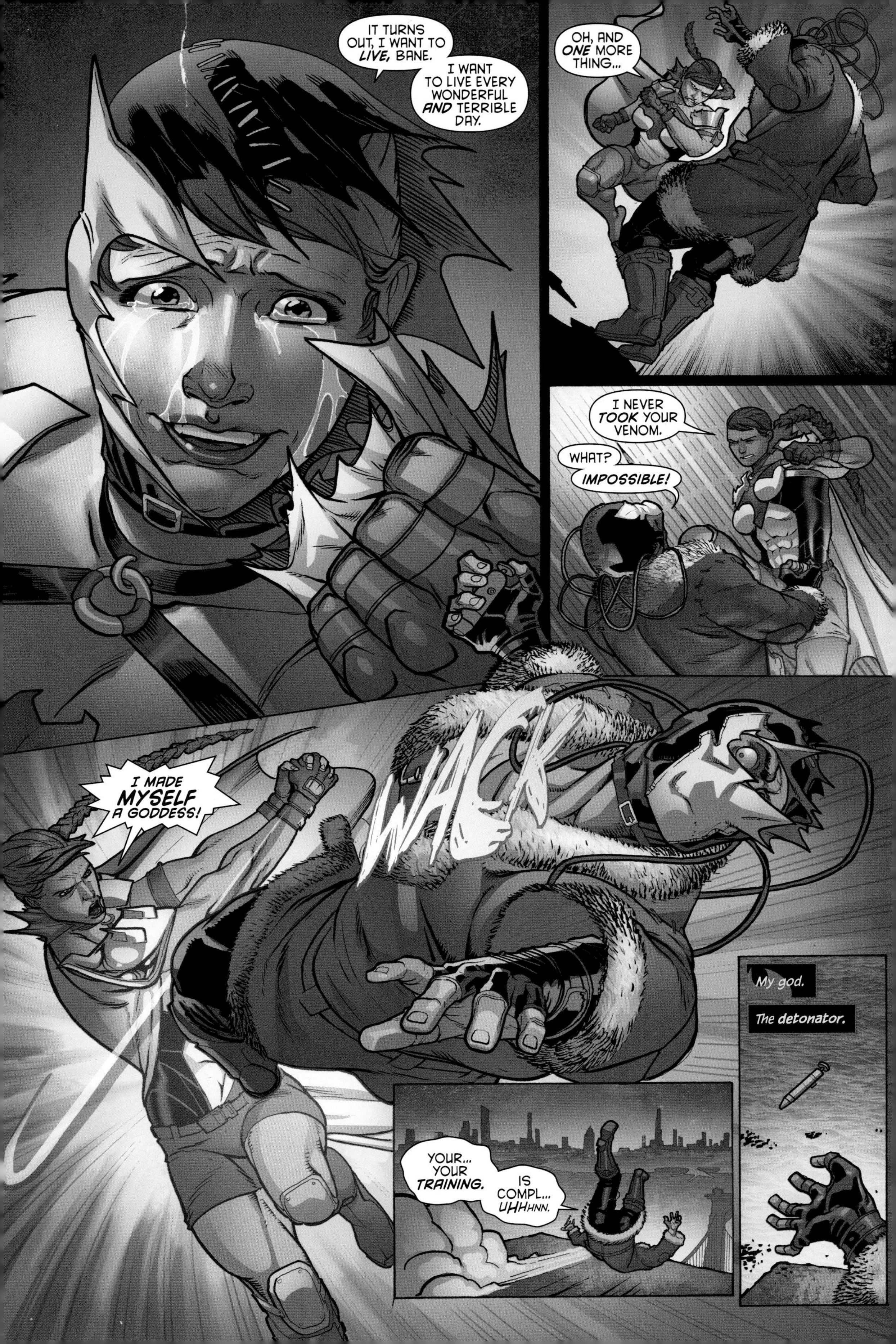
IT TURNS OUT, I WANT TO LIVE, BANE.
I WANT TO LIVE EVERY WONDERFUL AND TERRIBLE DAY.
OH, AND ONE MORE THING...
I NEVER TOOK YOUR VENOM.
WHAT? IMPOSSIBLE!
I MADE MYSELF A GODDESS!
WACK
YOUR... YOUR TRAINING.
IS COMPL... UHHHNN.
My god.
The detonator.

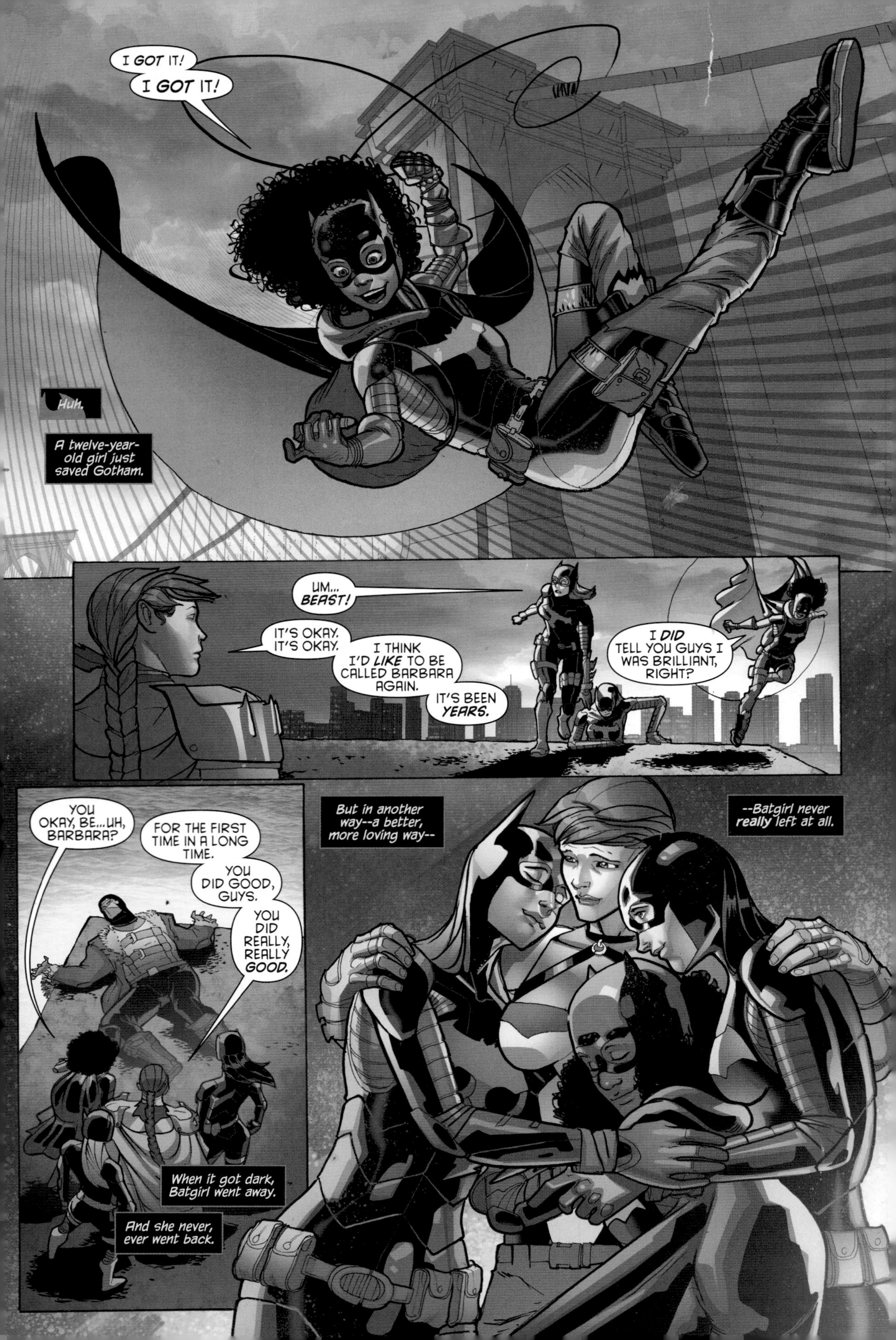
I GOT IT!
I GOT IT!
Huh.
A twelve-year-old girl just saved Gotham.
UM... BEAST!
IT'S OKAY. IT'S OKAY.
I THINK I'D LIKE TO BE CALLED BARBARA AGAIN.
IT'S BEEN YEARS.
I DID TELL YOU GUYS I WAS BRILLIANT, RIGHT?
YOU OKAY, BE...UH, BARBARA?
FOR THE FIRST TIME IN A LONG TIME.
YOU DID GOOD, GUYS.
YOU DID REALLY, REALLY GOOD.
When it got dark, Batgirl went away.
And she never, ever went back.
But in another way--a better, more loving way--
--Batgirl never really left at all.

VARIANT COVER GALLERY

BATGIRL 27
Scribblenauts variant cover by Jon Katz after Carmine Infantino

BATGIRL 28
Steampunk variant cover by J.G. Jones and Trish Mulvihill

BATGIRL 29
Robot Chicken variant cover by Adam Hughes and RC Stoodios

BATGIRL 30
MAD variant cover by Rick Tulka and Carl Peterson

BATGIRL 31
BATMAN '66 variant cover by Mike and Laura Allred

BATGIRL 32
DC Bombshell variant cover by Ant Lucia

BATGIRL 33
Batman 75th anniversary variant cover by Cliff Chiang and Mike Kaluta

BATGIRL 34
Selfie variant cover by Dave Johnson

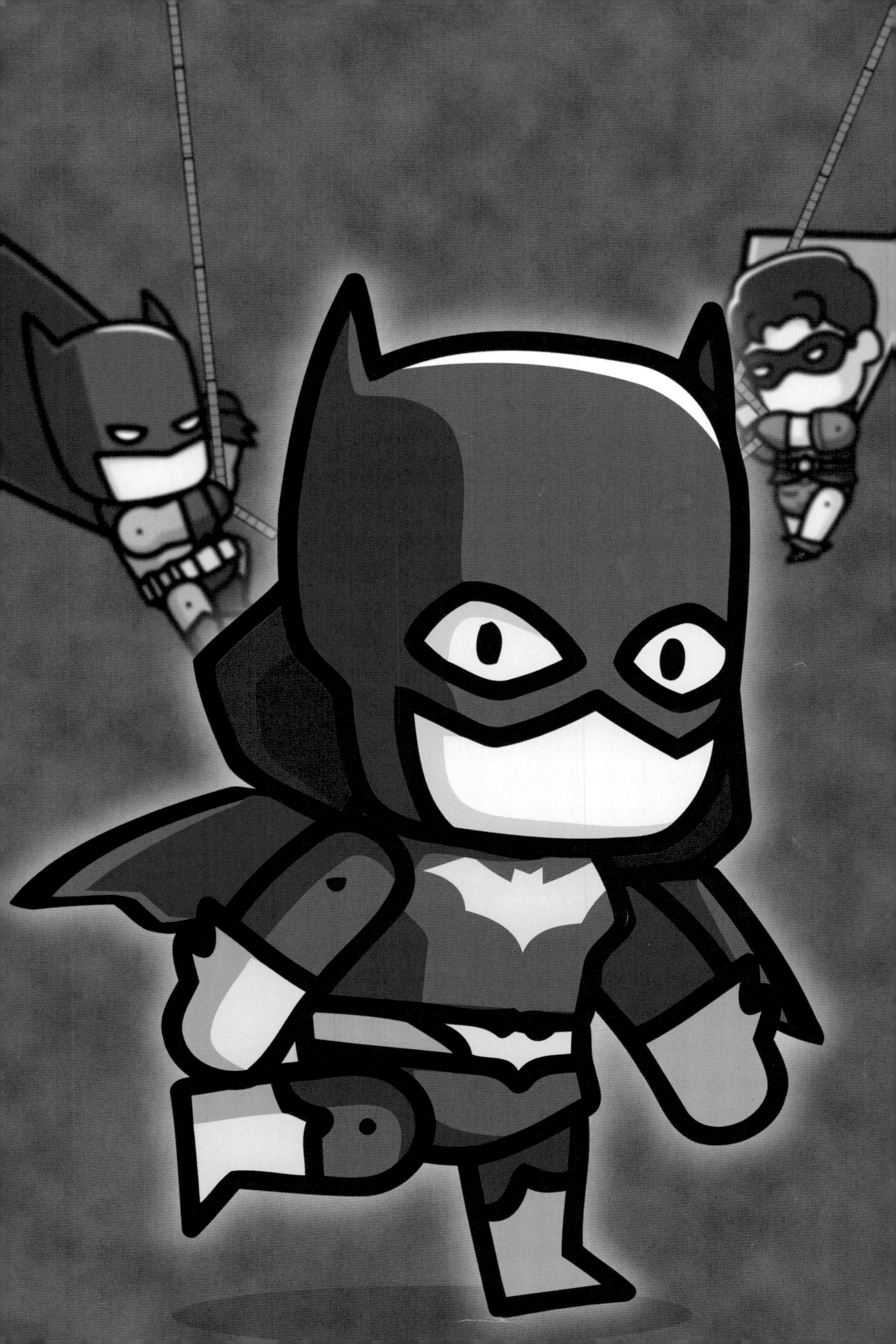

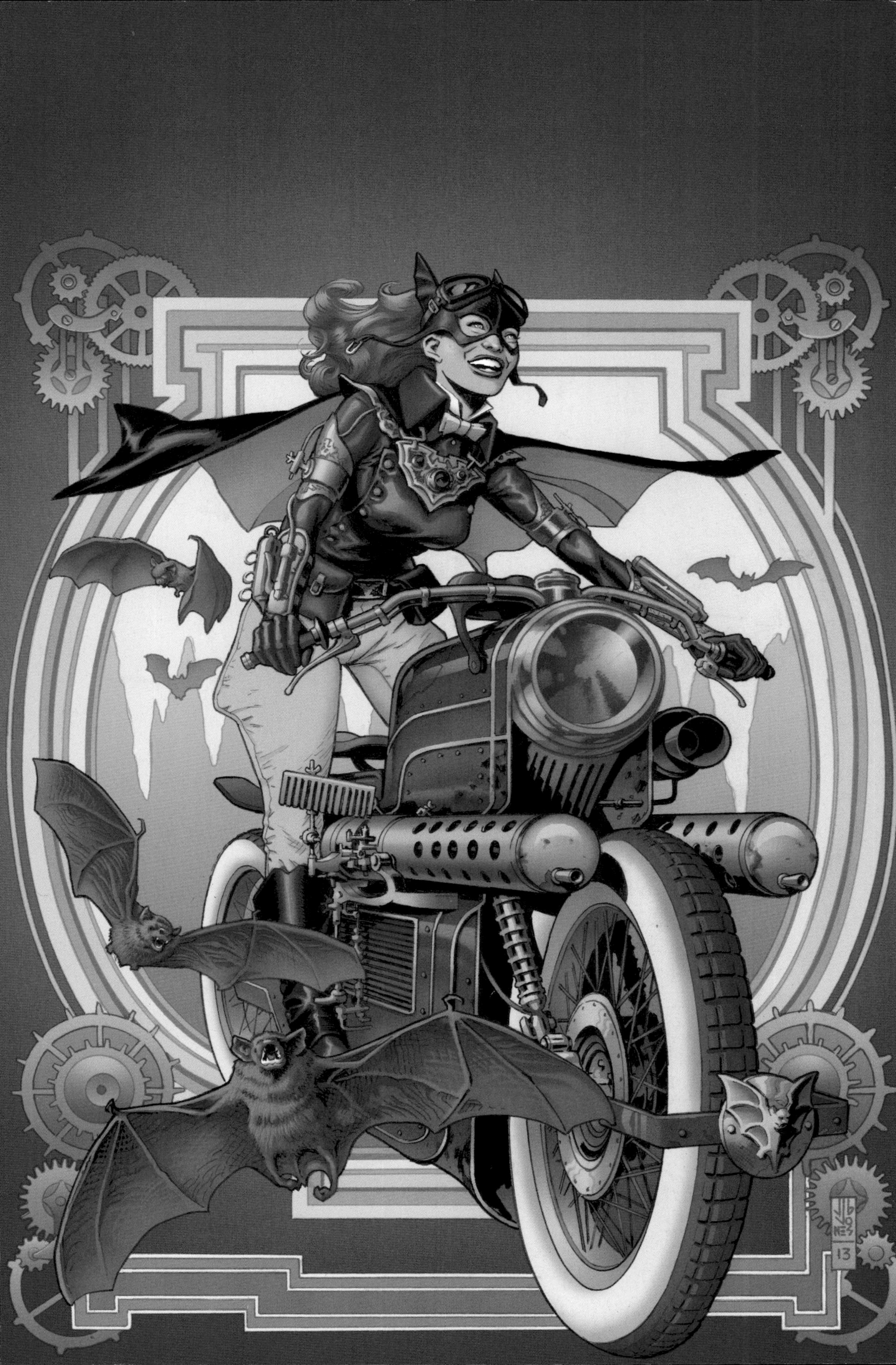

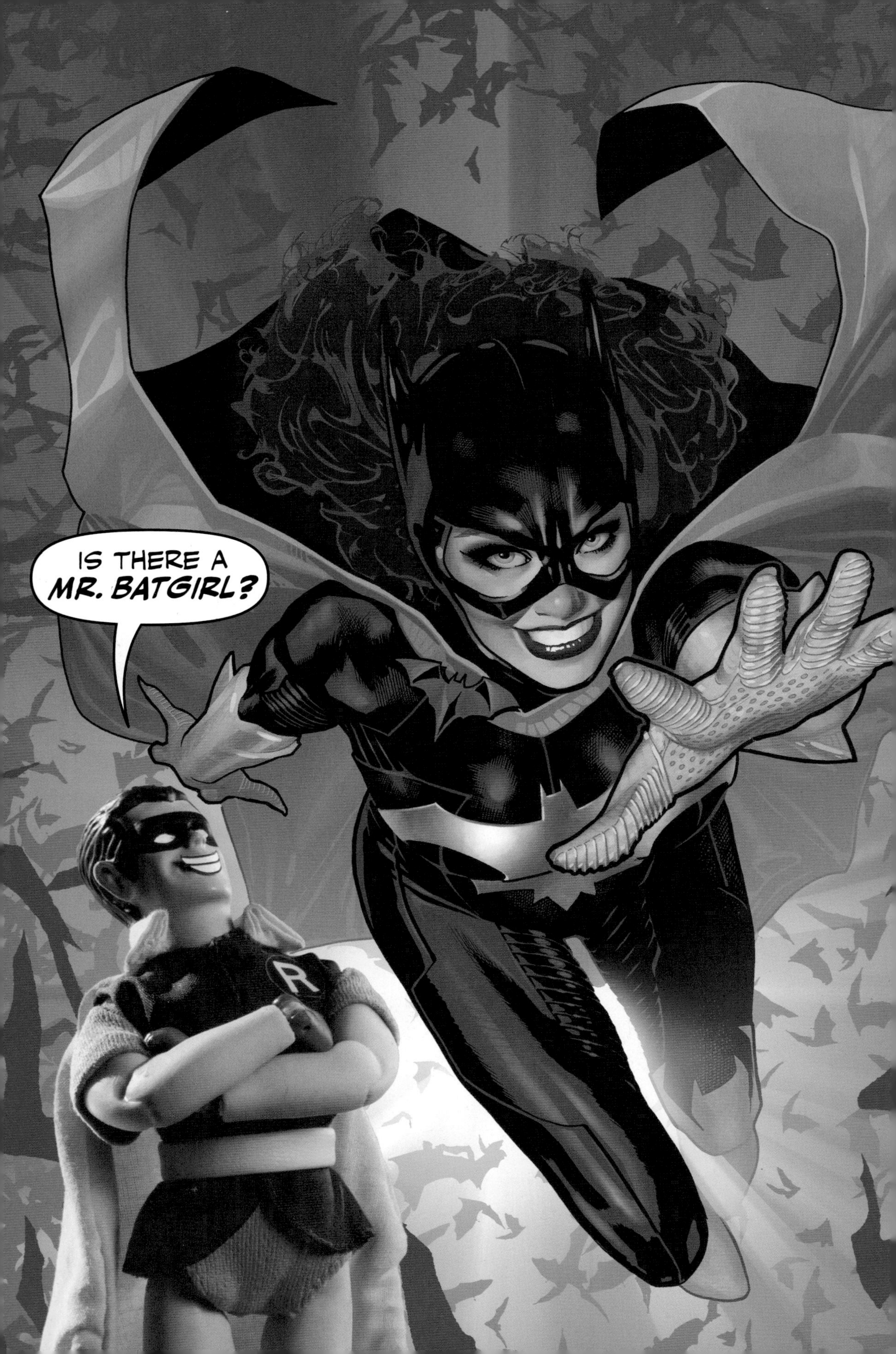
IS THERE A MR. BATGIRL?

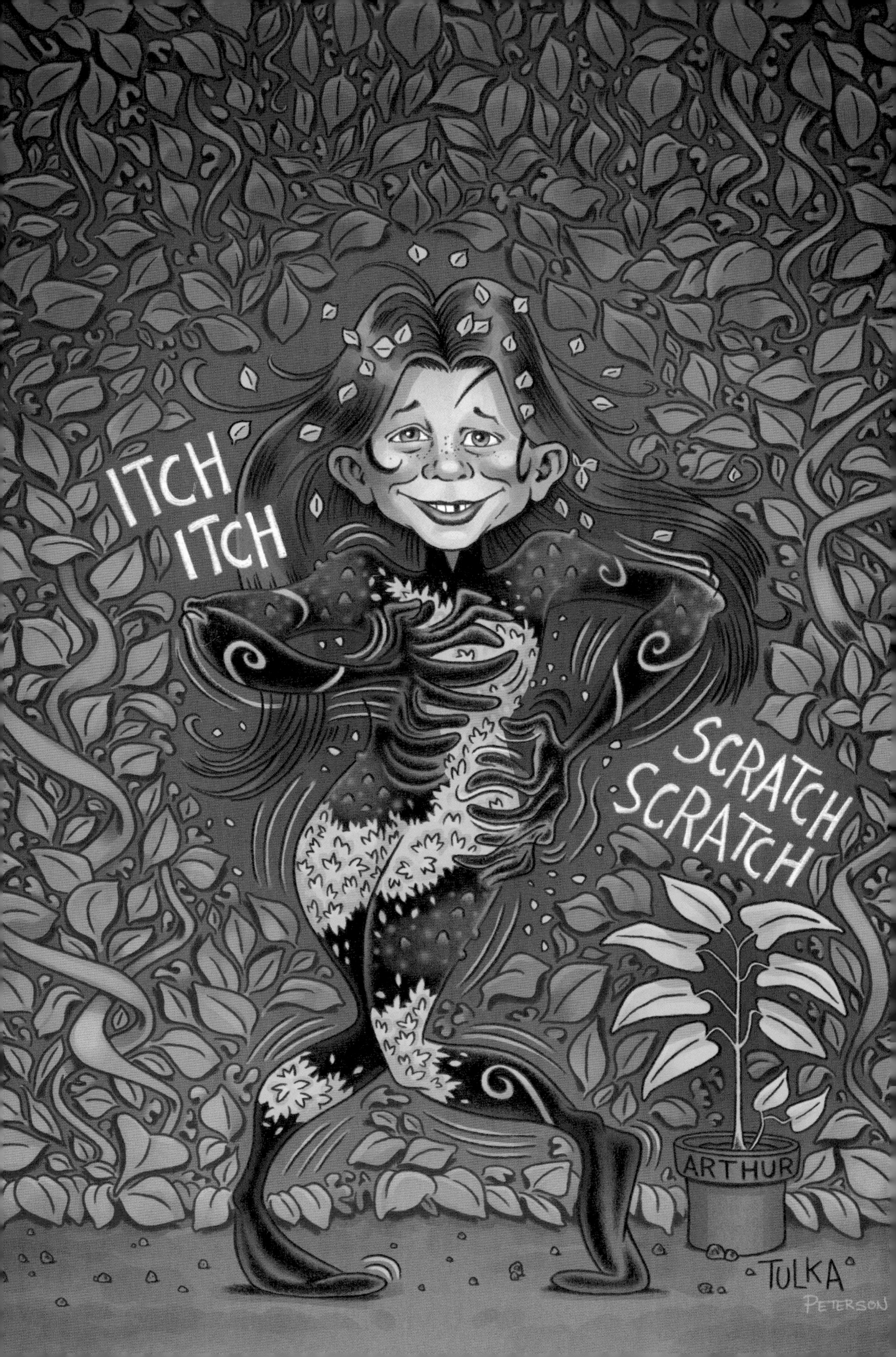
ITCH ITCH
SCRATCH SCRATCH
ARTHUR
TULKA
PETERSON

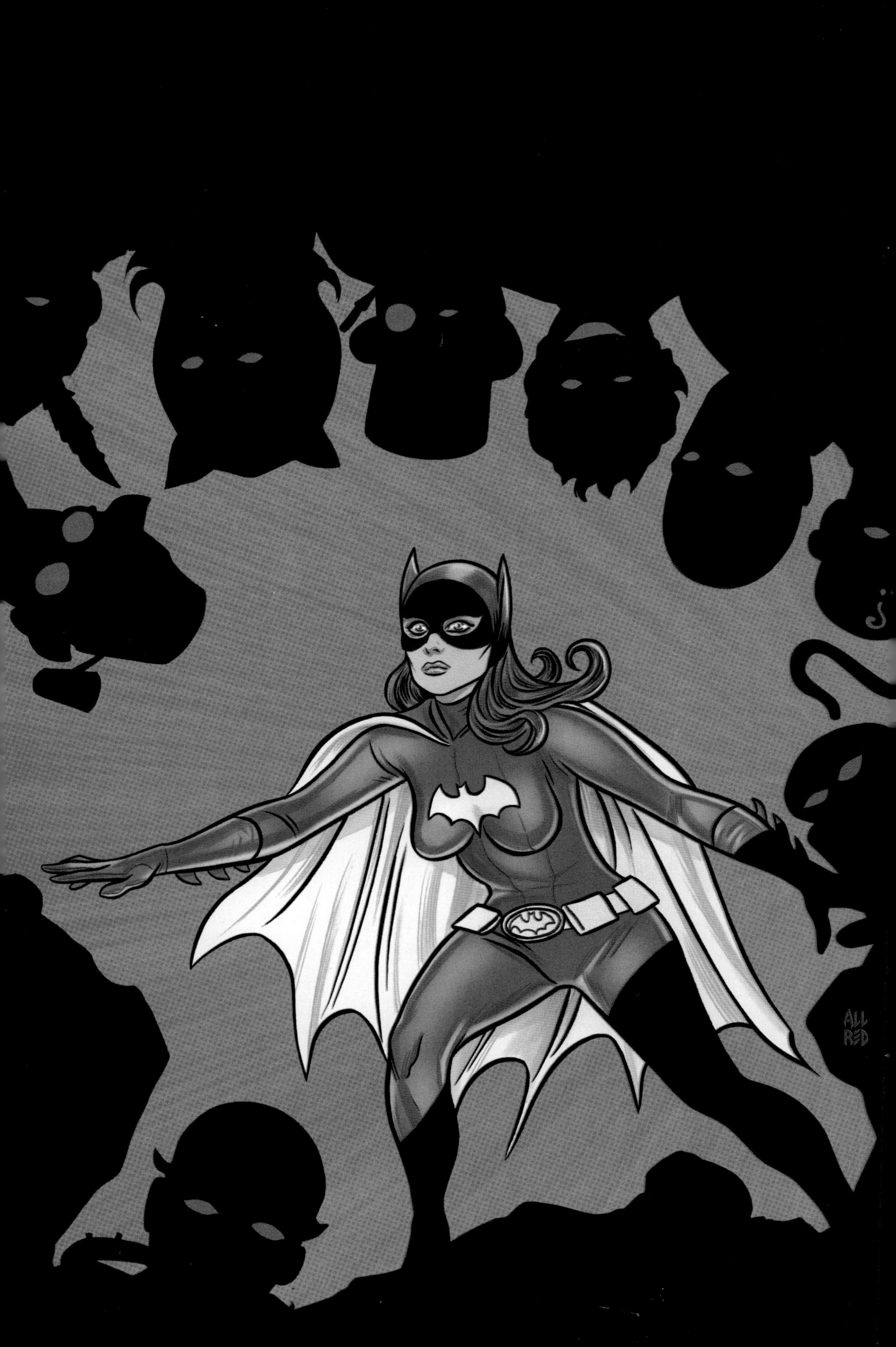
ALL
RED

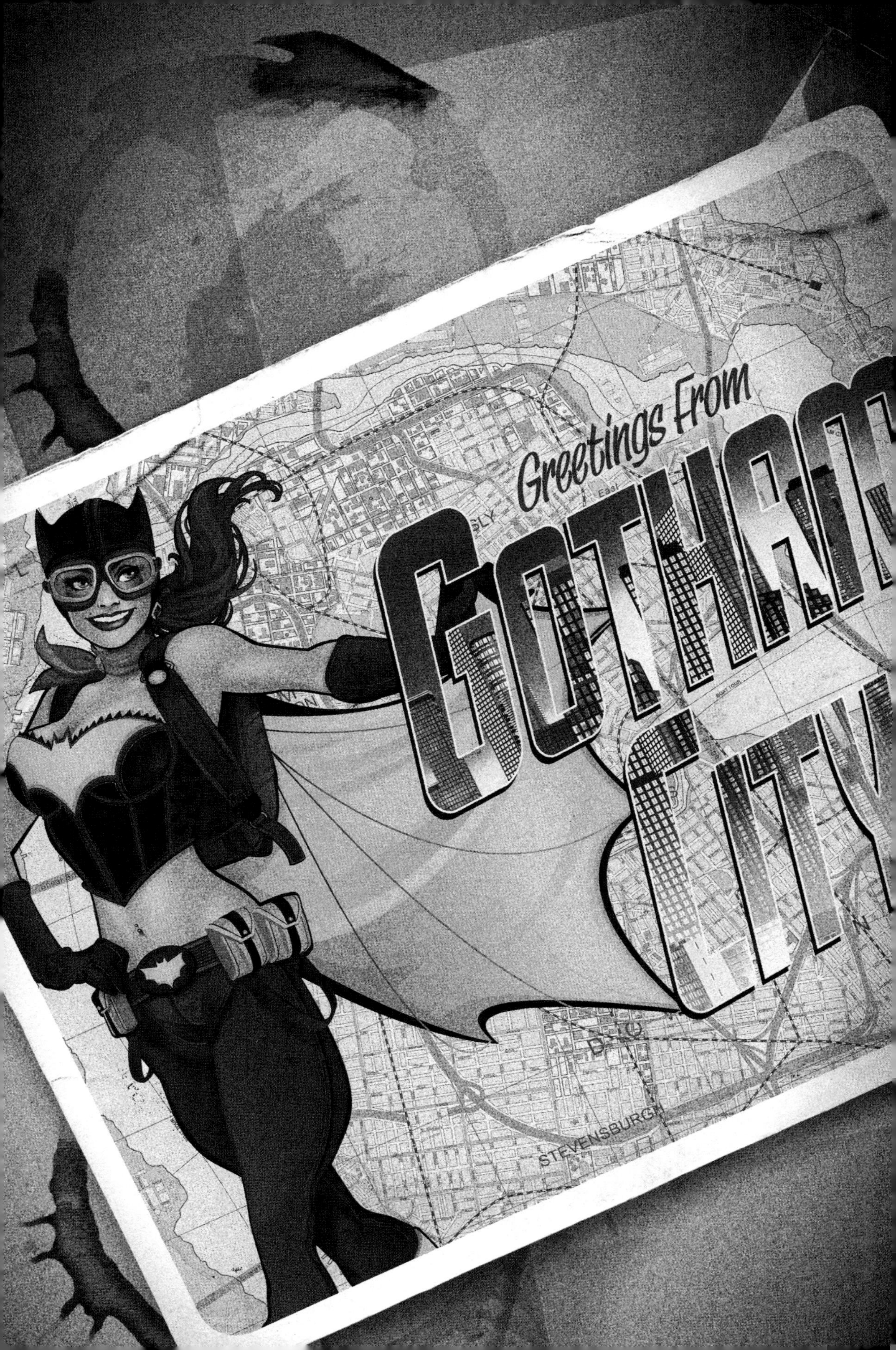
Greetings From
GOTHAM
CITY
STEVENSBURGH

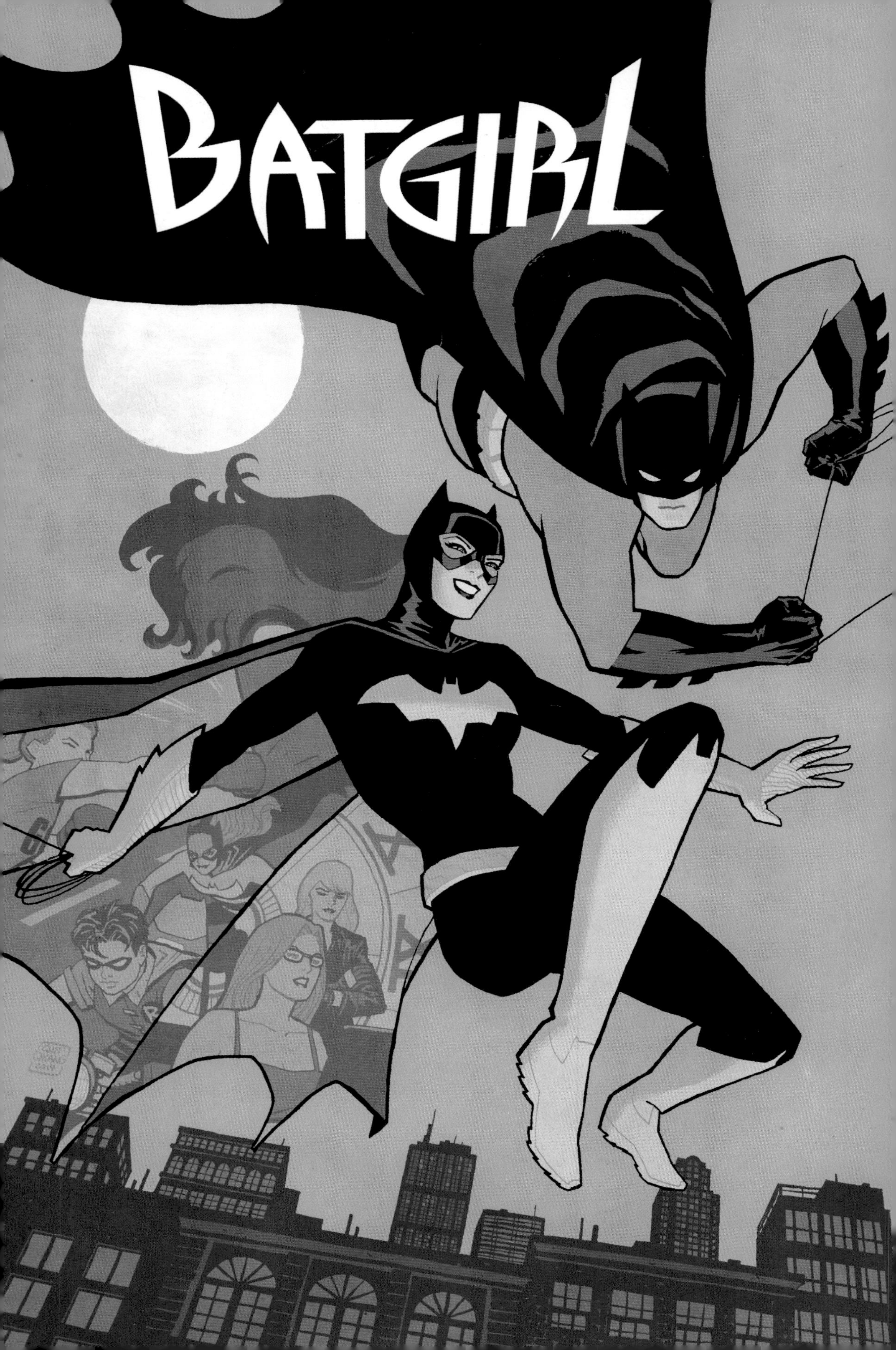
BATGIRL

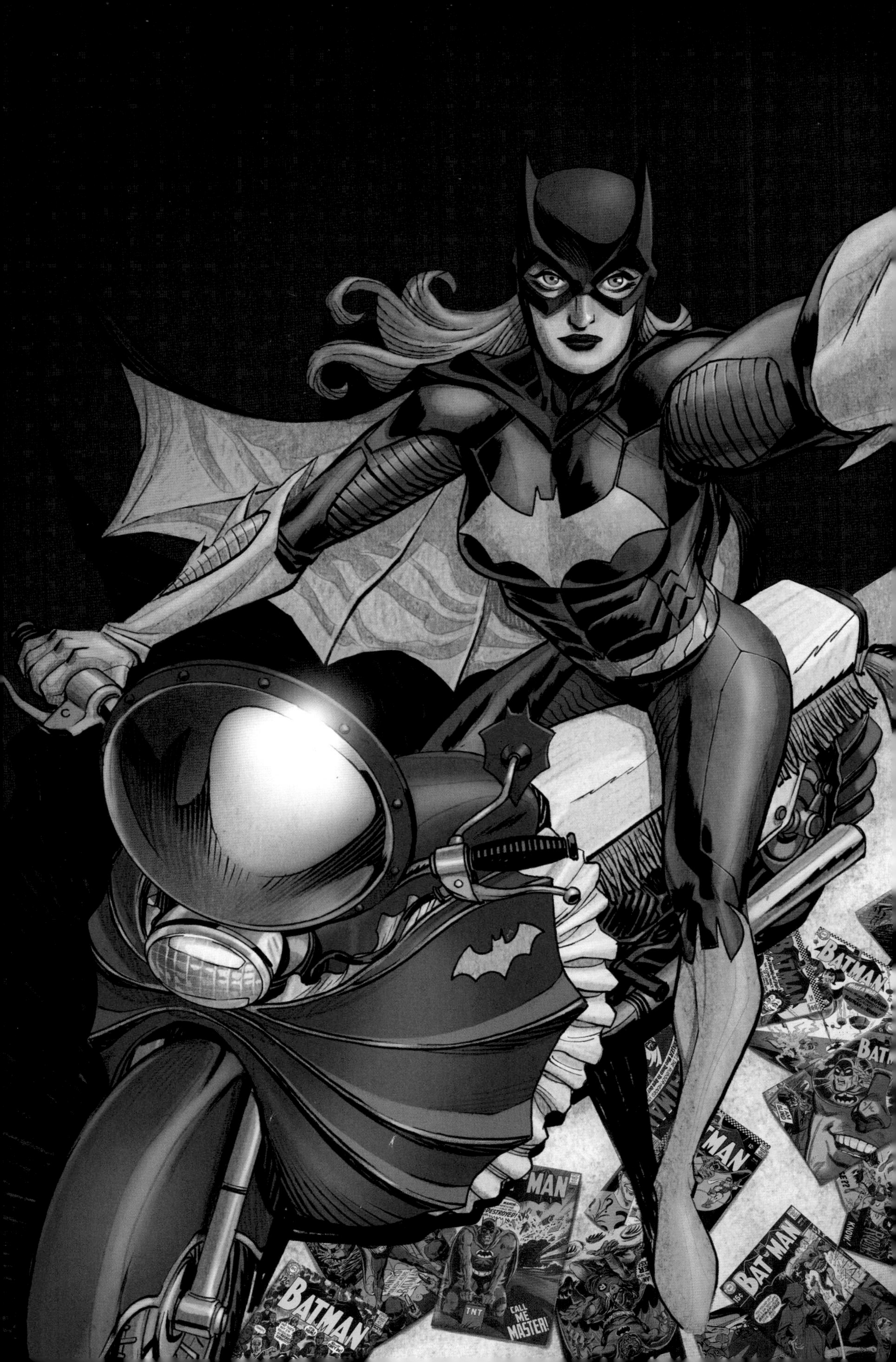
BATMAN
TNT
CALL ME MASTER!
BAT-MAN

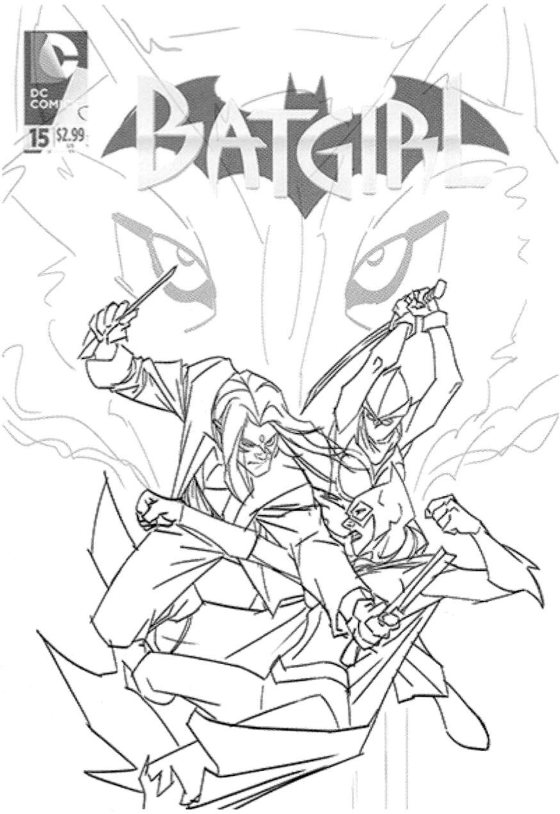
BATGIRL
15 $2.99

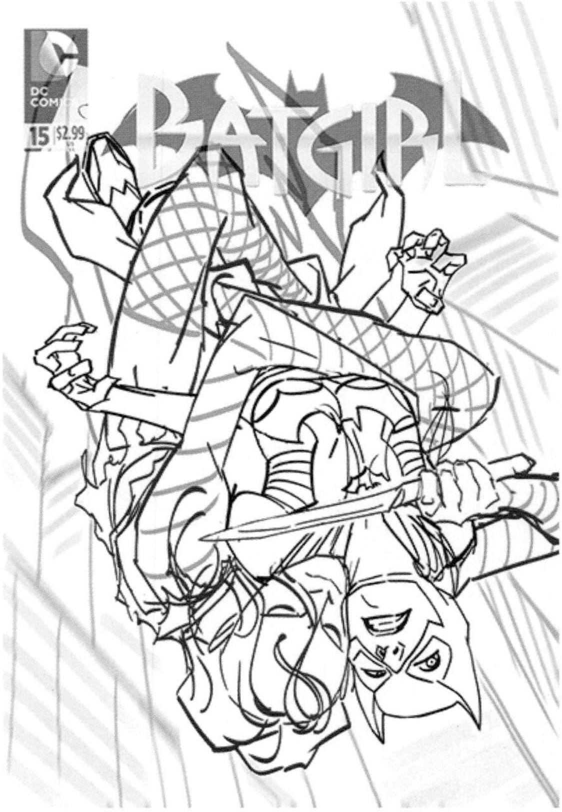
BATGIRL
15 $2.99

Cover sketches by Alex Garner for BATGIRL #29, 31 &33

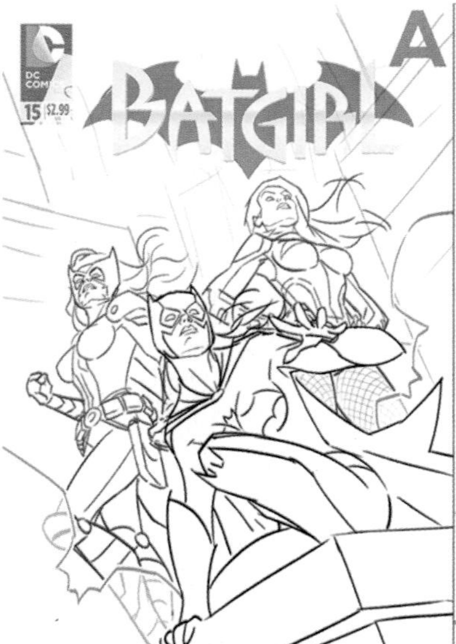
A
BATGIRL
15 $2.99

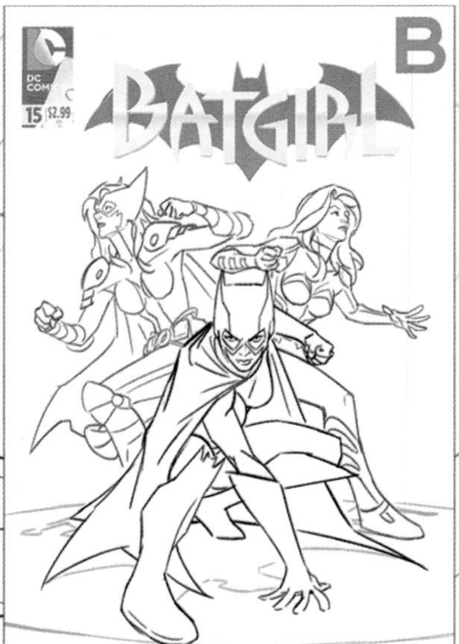
B
BATGIRL
15 $2.99

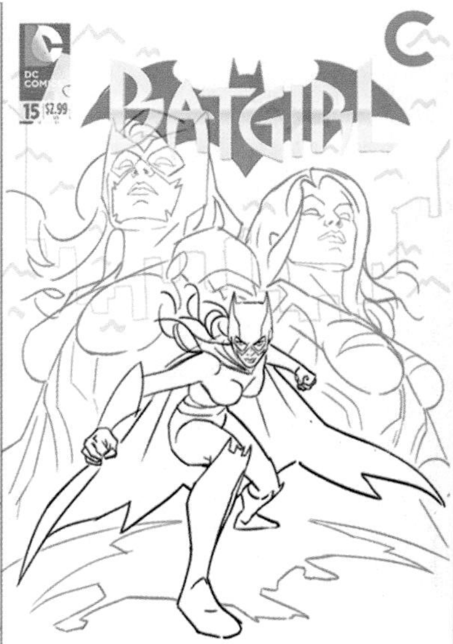
C
BATGIRL
15 $2.99

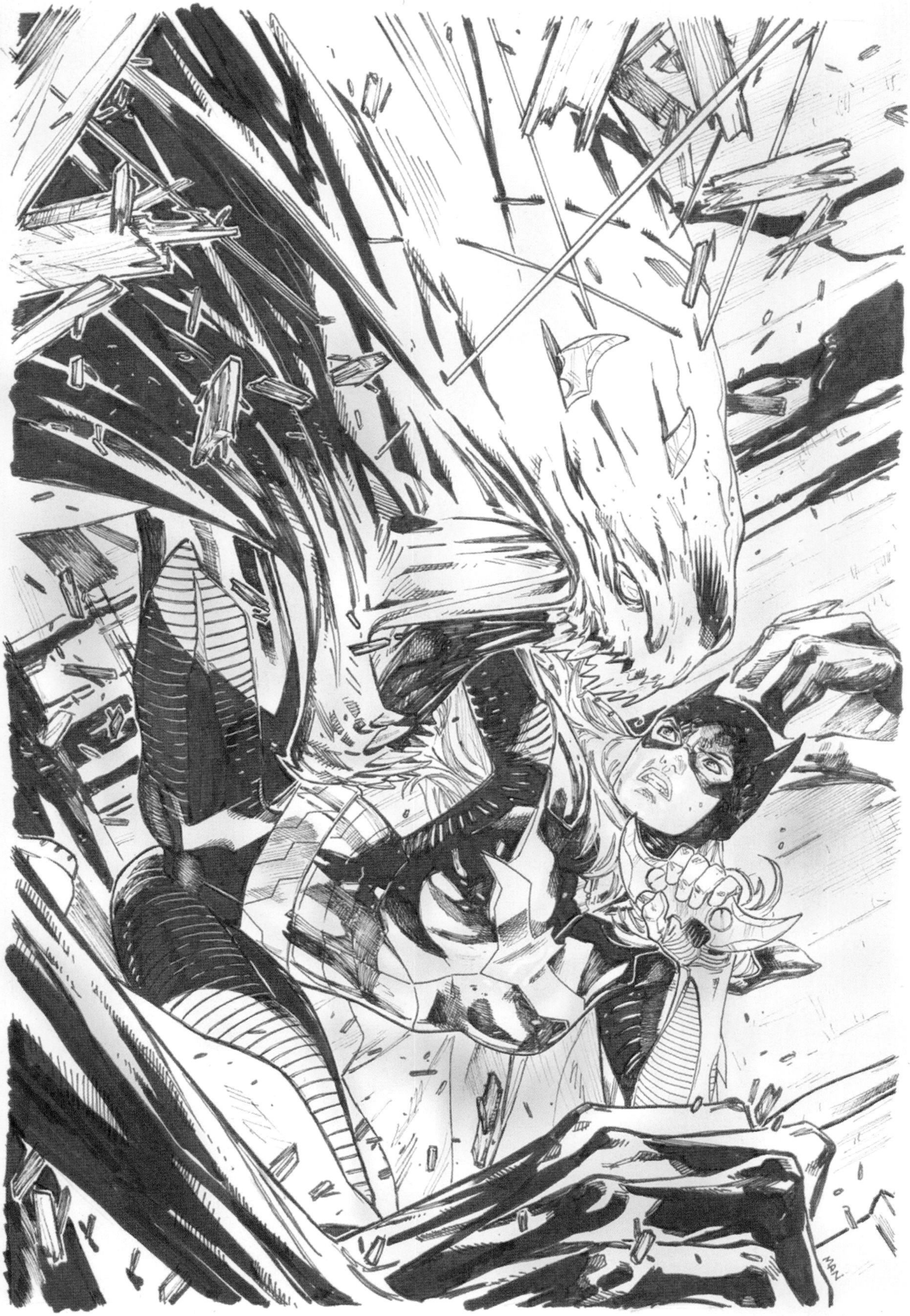
MANN

BATGIRL #30 cover pencils by Clay Mann

BATGIRL #27 thumbnail layouts

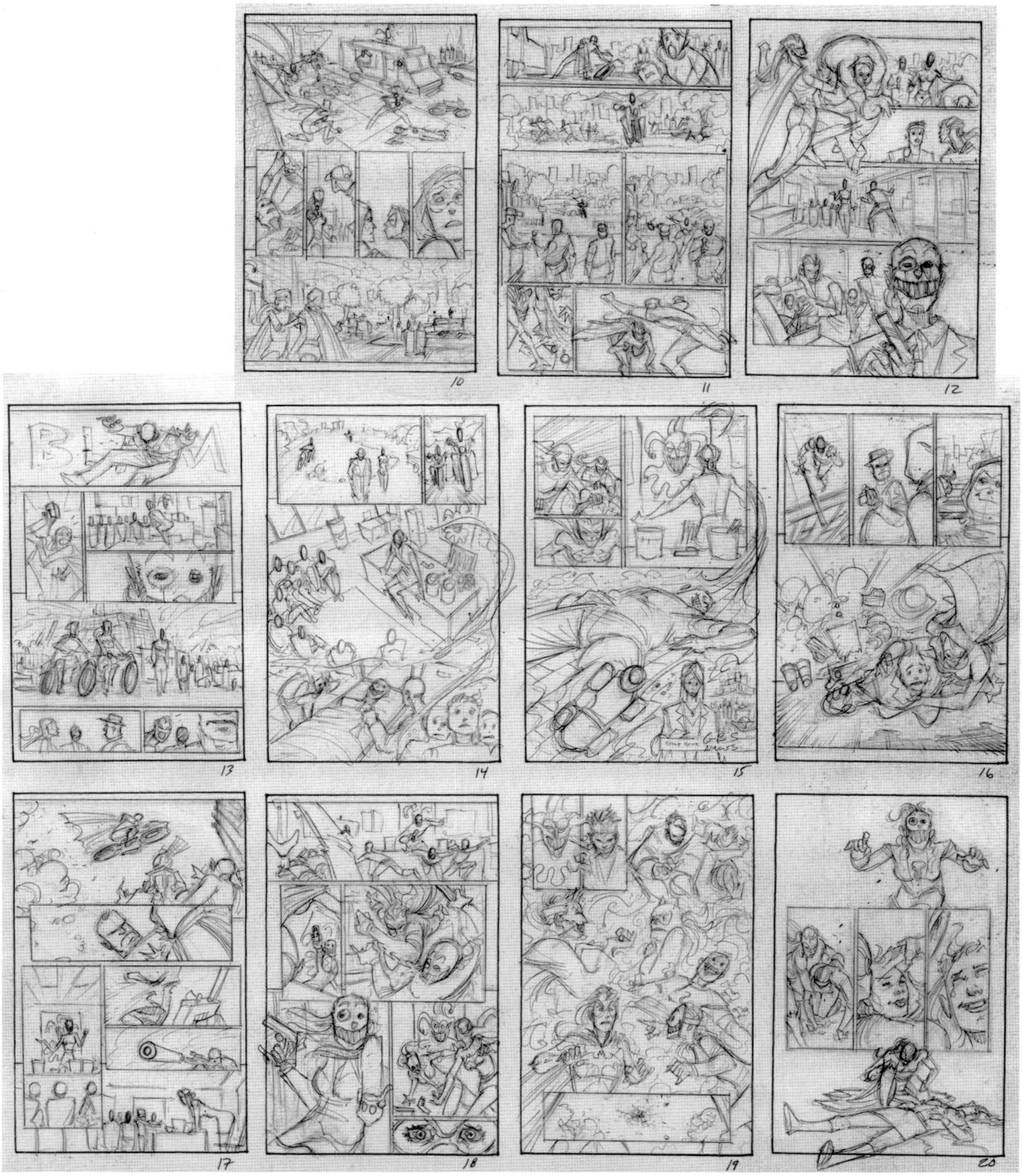
10
11
12
13
14
15
16
17
18
19
20

BATGIRL #30 thumbnail layouts

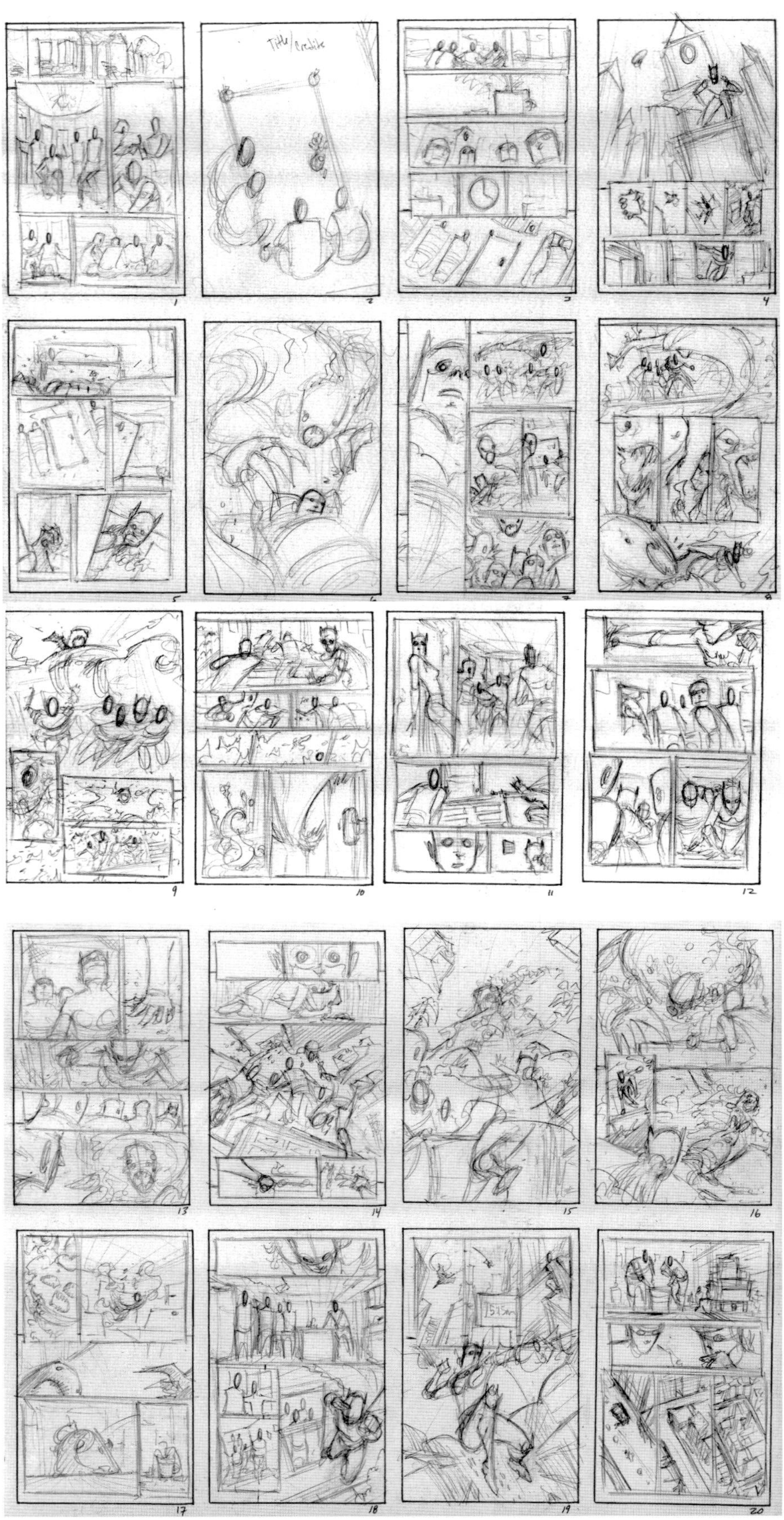
Title/Credits